ACCA

STUDY TEXT

Paper 2.4

Financial Management and Control

BPP's NEW STUDY TEXTS FOR ACCA's NEW SYLLABUS

- Targeted to the syllabus and study guide
- Quizzes and questions to check your understanding
- Clear layout and style designed to save you time
- Plenty of exam-style questions with new detailed guidance from BPP
- Chapter Roundups and summaries to help revision
- Mind Maps to integrate the key points
- BPP's **i-Learn** and **i-Pass** product also support this paper

FOR EXAMS IN DECEMBER 2002 AND JUNE 2003

BPP Publishing
June 2002

First edition February 2001
Second edition June 2002

ISBN 0 7517 0235 8 (Previous edition 0 7517 0730 9)

British Library Cataloguing-in-Publication Data
A catalogue record for this book
is available from the British Library

Published by

BPP Publishing Ltd
Aldine House, Aldine Place
London W12 8AW

www.bpp.com

Printed in Great Britain by WM Print
Frederick Street
Walsall
West Midlands

We are grateful to the Association of Chartered Certified Accountants for permission to reproduce past examination questions and questions from the pilot paper. The answers have been prepared by BPP Publishing Limited.

Page

THE BPP STUDY TEXT (v)

HELP YOURSELF STUDY FOR YOUR ACCA EXAMS (vii)
The right approach - developing your personal Study Plan - suggested study sequence

SYLLABUS (xii)

STUDY GUIDE (xvii)

THE EXAM PAPER (xxiii)

OXFORD BROOKES BSC (Hons) IN APPLIED ACCOUNTING (xxiv)

OXFORD INSTITUTE OF INTERNATIONAL FINANCE MBA (xxiv)

PART A: COSTING SYSTEMS AND TECHNIQUES

1	Cost and management accounting	3
2	Absorption and marginal costing	14
3	Other methods of cost accumulation	35
4	Specific order costing	54
5	Process costing and service costing	63

PART B: STANDARD COSTING

6	Introduction to standard costing	105
7	Basic variance analysis	117
8	Further variance analysis	141

PART C: BUDGETING

9	Budget planning and control	169
10	Budget preparation	184
11	Budgetary control and the behavioural implications of budgeting	210
12	Alternative budget systems	230
13	Quantitative aids in budgeting	240

PART D: DECISION MAKING

14	Decision making	267

PART E: THE FRAMEWORK OF FINANCIAL MANAGEMENT

15	Financial management and financial objectives	307
16	The financial management framework	330
17	Macroeconomic policy	350
18	Government intervention	372

PART F: WORKING CAPITAL MANAGEMENT

19	Management of working capital	385
20	The management of debtors and creditors	398
21	The management of stocks and cash	422

PART G: FINANCE AND INVESTMENT APPRAISAL

22 Equity financing 451
23 Debt and near debt financing 479
24 The capital structure decision 492
25 Financing of small and medium-sized enterprises 502
26 Investment decisions 514
27 Investment appraisal using DCF methods 528
28 Allowing for inflation and taxation 554
29 Project appraisal and risk 567
30 Capital rationing 584
31 Leasing decisions 593

APPENDIX: MATHEMATICAL TABLES 607

EXAM QUESTION BANK 611

EXAM ANSWER BANK 643

INDEX 723

REVIEW FORM & FREE PRIZE DRAW

ORDER FORM

THE BPP STUDY TEXT

Aims of this Study Text

To provide you with the knowledge and understanding, skills and application techniques that you need if you are to be successful in your exams

This Study Text has been written around the **Financial Management and Control** syllabus.

- It is **comprehensive**. It covers the syllabus content. No more, no less.
- It is written at the **right level**. Each chapter is written with the ACCA's **study guide** in mind.
- It is targeted to the **exam**. We have taken account of the **pilot paper**, questions put to the examiners at the recent ACCA conference and the assessment methodology.

To allow you to study in the way that best suits your learning style and the time you have available, by following your personal Study Plan (see page (ix))

You may be studying at home on your own until the date of the exam, or you may be attending a full-time course. You may like to (and have time to) read every word, or you may prefer to (or only have time to) skim-read and devote the remainder of your time to question practice. Wherever you fall in the spectrum, you will find the BPP Study Text meets your needs in designing and following your personal Study Plan.

To tie in with the other components of the BPP Effective Study Package to ensure you have the best possible chance of passing the exam (see page (vi))

Recommended period of use	Elements of the BPP Effective Study Package
From the outset and throughout	**Learning to learn accountancy** Read this invaluable book as you begin your studies and refer to it as you work through the various elements of the BPP Effective Study Package. It will help you to acquire knowledge, practice and revise, both efficiently and effectively.
Three to twelve months before the exam	**Study Text and i-Learn** Use the Study Text to acquire knowledge, understanding, skills and the ability to use application techniques. Use BPP's **i-Learn** product to reinforce your learning.
Throughout	**Virtual Campus** Study, practice, revise and take advantage of other useful resources with BPP's fully interactive e-learning site with comprehensive tutor support.
Throughout	**i-Pass** **i-Pass**, our computer-based testing package, provides objective test questions in a variety of formats and is ideal for self-assessment.
One to six months before the exam	**Practice & Revision Kit** Try the numerous examination-format questions, for which there are realistic suggested solutions prepared by BPP's own authors. Then attempt the two mock exams.
From three months before the exam until the last minute	**Passcards** Work through these short, memorable notes which are focused on what is most likely to come up in the exam you will be sitting.
One to six months before the exam	**Success Tapes** These audio tapes cover the vital elements of your syllabus in less than 90 minutes per subject. Each tape also contains exam hints to help you fine tune your strategy.
Three to twelve months before the exam	**Breakthrough Videos** Use a Breakthrough Video to supplement your Study Text. They give you clear tuition on key exam subjects and allow you the luxury of being able to pause or repeat sections until you have fully grasped the topic.

HELP YOURSELF STUDY FOR YOUR ACCA EXAMS

Exams for professional bodies such as ACCA are very different from those you have taken at college or university. You will be under **greater time pressure before** the exam - as you may be combining your study with work as well as in the exam room. There are many different ways of learning and so the BPP Study Text offers you a number of different tools to help you through. Here are some hints and tips: they are not plucked out of the air, but **based on research and experience.** (You don't need to know that long-term memory is in the same part of the brain as emotions and feelings - but it's a fact anyway.)

The right approach

1 **The right attitude**

Believe in yourself	Yes, there is a lot to learn. Yes, it is a challenge. But thousands have succeeded before and you can too.
Remember why you're doing it	Studying might seem a grind at times, but you are doing it for a reason: to advance your career.

2 **The right focus**

Read through the Syllabus and Study guide	These tell you what you are expected to know and are supplemented by Exam Focus Points in the text.
Study the Exam Paper section	The pilot paper is likely to be a reasonable guide of what you should expect in the exam.

3 **The right method**

The big picture	You need to grasp the detail - but keeping in mind how everything fits into the big picture will help you understand better. • The **Introduction** of each chapter puts the material in context. • The **Syllabus content, Study guide** and **Exam focus points** show you what you need to **grasp.** • **Mind Maps** show the links and key issues in key topics.
In your own words	To absorb the information (and to practise your written communication skills), it helps **put it into your own words.** • **Take notes.** • Answer the **questions** in each chapter. As well as helping you absorb the information you will practise your written communication skills, which become increasingly important as you progress through your ACCA exams. • Draw **mind maps**. We have some examples. • Try 'teaching' to a colleague or friend.

Give yourself cues to jog your memory	The BPP Study Text uses **bold** to **highlight key points** and **icons** to identify key features, such as **Exam focus points** and **Key terms.** • Try **colour coding** with a highlighter pen. • Write **key points** on cards.

4 **The right review**

Review, review, review	It is a **fact** that regularly reviewing a topic in summary form can **fix it in your memory**. Because **review** is so important, the BPP Study Text helps you to do so in many ways. • **Chapter roundups** summarise the key points in each chapter. Use them to recap each study session. • The **Quick quiz** is another review technique to ensure that you have grasped the essentials. • Go through the **Examples** in each chapter a second or third time.

Developing your personal Study Plan

One thing that the BPP Learning to learn accountancy book emphasises (see page (iv)) is the need to prepare (and use) a study plan. Planning and sticking to the plan are key elements of learning success.

There are four steps you should work through.

Step 1. How do you learn?

First you need to be aware of your style of learning. The BPP Learning to learn accountancy book commits a chapter to this **self-discovery**. What types of intelligence do you display when learning? You might be advised to brush up on certain study skills before launching into this Study Text.

> BPP's **Learning to Learn Accountancy** book helps you to identify what intelligences you show more strongly and then details how you can tailor your study process through your preferences. It also includes handy hints on how to develop intelligences you exhibit less strongly, but which might be needed as you study accountancy.

Are you a **theorist** or are you more **practical**? If you would rather get to grips with a theory before trying to apply it in practice, you should follow the study sequence on page X. If the reverse is true (you like to know why you are learning theory before you do so), you might be advised to flick through Study Text chapters and look at questions, case studies and examples (Steps 7, 8 and 9 in the **suggested study sequence**) before reading through the detailed theory.

Step 2. How much time do you have?

Work out the time you have available per week, given the following.

- The standard you have set yourself
- The time you need to set aside later for work on the Practice & Revision Kit and Passcards
- The other exam(s) you are sitting
- Very importantly, practical matters such as work, travel, exercise, sleep and social life

		Hours
Note your time available in box A.	A	

Step 3. Allocate your time

• Take the time you have available per week for this Study Text shown in box A, multiply it by the number of weeks available and insert the result in box B.	B	
• Divide the figure in Box B by the number of chapters in this text and insert the result in box C.	C	

Remember that this is only a rough guide. Some of the chapters in this book are longer and more complicated than others, and you will find some subjects easier to understand than others.

Step 4. Implement

Set about studying each chapter in the time shown in box C, following the key study steps in the order suggested by your particular learning style.

This is your personal **Study Plan**. You should try and combine it with the study sequence outlined below. You may want to modify the sequence a little (as has been suggested above) to adapt it to your **personal style**.

Suggested study sequence

Tackle the chapters in the order you find them in the Study Text. Taking into account your individual learning style, you could follow this sequence.

Key study steps	Activity
Step 1 **Topic list**	Each numbered topic is a numbered section in the chapter.
Step 2 **Introduction**	This gives you the **big picture** in terms of the **context** of the chapter. The content is referenced to the **Study Guide**, and **Exam Guidance** shows how the topic is likely to be examined. In other words, it sets your **objectives for study.**
Step 3 **Knowledge brought forward boxes**	In these we highlight information and techniques that it is assumed you have 'brought forward' with you from your earlier studies. If there are topics which have changed recently due to legislation for example, these topics are explained in more detail.
Step 4 **Explanations**	Proceed methodically through the chapter, reading each section thoroughly and making sure you understand.
Step 5 **Key terms and Exam focus points**	• **Key terms** can often earn you *easy marks* if you state them clearly and correctly in an appropriate exam answer (and they are indexed at the back of the text). • **Exam focus points** give you a good idea of how we think the examiner intends to examine certain topics.
Step 6 **Note taking**	Take brief notes if you wish, avoiding the temptation to copy out too much.
Step 7 **Examples**	Follow each through to its solution very carefully.
Step 8 **Case examples**	Study each one, and try to add flesh to them from your own experience - they are designed to show how the topics you are studying come alive (and often come unstuck) in the real world.
Step 9 **Questions**	Make a very good attempt at each one.
Step 10 **Answers**	Check yours against ours, and make sure you understand any discrepancies.
Step 11 **Chapter roundup**	Work through it very carefully, to make sure you have grasped the major points it is highlighting.
Step 12 **Quick quiz**	When you are happy that you have covered the chapter, use the **Quick quiz** to check how much you have remembered of the topics covered.

Key study steps	Activity
Step 13 **Question(s) in the Question bank**	Either at this point, or later when you are thinking about revising, make a full attempt at the **Question(s)** suggested at the very end of the chapter. You can find these at the end of the Study Text, along with the **Answers** so you can see how you did. We highlight those that are introductory, and those which are of the standard you would expect to find in an exam.

Short of time: *Skim study technique*?

You may find you simply do not have the time available to follow all the key study steps for each chapter, however you adapt them for your particular learning style. If this is the case, follow the **skim study** technique below (the icons in the Study Text will help you to do this).

- Study the chapters in the order you find them in the Study Text.
- For each chapter, follow the key study steps 1-3, and then skim-read through step 4. Jump to step 11, and then go back to step 5. Follow through steps 7 and 8, and prepare outline answers to questions (steps 9/10). Try the Quick quiz (step 12), following up any items you can't answer, then do a plan for the Question (step 13), comparing it against our answers. You should probably still follow step 6 (note-taking), although you may decide simply to rely on the BPP Passcards for this.

Moving on...

However you study, when you are ready to embark on the practice and revision phase of the BPP Effective Study Package, you should still refer back to this Study Text, both as a source of **reference** (you should find the list of key terms and the index particularly helpful for this) and as a **refresher** (the Chapter roundups and Quick quizzes help you here).

And remember to keep careful hold of this Study Text – you will find it invaluable in your work.

More advice on Study Skills can be found in the BPP **Learning to Learn Accountancy** book

SYLLABUS

Aim

To develop knowledge and understanding of financial management methods for analysing the benefits of various sources of finance and capital investment opportunities and of the application of management accounting techniques for business planning and control.

Objectives

On completion of this paper candidates should be able to:

- explain the role and purpose of financial management
- evaluate the overall management of working capital
- evaluate appropriate sources of finance for particular situations
- appraise capital investment through the use of appropriate methods
- identify and implement appropriate costing systems and techniques
- prepare budgets and use them to control and evaluate organisational performance
- critically assess the tools and techniques of financial management and control
- demonstrate the skills expected in Part 2

Position of the paper in the overall syllabus

Students must have a thorough knowledge of the material in Paper 1.2 **Financial Information for Management** and a good knowledge of other Part 1 papers.

Financial Management and Control is integrated with other Part 2 papers by providing a management decision framework within which some aspects of the Part 2 syllabus are developed. The effects of capital allowances and corporation tax on capital investment appraisal is examinable. Knowledge gained from Paper 2.3 **Business Taxation** (UK) will be useful in this respect.

Financial Management and Control is developed in Part 3 into advanced study of **Performance Management** (Paper 3.3) and **Strategic Financial Management** (Paper 3.7).

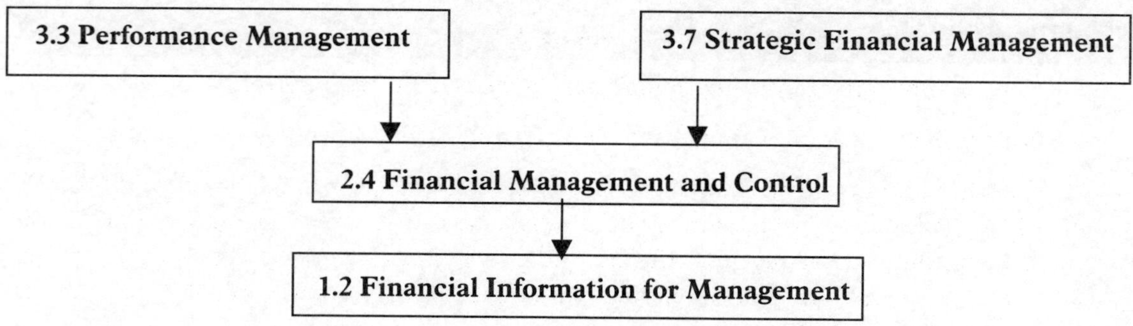

SYLLABUS

1 Financial management objectives

(a) The nature, purpose and scope of financial management.

(b) The relationship between financial management, management accounting and financial accounting.

(c) The relationship of financial objectives and organisational strategy.

(d) Problems of multiple stakeholders in financial management and the consequent multiple objectives.

(e) Objectives (financial and otherwise) in not-for-profit organisations.

2 The financial management environment

(a) Financial intermediation and credit creation.

(b) Money and capital markets.

(i) Domestic and international

(ii) Stock markets (both major markets and small firm markets).

(c) The Efficient Markets Hypothesis.

(d) Rates of interest and yield curves.

(e) The impact of fiscal and monetary policy on business.

(f) Regulation of business (for example, pricing restrictions, green policies and corporate governance).

3 Management of working capital

(a) The nature and scope of working capital management.

(b) Funding requirements for working capital.

(c) Working capital needs of different types of business.

(d) The relationship of working capital management to business solvency.

(e) Management of stock, debtors, short term funds, cash, overdrafts and creditors.

(f) Techniques of working capital management (including, *inter alia*, ratio analysis, EOQ, JIT, credit evaluation, terms of credit, cash discounts, factoring and invoice discounting, debtors cycles, efficient short term fund investing, cash forecasting and budgets, Miller-Orr models, basic foreign exchange methods, probabilities and risk assessment, terms of trade with creditors).

4 Sources of finance

(a) Sources and relative costs (including issue costs) of various types of finance and their suitability to different circumstances and organisations (large and small, listed and unlisted) including:

(i) access to funds and the nature of business risk

(ii) the nature and importance of internally generated funds

(iii) capital markets (types of share capital, new issues, rights issues, loan capital, convertibles, warrants)

(iv) the effect of dividend policy on financing needs

(v) bank finance (short, medium and long term, including leasing)

(vi) trade credit

(vii) government sources: grants, regional and national aid schemes and tax incentives

(viii) problems of small company financing (collateral, maturity funding gap, risk)

(ix) problems of companies with low initial earnings (R&D, Internet and other high-technology businesses)

(x) venture capital and financial sources particularly suited to the small company

(xi) international money and capital markets, including an introduction to international banking and the finance of foreign trade.

(b) Requirements of finance (for what purpose, how much and for how long) in relation to business operational and strategic objectives.

(c) The importance of the choice of capital structure: equity versus debt and basic analysis of the term profile of funds.

(d) Financial gearing and other key financial ratios and analysis of their significance to the organisation.

(e) Appropriate sources of finance, taking into account

(i) cost of finance
(ii) timing of cash payments
(iii) effect on gearing and other ratios
(iv) effect on company's existing investors.

5 Capital expenditure and investment

(a) Appraisal of domestic capital investment opportunities for profit and non-profit making organisations through the use of appropriate methods and techniques

(i) the risk return relationship
(ii) return on capital employed
(iii) payback
(iv) internal rate of return
(v) net present value
(vi) single and multi-period capital rationing
(vii) lease or buy decisions
(viii) asset replacement

Including (in categories (i) - (viii)) the effects of taxation, inflation, risk and uncertainty (probabilities, decision trees, sensitivity analysis, simulation).

6 Costing systems

(a) The purpose of costing as an aid to planning, monitoring and control of business activity.

(b) Information requirements of different approaches.

(c) Costing information requirements and limitations in not-for-profit organisations.

(d) Behavioural implications of different costing approaches including performance evaluation.

(e) Implications of costing approaches for profit reporting, the pricing of products and internal activities/services.

(f) The role of costing systems in performance evaluation and decision making.

7 Costing techniques

(a) Allocating/apportioning costs through the use of appropriate techniques

  (i) absorption, marginal and opportunity cost approaches to the accumulation of costs for specific orders (job, batch, contract) or operations (process, service)

  (ii) activity based costing: use of cost drivers and activities

  (iii) life cycle costing

  (iv) target costing.

8 Standard costing and variance analysis

(a) Standard costing

  (i) determination of standards

  (ii) identification and calculation of sales variances (including quantity and mix), cost variances (including mix and yield): absorption and marginal approaches

  (iii) significance and relevance of variances

  (iv) operating statements

  (v) interpretation and relevance of variance calculations to business performance.

(b) Planning and operational variances.

(c) Behavioural implications of standard costing and variance reporting.

9 Budgeting and budgetary control

(a) Objectives of budgetary planning and control systems including aspects of behavioural implications.

(b) Evaluation of budgetary systems such as fixed and flexible, zero based and incremental, periodic, continuous and activity based.

(c) Development, implementation and co-ordination of budgeting systems: functional, subsidiary and master/principal budgets (including cash budgeting): budget review.

(d) Calculation and cause of variances as aids to controlling performance.

(e) Quantitative aids to budgeting and the concepts of correlation, basic time series analysis (seasonality) and forecasting: use of computer based models.

(f) Implications of costing systems on profit reporting.

(g) Behavioural implications of budgeting and budgetary control.

Excluded topics

The following topics are specifically excluded from the syllabus:

- Calculations involving the derivation of cost of capital in discounting problems. Candidates will always be supplied with an appropriate discount rate.
- Calculations relating to Modigliani and Miller propositions.

Key areas of the syllabus

The core of the syllabus is aimed at developing the skills required in supporting managerial decision making. They reflect the core competencies needed for students to satisfy the aim of the paper identified above. The core areas are:

- financial management objectives
- management of working capital
- sources of finance
- capital expenditure and investment
- costing systems
- standard costing and variance analysis
- budgeting and budgetary control.

KEY SYLLABUS TOPICS ARE DEALT WITH FIRST IN THIS TEXT, SO THAT YOU CAN MOVE ON TO LESS IMPORTANT AREAS IF YOU HAVE TIME.

Paper 2.4(U)

Financial Management and Control
(United Kingdom)

Study Guide

1 THE ECONOMIC ENVIRONMENT 1

Macroeconomic Objectives

- Identify and explain the main macro-economic policy targets
- Explain how government economic policy may affect planning and decision-making in business
- Define and explain the role of fiscal, monetary, interest rate and exchange rate policy

Fiscal policy

- Identify the main tools of fiscal policy
- Explain how public expenditure is financed and the meaning of PSBR
- Explain how PSBR and taxation policy interact with other economic indicators
- Identify the implications of fiscal policy for business

2 THE ECONOMIC ENVIRONMENT II

Monetary, inflation and exchange rate policy

- Identify the main tools of monetary policy
- Identify the factors which influence inflation and exchange rates, including the impact of interest rates
- Identify the implications of monetary, inflation and exchange rate policy for business

Aspects of government intervention and regulation

- Explain the requirement for and the role of competition policy
- Explain the requirements for and the role of official aid intervention
- Explain the requirement for and the role of Green policies
- Identify examples of government intervention and regulation

3 THE NATURE AND SCOPE OF FINANCIAL MANAGEMENT

- Broadly describe the relationship between financial management, management accounting and financial accounting
- Discuss the nature and scope of financial objectives for private sector companies in the context of organisational objectives
- Discuss the role of social and non-financial objectives in private sector companies and identify their financial implications
- Identify objectives (financial and otherwise) in not-for-profit organisations and identify the extent to which they differ from private sector companies
- Discuss the problems of multiple stakeholders in financial management and the consequent multiple objectives and scope for conflict

4 THE FINANCIAL MANAGEMENT FRAMEWORK

- Identify the general role of financial intermediaries
- Explain the role of commercial banks as providers of funds (including the creation of credit)
- Discuss the risk/return trade-off
- Identify the international money and capital markets and outline their operation
- Explain the functions of a stock market and corporate bond market
- Explain the key features of different types of security in terms of the risk/return trade-off
- Outline the Efficient Markets Hypothesis and assess its broad implications for corporate policy and financial management
- Explain the Separation Theorem
- Explain the functions of and identify the links between the money and capital markets

5 **MANAGEMENT OF WORKING CAPITAL I**

General issues

- Explain the nature and scope of working capital management
- Distinguish between cash and flow and profits
- Explain the requirement for effective working capital management
- Explain the relationship between working capital management and business solvency
- Distinguish the working capital needs of different types of business

Management of stock

- Calculate and interpret stock ratios
- Explain the role of stock in the working capital cycle
- Apply the tools and techniques of stock management
- Analyse and evaluate the results of stock management techniques

6 **MANAGEMENT OF WORKING CAPITAL II**

Management of creditors

- Explain the role of creditors in the working capital cycle
- Explain the availability of credit and the role of the guarantee
- Identify the risks of taking increased credit and buying under extended credit terms
- Explain how methods of paying suppliers may influence cash flows of both parties
- Discuss the particular problems of managing overseas accounts payable
- Calculate and interpret creditor ratios
- Apply the tools and techniques of creditor management
- Analyse and evaluate the results of creditor management techniques

Management of debtors

- Explain the role of debtors in the working capital cycle
- Explain how the credit-worthiness of customers may be assessed
- Evaluate the balance of risks and costs of customer default against the profitability of marginal business
- Explain the role of factoring and invoice discounting
- Explain the role of settlement discounts
- Discuss the particular problems of managing overseas accounts receivable
- Calculate and interpret debtor ratios
- Apply the tools and techniques of debtor management
- Analyse and evaluate the results of debtor management techniques

7 **MANAGEMENT OF WORKING CAPITAL III**

Management of cash

- Explain the role of cash in the working capital cycle
- Calculate optimal cash balances
- Describe the functions of and evaluate the benefits from centralised cash control and Treasury Management
- Calculate and interpret cash ratios
- Apply the tools and techniques of cash management
- Analyse and evaluate the results of cash management techniques

8 **SOURCES OF FINANCE I: SMALL AND MEDIUM SIZED ENTERPRISES (SME'S)**

- Explain financing in terms of the risk/return trade-off
- Describe the requirements for finance of SME's (purpose, how much, how long)
- Describe the nature of the financing problem for small businesses in terms of the funding gap, the maturity gap and inadequate security
- Identify the role of risk and the lack of information on small companies to help explain the problem of SME financing
- Explain the role of information provision provided by financial statements
- Describe the particular financing problems of low-earning/high growth companies
- Describe the response of government agencies and financial institutions to the SME financing problem

- Explain what other measures may be taken to ease the financial problems of SME's such as trade creditors, factoring, leasing, hire purchase, AIM listing, business angels and venture capital
- Describe how capital structure decisions in SME's may differ from larger organisations
- Describe appropriate sources of finance for SME's
- Calculate and interpret appropriate ratios

9 SOURCE OF FINANCE II: EQUITY FINANCING

- Describe ways in which a company may obtain a stock market listing
- Describe how stock markets operate including AIM
- Explain the requirements of stock market investors in terms of returns on investment
- Calculate, analyse and evaluate appropriate financial ratios (eg EPS, PE, yield, etc)
- Outline and apply the dividend valuation model, including the growth adjustment
- Explain the importance of internally generated funds
- Describe the advantages and disadvantages of rights issues
- Calculate the price of rights
- Explain the purpose and impact of a bonus issue, scrip dividends and stock splits

10 SOURCE OF FINANCE III: DEBT AND NEAR-DEBT FINANCING

- Explain the features of different types of preference shares and the reasons for their issue
- Explain the features of different types of long-term straight debt and the reasons for their issue
- Explain the features of convertible debt and warrants and the reasons for their issue
- Broadly describe the reasons for the choice of financing between preference shares, debt and near-debt instruments in terms of the risk/return trade-off
- Assess the effect on EPS of conversion and option rights
- Broadly describe international debt markets and the financing of foreign trade
- Calculate and interpret appropriate ratios

11 SOURCE OF FINANCE IV: THE CAPITAL STRUCTURE DECISION

- Explain and calculate the level of financing gearing
- Distinguish between operational and financial gearing
- Outline the effects of gearing on the value of shares, company risk and required return
- Explain how a company may determine its capital structure in terms of interest charges, dividends, risk and redemption requirements
- Explain the role of short term financing in the capital structure decision
- Explain the relationship between the management of working capital and the long term capital structure decision
- Calculate and interpret appropriate ratios

12 INVESTMENT DECISIONS

- Define and distinguish between capital and revenue expenditure
- Compare and contrast fixed asset investment and working capital investment
- Describe the impact of investment projects on financial statements
- Calculate payback and assess its usefulness as a measure of investment worth
- Calculate ROCE and assess its usefulness as a measure of investment worth

13 INVESTMENT APPRAISAL USING DCF METHODS

- Explain the importance of the time value of money and the role of the cost of capital in appraising investments
- Identify and evaluate relevant cash flows of potential investments
- Calculate present values to derive the NPV and IRR measures of investment worth
- Explain the superiority of DCF methods over payback and ROCE
- Assess the merits of IRR and NPV

- Apply DCF methods to asset replacement decisions

14 PROJECT APPRAISAL ALLOWING FOR INFLATION AND TAXATION

Inflation

- Explain the relationship between inflation and interest rates, distinguishing between real and nominal rates
- Distinguish general inflation from specific price increases and assess their impact on cash flows
- Evaluate capital investment projects on a real terms basis
- Evaluate capital investment projects on a nominal terms basis

Taxation

- Calculate the effect of capital allowances and Corporation Tax on project cash flows
- Evaluate the profitability of capital investment projects on a post-tax basis

15 PROJECT APPRAISAL ALLOWING FOR RISK

- Distinguish between risk and uncertainty
- Identify the sources of risk affecting project profitability
- Evaluate the sensitivity of project NPV to changes in key variables
- Apply the probability approach to calculating expected NPV of a project and the associated standard deviation
- Apply decision tree analysis in project appraisal situations
- Explain the role of simulation in generating a probability distribution for the NPV of a project
- Identify risk reduction strategies for projects
- Evaluate the usefulness of risk assessment methods

16 CAPITAL RATIONING

- Distinguish hard and soft capital rationing
- Apply profitability index techniques for single period divisible projects
- Evaluate projects involving single and multi-period capital rationing

17 LEASING DECISIONS

- Distinguish between operating and finance leases
- Apply DCF methods to projects involving buy or lease problems
- Assess the relative advantages and disadvantages of different types of lease
- Describe the impact of leasing on company gearing

18 COSTING SYSTEMS: CONTEXT AND FRAMEWORK

- Outline and distinguish between the nature and scope of management accounting and the role of costing in meeting the needs of management
- Describe the purpose of costing as an aid to planning, monitoring and controlling business activity
- Explain the potential for different costing approaches to influence cost accumulation and profit reporting
- Describe the costing information requirements and limitations in not-for-profit organisations
- Broadly outline the implications of different costing approaches for performance evaluation
- Explain the role of costing systems in decision making

19 COST ACCUMULATION 1

- Explain the requirement to allocate overheads
- Describe, explain and apply absorption and marginal costing
- Reconcile the resulting profits/losses from absorption and marginal costing
- Describe, explain and apply opportunity and activity based costing
- Explain the impact of life cycle costing on cost accumulation
- Describe and apply target costing methods
- Describe the interaction between life cycle and target costing
- Evaluate the relative advantages and disadvantages of the different costing approaches

20 COST ACCUMULATION II

- Apply appropriate cost accumulation methods to problems of job, batch and contract costing
- Apply appropriate cost accumulation methods to problems of process costing
- Prepare statements which value losses in process and work in progress

- Calculate appropriate costs for joint products and prepare process costing statements which account for by-products
- Apply appropriate cost accumulation methods to problems of service costing
- Describe the difficulties of service costing in the not-for-profit sector
- Explain the difficulties in identifying relevant and accurate costs

21 STANDARD COSTING I

- Explain the uses of standard costs and the methods by which they are derived and subsequently reviewed
- Calculate and evaluate capacity limitations when setting standards
- Describe the types of standard (ideal, attainable, current and basic), and their behavioural implications
- Calculate basic labour, material, overhead (variable and fixed) and sales variances, including problems of labour idle time
- Explain the reasons for variances
- Assess appropriate management action arising from the variances identified

22 STANDARD COSTING II

- Prepare reconciliations using operating statements which
  - reconcile budgeted and actual profit figures, and/or
  - reconcile the actual sales less the standard cost of sales with the actual profit
- Calculate and explain operational and planning variances
- Demonstrate how absorption and marginal approaches can be used in standard costing
- Calculate mix and yield variances for materials
- Calculate mix and quantity variances for sales
- Demonstrate an understanding of the inter-relationship between variances
- Explain the reasons for variances
- Assess appropriate management action arising from the variance identified

23 BUDGET PLANNING AND CONTROL I

- Identify the purposes of budgetary planning and control systems
- Describe the planning and control cycle, and the control process
- Explain the implications of controllability for responsibility reporting
- Prepare, review and explain a budget preparation timetable
- Prepare and evaluate functional, subsidiary and master budgets, including cash budgeting
- Explain the processes involved with the development and implementation of budgets
- Explain the process of participation in budget setting and how this can address motivational problems

24 BUDGET PLANNING AND CONTROL II

- Prepare and evaluate fixed and flexible budgets and evaluate the resulting variances
- Prepare flexed budgets when standard fixed overhead absorption is employed
- Assess the behavioural implications of budget control and performance evaluation, including participation in budget setting

25 BUDGET PLANNING AND CONTROL III

- Describe and evaluate the main features of zero based budgeting systems
- Describe the areas/organisations in which zero based budgeting may be applied
- Describe and evaluate incremental budgeting and discuss the differences with zero based budgeting
- Describe and evaluate periodic and continuous budgeting systems

26 QUANTITATIVE AIDS TO BUDGETING

- Describe and apply the techniques of
  - least squares regression
  - scatter diagrams and correlation
  - forecasting with least squares regression
  - time series to identify trends and seasonality
  - forecasting with time series
- Evaluate the results of quantitative aids

27 COSTS AND DECISION MAKING

- Describe and distinguish between relevant and non-relevant costs
- Apply and evaluate limiting factor analysis
- Evaluate make or buy problems, shutdown decisions, additional shift decisions and overtime, accepting or rejecting special orders, and further processing
- Describe and apply cost-volume-profit analysis
- Describe and evaluate different product pricing approaches

28 REVISION

THE EXAM PAPER

Approach to examining the syllabus

The examination is a **three hour paper in two sections.** Financial management issues will always, but not exclusively, be examined in Section A. The Section A question will typically be a scenario based question. Most of the Section B questions will contain a mix of computation and discursive elements although it is intended that at least one question will be entirely discursive. The balance between computation and discursive elements will remain largely constant from one examination to the next.

		Number of marks
Section A:	One compulsory scenario-based question	50
Section B:	Choice of 2 from 4 question (25 marks each)	50
		100

Additional information

Present value and annuity tables will be provided in the examination. The Study Guide provides more detailed guidance on the syllabus.
The Study Guide provides more detailed guidance on the syllabus. Examinable documents are listed in the 'Exam Notes' section of the *Students' Newsletter*.

Analysis of past paper

Decermber 2001

Section A

1 Net present value; sensitivity analysis; business risk

Section B

2 Standard costing; non-financial objectives
3 Decision making involving opportunity costs; finance for small to medium-size enterprises
4 Working capital funding; factoring; credit control
5 Costing in a not-for-profit organisation

Pilot paper

Section A

1 Working capital management; cash budgeting; cash and treasury management

Section B

2 Assessment of growth and liquidity; sources of finance for small business
3 Replacement of assets; limitations of NPV
4 Basic and more complex variance analysis
5 Activity based costing

OXFORD BROOKES BSc (Hons) IN APPLIED ACCOUNTING

The standard required of candidates completing Part 2 is that required in the final year of a UK degree. Students completing Parts 1 and 2 will have satisfied the examination requirement for an honours degree in Applied Accounting, awarded by Oxford Brookes University.

To achieve the degree, you must also submit two pieces of work based on a **Research and Analysis Project.**

- A 5,000 word **Report** on your chosen topic, which demonstrates that you have acquired the necessary research, analytical and IT skills.
- A 1,500 word **Key Skills Statement,** indicating how you have developed your interpersonal and communication skills.

BPP was selected by the ACCA and Oxford Brookes University to produce the official text *Success in your Research and Analysis Project* to support students in this task. The book pays particular attention to key skills not covered in the professional examinations.

> AN ORDER FORM FOR THE NEW SYLLABUS MATERIAL, INCLUDING THE OXFORD BROOKES PROJECT TEXT, CAN BE FOUND AT THE END OF THIS STUDY TEXT.

OXFORD INSTITUTE OF INTERNATIONAL FINANCE MBA

The ACCA and Oxford Brookes University have set up the Oxford Institute of International Finance to provide an MBA programme. BPP has been appointed the provider of materials and electronic support. This new qualification has been available worldwide from January 2002.

The MBA is available to those who have completed the professional stage of the ACCA qualification (subject to when this was achieved), as the ACCA's Professional exams contribute credits towards the MBA award.

The qualification features an introductory module (*Markets, Management and Strategy*). This is followed by modules on *Global Business Strategy*, *Managing Self Development* and *Organisational Change and Transformation*. The MBA is completed by a *research dissertation*.

For further information, please see the Oxford Institute's website: **www.oxfordinstitute.org**

Part A

Costing systems and techniques

Chapter 1

COST AND MANAGEMENT ACCOUNTING

Topic list		Syllabus reference
1	**Management accounting and management**	**6(a)**
2	**Management accounting**	**6(a)**
3	**Cost accounting**	**6(a)**
4	**Costing**	**6(a)**

Introduction

Welcome to Financial Management and Control. As you will already be aware if you have read through the introduction to this Study Text (and if you have not you are strongly advised to do so before going any further), *Financial Management and Control* examines two related subjects, **management accounting** and **financial management**. We will be studying management accounting in the first fourteen chapters of this Study Text, financial management being the subject of the remaining part of the text.

This chapter serves as an introduction both to management accounting and the role of the management accountant.

In the following chapters we will be looking at the methods and techniques employed by the management accountant to fulfil that role.

Study guide

Section 18 – Costing systems: context and framework

- Outline and distinguish between the nature and scope of management accounting and the role of costing in meeting the needs of management
- Describe the purpose of costing as an aid to planning, monitoring and controlling business activity

Exam guide

This chapter serves as an introduction and framework for the remainder of your study of management accounting, but you could get a discursive Section B question on the role of management accounting in a particular type of organisation, say.

The issues covered in this chapter are useful background to the Oxford Brookes degree Research and Analysis Project Topic 10, which requires you to analyse how management accounting techniques are used to support decision making in organisations.

1 MANAGEMENT ACCOUNTING AND MANAGEMENT

The role of management

1.1 Have you ever wondered what those elevated beings do? You know who I mean. Elevated beings. Managers. So, what do they do? Difficult question if you are under their control. Easier, of course, if you just happen to be one of them.

1.2 If you are under their control you may think managers take long expensive lunches, have long exotic holidays, make long personal telephone calls, do little work, make little effort and treat you with little more than contempt. But if you are a manager, you probably think you work very hard, all you do is work very hard and nobody who works for you works very hard at all.

1.3 If you are having trouble defining the role of management, think about your management role. 'What role?', you may be thinking. Well, we are all managers of our lives. So what should we do to be effective managers of our lives?

You as a manager

1.4 Imagine your normal working day. There is little point in waking up each weekday and just hoping that you will find some washed and ironed clothes in your wardrobe, that some milk will have magically appeared in your fridge, that a bus which might happen to pass will get you to the office on time or that you will be able to fly off to the Caribbean on holiday. **You have to plan** for these things. They don't just happen. You have to plan to ensure that you have the appropriate resources (milk, clean and ironed clothes, timely transport and cash) to enable you to live.

1.5 What else do you do while managing your daily life? How many of us can afford to jump in a helicopter to go to work. Most of us are stuck with the bus, tube, train or car. What would happen if you decided to be extremely extravagant and chartered a helicopter every morning to take you to work. Your dream holiday to the Caribbean might then be out of the window. A lack of control over spending means that plans you might have made (for a holiday to the Caribbean) never come to fruition. So **you have to control what you do** to ensure that you can stick to your plans.

1.6 Suppose that you share a house with three other friends. What would happen if you made no decision as to who would do the cleaning, who would clean the toilet and who would put the bin bags out for the dustmen to collect. There would be chaos! Unless you like living in chaos, organisation is needed to share out household duties equally so that your house does not resemble the camel house at London Zoo. If you want to be able to walk around your home barefoot without worrying about what you might step in, **you need to organise yourself and others.**

1.7 Imagine you really fancy a few drinks in the pub after work. Your work colleagues are totally apathetic about the idea. They would rather go home and watch Coronation Street. How do you get them to do what you want them to do? You entice them with thoughts of good company, tomato juice and packets of crisps. You attempt to make them see that it really would be much better for them to accompany you to the pub than to slump in front of the television. In short **you motivate them.**

1.8 There is one common activity running through the various aspects of managing your life, however. You have to decide what mode of transport to take to work, where to go on holiday, who cleans the toilet and who washes up and what drink to have in the pub. A great part of managing your life obviously involves making decisions. Indeed, **it is difficult to plan, control, organise or motivate without making decisions.**

1.9 What does managing your life therefore involve?

- Planning
- Controlling
- Motivating
- Organising
- Decision making

1.10 This is exactly what those elevated beings have to do to manage you, your organisation's products, your organisation's financial position and your organisation's public image.

(a) **Planning**

Management have to **plan for both the short term and the long term.** A long-range plan is necessary in order to anticipate any future needs or opportunities that require action to be taken either now or in the near future. For example, management may need to consider building a new factory to meet future anticipated increased demand for a product. Management should constantly be **thinking ahead**. They should **never be surprised by any gradual developments.** The organisation's long-term objectives (such as building a new factory) are converted into a succession of short-term plans of action in the form of annual budgets.

(b) **Controlling**

Control enables management to see whether the organisation's long-term objectives are achievable and involves **comparing actual performance with the short-term plans** so that deviations from these short-term plans can be identified and corrective action taken to ensure that the long-term objectives are possible. If it is clear the long-term objectives are not achievable, the objectives can be changed before any serious damage to the company's future occurs.

(c) **Organising**

Organising involves establishing a **framework within which necessary activities can be performed,** designating an individual to be responsible for a particular activity and **defining managers' responsibilities**. It requires a breakdown of the organisation into manageable sections such as departments and the **coordination of activities** in these sections if the organisation's objectives are to be met.

(d) **Motivating**

Managers need to **influence employees to act in such a manner that the employees' objectives and the organisation's objectives are the same.**

(e) **Decision making**

Management is decision taking. Managers of all levels take decisions.

(i) Decisions taken at the **strategic level set or change the objectives or strategic targets of an organisation**. They include decisions about the selection of products and markets, the required levels of company profitability, the purchase or disposal of major fixed assets and so on.

(ii) **Tactical-level decisions** are concerned with the **efficient and effective use of an organisation's resources** (the '4Ms': men, materials, machines and money). They therefore include setting budgets for sales, production and so on and setting measures of performance by which results can be gauged.

(iii) **Operational-level decisions** are concerned with **ensuring that specific tasks are carried out effectively and efficiently**. They might include decisions concerning the allocation of particular staff to particular tasks or jobs.

Meeting the needs of management

1.11 Just as you manage your life so that you get what want (your objectives), managers manage the organisation so that the organisation's objectives are achieved. Having considered how the manager manages, let us look at how the management accountant can assist the manager to manage.

(a) **Assistance in planning**

The management accountant assists planning **by providing information**. This information may be about pricing, product costs or competition. In the short-term planning process of budgeting, the management accountant provides invaluable information on past costs and revenues and he is also deeply involved in the budgeting process itself. He establishes budget procedures, provides a budget timetable, coordinates and ensures the harmonisation of all subsidiary budgets and uses the subsidiary budgets to prepare the master budget.

(b) **Assistance in controlling**

The management accountant **supplies performance reports which compare actual performance with planned performance and which therefore highlight those activities which are not conforming to plan.**

(c) **Assistance in organising**

By **ensuring that the accounting system is tailored to the organisational structure**, the management accountant helps to reinforce the objectives of the organisational framework.

(d) **Assistance in motivating**

Because formalised targets are more likely to motivate than vague and uncertain comments, **budgets prepared by the management accountant should motivate managers and subordinates** to achieve the organisation's objectives. **Performance reports produced by the management accountant** for the control process are also intended to motivate individual performances by communicating performance information in relation to the targets which have been set. As we shall see, however, budgets and performance reports can cause serious behavioural problems and can be demotivating if used without knowledge of the problems which can occur.

(e) **Assistance in decision making**

The **management accountant collects data about the various options available and analyses that data into information so that management can make an informed decision about the most appropriate course of action.** For example, suppose a component that an organisation currently manufactures in-house can now be purchased from a supplier. The management accountant provides information about the various costs and benefits associated with each option so that management can choose whether to buy-in the component or manufacture it in-house.

1.12 We will be examining the way in which the management accountant provides this assistance in great detail and so you will have a much fuller understanding of how the management accountant fulfils his role by the time you have completed the text.

Question 1

Have a chat with some managers in your organisation. What do they do? Do they plan, control, organise, motivate and make decisions? How do they do this? Why do they do this? Are they successful in what they are doing and if not, why not?

2 MANAGEMENT ACCOUNTING

2.1 Having looked at how management accounting can meet the needs of management, we will now look at the discipline in more general terms.

KEY TERM

Management accounting is the application of the principles of accounting and financial management to create, protect, preserve and increase value so as to deliver that value to the stakeholders of profit and not-for-profit enterprises, both public and private.

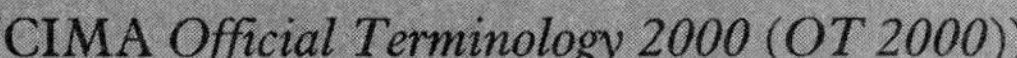

(CIMA *Official Terminology 2000* (*OT 2000*))

2.2 The *Official Terminology* continues as follows.

Management accounting is an integral part of management, requiring the identification, generation, presentation, interpretation and use of information relevant to:

- Formulating business strategy
- Planning and controlling activities
- Decision-making
- Efficient resource usage
- Performance improvement and value enhancement
- Safeguarding tangible and intangible assets
- Corporate governance and internal control

2.3 To assist with management planning, control and decision making, management accounting therefore deals principally with **gathering of data** from both internal and external sources and **analysing, processing, interpreting** and **communicating the resulting information.**

Exam focus point

In the exam you may be asked to describe the role of the management accountant within a particular setting.

3 COST ACCOUNTING

3.1 There are many different opinions on the distinction between management accounting and cost accounting.

(a) Drury (*Management and Cost Accounting)* claims that 'Cost accounting is concerned with cost accumulation for stock valuation to meet the requirements of external reporting, whereas management accounting relates to the provision of appropriate information for people within the organisation to help them make better decisions'.

(b) Lucey (*Costing*) states that 'there are similarities between the objectives of both management and cost accounting and indeed in practice there is no true dividing line. In general, management accounting is wider in scope and uses more advanced

techniques. However, a fundamental requirement for management accounting is the existence of a sound costing system to provide basic data'.

(c) Horngren, Foster, Datar (*Cost Accounting: A Managerial Emphasis*) are of the opinion that 'Cost accounting provides information for both management accounting and financial accounting. It measures and reports financial and non-financial information that relates to the cost of acquiring or consuming resources by an organisation. Cost accounting includes those parts of management accounting and financial accounting where cost information is collected or analysed'.

(d) CIMA in the *Official Terminology* provide a more detailed definition: 'The establishment of budgets, standard costs and actual costs of operations, processes, activities or products; and the analysis of variances, profitability or the social use of funds.'

3.2 There is therefore no right or wrong definition of cost accounting. Here's ours!

KEY TERM

Cost accounting is a management information system which analyses past, present and future data to provide a bank of data for the management accountant to use.

3.3 Cost accounting aims **to provide the answers to** the following types of questions.

(a) (i) **What has been the cost** of goods produced or services provided?
(ii) **What have revenues** been?

Knowing about costs and revenues that are being/have been incurred and earned **enables management** to do the following.

(i) **Assess the profitability** of a product, service or department.
(ii) **Set selling prices** with some regard for the costs of sale.
(iii) Put a **value to stocks of goods** that are still held in store at the end of a period.

(b) **What are the future costs of goods and services** (and operations and so on) likely to be? Costing is an integral part of budgeting (planning) for the future.

(c) **How do actual costs compare with budgeted costs?** If an organisation's revenues and costs turn out to be different from those planned, the differences can be measured and reported. Management can use these reports as a guide to whether corrective or 'control' action is needed to sort out a problem revealed by these differences. This is often referred to as budgetary control.

(d) **What information does management need in order to make sensible decisions about profits and costs?**

4 COSTING

4.1 Although CIMA in the *Official Terminology* warns that 'use of the term "costing" is not recommended except with a qualifying adjective eg standard costing', it does actually provide the following definition.

KEY TERM

Costing is the process of determining the costs of products, services or activities.

4.2 The *Official Terminology* then lists the following methods of costing, the vast majority of which we will be looking at in the remainder of the Study Text.

- Absorption costing (Chapter 2)
- Marginal costing (Chapter 2)
- Specific order costing (Chapter 4)
- Job costing (Chapter 4)
- Batch costing (Chapter 4)
- Contract costing (Chapter 4)
- Continuous operation/process costing (Chapter 5)
- Service/function costing (Chapter 5)
- Standard costing (Chapter 6)
- Uniform costing

4.3 Given the definition of cost accounting we have adopted above, **use of** the above **costing methods** to provide information (such as the estimated cost of job X) is part of **cost accounting. Use of that information** (such as whether or not to proceed with job X given estimated costs) is part of **management accounting.**

4.4 In your earlier studies you have seen how to use various costing methods. In this text we will be looking in more detail at how to use those costing methods and considering how to use the resulting information.

Exam focus point

One of the stated aims of the 2.4 syllabus is that you will be able to identify and implement appropriate costing methods. Work through Chapters 1 – 14 of this text and you will!

The importance of flexibility

4.5 The costing systems used by an organisation need to provide information for a **wide variety of purposes** in a **wide range of organisations** (including not-for-profit organisations, covered in Chapter 5).

Flexibility and cost accumulation and profit reporting

4.6 In Chapters 2 and 3 we will look at the costing approaches (absorption costing, marginal costing, activity based costing, opportunity costing) to accumulating costs and reporting profit and the impact that these can have on the figures produced.

Flexibility and decision making

4.7 Management face a wide variety of decisions on an hourly, daily, weekly and monthly basis.

(a) **Routine planning decisions**, for example, budgeting. Budgeting decisions commonly analyse fixed and variable costs, together with revenues, over a one-year period. They are also often concerned with how to make the best use of scarce resources.

(b) **Short-run problem decisions**, typically, unforeseen 'one-off' special decisions of a non-recurring nature, where the costs and benefits are all obtained within a relatively short period. For example, should a contract be accepted or rejected? What price should be quoted in the tender for a contract?

(c) **Investment or disinvestment decisions**, for example should an item of equipment be purchased? Should a department be shut down? Decisions of this nature often have long-term consequences, so that the 'time value of money' must be allowed for, and discounted cash flow techniques applied.

(d) **Longer-range decisions**, meaning decisions made once and reviewed infrequently, but which are intended to provide a continuing solution to a continuing or recurring problem. They include decisions about selling and distribution policies (such as whether goods should be sold through middlemen or direct to customers? What type of customer should the sales force attempt to attract? What should the company's discount policies be? Should a new product or service be launched?)

(e) **Control decisions**, for example, should disappointing performance be investigated, given that the benefits expected must exceed the costs from investigation and control?

It should be clear from the examples given that the management accountant will frequently be involved in providing information for business decisions of all kinds. Costing systems therefore need to be sufficiently flexible to provide the required information.

4.8 As we will see in Part D of this text, however, the accounting information required for decision making is different from the accounting information recorded in the books of financial accounts and conventional cost accounts. For cost accounting most UK companies still use **absorption costing** but this provides totally **misleading decision information.**

4.9 For example, suppose that a sales manager has an item of product which he is having difficulty in selling. Its historical full cost is £80, made up of variable costs of £50 and fixed costs of £30. A customer offers £60 for it.

(a) If there is no other customer for the product, **£60 would be better than nothing** and the product should be sold to improve income and profit by this amount.

(b) If the company has spare production capacity which would otherwise not be used, it would be profitable to continue making more of the same product, if customers are willing to pay £60 for each extra unit made. The additional costs are only £50 so that the profit would be increased marginally by £10 per unit produced.

(c) In **absorption costing terms**, the **product makes a loss of £20**, which would **discourage the sales manager from accepting a price of £60** from the customer. His decision would be a bad one.

(i) If the product is **not sold** for £60, it will presumably be scrapped eventually, so the **choice** is really between making a **loss in absorption costing terms of £20, or a loss of £80 when the stock is written off,** whenever this happens.

(ii) If there is **demand** for some extra units at £60 each, the absorption costing loss would be £20 per unit, but at the end of the year there would be an **additional contribution** to overheads and profit of £10 per unit. In terms of absorption costing the under-absorbed overhead would be reduced by £30 for each extra unit made and sold.

4.10 Thus, for **once-only decisions or decisions affecting the use of marginal spare capacity, absorption costing information about unit profits is irrelevant.** On the other hand, since total contribution must be sufficient to cover the fixed costs of the business, **marginal costing would be unsuitable as a basis for establishing long-term sales prices for all output.** In general, for decision-making purposes, **relevant costing** is required.

Flexibility and performance evaluation

4.11 Performance evaluation entails setting targets, recording actual performance and comparing this to target performance. This sounds straightforward enough, doesn't it? The **identification of appropriate performance measures** to affect the appropriate behavioural response is often **difficult,** however, and **costing systems** are often **unable to provide** the target and actual **information.** For example, if divisional management are appraised using a profit figure which includes non-controllable costs at division level and apportioned group costs and/or the costing system is unable to provide a figure for controllable profit, a negative motivational impact is likely. We consider these issues more fully throughout the text.

4.12 What should now be clear is that **costing systems** need to be **flexible** enough to provide **different costs for different purposes.**

Question 2

Wilton, Pearce & Co, a medium-sized firm of architects, are about to absorb Butcher & Partners, a similar sized firm. They have engaged you as management accountant. Part of your duties will be to review the cost and management accounting function of the combined practice and to recruit an assistant. You have an appointment with the senior partner to discuss these issues.

Required

Jot down notes to use in tomorrow's meeting which cover the following points.

(a) The functions of cost and management accounting
(b) The personal attributes you would expect the assistant management accountant to possess

Answer

(a) Cost and management accounting involve providing and interpreting internal accounting information for managers to use for the following purposes.

   (i) **Planning the organisation's activities in the short, medium and long term**. For example, the management accounting system should provide information which will allow management to plan the future activities of the new, larger business.

   (ii) **Controlling the activities of the organisation**. Management will have to learn to control a larger business. They will therefore need control reports so that they can compare actual results against plans or budgets. Action can then be taken to correct any differences between actual and plan and to help the organisation to continue in the direction set out by the plans.

   (iii) **Making decisions**. For example, information will be needed for pricing architectural contracts for tendering purposes.

   (iv) **Performance appraisal, both financial and non-financial**. For example, information on the percentage of jobs completed on time, percentage of successful tenders and so on should be provided.

(b) (i) Be training for or already possess a professional **qualification** in management accountancy.

   (ii) Be highly **numerate.**

   (iii) Have excellent knowledge of the cost and management accounting **information requirements** of a large architects' business.

   (iv) Be able to critically **appraise the existing systems and information** to ensure their relevance to the future.

   (v) Have excellent **communication skills**, particularly because of the uncertainty caused by the changes taking place. He must be able to explain and interpret management accounting information for employees who have little or no financial background.

   (vi) Be **flexible** and **self-motivating**. For example he/she must be willing to leave their office desk and visit sites when necessary.

(vii) Possess **management perspective** as well as being technically competent.

Of course you may have thought of completely different points to those noted above. The purpose of this question was to get you thinking about management accounting.

Chapter roundup

- **Management accounting** deals principally with the gathering of data from both internal and external sources and analysing, processing, interpreting and communicating the resulting information within the organisation to aid the management processes of planning, controlling, organising and motivating.
- **Cost accounting** provides a bank of data for the management accountant to use.
- **Costing** is the process of determining the costs of products, services or activities.
- **Costing systems** must be flexible enough to provide different costs for different purposes.

Quick quiz

1 *Match the type of decision with the appropriate description.*

Reasons

(a) Strategic level
(b) Tactical level
(c) Operational level

Descriptions

(1) Set or change the objectives of an organisation
(2) Ensure that specific tasks are carried out effectively and efficiently
(3) Concerned with the efficient and effective use of the '4 Ms'

2 Should the following tasks be classified as management accounting or cost accounting?

Tasks	*Management accounting*	*Cost accounting*
Valuation of stock using absorption costing		
Preparation of budgets		
Analysis of information about various decision options		
Valuation of output of a continuous process		
Setting of standard costs		
Preparation of performance reports		

3 Here are some terms you should have encountered in your earlier studies. *Match the term to the definition.*

Terms

Direct cost
Prime cost
Overhead
Classification by function
Fixed cost
Variable cost
Product cost
Avoidable cost
Controllable cost
Relevant cost
Cost centre
Cost unit

Definitions

(a) Specific costs of, say, an activity, which would not be incurred if the activity did not exist

(b) Total of direct costs

(c) Future cash flow which will be changed as the result of a decision

(d) Product produced by an organisation

(e) Dividing costs into production, administration, selling and distribution, research and development and financing costs

(f) Cost that can be traced in full to whatever is being costed

(g) Organisation's departments

(h) A cost that varies with the level of output

(i) A cost that is incurred in the course of making a product but which cannot be traced directly and in full to the product

(j) Cost that is incurred for a particular period of time and which, within certain activity levels, is unaffected by changes in the level of activity

(k) Cost identified with goods produced or purchased for resale and initially included in the value of stock

(l) Cost which can be influenced by management decisions and actions

Answers to quick quiz

1 (a) (1)
(b) (3)
(c) (2)

2

Tasks	*Management accounting*	*Cost accounting*
Valuation of stock using absorption costing		✓
Preparation of budgets	✓	
Analysis of information about various decision options	✓	
Valuation of output of a continuous process		✓
Setting of standard costs		✓
Preparation of performance reports	✓	

3

Direct cost	(f)
Prime cost	(b)
Overhead	(i)
Classification by function	(e)
Fixed cost	(j)
Variable cost	(h)
Product cost	(k)
Avoidable cost	(a)
Controllable cost	(l)
Relevant cost	(c)
Cost centre	(g)
Cost unit	(d)

Now try the question below from the Exam Question Bank

Question to try	Level	Marks	Time
1	Exam	25	45 mins

Chapter 2

ABSORPTION AND MARGINAL COSTING

	Topic list	Syllabus reference
1	**The problem of overheads**	**7(a)(i)**
2	**A revision of absorption costing**	**7(a)(i)**
3	**Overhead apportionment**	**7(a)(i)**
4	**Overhead absorption**	**7(a)(i)**
5	**Marginal costing**	**6(e), 6(f), 7(a)(i)**
6	**Reconciling the profit figures given by the two methods**	**7(a)(i)**
7	**Absorption costing and marginal costing compared**	**6(e), 6(f), 7(a)(i)**

Introduction

As we saw in the previous chapter, cost accounting is used to determine the cost of products, jobs or services (whatever the organisation happens to be involved in). Such costs have to be built up using a process known as **cost accumulation.**

In your earlier studies you will have learnt how to accumulate the various cost elements which make up total cost. If you have forgotten, the following diagram of an **absorption costing** cost accumulation system should jog your memory.

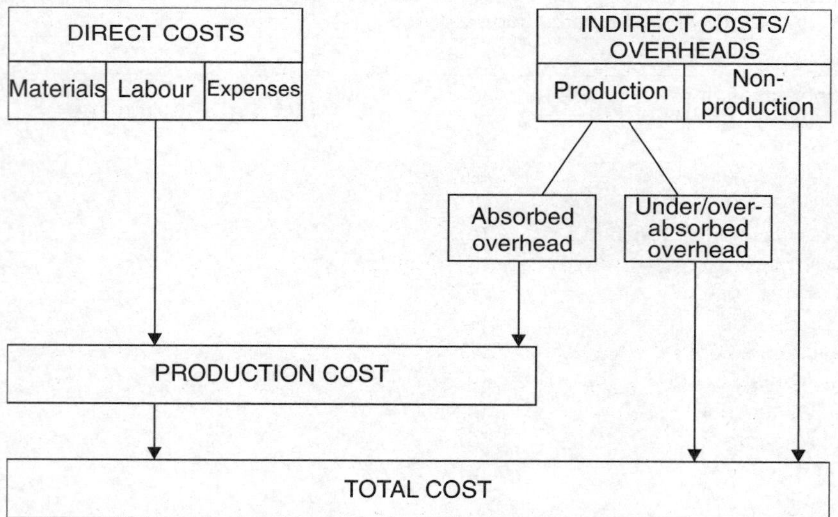

Remember that under a **marginal costing** system the production overhead absorbed would be variable production overhead only.

In this chapter we will be both building on your existing knowledge and seeing how the techniques which you have already learnt can be applied in more complex situations. This is quite a long chapter but much of what we cover will be familiar to you so working through it won't be too arduous.

In Chapter 3 we will be looking at some other techniques for allocating and apportioning costs.

Study guide

Section 18 – Costing systems: context and framework

- Explain the potential for different costing approaches to influence cost accumulation and profit reporting
- Explain the role of costing systems in decision making

Section 19 – Cost accumulation I

- Explain the requirement to allocate overheads
- Describe, explain and apply absorption and marginal costing
- Reconcile the resulting profits/losses from absorption and marginal costing
- Evaluate the relative advantages and disadvantages of different costing approaches

Exam guide

Absorption costing and marginal costing could appear in Section A (with other topics) or in Section B.

A Section B question might cover absorption costing or marginal costing or could ask you to compare and contrast the results of applying both methods. Alternatively they might need to be used as the appropriate cost accumulation methods within a question on another syllabus area.

1 THE PROBLEM OF OVERHEADS

1.1 If a company manufactures a product, the cost of the product will include the cost of the raw materials and components used in it and cost of the labour effort required to make it. These are **direct costs** of the product. The company would, however, incur many other costs in making the product, which are not directly attributable to a single product, but which are incurred generally in the process of manufacturing a large number of product units. These are **indirect costs** or **overheads**. Such costs include the following.

- Factory rent and rates
- Machine depreciation
- Supervision costs
- Heating and lighting

KEY TERMS

A **direct cost** is a cost that can be traced in full to the product, service or department that is being costed.

An **indirect cost** or **overhead** is a cost that is incurred in the course of making a product, providing a service or running a department, but which cannot be traced directly and in full to the product, service or department.

In some companies, the overheads cost might greatly exceed the direct production costs.

1.2 It might seem unreasonable to ignore indirect costs entirely when accumulating the costs of making a product, and yet there **cannot be a completely satisfactory way of sharing out indirect costs** between the many different items of production which benefit from them.

Using absorption costing to deal with the problem of overheads

1.3 Traditionally, the view has been that a fair share of overheads should be added to the cost of units produced. This fair share will **include a portion of all production overhead expenditure** and possibly administration and marketing overheads too. This is the view embodied in the principles of **absorption costing.**

1.4 The **theoretical justification** for using absorption costing is that all production overheads are incurred in the production of the organisation's output and so each unit of the product receives some benefit from these costs. Each unit of output should therefore be charged with some of the overhead costs.

1.5 The **practical reasons** for using absorption costing are as follows.

(a) **Stock valuations**

Stock in hand must be valued for two reasons.

(i) For the closing stock figure in the balance sheet
(ii) For the cost of sales figure in the profit and loss account

The valuation of stocks will affect profitability during a period because of the way in which the cost of sales is calculated.

	The cost of goods produced
+	the value of opening stocks
–	the value of closing stocks
=	the cost of goods sold.

(b) **Pricing decisions**

Many companies attempt to set selling prices **by calculating the full cost of production or sales** of each product, and then adding a margin for profit. 'Full cost plus pricing' can be particularly useful for companies which do jobbing or contract work, where each job or contract is different, so that a standard unit sales price cannot be fixed. Without using absorption costing, a full cost is difficult to ascertain.

(c) **Establishing the profitability of different products**

This argument in favour of absorption costing states that if a company sells more than one product, it will be difficult to judge **how profitable each individual product is,** unless overhead costs are shared on a fair basis and charged to the cost of sales of each product.

1.6 Of these three arguments, the problem of valuing stocks is perhaps the most significant. **Absorption costing is recommended in financial accounting** by the *Statement of standard accounting practice* on stocks and long-term contracts (SSAP 9). SSAP 9 deals with financial accounting systems and not with cost accounting systems. The cost accountant is (in theory) free to value stocks by whatever method seems best, but where companies integrate their financial accounting and cost accounting systems into a single system of accounting records, the valuation of closing stocks will be determined by SSAP 9.

1.7 SSAP 9 states that costs of all stocks should comprise those costs which have been incurred in the normal course of business in **bringing the product to its 'present location and condition'**. These costs incurred will include all related production overheads, even though these overheads may accrue on a time basis. In other words, in financial accounting, closing stocks should be valued at full factory cost, and it may therefore be convenient and appropriate to value stocks by the same method in the cost accounting system.

1.8 For many purposes absorption costing is, however, less useful as a costing method than marginal costing. In some situations, **absorption costing can be misleading** in the information it supplies.

Using marginal costing to deal with the problem of overheads

1.9 Advocates of **marginal costing** take the view that only the variable costs of making and selling a product or service should be identified. **Fixed costs should be dealt with separately** and treated as a cost of the accounting period rather than shared out somehow between units produced. Some overhead costs are, however, variable costs which increase as the total level of activity rises and so the marginal cost of production and sales should include an amount for variable overheads.

2 A REVISION OF ABSORPTION COSTING

KEY TERM

Absorption costing is a method of product costing which aims to include in the total cost of a product (unit, job and so on) an appropriate share of an organisation's total overhead, which is generally taken to mean an amount which reflects the amount of time and effort that has gone into producing the product.

2.1 You should have covered absorption costing in your earlier studies. We will therefore summarise the simpler points of the topic but will go into some detail on the more complex areas to refresh your memory.

Knowledge brought forward from earlier studies

Absorption costing

- Product costs are built up using absorption costing by a process of **allocation**, **apportionment** and **overhead absorption**.
- **Allocation** is the process by which whole cost items are charged directly to a cost unit or cost centre. **Direct costs** are allocated directly to cost units. **Overheads** clearly identifiable with cost centres are allocated to those cost centres but costs which cannot be identified with one particular cost centre are allocated to general overhead cost centres. The cost of a warehouse security guard would therefore be charged to the warehouse cost centre but heating and lighting costs would be charged to a general overhead cost centre.
- The **first stage of overhead apportionment** involves sharing out (or apportioning) the overheads within **general overhead cost centres** between the other cost centres using a fair basis of apportionment (such as floor area occupied by each cost centre for heating and lighting costs).
- The **second stage of overhead apportionment** is to apportion the costs of **service cost centres** (both directly allocated and apportioned costs) to production cost centres.
- The final stage in absorption costing is the **absorption** into product costs (using overhead absorption rates) of the overheads which have been allocated and apportioned to the production cost centres.
- Costs allocated and apportioned to non-production cost centres are usually deducted from the full cost of production to arrive at the cost of sales.

Question 1

Briefly discuss the type of factors which could affect the choice of the bases an organisation can use to apportion service department costs.

Answer

(a) The type of service being provided
(b) The amount of overhead expenditure involved
(c) The number of departments benefiting from the service
(d) The ability to be able to produce realistic estimates of the usage of the service
(e) The resulting costs and benefits

Question 2

A company is preparing its production overhead budgets and determining the apportionment of those overheads to products. Cost centre expenses and related information have been budgeted as follows.

	Total	*Machine shop A*	*Machine shop B*	*Assembly*	*Canteen*	*Mainten-ance*
	£	£	£	£	£	£
Indirect wages	78,560	8,586	9,190	15,674	29,650	15,460
Consumable materials	16,900	6,400	8,700	1,200	600	-
Rent and rates	16,700					
Buildings insurance	2,400					
Power	8,600					
Heat and light	3,400					
Depreciation (machinery)	40,200					
Value of machinery	402,000	201,000	179,000	22,000	-	-
Power usage (%)	100	55	40	3	-	2
Direct labour (hours)	35,000	8,000	6,200	20,800	-	-
Machine usage (hours)	25,200	7,200	18,000	-	-	-
Area (sq ft)	45,000	10,000	12,000	15,000	6,000	2,000

Required

Using the direct apportionment to production departments method and bases of apportionment which you consider most appropriate from the information provided, calculate overhead totals for the three production departments.

Answer

	Total	*A*	*B*	*Assembly*	*Canteen*	*Maintenance*	*Basis of apportionment*
	£	£	£	£	£	£	
Indirect wages	78,560	8,586	9,190	15,674	29,650	15,460	Actual
Consumable materials	16,900	6,400	8,700	1,200	600	-	Actual
Rent and rates	16,700	3,711	4,453	5,567	2,227	742	Area
Insurance	2,400	533	640	800	320	107	Area
Power	8,600	4,730	3,440	258	-	172	Usage
Heat and light	3,400	756	907	1,133	453	151	Area
Depreciation	40,200	20,100	17,900	2,200	-	-	Val of mach
	166,760	44,816	45,230	26,832	33,250	16,632	
Reallocate	-	7,600	5,890	19,760	(33,250)	-	Direct labour
Reallocate	-	4,752	11,880	-	-	(16,632)	Mach usage
Totals	166,760	57,168	63,000	46,592	-	-	

3 OVERHEAD APPORTIONMENT

3.1 In Question 2 above the costs of the canteen were allocated only to production departments, and not to maintenance, even though employees working in maintenance are as likely to use the canteen as anyone else and it is quite possible for the ovens and other machines in the kitchen to require maintenance.

3.2 It could therefore be argued that a **fair sharing** of service department costs is not possible unless consideration is given to the work done by each service department for other service department (**reciprocal services) are taken into account.**

3.3 For example, suppose a company has two production and two service departments. The following information about activity in the recent costing period is available.

	Production departments *A*	*B*	*Stores department*	*Maintenance department*
Overhead costs	£10,030	£8,970	£10,000	£8,000
Number of material requisitions	300	500	-	200
Maintenance hours needed	8,000	1,000	1,000	

If service department overheads were apportioned directly to production departments, the apportionment would be as follows.

Service department	*Basis of apportionment*	*Total cost*		*A*		*B*
		£		£		£
Stores	Material requisitions	10,000	(3/8)	3,750	(5/8)	6,250
Maintenance	Maintenance hours	8,000	(8/9)	7,111	(1/9)	889
		18,000		10,861		7,139
Overheads of departments A and B		19,000		10,030		8,970
		37,000		20,891		16,109

Suppose, however, recognition is made of the fact that the stores and maintenance department do work for each other, and the basis of apportionment remains the same.

	Dept A	*Dept B*	*Stores*	*Maint.*
Stores (100%)	30%	50%	-	20%
Maintenance (100%)	80%	10%	10%	-

3.4. This may be done using one of the following methods.

(a) **The repeated distribution method**
(b) **The simultaneous equation (algebraic) method**
(c) **The step-wise (elimination) method**

Repeated distribution method

3.5

	Dept A	*Dept B*	*Stores*	*Maint.*
	£	£	£	£
Overhead costs	10,030	8,970	10,000	8,000
Apportion stores costs * (30%/50%/20%)	3,000	5,000	(10,000)	2,000
			0	10,000
Apportion maintenance costs (80%/10%/10%)	8,000	1,000	1,000	(10,000)
			1,000	0
Repeat: Apportion stores	300	500	(1,000)	200
Repeat: Apportion maintenance	160	20	20	(200)
Repeat: Apportion stores	6	10	(20)	4
Repeat: Apportion maintenance **	4	-	-	(4)
	21,500	15,500	0	0

* The first apportionment could have been the costs of maintenance, rather than stores; there is no difference to the final results.

** When service department costs become small numbers (here £4) the final apportionment is an approximate rounding.

Simultaneous equation (algebraic) method

3.6 (a) Let S be the total stores department overhead for apportionment, after it has been apportioned overhead from Maintenance.

(b) Let M be the total of maintenance department overhead after it has been apportioned overhead from Stores.

We can set up our equations as follows.

$$S = 0.1M + £10{,}000 \quad (1)$$
$$M = 0.2S + £8{,}000 \quad (2)$$

Multiplying (2) by 5 gives us

$$5M = S + £40{,}000 \quad (3)\text{, which can be rearranged so that}$$
$$S = 5M - £40{,}000 \quad (4)$$

Subtracting (1) from (4)

$$S = 5M - £40{,}000 \quad (4)$$
$$S = 0.1M + £10{,}000 \quad (1)$$
$$0 = 4.9M - £50{,}000$$
$$M = £50{,}000/4.9 = £10{,}204$$

Substituting in (1)

$$S = 0.1 \times (£10{,}204) + £10{,}000 = £11{,}020$$

These overheads can be apportioned as follows, using the percentages in Paragraph 2.4.

	Dept A	*Dept B*	*Stores*	*Maintenance*
	£	£	£	£
Overhead costs	10,030	8,970	10,000	8,000
Apportion stores total	3,306	5,510	(11,020)	2,204
Apportion maintenance total	8,164	1,020	1,020	(10,204)
	21,500	15,500	-	-

This is the same result as the one we got using repeated distribution.

Step-wise (elimination) method

3.7 In examination questions you will be told which service department overheads to apportion first. We will start with stores.

	Dept A	*Dept B*	*Stores*	*Maintenance*
	£	£	£	£
Overhead costs	10,030	8,970	10,000	8,000
Apportion stores (30%/50%/20%)	3,000	5,000	(10,000)	2,000
	13,030	13,970	-	10,000
Apportion maintenance (8/9, 1/9)	8,889	1,111		(10,000)
	21,915	15,081		-

The service department **overheads apportioned first** (stores) **are apportioned across all the other departments**, both production and service. The **other service department's overheads** (maintenance) (which now include an apportionment of those of the stores department) are **apportioned to the production departments only in the ratio of use by**

the production departments. In our example the ratio is 80% to 10% or 8:1 or 8/9:1/9 (the denominator of 9 coming from 8 + 1). If the usage percentages had been 30% and 40% (with stores usage at 30%), the ratio would have been 3:4 or 3/7:4/7.

3.8 **Apportioning service department overheads is only useful if the resulting product costs reflect accurately the amounts expended by service departments.** If, however, the apportionment is arbitrary or ill-considered, the absorption of service department costs into product costs may be misleading.

Question 3

You are the cost accountant of an industrial concern and have been given the following budgeted information regarding the four cost centres within your organisation.

	Dept 1	*Dept 2*	*Maint. dept.*	*Canteen*	*Total*
	£	£	£	£	£
Indirect labour	60,000	70,000	25,000	15,000	170,000
Consumables	12,000	16,000	3,000	10,000	41,000
Heating and lighting					12,000
Rent and rates					18,000
Depreciation					30,000
Supervision					24,000
Power					20,000
					315,000

	Dept 1	*Dept 2*	*Maint. dept*	*Canteen*	*Total*
Floor space in sq. metres	10,000	12,000	5,000	3,000	30,000
Book value of machinery (£)	150,000	120,000	20,000	10,000	300,000
Number of employees	40	30	10		80
Kilowatt hours	4,500	4,000	1,000	500	10,000

You are also told that the canteen staff are outside contractors and that departments 1 and 2 are production cost centres and the maintenance department and canteen are service cost centres.

Required

(a) Provide an overhead statement showing the allocation of overheads and apportionment of general overheads to the four cost centres, showing the apportionment bases.

(b) Using the fact that the maintenance department provides 4,000 service hours to department 1, 3,000 service hours to department 2 and 1,000 hours for the canteen, apportion the overheads of the two service departments using the algebraic method.

(c) List the factors which should be considered when choosing bases of apportionment for apportioning the overheads of the service cost centres.

Answer

(a)

	Basis of apportionment	*Dept 1*	*Dept 2*	*Maintenance dept*	*Canteen*	*Total*
		£	£	£	£	£
Indirect labour	-	60,000	70,000	25,000	15,000	170,000
Consumables	-	12,000	16,000	3,000	10,000	41,000
Heat and light	Space	4,000	4,800	2,000	1,200	12,000
Rent and rates	Space	6,000	7,200	3,000	1,800	18,000
Depreciation	Book value	15,000	12,000	2,000	1,000	30,000
Supervision	Employees	12,000	9,000	3,000	-	24,000
Power	Kilowatt hrs	9,000	8,000	2,000	1,000	20,000
		118,000	127,000	40,000	30,000	315,000

(b) **Let C = canteen overhead including apportioned maintenance overhead.**
Let M = maintenance overhead including apportioned canteen overhead.

$C = 30{,}000 + \frac{1}{8}M$ (1)

$M = 40{,}000 + \frac{1}{8}C$ (2)

$8(M - 40{,}000) = C$ (3) (from (2))

$8(M - 40{,}000) = 30{,}000 + \frac{1}{8}M$ (4) (sub (1) into (3))

$8M - 320{,}000 = 30{,}000 + \frac{1}{8}M$

$7\frac{7}{8}M = 350{,}000$

$M = £44{,}444$

$C = 30{,}000 + \frac{1}{8}(44{,}444) = £35{,}556$

	Dept 1	*Dept 2*	*Maintenance*	*Canteen*
	£	£	£	£
Overheads	118,000	127,000	40,000	30,000
Apportion maintenance	22,222	16,666	(44,444)	5,556
Apportion canteen	17,778	13,334	4,444	(35,556)
Total	158,000	157,000	-	-

(c) (i) Services which the maintenance department and the canteen provide to each other, and to departments 1 and 2.

(ii) Selecting an appropriate basis of apportionment eg space, book value, employees.

(iii) The ability to produce accurate estimates about the usage of the maintenance department and the canteen by each other and by departments 1 and 2.

(iv) The cost of implementing the apportionment as compared with the resulting benefit.

(v) The value of the overhead expenditure incurred by the service and production departments, and how many departments used the service departments.

4 OVERHEAD ABSORPTION

4.1 Having allocated and/or apportioned all **overheads,** the next stage in absorption costing is to **add them to, or absorb them into,** the cost of production or sales.

Use of a predetermined absorption rate

Knowledge brought forward from earlier studies

Step 1. The overhead likely to be incurred during the coming year is estimated.

Step 2. The total hours, units or direct costs on which the overhead absorption rates are based (activity levels) are estimated.

Step 3. Absorption rate = estimated overhead ÷ budgeted activity level

Choosing the appropriate absorption base

Question 4

List as many possible bases of absorption (or 'overhead recovery rates') which you can think of.

Answer

(a) A percentage of direct materials cost
(b) A percentage of direct labour cost
(c) A percentage of prime cost
(d) A percentage of factory cost (for administration overhead)
(e) A percentage of sales or factory cost (for selling and distribution overhead)
(f) A rate per machine hour
(g) A rate per direct labour hour
(h) A rate per unit

4.2 The choice of an absorption basis is a **matter of judgement and common sense.** There are no strict rules or formulae involved. But the basis should realistically reflect the characteristics of a given cost centre, avoid undue anomalies and be 'fair'. The **choice will be significant in determining the cost of individual products, but the total cost of production overheads is the budgeted overhead expenditure, no matter what basis of absorption is selected.** It is the relative share of overhead costs borne by individual products and jobs which is affected.

Question 5

Using the information in and the results of Question 2, determine budgeted overhead absorption rates for each of the production departments using appropriate bases of absorption.

Answer

Machine shop A:	£57,168/7,200 = £7.94 per machine hour
Machine shop B:	£63,000/18,000 = £3.50 per machine hour
Assembly:	£46,592/20,800 = £2.24 per direct labour hour

Over and under absorption of overheads

4.3 The rate of overhead absorption is based on estimates (of both numerator and denominator) and it is quite likely that either one or both of the estimates will not agree with what actually occurs. Actual overheads incurred will probably be either greater than or less than overheads absorbed into the cost of production, and so it is almost inevitable that at the end of the accounting year there will have been an over absorption or under absorption of the overhead actually incurred.

- **Over absorption** means that the **overheads charged to the cost of sales are greater than the overheads actually incurred.**
- **Under absorption** means that **insufficient overheads have been included in the cost of sales.**

4.4 Suppose that the budgeted overhead in a production department is £80,000 and the budgeted activity is 40,000 direct labour hours, the overhead recovery rate (using a direct labour hour basis) would be £2 per direct labour hour. Actual overheads in the period are, say £84,000 and 45,000 direct labour hours are worked.

	£
Overhead incurred (actual)	84,000
Overhead absorbed (45,000 × £2)	90,000
Over-absorption of overhead	6,000

4.5 In this example, the cost of production has been charged with £6,000 more than was actually spent and so the cost that is recorded will be too high. The over-absorbed overhead will be an adjustment to the profit and loss account at the end of the accounting period to reconcile the overheads charged to the actual overhead

Question 6

The total production overhead expenditure of the company in Questions 2 and 5 was £176,533 and its actual activity was as follows.

	Machine shop A	*Machine shop B*	*Assembly*
Direct labour hours	8,200	6,500	21,900
Machine usage hours	7,300	18,700	-

Required

Using the information in and results of Questions 2 and 5, calculate the under- or over-absorption of overheads.

Answer

		£	£
Actual expenditure			176,533
Overhead absorbed			
Machine shop A	7,300 hrs × £7.94	57,962	
Machine shop B	18,700 hrs × £3.50	65,450	
Assembly	21,900 hrs × £2.24	49,056	
			172,468
Under-absorbed overhead			4,065

The reasons for under- /over-absorbed overhead

4.6 The overhead absorption rate is predetermined from budget estimates of overhead cost and activity level. Under or over recovery of overhead will occur in the following circumstances.

- Actual overhead costs are different from budgeted overheads.
- The actual activity level is different from the budgeted activity level.
- Actual overhead costs **and** actual activity level differ from those budgeted.

Question 7

Elsewhere Ltd has a budgeted production overhead of £180,000 and a budgeted activity of 45,000 machine hours.

Required

Calculate the under-/over-absorbed overhead, and note the reasons for the under-/over-absorption in the following circumstances.

(a) Actual overheads cost £170,000 and 45,000 machine hours were worked.
(b) Actual overheads cost £180,000 and 40,000 machine hours were worked.
(c) Actual overheads cost £170,000 and 40,000 machine hours were worked.

Answer

The overhead recovery rate is £180,000/45,000 = £4 per machine hour.

		£
(a)	Actual overhead	170,000
	Absorbed overhead (45,000 × £4)	180,000
	Over-absorbed overhead	10,000

Reason: Actual and budgeted machine hours are the same but actual overheads cost less than expected.

		£
(b)	Actual overhead	180,000
	Absorbed overhead (40,000 × £4)	160,000
	Under-absorbed overhead	20,000

Reason: Budgeted and actual overhead costs were the same but fewer machine hours were worked than expected.

		£
(c)	Actual overhead	170,000
	Absorbed overhead (40,000 × £4)	160,000
	Under-absorbed overhead	10,000

Reason: A combination of the reasons in (a) and (b).

Exam focus point

Absorption costing appeared in the first sitting of Paper 2.4. For three marks candidates were asked to briefly assess the reasonableness of particular allocation bases used for fixed and variable overheads.

5 MARGINAL COSTING

KEY TERMS

Marginal cost is the cost of one unit of a product/service which could be avoided if that unit were not produced/provided.

Contribution is the difference between sales revenue and variable (marginal) cost of sales.

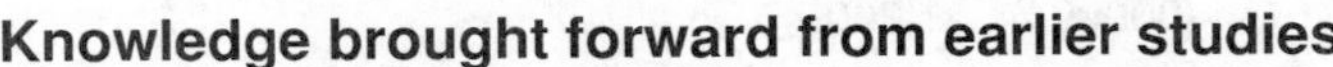

Marginal costing is an alternative to absorption costing. Only variable costs (marginal costs) are charged as a cost of sales. Fixed costs are treated as period costs and are charged in full against the profit of the period in which they are incurred.

Knowledge brought forward from earlier studies

Marginal costing

- In **marginal costing**, closing **stocks are valued at marginal (variable) production cost** whereas, in **absorption costing**, stocks are **valued at their full production cost** which includes absorbed fixed production overhead.
- If the opening and closing stock levels differ, the **profit reported** for the accounting period **under the two methods** of cost accumulation **will therefore be different**.
- But **in the long run, total profit for a company will be the same** whichever is used because, in the long run, total costs will be the same by either method of accounting. Different accounting conventions merely affect the profit of individual periods.

Question 8

A company makes and sells a single product. At the beginning of period 1, there are no opening stocks of the product, for which the variable production cost is £4 and the sales price £6 per unit. Fixed costs are £2,000 per period, of which £1,500 are fixed production costs. Normal output is 1,500 units per period. In period 1, sales were 1,200 units, production was 1,500 units. In period 2, sales were 1,700 units, production was 1,400 units.

Required

Prepare profit statements for each period and for the two periods in total using both absorption costing and marginal costing.

Answer

It is important to notice that although production and sales volumes in each period are different, over the **full period, total production equals sales volume**. The total cost of sales is the same and therefore the **total profit is the same by either method** of accounting. **Differences** in profit in any one period are merely **timing differences** which cancel out over a longer period of time.

(a) **Absorption costing.** The absorption rate for fixed production overhead is £1,500/1,500 units = £1 per unit. The fully absorbed cost per unit = £(4+1) = £5.

		Period 1		Period 2		Total	
		£	£	£	£	£	£
Sales			7,200		10,200		17,400
Production costs							
Variable		6,000		5,600		11,600	
Fixed		1,500		1,400		2,900	
		7,500		7,000		14,500	
Add opening stock b/f	(300×£5)	–		1,500		1,500	
		7,500		8,500		16,000	
Less closing stock c/f	(300×£5)	1,500		-		1,500	
Production cost of sales		6,000		8,500		14,500	
Under-absorbed o/hd		-		100		100	
Total costs			6,000		8,600		14,600
Gross profit			1,200		1,600		2,800
Other costs			(500)		(500)		((1,000)
Net profit			700		1,100		1,800

(b) **Marginal costing**

The marginal cost per unit = £4.

		Period 1		Period 2		Total	
		£	£	£	£	£	£
Sales			7,200		10,200		17,400
Variable production cost		6,000		5,600		11,600	
Add opening stock b/f	(300×£4)	-		1,200		1,200	
		6,000		6,800		12,800	
Less closing stock c/f	(300×£4)	1,200		-		1,200	
Variable prod. cost of sales			4,800		6,800		11,600
Contribution			2,400		3,400		5,800
Fixed costs			2,000		2,000		4,000
Profit			400		1,400		1,800

Question 9

RH Ltd makes and sells one product, which has the following standard production cost.

		£
Direct labour	3 hours at £6 per hour	18
Direct materials	4 kilograms at £7 per kg	28
Production overhead	Variable	3
	Fixed	20
Standard production cost per unit		69

Normal output is 16,000 units per annum. Variable selling, distribution and administration costs are 20 per cent of sales value. Fixed costs are £180,000 per annum. There are no units in finished goods stock at 1 October 20X2. The fixed overhead expenditure is spread evenly throughout the year. The selling price per unit is £140. Production and sales budgets are as follows.

	Six months ending 31 March 20X3	*Six months ending 30 September 20X3*
Production	8,500	7,000
Sales	7,000	8,000

Required

Prepare profit statements for each of the six-monthly periods, using the following methods of costing.

(a) Marginal costing
(b) Absorption costing

Answer

(a) **Profit statements for the year ending 30 September 20X3**
Marginal costing basis

	Six months ending 31 March 20X3		*Six months ending 30 September 20X3*	
	£'000	£'000	£'000	£'000
Sales at £140 per unit		980		1,120
Opening stock	-		73.5	
Std. variable prod. cost (at £49 per unit)	416.5		343.0	
	416.5		416.5	
Closing stock (W1)	73.5		24.5	
		343		392
		637		728
Variable selling and so on costs		196		224
Contribution		441		504
Fixed costs: production (W2)	160		160	
selling and so on	90		90	
		250		250
Net profit		191		254

(b) **Profit statements for the year ending 30 September 20X3**
Absorption costing basis

	Six months ending 31 March 20X3		*Six months ending 30 September 20X3*	
	£'000	£'000	£'000	£'000
Sales at £140 per unit		980		1,120
Opening stock	-		103.5	
Std. cost of prod. (at £69 per unit)	586.5		483.0	
	586.5		586.5	
Closing stock (W1)	103.5		34.5	
	483.0		552.0	
(Over-)/under-absorbed overhead (W3)	(10.0)		20.0	
		473		572
Gross profit		507		548
Selling and so on costs				
Variable	196		224	
Fixed	90		90	
		286		314
Net profit		221		234

Workings

1

	Six months ending 31 March 20X3	*Six months ending 30 September 20X3*
	Units	Units
Opening stock	-	1,500
Production	8,500	7,000
	8,500	8,500
Sales	7,000	8,000
Closing stock	1,500	500
Marginal cost valuation (× £49)	£73,500	£24,500
Absorption cost valuation (× £69)	£103,500	£34,500

2 Budgeted fixed production o/hd = 16,000 units × £20 = £320,000 pa = £160,000 per six months

3

	Six months ending 31 March 20X3		*Six months ending 30 September 20X3*	
Normal output (16,000 ÷ 2)	8,000	units	8,000	Units
Budgeted output	8,500	units	7,000	Units
Difference	500	units	1,000	Units
× std. fixed prod. o/hd per unit	× £20		× £20	
(Over-)/under-absorbed overhead	(£10,000)		£20,000	

6 RECONCILING THE PROFIT FIGURES GIVEN BY THE TWO METHODS

6.1 The **difference in profits** reported under the two costing systems is due to the **different stock valuation methods** used.

(a) **If stock levels increase** between the beginning and end of a period, **absorption costing will report the higher profit** because some of the fixed production overhead incurred during the period will be carried forward in closing stock (which reduces cost of sales) to be set against sales revenue in the following period instead of being written off in full against profit in the period concerned.

(b) **If stock levels decrease, absorption costing will report the lower profit** because as well as the fixed overhead incurred, fixed production overhead which had been carried forward in opening stock is released and is also included in cost of sales.

6.2 EXAMPLE: RECONCILING PROFITS

The profits reported for period 1 in Question 8 would be reconciled as follows.

	£
Marginal costing profit	400
Adjust for fixed overhead in stock (stock increase of 300 units × £1 per unit)	300
Absorption costing profit	700

Question 10

Reconcile the profits reported for period 2 of the example in Question 8.

Answer

	£
Marginal costing profit	1,400
Adjust for fixed overhead in stock (stock decrease of 300 units × £1 per unit)	(300)
Absorption costing profit	1,100

7 ABSORPTION COSTING AND MARGINAL COSTING COMPARED

Exam focus point

Remember that if opening stock values are greater than closing stock values, marginal costing shows the greater profit.

Marginal versus absorption costing: reporting to management

7.1 We know that the reported profit in any period is likely to differ according to the costing method used, but does one method provide a more reliable guide to management about the organisation's profit position.

7.2 **With marginal costing, contribution varies in direct proportion to the volume of units sold**. Profits will increase as sales volume rises, by the amount of extra contribution earned. Since fixed cost expenditure does not alter, marginal costing gives an accurate picture of how a firm's cash flows and profits are affected by changes in sales volumes.

7.3 **With absorption costing**, in contrast, **there is no clear relationship between profit and sales volume**, and as sales volume rises the total profit will rise by the sum of the gross profit per unit plus the amount of overhead absorbed per unit. Arguably this is a confusing and unsatisfactory method of monitoring profitability.

7.4 If sales volumes are the same from period to period, marginal costing reports the same profit each period (given no change in prices or costs). In contrast, using absorption costing, profits can vary with the volume of production, even when the volume of sales is constant. **Using absorption costing there is therefore the possibility of manipulating profit, simply by changing output and stock levels.**

7.5 EXAMPLE: MANIPULATING PROFITS

Gloom Ltd budgeted to make and sell 10,000 units of its product in 20X1. The selling price is £10 per unit and the variable cost £4 per unit. Fixed production costs were budgeted at £50,000 for the year. The company uses absorption costing and budgeted an absorption rate of £5 per unit. During 20X1, it became apparent that sales demand would only be 8,000 units. The management, concerned about the apparent effect of the low volume of sales on profits, decided to increase production for the year to 15,000 units. Actual fixed costs were still expected to be £50,000 in spite of the significant increase in production volume.

Required

Calculate the profit at an actual sales volume of 8,000 units, using the following methods.

(a) Absorption costing
(b) Marginal costing

7.6 SOLUTION

(a) **Absorption costing**

	£	£
Sales (8,000 × £10)		80,000
Cost of production (15,000 × £9)	135,000	
Less: over-absorbed overhead	(25,000)	
		(110,000)
		(30,000)
Closing stock (7,000 × £9)		63,000
Profit		33,000

(b) **Marginal costing**

	£	£
Sales		80,000
Cost of sales		
Cost of production (15,000 × £4)	60,000	
Closing stock (7,000 × £4)	28,000	
		32,000
Contribution		48,000
Fixed costs		50,000
Loss		(2,000)

7.7 The difference in profits of £35,000 is explained by the difference in the increase in stock values (7,000 units × £5 of fixed overhead per unit). With absorption costing, the expected profit will be higher than the original budget of (10,000 units × (£10 – 9)) £10,000 simply because £35,000 of fixed overheads will be carried forward in closing stock values. By producing to absorb overhead rather than to satisfy customers, stock levels will, of course, increase. Unless this stock is sold, however, there may come a point when production has to stop and the inventory has to be sold off at lower prices. Marginal costing would report a contribution of £6 per unit, or £48,000 in total for 8,000 units, which fails to cover the fixed costs of £50,000 by £2,000.

7.8 The argument above is not conclusive, however, because **marginal costing is not so useful when sales fluctuate from month to month because of seasonal variations in sales demand**, but production per month is held constant in order to arrange for an even flow of output (and thereby prevent the cost of idle resources in periods of low demand and overtime in periods of high demand).

7.9 EXAMPLE: SEASONAL VARIATIONS IN SALES DEMAND

H Ltd budgets to make and sell 3,600 units of its product during 20X2 at a selling price of £5. Production variable costs are £3 per unit and fixed costs for the year are budgeted as £5,400 (divisible equally between the 12 months of the year). Sales demand in the first six months of the year will be only 200 units per month, but monthly demand will double in the second six months. In order to save unnecessary production costs, the company has budgeted to spread production evenly over the year.

Required

Calculate the profits each month using the following costing methods.

(a) Absorption costing
(b) Marginal costing

7.10 SOLUTION

(a) **Absorption costing**

The fixed overhead absorption rate is £5,400/3,600 units = £1.50 per unit.

For each of the first six months of the year, profit per month would be as follows.

	£
Sales (200 units × £5)	1,000
Less full cost of sales (200 units × £4.50)	900
	100
Under-/over-absorbed overhead	0
Profit (£0.50 per unit)	100

For each of the second six months of the year, profit per month would be as follows.

	£
Sales (400 units × £5)	2,000
Less full cost of sales (400 units × £4.50)	1,800
	200
Under-/over-absorbed overhead	0
Profit (£0.50 per unit)	200

Total profit for the year would be 3,600 units × £0.50 = £1,800

(b) **Marginal costing**

For each of the first six months of the year, there would be a loss.

	£
Sales (200 units × £5)	1,000
Less variable cost of sales (200 units × £3)	600
Contribution (£2 per unit)	400
Less fixed costs	450
Loss	(50)

For each of the second six months of the year there would be a profit.

	£
Sales (400 units × £5)	2,000
Less variable cost of sales (400 units × £3)	1,200
Contribution (£2 per unit)	800
Less fixed costs	450
Profit	350

Total profit for the year would be £1,800

7.11 In this example it might be argued that in view of the deliberate policy of producing goods for stock in the first half of the year, and selling out of stock in the second half absorption costing would provide a better method of reporting profits month by month. At a profit of £0.50 per unit, total monthly profits double when sales double, which would conform to the expectations of the management of H Ltd.

7.12 In contrast, marginal costing would report a loss in each of the first six months and a misleadingly large jump into profitability in the second half of the year.

7.13 Other **arguments in favour of absorption costing for internal profit reporting** are as follows.

(a) **Marginal costing fails to recognise the importance of working to full capacity.** With absorption costing, the effect of higher production volumes is to reduce unit costs (because the fixed cost per unit is lower) and if sales prices are based on the 'cost-plus' method, the relevance of output capacity to cost/price/sales demand should be clear.

(b) **Selling prices based on marginal costing** might enable the firm to make a contribution on each unit of product it sells, but the **total contribution earned might be insufficient to cover all fixed costs.**

(c) **In the long run, all costs are variable**, and inventory values based on **absorption costing will give recognition to these long-run variable costs.**

7.14 There is a further **argument in favour of marginal costing for internal profit reporting: fixed costs** (such as depreciation, rent or salaries) **relate to a period of time and should be charged against the revenues of the period in which they are incurred.**

Marginal versus absorption costing: external reporting

7.15 It **might be argued that absorption costing is preferable** to marginal costing in management accounting, **in order to be consistent with the requirement of SSAP 9** to include production overhead in inventory values in published accounts. This argument might be especially relevant when a firm has an integrated or combined accounting system for its financial and management accounts.

7.16 The argument is, however, an unimportant one because it is quite easy for a firm to maintain its accounts on a marginal costing basis, and when financial accounts are prepared, to convert its stock values into fully absorbed costs.

Marginal versus absorption costing: decision-making information

7.17 Suppose that a sales manager has an item of product which he is having difficulty in selling. Its historical full cost is £80, made up of variable costs of £50 and fixed costs of £30. A customer offers £60 for it.

(a) If there is no other customer for the product, £60 would be better than nothing and the product should be sold to improve income and profit by this amount.

(b) If the company has spare production capacity which would otherwise not be used, it would be profitable to continue making more of the same product, if customers are willing to pay £60 for each extra unit made. This is because the additional costs are only £50 so that the profit would be increased marginally by £10 per unit produced.

(c) In absorption costing terms, the product makes a loss of £20, which would discourage the sales manager from accepting a price of £60. His decision would be a bad one.

   (i) If the product is not sold for £60, it will presumably be scrapped eventually, so the choice is really between making a loss in absorption costing terms of £20, or a loss of £80 when the stock is written off, whenever this happens.

   (ii) If there is demand for some extra units at £60 each, the absorption costing loss would be £20 per unit, but at the end of the year there would be an additional contribution to overheads and profit of £10 per unit. The under-absorbed overhead would be reduced by £30 (the fixed cost part of the product's full cost) for each extra unit made and sold.

7.18 **Absorption costing information** about unit profits is therefore **irrelevant in short-run decisions in which fixed costs do not change**. In such circumstances the decision rule is to choose the alternative which maximises contribution. We will be looking at this in more detail in Chapter 14.

Summary

7.19 **Although any technique can be used for internal purposes, absorption costing must be used for external reporting**. The use of marginal costing in an organisation for cost accumulation appears to be rare. But this does not mean that marginal costing techniques are unimportant. An understanding of the behaviour of cost and the implications of contribution is vital for accountants and managers, and the use of marginal costing for planning and decision making is universal.

Chapter roundup

- The traditional approach to dealing with overheads is **absorption costing**, the three stages of which are allocation, apportionment and absorption.
- **Apportionment** has two stages, general overhead apportionment and service department cost apportionment.
- There are three methods of **service department cost apportionment.**
  - Direct
  - Using algebra
  - Repeated distribution method
- After apportionment, overheads are **absorbed** into products using an appropriate **absorption rate** based on budgeted costs and budgeted activity levels.
- **Under-/over-absorbed overhead** occurs when overheads incurred do not equal overheads absorbed.
- In **marginal costing**, stocks are valued at variable production cost whereas in absorption costing they are valued at their full production cost.
- If opening and closing stock levels differ **profit reported under the two methods will be different.**
- In the long run, total profit will be the same whatever method is used.

Quick quiz

1 How is an overhead absorption rate calculated?

A Estimated overhead ÷ actual activity level
B Estimated overhead ÷ budgeted activity level
C Actual overhead ÷ actual activity level
D Actual overhead ÷ budgeted activity level

2 Over absorption means that the overheads charged to the cost of sales are greater than the overheads actually incurred. True or false?

3 *Fill in the blanks in the statements about marginal costing and absorption costing below.*

(a) If stock levels .... between the beginning and end of a period, absorption costing will report the higher profit.

(b) If stock levels decrease, ... costing will report the lower profit.

4 The overhead cost of service department A is £40,000, while that of B is £25,000. 15% of A's work is for B. 35% of B's work is for A. Which of the following sets of equations could be used to apportion the overhead costs?

(a) A = 40,000 – 0.35B B = 25,000 – 0.15A
(b) A = 40,000 – 0.15B B = 25,000 – 0.35A
(c) A = 40,000 + 0.35B B = 25,000 + 0.15A
(d) A = 40,000 + 0.15B B = 25,000 + 0.35A

5 *Fill in the following blanks with either 'marginal' or 'absorption'.*

(a) Using .... costing, profits can be manipulated simply by changing output and stock levels.

(b) Fixed costs are charged in full against the profit of the period in which they are incurred when .... costing is used.

(c) .... costing fails to recognise the importance of working to full capacity.

(d) .... costing could be argued to be preferable to .... costing in management accounting in order to be consistent with the requirements of SSAP9.

(e) .... costing should not be used when decision-making information is required.

6 Service department Y does 60% of its work for department A, 35% for department B and 5% for service department X. If the step-wise method of apportionment is used, and service department X costs are apportioned first, what proportion of Y's costs are apportioned to A?

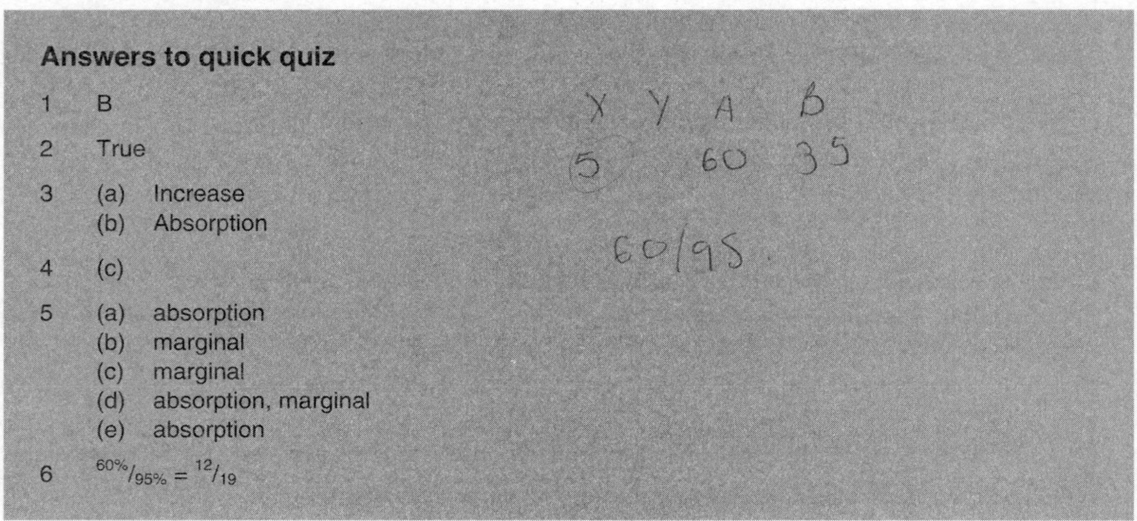

Answers to quick quiz

1 B

2 True

3 (a) Increase
  (b) Absorption

4 (c)

5 (a) absorption
  (b) marginal
  (c) marginal
  (d) absorption, marginal
  (e) absorption

6 $^{60\%}/_{95\%} = {}^{12}/_{19}$

Now try the question below from the Exam Question Bank

Question to try	Level	Marks	Time
2	Exam	25	45 mins

Chapter 3

OTHER METHODS OF COST ACCUMULATION

	Topic list	Syllabus reference
1	**Opportunity costing**	**6(e), 6(f), 7(a)(i)**
2	**Activity based costing**	**7(a)(ii)**
3	**Absorption costing versus ABC**	**6(e), 7(a)(ii)**
4	**Merits and criticisms of ABC**	**6(f), 7(a)(ii)**
5	**Life cycle costing**	**6(e), 7(a)(iii)**
6	**Target costing**	**6(e), 7(a)(iv)**

Introduction

In this chapter we will be looking at three more methods of cost accumulation.

- **Opportunity costing** is particularly useful for decision making.
- **Activity based costing** is a modern alternative to absorption costing.
- **Life cycle costing** accumulates costs over a product's life rather than on a periodic basis.

Target costing, the subject of Section 6, is a cost management process rather than a method of accumulating costs.

Study guide

Section 18 – Costing systems: context and framework

- Explain the potential for different costing approaches to influence cost accumulation and profit reporting
- Explain the role of costing systems in decision making

Section 19 – Cost accumulation I

- Describe, explain and apply opportunity and activity based costing
- Explain the impact of life cycle costing on cost accumulation
- Describe and apply target costing methods
- Describe the interaction between life cycle and target costing

Exam guide

You could face a Section B question on ABC or it could be examined with other subjects in Section A. The other topics covered in this chapter are likely to be examined with each other or with other topics in either Section A or Section B.

1 OPPORTUNITY COSTING

KEY TERM

The **opportunity cost** is the benefit forgone by choosing one opportunity instead of the next best alternative.

1.1 A common feature of both absorption costing and marginal costing is that the costs of the jobs or products or services are built up from the 'purchase' costs of the resources that are used up in making them. For example, suppose that a company manufactures a product at each of two sites, one in London and one in North East England. The factory rental in London is very cheap by London standards, because the company has occupied the premises for many years. The actual rental in London is £40,000 pa, which is exactly the same as for the similar-sized factory in the North East, where a full commercial rental is being paid. The company could sub-let the London factory, if it wished, for £100,000 pa.

(a) If absorption costing were used to cost the output from each factory, the rental cost allocated to production overhead would be £40,000 pa for each factory.

(b) If marginal costing were used instead, the rental cost of £40,000 pa at each factory would be charged as a period cost against profits.

1.2 **Neither method of costing recognises the opportunity cost of the London factory, which is the revenue that could be earned from sub-letting the factory** (but which has been sacrificed in favour of using the factory to make the company's own product). There is an argument that £100,000 should be charged as the cost of the London factory, to reflect the true value to the company of the resource - factory space - that it is using in London.

1.3 In a system of cost accumulation using **opportunity costing**, the **costs of resources consumed are valued at their opportunity cost rather than at the amount it actually costs to acquire them**.

(a) **If no alternative use for a resource exists then the opportunity cost is zero.**

(b) **If a resource is not scarce, no sacrifice exists from using the resource and so the opportunity cost is zero.**

1.4 **The main argument in favour of opportunity costing** is that management are made more aware of how well they are using resources to make products, and whether resources could be used better in other ways.

1.5 **The main drawback to opportunity costing** is a practical one. It is not always easy to recognise alternative uses for certain resources, nor to put an accurate value on opportunity cost. It is only likely to be accurate if resources have an alternative use which can be valued at an external market price, such as factory rental, or staff time in the case of professional firms of accountants and so on.

1.6 EXAMPLE: OPPORTUNITY COSTING

An information technology consultancy firm has been asked to do an urgent job by a client, for which a price of £2,500 has been offered. The job would require 30 hours' work from one member of staff, who is paid on an hourly basis, at a rate of £20 per hour, but who would normally be employed on work for clients where the charge-out rate is £45 per hour. No other member of staff is able to do the member of staff in question's work. The job would also require 5 hours of mainframe computer time, which the firm normally charges out to external users at a rate of £50 per hour. Mainframe computer time is currently used 24 hours a day, 7 days a week. Supplies and incidental expenses would be £200.

The opportunity cost of the job would be calculated as follows.

	£
Labour (30 hours × £45)	1,350
Computer time opportunity cost (5 hours × £50)	250
Supplies and expenses	200
	1,800

The opportunity cost of labour and computer time is the normal charge-out rate, of £45 and £50 per hour respectively. A further addition to cost might be added for 'general overhead' depending on the system of costing being used. The opportunity cost of the job shows that the firm would increase profits by accepting the job, by £(2,500 - 1,800) = £700.

Imputed interest (notional interest)

1.7 **There is a view that costs should include an interest charge which is based on the opportunity cost of the capital value of resources tied up**. For example, if a production department employs assets valued at £100,000, and the company's cost of borrowing is 12% pa, it might be considered appropriate to charge interest of £12,000 pa to the department, to reflect the cost of the assets.

1.8 Another reason for charging jobs or services with notional interest is to assist comparability. Suppose that there are two departments, A and B, each producing the same finished product with the same item of machinery. However, A has purchased its machine, whereas B leases its machine. Costs for period 1 are as follows.

	Dept A	*Dept B*
Output (units)	10,000	10,000
	£	£
Variable costs	10,000	10,000
Depreciation	2,000	-
Lease charge	-	2,500
Other fixed costs	8,000	8,000
	20,000	20,500

1.9 The costs in each department are identical, except that Dept A is charged with depreciation (a share of the original capital cost) whereas Dept B's lease charge will include an element for capital cost and an element for the finance or interest charge in the lease. To make the costs of the two departments properly comparable, it could be argued that Dept A ought to be charged a notional amount for interest on the capital value of its machine.

Opportunity costing and decision making

1.10 As we will see later in this Text, opportunity costing must be used for decision making.

2 ACTIVITY BASED COSTING

Reasons for the development of ABC

2.1 The traditional cost accumulation system of **absorption costing** was developed in a time when most organisations produced only a **narrow range of products** (so that products underwent **similar operations** and consumed **similar proportions of overheads**). And **overhead costs were only a very small fraction of total costs,** direct labour and direct material costs accounting for the largest proportion of the costs. The **benefits** of **more accurate systems for overhead allocation** would probably have been relatively **small.** In addition, **information processing costs were high.**

2.2 In **recent** years, however, there has been a **dramatic fall** in the **costs** of **processing information.** And, with the advent of **advanced manufacturing technology (AMT), overheads** are likely to be far **more important** and in fact direct labour may account for as little as 5% of a product's cost. It therefore now appears difficult to justify the use of direct labour or direct material as the basis for absorbing overheads or to believe that errors made in attributing overheads will not be significant.

2.3 Many resources are used in **non-volume related support activities,** (which have increased due to AMT) such as setting-up, production scheduling, inspection and data processing. These support activities assist the efficient manufacture of a wide range of products and are **not, in general, affected by changes in production volume**. They tend to **vary in the long term according to the range and complexity** of the products manufactured rather than the volume of output.

2.4 The wider the range and the more complex the products, the more support services will be required. Consider, for example, factory X which produces 10,000 units of one product, the Alpha, and factory Y which produces 1,000 units each of ten slightly different versions of the Alpha. Support activity costs in the factory Y are likely to be a lot higher than in factory X but the factories produce an identical number of units. For example, factory X will only need to set-up once whereas Factory Y will have to set-up the production run at least ten times for the ten different products. Factory Y will therefore incur more set-up costs for the same volume of production.

2.5 **Traditional costing systems,** which assume that all products consume all resources in proportion to their production volumes, tend to **allocate too great a proportion of overheads to high volume products** (which cause relatively little diversity and hence use fewer support services) and **too small a proportion of overheads to low volume products** (which cause greater diversity and therefore use more support services). **Activity based costing (ABC) attempts to overcome this problem.**

Definition of ABC

KEY TERM

Activity based costing (ABC) involves the identification of the factors which cause the costs of an organisation's major activities. Support overheads are charged to products on the basis of their usage of the factor causing the overheads.

2.6 The **major ideas** behind activity based costing are as follows.

(a) **Activities cause costs**. Activities include ordering, materials handling, machining, assembly, production scheduling and despatching.

(b) **Producing products creates demand for the activities.**

(c) **Costs** are **assigned** to a product **on the basis of the product's consumption of the activities.**

Outline of an ABC system

2.7 An ABC system operates as follows.

Step 1. Identify an organisation's major activities.

Step 2. Identify the **factors which determine the size of the costs of an activity/cause the costs of an activity**. These are known as **cost drivers.**

KEY TERM

A **cost driver** is a factor which causes a change in the cost of an activity.

Look at the following examples.

Costs	Possible cost driver
Ordering costs	Number of orders
Materials handling costs	Number of production runs
Production scheduling costs	Number of production runs
Despatching costs	Number of despatches

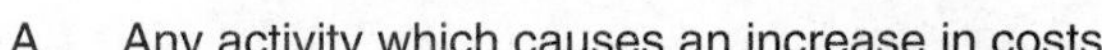

Step 3. Collect the **costs associated with each cost driver** into what are known as **cost pools.**

Step 4. Charge costs to products on the basis of their usage of the activity. A product's usage of an activity is measured by the number of the activity's cost driver it generates.

Question 1

Which of the following definitions best describes a cost driver?

A Any activity which causes an increase in costs
B A collection of costs associated with a particular activity
C A cost that varies with production levels
D Any factor which causes a change in the cost of an activity

Answer

The correct answer is D.

Cost drivers

2.8 For those **costs that vary with production levels in the short term,** ABC uses **volume-related cost drivers** such as labour or machine hours. The cost of oil used as a lubricant on the machines would therefore be added to products on the basis of the number of machine hours, since oil would have to be used for each hour the machine ran.

2.9 Kaplan and Cooper argue that long-term variable overhead costs are related to the transactions undertaken by the support departments where the costs are incurred.

(a) **Logistical transactions** are those activities concerned with organising the flow of resources throughout the manufacturing process.

(b) **Balancing transactions** are those activities which ensure that demand for and supply of resources are matched.

(c) **Quality transactions** are those activities which relate to ensuring that production is at the required level of quality.

(d) **Change transactions** are those activities associated with ensuring that customers' requirements (delivery date, changed design etc) are met.

These transactions in the support departments are the appropriate cost drivers to use.

Exam focus point

ABC is the topic of one the questions in the pilot paper.

3 ABSORPTION COSTING VERSUS ABC

3.1 The following example illustrates the point that traditional cost accounting techniques result in a misleading and inequitable division of costs between low-volume and high-volume products, and that ABC can provide a more meaningful allocation of costs.

3.2 EXAMPLE: ACTIVITY BASED COSTING

Suppose that Cooplan Ltd manufactures four products, W, X, Y and Z. Output and cost data for the period just ended are as follows.

	Output units	*Number of production runs in the period*	*Material cost per unit*	*Direct labour hours per unit*	*Machine hours per unit*
			£		
W	10	2	20	1	1
X	10	2	80	3	3
Y	100	5	20	1	1
Z	100	5	80	3	3
		14			

Direct labour cost per hour	£5
Overhead costs	£
Short run variable costs	3,080
Set-up costs	10,920
Expediting and scheduling costs	9,100
Materials handling costs	7,700
	30,800

Required

Prepare unit costs for each product using conventional costing and ABC.

3.3 SOLUTION

Using a **conventional absorption costing approach** and an absorption rate for overheads based on either direct labour hours or machine hours, the product costs would be as follows.

	W	*X*	*Y*	*Z*	*Total*
	£	£	£	£	£
Direct material	200	800	2,000	8,000	
Direct labour	50	150	500	1,500	
Overheads *	700	2,100	7,000	21,000	
	950	3,050	9,500	30,500	44,000
Units produced	10	10	100	100	
Cost per unit	£95	£305	£95	£305	

* £30,800 ÷ 440 hours = £70 per direct labour or machine hour.

Using **activity based costing** and assuming that the number of production runs is the cost driver for set-up costs, expediting and scheduling costs and materials handling costs and that machine hours are the cost driver for short-run variable costs, unit costs would be as follows.

	W	*X*	*Y*	*Z*	*Total*
	£	£	£	£	£
Direct material	200	800	2,000	8,000	
Direct labour	50	150	500	1,500	
Short-run variable overheads (W1)	70	210	700	2,100	
Set-up costs (W2)	1,560	1,560	3,900	3,900	
Expediting, scheduling costs (W3)	1,300	1,300	3,250	3,250	
Materials handling costs (W4)	1,100	1,100	2,750	2,750	
	4,280	5,120	13,100	21,500	44,000
Units produced	10	10	100	100	
Cost per unit	£428	£512	£131	£215	

Workings

1	£3,080 ÷ 440 machine hours =	£7 per machine hour
2	£10,920 ÷ 14 production runs =	£780 per run
3	£9,100 ÷ 14 production runs =	£650 per run
4	£7,700 ÷ 14 production runs =	£550 per run

Summary

Product	*Conventional costing unit cost*	*ABC unit cost*	*Difference per unit*	*Difference in total*
	£	£	£	£
W	95	428	+ 333	+3,330
X	305	512	+ 207	+2,070
Y	95	131	+ 36	+3,600
Z	305	215	– 90	–9,000

The figures suggest that the **traditional volume-based absorption costing system is flawed.**

(a) It **underallocates overhead costs to low-volume products** (here, W and X) and **over-allocates overheads to higher-volume products** (here Z in particular).

(b) It **underallocates overhead costs to smaller-sized products** (here W and Y with just one hour of work needed per unit) and **over allocates overheads to larger products** (here X and particularly Z).

ABC versus traditional costing methods

3.4 Both traditional absorption costing and ABC systems adopt the two stage allocation process.

Allocation of overheads

3.5 **ABC** establishes **separate cost pools for support activities** such as despatching. As the costs of these activities are assigned directly to products through cost driver rates, **reapportionment of service department costs is avoided.**

Absorption of overheads

3.6 The principal difference between the two systems is the way in which overheads are absorbed into products.

(a) **Absorption costing** most commonly uses two **absorption bases** (labour hours and/or machine hours) to charge overheads to products.

(b) **ABC** uses **many cost drivers** as absorption bases (number of orders, number of despatches and so on).

3.7 **Absorption rates** under **ABC** should therefore be **more closely linked to the causes of overhead costs.**

Cost drivers

3.8 The **principal idea** of ABC is to **focus attention on what causes costs to increase,** ie the **cost drivers.**

(a) Those **costs that do vary with production volume,** such as power costs, should be traced to products using production **volume-related cost drivers** as appropriate, such as direct labour hours or direct machine hours.

Overheads which do not **vary** with output but **with some other activity** should be traced to products using **transaction-based cost drivers,** such as number of production runs and number of orders received.

(b) Traditional costing systems allow overheads to be related to products in rather more arbitrary ways producing, it is claimed, less accurate product costs.

Question 2

A company manufactures two products, L and M, using the same equipment and similar processes. An extract of the production data for these products in one period is shown below.

	L	*M*
Quantity produced (units)	5,000	7,000
Direct labour hours per unit	1	2
Machine hours per unit	3	1
Set-ups in the period	10	40
Orders handled in the period	15	60

Overhead costs	£
Relating to machine activity	220,000
Relating to production run set-ups	20,000
Relating to handling of orders	45,000
	285,000

Required

Calculate the production overheads to be absorbed by one unit of each of the products using the following costing methods.

(a) A traditional costing approach using a direct labour hour rate to absorb overheads
(b) An activity based costing approach, using suitable cost drivers to trace overheads to products

Answer

(a) **Traditional costing approach**

		Direct labour hours
Product L = 5,000 units × 1 hour		5,000
Product M = 7,000 units × 2 hours		14,000
		19,000

∴ Overhead absorption rate	=	£285,000 / 19,000
	=	£15 per hour

Overhead absorbed would be as follows.

Product L	1 hour × £15	=	£15 per unit
Product M	2 hours × £15	=	£30 per unit

(b) **ABC approach**

		Machine hours
Product L	= 5,000 units × 3 hours	15,000
Product M	= 7,000 units × 1 hour	7,000
		22,000

Using ABC the overhead costs are absorbed according to the **cost drivers**.

	£			
Machine-hour driven costs	220,000	÷	22,000 m/c hours	= £10 per m/c hour
Set-up driven costs	20,000	÷	50 set-ups	= £400 per set-up
Order driven costs	45,000	÷	75 orders	= £600 per order

Overhead costs are therefore as follows.

		Product L		Product M
		£		£
Machine-driven costs	(15,000 hrs × £10)	150,000	(7,000 hrs × £10)	70,000
Set-up costs	(10 × £400)	4,000	(40 × £400)	16,000
Order handling costs	(15 × £600)	9,000	(60 × £600)	36,000
		163,000		122,000
Units produced		5,000		7,000
Overhead cost per unit		£32.60		£17.43

These figures suggest that product M absorbs an unrealistic amount of overhead using a direct labour hour basis. Overhead absorption should be based on the activities which drive the costs, in this case machine hours, the number of production run set-ups and the number of orders handled for each product.

4 MERITS AND CRITICISMS OF ABC

4.1 As you will have discovered when you attempted the question above, there is nothing difficult about ABC. Once the necessary information has been obtained it is similar to traditional absorption costing. This simplicity is part of its appeal. Further merits of ABC are as follows.

(a) The **complexity of manufacturing has increased**, with wider product ranges, shorter product life cycles and more complex production processes. **ABC recognises this complexity with its multiple cost drivers.**

(b) In a more competitive environment, companies must be able to assess product profitability realistically. **ABC facilitates a good understanding of what drives overhead costs.**

(c) In modern manufacturing systems, overhead functions include a lot of non-factory-floor activities such as product design, quality control, production planning and customer services. **ABC is concerned with all overhead costs** and so it takes management accounting beyond its 'traditional' factory floor boundaries.

Criticisms of ABC

4.2 It has been suggested by critics that **activity based costing has some series flaws.**

(a) Some measure of (arbitrary) cost apportionment may still be required at the cost pooling stage for items like rent, rates and building depreciation.

(b) Can a single cost driver explain the cost behaviour of all items in its associated pool?

(c) Unless costs are caused by an activity that is measurable in quantitative terms and which can be related to production output, cost drivers will not be usable. What drives the cost of the annual external audit, for example?

(d) ABC is sometimes introduced because it is fashionable, not because it will be used by management to provide meaningful product costs or extra information. If management is not going to use ABC information, an absorption costing system may be simpler to operate.

(e) The cost of implementing and maintaining an ABC system can exceed the benefits of improved accuracy.

(f) **Implementing** ABC is often **problematic**. Recent journal articles have highlighted the following issues.

(i) The incorrect belief that ABC can solve all an organisation's problems
(ii) Lack of the correct type of data
(iii) Difficulty in determining appropriate cost drivers

'World wide adoption rates for ABC have peaked at 20 per cent and a declining number of firms are giving it further consideration.' (Tom Kennedy, *Financial Management*, May 2000). Recent UK studies have found ABC usage rates of about 25%, with larger organisations and service sector companies being most likely to use it.

Other uses of ABC

4.3 The information provided by analysing activities can support the management functions of planning, control and decision making, provided it is used carefully and with full appreciation of its implications.

Planning

4.4 Before an ABC system can be implemented, management must analyse the organisation's activities, determine the extent of their occurrence and establish the relationships between activities, products/services and their cost.

4.5 The **information database** produced from such an exercise can then be **used as a basis for forward planning and budgeting**. For example, once an organisation has set its budgeted production level, the database can be used to determine the number of times that activities will need to be carried out, thereby establishing necessary departmental staffing and machine levels. Financial budgets can then be drawn up by multiplying the budgeted activity levels by cost per activity.

4.6 This activity-based approach may not produce the final budget figures but it can **provide the basis for different possible planning scenarios.**

Control

4.7 The information database also provides an **insight into the way in which costs are structured and incurred in service and support departments.** Traditionally it has been difficult to control the costs of such departments because of the lack of relationship between departmental output levels and departmental cost. With ABC, however, it is possible to **control or manage the costs by managing the activities which underlie them** by monitoring a number of key performance measures.

Decision making

4.8 Many of ABC's supporters claim that it can assist with decision making in a number of ways.

- **Provides accurate and reliable cost information**
- Establishes a long-run product cost
- Provides data which can be used to evaluate different ways of delivering business.

It is therefore particularly suited to the following types of decision.

- Pricing
- Promoting or discontinuing products or parts of the business
- Redesigning products and developing new products or new ways to do business

4.9 Note, however, that an ABC cost is **not a true cost,** it is **simply an average cost** because some costs such as depreciation are still arbitrarily allocated to products. An ABC cost is therefore **not a relevant cost** for all decisions.

4.10 The traditional cost behaviour patterns of fixed cost and variable cost are felt by advocates of ABC to be unsuitable for longer-term decisions, when resources are not fixed and changes in the volume or mix of business can be expected to have an impact on the cost of all resources used, not just short-term variable costs. A **five-level hierarchy** has therefore been suggested to facilitate the analysis of costs.

Level	Basis	Cost are dependent on ...	Example
1	Unit	volume of production	Machine power
2	Batch	number of batches	Set-up costs
3	Process	existence of a process	Quality control
4	Product	existence of a product group/line	Product management
5	Facility	existence of a production facility	Rent and rates

4.11 As Innes and Mitchell (*Activity Based Costing: A Review with Case Studies*, CIMA 1990) say:

> 'This analysis of cost highlights the decision level at which each element of cost can be influenced. For example, the reduction of production cost levels will not simply depend on a general reduction in output volumes, but also on reorganising production to perhaps increase *batch* size and reduce batch volume, on eliminating or modifying a *process*, on cutting out or merging product lines or on altering or removing *facility* capacity'.

4.12 Raiborn *et al* explain how a product cost is determined using such an analysis.

> 'Traditionally, accounting has assumed that if costs did not vary until changes in production at the unit level, those costs were fixed rather than variable. Such an assumption is not true. Batch level, product level, and organizational level costs are all variable, but these types of costs vary for reasons other than changes in production volume. For this reason, to determine an accurate estimate of product or service cost, **costs should be accumulated at each successively higher level of costs.** Because unit, batch and product level costs are all related to units of products (merely at different levels), these **costs can be gathered together at the product level to match with the revenues generated by product sales. Organisational level costs,** however, are not product related and, thus, should **only be subtracted in total from net product revenues.**'

Such an analysis provides an alternative method of determining product profitability which may be used for management decision making.

4.13 For example, suppose an organisation was deciding whether to withdraw a product. The withdrawal of the product could result in a **reduction in the number of some activities** and hence in a cost saving. This cost saving might **apply to unit level, batch level and product level costs but not to facility level costs,** which represent fixed infrastructure costs which would be incurred anyway.

Conclusion

4.14 The examiner of the equivalent paper to 2.4 under the old syllabus provided a useful conclusion to the ABC debate in a recent article. [Emphasis is BPP's own.]

> 'It can offer considerable benefits to some companies but a **decision to adopt ABC should not be taken lightly**. The staff time involved in developing and getting the system into operation is conservatively estimated at two person years, costs are at least £100,000 though it depends on the system being implemented and the size of the company.
>
> It requires **serious commitment of resources** and top management support.
>
> It is not a system that the accountant can do in his/her spare time.
>
> Indeed it is **not a system that should focus exclusively on the accountant**. It is common for a project team to develop the ABC system on which the accountant can play a part, but not necessarily a dominating part.
>
> Its **implementation** is not easy but is **made easier by the availability of IT support** within the organisation. Existing IT facilities can make it possible, at little extra cost, to obtain useful cost driver data. There is now a range of PC based packages on which to develop stand alone ABC systems, or they can be integrated with existing systems, though the former seem advisable at the prototype stage.
>
> There are cases of companies claiming significant benefit from adopting ABC (changing the way they do business) but also **examples of companies trying but rejecting the activity-based approach**.
>
> To be effective, cost management must be based on a sound knowledge of an organisation's cost structure, the proportion of its overheads, the degree of competition, its information needs within the organisation, an appreciation of how costs are determined and how they may be influenced. Only after **consideration of these factors can a judgement be made on the potential for an organisation of ABC**.'
>
> *Evaluating the Potential of Activity-Based Costing,* Mike Tayles, ACCA Students' Newsletter

Exam focus point

As well as being able to establish activity based costs, you must be prepared to answer a discursive question on ABC on, for example, its value in planning, control and decision making.

5 LIFE CYCLE COSTING

What are life cycle costs?

5.1 A product's life cycle costs are incurred **from its design stage through development to market launch, production and sales, and finally to its eventual withdrawal from the market**. The component elements of a product's cost over its life cycle could therefore include the following.

- **Research & development costs**
- The **cost of purchasing any technical data** required

- **Training costs** (including initial operator training and skills updating)
- **Production costs**
- **Distribution costs**
- **Marketing costs**
- **Inventory costs** (holding spare parts, warehousing and so on)
- **Retirement and disposal costs**

5.2 Life cycle costs can apply to services, customers and projects as well as to physical products.

5.3 **Traditional cost accumulation systems** are based on the financial accounting year and tend to dissect a product's life cycle into a series of 12-month periods. This means that traditional management accounting systems **do not accumulate costs over a product's entire life cycle** and **do not** therefore **assess a product's profitability over its entire life.** Instead they do it on a periodic basis.

5.4 **Life cycle costing,** on the other hand, **tracks and accumulates actual costs and revenues** attributable to each product **over the entire product life cycle.** Hence the total profitability of any given product can be determined.

KEY TERM

Life cycle costing is the accumulation of costs over a product's entire life.

The product life cycle

5.5 **Every product goes through a life cycle.**

(a) **Introduction**. The product is introduced to the market. Potential customers will be unaware of the product or service, and the organisation may have to spend further on advertising to bring the product or service to the attention of the market.

(b) **Growth**. The product gains a bigger market as demand builds up. Sales revenues increase and the product begins to make a profit.

(c) **Maturity**. Eventually, the growth in demand for the product will slow down and it will enter a period of relative maturity. It will continue to be profitable. The product may be modified or improved, as a means of sustaining its demand.

(d) **Decline**. At some stage, the market will have bought enough of the product and it will therefore reach 'saturation point'. Demand will start to fall. Eventually it will become a loss-maker and this is the time when the organisation should decide to stop selling the product or service.

5.6 The level of sales and profits earned over a life cycle can be illustrated diagrammatically as follows.

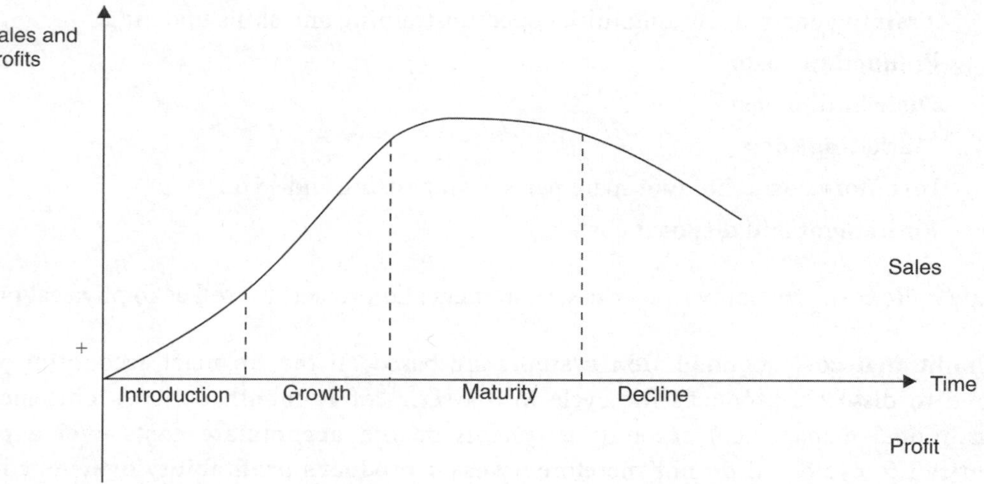

The horizontal axis measures the duration of **the life cycle**, which **can last** from, say, **18 months to several hundred years**. Children's crazes or fad products have very short lives while some products, such as binoculars (invented in the eighteenth century) can last a very long time.

Problems with traditional cost accumulation systems

5.7 Traditional cost accumulation systems do not tend to relate **research and development costs** to the products that caused them. Instead they **write off** these costs on an annual basis **against** the **revenue generated by existing products**. This makes the existing products seem **less profitable** than they really are. If research and development costs are not related to the causal product the true profitability of that product cannot be assessed.

5.8 Traditional cost accumulation systems usually **total all non-production costs** and record them as a **period expense**.

The value of life cycle costing

5.9 With life cycle costing, non-production costs are traced to individual products over complete life cycles.

(a) The total of these costs for each individual product can therefore be reported and compared with revenues generated in the future.

(b) The visibility of such costs is increased.

(c) **Individual product profitability can be more fully understood** by attributing *all* costs to products.

(d) As a consequence, **more accurate feedback information** is available on the organisation's success or failure in developing new products. In today's competitive environment, where the ability to produce new and updated versions of products is paramount to the survival of an organisation, this information is vital.

6 TARGET COSTING

6.1 To compete effectively in today's competitive market, organisations must continually redesign their products with the result that **product life cycles** have become much **shorter.** The **planning, development and design stage** of a product is therefore **critical** to an organisation's cost management process. Considering possible **cost reductions at this stage** of a product's life cycle (rather than during the production process) is now one of the most **important** issues facing management accountants in industry.

6.2 Here are some examples of **decisions made at the design stage** which directly **impact on the cost of a product.**

- The number of different components
- Whether the components are standard or not
- The ease of changing over tools

6.3 Japanese companies have developed **target costing** as a **response to the problem of controlling and reducing costs over the product life cycle.**

KEY TERMS

Target costing involves setting a target cost by subtracting a desired profit margin from a competitive market price.

Target cost is an estimate of a product cost which is determined by subtracting a desired profit margin from a competitive market price. This target cost may be less than the planned initial product cost but it is expected to be achieved by the time the product reaches the maturity stage of the product life cycle.

6.4 Target costing has its **greatest impact at the design stage** because a large percentage of a product's **life cycle costs are determined by decisions made early in its life cycle.**

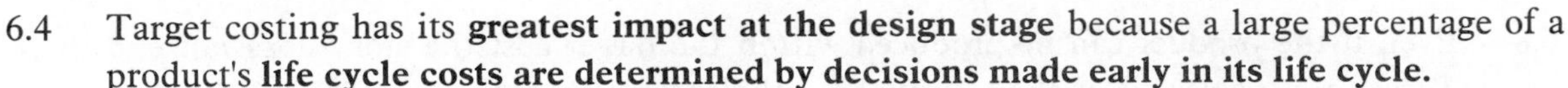

Case example

A number of countries, including Holland, Sweden and Norway, have passed or proposed legislation that will require manufacturers of certain goods to take back a product at the end of its life for safe disposal or salvage. The European Commission has also developed proposals to force manufacturers of electrical and electronic goods to take back obsolete products.

Any requirements to take back products will affect post-production costs and ultimately overall projected lifecycle costs. To cut these costs, the design could, for example, make the product easy to dismantle and its raw materials easy to recycle. Or it may be possible to design a product for use over several lifecycles rather than just one. (Xerox has been doing this for several years.)

6.5 The technique requires managers to **change** the way they think about the **relationship between cost, price and profit.**

(a) **Traditionally** the approach is to **develop a product, determine the production cost** of that product, **set a selling price,** with a **resulting profit** or loss.

(b) The **target costing approach** is to **develop a product, determine the market selling price and desired profit margin,** with a **resulting cost** which must be achieved.

6.6 In 'Product costing/pricing strategy' (*ACCA Students Newsletter*, August 1999), the examiner of the old syllabus Paper 9 provided a useful summary of the **steps in the implementation of the target costing process.**

Step 1. Determine a product specification of which an adequate sales volume is estimated.

Step 2. Set a selling price at which the organisation will be able to achieve a desired market share.

Step 3. Estimate the required profit based on return on sales or return on investment.

Step 4. Calculate the target cost = target selling price – target profit.

Step 5. Compile an estimated cost for the product based on the anticipated design specification and current cost levels.

Step 6. Calculate cost gap = estimated cost – target cost.

Step 7. Make efforts to close the gap. This is more likely to be successful if efforts are made to 'design out' costs prior to production, rather than to 'control out' costs during the production phase. (See Paragraph 6.7 below.)

Step 8. Negotiate with the customer before making the decision about whether to go ahead with the project.

6.7 When a product is first manufactured, its target cost may well be much lower than its currently-attainable cost, which is determined by current technology and processes. Management can then set **benchmarks for improvement** towards the target costs, by improving technologies and processes. Various techniques can be employed.

- Reducing the **number of components**
- Using **standard components** wherever possible
- **Training** staff in more efficient techniques
- Acquiring new, more efficient **technology**
- Cutting out **non-value-added activities** (identified using **activity analysis** etc)
- Using **different materials**
- Using **cheaper staff**

6.8 Even if the product can be produced within the target cost the story does not end there. Target costing can be applied throughout the entire life cycle. **Once the product goes into production target costs will therefore gradually be reduced.** These reductions will be **incorporated into the budgeting process**. This means that **cost savings** must be **actively sought** and made **continuously** over the life of the product.

Case examples

The following comments appeared in an article in the Financial Times in January 1993. (Emphasis is BPP's.)

'Mercedes-Benz, one of the world's most prestigious and tradition-laden carmakers, has taken its time to wake up to the daunting dimensions of the challenges it faces in the **rapidly-changing world car market** of the 1990s.

The company has accepted that radical changes in the world car market mean that Mercedes-Benz will no longer be able to demand premium prices for its products based on an image of effortless superiority and a content of the ultimate in automotive engineering.

Instead of developing the ultimate car and then charging a correspondingly sky-high price as in the past, Mercedes-Benz is taking the dramatic and radical step of moving to '**target pricing**'. **It will decide what the customer is willing to pay** in a particular product category - priced against its competitors - it will **add its profit margin** and then the real work will begin to **cost every part and component to bring in the vehicle at the target price**.

The following extracts are from an article which appeared three months later.

'The marketing motto for the Mercedes-Benz compact C-class is that it offers customers more car for their money.

It is the first practical example of the group's new pricing policy. The range embodies a principle new to Mercedes which states that **before any work starts a new product will be priced according to what the market will bear and what the company considers an acceptable profit. Then each component and manufacturing process will be costed to ensure the final product is delivered at the target price.**

Under the old system of building the car, adding up the costs and then fixing a price, the C-class would have been **between 15 per cent and 20 per cent dearer** than the 10-year-old outgoing 190 series, Mr Vöhringer said.

Explaining the practical workings of the new system, he explained that project groups for each component and construction process were instructed without exception to increase productivity by between 15 and 25 per cent. And they had to reach their targets in record time.

One result was that development time on the new models was cut to 40 months, about a third less than usual. But the most important effect, according to Mr Vöhringer, has been to **reduce** the **company's cost disadvantages vis-à-vis Japanese competitors in this class from 35 per cent to only 15 per cent**.'

Chapter roundup

- An **opportunity cost** is the value of the benefit sacrificed by not carrying out an alternative course of action.
- In a system of cost accumulation using opportunity costing, the costs of resources consumed are valued at their opportunity cost rather than at the amount it actually costs to acquire them.
- An alternative to absorption costing is **activity based costing (ABC).**
- ABC involves the identification of the factors **(cost drivers)** which cause the costs of an organisation's major activities. Support overheads are charged to products on the basis of their usage of an activity.
  - For costs that vary with production level in the short term, the cost driver will be volume related (labour or machine hours).
  - Overheads that vary with some other activity (and not volume of production) should be traced to products using transaction-based cost drivers such as production runs or number of orders received.
- **Life cycle costing** tracks and accumulates costs and revenues attributable to each product over the entire product life cycle.
- A **product life cycle** can be divided into four phases.
  - Introduction
  - Growth
  - Maturity
  - Decline
- **Target costing** involves setting a target cost by subtracting a desired profit margin from a competitive market price.

Quick quiz

1 Material X costs £20 per kg and is in short supply. 100 kgs are needed for job Y but those 100 kgs could be used on job Z, where they will earn contribution of £5 per kg. What is the opportunity cost per kg of using material X on job Y?

2 *Choose the correct phrases.*

Traditional costing systems tend to allocate **too great/too small** a proportion of overheads to high volume products and **too great/too small** a proportion of overheads to low volume products.

3 *Fill in the blanks.*

The major ideas behind ABC are as follows.

(a) Activities cause ....

(b) Producing products creates demand for the ....

(c) Costs are assigned to a product on the basis of the product's consumption of the ....

4 *Match the most appropriate cost driver to each cost.*

Costs	*Cost driver*
(a) Set-up costs	Number of machine hours
(b) Short-run variable costs	Number of production runs
(c) Materials handling and despatch	Number of orders executed

5 ABC recognises the complexity of modern manufacturing by the use of multiple cost pools. True or false?

6 *Match the following costs to the appropriate life cycle cost classification.*

Costs	*Classifications*
Design	Inventory costs
Energy costs	Acquisition costs
Warehousing	Maintenance costs
Transportation	Operation costs
Customer service	Product distribution costs

7 Life cycle costing is the profiling of cost over a product's production life.

☐ True

☐ False

8 *Fill in the blanks using words from the list (a) to (h).*

Target cost = ... minus ....

Cost gap = ... minus ....

(a) target cost
(b) cost gap
(c) budgeted selling price
(d) production cost
(e) target selling price
(f) estimated cost
(g) estimated selling price
(h) target profit

Answers to quick quiz

1 £(20 + 5) = £25

2 Too great
Too small

3 (a) Costs
(b) Activities
(c) Activities

4 (a) Number of production runs
(b) Number of machine hours
(c) Number of orders executed

5 False. Complexity is recognised by the use of multiple cost drivers.

6

Cost	*Classification*
Design	Acquisition costs
Energy costs	Operation costs
Warehousing	Inventory costs
Transportation	Product distribution costs
Customer service	Maintenance costs

7 False. It also looks at development costs and so on which are incurred prior to production, and any dismantling costs, which are incurred once production ceases.

8 Target cost = estimated selling price minus target profit
Cost gap = estimated cost – target cost

Now try the questions below from the Exam Question Bank

Question to try	Level	Marks	Time
3	Introductory	-	-
4	Exam	25	45 mins

Chapter 4

SPECIFIC ORDER COSTING

Topic list		Syllabus reference
1	**Job costing and batch costing**	6(e), 6(f), 7(a)(i)
2	**Contract costing**	6(e), 7(a)(i)

Introduction

In Chapter 2 and 3 we looked at some costing methods which can be used to accumulate the costs of a product or a service. This chapter describes the costing methods used to accumulate the costs of jobs, batches and contracts.

As you should know from your earlier studies, **costing methods** are **designed to suit the way goods are processed** or manufactured or the way that services are provided. **Each organisation's** costing method will therefore have **unique features**, but it is more than likely that costing methods of firms in the **same line of business** will have **features in common**. On the other hand, organisations involved in completely different activities, such as hospitals and car part manufacturers, will use very different costing methods.

In this chapter we will examine **job, batch and contract costing** (collectively known as **specific order costing**). Process costing and service costing are dealt with in the next chapter. You have already encountered all of these costing methods in your earlier studies but where necessary we have included 'Knowledge Brought Forward' boxes to remind you of important points.

Study guide

Section 20 – Cost accumulation II

- Apply appropriate cost accumulation methods to problems of job, batch and contract costing

Exam guide

You are unlikely to get a question entirely devoted to specific order costing but you may need to use job, batch or contract costing in both Section A and Section B questions.

1 JOB COSTING AND BATCH COSTING

KEY TERMS

Specific order costing should be used to cost separately identifiable contracts, jobs or batches.

Job costing is a form of specific order costing in which costs are attributed to individual jobs.

Batch costing is a form of specific order costing in which costs are attributed to batches of products.

Knowledge brought forward from earlier studies

Job costing and batch costing

- A **job** is a cost unit which consists of a single order or contract. **Job costing** is a costing method applicable where work is undertaken to customers' special requirements and each order is of comparatively short duration.
- Jobs move through processes and operations as a continuously identifiable unit, and because each job usually differs in one or more respects from every other job, a separate record must be maintained to show the details of a particular job.
- **Rectification costs** (costs of rectifying substandard work) can be either charged as a direct cost of the job concerned if not a frequent occurrence or treated as production overhead if regarded as a normal part of the work carried out generally.
- In general, the procedures for costing a **batch** (a group of similar articles which maintains its identity during one or more stages of production and is treated as a cost unit) are very similar to those for costing jobs. The batch is treated as a job during production. Once the batch is completed, the cost per unit is calculated as total batch cost ÷ number of units in the batch.

1.1 An example should remind you of the principles involved in job costing.

1.2 EXAMPLE: JOB COSTING

In order to identify the costs incurred in carrying out a range of work to customer specification in its factory, a company has a job costing system. This system identifies costs directly with a job where this is possible and reasonable. In addition, production overhead costs are absorbed into the cost of jobs at the end of each month, at an actual rate per direct labour hour for each of the two production departments.

One of the jobs carried out in the factory during the month just ended was Job No 123. The following information has been collected relating specifically to this job.

(a) 400 kilos of Material Y were issued from stores to Department A.

(b) 76 direct labour hours were worked in Department A at a basic wage of £4.50 per hour. Six of these hours were classified as overtime at a premium of 50%.

(c) 300 kilos of Material Z were issued from stores to Department B.

(d) Department B returned 30 kilos of material Z to the storeroom being excess to requirements for the job.

(e) 110 direct labour hours were worked in Department B at a basic wage of £4.00 per hour. 30 of these hours were classified as overtime at a premium of 50%. All overtime worked in Department B in the month is a result of the request of a customer for early completion of another job which had been originally scheduled for completion in the month following.

(f) Department B discovered defects in some of the work, which was returned to Department A for rectification. Three labour hours were worked in Department A on rectification (these are additional to the 76 direct labour hours in Department A noted above). Such rectification is regarded as a normal part of the work carried out generally in the department.

(g) Department B damaged five kilos of material Z which then had to be disposed of. Such losses of material are not expected to occur.

(h) Total costs incurred during the month on all jobs in the two production departments were as follows.

	Dept A	*Dept B*
	£	£
Direct materials issued from stores (note (i))	6,500	13,730
Direct materials returned to stores	135	275
Direct labour, at basic wage rate (note (ii))	9,090	11,200
Indirect labour, at basic wage rate	2,420	2,960
Overtime premium	450	120
Lubricants and cleaning compounds	520	680
Maintenance	720	510
Other	1,200	2,150

Notes

(i) This includes, in Department B, the scrapped Material Z. This was the only material scrapped in the month.

(ii) All direct labour in Department A is paid a basic wage of £4.50 per hour, and in Department B £4.00 per hour. Department A direct labour includes a total of 20 hours spent on rectification work.

(i) Materials are priced at the end of each month on a weighted average basis. Relevant information of material stock movements during the month, for Material Y and Z, is as follows.

	Material Y	*Material Z*
Opening stock	1,050 kilos (value £529.75)	6,970 kilos (value £9,946.50)
Purchases	600 kilos at £0.50 per kilo	16,000 kilos at £1.46 per kilo
	500 kilos at £0.50 per kilo	
	400 kilos at £0.52 per kilo	
Issues from stores	1,430 kilos	8,100 kilos
Returns to stores	-	30 kilos

Required

Prepare a list of the costs that should be assigned to Job No 123. Provide an explanation of your treatment of each item.

1.3 SOLUTION

Job 123: Costs	£
Materials	
Material Y (W1). The question states that this specifically relates to Job No 123.	202.00
Material Z (W2). As above. The figure takes account of the fact that of the 300 kilos initially issued to the job, 30 kilos were returned and are therefore not included. The lost five kilos are discussed in W2.	391.50
Labour	
Department A *(76 hrs × £4.50 per hr).* As material Y.	342.00
Department B *(110 hrs × £4 per hr).* As material Y. (Overtime is not a consideration at this stage.) In neither the case of dept A or dept B was the overtime worked specifically at the request of the Job 123 customer and so the overtime premium should not be a direct cost of Job 123.	440.00
Overheads	
Department A *(76 hrs × £2.70 per hour (W3)).* The explanation of items included in overheads, and the calculation of absorption rates, are shown at W3.	205.20
Department B *(110 hrs × £2.25 per hour (W3)).*	247.50

Workings

1 **Cost of material Y issued to Job 123**

This is priced at the month-end weighted average.

	kg	£
Balance b/f	1,050	529.75
plus, at 50p per kg	600	300.00
plus, at 50p per kg	500	250.00
plus, at 52p per kg	400	208.00
	2,550	1,287.75

Hence weighted average is £1,287.75/2,550 kg =50.5p per kg
So cost of stock issued to Job 123 is 400 kg × 50.5p per kg = £202

2 **Cost of material Z issued to Job 123**

Also priced at the month-end weighted average

	kg	£
Balance b/f	6,970	9,946.50
plus, at £1.46 per kg	16,000	23,360.00
	22,970	33,306.50

Hence weighted average is £33,306.50/22,970 = £1.45 per kg
So cost of stock issued to Job 123 is (300 – 30)kg × £1.45 per kg = £391.50

It is assumed that the five kilos damaged in Department B will be charged to Job 123, just as any adverse material usage would be charged to the job in hand. Alternatively the loss of the five kilos could be regarded as an exceptional item and charged as an overhead cost to an appropriate overhead cost centre (eg abnormal wastage in Department B).

3 **Rates of overhead absorption**

	Notes	*Dept A* £	*Dept B* £
Costs			
Rectification work (20 hrs × £4.50 per hr)	1	90	-
Indirect labour	2	2,420	2,960
Overtime premium	3	450	-
Lubricants	4	520	680
Maintenance	4	720	510
Other	4	1,200	2,150
		5,400	6,300

	Dept A Hrs	*Dept B* Hrs
Departmental direct labour hours		
£9,090/£4.50	2,020	
£11,200/£4.00		2,800
Less: Rectification work (included in overheads)	(20)	-
Direct labour hours	2,000	2,800

Absorption rates. Dept A: £5,400/2,000 hrs = £2.70 per hr
Dept B: £6,300/2,800 hrs = £2.25 per hr

Notes

1 Rectification is *normal* and part of work carried out *generally* in the dept.

2 Their time is not allocated to any particular job, but all jobs benefit indirectly.

3 The inclusion of overtime premium in overheads ensures that all jobs bear the same direct wage rate, regardless of whether they were performed in what is classified as overtime, or not. All overtime in Dept B, however, is specifically attributable to another job because the overtime was incurred at the specific request of the customer for the job.

4 Each job benefits from these in a general way.

Question 1

How can information concerning the cost of individual jobs be used?

Answer

(a) **To establish a price** which the customer should be charged for the job, in situations where the customer agrees to pay a price based on 'actual cost plus'. Because the job's share of fixed and variable production overhead has been included in the cost (in addition to, of course, the direct costs of the job), a selling price set in excess of total costs will ensure that all expenses have been covered, provided of course that the organisation works at budgeted capacity.

(b) **In budgeting for future periods.** If the work to customer specification forms any sort of a pattern, an analysis of previous years' jobs will provide a useful basis for the production of future periods' work.

(c) **For control purposes.** If an estimated cost for a job is produced, actual costs can be compared with estimate. Excess costs can be investigated with a view to control action.

(d) **To measure the actual profit or loss on each job** in cases where a customer is quoted a firm price before a job begins.

Job costing for internal services

1.4 It is possible to use a job costing system to control the costs of an internal service department, such as the maintenance department or the printing department. If a job costing system is used it is possible to **charge the user departments for the cost of specific jobs carried out, rather than apportioning the total costs of these service departments** to the user departments using an arbitrarily determined apportionment basis (as detailed in Chapter 2).

1.5 An internal job costing system for service departments will have the following advantages.

Advantages	Comment
Realistic apportionment	The identification of expenses with jobs and the subsequent charging of these to the department(s) responsible means that costs are borne by those who incurred them.
Increased responsibility and awareness	User departments will be aware that they are charged for the specific services used and may be more careful to use the facility more efficiently. They will also appreciate the true cost of the facilities that they are using and can take decisions accordingly.
Control of service department costs	The service department may be restricted to charging a standard cost to user departments for specific jobs carried out or time spent. The difference between the standard charges and the actual expenditure then gives a guide to the efficiency/ inefficiency of the service department.

2 CONTRACT COSTING

KEY TERM

Contract costing is a form of specific order costing in which costs are attributed to individual contracts.

Knowledge brought forward from earlier studies

Contract costing

- A **contract** is a cost unit or cost centre which is charged with the direct costs of production and an apportionment of head office overheads
- **Contract costing** is the name given to a method of job costing where the job to be carried out is of such magnitude that a formal contract is made between the customer and supplier. It applies where work is undertaken to customers' special requirements and each order is of long duration (compared with the time to which job costing applies). The work is usually constructional and *in general* the method is similar to job costing, although there are, of course, a few differences.
- Each contract is separately identifiable and is usually of a non-standard nature.
- Costs will need to be collected and charged to the contract's job/work in progress account.
- **Retention monies** are released by the customer when the contract is fully completed and is accepted by him/her.
- Much work may be done by **subcontractors**, the cost of which is treated as a direct expense.
- **Progress payments** (value of work done and certified – a retention – payments made to date) are likely to be made by the customer throughout the course of the contract work.

Question 2

Describe three methods of accounting for company-owned plant used in a contract.

Answer

(a) The contract may be charged depreciation on the plant.

(b) The contract may be charged with the current book value of the plant. On the receipt of the plant the contract account is debited with the current book value of the plant. At the end of an accounting period or when plant is returned from the site to head office (or another contract site) the contract account is credited with the written down value of the plant. The difference between the values on the debit and credit side of the account at the end of the year is the cost of the equipment to the contract for the year.

(c) A third method of accounting for plant costs is to open a *plant account*, which is debited with the depreciation costs and the running costs (repairs, fuel and so on) of the equipment. A notional hire charge is then made to contracts using the plant, at a rate of £x per day.

2.1 The problems which may arise in contract costing are as follows.

Problem	Comment
Identifying direct costs	Because of the large size of the job, many cost items which are usually thought of as production overhead are charged as direct costs of the contract (for example supervision, hire of plant, sub-contractors' fees or charges and so on).
Low indirect costs	For most contracts the only item of indirect cost would be a charge for head office expenses.
Difficulties of cost control	Because of the size of some contracts and some sites, there are often cost control problems (material losses, pilferage, labour supervision and utilisation, damage to and loss of plant and tools, vandalism and so on).
Dividing the profit between different accounting periods	When a contract covers two or more accounting periods, how should the profit (or loss) on the contract be divided between the periods?

Profits on contracts

2.2 Progress payments do not necessarily give rise to profit immediately because of retentions.

2.3 If a **contract is started and completed in the same accounting period**, the calculation of the **profit** is straightforward, **sales minus the cost of the contract**.

2.4 A more difficult problem emerges when a **contract is incomplete at the end of an accounting period**. The contractor may have spent considerable sums of money on the work, and received substantial progress payments, and even if the work is not finished, the **contractor will want to claim some profit on the work done so far.**

2.5 To make this point clearer, suppose that a company starts four new contracts in its accounting year to 31 December 20X1, but at the end of the year, none of them has been completed. All of the contracts are eventually completed in the first few months of 20X2 and they make profits of £40,000, £50,000, £60,000 and £70,000 respectively, £220,000 in total. If **profits are not taken until the contracts are finished**, the company would make no profits at all in 20X1, when most of the work was done, and £220,000 in 20X2. Such **violent fluctuations in profitability** would be confusing not only to the company's management, but also to shareholders and the investing public at large.

2.6 The **problem arises because contracts are for long-term work**, and it is a **well-established practice that some profits should be taken in an accounting period, even if the contract is incomplete.**

2.7 The method of calculating profit on an incomplete contract may vary. The **concept of prudence should always be applied**, however, and we suggest that the following guidelines are followed.

(a) If the contract is in its **early stages, no profit should be taken.** Profit should only be taken when the outcome of the contract can be assessed with reasonable accuracy.

(b) For a contract on which substantial costs have been incurred, but which is **not yet near completion** (that is, it is in the region of **35% to 85% complete**) a formula can be used to determine the profit to be taken.

(c) If the contract is **nearing completion**, the size of the eventual profit should be foreseeable with reasonable certainty and there is no need to be excessively prudent. Profit could be calculated as value of work certified to date minus the cost of work certified, for example.

Losses on incomplete contracts

2.8 At the end of an accounting period, it may be that instead of finding that the contract is profitable, a loss is expected. When this occurs, **the total expected loss should be taken into account as soon as it is recognised, even if the contract is not yet complete.** This means that in the next accounting period, the contract should break even, making neither a profit nor a loss, because the full loss has already been charged to the profit and loss account.

Exam focus point

The costing of specific orders was covered in detail in your earlier studies. A Paper 2.4 question on the topic might incorporate basic techniques and knowledge along with the more advanced Paper 2.4 aspects of absorption costing, stock valuation and decision making.

Chapter roundup

- You should be aware of the basics of job, batch and contract costing from your earlier studies but the main points are summarised below.
- **Job costing** is the costing method used where each cost unit is separately identifiable. The work is undertaken to customers' special requirements, is of comparatively short duration, is usually carried out within a factory or workshop and moves through processes and operations as a continuously identifiable unit.
- **Batch costing** is similar to job costing in that each batch of similar articles is separately identifiable. The cost per unit manufactured in a batch is the total batch cost divided by the number of units in the batch.
- **Contract costing** is the form of job costing which applies where the job is of a large scale and long duration. The majority of costs for a contract are direct costs.

Quick quiz

1 *Match the features to the costing method.*

Costing methods	*Features*
Job costing	(a) Work undertaken to customers' special requirements
	(b) Long duration
Contract costing	(c) Low indirect costs
	(d) Work usually of a non-standard nature
	(e) Short duration
	(f) Retention monies
	(g) Continuously identifiable unit
	(h) Separate records for each piece of work
	(i) Progress payments
	(j) High level of direct costs

2 *Choose from the list below to show how progress payments are calculated.*

+	cost of work certified
retention	payments made to date
progress payments	=
value of work done and certified	revenue
direct costs	depreciation
indirect costs	÷
deposit	x
–	profit
cost of work done	loss

3 *Match the correct profit with each type of contract.*

(a) Contract 35% to 85% complete	(1) Sales minus cost of the contract
(b) Contract started and completed in the same accounting period	(2) No profit should be taken
(c) Contract is in its early stages	(3) 10% of expected profit
(d) Contract nearing completion	(4) Appropriate formula
	(5) Value of work certified to date – cost of work certified
	(6) 35% to 85% expected profit
	(7) Sales – progress payments

Answers to quick quiz

1 Job costing (a), (e), (g), (h)
Contract costing (a), (b), (c), (d), (f), (g), (h), (i), (j)

2 Progress payments = value of work done and certified – retention – payments made to date

3 (a) (4)
(b) (1)
(c) (2)
(d) (5)

Now try the question below from the Exam Question Bank

Question to try	Level	Marks	Time
5	Exam	25	45 mins

Chapter 5

PROCESS COSTING AND SERVICE COSTING

	Topic list	Syllabus reference
1	**A framework for dealing with process costing questions**	**7(a)(i)**
2	**Losses in process**	**7(a)(i)**
3	**Valuing opening and closing work in progress**	**7(a)(i)**
4	**Changes in stock levels and losses**	**7(a)(i)**
5	**Losses/gains at different stages**	**7(a)(i)**
6	**Joint products and by-products**	**7(a)(i)**
7	**Service costing**	**7(a)(i)**
8	**Costing in not-for-profit organisations**	**6(b), 6(c)**
9	**Service costing for internal services**	**6(e)**

Introduction

In the previous chapter we looked at the three specific order costing methods. In this chapter we are going to consider process costing and service costing.

We begin the chapter with **process costing**, which you have already covered at an introductory level in your earlier studies. Here we will be building on your knowledge and considering some more complex applications.

In the second part of the chapter we turn our attention to **service costing** which is concerned with establishing the costs, not of items of production, but of services rendered. It is used by organisations operating in a service industry that wish to cost their services, and by organisations wishing to establish the cost of services carried out by some of their own departments. Basic service costing was also covered in your earlier studies but for Paper 2.4 we need to look at higher-level issues.

This is **quite a long chapter** but don't worry because you've **covered most of it at an introductory level**. You will probably be surprised by how much of it you already know.

Study guide

Section 18 – Costing systems: context and framework

- Describe the costing information requirements and limitations in not-for-profit organisations

Section 20 – Cost accumulation II

- Apply appropriate cost accumulation methods to problems of process costing
- Prepare statements which value losses in process and work in progress
- Calculate appropriate costs for joint products and prepare process costing statements which account for by-products
- Apply appropriate cost accumulation methods to problems of service costing
- Describe difficulties of service costing in the not-for-profit sector

Exam guide

A Section B question could well deal entirely with process costing. Service costing could appear with other topics. Both costing methods could appear in Section A questions.

KEY TERM

Process costing is a costing method used where it is not possible to identify separate units of production, or jobs, usually because of the continuous nature of the production processes involved.

Knowledge brought forward from earlier studies

Process costing

- It is common (but not essential) to **identify process costing with continuous production** such as oil refining, or the manufacture of soap, paint, textiles, paper, foods and drinks, many chemicals and so on. Process costing may also be associated with the continuous production of large volumes of low-cost items, such as cans or tins and with mass production industries such as car manufacturing.
- The **features** of process costing which make it different from job or batch costing are as follows.
  - The continuous nature of production in many processes means that there will usually be **opening and closing work in progress which must be valued**. In process costing it is not possible to build up cost records of the cost per unit of output or the cost per unit of closing stock because **production in progress is an indistinguishable homogeneous mass.**
  - There is often a **loss in process** due to spoilage, wastage, evaporation and so on.
  - Output from production may be a single product, but there may also be a **by-product** (or by-products) and/or **joint products**.
- The basic idea behind process costing is that, where a series of separate processes is required to manufacture the finished product, **the output of one process becomes the input to the next** until the final output is made in the final process. For example, if two processes are required the accounts would look like this.

PROCESS 1 ACCOUNT

	Units	£		Units	£
Direct materials	1,000	50,000	Output to process 2	1,000	90,000
Direct labour		20,000			
Production overhead		20,000			
	1,000	90,000		1,000	90,000

PROCESS 2 ACCOUNT

	Units	£		Units	£
Materials from process 1	1,000	90,000	Output to finished goods	1,500	150,000
Added materials	500	30,000			
Direct labour		15,000			
Production overhead		15,000			
	1,500	150,000		1,500	150,000

  - Direct labour and production overhead may be treated together in an examination question as '**conversion cost**'.
  - Added materials, labour and overhead in process 2 are added gradually throughout the process. Materials from process 1, in contrast, will be introduced in full at the start of process 2.
  - The 'units' columns in the process accounts are for memorandum purposes only and help you to ensure that you do not miss out any entries.

1 A FRAMEWORK FOR DEALING WITH PROCESS COSTING QUESTIONS

1.1 Process costing is centred around four key steps.

Step 1. **Determine output and losses.**

- Determine expected output.
- Calculate normal loss and abnormal loss and gain.
- Calculate equivalent units if there is closing or opening work in progress.

Step 2. **Calculate cost per unit of output, losses and WIP.**

- Calculate cost per unit or cost per equivalent unit.

Step 3. **Calculate total cost of output, losses and WIP.**

- In some examples this will be straightforward
- If there is closing and/or opening work-in-progress a **statement of evaluation** will have to be prepared.

Step 4. **Complete accounts.**

- Complete the process account.
- Write up the other accounts required such as abnormal loss/gain accounts.

Exam focus point

The exact work done at each step will depend on whether there are losses, opening stock, closing stock and so on, but this four-step approach can be adopted in any question.

2 LOSSES IN PROCESS

2.1 Losses during processing can happen through evaporation of liquids, wastage, or rejected units, and so the quantity of materials output from a process might be less than the quantities input. How would any losses be costed?

Three different ways of costing losses

2.2 One way of costing output is to say that the **cost per unit should be based on actual units produced (output), so that any lost units have no cost at all**. This would mean that the cost varies according to the actual loss in the period. If some loss in process is unavoidable, and if the amount of loss varies a little from period to period, this approach to costing will result in fluctuations in unit costs.

It might be more satisfactory to take a longer-term view of loss, and calculate average unit costs on the basis of average loss over a longer period of time. This would give greater stability and consistency to unit costs of production between one period and the next.

2.3 A second way of costing the output is to say that **lost units have a cost, which should be charged to the P & L account whenever they occur**. The cost per unit would then be **based on units of *input* rather than units of output.**

The main drawback to this method of costing is that **if some loss in processing is unavoidable** and to be expected, there would be **some cost of production unavoidably written off to the P & L account** in every period, and this is an unsatisfactory method of costing.

2.4 The third method of costing loss (described below and covered in your earlier studies) is a **compromise system,** which is based on the following view.

- **If some loss is to be expected, it should not be given a cost.**
- **If there is some loss that 'shouldn't happen', it ought to be given a cost.**

Normal loss and abnormal loss/gain

KEY TERMS

- **Normal loss** is the loss expected in the normal course of operations for unavoidable reasons.
- **Abnormal loss** is the loss resulting when actual loss is greater than the normal or expected loss.
- **Abnormal gain** is the gain resulting when actual loss is less than the normal or expected loss.

2.5 Normal loss is not given a cost.

Abnormal loss is given a cost.

Abnormal gain is given a 'cost', which is debited rather than credited to the process cost account: it is a 'negative' cost and so an item of gain.

Scrap value of loss

2.6 Loss or spoilage may have a scrap value.

(a) **The scrap value of normal loss is usually deducted from the cost of materials.**

(b) **The scrap value of abnormal loss (or abnormal gain) is usually set off against its cost, in an abnormal loss (abnormal gain) account.**

2.7 As the question that follows will show, the three steps to remember are these.

Firstly Separate the scrap value of normal loss from the scrap value of abnormal loss or gain.

Secondly In effect, subtract the scrap value of normal loss from the cost of the process, by crediting it to the process account (as a 'value' for normal loss).

Thirdly ***Either*** subtract the value of abnormal loss scrap from the cost of abnormal loss, by crediting the abnormal loss account.

or subtract the cost of the abnormal gain scrap from the value of abnormal gain, by debiting the abnormal gain account.

Question 1

Navigator Ltd has a factory which operates two production processes. Normal spoilage in each process is 10%, and scrapped units out of process 1 sell for 50p per unit whereas scrapped units out of process 2 sell for £3. Output from process 1 is transferred to process 2: output from process 2 is finished output ready for sale.

Relevant information about costs for period 5 are as follows.

	Process 1 Units	Process 1 £	Process 2 Units	Process 2 £
Input materials	2,000	£8,100		
Transferred to process 2	1,750			
Materials from process 1			1,750	
Added materials			1,250	£1,900
Labour and overheads		£10,000		£22,000
Output to finished goods			2,800	

Required

Prepare accounts for process 1, process 2, abnormal loss, abnormal gain and scrap.

Answer

(a) *Process 1*

***Step 1.* Determine output and losses**

The normal loss is 10% of 2000 units = 200 units, and the actual loss is (2000 - 1750) = 250 units. This means that there is abnormal loss of 50 units.

Actual output	1,750 units
Abnormal loss	50 units
Expected output (90% of 2,000)	1,800 units

***Step 2.* Calculate cost per unit of output and losses**

(i) The total value of scrap is 250 units at 50p per unit = £125. We must split this between the scrap value of normal loss and the scrap value of abnormal loss.

	£
Normal loss	100
Abnormal loss	25
Total scrap (250 units × 50p)	125

(ii) The scrap value of normal loss is first deducted from the materials cost in the process, in order to calculate the output cost per unit and then credited to the process account as a 'value' for normal loss. The cost per unit in process 1 is calculated as follows.

	Total cost		*Cost per expected unit of output*
	£		£
Materials	8,100		
Less normal loss scrap value *	100		
	8,000	(÷ 1,800)	4.44
Labour and overhead	10,000	(÷ 1,800)	5.56
Total	18,000	(÷ 1,800)	10.00

* It is usual to set this scrap value of normal loss against the cost of materials.

***Step 3.* Calculate total cost of output and losses**

		£
Output	(1,750 units × £10)	17,500
Normal loss	(200 units × £0.50)	100
Abnormal loss	(50 units × £10)	500
		18,100

***Step 4.* Complete accounts**

PROCESS 1 ACCOUNT

	Units	£		Units	£
Materials	2,000	8,100	Output to process 2*	1,750	17,500
Labour and Overhead		10,000	Normal loss (scrap a/c)	200	100
			Abnormal loss a/c	50	500
	2,000	18,100		2,000	18,100

* At £10 per unit.

(b) *Process 2*

***Step 1.* Determine output and losses**

The normal loss is 10% of the units processed = 10% of (1,750 + 1,250) = 300 units. The actual loss is (3,000 - 2,800) = 200 units, so that there is abnormal gain of 100 units. These are *deducted* from actual output to determine expected output.

	Units
Actual output	2,800
Abnormal gain	(100)
Expected output (90% of 3,000)	2,700

***Step 2.* Calculate cost per unit of output and losses**

(i) The total value of scrap is 200 units at £3 per unit = £600. We must split this between the scrap value of normal loss and the scrap value of abnormal gain. Abnormal gain's scrap value is 'negative'.

		£
Normal loss scrap value	300 units × £3	900
Abnormal gain scrap value	100 units × £3	(300)
Scrap value of actual loss	200 units × £3	600

(ii) The scrap value of normal loss is first deducted from the cost of materials in the process, in order to calculate a cost per unit of output, and then credited to the process account as a 'value' for normal loss. The cost per unit in process 2 is calculated as follows.

	Total cost £		*Cost per expected unit of output* £
Materials:			
Transferred from process 1	17,500		
Added in process 2	1,900		
	19,400		
Less scrap value of normal loss	900		
	18,500	(÷ 2,700)	6.85
Labour and overhead	22,000	(÷ 2,700)	8.15
	40,500	(÷ 2,700)	15.00

***Step 3.* Calculate total cost of output and losses**

		£
Output	(2,800 units × £15)	42,000
Normal loss	(300 units × £3)	900
		42,900
Abnormal gain	(100 units × £15)	(1,500)
		41,400

***Step 4.* Complete accounts**

PROCESS 2 ACCOUNT

	Units	£		Units	£
From process 1	1,750	17,500	Finished output *	2,800	42,000
Added materials	1,250	1,900			
Labour and overhead		22,000	Normal loss	300	900
	3,000	41,400	(scrap a/c)		
Abnormal gain a/c	100*	1,500			
	3,100	42,900		3,100	42,900

* At £15 per unit

(c) and (d)

Abnormal loss and abnormal gain accounts

For each process, one or the other of these accounts will record three items.

(i) The cost/value of the abnormal loss/gain (corresponding entry to that in the process account).

(ii) The scrap value of the abnormal loss or gain, to set off against it.

(iii) A balancing figure, which is written to the P&L a/c as an adjustment to the profit figure.

ABNORMAL LOSS ACCOUNT

	Units	£		£
Process 1	50	500	Scrap a/c (scrap value of ab. loss)	25
			Profit and loss a/c (balance)	475
		500		500

ABNORMAL GAIN ACCOUNT

	£		Units	£
Scrap a/c (scrap value of abnormal gain units)	300	Process 2	100	1,500
Profit & loss a/c (balance)	1,200			
	1,500			1,500

(e) **Scrap account**

This is credited with the cash value of actual units scrapped. The other entries in the account should all be identifiable as corresponding entries to those in the process accounts, and abnormal loss and abnormal gain accounts.

SCRAP ACCOUNT

	£		£
Normal loss:		Cash:	
Process 1 (200 × 50p)	100	sale of process 1 scrap (250 × 50p)	125
Process 2 (300 × £3)	900	sale of process 2 scrap (200 × £3)	600
Abnormal loss a/c	25	Abnormal gain a/c	300
	1,025		1,025

Losses with a disposal cost

2.8 The **basic calculations required** in such circumstances are as follows.

(a) Increase the process costs by the cost of disposing of the units of normal loss and use the resulting cost per unit to value good output and abnormal loss/gain.

(b) The normal loss is given no value in the process account.

(c) Include the disposal costs of normal loss on the debit side of the process account.

(d) Include the disposal costs of abnormal loss in the abnormal loss account and hence in the transfer of the cost of abnormal loss to the profit and loss account.

2.9 Suppose that input to a process was 1,000 units at a cost of £4,500. Normal loss is 10% and there are no opening and closing stocks. Actual output was 860 units and loss units had to be disposed of at a cost of £0.90 per unit.

Normal loss = 10% × 1,000 = 100 units and so abnormal loss = 900 – 860 = 40 units
Cost per unit = (£4,500 + (100 × £0.90))/900 = £5.10

2.10 The relevant accounts would be as follows.

PROCESS ACCOUNT

	Units	£		Units	£
Cost of input	1,000	4,500	Output	860	4,386
Disposal cost of			Normal loss	100	-
Normal loss		90	Abnormal loss	40	204
	1,000	4,590		1,000	4,590

ABNORMAL LOSS ACCOUNT

	£		£
Process a/c	204	Profit and loss a/c	240
Disposal cost (40 × £0.90)	36		
	240		240

3 VALUING OPENING AND CLOSING WORK IN PROGRESS

3.1 Suppose that we have the following process account for period 13.

PROCESS ACCOUNT

	Units	£		Units	£
Opening WIP	300	800			
Materials	700	5,400	Finished goods	800	?
Labour and overhead		2,850	Closing WIP	200	?
	1,000	9,050		1,000	9,050

How do we value the finished goods and closing work in process?

3.2 With any form of process costing involving closing WIP, we have to apportion costs between output and closing WIP. To apportion costs 'fairly' we make use of the concept of **equivalent units of production**.

Equivalent units

KEY TERM

Equivalent units are whole units of complete work equivalent to units of incomplete work. They are used in process costing to value opening and closing work in progress.

3.3 Let's suppose that in the example above the degree of completion is as follows.

(a) **Direct materials.** These are added in full at the start of processing, and so any opening WIP or closing WIP have 100% of their direct material content. (This is not always the case. Materials might be added gradually throughout the process, in which case opening stock will only be a certain percentage complete as to material content.)

(b) **Direct labour and production overhead.** These are usually assumed to be incurred at an even rate through the production process, so that when we refer to a unit that is 50% complete, we mean that it is half complete for labour and overhead, although it might be 100% complete for materials.

3.4 Continuing with the example, let us also make the following suppositions.

(a) The opening WIP is 100% complete for materials, and one-third complete for labour and overhead.

(b) The opening WIP's total cost of £800 consists of £550 direct materials and £250 labour and overhead.

(c) The closing WIP is 100% complete for materials and 25% complete for labour and overhead.

3.5 The cost of finished output and closing WIP will depend on the stock pricing method used, either FIFO or weighted average cost.

Equivalent units and FIFO

3.6 With **FIFO**, we take the following view.

(a) **Opening WIP is finished first**. It is part-costed at the start of the period (in our example, at £800). We must therefore calculate how much it has cost to complete the units during the current period. The total cost to completion of these units of opening stock is the sum of the cost brought forward as opening stock value plus the cost in the current period to complete the units.

(b) **Some units are started and finished in the period**, and so are 100% produced during the period. In our example, the total finished output in the period is 800 units, of which 300 units were opening stock, finished first, and so 500 units must have been started and finished in the period.

(c) **Some units are started and only part-completed**. These are the units of closing WIP.

3.7 Let's now use our four step approach.

Step 1. **Determine output and losses**. We know what the output is and there are no losses, but we need to calculate equivalent units.

		Equivalent units of work in the current period			
	Total units	*Materials*		*Labour and overhead*	
Opening WIP	300	0	(note (a))	200	(note (b))
Units started and finished in the period	500	500	(note (c))	500	(note (c))
Total finished output	800				
Closing WIP	200	200	(note (d))	50	(note (e))
	1,000	700		750	

Notes

(a) Opening WIP already 100% complete for materials, so no more cost to add

(b) Opening WIP one-third complete at the start of the period, and so two-thirds of work (labour and overhead) needed to complete in this period. Equivalent units = $^2/_3 \times 300 = 200$

(c) Units started and completed in this period are one equivalent unit each

(d) Closing WIP: 100% complete for materials

(e) Closing WIP: equivalent units of labour and overhead = 25% of 200 = 50

Step 2. **Calculate cost per unit of output, losses and WIP**. We can now calculate an average cost per equivalent unit.

	Materials	*Labour and overhead*
Costs incurred in the period	£5,400	£2,850
Equivalent units of work done	700	750
Cost per equivalent unit (approx)	£7.715	£3.80

Step 3. **Calculate total cost of output, losses and WIP**. These costs per equivalent unit can now be used to build up the total costs of finished output and closing WIP.

	Materials			*Labour and overhead*		*Total cost*
	Units		£	Units	£	£
Opening WIP cost b/f			550		250	800
Cost to complete			-	200 × £3.80	760	760
Total	300		550		1,010	1,560
Other finished units	500	× £7.715	3,857	500 × £3.80	1,900	5,757
Total finished output	800		4,407		2,910	7,317
Closing WIP	200	× £7.715	1,543	50 × £3.80	190	1,733
	1,000		5,950		3,100	9,050

Step 4. **Complete accounts**

PROCESS ACCOUNT

	£		£
Opening WIP	800	Finished goods	7,317
Materials	5,400		
Labour and overhead	2,850	Closing WIP	1,733
	9,050		9,050

Previous process costs

3.8 A common mistake made by students is to forget to include the costs of the previous process as an input cost in a subsequent process when dealing with production that passes through a number of processes (such as in the example in the 'knowledge brought forward' box).

3.9 Note that the **costs of the previous process** (Process 1 in the aforementioned box) are **combined together into a single cost of input in Process 2** and that we always **assume that the transfers into Process 2 are 100% complete with respect to Process 1 costs.** The cost of any additional materials added in Process 2 is treated separately from Process 1 costs.

Equivalent units and weighted average costing

3.10 If weighted average costing is used instead of FIFO, the equivalent units rules are the same, **except that** the **cost of opening WIP is not kept distinct from costs incurred in the current period.** We **add the costs brought forward in opening WIP to the costs incurred in the period,** and **treat all finished output as a full equivalent unit.**

3.11 Returning for a last time to our example, if we used weighted average costing instead of FIFO, our four-step approach would be as follows.

Step 1. **Determine output and losses**

		Equivalent units	
	Total units	*Materials*	*Labour and overhead*
Finished output	800	800	800
Closing WIP	200	200	50
Total	1,000	1,000	850

Step 2. **Calculate cost per unit of output, losses and WIP**

	Materials	*Labour and overhead*
Costs incurred in the period	£5,950*	£3,100**
Equivalent units of work done	1,000	850
Cost per equivalent unit (approx)	£5.95	£3.647

* £(550 + 5,400) **£(250 + 2,850)

Step 3. **Calculate total cost of output, losses and WIP**

	Units	*Materials* £	*Labour and overheads* £	*Total* £
Finished output	800	*4,760	**2,918	7,678
Closing WIP	200	1,190	182	1,372
	1,000	5,950	3,100	9,050

* 800 × £5.95 ** 800 × £3.647

Step 4. **Complete accounts**

PROCESS ACCOUNT

	£		£
Opening WIP	800	Finished output	7,678
Materials	5,400		
Labour and overhead	2,850	Closing WIP	1,372
	9,050		9,050

Which to use - FIFO or weighted average

3.12 **FIFO stock valuation is more common than the weighted average method, and should be used unless an indication is given to the contrary**. You may find that you are presented with limited information about the opening stock, however.

(a) If you are **told the degree of completion of each element in opening stock**, but not the value of each cost element, then you must use the **FIFO method**.

(b) If you are not given the degree of completion of each cost element in opening stock, but you are **given the value of each cost element**, then you must use the **weighted average method**.

4 CHANGES IN STOCK LEVELS AND LOSSES

4.1 The previous paragraphs have dealt separately with the following.

- The treatment of loss and scrap
- The use of equivalent units as a basis for apportioning costs between units of output and units of closing stock

We must now look at a situation where **both problems** occur together. We shall begin with an example where loss has no scrap value.

4.2 The rules are as follows.

(a) **Costs** should be **divided between finished output, closing stock and abnormal loss/gain** using **equivalent units** as a basis of apportionment.

(b) **Units of abnormal loss/gain** are often taken to be **one full equivalent unit each**, and are valued on this basis, ie they carry their full 'share' of the process costs.

(c) **Abnormal loss units are an addition** to the total equivalent units produced but **abnormal gain units are subtracted** in arriving at the total number of equivalent units produced.

(d) Units of **normal loss are valued at zero equivalent units**, ie they do not carry any of the process costs.

4.3 EXAMPLE: CHANGES IN STOCK LEVEL AND LOSSES

The following data have been collected for a process.

Opening stock	none	Output to finished goods	2,000 units
Input units	2,800 units	Closing stock	450 units, 70% complete
Cost of input	£16,695	Total loss	350 units
Normal loss	10%; nil scrap value		

Required

Prepare the process account for the period.

4.4 SOLUTION

Step 1. **Determine output and losses**

STATEMENT OF EQUIVALENT UNITS

	Total units		*Equivalent units of work done this period*
Completely worked units	2,000	(× 100%)	2,000
Closing stock	450	(× 70%)	315
Normal loss	280		0
Abnormal loss	70	(× 100%)	70
	2,800		2,385

Step 2. **Calculate cost per unit of output, losses and WIP**

STATEMENT OF COST PER EQUIVALENT UNIT

$$\frac{\text{Costs incurred}}{\text{Equivalent units of work done}} = \frac{16{,}695}{2{,}385}$$

Cost per equivalent unit = £7

Step 3. **Calculate total cost of output, losses and WIP**

STATEMENT OF EVALUATION

	Equivalent units	£
Completely worked units	2,000	14,000
Closing stock	315	2,205
Abnormal loss	70	490
	2,385	16,695

Step 4. **Complete accounts**

PROCESS ACCOUNT

	Units	£		Units	£
Opening stock	-	-	Normal loss	280	0
Input costs	2,800	16,695	Finished goods a/c	2,000	14,000
			Abnormal loss a/c	70	490
			Closing stock c/d	450	2,205
	2,800	16,695		2,800	16,695

4.5 EXAMPLE: MORE CHANGES IN STOCK LEVEL AND LOSSES

Consider the following information for a process.

	Units	*Degree of completion* *Materials*	*Conversion cost*	*Cost* £
Opening stock	700 units	100%	30%	6,400
Closing stock	300 units	100%	40%	
Costs of input:				
direct materials	4,000 units			£30,400
conversion costs				£16,440

Normal loss: 5% of input during the period
Output to next process: 4,300 units

Required

Prepare the process account for the period, using the FIFO method of valuation.

4.6 SOLUTION

Step 1. **Determine output and losses**

(a) Total loss = opening stock plus input minus (output plus closing stock)
= 700 + 4,000 – (4,300 + 300)
= 100 units

Normal loss = 200 units (5% of 4,000)

Abnormal gain = 100 units (200 –100)

Units of abnormal gain are subtracted in arriving at the total of equivalent units of production in the period.

(b) STATEMENT OF EQUIVALENT UNITS

	Total units		*Equivalent units* *Materials*		*Conversion costs*
Opening stock completed	700	(0%)	0	(70%)	490
Fully worked units	3,600		3,600		3,600
Output to next process	4,300		3,600		4,090
Normal loss	200		0		0
Closing stock	300	(100%)	300	(40%)	120
	4,800		3,900		4,210
Abnormal gain	(100)		(100)		(100)
Equivalent units	4,700		3,800		4,110

Step 2. **Calculate cost per unit of output, losses and WIP**

STATEMENT OF COSTS PER EQUIVALENT UNIT

	Materials	*Conversion costs*
Costs incurred during the period	£30,400	£16,440
Equivalent units of production	3,800 units	4,110 units
Cost per equivalent unit	£8	£4

Step 3. **Calculate total cost of output, losses and WIP**

STATEMENT OF EVALUATION

	Materials Units	£	*Conversion costs* Units	£	*Total* £
Opening stock b/f					6,400
Work this period	0	0	490	1,960	1,960
					8,360
Fully worked units	3,600	28,800	3,600	14,400	43,200
Closing stock	300	2,400	120	480	2,880
Abnormal gain	(100)	(800)	(100)	(400)	(1,200)
	3,800	30,400	4,110	16,440	53,240

Step 4. **Complete accounts**

PROCESS ACCOUNT

	Units	£		Units	£
Opening stock	700	6,400	Normal loss	200	0
Direct materials	4,000	30,400	Output to next process:		
Conversion costs		16,440	Opening stock completed	700	8,360
	4,700	53,240	Fully worked units	3,600	43,200
Abnormal gain	100	1,200	Closing stock	300	2,880
	4,800	54,440		4,800	54,440

Changes in stock levels, loss and scrap

4.7 When loss has a scrap value, the accounting procedures are the same as those previously described, and changes in stock levels during a period do not affect these procedures in any way. However, if the **equivalent units are a different percentage** (of the total units) for **materials, labour and overhead,** it is a convention that the **scrap value of normal loss is deducted from the cost of materials before a cost per equivalent unit is calculated.** This point will be illustrated in the following example.

4.8 EXAMPLE: STOCK, LOSS AND SCRAP

The following information relates to process 2 of a three-stage production process for period 8.

Material input from process 1	5,000 units at £1.85 per unit	
Material added	£2,245	
Labour	£4,320	
Overhead	£3,090	
Number of units scrapped	800 units	
Opening stock was 600 units, complete as to:		
		£
material from process 1	100%, cost	945
material added	60%, cost	180
labour	30%, cost	405
overhead	30%, cost	135
		1,665
Work in progress at period end	1,000 units	
Complete as to:		
material from process 1	100%	
material added	75%	
labour	40%	
overhead	20%	

Normal loss is taken as 10% of input during the period. Scrap value of any loss is 50p per unit.

Required

Prepare the process account and the abnormal loss account.

4.9 SOLUTION

Normal loss is 10% of 5,000 units = 500 units. The normal loss on the opening stock of 600 units was accounted for in the previous period, period 7, and should not be calculated a second time in period 8.

Step 1. **Determine output and losses**

	Units	
(a) *Input*		
Opening stock		600
Input materials		5,000
		5,600
Output		
Opening stock completed	600	
Normal loss	500	
Abnormal loss (800 – 500)	300	
Closing stock	1,000	
		2,400
Units started and finished in period 8		3,200

(b) STATEMENT OF EQUIVALENT UNITS

		Equivalent units			
	Total units	Process 1 material	Added material	Labour	Overhead
Normal loss	500	0	0	0	0
Abnormal loss	300	300	300	300	300
Opening stock completed	600	0	240	420	420
Fully worked units	3,200	3,200	3,200	3,200	3,200
Closing stock	1,000	1,000	750	400	200
	5,600	4,500	4,490	4,320	4,120

Step 2. **Calculate cost per unit of output, losses and WIP**

STATEMENT OF COST PER EQUIVALENT UNIT

	Total	Equivalent units	Cost per equivalent unit
	£		£
Material from process 1	* 9,000	4,500	2.00
Added material	2,245	4,490	0.50
Labour	4,320	4,320	1.00
Overhead	3,090	4,120	0.75

* (5,000 units × £1.85 less scrap value of normal loss = £9,250 – £250 = £9,000)

It is a convention that the **scrap value of normal** loss should be **deducted from the cost of materials** and more specifically, where appropriate, **from the cost of materials input from the previous process.**

Step 3. **Calculate the total cost of output, losses and WIP**

STATEMENT OF EVALUATION

	Opening stock completed	Fully worked units	Abnormal loss	Closing stock
	£	£	£	£
Material from process 1 (at £2)	0	6,400	600	2,000
Added material (at £0.50)	120	1,600	150	375
Labour (at £1)	420	3,200	300	400
Overhead (at £0.75)	315	2,400	225	150
	855	13,600	1,275	2,925

The cost of work to complete the opening stock was £855 in period 8. Period 7 costs were £1,665. Total costs of these units were therefore £(855 + 1,665) = £2,520.

Step 4. **Complete accounts**

(a) PROCESS 2 ACCOUNT - PERIOD 8

	Units	£		Units	£
Opening stock	600	1,665	Normal loss (scrap a/c)	500	250
Material from process 1	5,000	9,250	Abnormal loss a/c	300	1,275
Added materials		2,245	Process 3:		
Labour		4,320	Opening stock finished	600	2,520
Overhead		3,090	Other units	3,200	13,600
			Closing stock c/d	1,000	2,925
	5,600	20,570		5,600	20,570

(b) ABNORMAL LOSS ACCOUNT

	£		£
Process 2 a/c	1,275	Scrap a/c (300 units × 50p)	150
		Profit and loss account	1,125
	1,275		1,275

4.10 Where stocks are valued, not on a FIFO basis, but on a **weighted average basis**, the value of opening stock is added to the costs in period 8, and completed units of opening stock are each given a value of one full equivalent unit of production.

In the previous example, the cost per equivalent unit would have been as follows.

STATEMENT OF COST PER EQUIVALENT UNIT

	Process 1 material	*Added material*	*Labour*	*Overhead*
	£	£	£	£
Period 8 costs	9,000(net)	2,245	4,320	3,090
Value of opening stock	945	180	405	135
	9,945	2,425	4,725	3,225
Equivalent units: as before	4,500	4,490	4,320	4,120
Opening stock	600	360	180	180
	5,100	4,850	4,500	4,300
Costs per equivalent unit	£1.95	£0.50	£1.05	£0.75

Total cost per equivalent unit = £4.25

Evaluation would be as follows.

STATEMENT OF EVALUATION

			£
(a)	Output to Process 3	3,800 units × £4.25	16,150
(b)	Abnormal loss	300 units × £4.25	1,275
(c)	Closing stock	(1,000 × £1.95 plus 750 × £0.50 plus 400 × £1.05 plus 200 × £0.75)	2,895
			20,320

Question 2

Use the statement of evaluation above to re-state the process account using the weighted average basis of stock valuation.

Answer

PROCESS 2 ACCOUNT - PERIOD 8
(using weighted average basis)

	Units	£		Units	£
Opening stock	600	1,665	Normal loss (scrap a/c)	500	250
Material from Process 1	5,000	9,250	Abnormal loss	300	1,275
Added materials		2,245	Process 3	3,800	16,150
Labour		4,320	Closing stock c/d	1,000	2,895
Overhead		3,090			
	5,600	20,570		5,600	20,570

5 LOSSES/GAINS AT DIFFERENT STAGES

5.1 In our previous examples, we have assumed that loss **occurs at the completion of processing,** so that **units of abnormal loss or abnormal gain** count as a **full equivalent unit of production**. It may be, however, that **units are rejected as scrap or 'loss' at an inspection stage before the completion of processing**. When this occurs, **units of abnormal loss should count as a proportion of an equivalent unit,** according to the volume of work done and materials added up to the point of inspection. An example may help as an illustration.

5.2 EXAMPLE: INCOMPLETE REJECTED ITEMS

Koffee Ltd is a manufacturer of processed goods, and the following information relates to process 2 during September 20X2.

During the month 1,600 units were transferred from process 1, at a valuation of £10,000. Other costs in process 2 were as follows.

Added materials	£4,650
Labour and overhead	£2,920

Units are inspected in process 2 when added materials are 50% complete and conversion cost 30% complete. No losses are normally expected, but during September 20X2, actual loss at the inspection stage was 200 units, which were sold as scrap for £2 each.

The company uses a FIFO method of stock valuation.

Required

Prepare the process 2 account and abnormal loss account for September 20X2.

5.3 SOLUTION

Step 1. **Determine output and losses**

STATEMENT OF EQUIVALENT UNITS

			Equivalent units	
	Total	*Process 1*	*Added*	*Conversion*
Item	*units*	*material*	*material*	*costs*
Units from process 1	1,600			
Abnormal loss	(200)	200	(50%) 100	(30%) 60
Fully worked units, Sept 20X2	1,400	1,400	1,400	1,400
		1,600	1,500	1,460

Step 2. **Calculate cost per unit of output and losses**

STATEMENT OF COST PER EQUIVALENT UNIT

Costs incurred, Sept 20X2	£10,000	£4,650	£2,920
Equivalent units	1,600	1,500	1,460
Cost per equivalent unit	£6.25	£3.10	£2

Step 3. **Calculate the total cost of output and losses**

STATEMENT OF EVALUATION

	Process 1 material	*Added material*	*Conversion cost*	*Total*
	£	£	£	£
Fully worked units	8,750	4,340	2,800	15,890
Abnormal loss	1,250	310	120	1,680
	10,000	4,650	2,920	17,570

The only difference between this example and earlier examples is that abnormal loss has been valued at less than one equivalent unit, for added materials and conversion costs.

Step 4. **Complete accounts**

PROCESS 2 ACCOUNT

	Units	£		Units	£
Process 1	1,600	10,000	Good units	1,400	15,890
Added materials	-	4,650	Abnormal loss	200	1,680
Labour and overhead	-	2,920			
	1,600	17,570		1,600	17,570

ABNORMAL LOSS ACCOUNT

	£		£
Process 2 account	1,680	Cash (sale of scrap)	400
		Profit and loss a/c	1,280
	1,680		1,680

Losses in process: gradual loss

5.4 When the loss during process occurs continuously the calculation of equivalent units is a little more tricky if we want the apportionment of the process costs to be as 'fair' as possible.

5.5 If it is possible physically to distinguish opening work in progress from material input in a period, and to distinguish output from closing work in progress, then these **items can be treated separately in the equivalent units calculations**.

(a) For example, in a continuous process (such as a chemical process) a loss may be the result of evaporation, so that work in progress may be of a significantly higher concentration than input (and kept in different tanks).

(b) Alternatively, if a large number of small objects (like confectionery) are produced in a process, objects at the end of the process may be more advanced (for example if chocolate has been moulded or shaped) than at the beginning.

The fact that loss is continuous does not therefore mean that work in progress at the beginning of a period, and materials input during the period need to be aggregated either physically, or in the calculation of equivalent units.

6 JOINT PRODUCTS AND BY-PRODUCTS

KEY TERMS

- **Joint products** are two or more products which are output from the same processing operation, but which are indistinguishable from each other (that is, they are the same commonly processed materials) up to their point of separation. Joint products have a substantial sales value (or a substantial sales value after further, separate, processing has been carried out to make them ready for sale).
- A **by-product** is a product which is similarly produced at the same time and from the same common process as the 'main product' or joint products. The distinguishing feature of a by-product is its relatively low sales value in comparison to the large value of the main product.

Knowledge brought forward from earlier studies

Joint and by products

- **Joint products** are not separately identifiable until the **separation point** or **split-off point** is reached.
- Costs incurred before this point are common or joint costs and must be apportioned in some manner to the various joint products.
- There are four principal methods of apportioning the joint costs.
  - **Physical measurement** (common costs are apportioned on the basis of the proportion that the output of each joint product bears by weight or volume to total output)
  - **Sales value at split-off point** (common costs are apportioned according to each product's ability to produce income)
  - **Sales value where no market value at split-off point exists** (common costs are apportioned according to each product's residual sales value or net realisable value (final sales value less post-separation processing and selling costs))
  - **Weighted average** (common costs are apportioned using units of each joint product multiplied by a weighting factor as the basis)
- **By-products** are not costed but there are three alternative approaches to dealing with by-product net realisable income (sales value less post-separation costs).
  - Treat as a separate, incidental source of income
  - Deduct from the total cost of sales
  - Deduct from the cost of production (thereby affecting stock valuation)

  The third method is arguably the most 'correct' but the choice of method will be influenced by practicality as well as by conceptual correctness.

Question 3

Three products are produced from a single process. During one period in which the process costs are expected to be £200,000, the following outputs are expected.

	Output	*Selling price*
Product A	8,000 tonnes	£5 per tonne
Product B	20,000 tonnes	£5 per tonne
Product C	25,000 tonnes	£10 per tonne

Required

(a) Calculate the apportionment of joint costs using the physical measurement method
(b) Calculate the apportionment using the relative sales value apportionment method.
(c) Why might the sales value method be considered fairer of the two?

Answer

(a) **Physical measurement**

Product	*A*	*B*	*C*	*Total*
Output (tonnes)	8,000	20,000	25,000	53,000
Proportion of joint cost allocated	8/53	20/53	25/53	
Joint costs	£30,188	£75,472	£94,340	

(b) **Relative sales value apportionment**

Product	*A*	*B*	*C*	*Total*
Sales value	(8,000 × £5) £40,000	(20,000 × £5) £100,000	(25,000 × £10) £250,000	£390,000
Proportion of joint cost allocated	4/39	10/39	25/39	
Joint costs	£20,513	£51,282	£128,205	

(c) A comparison of the gross profit margins illustrates that the relative sales value apportionment method could be regarded as the 'fairer' of the two, by ensuring that each joint product makes the

same gross profit margin after deducting the product's share of the common costs. In contrast, the physical measurement basis of apportionment could result in high gross profits for some joint products and low gross profits - even losses - for others.

Question 4

John Tellymade Ltd has a factory where four products are originated in a common process. During period 4, the costs of the common process were £16,000. Output was as follows.

	Units made	*Units sold*	*Sales value per unit*
Product P1	600		
Product Q1	400		
Product R	500	400	£ 7
Product S	600	450	£10

Products P1 and Q1 are further processed, separately, to make end-products P2 and Q2.

	Units processed	*Units sold*	*Cost of further processing*	*Sales value per unit*
Product P1/P2	600	600	£1,000	(P2) - £10
Product Q1/Q2	400	300	£2,500	(Q2) - £20

Required

Calculate each joint product's costs and their profit in period 4. There were no opening stocks.

Answer

(a)

	P2	*Q2*
	£	£
Sales value of production	6,000	8,000
Less further processing costs	1,000	2,500
Assumed sales value for P1 and Q1	5,000	5,500

(b) **Joint products**

	Sales value		*Allocation of joint costs*
	£	%	£
P1	5,000	25	4,000
Q1	5,500	27½	4,400
R	3,500	17½	2,800
S	6,000	30	4,800
	20,000	100	16,000

(c) **Profit statement**

	P1/2	*Q1/2*	*R*	*S*	*Total*
	£	£	£	£	£
Joint costs	4,000	4,400	2,800	4,800	16,000
Further processing	1,000	2,500	-	-	3,500
Cost of production	5,000	6,900	2,800	4,800	19,500
Less closing stock	0	1,725	560	1,200	3,485
Cost of sales	5,000	5,175	2,240	3,600	16,015
Sales	6,000	6,000	2,800	4,500	19,300
Profit	1,000	825	560	900	3,285
Profit/sales ratio	17%	14%	20%	20%	

Question 5

Three joint products are made from a common process costing £24,000. Output of JP1 is 2,000 kilograms, JP2 is 5,000 litres and JP3 is 14,000 litres. Weightings of 6, 4 and 2 are given to JP1, JP2 and JP3 respectively.

Required

Determine the costs of each joint product.

Answer

Output	*Product*	*Weighting*	*Weighted output*		*Share of joint costs*
	Units		Units	%	£
JP1	2,000 kg	6	12,000	20	4,800
JP2	5,000 litres	4	20,000	33 1/3	8,000
JP3	14,000 litres	2	28,000	46 2/3	11,200
			60,000	100	24,000

6.1 Note that we will be looking at joint product decisions in Chapter 14.

By-products and process costing statements

6.2 The following example illustrates how to incorporate by-product information into process costing statements.

6.3 EXAMPLE: WASTE AND LOSSES

The relevant data for process 3 of the manufacturing operations of Kie plc, a chemical company, in period 6 are as follows.

Opening and closing stocks	Nil
Materials transferred from process 2	20,000 litres at £5 per litre
Conversion costs	£67,000
Output	
Finished production	12,500 litres
By-product	3,000 litres
Waste	2,500 litres

Wasted units are the same chemical as finished output, except that they have been polluted during the process. They must be disposed of at a cost of £2 per litre.

The by-product is packed at a further cost of £2 per litre. Its selling price is £3 per litre. The net realisable value of the by-product produced in a period is credited to the process 3 account during that period. During period 6, 2,000 litres of by-product were sold.

The normal output from the process per 1,000 litres of input is as follows.

Finished production	700 litres
By-product	150 litres
Waste	100 litres
Loss through evaporation	50 litres

Required

Prepare the process 3 account, the by-product account, the waste account and the abnormal loss/gain account for period 6.

6.4 SOLUTION

There are two types of loss in this example: evaporation and waste. In each case it is necessary to distinguish between normal waste loss and normal evaporation loss on the one hand, and abnormal loss or gain on the other.

Another point to note about normal waste is that instead of having a scrap value to be credited to the process account, it has a disposal cost. The disposal cost of normal waste is **debited** to the process account.

Step 1. **Determine output and losses**

	Litres	*Equivalent units*
Finished output	12,500	12,500
By-product	3,000	0
Normal waste (20 × 100)	2,000	0
Abnormal waste (2,500 – 2,000)	500	500
Normal loss through evaporation (20 × 50)	1,000	0
Abnormal loss (balance)-evaporation	1,000	1,000
Total input units	20,000	14,000

Step 2. **Calculate cost per unit of output and losses**

	£
Materials from process 2	100,000
Conversion costs	67,000
Normal waste: disposal costs (2,000 × £2)	4,000
	171,000
Less net realisable value of by-product *(3,000 litres × £1)	3,000
	168,000

* Units sold are irrelevant, given the wording of the question.

Cost per equivalent unit = £168,000 ÷ 14,000 = £12

Steps 3 and 4. **Calculate total cost of output and losses and complete accounts**

PROCESS 3 ACCOUNT

	£		£
Process 2 materials	100,000	By-product: net realisable value	3,000
Conversion costs	67,000	Finished production	
Normal waste disposal costs	4,000	(12,500 × £12)	150,000
		Abnormal loss - evaporation	
		(1,000 × £12)	12,000
		Abnormal loss - waste	
		(500 × £12)	6,000
	171,000		171,000

BY - PRODUCT ACCOUNT

	£		£
Cash		Cash	
(packing costs, 2,000 × £2)	4,000	(sales of 2,000 litres)	6,000
Process account		Closing stock (1,000 litres)	
(3,000 litres × £1)	3,000	(balancing figure)	1,000
	7,000		7,000

It is assumed that the unsold by-product has not yet been packed. (The closing stock, if not yet packed, is valued at its net realisable value.)

NORMAL WASTE ACCOUNT

	£		£
Cash		Process 3 account	
(Disposal costs paid for)	4,000	(Disposal cost of normal waste)	4,000

Normal waste disposal costs are 2,000 litres × £2

ABNORMAL LOSS (WASTE) ACCOUNT

	£		£
Cash		Profit and loss account	7,000
(Disposal costs 500 litres × £2)	1,000		
Process a/c (abnormal loss of waste)	6,000		
	7,000		7,000

ABNORMAL LOSS (EVAPORATION) ACCOUNT

	£		£
Process account (1,000 × £12)	12,000	Profit and loss account	12,000

7 SERVICE COSTING

What are service organisations?

7.1 **Service organisations do not make or sell tangible goods.** Profit-seeking service organisations include accountancy firms, law firms, management consultants, transport companies, banks, insurance companies and hotels. Almost all non-profit-seeking organisations - hospitals, schools, libraries and so on - are also service organisations.

KEY TERM

Service/function costing is the application of cost accounting principles and techniques to services and functions.

7.2 **Service costing differs from the other costing methods** (product costing methods) for a number of reasons.

(a) With many services, the **cost of direct materials** consumed will be **relatively small** compared to the labour, direct expenses and overheads cost. In product costing the direct materials are often a greater proportion of the total cost. Catering and hospitality is a service, however, but in restaurants and canteens up to 40% of the cost relates to materials (food). And hospitals hold large stocks of medicines, equipment and consumables.

(b) The **output** of most service organisations is **difficult to define** and hence a **unit cost is difficult to calculate.**

(c) The service industry includes such a **wide range of organisations** which provide such different services and have such **different cost structures** that costing will vary considerably from one to another.

7.3 Tom Sheridan, in his article 'Costing in the service sector' (*Management Accounting*, May 1996), expands on these differences between service costing and product costing.

> 'Britain has a powerful service economy but nonetheless costing has only become a talking point in the service sector in the last decade. The service sector is wide-ranging. It not only covers a whole variety of business areas but also includes the head office administrative element of manufacturing companies...
>
> **In theory costing should be easier in the service sector**: there are **no stocks** or work-in-progress to be valued while, secondly, being a Johnny-come-lately in costing, it has been possible to ... **take advantage of the new concepts** ... Not a few new businesses in the service sector have been able to introduce ABC or incorporate ABC concepts, right from the start without going through the trauma and expense of dismantling their previous costing systems.

> **But there are disadvantages too**. The products are so **subjective**. **Simultaneity** and **perishability** are also key factors. One cannot build for stock. A lawyer without clients loses billable time for ever, a hotel with rooms unoccupied or an airline with seats unsold cannot recoup the costs after the event...
>
> If management's bottom-line objective is - as it usually is - cost management through cost understanding and traceability, the task is not made any easier because in most service industries one is dealing with intangibles. Everything is **intangible**. You cannot touch the product as you can in manufacturing. So, how do you measure it? How does one define a product or service? How does one cost IT? Everything seems to be an overhead and therefore, try as one will, one cannot get away from that bugbear of the management accountant's life - allocations ...
>
> A key to unravelling the complexities is to **take an ABC approach** ...'

Cost control and service organisations

7.4 The cost control techniques used by manufacturing organisations may not be entirely suitable for service organisations due to difficulties set out in Paragraph 7.2 and to the following service organisation characteristics.

Characteristic	Example
Most services are intangible	The customer on an aeroplane will be influenced by the comfort of the seat, the meal served, the attitudes of the cabin staff, the boarding process and so on. Managing and controlling the operation is therefore complex because it is difficult to establish exactly what the customer is buying, the journey or the treatment.
Service outputs vary from day to day	Services are provided by individuals whose performance can affect the quality of service provided, such as the service provided by hairdressers.
Production and consumption of many services are inseparable	A plane journey is produced and consumed simultaneously.
Services are perishable and cannot be stored	If an airline seat is unoccupied, the sales opportunity is lost forever and the service is wasted.

Unit cost measures

7.5 We mentioned above that the output of most service organisations is difficult to define. This is a particular problem with service costing: the difficulty in defining a realistic cost unit that represents a suitable measure of the service provided. Frequently, a **composite cost unit may be deemed more appropriate** if the service is a function of two activity variables. Hotels, for example, may use the 'occupied bed night' as an appropriate unit for cost ascertainment and control.

7.6 Typical cost units used by companies operating in a service industry are shown as follows.

Service	Cost unit
Road, rail and air transport services	Passenger/kilometre
Hotels	Occupied bed-night
Education	Full-time student
Hospitals	Patient

7.7 Each organisation will need to ascertain the cost unit most appropriate to its activities. If a number of organisations within an industry use a common cost unit, valuable comparisons can be made between similar establishments. This is particularly applicable to hospitals, educational establishments and local authorities.

Management accounting in service industries

7.8 The difficulties of costing service businesses that we have been looking at mean that attention should be directed on to other measures rather than the traditional 'cost per unit'.

(a) **Competitive performance** should focus on factors such as sales growth and market share.

(b) Like any other business, a service business needs to monitor its **financial performance** and to plan, and its short-term plans can be drawn up for service activities in the form of a budget. (Budgeting is covered in Chapters 9 to 13.)

   (i) There might be a budgeted expenditure limit for activities within the business.
   (ii) Standard performance measures can be established as targets for efficiency.

(c) **Service quality** is measured principally by qualitative measures, although quantitative measures are used by some businesses. If it were able to obtain the information, a retailer, for example, might use number of lost customers in a period as an indicator of service quality. Lawyers use the proportion of time spent with clients.

(d) **Flexibility** has three aspects.

   (i) **Speed of delivery** in the sense of punctuality is vital in some service industries like passenger transport: indeed punctuality is currently one of the most widely-publicised performance measures in the UK, because organisations like London Underground are making a point of it. Measures include waiting time in queues, as well as late trains.

   (ii) The **ability** of a service organisation **to respond to customers' specifications** is vital in a professional service such as legal advice where assistance must be tailored exactly to the customers' needs.

   (iii) **Coping with demand** is clearly measurable in quantitative terms in a mass service like London Underground which can ascertain the extent of overcrowding. It can also be very closely monitored in service shops: customer queuing time can be measured for example, and this is highly relevant for banks.

(e) **Resource utilisation** is usually measured in terms of productivity, which is the ratio of inputs to outputs. As usual, the ease with which this may be measured varies according to the service being delivered.

   (i) The main resource of a firm of accountants, for example, is the *time* of various grades of staff. The main output of an accountancy firm is chargeable hours.

   (ii) In a restaurant it is not nearly so straightforward. Inputs are the ingredients for the meal, the chef's time and expertise, the waiter's time and expertise, the surroundings, the other customers, and the customers' own likes and dislikes. A customer attitude survey might show whether or not a customer enjoyed the food, but it could not ascribe the enjoyment or lack of it to the quality of the ingredients, say, rather than the skill of the chef or the speed of the waiter.

(f) Companies do not have to **innovate** to be successful, but it helps! Others will try to steal their market, and so others' innovations must at least be matched. In a modern environment in which product quality, product differentiation and continuous improvement are the order of the day, a company that can find innovative ways of satisfying customers' needs has an important competitive advantage.

Non-financial indicators

7.9 There is a danger in service organisations of focusing excessively on financial performance measures, which can be easily quantified, thus placing an undue emphasis on maximising short-term performance even if this conflicts with maximising long-term performance. It is therefore more important in service organisations that a range of **non-financial indicators** be developed to provide better predictors for the attainment of long-term profitability goals. Here are some examples.

- Quality
- Number of customer complaints
- Lead times
- Delivery to time
- Non-productive hours
- System (machine) down time, and so on

7.10 Unlike traditional variance reports, measures such as these can be **provided quickly** for managers, per shift or on a daily or hourly basis. They are likely to be **easy to calculate**, and **easier** for non-financial managers **to understand** and therefore to use effectively.

7.11 The beauty of non-financial indicators is that **anything can be compared if it is meaningful to do so**. The measures should be **tailored to the circumstances** so that number of coffee breaks per 20 pages of text might indicate to you how hard you are studying!

7.12 Some service organisations, notably banks, are using **activity-based profitability analysis** to analyse and thus measure profits of different segments of the business.

The balanced scorecard

7.13 A popular approach in current management thinking to performance measurement (for service *and* non-service organisations) is the use of what is called a **'balanced scorecard'.**

KEY TERM

The **balanced scorecard approach** aims to provide management with information covering all relevant areas of performance. The information provided may include both financial and non-financial elements.

7.14 The balanced scorecard focuses on four different perspectives, as follows.

Perspective	Question
Customer	What do existing and new **customers** value from us? This perspective gives rise to targets that matter to customers: cost, quality and so on.
Internal	What **processes** must we excel at to achieve our financial and customer objectives? This perspective aims to improve internal processes and decision making.
Innovation and learning	Can we continue to **improve** and create future value? This perspective considers the business's capacity to maintain its competitive position by acquiring new skills and developing new products.

Financial	How do we create **value** for our shareholders? This perspective covers traditional measures such as growth, profitability and shareholder value but these are set through talking to the shareholder or shareholders direct.

7.15 **Performance targets** are set once the key areas for improvement have been identified, and the balanced scorecard is the main monthly report.

7.16 The scorecard is '**balanced**' in the sense that managers are required to think in terms of **all four** perspectives, to prevent improvements being made in one area at the expense of another. The method had the advantages of looking at both **internal and external** matters concerning the organisation and of linking together **financial and non-financial** measures.

8 COSTING IN NOT-FOR-PROFIT ORGANISATIONS

8.1 Not-for-profit organisations include private sector organisations like **charities** and **churches** and much of the **public sector**.

8.2 The **purpose** of such organisations is to **serve the broader community interests** rather than to pursue profit. Commercial organisations generally have market competition and the profit motive to guide the process of managing resources economically, efficiently and effectively. Not-for-profit organisations **cannot by definition be judged by profitability nor do they generally have to be successful against competition**. They are more concerned with providing an appropriate level of service. They therefore tend to use **non-financial indicators** as measures, profit margin and return on capital employed having little relevance.

8.3 A major problem with many not-for-profit organisations, particularly government bodies, is that it is extremely **difficult to define their objectives** at all, let alone find *one* which can serve as a yardstick function in the way that profit does for commercial bodies. This is in part due to the fact that they usually need to **satisfy** a **wide group** of people (**stakeholders).** A hospital, for example, has stakeholders which include the government (the provider of funds), the employees (the providers of services) and the general public (the customers).

How can performance be measured?

8.4 It is reasonable to argue that such organisations **best serve society's interests** when the **gap** between the **benefits** they provide and **the cost** of providing those benefits is **greatest**. This is commonly termed '**value for money**' and is not dissimilar from the concept of profit maximisation, apart from the fact that society's interests are being maximised rather than profit.

8.5 Value for money can be defined as '**getting the best possible combination of services from the least resources'**, which means maximising the benefits for the lowest possible cost. This is usually accepted as requiring the application of economy, effectiveness and efficiency.

(a) **Economy** (spending money frugally)
(b) **Efficiency** (getting out as much as possible for what goes in)
(c) **Effectiveness** (getting done, by means of (a) and (b), what was supposed to be done)

8.6 More formally, these criteria can be defined as follows.

KEY TERMS

Effectiveness is the extent to which declared objectives/goals are met.

Efficiency is the relationship between inputs and outputs.

Economy is attaining the appropriate quantity and quality of inputs at lowest cost to achieve a certain level of outputs.

8.7 EXAMPLE: ECONOMY, EFFICIENCY, EFFECTIVENESS

(a) **Economy.** The economy with which a school purchases equipment can be measured by comparing actual costs with budgets, with costs in previous years, with government/ local authority guidelines or with amounts spent by other schools.

(b) **Efficiency.** The efficiency with which a school's IT laboratory is used might be measured in terms of the proportion of the school week for which it is used.

(c) **Effectiveness.** The effectiveness of a school's objective to produce quality teaching could be measured by the proportion of students going on to higher or further education.

8.8 **Value for money** as a concept **assumes** that there is a **yardstick** against which to measure the achievement of objectives. It can be **difficult to determine where there is value for money**, however.

(a) Not-for-profit organisations tend to have **multiple objectives**, so that even if they can all be clearly identified it is impossible to say which is the overriding objective.

(b) **Outputs can seldom be measured** in a way that is generally agreed to be meaningful. (Are good exam results alone an adequate measure of the quality of teaching? How does one quantify the easing of pain following a successful operation?) For example, in the National Health Service success is measured in terms of fewer patient deaths per hospital admission, shorter waiting lists for operations, average speed of patient recovery and so on.

8.9 Here are a number of possible solutions to these problems.

(a) Performance can be judged in terms of **inputs**. This is very common in everyday life. If somebody tells you that their suit cost £750, for example, you would generally conclude that it was an extremely well-designed and good quality suit, even if you did not think so when you first saw it. The **drawback**, of course, is that you might also conclude that the person wearing the suit had been cheated or was a fool, or you may think that no piece of clothing is worth £750. So it is with the inputs and outputs of a non-profit-seeking organisation.

(b) Accept that performance measurement must to some extent be subjective. **Judgements** can be made **by experts**.

(c) Most not-for-profit organisations do not face competition but this does not mean that they are all unique. Bodies like local governments, health services and so on can **compare** their performance **against each other** and **against the historical results** of their predecessors. **Unit cost measurements** like 'cost per patient day' or 'cost of borrowing one library book' can be established to allow organisations to assess whether they are doing better or worse than their counterparts. Care must be taken not to read too much into limited information, however.

Performance measures

8.10 Although output of not-for-profit organisations can seldom be measured in a way that is generally agreed to be meaningful, outputs of a university might be measured in terms of the following.

Broader performance measures

- Proportion of total undergraduate population attending the university (by subject)
- Proportion of students graduating and classes of degrees obtained
- Amount of private sector research funds attracted
- Number of students finding employment after graduation
- Number of publications/articles produced by teaching staff

Operational performance measures

- Unit costs for each operating 'unit'
- Staff: student ratios; staff workloads
- Class sizes
- Availability of computers; good library stock
- Courses offered

8.11 EXAMPLE: COSTING AN EDUCATIONAL ESTABLISHMENT

A university organisation structure consists of three faculties each with a number of teaching departments. In addition, there is a university administrative/management function and a central services function.

(a) The following cost information is available for the year ended 30 June 20X3.

(i) **Occupancy costs.** Costs of £1,500,000 are apportioned on the basis of area used, which is as follows.

	Square metres
Faculties	7,500
Teaching departments	20,000
Administration/management	7,000
Central services	3,000

(ii) **Administrative/management costs.** Direct costs of £1,775,000 and indirect costs (an apportionment of occupancy costs) are charged to degree courses on a percentage basis.

(iii) **Faculty costs.** Direct costs of £700,000 and indirect costs (an apportionment of occupancy costs and central service costs) are charged to teaching departments.

(iv) **Teaching departments.** Direct costs of £5,525,000 and indirect costs (an apportionment of occupancy costs and central service costs plus all faculty costs) are charged to degree courses on a percentage basis.

(v) **Central services.** Direct costs total £1,000,000. Indirect costs are an apportionment of occupancy costs.

(b) Direct and indirect costs of central services have been charged to users on a percentage basis. A recent study has estimated what user areas would have paid external suppliers for the same services on an individual basis. For the year ended 30 June 20X3, the apportionment of the central services cost is to be recalculated in a manner which recognises the cost savings achieved by using the central services facilities instead of using external service companies. This is to be done by apportioning the overall savings to user areas in proportion to their share of the estimated external costs, which are as follows.

	£'000
Faculties	240
Teaching departments	800
Degree courses:	
Business studies	32
Mechanical engineering	48
Catering studies	32
All other degrees	448
	1,600

(c) Additional data relating to the degree courses is as follows.

	Degree course		
	Business studies	*Mechanical engineering*	*Catering studies*
Number of graduates	80	50	120
Apportioned costs (as % of totals)			
Teaching departments	3.0%	2.5%	7%
Administration/management	2.5%	5.0%	4%

Central services are to be apportioned as detailed in (a)(v) above. The total number of undergraduates from the university in the year to 30 June 20X3 was 2,500.

Required

(a) Calculate the average cost per undergraduate for the year ended 30 June 20X3 and discuss the relevance of this information to the university management.

(b) Calculate the average cost per undergraduate for each of the three degrees detailed, showing all relevant cost analysis.

(c) Suggest reasons for any differences in the average cost per undergraduate from one degree to another, and discuss briefly the usefulness of such information to the university management.

8.12 SOLUTION

(a) The **average cost per undergraduate** is as follows.

	Total costs
	£'000
Occupancy	1,500
Admin/management	1,775
Faculty	700
Teaching departments	5,525
Central services	1,000
	10,500
Number of undergraduates	2,500
Average cost per undergraduate for year ended 30 June 20X3	£4,200

The average cost per undergraduate is not particularly relevant for the university management. It is a figure that can be monitored from year to year. If it becomes too high then control action needs to be taken to bring costs down.

(b) **Average cost per undergraduate for specified course** is as follows.

	Business Studies £	Mechanical engineering £	Catering studies £
Teaching department costs (W1 and using % in question)	241,590	201,325	563,710
Admin/management costs (W1 and using % in question)	51,375	102,750	82,200
Central services (W2)	22,400	33,600	22,400
	315,365	337,675	668,310
Number of undergraduates	80	50	120
Average cost per undergraduate for year ended 30 June 20X3	£3,942	£6,754	£5,569

Workings

1 **Cost allocation and apportionment**

Cost item	Basis of apportionment	Teaching departments £'000	Admin/ management £'000	Central services £'000	Faculties £'000
Direct costs	allocation	5,525	1,775	1,000	700
Occupancy costs	area used	800	280	120	300
Central services Reapportioned	(W2)	560	-	(1,120)	168
Faculty costs Reallocated	allocation	1,168	-	-	(1,168)
		8,053	2,055	-	-

2 Apportioning savings to user areas on the basis given in the question gives the same result as apportioning internal costs in proportion to the external costs.

	External costs £'000	Apportionment of internal central service costs £'000
Faculties	240	168.0
Teaching	800	560.0
Degree courses:		
Business studies	32	22.4
Mechanical engineering	48	33.6
Catering studies	32	22.4
All other degrees	448	313.6
	1,600	1,120.0

(c) **Possible reasons for the differences in the average cost per undergraduate**

(i) Some of the courses may require lecturers of greater skill, who command higher rates of pay.

(ii) Teaching methods may be different on the various courses. Some may be split into small groups, each needing a separate tutor. Others may be taught by one lecturer in a large group, or two or more lecturers simultaneously.

(iii) Teaching aids in use will vary from course to course. Both mechanical engineering and catering studies require specialist equipment.

(iv) Some courses may take longer to complete than others.

(v) Some courses may feature intensive one-to-one tuition as a matter of routine, whereas others will operate on the basis of seminars or lectures.

(vi) Management and administration charges will vary from course to course. Catering studies is likely to require extensive space for kitchens.

(vii) The students for each course may be drawn from different years. The overall size of each year may be different.

Usefulness of the information

(i) Monitoring the cost per graduate for each degree course on a year by year basis will prove useful. Such information will allow an assessment of how well the costs relating to particular disciplines are being controlled.

(ii) Consideration should be given to the costs actually included in the analysis. The management should consider whether unavoidable costs should be incorporated.

(iii) The information may prove more useful if it is used in conjunction with qualitative information such as pass rates and student satisfaction.

8.13 The key findings of Paul Cropper and Professor Colin Drury's recent survey of management accounting practices within UK university management are as follows.

(a) 'The costing method considered the most appropriate for determining the cost of running *degree courses* was identified as the calculation of '**full costs**' (35 per cent of institutions favoured this method). A significant number of institutions (27 per cent) stated that they believed '**activity-based costing**' was the most appropriate method. 'Direct cost plus a fixed percentage overhead' was preferred by only 21 per cent of institutions despite the fact that 56 per cent of respondents said they currently used this method 'often or always'.

These findings indicate that institutions would like to move towards a **more accurate basis for costing their principal activities**.'

(b) '... 100 per cent of higher-education institutions indicating that they operated a system of **budgetary control** ... where the cost estimates submitted by managers were perceived to be excessive, 57 per cent of respondents indicated that budgets were reduced through negotiation. A further 9 per cent said that a reduction was achieved through a combination of negotiation and cuts deemed appropriate by upper management. ... Of the budgetary control methods available, by far the most popular were '**previous year plus inflation**' and '**incremental budgeting**'.'

(c) 'The majority of respondents (73 per cent) do place a strong emphasis on a manager's ability to attain the budget as a major factor in judging performance ... **non-financial measures** are used and that institutions do attempt to measure student/customer satisfaction and student achievement on a regular basis ... Most respondents placed an emphasis on **measuring and evaluating their performance relative to that of other institutions**.'

('Management Accounting Practices in Universities', *Management Accounting,* February 1996)

9 SERVICE COSTING FOR INTERNAL SERVICES

9.1 Service costing can be used to establish a **specific cost for an 'internal service'** which is a service provided by one department for another, rather than sold externally. Service departments therefore include canteens and data processing departments.

The purposes of service costing for internal services

9.2 (a) **To control the costs and efficiency in the service department**. If we establish a distribution cost per tonne/km, a canteen cost per employee or a mainframe computer operating cost per hour, we can do the following.

(i) Compare actual costs against a target or standard

(ii) Compare actual costs in the current period against the in previous periods

(b) **To control the costs of the user departments, and prevent the unnecessary use of services.** If the costs of services are charged to the user departments so that the charges reflect the use actually made by each user department of the services then the following will occur.

(i) The overhead costs of user departments will be established more accurately. Variable costs might be identified as costs which are directly attributable to the user department.

(ii) If the service department's charges for a user department are high, the user department might consider it is making an excessively costly and wasteful use of the service department's service.

(iii) The user department might decide that it can obtain a similar service at a lower cost from an external service company. This is clearly not satisfactory from the point of view of the organisation as a whole.

9.3 Service costing also provides a **fairer basis for charging service costs to user departments,** instead of charging service costs as overheads on a broad direct labour hour basis, or similar arbitrary apportionment basis. This is because service **costs are related more directly to use,** particularly if an **ABC** system is used.

(a) If repair costs in a factory are costed as jobs with each bit of repair work being given a job number and costed accordingly, repair costs can be charged to the departments on the basis of repair jobs actually undertaken, instead of on a more generalised basis, such as apportionment according to machine hour capacity in each department. Departments with high repair costs could then consider their high incidence of repairs, the age and reliability of their machines, or the skills of the machine operators.

(b) If mainframe computer costs are charged to a user department on the basis of a cost per hour, the user department would make the following assessment.

(i) Whether it was getting good value from its use of the mainframe computer

(ii) Whether it might be better to hire the service of a computer bureau, or perhaps install a stand-alone microcomputer system in the department

The bases for charging service costs to user departments

9.4 The 'cost' of support services charged to user departments could be based on any of the following.

(a) **No charge at all**

Service costs are either apportioned on a more arbitrary basis between production departments in a system of absorption costing, or charged against profit as a period charge in a system of marginal costing, without any attempt to recognise that some departments might be using services more than others.

(b) **Total actual cost**

The total costs of the service department are accumulated over a period of time. No distinction is made between fixed and variable costs in the department. The charge to the user departments is then:

(total actual cost/total activity (eg hours worked)) $\times$ work done for user department

This method might be suitable if it is difficult to separate fixed and variable costs or if it is difficult to establish standard costs, but there are several problems associated with it.

(i) User departments are charged for any overspending and inefficiency in the service departments.

(ii) If the service department is not working at full capacity, the charge per unit of service is higher than if the department is more busy. This might discourage user departments from using the service, to avoid high service charges.

(iii) The fluctuating charges which can result from the use of actual costs could make it difficult for the user departments to plan and control costs.

(c) **Standard absorption cost**

The charge to user departments is based on a standard, predetermined cost for the service, consisting of the service department's variable costs plus a share of its fixed costs. The standard cost is based on (standard total costs ÷ standard (budgeted) service activity). The user departments are therefore *not* penalised for either overspending and inefficiency or under-capacity in the service department. There are, however, two problems with this method.

(i) It is necessary to review the standard cost regularly and frequently, so that user departments do not get a false impression of the cost of the service.

(ii) There is a problem in deciding what the standard activity level ought to be.

(d) **Variable cost**

Support services are costed at marginal or variable cost only. This could be either standard or actual variable cost. The advantage of this method is that user departments are charged for the extra costs incurred by using more of the service. There are, however, a number of weaknesses or problems with this system.

(i) The user departments are under a false impression as to the true full cost of the service, because they are charged with just the marginal costs.

(ii) If actual variable costs are used, there is no control of overspending and inefficiency in the service department because the service department simply 'passes on' its overspending in higher charges to the user department.

(iii) If standard costs are used, the standard needs to be revised regularly.

(e) **Opportunity cost**

This method is appropriate if the service department is working at full capacity and is also providing services outside the company. This means that profit is forgone every time the service department provides a service internally, which should be reflected in an opportunity cost charge. The main problem associated with this method is that it is difficult to establish the opportunity cost.

Question 6

Identify three different reasons for the charging of service department costs to user departments and comment on the charging methods which may be relevant in the case of maintenance, computer services, and health, safety and welfare service departments.

Answer

Service department costs are charged to user departments for the following **reasons**.

(a) User departments which use most of the services are made responsible for them.
(b) Service costs are included in production costs, where appropriate.
(c) The 'true' cost of each user department is known to management.
(d) User departments are encouraged to use the service as opposed to external contractors.

Maintenance might be easy to allocate. The machines are in definite locations, and there is a distinct chain of responsibility. Maintenance costs could be charged out in the budget as part of production overhead at a predetermined rate, or in an activity based costing system. This would be for budgetary purposes only. In practice, during the budget period, maintenance jobs could be charged out on an individual basis, directly to user departments.

Computer services cost would be charged on the basis of computer time for normal processing, and any computer projects which are directly attributable to user departments would be charged directly. Some estimate would be needed of any system enhancements required during the year.

The **health, safety and welfare department's** cost will be allocated to user departments on a basis of employee numbers in the case of nursing care, or floorspace in the case of fire prevention equipment, alarm systems and so forth. Both the number of employees and the floor area might therefore be a means of allocating the cost.

Exam focus point

Service costing was examined in the first sitting of the 2.4 syllabus. A fee charging hospital provided the scenario and candidates were required to prepare budgeted profit/loss statements and to evaluate a proposal. Neither requirement demanded more than the most basic of techniques or knowledge.

Chapter roundup

- This was a long chapter which covered a lot of ground. The majority of the points covered should not, however, have been new to you and your memory should now be fully refreshed.
- Losses may occur in process. If a certain level of loss is expected, this is known as **normal loss**. If losses are greater than expected, the extra loss is **abnormal loss**. If losses are less than expected, the difference is known as **abnormal gain**.
- It is conventional for the **scrap value of normal loss to be deducted from the cost of materials** before a cost per equivalent unit is calculated.
- **Abnormal losses and gains never affect the cost of good units of production.** The scrap value of abnormal losses is not credited to the process account, and abnormal loss and gain units carry the same full cost as a good unit of production.
- When units are partly completed at the end of a period, it is necessary to calculate the **equivalent units of production** in order to determine the cost of a completed unit.
- Stocks in process can be valued using either the **FIFO** method or the **weighted average cost** method.
- When there is **opening and/or closing WIP and losses** (at the end of processing), make the following assumptions.
    - Unit of normal loss counts as no equivalent units
    - Unit of abnormal loss counts as one equivalent unit extra
    - Unit of abnormal gain counts as minus one equivalent unit
- **Joint products** are two or more products separated in a process, each of which has a significant value compared to the other. A **by-product** is an incidental product from a process and has an insignificant value compared to the main product.
- There are four methods of apportioning joint costs, each of which can produce significantly different results. These methods are **physical measurement** method, **sales value at split-off point** apportionment method, **sales value of end product less further processing costs after split-off point** apportionment method and **weighted average** method.
- The most common method of **accounting for by-products** is to deduct the net realisable value of the by-product from the cost of the main products.
- **Service costing** can be used by companies operating in a service industry or by companies wishing to establish the cost of services carried out by some of their departments.
- **Service costing for internal services** adds to the administrative burdens of an organisation because it costs time and money. The benefits of the system should therefore exceed the costs of its operation.

Quick quiz

1 Fill in the blanks in the four steps to dealing with process costing questions using some of the words from the list below and then put the steps in the correct order.

Steps

(a) Complete ………………………

(b) Determine ……………………… and ………………………

(c) Calculate ……………………… of output, losses and WIP

(d) Calculate ……………………… of output losses and WIP

Possible missing words

abnormal loss	losses
accounts	output
cost per unit	total cost
normal loss	abnormal gain
WIP	

2 What is the correct way to record the scrap value of normal loss?

A DR Scrap a/c
 CR Process a/c ('value' for normal loss)

B DR Normal loss a/c
 CR Scrap a/c

C DR Process a/c ('value' for normal loss)
 CR Scrap a/c

D DR Scrap a/c
 CR Cash a/c

3 *Record the following entries correctly in the appropriate accounts below.*

Entries

Materials	Finished output
Labour and overhead	Scrap value of normal loss
Abnormal loss	Profit/loss
Abnormal gain	Scrap value of abnormal gain
Profit/loss	Abnormal gain
Scrap value of normal loss	Scrap value of abnormal loss
Abnormal loss	Scrap value of abnormal gain
Scrap value of abnormal loss	Cash

PROCESS A/C

	£		£

ABNORMAL LOSS A/C

	£		£

ABNORMAL GAIN A/C

	£		£

SCRAP A/C

	£		£

4 Consider the following process account.

PROCESS A

	Units		Units
Opening WIP	25	Finished goods	70
Materials	100	Closing WIP	55
	125		125

Opening WIP is 20% complete for labour and overhead, 100% complete for material. Closing WIP is 20% complete for labour and overhead, 100% complete for material.

Calculate the equivalent units for material and for labour and overhead using both FIFO and weighted average.

5 *Match the correct statement to the appropriate method of valuing joint products.*

Statement 1

Widely used because the assumption that some profit margin should be attained for all products under normal marketing conditions is satisfied

Statement 2

Unsuitable where the products separate during processing into different states

Statement 3

Useful if the units of joint product are not comparable in physical resemblance or physical weight

Statement 4

Suitable if products require further processing after the point of separation.

Valuation methods

(a) Physical measurement
(b) Sales value at split-off point
(c) Sales value minus further processing costs
(d) Weighted average

6 *Choose the four perspectives of the balanced scorecard from the list below.*

Quality	Financial	Competitive	Innovation and learning
Internal	Speed	Customer	Resource utilisation

7 Which of the following are the three 'Es' often used to assess the performance of not-for-profit organisations?

Effort	Efficiency	Earnings	Ease	Economy	Efficacy
Effusiveness	Elementalism	Emotiveness	Effectiveness	Endurability	

8 Suggest five bases for charging service costs to user departments.

Answers to quick quiz

1 Determine output and losses.
Calculate total cost of output, losses and WIP.
Calculate cost per unit of output, losses and WIP.
Complete accounts.

2 A

3

PROCESS A/C

	£		£
Materials		Finished output	
Labour and o/hd		Abnormal loss	
Abnormal gain		Scrap value of normal loss	

ABNORMAL LOSS A/C

	£		£
Abnormal loss		Scrap value of abnormal loss	
		Profit/loss	

ABNORMAL GAIN A/C

	£		£
Scrap value of abnormal gain		Abnormal gain	
Profit/loss			

SCRAP A/C

	£		£
Scrap value of normal loss		Cash	
Scrap value of abnormal loss		Scrap value of abnormal gain	

4 **FIFO**

	Total	*Materials*	*Labour & o/hd*
Opening WIP	25	0	20
Units started/finished	45	45	45
Total finished	70	45	65
Closing WIP	55	55	11
	125	100	76

Weighted average

	Total	*Materials*	*Labour & o/hd*
Finished output	70	70	70
Closing WIP	55	55	11
	125	125	81

5

Statement	*Method*
1	(b)
2	(a)
3	(d)
4	(c)

6 Internal
Financial
Customer
Innovation and learning

7 Economy
Efficiency
Effectiveness

8 No charge at all
Total actual cost
Standard absorption cost
Variable cost
Opportunity cost

Now try the questions below from the Exam Question Bank

Question to try	Level	Marks	Time
6	Introductory	-	-
7	Exam	25	45 mins

Part B

Standard costing

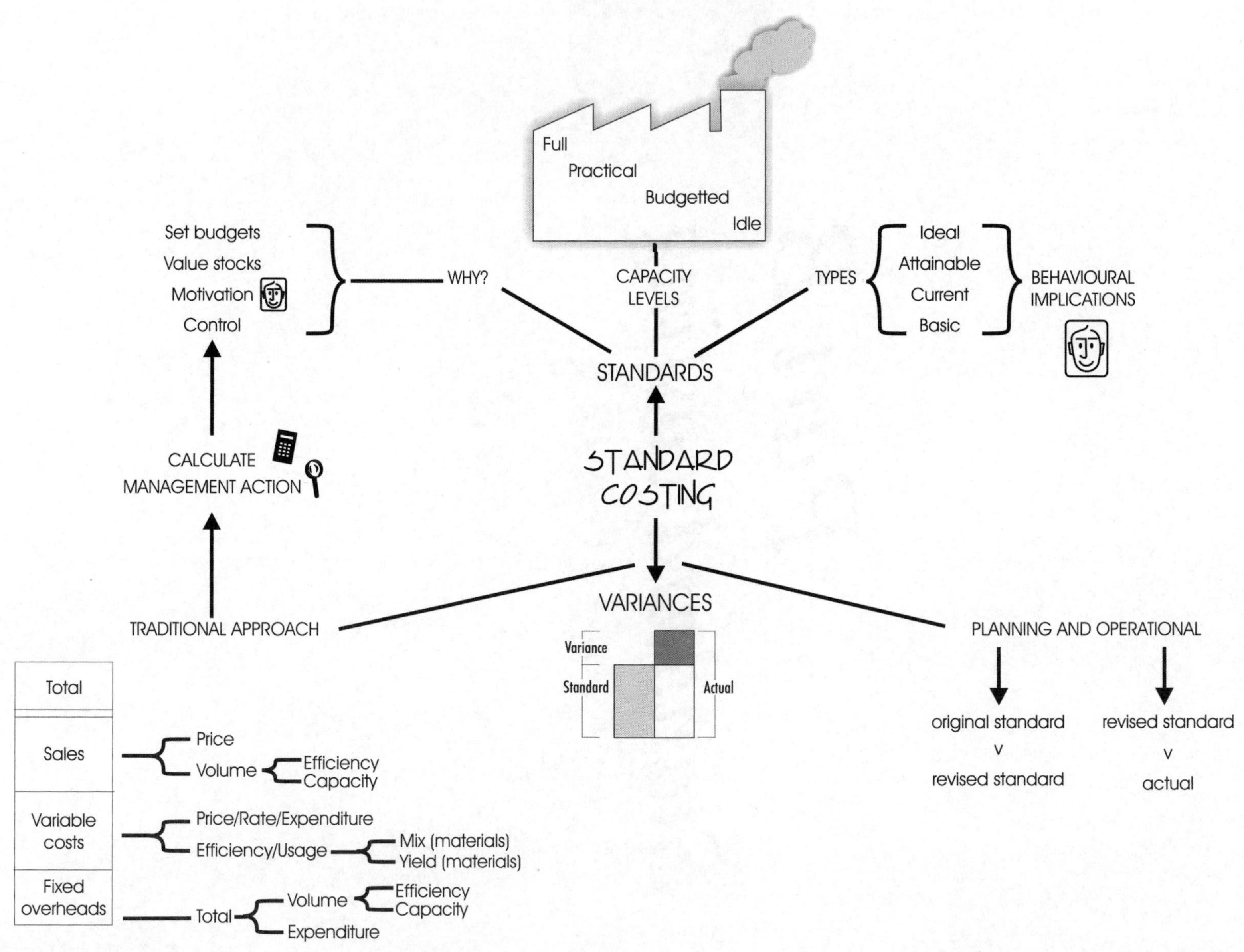
Full
Practical
Budgetted
Idle
Set budgets
Value stocks
Motivation
Control
WHY?
CAPACITY LEVELS
TYPES
Ideal
Attainable
Current
Basic
BEHAVIOURAL IMPLICATIONS
STANDARDS
CALCULATE
MANAGEMENT ACTION
STANDARD COSTING
VARIANCES
TRADITIONAL APPROACH
PLANNING AND OPERATIONAL
Variance
Standard
Actual
Total
Sales
Price
Volume
Efficiency
Capacity
Variable costs
Price/Rate/Expenditure
Efficiency/Usage
Mix (materials)
Yield (materials)
Fixed overheads
Total
Volume
Efficiency
Capacity
Expenditure
original standard
v
revised standard
revised standard
v
actual

Chapter 6

INTRODUCTION TO STANDARD COSTING

	Topic list	Syllabus reference
1	**Standard costs**	**8(a)(i)**
2	**Standard costing**	**8(a)(i)**
3	**Deriving standards**	**8(a)(i)**
4	**Types of standard and their behavioural impact**	**6(d), 8(a)(i), 8(c)**
5	**Reviewing standards**	**8(a)(i)**

Introduction

Just as there are standards for most things in our daily lives (cleanliness in hamburger restaurants, educational achievement of nine year olds, number of underground trains running on time) there are **standards** for the costs of products and services. And just as the standards in our daily lives are not always met, the standards for the costs of products and services are not always met. We will not, however, be considering the cleanliness of hamburger restaurants in this chapter but we will be looking at standard costs and standard costing.

In the next chapter we will see how standard costing forms the basis of a process called **variance analysis**, a vital management control tool.

Study guide

Section 21 – Standard costing I

- Explain the uses of standard costs and the methods by which they are derived and subsequently reviewed
- Calculate and evaluate capacity limitations when setting standards
- Describe the types of standard (ideal, attainable current and basic) and their behavioural implications

Exam guide

The contents of this chapter are likely to be examined in conjunction with variance analysis, covered in Chapters 7 and 8.

1 STANDARD COSTS

KEY TERM

A **standard cost** is an estimated unit cost.

1.1 The standard cost of product 12345 is set out below on a **standard cost card.**

STANDARD COST CARD
Product: the Splodget, No 12345

	Cost	*Requirement*	£	£
Direct materials				
A	£2.00 per kg	6 kgs	12.00	
B	£3.00 per kg	2 kgs	6.00	
C	£4.00 per litre	1 litre	4.00	
Others			2.00	
				24.00
Direct labour				
Grade I	£4.00 per hour	3 hrs	12.00	
Grade II	£5.40 per hour	5 hrs	27.00	
				39.00
Variable production overheads	£1.00 per hour	8 hrs		8.00
Fixed production overheads	£3.00 per hour	8 hrs		24.00
Standard full cost of production				95.00

1.2 Notice how it is **built up from standards for each cost element:** standard quantities of materials at standard prices, standard quantities of labour time at standard rates and so on. It is therefore determined by management's estimates of the following.

- The expected prices of materials, labour and expenses
- Efficiency levels in the use of materials and labour
- Budgeted overhead costs and budgeted volumes of activity

We will see how management arrives at these estimates later in the chapter.

1.3 But why should management want to prepare standard costs? Obviously to assist with standard costing, but what is the point of standard costing?

2 STANDARD COSTING

The uses of standard costing

2.1 **Standard costing** has two principal **uses.**

- **To value stocks and cost production** for cost accounting purposes. It is an alternative method of valuation to methods like FIFO and LIFO which you will have covered in your earlier studies.

- **To act as a control device** by establishing standards (expected costs) and comparing actual costs with the expected costs, thus highlighting areas of the organisation which may be out of control

2.2 It can also be used in the following circumstances.

(a) To assist in setting **budgets** and **evaluating managerial performance**.

(b) To enable the principle of '**management by exception**' to be practised. A standard cost, when established, is an average expected unit cost. Because it is only an average, actual results will vary to some extent above and below the average. Only significant differences between actual and standard should be reported.

(c) To provide a prediction of future costs to be used in **decision-making** situations.

(d) To **motivate** staff and management by the provision of challenging targets.

(e) To provide guidance on possible ways of **improving efficiency**.

Exam focus point

An outline of the uses of standard costing was worth eight marks in the December 2001 exam.

2.3 Although the various uses of standard costing should not be overlooked, we will be concentrating on the control aspect.

Standard costing as a control technique

KEY TERMS

Standard costing involves the establishment of predetermined estimates of the costs of products or services, the collection of actual costs and the comparison of the actual costs with the predetermined estimates. The predetermined costs are known as standard costs and the difference between standard and actual cost is known as a **variance**. The process by which the total difference between standard and actual results is analysed in known as **variance analysis**.

Question 1

What are the possible advantages for the control function of an organisation of having a standard costing system?

Answer

(a) Carefully planned standards are an aid to more accurate **budgeting**.

(b) Standard costs provide a **yardstick** against which actual costs can be measured.

(c) The setting of standards involves determining the **best** materials and methods which may lead to economies.

(d) A **target of efficiency** is set for employees to reach and **cost-consciousness** is stimulated.

(e) Variances can be calculated which enable the principle of '**management by exception**' to be operated. Only the variances which exceed acceptable tolerance limits need to be investigated by management with a view to control action.

(f) Standard costs and variance analysis can provide a way of **motivation** to managers to achieve better performance. However, care must be taken to distinguish between controllable and non-controllable costs in variance reporting.

Where standard costing should be used

2.4 Although standard costing can be used in a variety of costing situations (batch and mass production, process manufacture, jobbing manufacture (where there is standardisation of parts) and service industries (if a realistic cost unit can be established)), the **greatest benefit from its use can be gained if there is a degree of repetition in the production process** so that average or expected usage of resources can be determined. It is therefore **most suited to mass production and repetitive assembly work** and less suited to organisations which produce to customer demand and requirements.

Question 2

Can you think of a service organisation that could apply standard costing?

Answer

In an *ACCA Students' Newsletter* article (December 1998), the examiner of the equivalent paper under the old syllabus provided the example of restaurants which deal with standard recipes for meals. If a large number of meals are produced, say, for conference delegates, mass production systems will apply. Standards may not be calculated with the same accuracy as in manufacturing environments, but the principles are still relevant. Other examples are equally valid.

3 DERIVING STANDARDS

3.1 The **responsibility for deriving standard costs** should be shared between **managers able to provide the necessary information** about levels of expected efficiency, prices and overhead costs.

Setting standards for materials costs

3.2 Direct materials costs per unit of raw material will be estimated by the purchasing department from their knowledge of the following.

- Purchase contracts already agreed
- Pricing discussions with regular suppliers
- The forecast movement of prices in the market
- The availability of bulk purchase discounts
- The quality of material required by the production departments

3.3 The standard cost ought to include an allowance for **bulk purchase discounts**, if these are available on all or some of the purchases, and it may have to be a weighted average price of the differing prices charged for the same product by alternative suppliers.

3.4 A decision must also be taken as to how to deal with price **inflation**. Suppose that a material costs £10 per kilogram at the moment, and during the course of the next 12 months, it is expected to go up in price by 20% to £12 per kilogram. What standard price should be selected?

(a) If the **current price** of £10 per kilogram **were used in the standard**, the reported price variance would become adverse as soon as prices go up, which might be very early in the year. If prices go up gradually rather than in one big jump, it would be difficult to select an appropriate time for revising the standard.

(b) If an **estimated mid-year price** of, say, £11 per kilogram **were used**, price variances should be favourable in the first half of the year and adverse in the second half, again assuming that prices go up gradually. Management could only really check that in any month, the price variance did not become excessively adverse (or favourable) and that the price variance switched from being favourable to adverse around month six or seven and not sooner.

3.5 Standard costing is therefore more **difficult in times of inflation but it is still worthwhile.**

- Usage and efficiency variances will still be meaningful.
- Inflation is measurable: there is no reason why its effects cannot be removed.
- Standard costs can be revised, so long as this is not done too frequently.

Setting standards for labour costs

3.6 Direct labour rates per hour will be set by reference to the payroll and to any agreements on pay rises with trade union representatives of the employees. A separate hourly rate or weekly wage will be set for each different labour grade/type of employee and an average hourly rate will be applied for each grade (even though individual rates of pay may vary according to age and experience).

3.7 Similar problems to those which arise when setting material standards in times of high inflation can be met when setting labour standards.

Setting standards for material usage and labour efficiency

3.8 To estimate the materials required to make each product (material usage) and also the labour hours required (labour efficiency), technical specifications must be prepared for each product by production experts (either in the production department or the work study department).

Setting standards for overheads

3.9 When standard costs are fully absorbed costs (standard costs can be used in both marginal and absorption costing systems), the **absorption rate** of fixed production overheads will be **predetermined** and **based on budgeted** fixed production **overhead** and planned **production volume.**

3.10 **Production volume will depend on two factors.**

(a) **Production capacity** (or '**volume capacity**') measured perhaps in standard hours of output (a standard hour being the amount of work achievable at standard efficiency levels in an hour), which in turn reflects direct production labour hours.

(b) **Efficiency of working,** by labour or machines, allowing for rest time and contingency allowances.

3.11 Suppose that a department has a work force of ten men, each of whom works a 36 hour week to make standard units, and each unit has a standard time of two hours to make. The expected efficiency of the work-force is 125%.

(a) Budgeted capacity, in direct labour hours, would be $10 \times 36 = 360$ production hours per week.

(b) Budgeted efficiency is 125% so that the work-force should take only 1 hour of actual production time to produce 1.25 standard hours of output.

(c) This means in our example that budgeted output is 360 production hours × 125% = 450 standard hours of output per week. At 2 standard hours per unit, this represents production activity or volume of 225 units of output per week.

Question 3

ABC Ltd carries out routine office work in a sales order processing department, and all tasks in the department have been given standard times. There are 40 clerks in the department who work on average 140 hours per month each. The efficiency ratio of the department is 110%.

Required

Calculate the budgeted output in the department.

Answer

Capacity	=	40 × 140 = 5,600 hours per month
Efficiency	=	110%
Budgeted output	=	5,600 × 110% = 6,160 standard hours of work per month.

Capacity levels

3.12 Capacity levels are needed to establish a standard absorption rate for production overhead, when standard absorption costing is used.

KEY TERMS

- **Full capacity** is the theoretical capacity, assuming continuous production without any stoppages due to factors such as machine downtime, supply shortages or labour shortages. Full capacity would be associated with ideal standards.
- **Practical capacity** is an output level below full capacity, and is associated with attainable standards, since it takes account of known, unavoidable stoppages.
- **Budgeted capacity** is the capacity (labour hours, machine hours) needed to produce the budgeted output. It is associated with current standards, which relate to current conditions but may not be representative of normal practical capacity over a longer period of time.
- **Idle capacity** is the practical capacity in a period less the budgeted capacity measured in standard hours of output. It represents unused capacity that ought to be available, but which is not needed because the budgeted volume is lower than the practicable volume that could be achieved.

3.13 **Capacity ratios** can be calculated.

Question 4

Given the following information, calculate an idle capacity ratio, a production volume/ratio, a capacity ratio and an efficiency ratio and explain their meanings.

Full capacity	10,000 standard hours
Practical capacity	8,000 standard hours
Budgeted capacity	7,500 standard hours
Standard hours produced	6,500
Actual hours worked	7,000

Answer

Idle capacity ratio = ((practical capacity – budgeted capacity)/practical capacity) × 100%
= ((8,000 – 7,500)/8,000) × 100% = 6.25%.

This means that 6.25% of practical capacity will be unused because budgeted volume is lower than the volume that could be achieved.

Production volume ratio = (actual output measured in expected or standard hours/budgeted capacity) × 100%

= (6,500/7,500) × 100% = 86.67%

This means actual output was only 86.67% of budgeted output.

Capacity ratio = (actual hours worked/budgeted capacity) x 100%

= (7,000/7,500) × 100% = 93.33%

This means that only 93.33% of budgeted capacity was actually used.

Efficiency ratio = (actual output measured in standard or expected hours/actual hours worked) × 100%

= (6,500/7,000) × 100% = 92.86%

This means that the labour force were working at 92.86% efficiency.

3.14 The production volume ratio shows the overall effect of the capacity and efficiency ratio. In the question above we have:

Production volume ratio	=	**capacity ratio**	×	**efficiency ratio**
ie 86.67%	=	93.33%	×	92.86%

Setting standards for sales price and margin

3.15 The **standard selling price** will depend on a number of factors including the following.

- Anticipated market demand
- Competing products
- Manufacturing costs
- Inflation estimates

3.16 The **standard sales margin** is the difference between the standard cost and the standard selling price.

Question 5

What problems do you think could occur when standards are being set?

Answer

The following problems can occur when setting standards.

(a) Deciding how to incorporate **inflation** into planned unit costs

(b) Agreeing on a **performance standard** (attainable or ideal)

(c) Deciding on the **quality** of materials to be used (a better quality of material will cost more, but perhaps reduce material wastage)

(d) Estimating materials prices where **seasonal price variations** or **bulk purchase discounts** may be significant

(e) Finding sufficient **time** to construct standards as standard setting can be time consuming

(f) Incurring the **cost** of setting up and maintaining a system for establishing standards

---

4 TYPES OF STANDARD AND THEIR BEHAVIOURAL IMPACT

4.1 How demanding should a standard be? Should the standard represent perfect performance or easily attainable performance? There are four types of standard.

KEY TERMS

- An **ideal standard** is a standard which can be attained under perfect operating conditions: no wastage no inefficiencies, no idle time, no breakdowns.
- An **attainable standard** is a standard which can be attained if production is carried out efficiently, machines are properly operated and/or materials are properly used. Some allowance is made for wastage and inefficiencies.
- A **current standard** is standard based on current working conditions (current wastage, current inefficiencies).
- A **basic standard** is a long-term standard which remains unchanged over the years and is used to show trends.

4.2 The **different types of standard have a number of advantages and disadvantages.**

(a) Ideal standards can be seen as long-term targets but are not very useful for day-to-day control purposes.

(b) Ideal standards cannot be achieved. If such standards are used for budgeting, an allowance will have to be included to make the budget realistic and attainable.

(c) Attainable standards can be used for product costing, cost control, stock valuation, estimating and as a basis for budgeting.

(d) Current standards or attainable standards provide the best basis for budgeting, because they represent an achievable level of productivity.

(e) Current standards do not attempt to improve on current levels of efficiency.

(f) Current standards are useful during periods when inflation is high. They can be set on a month by month basis.

(g) Basic standards are used to show changes in efficiency or performance over a long period of time. They are perhaps the least useful and least common type of standard in use.

The impact on employee behaviour of the type of standard set

4.3 The type of standard set can have an impact on the behaviour of the employees trying to achieve those standards.

Type of standard	Impact
Ideal	Some say that they provide employees with an **incentive to be more efficient** even though it is highly unlikely that the standard will be achieved. Others argue that they are likely to have an unfavourable effect on employee motivation because the differences between standards and actual results will always be adverse. The **employees may feel that the goals are unattainable** and so **they will not work so hard.**
Attainable	Might be an **incentive to work harder** as they provide a **realistic but challenging target of efficiency.**
Current	**Will not motivate employees to do anything more than they are currently doing.**

Basic	May have an **unfavourable impact** on the motivation of employees. Over time they will discover that they are easily able to achieve the standards. They may become bored and lose interest in what they are doing if they have nothing to aim for.

Exam focus point

We will return to the behavioural implications of different costing approaches in Chapter 11 so try to link what you have covered here with the behavioural aspects of budgetary control systems when you get to that point in the Text.

5 REVIEWING STANDARDS

5.1 Although standards are developed from past and current information, they should reflect technical and current factors expected for the period in which the standards are to be applied. Management should not think that once standards are set they will remain useful for ever. **Standards must evolve to reflect an organisation's changing methods and processes**. Comparing out-of-date standards with actual results will provide misleading information.

5.2 Consider a computer manufacturer. Suppose that the standard price for computer chips was set in 1995 and not changed until 2001. In the six-year period, however, the price of chips would have dramatically decreased. Consistently favourable material price variances would have been reported, giving the appearance that the purchasing department was performing very well, buying chips at well below the standard price. What's more, if stocks are valued at standard cost, the stock value of the chips would have been too high. The price reductions occurring since the standard was set would therefore render the standard obsolete and worthless.

5.3 It has also been argued that **standard costing is unhelpful and potentially misleading in the modern organisation**, and causes managers to focus their attention on the wrong issues. **Continuous improvement and cost reduction programmes** are widespread but can they co-exist with systems of standard costing?

(a) Efforts to improve the efficiency of operations or reduce costs will alter quantities of inputs, prices and so on whereas standard costing is best used in a stable, standardised, repetitive environment.

(b) Predetermined standards conflict with a philosophy of continual improvement.

(c) Standard costs often incorporate a planned level of scrap in material standards. This is at odds with the aim of 'zero defects' inherent in continuous improvement programmes.

5.4 If standard costing is to be adopted in conjunction with cost reduction and continuous improvement programmes it is therefore vital that management **review standards on a regular basis and revise them if necessary.**

5.5 **Some argue that standards should be revised as soon as there is any change in the basis upon which they were set**. Clearly, if a standard is based on the cost of a material that is no longer available, it is meaningless to compare actual performance using a new material with the old standard. Or if an existing standard is discovered to be incorrectly set, the use of the incorrect standard is pointless.

5.6 **Others people believe that frequent changes in standards make them ineffective as motivators and measures of performance**, since those trying to achieve the targets will believe the target setters are constantly **'moving the goal posts'**. It has also been argued that frequent changes to standards are **too time-consuming** from the point of view of administration, although the introduction of computer systems makes this objection less forceful.

5.7 In practice, standard costs are **usually revised once a year** to allow for the new overheads budget, inflation in prices and wage rates, and any changes in expected efficiency of material usage, labour or machinery. One research study showed that most organisations revise their standards annually.

5.8 The **most suitable approach** would therefore appear to be a policy of **revising the standards whenever changes of a permanent and reasonably long-term nature occur,** but not in response to temporary 'blips' in price or efficiency.

Exam focus point

There were eight marks available in the December 2001 exam for a discussion on the reasons why standards have to be reviewed.

Chapter roundup

- A **standard cost** is an estimated unit cost.
- A standard cost is built up of standards for each cost element (standard resource price and standard resource usage).
- **Standard costing** is principally used to value stocks and cost production and to act as a control device.
- Standard costing is most suited to mass production and repetitive assembly work.
- The responsibility for setting standards should be shared between the managers able to provide the necessary information about levels of expected efficiency, prices and overhead costs.
- There are four **capacity levels** you need to be aware of.
  - Full
  - Practical
  - Budgeted
  - Idle
- There are four **types of standard: ideal, attainable, current** and **basic**. These can have an impact on employee motivation.
- Standards should be revised whenever there are changes of a permanent and reasonably long-term nature.

Quick quiz

1 Choose the appropriate words from those highlighted.

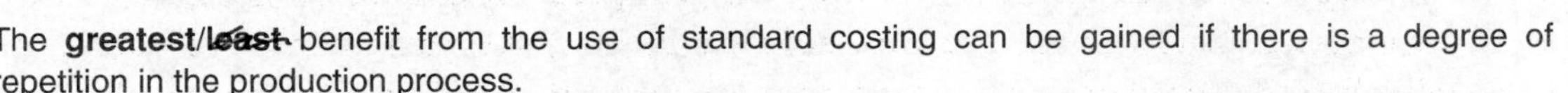

The **greatest/least** benefit from the use of standard costing can be gained if there is a degree of repetition in the production process.

Standard costing is therefore **most/less** suited to organisations which produce to customer demand and requirements and **most/less** suited to mass production.

2 Fill in the blanks using phrases from the list below.

(a) Idle capacity ratio = ((…………………….. – ……………………..)/……………………..) x 100%

(b) Production volume ratio = (………………………./……………………….) × 100%

(c) Capacity ratio = (………………………./……………………….) × 100%

(d) Efficiency ratio = (………………………./……………………….) × 100%

Missing phrases

Actual hours worked
Budgeted capacity
Practical capacity
Actual hours worked
Actual output measured in standard hours
Budgeted capacity
Practical capacity
Budgeted capacity
Actual output measured in expected hours

3 *Match the type of standard with the correct definition.*

Types of standard

Ideal a
Attainable b
Current c
Basic d

Definitions

(a) Can be attained under perfect operating conditions

(b) Can be attained if production is carried out efficiently, machines are properly operated and/or materials are properly used

(c) Based on current working conditions

(d) Remains unchanged over the years and is used to show trends

4 *Fill in the blanks.*

Standard costing is difficult in times of inflation but it is still worthwhile.

- ..wage....... and ..efficiency....... variances will still be meaningful.
- Inflation is ..measurable.......: there is no reason why its effects cannot be removed.
- Standard costs can be ..revised......, as long as this is not done ..often...... .

5 Provide three reasons why standard costing conflicts with schemes of continuous improvement and cost reduction programmes.

Answers to quick quiz

1 greatest
less
most

2 (a) ((practical capacity – budgeted capacity)/practical capacity) x 100%
(b) (actual output measured in expected hours/budgeted capacity) x 100%
(c) (actual hours worked/budgeted capacity) x 100%
(d) (actual output measured in standard hours/actual hours worked) x 100%

3 Ideal (a)
Attainable (b)
Current (c)
Basic (d)

4 (a) Usage and efficiency variances will still be meaningful.

(b) Inflation is measurable: there is no reason why its effects cannot be removed.

(c) Standard costs can be reviewed, as long as this is not done too frequently.

5 (a) Efforts to improve the efficiency of operations or reduce costs will alter quantities of inputs, prices and so on whereas standard costing is best used in a stable, standardised, repetitive environment.

(b) Predetermined standards conflict with a philosophy of continual improvement.

(c) Standard costs often incorporate a planned level of scrap in material standards. This is at odds with the aim of 'zero defects' inherent in continuous improvement programmes.

Now try the question below from the Exam Question Bank

Question to try	Level	Marks	Time
8	Exam	25	45 mins

Chapter 7

BASIC VARIANCE ANALYSIS

	Topic list	Syllabus reference
1	**Variances**	8(a)(ii)
2	**Material variances**	8(a)(ii)
3	**Labour variances**	8(a)(ii)
4	**Variable production overhead variances**	8(a)(ii)
5	**Fixed production overhead variances**	8(a)(ii)
6	**Sales variances**	8(a)(ii)
7	**Working backwards approach**	8(a)(ii)
8	**The reasons for variances**	8(a)(iii), (v)
9	**Investigating variances**	8(a)(iii), (v)

Introduction

The **actual results** achieved by an organisation will, more than likely, be **different from the expected results** (the expected results being the standard costs and revenues which we looked at in the previous chapter). Such differences may occur between individual items, such as the cost of labour or the volume of sales, and between the total expected profit/contribution and the total actual profit/contribution. These differences are **variances**.

In this chapter and the next we will be looking at the way in which variances are calculated and analysed.

Study guide

Section 21 – Standard costing I

- Calculate basic labour, material, overhead (variable and fixed) and sales variances, including problems of labour idle time
- Explain the reasons for variances
- Assess appropriate management action arising from the variances identified

Section 22 – Standard costing II

- Demonstrate an understanding of the inter-relationships between variances

Exam guide

Expect to see Section B questions based entirely on the contents of this chapter. Of course, Section A questions could also include variance analysis.

1 VARIANCES

KEY TERMS

- A **variance** is the difference between an actual result and an expected result.
- **Variance analysis** is the process by which the *total* difference between standard and actual results is analysed.

1.1 When actual results are better than expected results, we have a **favourable variance (F)**. If actual results are worse than expected results, we have an **adverse variance (A)**.

2 MATERIAL VARIANCES

KEY TERMS

- The **material total variance** is the difference between what the output actually cost and what it should have cost, in terms of material. It can be divided into the following two sub-variances.
- The **material price variance** is the difference between what the material did cost and what it should have cost.
- The **material usage variance** is the difference between the standard cost of the material that should have been used and the standard cost of the material that was used.

2.1 EXAMPLE: MATERIAL VARIANCES

Product X has a standard direct material cost of 10 kilograms of material Y at £10 per kilogram (= £100 per unit of X). During period 4, 1,000 units of X were manufactured, using 11,700 kilograms of material Y which cost £98,600.

Required

Calculate the following variances.

(a) The material total variance
(b) The material price variance
(c) The material usage variance

2.2 SOLUTION

(a) The **material total variance.** This is the difference between what 1,000 units should have cost and what they did cost.

	£
1,000 units should have cost (× £100)	100,000
but did cost	98,600
Material total variance	1,400 (F)

The variance is favourable because the units cost less than they should have cost.

(b) The **material price variance**. This is the difference between what 11,700 kgs should have cost and what 11,700 kgs did cost.

	£
11,700 kgs of Y should have cost (× £10)	117,000
but did cost	98,600
Material Y price variance	18,400 (F)

The variance is favourable because the material cost less than it should have.

(c) The **material usage variance.** This is the difference between how many kilograms of Y should have been used to produce 1,000 units of X and how many kilograms were used, valued at the standard cost per kilogram.

1,000 units should have used (× 10 kgs)	10,000 kgs
but did use	11,700 kgs
Usage variance in kgs	1,700 kgs (A)
× standard cost per kilogram	× £10
Usage variance in £	£17,000 (A)

The variance is adverse because more material than should have been used was used.

(d) **Summary**

	£
Price variance	18,400 (F)
Usage variance	17,000 (A)
Total variance	1,400 (F)

Materials variances and opening and closing stock

2.3 Suppose that raw material P has a standard price of £3 per metre. During one month 6,000 metres are bought for £18,600, and 5,000 metres are used in production. At the end of the month, stock will have been increased by 1,000 metres. Should the material price variance be calculated on the basis of materials purchased (6,000 metres) or on the basis of materials used (5,000 metres)?

2.4 The answer depends on how **closing stocks** of the raw materials will be valued.

(a) If they are **valued at standard cost,** (1,000 units at £3 per unit) the **price variance** is **calculated on material purchases** in the period.

(b) If they are **valued at actual cost** (FIFO) (1,000 units at £3.10 per unit) the **price variance is calculated on materials used in production** in the period.

2.5 A full standard costing system is usually in operation and therefore the price variance is calculated on purchases in the period. The variance on the full 6,000 metres will be written off to the costing profit and loss account, even though only 5,000 metres are included in the cost of production.

2.6 There are two main **advantages** in extracting the material price variance at the time of receipt.

(a) Variances will be brought to the attention of managers earlier than if they are extracted as the material is used. If it is necessary to correct any variances then management action can be more timely.

(b) All stocks will be valued at standard price. This is administratively easier than using FIFO, LIFO or a weighted average method and it means that all issues from stocks can be made at standard price. If stocks are held at actual cost it is necessary to calculate a separate price variance on each batch as it is issued. This can be a time consuming task, especially with a manual system.

2.7 The price variance would be calculated as follows.

	£	
6,000 metres of material P purchased should cost (× £3)	18,000	
but did cost	18,600	
Price variance	600	(A)

2.8 Note that there are **disadvantages** to doing this, however.

(a) If variances are extracted at the time of receipt, revenues will be matched with the standard cost of the materials used plus the variances on the materials purchased rather than the true cost of sales, which does not comply with the matching concept.

(b) The usage variance may be calculated on a different amount to that on which the price variance is calculated and so the two variances may not sum to the materials total variance.

(c) SSAP 9 requires that stocks are valued at the lower of cost and net realisable value but by extracting variances upon receipt stocks are valued at standard. This may require an inventory adjustment for financial accounting purposes.

2.9 **In practice**, most organisations calculate materials price variances **when the material is purchased**. As far as your exam is concerned, David Cornes provides the following guidance in the June 1996 edition of *ACCA Students' Newsletter*.

> 'In examination questions the wording of the question should make clear what method is to be used. If both variances are to be calculated on the same quantity the examiner may say that the company uses a method of just-in-time purchasing or even that a system of Backflush Accounting ensures that purchases are not accounted for until the materials are used.'

3 LABOUR VARIANCES

KEY TERMS

- The **labour total variance** is the difference between what the output should have cost and what it did cost, in terms of labour. It can be divided into two sub-variances.
- The **labour rate variance** is the difference between what the labour did cost and what it should have cost.
- The **labour efficiency variance** is the difference between the standard cost of the hours that should have been worked and the standard cost of the hours that were worked.

3.1 The calculation of labour variances is very similar to the calculation of material variances. The calculation of the labour rate variance is similar to that for the material price variance while the calculation of the labour efficiency variance is similar to that for the material usage variance.

3.2 EXAMPLE: LABOUR VARIANCES

The standard direct labour cost of product X is 2 hours of grade Z labour at £5 per hour (= £10 per unit of product X). During period 4, 1,000 units of product X were made, and the direct labour cost of grade Z labour was £8,900 for 2,300 hours of work.

Required

Calculate the following variances.

(a) The labour total variance
(b) The labour rate variance
(c) The labour efficiency (productivity) variance

3.3 SOLUTION

(a) **The labour total variance.** This is the difference between what 1,000 units should have cost and what they did cost.

	£
1,000 units should have cost (× £10)	10,000
but did cost	8,900
Labour total variance	1,100 (F)

The variance is favourable because the units cost less than they should have done.

(b) **The labour rate variance.** This is the difference between what 2,300 hours should have cost and what 2,300 hours did cost.

	£
2,300 hours of work should have cost (× £5 per hr)	11,500
but did cost	8,900
Labour rate variance	2,600 (F)

The variance is favourable because the labour cost less than it should have cost.

(c) **The labour efficiency variance.** This is the difference between the number of hours it should have taken to produce 1,000 units of X, and the number of hours it did take, valued at the standard rate per hour.

1,000 units of X should have taken (× 2 hrs)	2,000 hrs
but did take	2,300 hrs
Efficiency variance in hours	300 hrs (A)
× standard rate per hour	× £5
Efficiency variance in £	£1,500 (A)

The variance is adverse because more hours were worked than should have been worked.

(d) **Summary**

	£
Rate variance	2,600 (F)
Efficiency variance	1,500 (A)
Total variance	1,100 (F)

Idle time variance

KEY TERM

The **idle time variance** is the number of hours that labour were idle valued at the standard rate per hour.

3.4 Idle time may be caused by machine breakdowns or not having work to give to employees, perhaps because of bottlenecks in production or a shortage of orders from customers. When it occurs, the labour force is still paid wages for time at work, but no actual work is done. Such time is unproductive and therefore inefficient. **In variance analysis, idle time is an adverse efficiency variance.**

3.5 The idle time variance is shown as a separate part of the total labour efficiency variance. The remaining **efficiency variance will then relate only to the productivity of the labour force during the hours spent actively working.**

3.6 EXAMPLE: LABOUR VARIANCES WITH IDLE TIME

During period 5, 1,500 units of product X were made and the cost of grade Z labour was £17,500 for 3,080 hours. During the period, however, there as a shortage of customer orders and 100 hours were recorded as idle time.

Required

Calculate the following variances.

(a) The labour total variance
(b) The labour rate variance
(c) The idle time variance
(d) The labour efficiency variance

3.7 SOLUTION

(a) **The labour total variance**

	£
1,500 units of product X should have cost (× £10)	15,000
but did cost	17,500
Labour total variance	2,500 (A)

Actual cost is greater than standard cost. The variance is therefore adverse.

(b) **The labour rate variance.** This is a comparison of what the hours paid should have cost and what they did cost.

	£
3,080 hours of grade Z labour should have cost (× £5)	15,400
but did cost	17,500
Labour rate variance	2,100 (A)

Actual cost is greater than standard cost. The variance is therefore adverse.

(c) **The idle time variance.** This is the hours of idle time, valued at the standard rate per hour. Idle time is *always* an adverse variance.

Idle time variance = 100 hours (A) × £5 = £500 (A)

(d) **The labour efficiency variance.** This considers the hours actively worked (the difference between hours paid for and idle time hours) and is calculated by taking the amount of output produced and comparing the time it should have taken to make them, with the actual time spent *actively* making them (3,080 – 100 = 2,980 hours). The variance in hours is valued at the standard rate per labour hour.

1,500 units of product X should take (× 2 hrs)	3,000 hrs
but did take (3,080 – 100)	2,980 hrs
Labour efficiency variance in hours	20 hrs (F)
× standard rate per hour	× £5
Labour efficiency variance in £	£100 (F)

(e) **Summary**

	£
Labour rate variance	2,100 (A)
Idle time variance	500 (A)
Labour efficiency variance	100 (F)
Labour total variance	2,500 (A)

3.8 Remember that, if idle time is recorded, the actual hours used in the efficiency variance calculation are the hours worked and not the hours paid for.

4 VARIABLE PRODUCTION OVERHEAD VARIANCES

4.1 Suppose that the variable production overhead cost of product X is 2 hours at £1.50 (= £3 per unit). During period 6, 400 units of product X were made. The labour force worked 820 hours, of which 60 hours were recorded as idle time. The variable overhead cost was £1,230.

Required

Calculate the following variances.

(a) The variable production overhead total variance

(b) The variable production overhead expenditure variance

(c) The variable production overhead efficiency variance

4.2 Since this **example relates to variable production costs, the total variance is based on actual units of production**. (If the overhead had been a variable selling cost, the variance would be based on sales volumes.)

	£
400 units of product X should cost (× £3)	1,200
but did cost	1,230
Variable production overhead total variance	30 (A)

4.3 In many variance reporting systems, the variance analysis goes no further, and expenditure and efficiency variances are not calculated. However, the adverse variance of £30 may be explained as the sum of two factors.

(a) The **hourly rate of spending on variable production overheads was higher** than it **should have been**, that is there is an **expenditure variance**.

(b) The **labour force worked inefficiently**, and took longer to make the output than it should have done. This means that spending on variable production overhead was higher than it should have been, in other words there is an **efficiency (productivity) variance**. The **variable production overhead efficiency variance is exactly the same, in hours, as the direct labour efficiency variance, and occurs for the same reasons.**

4.4 It is usually **assumed that variable overheads are incurred during active working hours,** but are not incurred during idle time (for example the machines are not running, therefore power is not being consumed). This means in our example that although the labour force was paid for 820 hours, they were actively working for only 760 of those hours, therefore variable production overhead spending occurred during 760 hours.

KEY TERMS

- The **variable production overhead total variance** is the difference between what the output should have cost and what it did cost, in terms of variable production overhead. It can be divided into two sub-variances.
- The **variable production overhead expenditure variance** is the difference between the amount of variable production overhead that should have been incurred in the actual hours actively worked, and the actual amount of variable production overhead incurred.
- The **variable production overhead efficiency variance** is the difference between the standard cost of the hours that should have been worked for the number of units actually produced, and the standard cost of the actual number of hours worked.

4.5 In our example, the expenditure and efficiency variances would be as follows.

		£
(a)	760 hours of variable production overhead should cost (× £1.50)	1,140
	but did cost	1,230
	Variable production overhead expenditure variance	90 (A)
(b)	400 units of product X should take (× 2 hrs)	800 hrs
	but did take (active hours)	760 hrs
	Variable production overhead efficiency variance in hours	40 hrs (F)
	× standard rate per hour	× £1.50
	Variable production overhead efficiency variance in £	£60 (F)
(c)	*Summary*	£
	Variable production overhead expenditure variance	90 (A)
	Variable production overhead efficiency variance	60 (F)
	Variable production overhead total variance	30 (A)

4.6 Note that **if variances change in line with production volume rather than labour hours, only a total variance can be calculated.**

5 FIXED PRODUCTION OVERHEAD VARIANCES

5.1 You may have noticed that the method of calculating cost variances for variable cost items is essentially the same for labour, materials and variable overheads. Fixed production overhead variances are very different. In an absorption costing system, they are simply an **attempt to explain the under or over absorption of fixed overheads.**

5.2 The **fixed production overhead total variance may be broken down into two parts** as usual.

(a) An **expenditure variance**

(b) A **volume variance**. This in turn may be split into two parts.

 (i) **A volume efficiency variance**

 (ii) **A volume capacity variance**

5.3 The fixed production overhead volume variance sometimes causes confusion and may need more explanation. The most important point is that the volume variance applies to fixed production overhead costs only and not to variable production overheads.

(a) Variable production overheads incurred change with the volume of activity. If the master budget is to work for 300 hours and variable production overheads are incurred and absorbed at a rate of £6 per hour, the variable production overhead budget will be £1,800. If only 200 hours are actually worked, the variable production overhead absorbed will be £1,200, but the expected expenditure will also be £1,200, so that there will be no under- or over-absorption of production overhead because of volume changes.

(b) Fixed production overheads are different because the level of expenditure does not change as the number of hours worked varies. If the master budget is to work for 300 hours and fixed production overheads are budgeted to be £2,400, the fixed production overhead absorption rate will be £8 per hour. If actual hours worked are only 200 hours, the fixed production overhead absorbed will be £1,600, whereas expected expenditure will be unchanged at £2,400. There is an under-absorption of £800 because of the volume variance of 100 hours shortfall multiplied by the absorption rate of £8 per hour.

5.4 You will find it easier to calculate and understand fixed production overhead variances if you keep in mind the whole time the fact that you are trying to explain the reasons for any under- or over-absorbed production overhead. Remember that the absorption rate is calculated as (budgeted fixed production overhead ÷ budgeted level of activity).

Generally the level of activity used in the overhead absorption rate will be units of production or hours of activity. More often than not, if just one product is being produced, the level of activity is in terms of units produced. If, however, more than one product is produced, units of output are converted to standard hours.

5.5 As you should remember, if either the budgeted overhead or the budgeted activity level or both are incorrect then we will have under- or over-absorbed fixed production overhead.

(a) The fixed production overhead **expenditure variance** measures the under- or over-absorption caused by the **actual production overhead expenditure being different from budget**.

(b) There are two reasons why the actual production or hours of activity may be different from the budgeted production or budgeted number of hours used in calculating the absorption rate.

(i) The **work force may have been working at a more or less efficient rate than standard** to produce a given output. This is measured by the fixed production overhead **volume efficiency variance**, which is similar to the variable production overhead efficiency variance.

(ii) Regardless of the level of efficiency, the **total number of hours worked could have been less or more than was originally budgeted** (employees may have worked a lot of overtime or there may have been a strike). Other things being equal, this could lead to under- or over-absorbed fixed overhead and the effect is measured by the fixed production overhead **volume capacity variance**.

How to calculate the variances

KEY TERMS

- **Fixed production overhead total variance** is the difference between fixed production overhead incurred and fixed production overhead absorbed. In other words, it is the under- or over-absorbed fixed production overhead.
- **Fixed production overhead expenditure variance** is the difference between the budgeted fixed production overhead expenditure and actual fixed production overhead expenditure.
- **Fixed production overhead volume variance** is the difference between actual and budgeted production/volume multiplied by the standard absorption rate per *unit*.
- **Fixed production overhead volume efficiency variance** is the difference between the number of hours that actual production should have taken, and the number of hours actually taken (that is, worked) multiplied by the standard absorption rate per *hour*.
- **Fixed production overhead volume capacity variance** is the difference between budgeted hours of work and the actual hours worked, multiplied by the standard absorption rate per *hour*.

5.6 EXAMPLE: FIXED PRODUCTION OVERHEAD VARIANCES

Suppose that a company budgets to produce 1,000 units of product E during August. The expected time to produce a unit of E is five hours, and the budgeted fixed production overhead is £20,000. The standard fixed production overhead cost per unit of product E will therefore be 5 hours at £4 per hour (= £20 per unit). Actual fixed production overhead expenditure in August turns out to be £20,450. The labour force manages to produce 1,100 units of product E in 5,400 hours of work.

Required

Calculate the following variances.

(a) The fixed production overhead total variance
(b) The fixed production overhead expenditure variance
(c) The fixed production overhead volume variance
(d) The fixed production overhead volume efficiency variance
(e) The fixed production overhead volume capacity variance

5.7 SOLUTION

(a) **Fixed production overhead total variance**

	£
Fixed production overhead incurred	20,450
Fixed production overhead absorbed (1,100 units × £20 per unit)	22,000
Fixed production overhead expenditure variance (= under-/over-absorbed overhead)	1,550 (F)

The variance is favourable because more overheads were absorbed than budgeted.

(b) **Fixed production overhead expenditure variance**

	£
Budgeted fixed production overhead expenditure	20,000
Actual fixed production overhead expenditure	20,450
Fixed production overhead expenditure variance	450 (A)

The variance is adverse because actual expenditure was greater than budgeted.

(c) **Fixed production overhead volume variance**. The production volume achieved was greater than expected. The fixed production overhead volume variance measures the difference at the standard rate.

	£
Actual production at standard rate (1,100 × £20 per unit)	22,000
Budgeted production at standard rate (1,000 × £20 per unit)	20,000
Fixed production overhead volume variance	2,000 (F)

The variance is favourable because output was greater than expected.

(i) The labour force may have worked efficiently, and produced output at a faster rate than expected. More overhead will be absorbed if units are produced more quickly. This **efficiency variance** is exactly the same in hours as the direct labour efficiency variance (and the variable production overhead efficiency variance), but is valued in £ at the standard absorption rate for fixed overhead.

(ii) The labour force may have worked longer hours than budgeted, and therefore produced more output, so there may be a *capacity variance*.

(d) **Fixed production overhead volume efficiency variance.** The volume efficiency variance is calculated in the same way as the labour efficiency variance.

1,100 units of product E should take (× 5 hrs)	5,500 hrs
but did take	5,400 hrs
Fixed overhead production volume efficiency variance in hours	100 hrs (F)
× standard fixed production overhead absorption rate per hour	× £4
Fixed production overhead volume efficiency variance in £	£400 (F)

The labour force has produced 5,500 standard hours of work in 5,400 actual hours and so output is 100 standard hours (or 20 units of product E) higher than budgeted for this reason and the variance is favourable.

(e) **Fixed production overhead volume capacity variance.** The volume capacity variance is the difference between the budgeted and actual active hours of work (excluding any idle time).

Budgeted hours of work	5,000 hrs
Actual hours of work	5,400 hrs
Fixed production overhead volume capacity variance	400 hrs (F)
× standard fixed production overhead absorption rate per hour	× £4
Fixed production overhead volume capacity variance in £	£1,600 (F)

Since the labour force worked 400 hours longer than budgeted, we should expect output to be 400 standard hours (or 80 units of product E) higher than budgeted and hence the variance is favourable.

Question 1

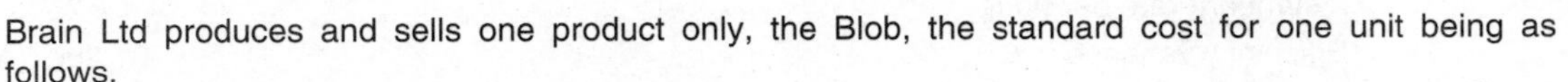

Brain Ltd produces and sells one product only, the Blob, the standard cost for one unit being as follows.

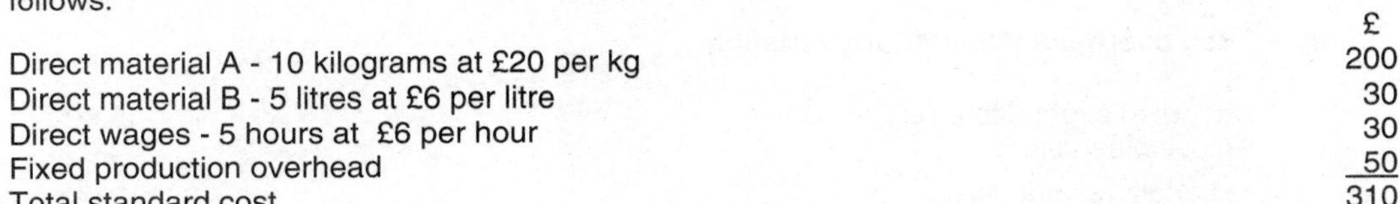

	£
Direct material A - 10 kilograms at £20 per kg	200
Direct material B - 5 litres at £6 per litre	30
Direct wages - 5 hours at £6 per hour	30
Fixed production overhead	50
Total standard cost	310

The fixed overhead included in the standard cost is based on an expected monthly output of 900 units. Fixed production overhead is absorbed on the basis of direct labour hours.

During April the actual results were as follows.

Production	800 units
Material A	7,800 kg used, costing £159,900
Material B	4,300 litres used, costing £23,650
Direct wages	4,200 hours worked for £24,150
Fixed production overhead	£47,000

Required

(a) Calculate price and usage variances for each material.

(b) Calculate labour rate and efficiency variances.

(c) Calculate fixed production overhead expenditure and volume variances and then subdivide the volume variance.

Answer

(a) **Price variance - A**

	£
7,800 kgs should have cost (× £20)	156,000
but did cost	159,900
Price variance	3,900 (A)

Usage variance - A

800 units should have used (× 10 kgs)	8,000 kgs
but did use	7,800 kgs
Usage variance in kgs	200 kgs (F)
× standard cost per kilogram	× £20
Usage variance in £	£4,000 (F)

Price variance - B

	£
4,300 litres should have cost (× £6)	25,800
but did cost	23,650
Price variance	2,150 (F)

Usage variance - B

800 units should have used (× 5 l)	4,000 l
but did use	4,300 l
Usage variance in litres	300 (A)
× standard cost per litre	× £6
Usage variance in £	£1,800 (A)

(b) **Labour rate variance**

	£
4,200 hours should have cost (× £6)	25,200
but did cost	24,150
Rate variance	1,050 (F)

Labour efficiency variance

800 units should have taken (× 5 hrs)	4,000 hrs
but did take	4,200 hrs
Efficiency variance in hours	200 hrs (A)
× standard rate per hour	× £6
Efficiency variance in £	£1,200 (A)

(c) **Fixed overhead expenditure variance**

	£
Budgeted expenditure (£50 × 900)	45,000
Actual expenditure	47,000
Expenditure variance	2,000 (A)

Fixed overhead volume variance

	£
Budgeted production at standard rate (900 × £50)	45,000
Actual production at standard rate (800 × £50)	40,000
Volume variance	5,000 (A)

Fixed overhead volume efficiency variance

	£
800 units should have taken (× 5 hrs)	4,000 hrs
but did take	4,200 hrs
Volume efficiency variance in hours	200 hrs
× standard absorption rate per hour	× £10
Volume efficiency variance	£2,000 (A)

Fixed overhead volume capacity variance

Budgeted hours	4,500 hrs
Actual hours	4,200 hrs
Volume capacity variance in hours	300 hrs (A)
× standard absorption rate per hour (£50 ÷ 5)	× £10
	£3,000 (A)

6 SALES VARIANCES

Selling price variance

> **KEY TERM**
>
> The **selling price variance** is a measure of the effect on expected profit of a different selling price to standard selling price. It is calculated as the difference between what the sales revenue should have been for the actual quantity sold, and what it was.

6.1 Suppose that the standard selling price of product X is £15. Actual sales in March were 2,000 units at £15.30 per unit. The selling price variance is calculated as follows.

	£
Revenue from 2,000 units should be (× £15)	30,000
but was (× £15.30)	30,600
Selling price variance	600 (F)

The variance is favourable because the price was higher than expected.

Sales volume variance

> **KEY TERM**
>
> The **sales volume variance** measures the increase or decrease in expected profit as a result of the sales volume being higher or lower than budgeted.

6.2 Suppose that a company budgets to sell 8,000 units of product J for £12 per unit. The standard full cost per unit is £7. Actual sales were 7,700 units, at £12.50 per unit. The sales volume variance is calculated as follows.

Budgeted sales volume	8,000 units
Actual sales volume	7,700 units
Sales volume variance in units	300 units (A)
× standard profit per unit (£(12–7))	× £5
Sales volume variance	£1,500 (A)

The variance is adverse because actual sales were less than budgeted.

6.3 EXAMPLE: SALES VARIANCES

Jasper Ltd has the following budget and actual figures for May.

	Budget	*Actual*
Sales units	600	620
Selling price per unit	£30	£29

Standard full cost of production = £28 per unit.

Required

Calculate the selling price variance and the sales volume variance.

6.4 SOLUTION

(a)

	£
Sales revenue for 620 units should have been (× £30)	18,600
but was (× £29)	17,980
Selling price variance	620 (A)

(b)

Budgeted sales volume	600 units
Actual sales volume	620 units
Sales volume variance in units	20 units (F)
× standard profit per unit (£(30 – 28))	× £2
Sales volume variance	£40 (F)

Exam focus point

A common mistake when computing the sales volume variance is to multiply the variance in units by the standard selling price rather than by the standard profit per unit. In effect this is calculating the sales value variance.

7 WORKING BACKWARDS APPROACH

7.1 Exam questions often provide you with data about expected and actual results and you have to calculate variances. One way in which your understanding of the topic can be tested, however, is if you are provided with **information about variances from which you have to 'work backwards' to determine the expected and actual results.**

7.2 EXAMPLE: WORKING BACKWARDS

The standard direct material cost of Product X is £96 (16 kgs × £6 per kg) and the standard direct labour cost is £72 (6 hours × £12 per hour). The following variances were among those reported in control period 10 in relation to Product X.

Direct material price: £18,840 favourable
Direct material usage: £480 adverse
Direct labour rate: £10,598 adverse
Direct labour efficiency: £8,478 favourable

Actual direct wages cost £171,320 and £5.50 was paid for each kg of direct material. There was no opening or closing stocks of the material.

Required

Calculate the following.

(a) Actual output
(b) Actual hours worked
(c) Average actual wage rate per hour
(d) Actual number of kilograms purchased and used

7.3 SOLUTION

(a)

	£
Total direct wages cost	171,320
Adjust for variances:	
labour rate	(10,598)
labour efficiency	8,478
Standard direct wages cost	169,200

∴ Actual output = Total standard cost ÷ unit standard cost
= £169,200 ÷ £72
= 2,350 units

(b)

	£
Total direct wages cost	171,320.0
Less rate variance	(10,598.0)
Standard rate for actual hours	160,722.0
÷ standard rate per hour	÷ £12.0
Actual hours worked	13,393.5 hrs

(c) Average actual wage rate per hour = actual wages/actual hours = £171,320/13,393.5 = £12.79 per hour.

(d) Number of kgs purchased and used = x

	£
x kgs should have cost (× £6)	6.0x
but did cost (× £5.50)	5.5x
Direct material price variance	0.5x

∴ £0.5x = £18,840
∴ x = 37,680 kgs

Question 2

XYZ Ltd uses standard costing. The following data relates to labour grade II.

Actual hours worked = 10,400 hours
Standard allowance for actual production = 9,800 hours
Standard rate per hour = £5
Rate variance (adverse) = £416

What was the actual rate of pay per hour?

Answer

Rate variance per hour worked = £416/10,400 = £0.04(A)

Actual rate per hour = £(5.00 + 0.04) = £5.04

8 THE REASONS FOR VARIANCES

Exam focus point

In an examination, always be prepared to be able to explain the reasons why variances have occurred, and their significance.

8.1 There now follows a list of a few possible causes of variances. This is not an exhaustive list and in an examination question you should review the information given and use your imagination and common sense to suggest possible reasons for variances.

Variance	Favourable	Adverse
Material price	Unforeseen discounts received Greater care in purchasing Change in material standard	Price increase Careless purchasing Change in material standard
Material usage	Material used of higher quality than standard More effective use made of material Errors in allocating material to jobs	Defective material Excessive waste Theft Stricter quality control Errors in allocating material to jobs
Labour rate	Use of workers at a rate of pay lower than standard	Wage rate increase
Idle time	*The idle time variance is always adverse.*	Machine breakdown Non-availability of material Illness or injury to worker
Labour efficiency	Output produced more quickly than expected, because of work motivation, better quality of equipment or materials Errors in allocating time to jobs	Lost time in excess of standard allowed Output lower than standard set because of lack of training, sub-standard material etc Errors in allocating time to jobs
Overhead expenditure	Savings in costs incurred More economical use of services	Increase in cost of services Excessive use of services Change in type of services used
Overhead volume	Production or level of activity greater than budgeted	Production or level of activity less than budgeted
Selling price	Unplanned price increase	Unplanned price reduction
Sales volume	Additional demand	Unexpected fall in demand Production difficulties

9 INVESTIGATING VARIANCES

9.1 Before management decide whether or not to investigate the reasons for the occurrence of a particular variance, there are a number of factors which should be considered in assessing the significance of the variance.

9.2 **Materiality**

Because a standard cost is really only an *average* expected cost, small variations between actual and standard are bound to occur and are unlikely to be significant. Obtaining an 'explanation' of the reasons why they occurred is likely to be time consuming and irritating for the manager concerned. The explanation will often be 'chance', which is not, in any case, particularly helpful. For such variations **further investigation is not worthwhile** since such variances are not controllable.

9.3 **Controllability**

This must also influence the decision about whether to investigate. If there is a general worldwide increase in the price of a raw material there is nothing that can be done internally to control the effect of this. If a central decision is made to award all employees a 10% increase in salary, staff costs in division A will increase by this amount and the variance is not controllable by division A's manager. **Uncontrollable variances call for a change in the plan, not an investigation into the past.**

9.4 The type of standard being used

The efficiency variance reported in any control period, whether for materials or labour, will depend on the **efficiency level set**. If, for example, an ideal standard is used, variances will always be adverse. A similar problem arises if average price levels are used as standards. If **inflation** exists, favourable price variances are likely to be reported at the beginning of a period, to be offset by adverse price variances later in the period.

9.5 Variance trend

Although small variations in a single period are unlikely to be significant, small variations that occur consistently may need more attention. Variance trend is probably more important that a single set of variances for one accounting period. The trend **provides an indication of whether the variance is fluctuating within acceptable control limits or becoming out of control.**

(a) If, say, an efficiency variance is £1,000 adverse in month 1, the obvious conclusion is that the process is out of control and that corrective action must be taken. This may be correct, but what if the same variance is £1,000 adverse every month? The *trend* indicates that the process is in control and the standard has been wrongly set.

(b) Suppose, though, that the same variance is consistently £1,000 adverse for each of the first six months of the year but that production has steadily fallen from 100 units in month 1 to 65 units by month 6. The variance trend in absolute terms is constant, but relative to the number of units produced, efficiency has got steadily worse.

Individual variances should therefore not be looked at in isolation; variances should be scrutinised for a number of successive periods if their full significance is to be appreciated.

9.6 Interdependence between variances

Individual variances should not be looked at in isolation. One variance might be inter-related with another, and much of it might have occurred only because the other variance occurred too. **When two variances are interdependent (interrelated) one will usually be adverse and the other one favourable.** Here are some examples.

Interrelated variances	Explanation
Materials price and usage	If cheaper materials are purchased for a job in order to obtain a favourable price variance, materials wastage might be higher and an adverse usage variance may occur. If the cheaper materials are more difficult to handle, there might be an adverse labour efficiency variance too. If more expensive materials are purchased, the price variance will be adverse but the usage variance might be favourable if the material is easier to use or of a higher quality.
Labour rate and efficiency	If employees are paid higher rates for experience and skill, using a highly skilled team might lead to an adverse rate variance and a favourable efficiency variance (experienced staff are less likely to waste material, for example). In contrast, a favourable rate variance might indicate a larger-than-expected proportion of inexperienced workers, which could result in an adverse labour efficiency variance, and perhaps poor materials handling and high rates of rejects too (and hence an adverse materials usage variance).

Interrelated variances	Explanation
Selling price and sales volume	A reduction in the selling price might stimulate bigger sales demand, so that an adverse selling price variance might be counterbalanced by a favourable sales volume variance. Similarly, a price rise would give a favourable price variance, but possibly cause an adverse sales volume variance.

9.7 **Costs of investigation**

The costs of an investigation should be weighed against the benefits of correcting the cause of a variance.

Exam focus point

When asked to provide a commentary on variances you have calculated, make sure that you *interpret* your calculations rather than simply detail them.

Variance investigation models

Rule-of-thumb model

9.8 This involves **deciding a limit** and if the size of a **variance is within the limit,** it should be considered **immaterial.** Only if it exceeds the limit is it considered materially significant, and worthy of investigation.

9.9 In practice many managers believe that this approach to deciding which variances to investigate is perfectly adequate. However, it has a number of **drawbacks**.

(a) Should variances be investigated if they exceed 10% of standard? Or 5%? Or 15%?

(b) Should a **different fixed percentage be applied to favourable and unfavourable variances**?

(c) Suppose that the fixed percentage is, say, 10% and an important category of expenditure has in the past been very closely controlled so that adverse variances have never exceeded, say, 2% of standard. Now if adverse variances suddenly shoot up to, say, **8% or 9%** of standard, there might well be **serious excess expenditures incurred that ought to be controlled,** but with the fixed percentage limit at 10%, the variances would not be 'flagged' for investigation.

(d) **Unimportant categories** of low-cost expenditures might be loosely controlled, with variances commonly exceeding 10% in both a favourable and adverse direction. These would be regularly - and **unnecessarily - flagged for investigation.**

(e) Where actual expenditures have **normal and expected wide fluctuations** from period to period, but the 'standard' is a fixed expenditure amount, variances will be **flagged for investigation unnecessarily often.**

(f) There is **no attempt to consider the costs and potential benefits of investigating variances** (except insofar as the pre-set percentage is of 'material significance').

(g) The **past history of variances in previous periods is ignored**. For example, if the pre-set percentage limit is set at 10% and an item of expenditure has regularly exceeded the standard by, say, 6% per month for a number of months in a row, in all probability there is a situation that ought to warrant control action. Using the pre-set percentage rule, however, the variance would never be flagged for investigation in spite of the cumulative adverse variances.

9.10 Some of the difficulties can be overcome by **varying the pre-set percentage from account to account** (for example 5% for direct labour efficiency, 2% for rent and rates, 10% for salesmen's expenditure, 15% for postage costs, 5% for direct materials price, 3% for direct materials usage and so on). On the other hand, some difficulties, if they are significant, can only be overcome with a different cost-variance investigation model.

Statistical significance model

9.11 Historical data are used to **calculate** both a standard as **an expected average** and the **expected standard deviation** around this average when the process is under control. An **in-control process** (process being material usage, fixed overhead expenditure and so on) is one in which any resulting **variance is simply due to random fluctuations** around the expected outcome. An **out-of-control process,** on the other hand, is one in which **corrective action can be taken to remedy any variance.**

9.12 By assuming that variances that occur are normally distributed around this average, a **variance will be investigated if it is *more* than a distance from the expected average that the estimated normal distribution suggests is likely if the process is in control.** (Note that such a variance would be deemed significant.)

(a) A 95% or 0.05 significance level rule would state that variances should be investigated if they exceed 1.96 standard deviations from the standard.

(b) A 99% or 0.01 significance level rule would state that variances should be investigated if they exceed 2.58 standard deviations from the standard. This is less stringent than a 0.05 significance level rule.

(c) For simplicity, 1.96 and 2.58 standard deviations can be rounded up to 2 and 3 standard deviations respectively.

9.13 For example data could be collected and analysed to reveal the following pattern.

Standard hours per unit	6 hours
Standard deviation per unit	0.5 hours

Assume that a **0.05 significance level** rule is in use.

Suppose that 100 units are made and take 640 hours. The efficiency variance would be 40 hours (A). The standard deviation is 0.5 hours for one unit and $0.5 \times \sqrt{100} = 5$ hours for 100 units. Since 40 hours (A) is **8 standard deviations** from the standard of 600 hours, the efficiency variance should be **investigated.**

Question 3

Data has been collected and analysed and reveals that transport costs per month are £25,000, with a standard deviation of £2,000. A 0.01 significance rule is in use. Actual travel expenses are £28,750. Should the resulting variance be investigated?

Answer

Variance = £3,750 (A) = 1.875 standard deviations

The variance would not be investigated.

9.14 The statistical significance rule has two principal **advantages** over the rule of thumb approach.

(a) **Important costs** that normally vary by only a small amount from standard will be **signalled for investigation if variances increase significantly**.

(b) Costs that **usually fluctuate by large amounts will not be signalled** for investigation unless variances are extremely large.

9.15 The main **disadvantage** of the statistical significance rule is the problem of assessing standard deviations in expenditure.

Statistical control charts

9.16 By marking variances and control limits on a control chart, **investigation** is signalled not only when a particular **variance exceeds the control limit** (since it would be non-random and worth investigating) but also when the **trend of variances shows a progressively worsening movement** in actual results (even though the variance in any single control period has not yet overstepped the control limit).

9.17 The **$\bar{x}$ control chart** is based on the principle of the statistical significance model. For each cost item, a chart is kept of monthly variances and **tolerance limits are set at 1, 2 or 3 standard deviations.**

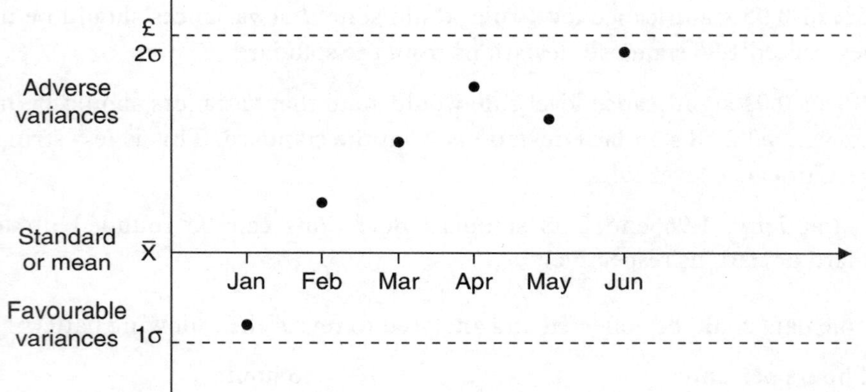

In this example, variances do not exceed the tolerance limits in any month, but the chart shows a worsening of variances over time, and so management might decide that an investigation is warranted, perhaps when it exceeds an inner warning limit.

9.18 Using a **cusum chart, the cumulative sum of variances** over a long period of time **is plotted**. If the variances are not significant, these 'sums' will simply fluctuate in a random way above and below the average to give a total or cumulative sum of zero. But if significant variances occur, the cumulative sum will start to develop a positive or negative drift, and when it exceeds a set tolerance limit, the situation must be investigated.

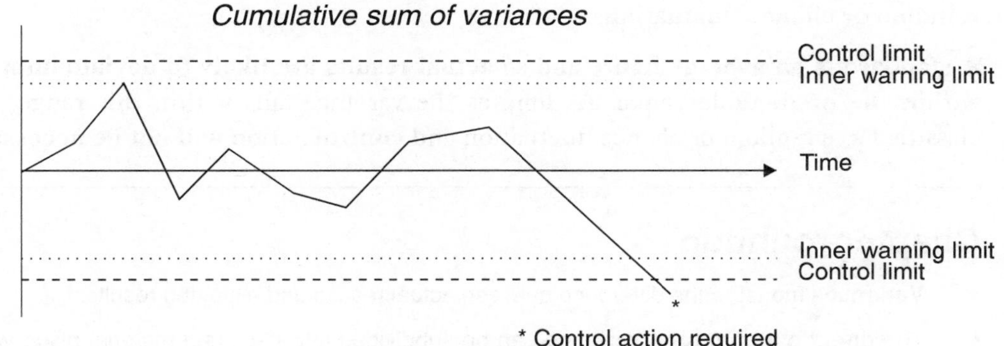

9.19 The **advantage** of the multiple period approach over the single period approach is that **trends are detectable earlier,** and control action would be introduced sooner than might have been the case if only current-period variances were investigated.

Possible control action

9.20 There are few basic reasons why variances occur and the **control action which may be taken will depend on the reason why the variance occurred.**

9.21 Measurement errors

In exam questions there is generally no question of the information that you are given being wrong. In practice, however, it may be extremely difficult to establish that 1,000 units of product A used 32,000 kg of raw material X. Scales may be misread, the pilfering or wastage of materials may go unrecorded, items may be wrongly classified (as material X3, say, when material X8 was used in reality), or employees may make 'cosmetic' adjustments to their records to make their own performance look better than it really was. An investigation may show that **control action is required to improve the accuracy of the recording system** so that measurement errors do not occur.

9.22 Out of date standards

Price standards are likely to become out of date quickly when frequent changes to the costs of material, power, labour and so on occur, or in **periods of high inflation**. In such circumstances an **investigation of variances is likely to highlight a general change in market prices** rather than efficiencies or inefficiencies in acquiring resources. Standards may also be out of date where operations are subject to **technological development** or if **learning curve effects** have not been taken into account. Investigation of this type of variance will provide information about the inaccuracy of the standard and **highlight the need to frequently review and update standards.**

9.23 Efficient or inefficient operations

Spoilage and better quality material/more highly skilled labour than standard are all likely to affect the efficiency of operations and hence cause variances. **Investigation** of variances in this category should **highlight the cause of the inefficiency or efficiency and will lead to control action to eliminate the inefficiency being repeated** or action to **compound the benefits of the efficiency**. For example, stricter supervision may be required to reduce wastage levels and the need for overtime working. The purchasing department could be encouraged to continue using suppliers of good quality materials.

9.24 **Random or chance fluctuations**

A standard is an average figure and so **actual results are likely to deviate unpredictably within the predictable range.** As long as the variance falls within this range, it will be classified as a random or chance fluctuation and **control action will not be necessary.**

Chapter roundup

- **Variances** measure the difference between actual results and expected results.
- The **direct material total variance** can be subdivided into the direct material **price** variance and the direct material **usage** variance. Direct material price variances are extracted at the time of receipt of the materials, not the time of usage.
- The **direct labour total variance** can be subdivided into the direct labour **rate** variance and the direct labour **efficiency** variance.
- If idle time arises, it is usual to calculate a separate **idle time variance**, and to base the calculation of the efficiency variance on active hours (when labour actually worked) only. It is always an adverse variance.
- The **variable production overhead total variance** can be subdivided into the variable production overhead **expenditure** variance and the variable production overhead **efficiency** variance (based on active hours).
- The **fixed production overhead total variance** can be subdivided into an **expenditure** variance and a volume variance. The volume variance can be subdivided into an **efficiency** variance and a **capacity** variance.
- The **selling price variance** measures the effect on profit of a different selling price to standard selling price.
- The **sales volume variance** measures the effect on profit of actual sales volume being different to budgeted sales volume.
- **Materiality**, **controllability**, the **type** of standard being used, variance **trend**, **interdependence** and **costs** should be taken into account when deciding on the significance of a variance.
- The **rule-of-thumb** and **statistical significance** variance investigation models and/or statistical **control charts** can be used to determine whether a variance should be investigated.
- **Measurement errors** and **out of date standards**, as well as **efficient/inefficient operations** and **random fluctuations**, can cause differences between standard and actual performance.

Quick quiz

1 *Fill in the blanks.*

The material price variance is the difference between .... and ....

The material usage variance is the difference between .... and ....

2 If closing stocks of raw materials are valued at standard cost, the material price variance is calculated on material purchases in the period. True or false?

3 *Choose the appropriate words from those highlighted.*

The idle time variance is an **efficiency/price** variance which is **adverse/favourable**.

4 Are variable production overhead variances based on hours paid or hours worked?

5 *Fill in the boxes in the diagram with the names of the variances and add the appropriate definition number from the list below.*

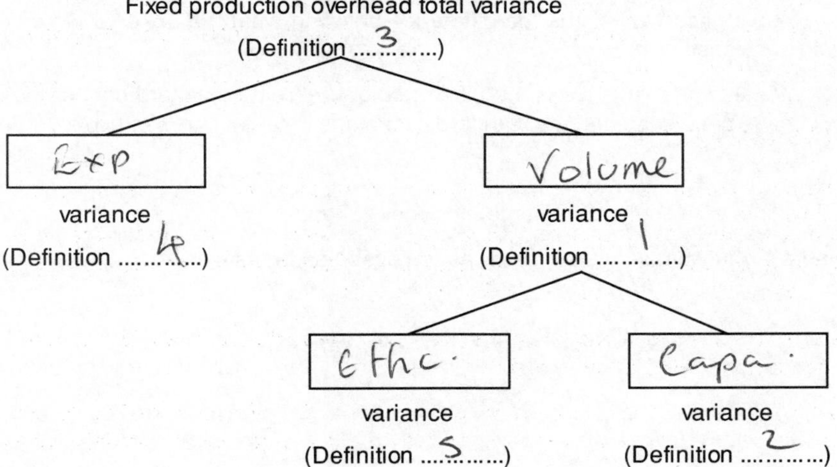

Definitions

1 The difference between actual and budgeted production, multiplied by the standard absorption rate per unit

2 The difference between budgeted hours of work and the actual hours worked, multiplied by the standard absorption rate per hour

3 The under or over absorption of fixed production overhead

4 The difference between budgeted fixed production overhead expenditure and actual fixed production overhead expenditure

5 The difference between the number of hours that actual production should have taken, and the number of hours actually taken, multiplied by the standard absorption rate per hour

6 The sales volume variance is valued at the standard selling price per unit.

☐ True

☐ False

7 *Match the following causes of variances to the appropriate variance.*

Variances	*Causes*
(a) Favourable labour efficiency	(1) Inexperienced staff in the purchasing department
(b) Adverse sales volume	(2) Materials of higher quality than standard
(c) Adverse material price	(3) Unexpected slump in demand
(d) Adverse selling price	(4) Production difficulties
(e) Adverse fixed production overhead volume	(5) Strike
(f) Idle time	(6) Poor machine maintenance

8 *Match the three pairs of interrelated variances.*

(a) Adverse selling price
(b) Favourable labour rate
(c) Adverse materials usage
(d) Favourable sales volume
(e) Adverse materials price
(f) Favourable materials usage
(g) Adverse sales volume
(h) Idle time

Answers to quick quiz

1 The material price variance is the difference between what the material did cost and what it should have cost.

The material usage variance is the difference between the standard cost of the material that should have been used and the standard cost of the material that was used.

2 True

3 The idle time variance is an adverse efficiency variance.

4 Variable production overhead variances are based on hours worked.

5

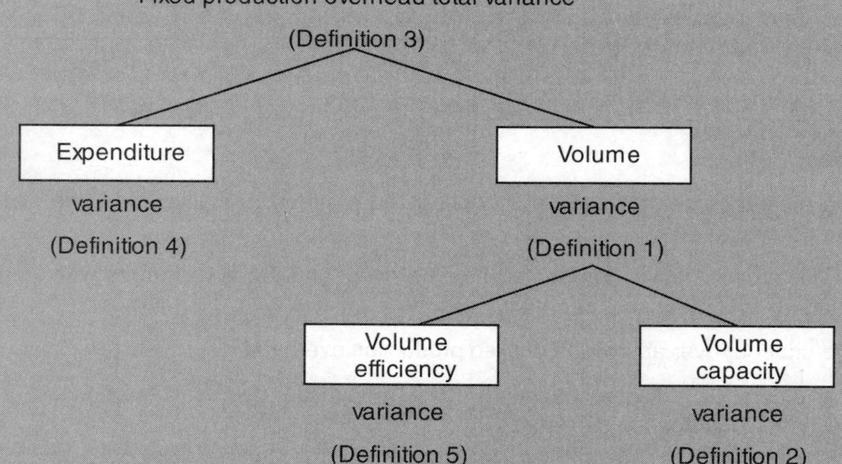

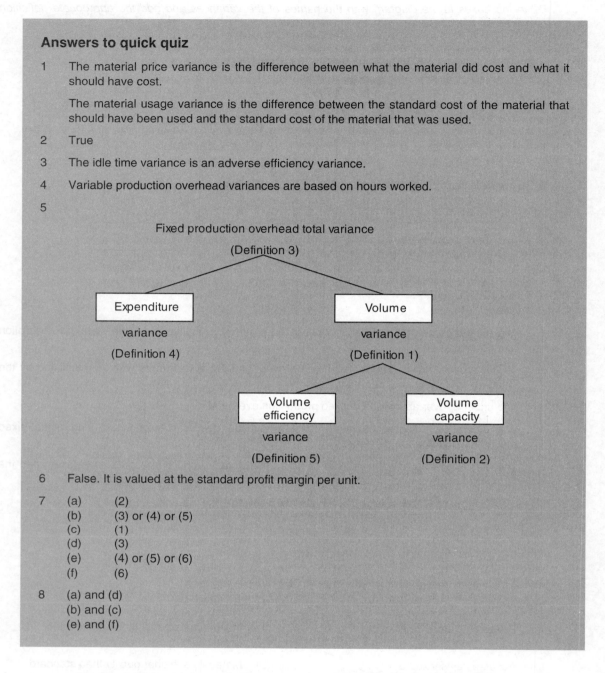

6 False. It is valued at the standard profit margin per unit.

7 (a) (2)
(b) (3) or (4) or (5)
(c) (1)
(d) (3)
(e) (4) or (5) or (6)
(f) (6)

8 (a) and (d)
(b) and (c)
(e) and (f)

Now try the questions below from the Exam Question Bank

Question to try	Level	Marks	Time
9	Exam	25	45 mins
10	Exam	25	45 mins

Chapter 8

FURTHER VARIANCE ANALYSIS

Topic list		Syllabus reference
1	Operating statements	8(a)(iv)
2	Variances in a standard marginal costing system	8(a)(ii)
3	Materials mix and yield variances	8(a)(ii)
4	Sales mix and quantity variances	8(a)(ii)
5	Planning and operational variance	8(b)

Introduction

In this chapter we build on the knowledge you have gained from Chapters 6 and 7 and examine a number of further variance analysis topics. We begin by considering the way in which individual variances can be **summarised** so as to show how budgeted profit/contribution differs from actual profit/contribution.

We then move on to looking at the **differences** between variances in an **absorption** costing system (which we have been concentrating on so far) and those in a **marginal** costing system.

The final three topics of the chapter deal with slightly more complex variance analysis.

When a product requires two or more materials in its make-up the **materials usage variance** can be split into a materials **mix variance** and a materials **yield variance**. Likewise, if a company sells more than one product, it is possible to analyse the overall **sales volume variance** into a sales **mix variance** and a sales **quantity variance**. Don't be put off by these new terms. The basic principles of variance calculation covered in the previous chapter still applies: an actual result is compared with an original standard result.

In the last section of the chapter we will be moving away from this approach to variance calculation with a study of **planning and operational variances.**

Study guide

Section 22 – Standard costing II

- Prepare reconciliations using operating statements which reconcile budgeted and actual profit figures, and/or reconcile the actual sales less the standard cost of sales with the actual profit
- Demonstrate how absorption and marginal approaches can be used in standard costing
- Calculate mix and yield variances for materials
- Calculate mix and quantity variances for sales
- Calculate and explain operational and planning variances
- Demonstrate an understanding of the inter-relationships between variances
- Explain the reasons for variances
- Assess appropriate management action arising from the variances identified

Exam guide

Expect to encounter Section B questions on the topics covered in this chapter, either on their own or in conjunction with more straightforward variance analysis covered in Chapter 7. Section A questions might include this chapter's topics.

1 OPERATING STATEMENTS

1.1 So far, we have considered how variances are calculated without considering how they combine to reconcile the difference between budgeted profit and actual profit during a period. This reconciliation is usually presented as a report to senior management at the end of each control period. The report is called an **operating statement** or **statement of variances.**

KEY TERM

An **operating statement** is a regular report for management which compares actual costs and revenues with budgeted figures and shows variances.

1.2 An extensive example will now be introduced, both to revise the variance calculations already described, and also to combine them into an operating statement.

1.3 EXAMPLE: VARIANCES AND OPERATING STATEMENTS

Armoured Kangaroo Ltd manufactures one product, and the entire product is sold as soon as it is produced. There are no opening or closing stocks and work in progress is negligible. The company operates a standard costing system and analysis of variances is made every month. The standard cost card for the product, a boomerang, is as follows.

STANDARD COST CARD - BOOMERANG

		£
Direct materials	0.5 kilos at £4 per kilo	2.00
Direct wages	2 hours at £2.00 per hour	4.00
Variable overheads	2 hours at £0.30 per hour	0.60
Fixed overhead	2 hours at £3.70 per hour	7.40
Standard cost		14.00
Standard profit		6.00
Standing selling price		20.00

Budgeted output for June was 5,100 units. Actual results for June were as follows.

Production of 4,850 units was sold for £95,600
Materials consumed in production amounted to 2,300 kilos at a total cost of £9,800
Labour hours paid for amounted to 8,500 hours at a cost of £16,800
Actual operating hours amounted to 8,000 hours
Variable overheads amounted to £2,600
Fixed overheads amounted to £42,300

Required

Calculate all variances and prepare an operating statement for June.

1.4 SOLUTION

		£
(a)	2,300 kg of material should cost (× £4)	9,200
	but did cost	9,800
	Material price variance	600 (A)
(b)	4,850 boomerangs should use (× 0.5 kgs)	2,425 kg
	but did use	2,300 kg
	Material usage variance in kgs	125 kg (F)
	× standard cost per kg	× £4
	Material usage variance in £	£ 500 (F)

(c)	8,500 hours of labour should cost (× £2)	17,000
	but did cost	16,800
	Labour rate variance	200 (F)
(d)	4,850 boomerangs should take (× 2 hrs)	9,700 hrs
	but did take (active hours)	8,000 hrs
	Labour efficiency variance in hours	1,700 hrs (F)
	× standard cost per hour	× £2
	Labour efficiency variance in £	£3,400 (F)
(e)	Idle time variance 500 hours (A) × £2	£1,000 (A)
		£
(f)	8,000 hours incurring variable o/hd expenditure should cost (× £0.30)	2,400
	but did cost	2,600
	Variable overhead expenditure variance	200 (A)
(g)	Variable overhead efficiency variance is the same as the labour efficiency variance:	
	1,700 hours (F) × £0.30 per hour	£ 510 (F)
		£
(h)	Budgeted fixed overhead (5,100 units × 2 hrs × £3.70)	37,740
	Actual fixed overhead	42,300
	Fixed overhead expenditure variance	4,560 (A)
		£
(i)	Actual production at standard rate (4,850 units × £7.40)	35,890
	Budgeted production at standard rate (5,100 units × £7.40)	37,740
	Fixed overhead volume variance	1,850 (A)
		£
(j)	4,850 boomerangs should have sold for (× £20)	97,000
	but did sell for	95,600
	Selling price variance	1,400 (A)
(k)	Budgeted sales volume	5,100 units
	Actual sales volume	4,850 units
	Sales volume variance in units	250 units
	× standard profit per unit	× £6 (A)
	Sales volume variance in £	£1,500 (A)

There are several ways in which an operating statement may be presented. Perhaps the most **common format** is one which **reconciles budgeted profit to actual profit. Sales variances are reported first,** and the **total of the budgeted profit and the two sales variances** results in a figure for '**actual sales minus the standard cost of sales' as follows.**

	£	£
Budgeted profit (5,100 units × £6 profit)		30,600
Selling price variance	1,400 (A)	
Sales volume variance	1,500 (A)	
		2,900 (A)
Actual sales (£95,600) less the standard cost of sales (4,850 × £14)		27,700

The cost variances are then reported, and an actual profit calculated.

ARMOURED KANGAROO LTD - OPERATING STATEMENT FOR JUNE

		£	£	£
Budgeted profit				30,600
Sales variances:	price		1,400 (A)	
	volume		1,500 (A)	
				2,900 (A)
Actual sales minus the standard cost of sales				27,700
Cost variances		(F)	(A)	
Material price			600	
Material usage		500		
Labour rate		200		
Labour efficiency		3,400		
Labour idle time			1,000	
Variable overhead expenditure			200	
Variable overhead efficiency		510		
Fixed overhead expenditure			4,560	
Fixed overhead volume			1,850	
		4,610	8,210	3,600 (A)
Actual profit for June				24,100

Check	£	£
Sales		95,600
Materials	9,800	
Labour	16,800	
Variable overhead	2,600	
Fixed overhead	42,300	
		71,500
Actual profit		24,100

1.5 Another way in which an operating statement can be presented is to reconcile the actual sales minus the standard cost of sales with the actual profit. In other words, only the cost variances are shown on the face of the operating statement.

2 VARIANCES IN A STANDARD MARGINAL COSTING SYSTEM

Exam focus point

Before tackling variances in a standard marginal costing system, it is vital that you are happy with the principles of marginal costing.

2.1 If an organisation uses standard marginal costing instead of standard absorption costing, there will be two differences in the way the variances are calculated.

(a) In marginal costing, fixed costs are not absorbed into product costs and so there are no fixed cost variances to explain any under- or over-absorption of overheads. There will, therefore, be ***no* fixed overhead volume variance.** There will be a fixed overhead expenditure variance which is calculated in exactly the same way as for absorption costing systems.

(b) The **sales volume variance will be valued at standard contribution margin, not standard profit margin** (that is, sales price per unit minus variable costs of sale per unit).

2.2 EXAMPLE: MARGINAL COSTING OPERATING STATEMENT

Returning once again to the example of Armoured Kangaroo Ltd, the variances in a system of standard marginal costing would be as follows.

(a) There is no fixed overhead volume variance.

(b) The standard contribution per unit of boomerang is £(20 – 6.60) = £13.40, therefore the sales volume variance of 250 units (A) is valued at (× £13.40) = £3,350 (A).

The other variances are unchanged, therefore an operating statement might appear as follows.

ARMOURED KANGAROO - OPERATING STATEMENT FOR JUNE

		£	£	£
Budgeted profit				30,600
Budgeted fixed production costs				37,740
Budgeted contribution				68,340
Sales variances:	volume		3,350 (A)	
	price		1,400 (A)	
				4,750 (A)
Actual sales (£95,600) minus the standard variable cost of sales (4,850 × £6.60)				63,590
Variable cost variances		(F)	(A)	
Material price			600	
Material usage		500		
Labour rate		200		
Labour efficiency		3,400		
Labour idle time			1,000	
Variable overhead expenditure			200	
Variable overhead efficiency		510		
		4,610	1,800	
				2,810 (F)
Actual contribution				66,400
Budgeted fixed production overhead			37,740	
Expenditure variance			4,560 (A)	
Actual fixed production overhead				42,300
Actual profit				24,100

Note. The profit here is the same on the profit calculated by standard absorption costing because there were no changes in stock levels. Absorption costing and marginal costing do not always produce an identical profit figure.

Question 1

Hides of March Ltd manufacture a standard leather walking boot, model number M25, for which the standard unit cost and selling price are as follows.

		£
Direct materials		
Leather	3 units at £5 per unit	15
Other materials		3
		18
Direct labour	1½ hours at £4 per hour	6
Variable production overheads	1½ hours at £2 per hour	3
Fixed production overheads	1½ hours at £6 per hour	9
Standard cost		36
Selling price		48
Standard profit, before marketing and administrative expenses		12

Budgeted production and sales for period 7 of 20X8 were 3,000 units of M25.

During period 7 the actual results were as follows.

Production of M25		3,200 units
Sales of M25		2,850 units
Sales revenue		£141,000
Leather purchased:	quantity	9,200 units
	cost	£45,400
Leather used		9,750 units
Other materials purchased and used		£9,500
Direct labour:	hours paid for	5,850 hours
	production time	5,100 hours
	labour cost	£24,100
Variable production overheads		£10,650
Fixed production overheads		£31,500

Stocks of leather are valued at standard cost, and stocks of finished goods are valued at standard full production cost.

Required

Prepare an operating statement for period 7 reconciling budgeted and actual profit and specifying all the relevant variances. Ignore marketing and administration costs.

Answer and discussion

Budgeted profit. This is clearly 3,000 units × standard profit of £12 per unit = £36,000.

(a) Stocks are valued at standard costs, and so price variances must be calculated on quantities purchased, rather than quantities used.

	£
9,200 units of leather were purchased and cost	45,400
but should cost (× £ 5)	46,000
Leather price variance	600 (F)

(b)

3,200 units of M25 were made and used	9,750 units of materials
but 3,200 units should use (× 3)	9,600 units of materials
Usage variance in units	150 units (A)
× standard cost per unit of leather	× £5
Leather usage variance in £	£750 (A)

(c) **Other materials**. We are not given a breakdown into units of material and price per unit of material, and so the only materials variance we can calculate is the total cost variance.

	£
3,200 units of M25 did cost	9,500 in other materials
but should cost (× £3)	9,600
Other materials cost variance	100 (F)

(d)

	£
5,850 hours were paid for and cost	24,100
but should cost (× £4)	23,400
Direct labour rate variance	700 (A)

(e) The efficiency variance is based on production hours, excluding idle time.

3,200 units of M25 took	5,100 hours
but should take (× 11/2 hrs)	4,800 hours
Efficiency variance, in hours	300 hours (A)
× standard cost per labour hour	× £4
Direct labour efficiency variance in £	£1,200 (A)

(f) **Idle time variance** = 750 hours × £4 per hr = £3,000 (A)

This is a large variance compared to the others calculated so far, and the existence of this variance would raise control questions about how such a large amount of idle time occurred, and if it is normal downtime, why an allowance for idle time has not been built into the standard cost itself.

(g)

	£	
5,100 hours of working did cost	10,650	
but should cost (× £2)	10,200	
Variable overhead expenditure variance	450	(A)

(h) The **variable overhead efficiency variance** is exactly the same in hours as the direct labour efficiency variance, ignoring idle time hours = 300 hours (A) × £2 per hour = £600 (A).

(i)

	£	
Actual fixed overheads absorbed (3,200 × £9)	28,800	
Actual fixed overheads incurred	31,500	
Total fixed overhead variance	2,700	(A)

(j) **Fixed overhead expenditure variance.** This is under- or over-absorption of overhead because actual fixed overhead expenditure differed from budgeted expenditure.

	£	
Budgeted fixed overhead	27,000	
Actual fixed overhead	31,500	
Expenditure variance	4,500	(A)

The expenditure variance also indicates over-spending above budget by £4,500, and a control report should attempt to pinpoint the source of this excessive overhead spending more specifically.

(k) **Fixed overhead volume variance.** This is under- or over-absorbed overhead caused by a difference between actual and budgeted production volume.

	In terms of units	*Alternatively standard hours*
Budgeted production volume of M25	3,000 (× 1.5)	4,500
Actual production volume	3,200 (× 1.5)	4,800
Total volume variance, in units or std hours	200 (F)	300 (F)
× standard fixed overhead cost per unit or per std hr	× £9	× £6
Total **volume variance** in £	£1,800 (F)	£1,800 (F)

Producing a bigger quantity than budgeted will create over absorption of fixed overhead, and so is a favourable variance. The fixed overhead total volume variance of 300 standard hours (F) means that the company produced 300 standard hours worth of output more than budgeted in period 7. The reason for this must have been either working more efficiently than expected (a volume efficiency variance) or working more production hours than expected (a volume capacity variance).

(l) **Fixed overhead volume efficiency variance.** This is the same variance in hours as the direct labour efficiency variance (ignoring idle time) = 300 hrs (A) × £6 per hour = £1,800 (A)

(m) **Fixed overhead volume capacity variance.** This is the difference between actual and budgeted production hours.

Budgeted production hours (3,000 units × 1.5 hrs)	4,500 hours
Actual production hours, ignoring idle time	5,100 hours
Volume capacity variance in hours	600 hours (F)
× standard fixed overhead rate per hour	× £6
Volume capacity variance in £	£3,600 (F)

The capacity and efficiency variances add up to the total volume variance of £1,800(F).

(n)

	£	
2,850 units of M25 should have sold for (× £48)	136,800	
but did sell for	141,000	
Selling price variance	4,200	(F)

(o)

Budgeted sales volume of M25	3,000 units
Actual sales volume	2,850 units
Sales volume variance	150 units (A)
× standard profit margin per unit	× £12
Sales volume variance	£1,800 (A)

The variances can now be summarised in an operating statement.

HIDES OF MARCH LTD
OPERATING STATEMENT FOR PERIOD 7

		£	£	£
Budgeted profit				36,000
Sales variances:	price variance		4,200 (F)	
	volume variance		1,800 (A)	
				2,400 (F)
				38,400
Cost variances		(F)	(A)	
Leather: price		600		
usage			750	
Other materials		100		
Direct labour:	rate		700	
	efficiency		1,200	
Idle time			3,000	
Variable overhead expenditure			450	
Variable overhead efficiency			600	
Fixed overhead expenditure			4,500	
Fixed overhead volume		1,800		
		2,500	11,200	
Total cost variances				8,700 (A)
Actual profit				29,700

3 MATERIALS MIX AND YIELD VARIANCES

Exam focus point

Mix and yield variances appear in the pilot paper.

3.1 When a product requires two or more raw materials in its make-up, it is often possible to **sub-analyse the materials usage variance into a materials mix and a materials yield variance.**

3.2 Adding a greater proportion of one material (therefore a smaller proportion of a different material) might make the materials mix cheaper or more expensive. For example the standard mix of materials for a product might consist of the following.

	£
(2/3) 2 kg of material A at £1.00 per kg	2.00
(1/3) 1 kg of material B at £0.50 per kg	0.50
	2.50

It may be possible to change the mix so that one kilogram of material A is used and two kilograms of material B. The new mix would be cheaper.

	£
(1/3) 1 kg of material A	1
(2/3) 2 kg of material B	1
	2

3.3 By changing the proportions in the mix, the efficiency of the combined material usage may change. In our example, in making the proportions of A and B cheaper, at 1:2, the product may now require more than three kilograms of input for its manufacture, and the new materials requirement per unit of product might be 3.6 kilograms.

	£
(1/3) 1.2 kg of material A at £1.00 per kg	1.20
(2/3) 2.4 kg of material B at £0.50 per kg	1.20
	2.40

3.4 In establishing a materials usage standard, management may therefore have to balance the cost of a particular mix of materials with the efficiency of the yield of the mix.

3.5 Once the standard has been established it may be possible for management to exercise control over the materials used in production by calculating and reviewing mix and yield variances.

KEY TERMS

A **mix variance** occurs when the materials are not mixed or blended in standard proportions and it is a measure of whether the actual mix is cheaper or more expensive than the standard mix.

A **yield variance** arises because there is a difference between what the input should have been for the output achieved and the actual input.

Calculating the variances

3.6 The **mix variance** is calculated as the **difference between** the **actual total quantity used** in **the standard mix** and the **actual quantities used in the actual mix, valued at standard costs.**

3.7 The **yield variance** is calculated as the **difference between the standard input for what was actually output, and the actual total quantity input (in the standard mix), valued at standard costs.**

When to calculate the mix and yield variance

3.8 A mix variance and yield variance are only appropriate in the following situations.

(a) **Where proportions of materials in a mix are changeable and controllable**

(b) Where the **usage variance of individual materials is of limited value because of the variability of the mix,** and a combined yield variance for all the materials together is more helpful for control

3.9 It would be totally inappropriate to calculate a mix variance where the materials in the 'mix' are discrete items. A chair, for example, might consist of wood, covering material, stuffing and glue. These materials are separate components, and it would not be possible to think in terms of controlling the proportions of each material in the final product. The usage of each material must be controlled separately.

3.10 EXAMPLE: MATERIALS USAGE, MIX AND YIELD VARIANCES

A company manufactures a chemical, Dynamite, using two compounds Flash and Bang. The standard materials usage and cost of one unit of Dynamite are as follows.

		£
Flash	5 kg at £2 per kg	10
Bang	10 kg at £3 per kg	30
		40

In a particular period, 80 units of Dynamite were produced from 500 kg of Flash and 730 kg of Bang.

Required

Calculate the materials usage, mix and yield variances.

3.11 SOLUTION

(a) **Usage variance**

	Std usage for actual output	*Actual usage*	*Variance*	*Standard cost per kg*	*Variance*
	kgs	kgs	kgs	£	£
Flash	400	500	100 (A)	2	200 (A)
Bang	800	730	70 (F)	3	210 (F)
	1,200	1,230	30 (A)		10 (F)

The total usage variance of £10 (F) can be analysed into a mix variance and a yield variance.

(b) **Mix variance**

To calculate the mix variance, it is first necessary to decide how the total quantity of materials used (500 kg + 730 kg) should have been divided between Flash and Bang. In other words, we need to **calculate the standard mix of the actual quantity of materials used.**

		kg
Total quantity used (500 + 730)		1,230

		kg
Standard mix of actual use:	1/3 Flash	410
	2/3 Bang	820
		1,230

The differences between what should have been used in the mix (as calculated above) and what was actually used is the mix variance (in kg) which should be converted into money values at standard cost.

	Mix should have been	*but mix was*	*Variance*	*Standard cost per kg*	*Variance*
	kgs	kgs	kgs	£	£
Flash	410	500*	90 (A)	2	180 (A)
Bang	820	730	90 (F)	3	270 (F)
	1,230	1,230	-		90 (F)

* When actual use exceeds standard use the variance is always adverse.

Note that the **total mix variance in quantity is zero.** This must always be the case since the expected mix is based on the total quantity actually used and hence the difference between the total expected and total actual is zero.

The favourable money variance is due to the greater use in the mix of the relatively cheap material, Flash.

(c) **Yield variance**

The yield variance can be calculated in total or for each individual material input.

In total

Each unit of output (Dynamite) requires	5 kg	of Flash, costing	£10
	10 kg	of Bang, costing	£30
	15 kg		£40

1,230 kg should have yielded (÷ 15 kg)	82 units of Dynamite
but did yield	80 units of Dynamite
Yield variance in units	2 units (A)
× standard cost per unit of output	×£40
Yield variance in £	£80 (A)

The adverse yield variance is due to the output from the input being less than standard.

For individual materials

This is calculated as the **difference between what the usage should have been for the output actually achieved and the actual usage in the standard mix,** converted into money values at standard cost.

	Standard usage for actual output	*Actual usage in standard mix*	*Variance*	*Standard cost per kg*	*Variance*
	kgs	kgs	kgs	£	£
Flash	400	410	10 (A)	2	20 (A)
Bang	800	820	20 (A)	3	60 (A)
	1,200	1,230	30 (A)		80 (A)

Question 2

The standard materials cost of product D456 is as follows.

		£
Material X	3 kg at £2.00 per kg	6
Material Y	5 kg at £3.60 per kg	18
		24

During period 2, 2,000 kgs of material X (costing £4,100) and 2,400 kgs of material Y (costing £9,600) were used to produce 500 units of D456.

Required

Calculate the following variances.

(a) Price variances
(b) Mix variances
(c) Yield variances – in total and for each individual material

Answer

(a)

	£
2,000 kg of X should cost (× £2)	4,000
but did cost	4,100
Material X price variance	100 (A)

	£
2,400 kg of Y should cost (× £3.60)	8,640
but did cost	9,600
Material Y price variance	960 (A)

(b)

		kg
Total quantity used (2,000 + 2,400) kgs		4,400
		kg
Standard mix for actual use:	3/8 X	1,650
	5/8 Y	2,750
		4,400

	Mix should have been	*but mix was*	*Variance*	*Standard cost per kg*	*Variance*
	kgs	kgs	kgs	£	£
X	1,650	2,000	350 (A)	2.00	700 (A)
Y	2,750	2,400	350 (F)	3.60	1,260 (F)
	4,400	4,400	-		560 (F)

(c) **In total**

Each unit of D456 requires	3 kg of X, costing	£6
	5 kg of Y, costing	£18
	8 kg	£24

4,400 kg should have yielded (÷ 8 kg)	550 units
But did yield	500 units
Yield variance in units	50 units (A)
× standard cost per unit of output	× £24
Yield variance in £	£1,200 (A)

For individual materials

	Std usage for actual output	*Actual usage in std mix*	*Variance*	*Standard cost per kg*	*Variance*
	kgs	kgs	kgs	£	£
X	1,500	1,650	150 (A)	2.00	300 (A)
Y	2,500	2,750	250 (A)	3.60	900 (A)
	4,000	4,400	400 (A)		1,200 (A)

Exam focus point

With all variance calculations, it is vital that you do not simply learn formulae. You must have a thorough understanding of what your calculations are showing. This is especially true of the variances we will look at in this section and in Section 4.

3.12 The next example is similar to the pilot paper question in that it incorporates losses.

3.13 EXAMPLE: LOSSES, MIX AND YIELD

Coope and Sorcerer Ltd make product T42 in a continuous process, for which standard and actual quantities in month 10 were as follows.

	Standard			*Actual*		
	Quantity	*Price per kg*	*Value*	*Quantity*	*Price per kg*	*Std cost of actual usage*
	kg	£	£	kg	£	£
Material P	40,000	2.50	100,000	34,000	2.50	85,000
Material Q	20,000	4.00	80,000	22,000	4.00	88,000
	60,000		180,000	56,000		173,000

Losses occur at an even rate during the processing operation and are expected to be 10% of materials input. Actual output during the month was 53,000 kgs.

Required

Calculate total usage, mix and yield variances.

3.14 SOLUTION

Usage variance

Output of 53,000 kgs should have used input of 53,000/90% = 58,889 kgs.

∴ Standard input should have been as follows.

			Kgs
P	$^2/_3 \times 58{,}889$	=	39,259
Q	$^1/_3 \times 58{,}889$	=	19,630
			58,889

	P		*Q*
53,000 kg of T42 should need	39,259 kg		19,630 kg
but did need	34,000 kg		22,000 kg
Usage variance in kg	5,259 kg (F)		2,370 kg (A)
× standard price per kg	× £2.50		× £4
Usage variance in £	£13,148 (F)		£9,480 (A)
Total usage variance		£3,668 (F)	

Yield variance

Each kg of T42 requires ($1 \times {}^{100}/_{90}$) kg of input costing £3.33 (£180,000/(60,000 × 90%))

56,000 kg should have yielded (÷ 100/90)	50,400 kgs
but did yield	53,000 kgs
Yield variance in kgs	2,600 kgs (F)
× standard cost per kg of T42	× £3.33
Yield variance in £	£8,667 (F)

Mix variance

		Kg
Total quantity used		56,000.00
		Kg
Standard mix for actual use:	$^2/_3$ P	37,333.33
	$^1/_3$ Q	18,666.67
		56,000.00

	P		*Q*
Mix should have been	37,333.33 kgs		18,666.67 kgs
but was	34,000.00 kgs		22,000.00 kgs
Mix variance in kgs	3,333.33 kgs (F)		3,333.33 kgs (A)
× standard cost per kg	× £2.50		× £4.00
Mix variance in £	£8,333.00 (F)		£13,333.00 (A)
Total mix variance		£5,000 (A)	

(Note that there is a difference between the sum of the mix and yield variances and the usage variance due to rounding.)

4 SALES MIX AND QUANTITY VARIANCES

4.1 Just as it is possible to subdivide the materials usage variance into mix and yield variances, the **sales volume variance** can be subdivided into a **mix variance** and a **quantity variance**.

4.2 If a company sells more than one product, the **volume variance can be caused by two factors.**

(a) The **quantity** of product sold is **different than budgeted**. For example, suppose Nilats Ltd sells two products, the Trot and the Sky.

	Budget	*Actual*
	Units	Units
Trots	100 (50%)	175 (70%)
Skys	100 (50%)	75 (30%)
	200	250

Notice that the total quantity is 50 greater than budget and that the relative proportions of the products to the total are also different than budgeted.

(b) The **mix** of products sold can be **different than budgeted**. For example if product A earned a standard profit of £10 per unit and product B earned a standard profit of £8 a unit, a change in the relative numbers of each product sold will change the total profit.

	Budgeted sales		*Actual sales*	
	Units	£	Units	£
A	100	1,000	75	750
B	50	400	75	600
	150	1,400	150	1,350

4.3 **If management cannot control the proportions** of products sold then there is **little point in calculating sales mix and sales quantity variances** since their causes are uncontrollable.

4.4 EXAMPLE: SALES QUANTITY AND SALES MIX VARIANCES

Tardis Ltd manufactures three products, the Dalek, the Yeti and the Cyberman. The budget relating to period 1 is given below.

	Unit sales price	*Unit full cost of product*	*Profit per unit*	*Budgeted sales*	*Standard mix*
	£	£	£	Units	%
Dalek	5	3	2	500	50
Yeti	7	4	3	300	30
Cyberman	10	6	4	200	20

Actual sales in period 1 were as follows.

	Units	%
Dalek	700	46.7
Yeti	300	20.0
Cyberman	500	33.3
	1,500	100.0

4.5 SOLUTION

(a) **Sales quantity variance**

Product	*Actual sales in standard mix*	*Budgeted sales*	*Variance*	*Standard profit per unit*	*Variance*
	Units	Units	Units	£	£
Dalek	750	500	250 (F)	2	500 (F)
Yeti	450	300	150 (F)	3	450 (F)
Cyberman	300	200	100 (F)	4	400 (F)
	1,500	1,000	500 (F)		1,350 (F)

(b) **Sales mix variance**

Product		Mix should have been	but mix was	Variance	Standard profit per unit	Variance
		Units	Units	Units	£	£
Dalek	(1,500 × 50%) =	750	700	(50) (A)	2	(100) (A)
Yeti	(1,500 × 30%) =	450	300	(150) (A)	3	(450) (A)
Cyberman	(1,500 × 20%) =	300	500	200 (F)	4	800 (F)
		1,500	1,500	0		250 (F)

(c) **Total sales volume variance**

			£
Dalek	£500(F) quantity + £100(A) mix	=	400 (F)
Yeti	£450(F) quantity + £450(A) mix	=	0
Cyberman	£400(F) quantity + £800(F) mix	=	1,200 (F)
Total sales volume variance			1,600 (F)

5 PLANNING AND OPERATIONAL VARIANCES

5.1 So far in this text we have been looking at variances which are calculated using what we will call the conventional approach to variance analysis, whereby an actual cost is compared with an original standard cost. In this section of the chapter we will be examining planning and operational variances. They are not really alternatives to the conventional approach, they merely provide a much more detailed analysis.

5.2 Basically, the planning and operational approach attempts to divide a total variance (which has been calculated conventionally) into a group of variances which have arisen because of inaccurate planning or faulty standards (planning variances) and a group of variances which have been caused by adverse or favourable operational performance (operational variances, surprisingly enough!).

5.3 Planning and operational variances may seem confusing if you do not have a really good grasp of the conventional approach and so, before you go any further, make sure that you understand everything that we covered so far in this Text. Go back over any areas you are unsure about. Only when you are happy that you have mastered the basics should you begin on this section.

KEY TERMS

A **planning variance** (or **revision variance**) compares an original standard with a revised standard that should or would have been used if planners had known in advance what was going to happen.

An **operational variance** (or **operating variance**) compares an actual result with the revised standard.

5.4 Planning and operational variances are based on the principle that variances ought to be reported by taking as the **main starting point**, not the original standard, but a **standard** which can be seen, in hindsight, to be the **optimum** that should have been **achievable**.

5.5 Exponents of this approach argue that the monetary value of variances ought to be a realistic reflection of what the **causes** of the variances have cost the organisation. In other words they should show the cash (and profit) gained or lost as a consequence of operating results being different to what should have been achieved. Variances can be valued in this

way by **comparing actual results with a realistic standard or budget**. Such variances are called **operational variances**.

5.6 **Planning variances** arise because the **original standard and revised more realistic standards are different** and have nothing to do with operational performance. In most cases, it is unlikely that anything could be done about planning variances: they are **not controllable by operational managers but by senior management**.

5.7 In other words the **cause of a total variance** might be one or both of:

- Adverse or favourable operational performance (**operational variance**)
- Inaccurate planning, or faulty standards (**planning variance**)

Calculating total planning and operational variances

5.8 We will begin by looking at how to split a total cost variance into its planning and operational components.

5.9 EXAMPLE: TOTAL COST PLANNING AND OPERATIONAL VARIANCES

At the beginning of 20X0, WB Ltd set a standard marginal cost for its major product of £25 per unit. The standard cost is recalculated once each year. Actual production costs during August 20X0 were £304,000, when 8,000 units were made.

With the benefit of hindsight, the management of WB Ltd realises that a more realistic standard cost for current conditions would be £40 per unit. The planned standard cost of £25 is unrealistically low.

Required

Calculate the planning and operational variances.

5.10 SOLUTION

With the benefit of hindsight, the **realistic standard should have been £40.** The variance caused by favourable or adverse **operating** performance should be calculated by comparing actual results against this realistic standard.

	£
Revised standard cost of actual production (8,000 × £40)	320,000
Actual cost	304,000
Total **operational** variance	16,000 (F)

The variance is favourable because the actual cost was lower than would have been expected using the revised basis.

The **planning** variance reveals the extent to which the original standard was at fault.

Revised standard cost	8,000 units × £40 per unit	320,000
Original standard cost	8,000 units × £25 per unit	200,000
Planning variance		120,000 (A)

It is an adverse variance because the original standard was too optimistic, overestimating the expected profits by understating the standard cost. More simply, it is adverse because the revised cost is much higher than the original cost.

	£
Planning variance	120,000 (A)
Operational variance	16,000 (F)
Total	104,000 (A)

If **traditional variance analysis** had been used, the total cost variance would have been the same, but **all the 'blame' would appear to lie on actual results** and operating inefficiencies (rather than some being due to faulty planning).

	£
Standard cost of 8,000 units (× £25)	200,000
Actual cost of 8,000 units	304,000
Total cost variance	104,000 (A)

Question 3

Suppose a budget is prepared which includes a raw materials cost per unit of product of £2 (2 kg of copper at £1 per kg). Due to a rise in world prices for copper during the year, the average market price of copper rises to £1.50 per kg. During the year, 1,000 units were produced at a cost of £3,250 for 2,200 kg of copper.

What are the planning and operational variances?

Answer

Operational variance

	£
Actual cost (for 1,000 units)	3,250
Revised standard cost (for 1,000 units) (2,000 kg × £1.50)	3,000
Total operational variance	250 (A)

Planning variance

	£
Revised standard cost (1,000 × 2 kg × £1.50)	3,000
Original standard cost (1,000 × 2 kg × £1)	2,000
Total planning variance	1,000 (A)

Operational price and usage variances

5.11 So far we have only considered planning and operational variances in total, without carrying out the usual two-way split. In Question 3, for instance, we identified a total operational variance for materials of £250 without considering whether this operational variance could be split between a usage variance and a price variance.

5.12 This is not a problem so long as you retain your grasp of knowledge you already possess. You know that a **price** variance measures the difference between the actual amount of money paid and the amount of money that should have been paid for that quantity of materials (or whatever). Thus, in our example:

	£
Actual price of actual materials (2,200 kg)	3,250
Revised standard price of actual materials (£1.50 × 2,200 kg)	3,300
Operational price variance	50 (F)

The variance is favourable because the materials were purchased more cheaply than would have been expected.

5.13 Similarly, a **usage** variance measures the difference between the actual physical quantity of materials used or hours taken and the quantities that should have been used or taken for the actual volume of production. Those physical differences are then converted into money values by applying the appropriate standard cost.

5.14 In our example we are calculating **operational variances**, so we are not interested in planning errors. This means that the **appropriate standard cost is the revised standard cost** of £1.50.

Actual quantity should have been	2,000 kgs
but was	2,200 kgs
Operational usage variance in kgs	200 kgs (A)
× revised standard cost per kg	× £1.50
Operational usage variance in £	£300 (A)

5.15 The two variances of course reconcile to the total variance as previously calculated.

	£
Operational price variance	50 (F)
Operational usage variance	(300) (A)
Total operational variance	250 (A)

Operational variances for labour and overheads

5.16 Precisely the same argument applies to the calculation of operational variances for labour and overheads, and the examples already given should be sufficient to enable you to do Question 4.

Question 4

A new product requires three hours of labour per unit at a standard rate of £6 per hour. In a particular month the budget is to produce 500 units. Actual results were as follows.

Hours worked	1,700
Production	540 units
Wages cost	£10,500

Within minutes of production starting it was realised that the job was extremely messy and the labour force could therefore claim an extra 25p per hour in 'dirty money'.

Required

Calculate planning and operational variances in as much detail as possible.

Answer

Keep calm and calculate the *total* variance in the normal way to begin with. Then you will understand what it is that you have to analyse. Next follow through the workings shown above, substituting the figures in the exercise for those in the example.

Total labour variance	£
540 units should have cost (× 3 hrs × £6)	9,720
but did cost	10,500
	780 (A)

Planning variance	£
Revised standard cost (540 × 3 hrs × £6.25)	10,125
Original standard cost (540 × 3 hrs × £6.00)	9,720
	405 (A)

Operational rate variance	£
Actual cost of actual units	10,500
Revised cost of actual units (1,700 × £6.25)	10,625
	125 (F)

Operational efficiency variance

540 units should have taken (× 3 hrs)	1,620 hrs
but did take	1,700 hrs
Operational efficiency variance in hours	80 hrs
× revised standard rate per hour	× £6.25
Operational efficiency variance in £	£500 (A)

Planning variances and sub-variances

5.17 In the examples described so far, there has only been one 'planning error' in the standard cost. When two planning errors occur, there may be some difficulty in deciding how much of the total planning variance is due to each separate error.

5.18 EXAMPLE: TWO PLANNING ERRORS

A company estimates that the standard direct labour cost for a product should be £20 (4 hours × £5 per hour). Actual production of 1,000 units took 6,200 hours at a cost of £23,800. In retrospect, it is realised that the standard cost should have been 6 hours × £4 per hour = £24 per unit.

Required

Calculate the planning and operational variances.

5.19 SOLUTION

(a) **Operational variances**

(i)	1,000 units should take (× 6 hours)	6,000 hrs
	but did take	6,200 hrs
	Efficiency variance in hours	200 hrs (A)
	× revised standard cost per hour	× £4 (A)
	Efficiency variance in £	£800 (A)
		£
(ii)	6,200 hours should cost (× £4)	24,800
	but did cost	23,800
	Rate variance	1,000 (F)
(iii)	*Check:*	£
	Actual costs	23,800
	Revised standard cost (1,000 units × £24)	24,000
	Total operational variance (800 (A) + 1,000 (F))	200 (F)

(b) **Planning variance**

	£
Revised standard cost 1,000 units × 6 hours × £4	24,000
Original standard cost 1,000 units × 4 hours × £5	20,000
Planning variance	4,000 (A)

Commentary

Within the total planning variance, there are two separate variances.

- A **planning efficiency variance** of 1,000 units × (6 – 4) hours or 2,000 hours (A).
- A **planning rate variance** of £1 per hour (F).

The problem, however, is to put a **value** to these sub-variances. This can be done in either of **two ways**.

			£
(a)	Planning efficiency variance	2,000 hours (A) × original price of £5	10,000 (A)
	Planning rate variance	£1 per hour (F) × revised standard efficiency of 6,000 hours	6,000 (F)
	Total		4,000 (A)

			£
(b)	Planning efficiency variance	2,000 hours (A) × revised rate of £4	8,000 (A)
	Planning rate variance	£1 per hour (F) × original efficiency of 4,000 hours	4,000 (F)
	Total		4,000 (A)

5.20 Since the analysis can be done either way, it is **doubtful whether there is much value in splitting the total planning variance.** However, this point may be examinable and is worth learning. The following exercise provides an example of when there may be some point in carrying out the analysis.

Question 5

The standard materials cost of a product is 3 kg × £1.50 per kg = £4.50. Actual production of 10,000 units used 28,000 kg at a cost of £50,000. In retrospect it was realised that the standard materials cost should have been 2.5 kg per unit at a cost of £1.80 per kg (so that the *total* cost per unit was correct).

Required

Calculate the planning and operational variances in as much detail as possible, giving alternative analyses of planning variances.

Answer

As always, calculate the *total* materials variance first, to give you a point of reference. Then follow through the workings above.

Total materials variance	£
10,000 units should have cost (× £4.50)	45,000
but did cost	50,000
	5,000 (A)

Operational price variance	£
28,000 kg should cost (× £1.80)	50,400
but did cost	50,000
	400 (F)
Operational usage variance	
10,000 units should use (× 2.5 kgs)	25,000 kgs
but did use	28,000 kgs
	3,000 kgs (A)
× standard rate per kg	× £1.80
	£5,400 (A)

Planning variance

Either	£
Planning usage variance (5,000 kgs (F) × £1.50)	7,500 (F)
Planning price variance (£0.30(A) × 25,000 kgs)	7,500 (A)
	-

or	£
Planning usage variance (5,000 kgs (F) × £1.80)	9,000 (F)
Planning price variance (£0.30 (A) × 30,000 kgs)	9,000 (A)
	-

Planning and operational sales variances

5.21 Our final calculations in this section deal with planning and operational sales variances.

5.22 EXAMPLE: PLANNING AND OPERATIONAL SALES VARIANCES

Dimsek Ltd budgeted to make and sell 400 units of its product, the role, in the four-week period no 8, as follows.

	£
Budgeted sales (100 units per week)	40,000
Variable costs (400 units × £60)	24,000
Contribution	16,000
Fixed costs	10,000
Profit	6,000

At the beginning of the second week, production came to a halt because stocks of raw materials ran out, and a new supply was not received until the beginning of week 3. As a consequence, the company lost one week's production and sales. Actual results in period 8 were as follows.

	£
Sales (320 units)	32,000
Variable costs (320 units × £60)	19,200
Contribution	12,800
Fixed costs	10,000
Actual profit	2,800

In retrospect, it is decided that the optimum budget, given the loss of production facilities in the third week, would have been to sell only 300 units in the period.

Required

Calculate appropriate planning and operational variances.

5.23 SOLUTION

The **planning** variance **compares the revised budget** with the **original budget**.

Revised sales volume, given materials shortage	300 units
Original budgeted sales volume	400 units
Planning variance in units of sales	100 units(A)
× standard contribution per unit	× £40
Planning variance in £	£4,000 (A)

Arguably, **running out of raw materials is an operational error** and so the loss of sales volume and contribution from the materials shortage is an opportunity cost that could have been avoided with better purchasing arrangements. The operational variances are variances calculated in the usual way, except that actual results are compared with the revised standard or budget. There is a sales volume variance which is an **operational variance**, as follows.

Actual sales volume	320 units
Revised sales volume	300 units
Operational sales volume variance in units	20 units (F)
(possibly due to production efficiency or marketing efficiency)	
× standard contribution per unit	× £40
	£800 (F)

These variances can be used as **control information** to reconcile budgeted and actual profit.

	£	£
Operating statement, period 8		
Budgeted profit		6,000
Planning variance	4,000 (A)	
Operational variance - sales volume	800 (F)	
		3,200 (A)
Actual profit in period 8		2,800

5.24 You will have noticed that in this example sales volume variances were **valued at contribution forgone,** and there were no fixed cost volume variances. This is because contribution forgone, in terms of lost revenue or extra expenditure incurred, is the nearest equivalent to **opportunity cost** which is readily available to management accountants (who assume linearity of costs and revenues within a relevant range of activity).

Question 6

KSO Ltd budgeted to sell 10,000 units of a new product during 20X0. The budgeted sales price was £10 per unit, and the variable cost £3 per unit.

Although actual sales in 20X0 were 10,000 units and variable costs of sales were £30,000, sales revenue was only £5 per unit. With the benefit of hindsight, it is realised that the budgeted sales price of £10 was hopelessly optimistic, and a price of £4.50 per unit would have been much more realistic.

Required

Calculate planning and operational variances.

Answer

The only variances are selling price variances.

Planning (selling price) variance

	Total £
Revised budget (10,000 × £4.50)	45,000
Original budget (10,000 × £10.00)	100,000
Planning variance	55,000 (A)

The original variance was too optimistic and so the planning variance is an adverse variance.

Operational (selling price) variance

	£
Actual sales (10,000 × £5)	50,000
Revised sales (10,000 × £4.50)	45,000
Operational (selling price) variance	5,000 (F)

The total difference between budgeted and actual profit of £50,000 (A) is therefore analysed as follows.

	£
Operational variance (selling price)	5,000 (F)
Planning variance	55,000 (A)
	50,000 (A)

The value of planning and operational variances

5.25 **Advantages of a system of planning and operational variances**

- The analysis highlights those variances which are **controllable** and those which are **non-controllable.**

- **Managers' acceptance** of the use of variances for performance measurement, and their **motivation**, is likely to increase if they know they will not be held responsible for poor planning and faulty standard setting.
- The **planning and standard-setting processes** should improve; standards should be more accurate, relevant and appropriate.
- Operational variances will provide a **'fairer' reflection of actual performance**.

5.26 **The limitations of planning and operational variances, which must be overcome if they are to be applied in practice.**

- It is difficult to **decide in hindsight** what the **realistic standard** should have been.
- It may become **too easy to justify all the variances as being due to bad planning**, so no operational variances will be highlighted.
- Establishing realistic revised standards and analysing the total variance into planning and operational variances can be a **time consuming** task, even if a spreadsheet package is devised.
- Even though the intention is to provide more meaningful information, **managers may be resistant** to the very idea of variances and refuse to see the virtues of the approach. Careful presentation and explanation will be required until managers are used to the concepts.

Management reports involving planning and operational variances

5.27 The format of a management report that includes planning and operational variances should be tailored to the information requirements of the managers who receive it.

5.28 From the **point of view of senior management** reviewing performance as a whole, a layout that identifies **all of the planning variances together**, and then **all of the operational variances** may be most illuminating. The difference due to planning is the responsibility of the planners, and the remainder of the difference is due to functional managers.

5.29 One possible layout is shown below.

X LTD OPERATING STATEMENT PERIOD 1

	£	£
Original budget contribution		X
Planning variances		
Material usage	X	
Material price	X	
Labour efficiency	X	
Labour idle time	X	
Labour rate	X	
Selling price	X	
		X
Revised budget contribution		X
Sales volume variance		X
Revised standard contribution from sales achieved		X
Operational variances	X	
Selling price	X	
Material usage	X	
Material price	X	
Labour efficiency	X	
Labour rate	X	
Variable overhead expenditure	X	
Variable overhead efficiency	X	
		X
Actual contribution		X
Less: fixed costs budget	X	
expenditure variance	X	
		X
Actual margin		X

Chapter roundup

- **Operating statements** show how cost and revenue variances combine to reconcile budgeted profit to actual profit.
- There are two main differences between the variances calculated in an absorption costing system and the **variances calculated in a marginal costing system**. In a marginal costing system the only fixed overhead variance is an expenditure variance and the sales volume variance is valued at standard contribution margin, not standard profit margin.
- The **materials usage variance** can be subdivided into a materials **mix** variance and a materials **yield** variance.
- The **sales volume variance** can be subdivided into a **mix** variance and a **quantity** variance.
- A planning and operational approach to variance analysis divides the total variance into those variances which have arisen because of inaccurate planning or faulty standards (**planning variances**) and those variances which have been caused by adverse or favourable operational performance, compared with a standard which has been revised in hindsight (**operational variances**).

Quick quiz

1 By what two variances does budgeted profit need to be adjusted to get actual sales minus the standard cost of sales?

2 *Fill in the blanks.*

If an organisation uses standard marginal costing, there will be no .... variance and the .... variance will be valued at ....

3 *Choose the appropriate words from those highlighted.*

The materials mix variance is calculated as the difference between the **standard/actual** total quantity used in the **standard/actual** mix and the **standard/actual** quantities used in the **standard/actual** mix, valued at **standard/actual** costs.

The materials yield variance is calculated on the difference between the **standard/actual** input for **standard/actual** output, and the **standard/actual** total quantity input (in the **standard/actual** mix), valued at **standard/actual** costs.

4 The total yield variance in quantity is zero. True or false?

5 *Fill in the boxes using three of the following words.*

Possible words

quantity, rate, mix, volume, price, efficiency, usage, total

	Sales		variance
+	Sales		variance
=	Sales		variance

6 A revision variance compares what with what?

7 If a planning efficiency variance is valued at an original standard rate, the planning rate variance is valued at the original efficiency level. True or false?

Answers to quick quiz

1 Sales volume and selling price

2 There will be no fixed production overhead volume variance and the sales volume variance will be valued at standard contribution margin.

3 The materials mix variance is calculated as the difference between the actual total quantity used in the standard mix, and the actual quantities used in the actual mix, valued at standard costs.

The materials yield variance is calculated as the difference between the standard input for actual output, and the actual total quantity input (in the standard mix), valued at standard costs.

4 False. It is the total mix variance in quantity which is zero.

5

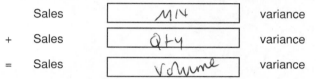

	Sales	mix	variance
+	Sales	quantity	variance
=	Sales	volume	variance

6 A revision or planning variance compares an original standard with a revised standard that should or would have been used if planners had known in advance what was going to happen.

7 False. It is valued at the revised efficiency level.

Now try the question below from the Exam Question Bank

Question to try	Level	Marks	Time
11	Exam	25	45 mins
38	Exam	25	45 mins

Question 38 has been fully analysed to help you get to grips with the more complex aspects of variance analysis.

Part C
Budgeting

Chapter 9

BUDGET PLANNING AND CONTROL

	Topic list	Syllabus reference
1	The planning and control cycle	9(a)
2	The control process	9(a)
3	Feedback and feedforward control	9(a)
4	Controllability and responsibility reporting	9(a)
5	Budgetary planning and control systems	9(a)

Introduction

This chapter serves as an **introduction** to Part C of the Study Text and looks at the **overall planning and control system**. It should help you to put your knowledge of budgeting from earlier studies into a **wider context.**

In the next chapter we go on to consider budget preparation.

Study guide

Section 23 – Budget planning and control I

- Describe the planning and control cycle, and the control process
- Explain the implications of controllability for responsibility reporting
- Identify the purposes of budgetary planning and control systems

Exam guide

Topics covered in this chapter could form the basis of part or all of a Section B discursive question. Section A questions could well require you to apply what you learn in this chapter given the wide context of the subject.

1 THE PLANNING AND CONTROL CYCLE

1.1 The diagram below represents the planning and control cycle. The first five steps cover the planning process. **Planning** involves making choices between alternatives and is primarily a decision-making activity. The last two steps cover the **control** process, which involves measuring and correcting actual performance to ensure that the alternatives that are chosen and the plans for implementing them are carried out.

The planning and control cycle

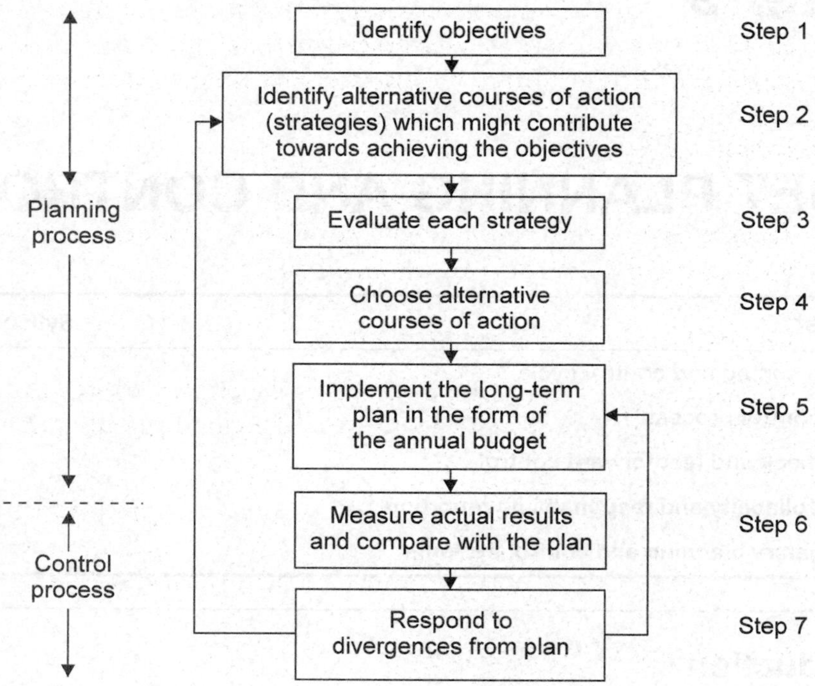

Planning process	Identify objectives	Step 1
	Identify alternative courses of action (strategies) which might contribute towards achieving the objectives	Step 2
	Evaluate each strategy	Step 3
	Choose alternative courses of action	Step 4
	Implement the long-term plan in the form of the annual budget	Step 5
Control process	Measure actual results and compare with the plan	Step 6
	Respond to divergences from plan	Step 7

Step 1. **Identify objectives**

Objectives establish the direction in which the management of the organisation wish it to be heading. Typical objectives include the following.

- To maximise profits
- To increase market share
- To produce a better quality product than anyone else

Objectives answer the question: **'where do we want to be?'**

Step 2. **Identify potential strategies**

Once an organisation has decided 'where it wants to be', the next step is to identify a range of possible courses of action or **strategies that might enable the organisation to get there.** The organisation must therefore carry out an **information-gathering exercise** to ensure that it has a full **understanding of where it is now.** This is known as a '**position audit**' or **'strategic analysis'** and involves **looking** both **inwards** and **outwards.**

(a) The organisation must **gather information from all of its internal parts** to find out what resources it possesses: what its manufacturing capacity and capability is, what is the state of its technical know-how, how well it is able to market itself, how much cash it has in the bank and so on.

(b) It must also **gather information externally** so that it can assess its position in the environment. Just as it has assessed its **own strengths and weaknesses,** it must do likewise for its competitors (**threats**). Current and potential markets must be analysed to identify possible new **opportunities**. The 'state of the world' must be considered. Is it in recession or is it booming? What is likely to happen in the future?

Having carried out a strategic analysis, alternative strategies can be identified. An organisation might decide to be the lowest cost producer in the industry, perhaps by withdrawing from some markets or developing new products for sale in existing markets. This may involve internal development or a joint venture.

Step 3. **Evaluate strategies**

The strategies must then be evaluated **in terms of suitability, feasibility and acceptability**. Management should select those strategies that have the greatest potential for achieving the organisation's objectives.

Step 4. **Choose alternative courses of action**

The next step in the process is to collect the **chosen strategies** together and **co-ordinate them into a long-term financial plan.** Typically this would show the following.

- Projected cash flows
- Capital expenditure plans
- Projected long-term profits
- Balance sheet forecasts
- A description of the long-term objectives and strategies in words

Step 5. **Implement the long-term plan**

The **long-term plan** should then be **broken down into smaller parts**. It is unlikely that the different parts will fall conveniently into successive time periods. Strategy A may take two and a half years, while Strategy B may take five months, but not start until year three of the plan. It is usual, however, to break down the plan as a whole into equal time periods (usually one year). The resulting **short-term plan** is called a **budget**.

Question 1

Is your organisation's planning and control cycle similar to the one described here? If it differs, how does it differ? Why does it differ? Try to find out your organisation's objectives and the strategies being adopted to attain these objectives.

Answers to this question could be usefully employed in the exam.

---

2 THE CONTROL PROCESS

2.1 Control is achieved through what is known as a control cycle. The elements in the control cycle, illustrated in the diagram, are as follows.

Step 1. **Plans and targets are set for the future**. These could be long-, medium- or short-term plans. Examples include budgets, profit targets and standard costs.

Step 2. **Plans are put into operation.** As a consequence, materials and labour are used, and other expenses are incurred.

Step 3. **Actual results are recorded and analysed.**

Step 4. **Information about actual results is fed back** to the management concerned, often in the form of accounting reports. This reported information is **feedback.**

Step 5. **The feedback is used by management to compare** actual results with the plan or targets (what should be or should have been achieved).

Step 6. By comparing actual and planned results, management can then do one of three things, depending on how they see the situation.

(a) **They can take control action**. By identifying what has gone wrong, and then finding out why, corrective measures can be taken.

(b) **They can decide to do nothing**. This could be the decision when actual results are going better than planned, or when poor results were caused by something which is unlikely to happen again in the future.

(c) **They can alter the plan or target** if actual results are different from the plan or target, and there is nothing that management can do (or nothing, perhaps, that they want to do) to correct the situation.

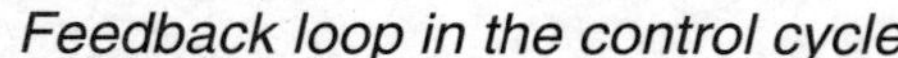

Feedback loop in the control cycle

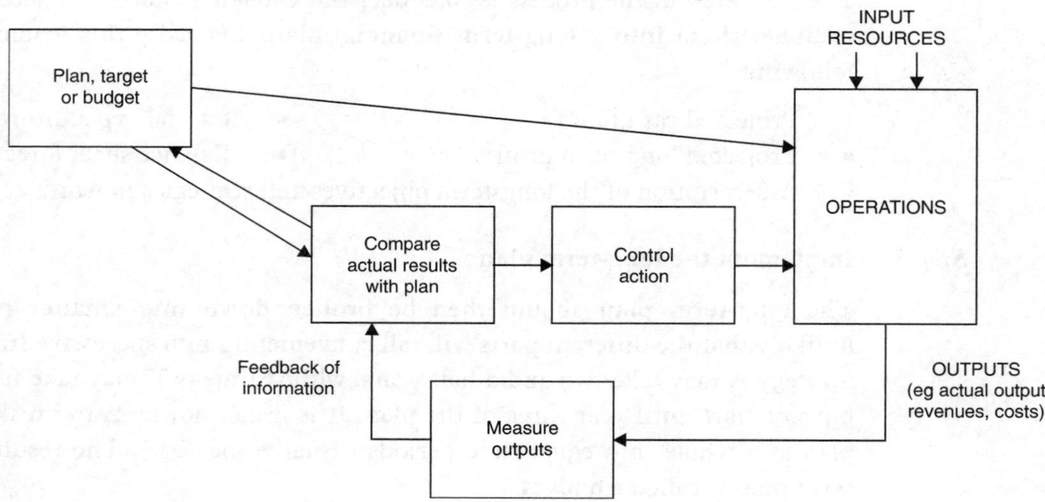

2.2 It may be helpful at this stage to relate the control system to a **practical example, such as monthly sales.**

Step 1. A **sales budget** or plan is prepared for the year.

Step 2. Management **organises the business's resources** to achieve the budget targets.

Step 3. At the end of each month, **actual results** are **reported back to management.**

Step 4. Managers **compare actual results against the plan.**

Step 5. Where necessary, they **take corrective action to adjust the workings of the system,** probably by amending the inputs to the system.

- Salesmen might be asked to work longer hours.
- More money might be spent on advertising.
- Some new price discounts might be decided.
- Delivery periods to customers might be reduced by increasing output.

Where appropriate the sales plan may be revised, up or down.

2.3 In this example, however, we have **not allowed for several factors.**

(a) The **influence of the environment** (such as government legislation about safety standards, changing consumer demand, an unexpected rise in raw material prices, or a long strike in a supplier industry).

(b) **Whether control action is possible.** A sales manager might not be able to increase sales if the production department can't produce the desired output fast enough.

(c) **How much information should be measured and compared with planned results.** Not all output is measured, either because it would not have any useful value, or because the system does not provide for its measurement. The reasons why customers buy or don't buy from the company might be reported back, but they might not.

(d) The **plan might need to be changed** and a **comparison of actual results against the existing plan might be invalid.** Environmental influences could be responsible for the need to change the sales plan.

(e) **Not all inputs to the system are controllable**; a rise in raw material prices is outside the scope of management control. Other inputs might be controllable, but are **not controlled due to lax or inattentive management** (for example poor labour morale and a high labour turnover amongst sales staff).

2.4 In an article in the *ACCA Students' Newsletter* ('Budgetary control - the organisational aspects, December 1998), the examiner of the equivalent paper under the old syllabus provided the following diagram of the management control process.

Phases of management control

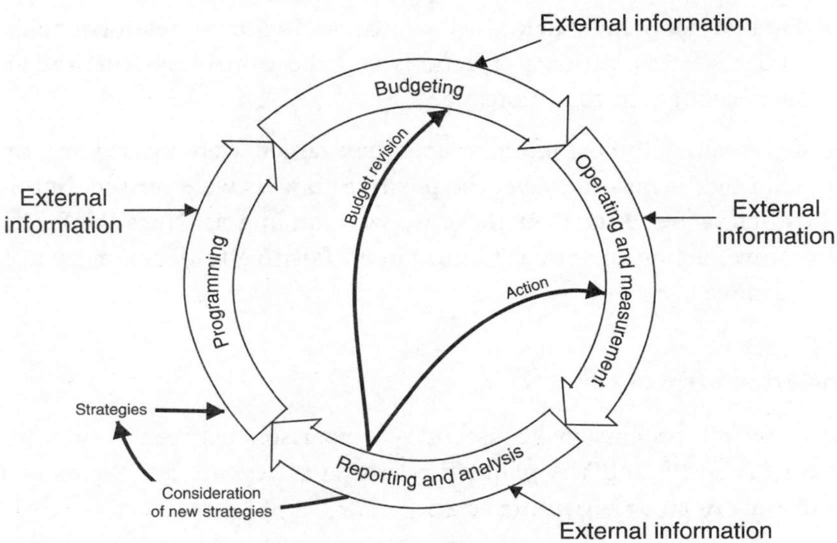

'To elaborate on the features of [the diagram] *programming* is the link with strategic planning. It identifies the products a company intends to develop, projects which management intend to pursue to meet the organisation's overall goals. *Budgets* are derived from these and are specified in terms of a manager's responsibility. *Operating and measurement* is the collecting of actual costs and outcomes identified to both programmes and responsibility centres. Finally, *reporting and analysis* takes place as a basis for control to the budget, for the co-ordination of activities and as a basis for future decisions perhaps to change the original plan.

Budgets as they are generally understood form the cornerstone of management control and the management control system...'

3 FEEDBACK AND FEEDFORWARD CONTROL

Feedback

KEY TERM

Feedback is both the process of reporting back control information to management and the control information itself. In a business organisation, it is information produced from within the organisation (management control reports) with the purpose of helping management and other employees with control decisions.

3.1 (a) **Single loop feedback**, normally expressed as feedback, is the feedback of relatively small variations between actual and plan in order that corrective action can bring performance in line with planned results. This implies that the existing plans will not change. This type of feedback is associated with budgetary control and standard costing.

(b) **Double loop feedback**, also known as **higher level feedback**, ensures that plans, budgets, organisational structures and the control systems themselves are revised to meet changes in conditions.

(c) Feedback will most often be **negative:** targets were missed and this was **not** what was required. It may, however, be **positive:** targets were missed, but other targets were hit which were better than those we were aiming at. Negative feedback would result in control action to get back onto target. Positive feedback means that the target should be moved.

Feedforward control

3.2 Most control systems make use of a comparison between results of the current period (historical costs) and the planned results. Past events are therefore used as a means of controlling or adjusting future activity.

3.3 Consider, however, a **cash budget** (which we cover in depth in the next chapter). This is used to identify likely peaks and troughs in cash balances, and if it seems probable that, say, a higher overdraft facility will be needed later in the year, control action will be taken in advance of the actual need, to make sure that the facility will be available. This is an example of **feedforward control**

KEY TERM

Feedforward control is control based on comparing original targets or actual results with a forecast of future results.

3.4 The 'information revolution', which has arisen from computer technology, management information systems theory and the growing use of quantitative techniques has widened the scope for the use of this control technique. Forecasting models can be constructed which enable regular revised forecasts to be prepared about what is now likely to happen in view of changes in key variables (such as sales demand, wage rates and so on).

3.5 If regular forecasts are prepared, managers will have both the current forecast and the original plan to guide their action. The original plan may or may not be achievable in view of the changing circumstances. The current forecast indicates what is expected to happen in view of these circumstances.

3.6 **Examples of control comparisons**

Step 1. **Current forecast versus plan.** What action must be taken to get back to the plan, given the differences between the current forecast and the plan? Is any control action worthwhile?

Step 2. If **control action** is **planned,** the current forecast will need to be amended to take account of the effects of the control action and a **revised forecast** prepared.

Step 3. The next comparison should then be **revised forecast versus plan** to determine whether the plan is now expected to be achieved.

Step 4. A comparison between the **original current forecast** and the **revised forecast** will show what the expected effect of the control action will be.

Step 5. At the **end of a control period,** actual results will be analysed and two comparisons may be made.

- **Actual results versus the revised forecast.** Why did differences between the two occur?
- **Actual results so far in the year versus the plan.** How close are actual results to the plan?

Step 6. At the same time, a **new current forecast** should be prepared, and the cycle of comparisons and control action may begin again.

It is in this way that costs are constantly controlled and monitored.

4 CONTROLLABILITY AND RESPONSIBILITY REPORTING

4.1 In order to prepare a budget for an organisation as a whole, individual budgets have to be prepared for sub-sections of the organisation, such as individual subsidiaries within the group and individual departments, products or activities within each subsidiary.

KEY TERM

Each section of an organisation for which a budget is prepared is a **budget centre**.

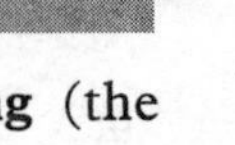

Since budgets will be made for each of these budget centres, **control reporting** (the comparison of actual results against plan) will also be **based on budget centres.**

4.2 The **selection of budget centres** in an organisation is therefore a **key first step in setting up a control system**. What should the budget centres be? What income, expenditure and/or capital employment plans should each budget centre prepare? And how will measures of performance for each budget centre be made?

4.3 **A well-organised system of control should have the following features.**

Feature	Explanation
A hierarchy of budget centres	If the organisation is quite large a hierarchy is needed. Subsidiary companies, departments and work sections might be budget centres. Budgets of each section would then be consolidated into a departmental budget, departmental budgets in turn would be consolidated into the subsidiary's budget, and the budgets of each subsidiary would be combined into a master budget for the group as a whole.
Clearly identified responsibilities for achieving budget targets	Individual managers should be made responsible for achieving the budget targets of a particular budget centre.
Responsibilities for revenues, costs and capital employed	Budget centres should be organised so that all the revenues earned by an organisation, all the costs it incurs, and all the capital it employs are made the responsibility of someone within the organisation, at an appropriate level of authority in the management hierarchy.

Exam focus point

A description of these features was worth up to six marks in the December 2001 exam.

4.4 Budgetary control and budget centres are therefore part of the overall system of **responsibility accounting** within an organisation.

KEY TERMS

Responsibility accounting is a system of accounting that segregates revenue and costs into areas of personal responsibility in order to monitor and assess the performance of each part of an organisation.

A **responsibility centre** is a unit of an organisation headed by a manager who has direct responsibility for its performance.

4.5 Responsibility centres might be a mixture of cost centres, profit centres and investment centres.

4.6 The following table should help to highlight the differences between cost centres, profit centres and investment centres.

Type of responsibility centre	Manager has control over . . .	Principal performance measure
Cost centre	Controllable costs	Variance analysis
Profit centre	Controllable costs Sales volumes Sales prices	Profit
Investment centre	Controllable costs Sales prices Output volumes Investment in fixed and current assets	Return on investment and residual income

Question 2

Find out if your organisation has a system of cost, profit and investment centres. What is the scope of planning and control within each centre?

Exam focus point

The difficulty in implementing responsibility accounting in not-for-profit organisations was examined in December 2001. Would you have been able to earn the possible six marks available? Try the question below to find out. You may need to refer back to Chapter 5.

Question 3

Why might responsibility accounting be difficult to implement in a not-for-profit organisation?

Answer

(a) Objectives are often unclear, so there is no obvious link between inputs and outputs. Responsibility is then hard to define.

(b) Budget holders may have to monitor costs rather than control them. For example, budget holders in a hospital are often not medical staff but medical decisions control the extent to which costs are incurred.

(c) The value for money objective of effectiveness is not measurable in money terms.

Controllable and non-controllable costs

KEY TERM

Controllable costs are items of expenditure which can be directly influenced by a given manager within a given time span.

4.7 **A cost which is not controllable by a junior manager might be controllable by a senior manager**. For example, there may be high direct labour costs in a department caused by excessive overtime working. The junior manager may feel obliged to continue with the overtime to meet production schedules, but his senior may be able to reduce costs by hiring extra full-time staff, thereby reducing the requirements for overtime.

A cost which is not controllable by a manager in one department may be controllable by a manager in another department. For example, an increase in material costs may be caused by buying at higher prices than expected (controllable by the purchasing department) or by excessive wastage (controllable by the production department) or by a faulty machine producing rejects (controllable by the maintenance department).

4.8 Some costs are **non-controllable**, such as increases in expenditure items due to inflation. Other costs are **controllable, but in the long term rather than the short term.** For example, production costs might be reduced by the introduction of new machinery and technology, but in the short term, management must attempt to do the best they can with the resources and machinery at their disposal.

The controllability of fixed costs

4.9 It is often assumed that all fixed costs are non-controllable in the short run. This is not so.

(a) **Committed fixed costs** are those costs arising from the possession of plant, equipment, buildings and an administration department to **support the long-term needs of the business**. These costs (depreciation, rent, administration salaries) are largely **non-controllable in the short term** because they have been committed by longer-term decisions affecting longer-term needs. When a company decides to cut production drastically, the long-term committed fixed costs will be reduced, but only after redundancy terms have been settled and assets sold.

(b) **Discretionary fixed costs**, such as advertising and research and development costs, are incurred as a result of a top management decision, but could be **raised or lowered at fairly short notice** (irrespective of the actual volume of production and sales).

Controllability and apportioned costs

4.10 **Managers should only be held accountable for costs over which they have some influence**. This may seem quite straightforward in theory, but it is not always so easy in practice to distinguish controllable from uncontrollable costs. **Apportioned overhead costs provide a good example**.

4.11 Suppose that a manager of a production department in a manufacturing company is made responsible for the costs of his department. These costs include **directly attributable overhead items** such as the costs of indirect labour employed in the department and indirect materials consumed in the department. The department's overhead costs also include an apportionment of costs from other costs centres, such as rent and rates for the building it shares with other departments and a share of the costs of the maintenance department.

4.12 Should the production manager be held accountable for any of these apportioned costs?

(a) Managers should not be held accountable for costs over which they have no control. In this example, apportioned rent and rates costs would not be controllable by the production department manager.

(b) Managers should be held accountable for costs over which they have some influence. In this example, it is the responsibility of the maintenance department manager to keep maintenance costs within budget. But their costs will be partly variable and partly fixed, and the variable cost element will depend on the volume of demand for their services. If the production department's staff treat their equipment badly we might expect higher repair costs, and the production department manager should therefore be made accountable for the repair costs that his department makes the maintenance department incur on its behalf.

Question 4

Try to discover some of your organisation's committed fixed costs and discretionary fixed costs. You will then be able to use them as examples in the exam.

Controllability and dual responsibility

4.13 Quite often a particular cost might be the **responsibility of two or more managers**. For example, raw materials costs might be the responsibility of the purchasing manager (prices) and the production manager (usage). A **reporting system must allocate responsibility appropriately**. The purchasing manager must be responsible for any increase in raw materials prices whereas the production manager should be responsible for any increase in raw materials usage.

Control reporting

4.14 Feedback periods ought to be planned, especially for routine control reporting.

(a) It is important to **avoid excessive reporting**. There is no point in producing control reports weekly if it takes several days to find out the cause of a variance and put it right. There has to be a reasonable interval between control reports so that managers can make a reasonable judgement about the effects of their past control actions. If reports are too frequent, they might well be thrown into the wastepaper basket unread.

(b) It is also important to **avoid unnecessary delays** in control reporting, by making the feedback period too long, or by taking too much time to put a feedback report together.

The most suitable frequency of routine control reporting will vary from operation to operation.

4.15 Control reports should be **clear** and **understandable** to the person receiving them. **Highlighting key results** and **exception reporting** are ways of improving clarity. Several reports will be prepared, all relating in some way to the same actual results. This is because reports will go to managers at different levels in the chain of command.

5 BUDGETARY PLANNING AND CONTROL SYSTEMS

5.1 A budgetary planning and control system is essentially a system for ensuring **communication, coordination** and **control** within an organisation. Communication, coordination and control are general objectives: more information is provided by an inspection of the specific objectives of a budgetary planning and control system.

Objective	Comment
Ensure the achievement of the organisation's objectives	Objectives are set for the organisation as a whole, and for individual departments and operations within the organisation. Quantified expressions of these objectives are then drawn up as targets to be achieved within the timescale of the budget plan.

Objective	Comment
Compel planning	This is probably the most important feature of a budgetary planning and control system. Planning forces management to look ahead, to set out detailed plans for achieving the targets for each department, operation and (ideally) each manager and to anticipate problems. It thus prevents management from relying on ad hoc or uncoordinated planning which may be detrimental to the performance of the organisation.
Communicate ideas and plans	A formal system is necessary to ensure that each person affected by the plans is aware of what he or she is supposed to be doing. Communication might be one-way, with managers giving orders to subordinates, or there might be a two-way dialogue and exchange of ideas.
Coordinate activities	The activities of different departments or sub-units of the organisation need to be coordinated to ensure maximum integration of effort towards common goals. This concept of coordination implies, for example, that the purchasing department should base its budget on production requirements and that the production budget should in turn be based on sales expectations. Although straightforward in concept, coordination is remarkably difficult to achieve, and there is often '**sub-optimality**' and conflict between departmental plans in the budget so that the efforts of each department are not fully integrated into a combined plan to achieve the company's best targets.
Provide a framework for responsibility accounting	Budgetary planning and control systems require that managers of **budget centres** are made responsible for the achievement of budget targets for the operations under their personal control.
Establish a system of control	A budget is a **yardstick** against which actual performance is measured and assessed. Control over actual performance is provided by the comparisons of actual results against the budget plan. Departures from budget can then be investigated and the reasons for the departures can be divided into **controllable** and **uncontrollable** factors.
Motivate employees to improve their performance	The interest and commitment of employees can be retained via a system of feedback of actual results, which lets them know how well or badly they are performing. The identification of controllable reasons for departures from budget with managers responsible provides an incentive for improving future performance.

Exam focus point

An exam question could well ask you to explain a number of these objectives in the context of a particular scenario such as a not-for-profit organisation.

Chapter roundup

- **Planning** involves making choices between alternatives and is primarily a decision-making activity.
- The **planning and control cycle** has seven steps.
    - *Step 1.* Identify **objectives**
    - *Step 2.* Identify potential **strategies**
    - *Step 3.* Evaluate strategies
    - *Step 4.* Choose alternative courses of action
    - *Step 5.* Implement the long-term plan
- **Control** is achieved through the **control cycle**. Actual performance is compared with planned performance and the appropriate action is taken for those items that are not proceeding according to plan.
- **Feedback** is the process of reporting back control information to management and the control information itself.
- **Feedforward control** is control based on comparing original targets or actual results with a forecast of future results.
- The selection of **budget centres** in an organisation is a key first step in setting up a control system. A system of **responsibility accounting** must be established.
- **Responsibility centres** include **cost centres**, **profit centres** and **investment centres**.
- **Controllable costs** are items of expenditure which can be directly influenced by a given manager within a given time span.
- A particular cost might be the responsibility of two or more managers (**dual responsibility**). A reporting system must allocate responsibility appropriately.
- Here are the **objectives of a budgetary planning and control system.**
    - Ensure the achievement of the organisation's objectives
    - Compel planning
    - Communicate ideas and plans
    - Coordinate activities
    - Provide a framework for responsibility accounting
    - Establish a system of control
    - Motivate employees to improve their performance

Quick quiz

1. *Put the following steps in the planning and control cycle in the correct order. (Don't cheat by looking at the roundup above!)*
    - Evaluate strategies
    - Implement the long-term plan
    - Identify objectives
    - Choose alternative courses of action
    - Identify potential strategies
2. A 'strategic audit' or 'position analysis' is an information gathering exercise carried out by an organisation to ensure that it has a full understanding of where it is now. True or false?
3. What questions do objectives answer?

4 *Complete the following steps in the control cycle.*

Step 1. ....

Step 2. ....

Step 3. ....

Step 4. ....

Step 5. ....

Step 6. ....

(a) ....

(b) ....

(c) ....

5 *Match the following terms to the correct description.*

Terms

- Programming
- Operating and measurement
- Reporting and analysis
- Feedback
- Budgets

Descriptions

(a) The cornerstone of management control and the management control system

(b) Collection of actual costs and outcomes identified to both programmes and responsibility centres

(c) Identification of the products a company intends to develop and projects which management intend to pursue to meet the organisation's overall goals

(d) Used to compare actual results with targets

(e) Used as a basis for control, for the coordination of activities and as a basis for future decisions perhaps to change the original plan

6 *Fill in the blanks.*

A well-organised system of control should have the following features.

(a) A hierarchy of ....

(b) Clearly identified .... for achieving budget targets

(c) Responsibilities for ...., ... and ....

7 Which of the following are not controllable by a production department manager?

(a) Direct labour rate

(b) Variable production overheads

(c) Apportioned canteen costs

(d) Increases in raw material costs due to inflation

(e) Increases in overall material costs due to high levels of wastage caused by poor supervision of production workers

(f) An increase in the level of idle time because of poorly-maintained machines

(g) Depreciation

(h) Advertising for production workers

(i) Share of the costs of maintenance department

Answers to quick quiz

1 Identify objectives
Identify potential strategies
Evaluate strategies
Choose alternative courses of action
Implement the long-term plan

2 False. A 'position audit' or 'strategic analysis' is being described.

3 'Where do we want to be?'

4 *Step 1.* Plans and targets are set for the future.

Step 2. Plans are put into operation.

Step 3. Actual results are recorded and analysed.

Step 4. Information about actual results is fed back to management.

Step 5. Management uses the feedback to compare actual results and targets.

Step 6. The comparison leads management to do one of three things.

(a) Take control action
(b) Decide to do nothing
(c) Alter the plan or target

5

Programming	(c)
Operating and measurement	(b)
Reporting and analysis	(e)
Feedback	(d)
Budgets	(a)

6 (a) budget centres

(b) responsibilities

(c) revenues
costs
capital employed

7 (a)
(c)
(d)
(f) (if there is a maintenance department)
(g)
(h)

Now try the question below from the Exam Question Bank

Question to try	Level	Marks	Time
12	Exam	25	45 mins

Chapter 10

BUDGET PREPARATION

Topic list		Syllabus reference
1	Administration of the budget	9(c)
2	The budget preparation timetable	9(c)
3	Functional budgets	9(c)
4	Cash budgets	9(c)
5	Budgeted P&L account and balance sheet	9(c)
6	The master budget	9(c)

Introduction

In Chapter 9 we looked at how **budgeting** fits into organisational planning. Budgeting is a topic which you will meet at all stages of your examination studies and so it is vital that you get a firm grasp of the basics now.

The chapter begins by looking at the **budgeting process**. The process is broken down and the individual stages looked at in detail. We will see how the sales budget and the production and related budgets (the **functional budgets**) are prepared, as well as the **cash budget.** The culmination of the budget process is the **master budget**, which comprises the budgeted profit and loss account, budgeted balance sheet and the cash budget. You will have the opportunity to see how a master budget is prepared in Section 6 of the chapter.

Chapter 11 builds on the general awareness of budgeting which you will have gained in this chapter and considers the control function of budgets.

Study guide

Section 23 – Budget planning and control I

- Prepare, review and explain a budget preparation timetable
- Prepare and evaluate functional, subsidiary and master budgets, including cash budgeting
- Explain the processes involved with the development and implementation of budgets

Exam guide

As well as discursive questions on the topics of this chapter, Section B questions could require you to prepare budgets including various functional budgets, a master budget and/or a cash budget.

Budget preparation may also appear in conjunction with financial management topics in Section A.

1 ADMINISTRATION OF THE BUDGET

KEY TERM

A **budget** is an organisation's plan for a forthcoming period, expressed in money term.

1.1 Having seen why organisations prepare budgets in the previous chapter, we will now turn our attention to the administrative procedures that ensure that the budget process works effectively.

The budget period

KEY TERM

The **budget period** is the time period to which the budget relates.

1.2 Except for capital expenditure budgets, the budget period is commonly the accounting year (sub-divided into 12 or 13 control periods).

Budget documentation: the budget manual

KEY TERM

The **budget manual** is a collection of instructions governing the responsibilities of persons and the procedures, forms and records relating to the preparation and use of budgetary data.

1.3 As one of the functions of the budget is to improve communication, a manual should be produced so that everyone can refer to it for information and guidance about the budgeting process. The budget manual does *not* contain the actual budgets for the forthcoming period; it is more of an **instruction/information manual about the way budgeting operates** in a particular organisation.

1.4 A budget manual will usually be prepared by the management accountant and although its contents will vary from organisation to organisation, it may contain the following.

Content	Detail
Explanation of the objectives of the budgeting process	• The purpose of budgetary planning and control • The objectives of the various stages of the budgeting process • The importance of budgets in the long-term planning and administration of the enterprise
Organisational structures	• An organisation chart • A list of staff holding budget responsibilities
Outline of the principal budgets	• Relationship between them
Administrative details	• Membership, and terms of reference, of the budget committee • Sequence in which budgets are to be prepared • A timetable
Procedural matters	• Specimen forms and instructions for completing them • Specimen reports • Account codes (or a chart of accounts) • Budget officer to whom to send enquiries

Responsibility for the preparation of budgets

1.5 Ideally the **managers (and their subordinates) responsible for preparing budgets should be the managers (and their subordinates) who are responsible for carrying out the budgets**. For example, the sales manager should draft the sales budget and selling overhead cost centre budget and the purchasing manager should draft the material purchases budget.

Budget committee

1.6 The **coordination** and **administration of budgets** is usually the **responsibility of a budget committee** (with the managing director as chairman). The budget committee is **assisted by a budget officer** who is usually an accountant. Every part of the organisation should be represented on the committee, so there should be a **representative from sales, production, marketing** and so on. Functions of the budget committee include the following.

- Coordination of budget preparation, including the issue of the budget manual
- Issuing of timetables for the preparation of functional budgets
- Allocation of responsibilities for the preparation of functional budgets
- Provision of information to assist in the preparation of budgets
- Communication of final budgets to the appropriate managers
- Comparison of actual results with budget and the investigation of variances
- Continuous assessment of the budgeting and planning process

2 THE BUDGET PREPARATION TIMETABLE

2.1 Let us now look at the steps involved in the **development, preparation and implementation of a budget**. The procedures will differ from organisation to organisation, but the step-by-step approach described here is indicative of the steps followed by many organisations. The preparation of a budget may take weeks or months and the budget committee may meet several times before an organisation's budget is finally agreed.

Step 1. **Communicating details of the budget policy and budget guidelines**

The long-term plan is the starting point for the preparation of the annual budget. Managers responsible for preparing the budget must be aware of the way it is affected by the long-term plan so that it becomes part of the process of meeting the organisation's objectives. For example, if the long-term plan calls for a more aggressive pricing policy, the budget must take this into account. Managers should also be provided with important guidelines for wage rate increases, changes in productivity and so on, as well as information about industry demand and output.

Step 2. **Determining the factor that restricts output**

KEY TERM

The **principal budget factor** (or **key budget factor** or **limiting budget factor)** is the factor that limits an organisation's performance for a given period and is often the starting point in budget preparation.

For example, a sales department might estimate that it could sell 1,000 units of product X, which would require 5,000 hours of grade A labour. If there are no units of product X already in stock, and only 4,000 hours of grade A labour available in the period, the company would be unable to sell 1,000 units of X because of the shortage of labour hours. Grade A labour would be a limiting budget factor, and management must choose one of the following options.

- Reduce budgeted sales by 20%
- Try to increase the availability of grade A labour by 1,000 hours (25%) by recruitment or overtime working
- Try to sub-contract the production of 1,000 units to another manufacturer, but still profit on the transaction

In most organisations the principal budget factor is sales demand: a company is usually restricted from making and selling more of its products because there would be no sales demand for the increased output at a price which would be acceptable to the company. The principal budget factor may also be machine capacity, distribution and selling resources, the availability of key raw materials or cash. Once this factor is defined then the rest of the budget can be prepared. For example, if sales are the principal budget factor then the production manager can only prepare his budget after the sales budget is complete.

Management may not know what the limiting budget factor is until a draft budget has been attempted. The first draft budget will therefore usually begin with the preparation of a draft sales budget.

If an organisation produces **two or more products** and the **principal budget factor is *not* sales demand,** a technique known as **limiting factor analysis** must be used to determine the most profitable production plan. We will be looking at this technique in Chapter 14.

Step 3. **Preparation of the sales budget**

We have already established that, for many organisations, the principal budget factor is sales volume. The sales budget is therefore often the primary budget from which the majority of the other budgets are derived. Before the sales budget can be prepared a **sales forecast** has to be made. Sales forecasting is complex and difficult and involves the consideration of a number of factors.

- Past sales patterns
- The economic environment
- Results of market research
- Anticipated advertising
- Competition
- Changing consumer taste
- New legislation
- Distribution
- Pricing policies and discounts offered
- Legislation
- Environmental factors

As well as bearing in mind the above factors, management can use a number of forecasting methods, which we will return to in Chapter 13.

On the basis of the sales forecast and the production capacity of the organisation, a sales budget will be prepared. This may be subdivided, possible subdivisions being by product, by sales area, by management responsibility and so on.

Step 4. **Initial preparation of budgets**

Budget	Detail
Finished goods stock budget	Decides the planned increase or decrease in finished stock levels.
Production budget	Stated in units of each product and is the sales budget in units plus the budgeted increase in finished goods stocks **or** minus the budgeted decrease in finished goods stocks.
Budgets of resources for production	**Materials usage budget** is stated in quantities and perhaps cost for each type of material used. It should take into account budgeted losses in production.
	Machine utilisation budget shows the operating hours required on each machine or group of machines.
	Labour budget or wages budget will be expressed in hours for each grade of labour and in terms of cost. It should take into account budgeted idle time.
Overhead cost budgets	**Production, administration, selling and distribution and research and development department overheads**
Raw materials stock budget	Decides the planned increase or decrease of the level of stocks.
Raw materials purchase budget	Can be prepared in quantities and value for each type of material purchased once the raw material usage requirements and the raw materials stock budget are known.
Overhead absorption rate	Can be calculated once the production volumes are planned, and the overhead cost centre budgets prepared.

Step 5. **Negotiation of budgets with superiors**

Once a manager has prepared his draft budget he should submit it to his superior for approval. The superior should then incorporate this budget with the others for which he or she is responsible and then submit this budget for approval to his or her superior. This process continues until the final budget is presented to the budget committee for approval.

At each stage, the **budget** would be **negotiated between the manager who had prepared the budget and his/her superior** until agreed by both parties.

Step 6. **Co-ordination of budgets**

Remember that it is unlikely that the execution of the above steps will be problem-free. The budgets must be reviewed in relation to one another. Such a **review may indicate that some budgets are out of balance with others and need modifying** so that they will be compatible. The budget officer must identify such inconsistencies and bring them to the attention of the manager concerned. The **revision of one budget may lead to the revision of all budgets**. During this process the budgeted profit and loss account and budgeted balance sheet and cash budget should be prepared to ensure that all of the individual parts of the budget combine into an acceptable master budget.

Step 7. **Final acceptance of the budget**

When all the budgets are in harmony with one another they are summarised into a **master budget** consisting of a budgeted profit and loss account, budgeted balance sheet and cash budget.

Step 8. **Budget review**

The budgeting process does not stop once the budgets have been agreed. Actual results should be compared on a regular basis with the budgeted results. Management should receive a report detailing the differences and should investigate the reasons for the differences. **If the differences are within the control of management, corrective action should be taken** to bring the reasons for the difference under control and to ensure that such inefficiencies do not occur in the future.

The **differences may have occurred, however, because the budget was unrealistic to begin with or because the actual conditions did not reflect those anticipated (or could have possibly been anticipated).** This would therefore invalidate the remainder of the budget.

The **budget committee**, who should meet periodically to evaluate the organisation's actual performance, **may need to reappraise the organisation's future plans in the light of changes to anticipated conditions and to adjust the budget to take account of such changes.**

The important point to note is that the budgeting process does not end for the current year once the budget period has begun: budgeting should be seen as a continuous and dynamic process.

Question 1

A company that manufactures and sells a range of products, with sales potential limited by market share, is considering introducing a system of budgeting.

Required

(a) List (in order of preparation) the functional budgets that need to be prepared.

(b) State which budgets the master budget will comprise.

(c) Consider how the work outlined in (a) and (b) can be coordinated in order for the budgeting process to be successful.

Answer

(a) The **sequence** of budget preparation will be roughly as follows.

(i) **Sales budget**. (The market share limits demand and so sales is the principal budget factor. All other activities will depend upon this forecast.)

(ii) **Finished goods stock budget** (in units)

(iii) **Production budget** (in units)

(iv) **Production resources budgets** (materials, machine hours, labour)

(v) **Overhead budgets** for production, administration, selling and distribution, research and development and so on

Other budgets required will be the capital expenditure budget, and, very importantly, the cash budget.

(b) The master budget is the summary of all the functional budgets. It often includes a **summary profit and loss account and balance sheet.**

(c) Procedures for preparing budgets can be contained in a **budget manual** which shows which budgets must be prepared when and by whom, what each functional budget should contain and detailed directions on how to prepare budgets including, for example, expected price increases, rates of interest, rates of depreciation and so on.

The formulation of budgets can be coordinated by a **budget committee** comprising the senior executives of the departments responsible for carrying out the budgets: sales, production, purchasing, personnel and so on.

The budgeting process may also be assisted by the use of a **spreadsheet/computer budgeting package**.

3 FUNCTIONAL BUDGETS

Exam focus point

You must be able to prepare budgets from information provided in examination questions and comment on those budgets, perhaps giving recommendations about management action required.

KEY TERM

Functional (or **departmental**) **budgets** are the budgets for the various functions and departments of an organisation. They therefore include production budgets, marketing budgets, sales budgets, personnel budgets, purchasing budgets and research and development budgets.

3.1 We will look at the preparation of a number of types of functional budget in this chapter but the general principles covered can be applied in most situations.

Production cost budget

3.2 If the principal budget factor was production capacity then the production cost budget would be the first to be prepared.

3.3 To assess whether production is the principal budget factor, the **production capacity available** must be determined. This should take into account the following factors.

- **Available labour**, including idle time, overtime and standard output rates per hour
- **Availability of raw materials** including allowances for losses during production
- **Maximum machine hours available**, including expected idle time and expected output rates per machine hour

It is, however, normally sales volume that is the constraint and therefore the production budget is prepared after the sales budget and the finished goods stock budget.

3.4 The **production cost budget** will show the **quantities** and **costs** for **each product** and product group and will tie in with the sales and stock budgets. This co-ordinating process is likely to show any shortfalls or excesses in capacity at various times over the budget period. If there is likely to be a shortfall then consideration should be given to overtime, subcontracting, machine hire, new sources of raw materials or some other way of increasing output. A significant shortfall means that production capacity is, in fact, the limiting factor. If capacity exceeds sales volume for a length of time then consideration should be given to product diversification, a reduction in selling price (if demand is price elastic) and so on.

3.5 Once the production budget has been finalised, the labour, materials and machine budgets can be drawn up. These budgets will be based on budgeted activity levels, existing stock positions and projected labour and material costs.

3.6 EXAMPLE: THE PREPARATION OF THE PRODUCTION BUDGET AND DIRECT LABOUR BUDGET

Pearson Ltd manufactures two products, P and L, and is preparing its budget for 20X3. Both products are made by the same grade of labour, grade G. The company currently holds 800 units of P and 1,200 units of L in stock, but 250 of these units of L have just been discovered to have deteriorated in quality, and must therefore be scrapped. Budgeted sales of P are 3,000 units and of L 4,000 units, provided that the company maintains finished goods stocks at a level equal to three months' sales.

Grade G labour was originally expected to produce one unit of P in two hours and one unit of L in three hours, at an hourly rate of £2.50 per hour. In discussions with trade union negotiators, however, it has been agreed that the hourly wage rate should be raised by 50p per hour, provided that the times to produce P and L are reduced by 20%.

Required

Prepare the production budget and direct labour budget for 20X3.

3.7 SOLUTION

The expected time to produce a unit of P will now be 80% of 2 hours = 1.6 hours, and the time for a unit of L will be 2.4 hours. The hourly wage rate will be £3, so that the direct labour cost will be £4.80 for P and £7.20 for L (thus achieving a saving for the company of 20p per unit of P produced and 30p per unit of L).

(a) **Production budget**

		Product P			*Product L*	
		Units	Units		Units	Units
Budgeted sales			3,000			4,000
Closing stocks	($^3/_{12}$ of 3,000)	750		($^3/_{12}$ of 4,000)	1,000	
Opening stocks (minus stocks scrapped)		800			950	
(Decrease)/increase in stocks			(50)			50
Production			2,950			4,050

BPP PUBLISHING

(b) **Direct labour budget**

	Grade G Hours	*Cost* £
2,950 units of product P	4,720	14,160
4,050 units of product L	9,720	29,160
Total	14,440	43,320

It is assumed that there will be no idle time among grade G labour which, if it existed, would have to be paid for at the rate of £3 per hour.

Labour budget

3.8 A useful concept in budgeting for labour requirements is the standard hour.

KEY TERM

A **standard hour** is the quantity of work achievable at standard performance, expressed in terms of a standard unit of work done in a standard period of time.

3.9 Budgeted output of different products or jobs in a period can be converted into standard hours of production, and a labour budget constructed accordingly.

3.10 Standard hours are particularly useful when management wants to monitor the production levels of a variety of dissimilar units. For example product A may take five hours to produce and product B, seven hours. If four units of each product are produced, instead of saying that total output is eight units, we could state the production level as $(4 \times 5) + (4 \times 7)$ standard hours = 48 standard hours.

3.11 EXAMPLE: DIRECT LABOUR BUDGET BASED ON STANDARD HOURS

Canaervon Ltd manufactures a single product, the close, with a single grade of labour. Its sales budget and finished goods stock budget for period 3 are as follows.

Sales	700 units
Opening stocks, finished goods	50 units
Closing stocks, finished goods	70 units

The goods are inspected only when production work is completed, and it is budgeted that 10% of finished work will be scrapped. The standard direct labour hour content of the close is three hours. The budgeted productivity ratio for direct labour is only 80% (which means that labour is only working at 80% efficiency). The company employs 18 direct operatives, who are expected to average 144 working hours each in period 3.

Required

(a) Prepare a production budget.

(b) Prepare a direct labour budget.

(c) Comment on the problem that your direct labour budget reveals, and suggest how this problem might be overcome.

3.12 SOLUTION

(a) **Production budget**

	Units
Sales	700
Add closing stock	70
	770
Less opening stock	50
Production required of 'good' output	720
Wastage rate	10%

Total production required* = 720/0.9 = 800 units

* Output = 90% × input and so 720 = 0.9 × input and therefore 720/0.9 = input.

(b) Now we can prepare the **direct labour budget.**

Standard hours per unit		3
Total standard hours required	= 800 units × 3 hours	2,400 hours
Productivity ratio		80%
Actual hours required	= 2,400/0.8 = 3,000 hours	

(c) If we look at the direct labour budget against the information provided, we can identify the **problem**.

	Hours
Budgeted hours available (18 operatives × 144 hours)	2,592
Actual hours required	3,000
Shortfall in labour hours	408

The (draft) budget indicates that there will not be enough direct labour hours to meet the production requirements. This problem might be **overcome** in one, or a combination, of the following ways.

(i) Reduce the closing stock requirement below 70 units. This would reduce the number of production units required.

(ii) Persuade the workforce to do some overtime working.

(iii) Perhaps recruit more direct labour if long-term prospects are for higher production volumes.

(iv) Discuss with the workforce (or their union representatives) the following possibilities.

(1) Improve the productivity ratio, and so reduce the number of hours required to produce the output.

(2) If possible, reduce the wastage rate below 10%.

Cost of sales budget

3.13 This is based on the **production cost budget** but **adjusted by the opening and closing stock positions.**

Coordination of functional budgets

3.14 **It is vital that the functional budgets are prepared in the correct order** (for example, the material usage budget should be prepared after the production budget) and that the **overall process is coordinated** to ensure that the budgets are all in balance with each other. There is little point in the material usage budget being based on a budgeted production level of 10,000 units if the budgeted production level specified in the production budget is 15,000 units.

4 CASH BUDGETS

KEY TERM

A **cash budget** is a detailed budget of cash inflows and outflows incorporating both revenue and capital items.

4.1 A cash budget is thus a statement in which estimated future cash receipts and payments are tabulated in such a way as to show the forecast cash balance of a business at defined intervals. For example, in December 20X2 an accounts department might wish to estimate the cash position of the business during the three following months, January to March 20X3. A cash budget might be drawn up in the following format.

	Jan	*Feb*	*Mar*
	£	£	£
Estimated cash receipts			
From credit customers	14,000	16,500	17,000
From cash sales	3,000	4,000	4,500
Proceeds on disposal of fixed assets		2,200	
Total cash receipts	17,000	22,700	21,500
Estimated cash payments			
To suppliers of goods	8,000	7,800	10,500
To employees (wages)	3,000	3,500	3,500
Purchase of fixed assets		16,000	
Rent and rates			1,000
Other overheads	1,200	1,200	1,200
Repayment of loan	2,500		
	14,700	28,500	16,200
Net surplus/(deficit) for month	2,300	(5,800)	5,300
Opening cash balance	1,200	3,500	(2,300)
Closing cash balance	3,500	(2,300)	3,000

4.2 In the example above (where the figures are purely for illustration) the accounts department has calculated that the cash balance at the beginning of the budget period, 1 January, will be £1,200. Estimates have been made of the cash which is likely to be received by the business (from cash and credit sales, and from a planned disposal of fixed assets in February). Similar estimates have been made of cash due to be paid out by the business (payments to suppliers and employees, payments for rent, rates and other overheads, payment for a planned purchase of fixed assets in February and a loan repayment due in January).

4.3 From these estimates it is a simple step to calculate the excess of cash receipts over cash payments in each month. In some months cash payments may exceed cash receipts and there will be a deficit for the month; this occurs during February in the above example because of the large investment in fixed assets in that month.

4.4 The last part of the cash budget above shows how the business's estimated cash balance can then be rolled along from month to month. Starting with the opening balance of £1,200 at 1 January a cash surplus of £2,300 is generated in January. This leads to a closing January balance of £3,500 which becomes the opening balance for February. The deficit of £5,800 in February throws the business's cash position into overdraft and the overdrawn balance of £2,300 becomes the opening balance for March. Finally, the healthy cash surplus of £5,300 in March leaves the business with a favourable cash position of £3,000 at the end of the budget period.

Exam focus point

When preparing budgets, it is vital that your work is clearly laid out, and referenced to workings if necessary.

The usefulness of cash budgets

4.5 The cash budget is one of the most important planning tools that an organisation can use. It shows the cash effect of all plans made within the budgetary process and hence its preparation can lead to a modification of budgets if it shows that there are insufficient cash resources to finance the planned operations.

4.6 It can also **give management an indication of potential problems that could arise and allows them the opportunity to take action to avoid such problems.** A cash budget can show four positions. Management will need to take appropriate action depending on the potential position.

Cash position	Appropriate management action
Short-term surplus	Pay creditors early to obtain discount Attempt to increase sales by increasing debtors and stocks Make short-term investments
Short-term deficit	Increase creditors Reduce debtors Arrange an overdraft
Long-term surplus	Make long-term investments Expand Diversify Replace/update fixed assets
Long-term deficit	Raise long-term finance (such as via issue of share capital) Consider shutdown/disinvestment opportunities

Exam focus point

A cash budgeting question in an examination could ask you to recommend appropriate action for management to take once you have prepared the cash budget. Ensure your advice takes account both of whether there is a surplus or deficit and whether the position is long or short term.

What to include in a cash budget

4.7 A cash budget is prepared to show the **expected receipts of cash and payments of cash** during a budget period.

4.8 It should be obvious that the **profit or loss made by an organisation during an accounting period does not reflect its cash flow position for the following reasons.**

(a) Not all cash receipts affect profit and loss account income.

(b) Not all cash payments affect profit and loss account expenditure.

(c) Some costs in the profit and loss account such as profit or loss on sale of fixed assets or depreciation are not cash items but are costs derived from accounting conventions.

(d) The timing of cash receipts and payments may not coincide with the recording of profit and loss account transactions. For example, a dividend might be declared in the results for 20X6 and shown in the profit and loss account for that year, but paid in 20X7.

4.9 To ensure that there is sufficient cash in hand to cope adequately with budgeted activities, management should therefore prepare and pay close attention to a cash budget rather than a profit and loss account. Cash budgets are most effective if they are treated as rolling budgets. **Rolling budgets** involve a process of continuous budgeting whereby regularly each period (week month, quarter) a new future period is added to the budget whilst the earliest period is deleted. In this way the budget is **constantly revised** to reflect the most up to date position. We consider rolling budgets in Chapter 12.

4.10 EXAMPLE: CASH BUDGET

Peter Blair has worked for some years as a sales representative, but has recently been made redundant. He intends to start up in business on his own account, using £15,000 which he currently has invested with a building society. Peter maintains a bank account showing a small credit balance, and he plans to approach his bank for the necessary additional finance. Peter provides the following additional information.

(a) Arrangements have been made to purchase fixed assets costing £8,000. These will be paid for at the end of September and are expected to have a five-year life, at the end of which they will possess a nil residual value.

(b) Stocks costing £5,000 will be acquired on 28 September and subsequent monthly purchases will be at a level sufficient to replace forecast sales for the month.

(c) Forecast monthly sales are £3,000 for October, £6,000 for November and December, and £10,500 from January 20X4 onwards.

(d) Selling price is fixed at the cost of stock plus 50%.

(e) Two months' credit will be allowed to customers but only one month's credit will be received from suppliers of stock.

(f) Running expenses, including rent but excluding depreciation of fixed assets, are estimated at £1,600 per month.

(g) Blair intends to make monthly cash drawings of £1,000.

Required

Prepare a cash budget for the six months to 31 March 20X4.

4.11 SOLUTION

The opening cash balance at 1 October will consist of Peter's initial £15,000 less the £8,000 expended on fixed assets purchased in September. In other words, the opening balance is £7,000. Cash receipts from credit customers arise two months after the relevant sales.

Payments to suppliers are a little more tricky. We are told that cost of sales is 100/150 × sales. Thus for October cost of sales is 100/150 × £3,000 = £2,000. These goods will be purchased in October but not paid for until November. Similar calculations can be made for later months. The initial stock of £5,000 is purchased in September and consequently paid for in October.

Depreciation is not a cash flow and so is *not* included in a cash budget.

4.12 The cash budget can now be constructed.

CASH BUDGET FOR THE SIX MONTHS ENDING 31 MARCH 20X4

	Oct	*Nov*	*Dec*	*Jan*	*Feb*	*Mar*
	£	£	£	£	£	£
Payments						
Suppliers	5,000	2,000	4,000	4,000	7,000	7,000
Running expenses	1,600	1,600	1,600	1,600	1,600	1,600
Drawings	1,000	1,000	1,000	1,000	1,000	1,000
	7,600	4,600	6,600	6,600	9,600	9,600
Receipts						
Debtors	-	-	3,000	6,000	6,000	10,500
Surplus/(shortfall)	(7,600)	(4,600)	(3,600)	(600)	(3,600)	900
Opening balance	7,000	(600)	(5,200)	(8,800)	(9,400)	(13,000)
Closing balance	(600)	(5,200)	(8,800)	(9,400)	(13,000)	(12,100)

Cash budgets and an opening balance sheet

4.13 You might be given a cash budget question in which you are required to analyse an opening balance sheet to decide how many outstanding debtors will pay what they owe in the first few months of the cash budget period, and how many outstanding creditors must be paid.

4.14 Suppose that a balance sheet as at 31 December 20X4 shows debtors of £150,000 and trade creditors of £60,000. The following information is also relevant.

- Debtors are allowed two months to pay.
- $1^1/_2$ months' credit is taken from trade creditors.
- Sales and materials purchases were both made at an even monthly rate .

Let's try to ascertain the months of 20X5 in which the debtors will eventually pay and the creditors will be paid.

(a) Since debtors take two months to pay, the £150,000 of debtors in the balance sheet represents credit sales in November and December 20X4, who will pay in January and February 20X5 respectively. Since sales in 20X4 were at an equal monthly rate, the cash budget should plan for receipts of £75,000 each month in January and February from the debtors in the opening balance sheet.

(b) Similarly, since creditors are paid after $1^1/_2$ months, the balance sheet creditors will be paid in January and the first half of February 20X5, which means that budgeted payments will be as follows.

	£
In January (purchases in 2nd half of Nov. and 1st half of Dec.20X4)	40,000
In February (purchases in 2nd half of December 20X4)	20,000
Total creditors in the balance sheet	60,000

(The balance sheet creditors of £60,000 represent $1^1/_2$ months' purchases, so that purchases in 20X4 must be £40,000 per month, which is £20,000 per half month.)

4.15 EXAMPLE: A MONTH BY MONTH CASH BUDGET

From the following information which relates to George and Zola Ltd you are required to prepare a month by month cash budget for the second half of 20X5 and to append such brief comments as you consider might be helpful to management.

(a) The company's only product, a vest, sells at £40 and has a variable cost of £26 made up of material £20, labour £4 and overhead £2.

(b) Fixed costs of £6,000 per month are paid on the 28th of each month.

(c) Quantities sold/to be sold on credit

May	*June*	*July*	*Aug*	*Sept*	*Oct*	*Nov*	*Dec*
1,000	1,200	1,400	1,600	1,800	2,000	2,200	2,600

(d) Production quantities

May	*June*	*July*	*Aug*	*Sept*	*Oct*	*Nov*	*Dec*
1,200	1,400	1,600	2,000	2,400	2,600	2,400	2,200

(e) Cash sales at a discount of 5% are expected to average 100 units a month.

(f) Customers settle their accounts by the end of the second month following sale.

(g) Suppliers of material are paid two months after the material is used in production.

(h) Wages are paid in the same month as they are incurred.

(i) 70% of the variable overhead is paid in the month of production, the remainder in the following month.

(j) Corporation tax of £18,000 is to be paid in October.

(k) A new delivery vehicle was bought in June. It cost £8,000 and is to be paid for in August. The old vehicle was sold for £600, the buyer undertaking to pay in July.

(l) The company is expected to be £3,000 overdrawn at the bank at 30 June 20X5.

(m) No increases or decreases in raw materials, work in progress or finished goods are planned over the period.

(n) No price increases or cost increases are expected in the period.

4.16 SOLUTION

Cash budget for 1 July to 31 December 20X5

	July	*Aug*	*Sept*	*Oct*	*Nov*	*Dec*	*Total*
	£	£	£	£	£	£	£
Receipts							
Credit sales	40,000	48,000	56,000	64,000	72,000	80,000	360,000
Cash sales	3,800	3,800	3,800	3,800	3,800	3,800	22,800
Sale of vehicle	600	-	-	-	-	-	600
	44,400	51,800	59,800	67,800	75,800	83,800	383,400
Payments							
Materials	24,000	28,000	32,000	40,000	48,000	52,000	224,000
Labour	6,400	8,000	9,600	10,400	9,600	8,800	52,800
Variable overhead (W)	3,080	3,760	4,560	5,080	4,920	4,520	25,920
Fixed costs	6,000	6,000	6,000	6,000	6,000	6,000	36,000
Corporation tax				18,000			18,000
Purchase of vehicle		8,000					8,000
	39,480	53,760	52,160	79,480	68,520	71,320	364,720
Receipts less payments	4,920	(1,960)	7,640	(11,680)	7,280	12,480	18,680
Balance b/f	(3,000)	1,920	(40)	7,600	(4,080)	3,200	(3,000)
Balance c/f	1,920	(40)	7,600	(4,080)	3,200	15,680	15,680

Working

	June	*July*	*Aug*	*Sept*	*Oct*	*Nov*	*Dec*
	£	£	£	£	£	£	£
Variable overhead production cost	2,800	3,200	4,000	4,800	5,200	4,800	4,400
70% paid in month		2,240	2,800	3,360	3,640	3,360	3,080
30% in following month		840	960	1,200	1,440	1,560	1,440
		3,080	3,760	4,560	5,080	4,920	4,520

Comments

(a) There will be a small overdraft at the end of August but a much larger one at the end of October. It may be possible to delay payments to suppliers for longer than two months or to reduce purchases of materials or reduce the volume of production by running down existing stock levels.

(b) If neither of these courses is possible, the company may need to negotiate overdraft facilities with its bank.

(c) The cash deficit is only temporary and by the end of December there will be a comfortable surplus. The use to which this cash will be put should ideally be planned in advance.

Question 2

You are presented with the following budgeted cash flow data for your organisation for the period November 20X1 to June 20X2. It has been extracted from functional budgets that have already been prepared.

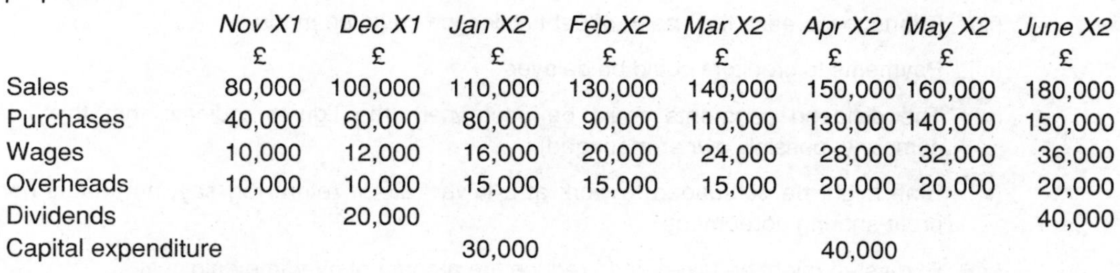

	Nov X1	*Dec X1*	*Jan X2*	*Feb X2*	*Mar X2*	*Apr X2*	*May X2*	*June X2*
	£	£	£	£	£	£	£	£
Sales	80,000	100,000	110,000	130,000	140,000	150,000	160,000	180,000
Purchases	40,000	60,000	80,000	90,000	110,000	130,000	140,000	150,000
Wages	10,000	12,000	16,000	20,000	24,000	28,000	32,000	36,000
Overheads	10,000	10,000	15,000	15,000	15,000	20,000	20,000	20,000
Dividends		20,000						40,000
Capital expenditure			30,000			40,000		

You are also told the following.

(a) Sales are 40% cash 60% credit. Credit sales are paid two months after the month of sale.
(b) Purchases are paid the month following purchase.
(c) 75% of wages are paid in the current month and 25% the following month.
(d) Overheads are paid the month after they are incurred.
(e) Dividends are paid three months after they are declared.
(f) Capital expenditure is paid two months after it is incurred.
(g) The opening cash balance is £15,000.

The managing director is pleased with the above figures as they show sales will have increased by more than 100% in the period under review. In order to achieve this he has arranged a bank overdraft with a ceiling of £50,000 to accommodate the increased stock levels and wage bill for overtime worked.

Required

(a) Prepare a cash budget for the six-month period January to June 20X2.

(b) Comment on your results in the light of the managing director's comments and offer advice.

Answer

(a)

	January	February	March	April	May	June
	£	£	£	£	£	£
Cash receipts						
Cash sales	44,000	52,000	56,000	60,000	64,000	72,000
Credit sales	48,000	60,000	66,000	78,000	84,000	90,000
	92,000	112,000	122,000	138,000	148,000	162,000
Cash payments						
Purchases	60,000	80,000	90,000	110,000	130,000	140,000
Wages: 75%	12,000	15,000	18,000	21,000	24,000	27,000
Wages: 25%	3,000	4,000	5,000	6,000	7,000	8,000
Overheads	10,000	15,000	15,000	15,000	20,000	20,000
Dividends			20,000			
Capital expenditure			30,000			40,000
	85,000	114,000	178,000	152,000	181,000	235,000
b/f	15,000	22,000	20,000	(36,000)	(50,000)	(83,000)
Net cash flow	7,000	(2,000)	(56,000)	(14,000)	(33,000)	(73,000)
c/f	22,000	20,000	(36,000)	(50,000)	(83,000)	(156,000)

(b) The overdraft arrangements are quite inadequate to service the cash needs of the business over the six-month period. If the figures are realistic then action should be taken now to avoid difficulties in the near future. The following are **possible courses of action**.

(i) Activities could be curtailed.

(ii) Other sources of cash could be explored, for example a long-term loan to finance the capital expenditure and a factoring arrangement to provide cash due from debtors more quickly.

(iii) Efforts to increase the speed of debt collection could be made.

(iv) Payments to creditors could be delayed.

(v) The dividend payments could be postponed (the figures indicate that this is a small company, possibly owner-managed).

(vi) Staff might be persuaded to work at a lower rate in return for, say, an annual bonus or a profit-sharing agreement.

(vii) Extra staff might be taken on to reduce the amount of overtime paid.

(viii) The stockholding policy should be reviewed; it may be possible to meet demand from current production and minimise cash tied up in stocks.

5 BUDGETED P&L ACCOUNT AND BALANCE SHEET

5.1 As well as wishing to forecast its cash position, a business might want to estimate its profitability and its financial position for a coming period. This involves the preparation of a budgeted P&L account and balance sheet, along with the cash budget which form the master budget.

5.2 Just like historical financial statements, **budgeted accounts are based on the accruals concept**. The example of Peter Blair above will be used to illustrate the procedure.

5.3 EXAMPLE: PREPARING A BUDGETED P&L ACCOUNT AND BALANCE SHEET

Using the information in the Peter Blair example, prepare Peter Blair's budgeted P&L account for the six months ending on 31 March 20X4 and a budgeted balance sheet as at that date.

5.4 SOLUTION

The profit and loss account is straightforward. The first figure is sales, which can be computed very easily from the information in Paragraph 4.10(c). It is sufficient to add up the monthly sales figures given there; for the profit and loss account there is no need to worry about any closing debtor. Similarly, cost of sales is calculated directly from the information on gross margin contained in Paragraph 4.10(d).

FORECAST TRADING AND PROFIT AND LOSS ACCOUNT
FOR THE SIX MONTHS ENDING 31 MARCH 20X4

	£	£
Sales (3,000 + (2 × 6,000) + (3 × 10,500))		46,500
Cost of sales (2/3 × £46,500)		31,000
Gross profit		15,500
Expenses: Running expenses (6 × £1,600)	9,600	
Depreciation (£8,000 × 20% × 6/12)	800	
		10,400
Net profit		5,100

Items will be shown in the balance sheet as follows.

(a) Stock will comprise the initial purchases of £5,000.
(b) Debtors will comprise sales made in February and March (paid in April and May).
(c) Creditors will comprise purchases made in March (not paid for until April).
(d) The bank overdraft is the closing cash figure computed in the cash budget.

FORECAST BALANCE SHEET AT 31 MARCH 20X4

	£	£
Fixed assets £(8,000 – 800)		7,200
Current assets		
Stocks	5,000	
Debtors (2 × £10,500)	21,000	
	26,000	
Current liabilities		
Bank overdraft	12,100	
Trade creditors (March purchases)	7,000	
	19,100	
Net current assets		6,900
		14,100
Proprietor's interest		
Capital introduced		15,000
Profit for the period	5,100	
Less drawings	6,000	
Deficit retained		(900)
		14,100

5.5 Budget questions are often accompanied by a large amount of sometimes confusing detail. This should not blind you to the fact that many figures can be entered very simply from the logic of the trading situation described. For example in the case of Blair you are told that debtors take two months to pay. Closing debtors will equal total credit sales in the last two months of the period.

5.6 Similarly, you may be given a simple statement that a business pays rates at £1,500 a year, followed by a lot of detail to enable you to calculate a prepayment at the beginning and end of the year. If you are preparing a budgeted profit and loss account for the year the rates expense can be entered as £1,500 without any calculation at all.

6 THE MASTER BUDGET

KEY TERM

When all the functional budgets have been prepared, they are summarised and consolidated into a **master budget** which consists of the budgeted profit and loss account, budgeted balance sheet and cash budget and which provides the overall picture of the planned performance for the budget period.

6.1 EXAMPLE: A MASTER BUDGET

Plagued Engineering Limited produces two products, Niks and Args. The budget for the forthcoming year to 31 March 20X8 is to be prepared. Expectations for the forthcoming year include the following.

(a) **PLAGUED ENGINEERING LTD**
BALANCE SHEET AS AT 1 APRIL 20X7

	£	£
Fixed assets		
Land and buildings		45,000
Plant and equipment at cost	187,000	
Less accumulated depreciation	75,000	
		112,000
Current assets		
Raw materials	7,650	
Finished goods	23,600	
Debtors	19,500	
Cash	4,300	
	55,050	
Current liabilities		
Creditors	6,800	
		48,250
		205,250
Financed by		
Share capital		150,000
Retained profit		55,250
		205,250

(b) **Finished products**

The sales director has estimated the following.

		Niks	*Args*
(i)	Demand for the company's products	4,500 units	4,000 units
(ii)	Selling price per unit	£32	£44
(iii)	Closing stock of finished products at 31 March 20X8	400 units	1,200 units
(iv)	Opening stock of finished products at 1 April 20X7	900 units	200 units
(v)	Unit cost of this opening stock	£20	£28
(vi)	Amount of plant capacity required for each unit of product		
	Machining	15 min	24 min
	Assembling	12 min	18 min
(vii)	Raw material content per unit of each product		
	Material A	1.5 kilos	0.5 kilos
	Material B	2.0 kilos	4.0 kilos

		Niks	Args
(viii)	Direct labour hours required per unit of each product	6 hours	9 hours

Finished goods are valued on a FIFO basis at full production cost.

(c) **Raw materials**

		Material A	*Material B*
(i)	Closing stock requirement in kilos at 31.3.X8	600	1,000
(ii)	Opening stock at 1 April 20X7 in kilos	1,100	6,000
(iii)	Budgeted cost of raw materials per kilo	£1.50	£1.00

Actual costs per kilo of opening stocks are as budgeted cost for the coming year.

(d) **Direct labour**

The standard wage rate of direct labour is £1.60 per hour.

(e) **Production overhead**

Production overhead is absorbed on the basis of machining hours, with separate absorption rates for each department. Overheads in the machining department are anticipated to be £39,500, while in the assembling department they are anticipated to be £18,650.

Depreciation is taken at 5% straight line on plant and equipment. A machine costing the company £20,000 is due to be installed on 1 October 20X7 in the machining department, which already has machinery installed to the value of £100,000 (at cost). Land worth £180,000 is to be acquired in December 20X7.

(f) Selling and administration expenses are expected to be £30,400.

(g) There is no opening or closing work in progress and inflation should be ignored.

(h) **Budgeted cash flows** are as follows.

	Quarter 1	*Quarter 2*	*Quarter 3*	*Quarter 4*
Receipts from customers	70,000	100,000	100,000	40,000
Payments:				
Materials	7,000	9,000	10,000	5,000
Wages	33,000	20,000	11,000	15,000
Other costs and expenses	10,000	100,000	205,000	5,000

Required

Prepare the following for the year ended 31 March 20X8 for Plagued Engineering Ltd.

(a) Sales budget
(b) Production budget (in quantities)
(c) Plant utilisation budget
(d) Direct materials usage budget
(e) Direct labour budget
(f) Production overhead budget
(g) Computation of the factory cost per unit for each product
(h) Direct materials purchases budget
(i) Cost of goods sold budget
(j) Master budget

6.2 SOLUTION

(a) **Sales budget**

	Market demand	*Selling price*	*Sales value*
	Units	£	£
Niks	4,500	32.00	144,000
Args	4,000	44.00	176,000
			320,000

(b) **Production budget**

	Niks	*Args*
	Units	Units
Sales requirement	4,500	4,000
(Decrease)/increase in finished goods stock	(500)	1,000
Production requirement	4,000	5,000

(c) **Plant utilisation budget**

Product		*Machining*		*Assembling*	
	Units	Hours per unit	Total hours	Hours per unit	Total hours
Niks	4,000	0.25	1,000	0.20	800
Args	5,000	0.40	2,000	0.30	1,500
			3,000		2,300

(d) **Direct materials usage budget**

	Material A	*Material B*
	kg	kg
Required for production:		
Niks: 4,000 × 1.5 kilos	6,000	-
4,000 × 2.0 kilos	-	8,000
Args: 5,000 × 0.5 kilos	2,500	-
5,000 × 4.0 kilos	-	20,000
Material usage	8,500	28,000
Unit cost	£1.50 per kilo	£1.00 per kilo
Cost of materials used	£12,750	£28,000

(e) **Direct labour budget**

Product	*Production*	*Hours required per unit*		*Rate per hour*	*Cost*
	Units		Total hours	£	£
Niks	4,000	6	24,000	1.60	38,400
Args	5,000	9	45,000	1.60	72,000
				Total direct wages	110,400

(f) **Production overhead budget**

	Machining dept	*Assembling dept*
	£	£
Production overhead allocated and apportioned (excluding depreciation)	39,500	18,650
Depreciation costs		
(i) Existing plant: (5% of £100,000 in machining)	5,000	
(5% of £87,000 in assembly)		4,350
(ii) Proposed plant: (5% of $^{6}/_{12}$ × £20,000)	500	
Total production overhead	45,000	23,000
Total machine hours (see (c))	3,000 hrs	2,300 hrs
Absorption rate per machine hour	£15	£10

(g) **Cost of finished goods**

			Niks		Args
			£		£
Direct material	A	1.5 kg × £1.50	2.25	0.5 kg × £1.50	0.75
	B	2.0 kg × £1.00	2.00	4.0 kg × £1.00	4.00
Direct labour		6 hrs × £1.60	9.60	9 hrs × £1.60	14.40
Production overhead					
Machining department		15 mins at £15 per hr	3.75	24 min at £15 per hr	6.00
Assembling department		12 mins at £10 per hr	2.00	18 mins at £10 per hr	3.00
Production cost per unit			19.60		28.15

(h) **Direct material purchases budget**

	A	B
	kg	kg
Closing stock required	600	1,000
Production requirements	8,500	28,000
	9,100	29,000
Less opening stock	1,100	6,000
Purchase requirements	8,000	23,000
Cost per unit	£1.50	£1.00
Purchase costs	£12,000	£23,000

(i) **Cost of goods sold budget** (Using FIFO)

	Niks			Args		
	Units		£	Units		£
Opening stocks	900	(× £20.00)	18,000	200	(× £28.00)	5,600
Cost of production	4,000	(× £19.60)	78,400	5,000	(× £28.15)	140,750
	4,900		96,400	5,200		146,350
Less closing stocks	400	(× £19.60)	7,840	1,200	(× £28.15)	33,780
Cost of sales	4,500		88,560	4,000		112,570

Notes

(i) The cost of sales of Niks = 900 units at £20 each plus 3,600 units at £19.60 each.

(ii) The cost of sales of Args = 200 units at £28 each plus 3,800 units at £28.15 each.

(j) **MASTER BUDGET**

Cash budget for year to 31.3.X8

	Quarter 1	Quarter 2	Quarter 3	Quarter 4	Total
	£	£	£	£	£
Receipts	70,000	100,000	100,000	40,000	310,000
Payments					
Materials	7,000	9,000	10,000	5,000	31,000
Labour	33,000	20,000	11,000	15,000	79,000
Other costs and expenses	10,000	100,000	205,000	5,000	320,000
	50,000	129,000	226,000	25,000	430,000
Receipts less payments	20,000	(29,000)	(126,000)	15,000	(120,000)
Opening cash balance b/f	4,300	24,300	(4,700)	(130,700)	4,300
Closing cash balance c/f	24,300	(4,700)	(130,700)	(115,700)	(115,700)

Budgeted profit and loss account for year to 31.3.X8

	Niks	Args	Total
	£	£	£
Sales	144,000	176,000	320,000
Less cost of sales	88,560	112,570	201,130
Gross profit	55,440	63,430	118,870
Less selling and administration			30,400
Net profit			88,470

Note. There will be no under-/over-absorbed production overhead in the budgeted profit and loss account.

Budgeted balance sheet at 31.3.X8

	£	£	£
Fixed assets			
Land and buildings (W1)			225,000
Plant and equipment at cost (W2)		207,000	
Less accumulated depreciation (W3)		84,850	
			122,150
			347,150
Current assets			
Raw materials (W4)		1,900	
Finished goods (W5)		41,620	
Debtors (W6)		29,500	
		73,020	
Current liabilities			
Creditors (W7)	10,750		
Bank overdraft (W8)	115,700		
		126,450	
Net current liabilities			(53,430)
			293,720
			£
Financed by			
Share capital			150,000
Retained profit (W9)			143,720
			293,720

Workings

1 Opening balance at 1.4.X7 + addition = cost at 31.3.X8
$\therefore$£(45,000 + 180,000) = £225,000

2 Opening balance at 1.4.X7 + addition = cost at 31.3.X8
$\therefore$£(187,000 + 20,000) = £207,000

3 Opening balance at 1.4.X7 + addition in period ((f)(i) and (ii) of solution) = accumulated depreciation at 31.3.X8
$\therefore$£(75,000 + 5,000 + 4,350 + 500) = £84,850

4

	A	*B*	*Total*
Closing stock (kgs)	600	1,000	
Cost per kg	× £1.50	× £1.00	
Value of closing stock	£900	£1,000	£1,900

5

	Niks	*Args*	*Total*
Closing stock (units)	400	1,200	
Cost per unit ((g) of solution)	× £19.60	× £28.15	
	£7,840	£33,780	£41,620

6 Opening balance + sales ((a) of solution) – receipts (from cash budget) = closing balance
$\therefore$ £(19,500 + 320,000 – 310,000) = £29,500

7

		£	£
Opening balance at 1.4.X7			6,800
Land		180,000	
Machine		20,000	
Labour		110,400	
Production overhead	39,500		
	18,650		
		58,150	
Materials	12,000		
	23,000		
		35,000	
Expenses		30,400	
			433,950
			440,750
Cash payments (from cash budget)			(430,000)
Closing balance at 31.3.X8			10,750

8 From cash budget £115,750 overdrawn

9 Retained profit b/f + profit for year = retained profit c/f
∴ £(55,250 + 88,470) = £143,720.

Exam focus point

You need to be able to transfer **accurate** information **quickly** when building up a master budget, so make sure that you are happy with the techniques covered in this section.

Chapter roundup

- A budget is a **quantified plan of action** for a forthcoming accounting period.
- The **budget manual** is a collection of instructions governing the responsibilities of persons and the procedures, forms and records relating to the preparation and use of budgetary data.
- The **budget committee** is the coordinating body in the preparation and administration of budgets.
- The **budget preparation process** is as follows.
  - Communicating details of the budget policy and budget guidelines.
  - Determining the factor that restricts output
  - Preparation of the sales budget
  - Initial preparation of budgets
  - Negotiation of budgets with superiors
  - Coordination and review of budgets
  - Final acceptance of the budgets
  - Budget review
- The **principal budget factor** should be identified at the beginning of the budgetary process, and the budget for this is prepared before all the others.
- Once prepared, the **subsidiary budgets** must be reviewed to ensure they are consistent with one another.
- **Cash budgets** show the expected receipts and payments during a budget period and are a vital management control tool, especially during times of recession.
- The profit or loss made by an organisation during an accounting period does not reflect its cash flow position.
- The **master budget** consists of a budgeted profit and loss account, a budgeted balance sheet and a cash budget.

Quick quiz

1 List six functions of the budget committee.

2 *Put the following steps involved in the preparation of a budget in the correct order.*

- Negotiation of budgets with superiors
- Determining the factor that restricts output
- Final acceptance of the budget
- Initial preparation of other budgets
- Communicating details of budget policy and budget guidelines
- Preparation of the budget for the principal budget factor
- Coordination of budgets
- Budget review

3 Which of the following could not be a principal budget factor?

(a) Cash
(b) Machine capacity
(c) Sales demand
(d) Selling price
(e) Labour
(f) Premises

4 *Fill in the blanks.*

When preparing a production budget, the quantity to be produced is equal to sales .... opening stock .... closing stock.

5 A production process is set up to manufacture product X. 10% of total output is rejected because of quality problems. Sales demand is 17,500 units. How many units must be produced?

6 Which of the following should be included in a cash budget?

	Include	Do not include
Funds from the issue of share capital		
Revaluation of a fixed asset		
Receipts of dividends from outside the business		
Depreciation of production machinery		
Bad debts written off		
Repayment of a bank loan		

7 *Match the appropriate management action to the cash position shown by a cash budget.*

Position

(a) Short-term surplus
(b) Short-term deficit
(c) Long-term surplus
(d) Long-term deficit

Action

1 Diversity
2 Issue share capital
3 Reduce debtors
4 Increase debtors
5 Increase creditors
6 Expand

Answers to quick quiz

1
- Coordination of budget preparation, including the issue of the budget manual
- Issuing of timetables for the preparation of functional budgets
- Allocation of responsibilities for the preparation of functional budgets
- Provision of information to assist in the preparation of budgets
- Communication of final budgets to the appropriate managers
- Comparison of actual results with budget and the investigation of variances
- Continuous assessment of the budgeting and planning process

2
- Communicating details of budget policy and budget guidelines
- Determining the factor that restricts output
- Preparation of the budget for the principal budget factor
- Initial preparation of other budgets
- Negotiation of budgets with superiors
- Coordination of budgets
- Final acceptance of the budget
- Budget review

3 (d)

4 Quantity to be produced = sales – opening stock + closing stock

5 Good output = 90% of total production
∴ 17,500 = 0.9 x total production
∴ 17,500/0.9 = total production
∴ 19,445 units = total production

6

	Include	Do not include
Funds from the issue of share capital	✓	
Revaluation of a fixed asset		✓
Receipts of dividends from outside the business	✓	
Depreciation of production machinery		✓
Bad debts written off		✓
Repayment of a bank loan	✓	

7 (a) 4
(b) 3, 5
(c) 1, 6
(d) 2

Now try the question below from the Exam Question Bank

Question to try	Level	Marks	Time
13	Exam	25	45 mins

Chapter 11

BUDGETARY CONTROL AND THE BEHAVIOURAL IMPLICATIONS OF BUDGETING

	Topic list	Syllabus reference
1	Fixed and flexible budgets	9(b)
2	Flexible budgets and budgetary control	9(b), 9(d), 9(f)
3	Behavioural implications of budgeting	6(d), 6(f), 9(g)
4	Participation and performance evaluation	6(d), 6(f), 9(g)
5	The use of budgets as targets	6(d), 6(f), 9(g)
6	The management accountant and motivation	6(d), 6(f), 9(g)

Introduction

You should now be able to prepare functional budgets and a master budget and have a firm grasp of the budgeting process. This chapter continues the budgeting theme and looks at two particular issues.

Flexible budgets are vital in management planning and control and this chapter shows how they are constructed and their use in the overall budgetary control process.

The chapter then moves on to consider the **behavioural implications** of operating a budgetary control system. There has been a great deal of research into the behavioural implications of budgeting and, as in all studies of human behaviour, it is difficult to draw concrete conclusions. There is, however, one point which is agreed: budgeting is more than a mathematical technique.

While Chapter 13 details the **quantitative techniques** which the management accountant can use in the budgeting process, Chapter 12 examines alternative budgeting systems to the traditional one outlined in Chapter 10.

Study guide

Section 18 – Costing systems: context and framework

- Broadly outline the implications of different costing approaches for performance evaluation

Section 23 – Budget planning and control I

- Explain the process of participation in budget setting and how this can address motivational problems

Section 24 – Budget planning and control II

- Prepare and evaluate fixed and flexible budgets and evaluate the resulting variances
- Prepare flexed budgets when standard fixed overhead absorption is employed
- Assess the behavioural implications of budget control and performance evaluation, including participation in budget setting

Exam guide

Given that the behavioural implications of budgeting and budgetary control is a key area of the syllabus, a discursive Section B question could focus on the behavioural aspects of budgeting. A computational question could require you to produce a flexible budget.

1 FIXED AND FLEXIBLE BUDGETS

Fixed budgets

KEY TERM

A **fixed budget** is a budget which is designed to remain unchanged regardless of the volume of output or sales achieved.

1.1 The master budget prepared before the beginning of the budget period is known as the **fixed budget**. The term 'fixed' means the following.

(a) The budget is **prepared on the basis of an estimated volume of production** and an **estimated volume of sales**, but no plans are made for the event that actual volumes of production and sales may differ from budgeted volumes.

(b) When actual volumes of production and sales during a control period (month or four weeks or quarter) are achieved, a fixed budget is **not adjusted (in retrospect) to the new levels of activity.**

1.2 The major purpose of a fixed budget is at the planning stage, when it seeks to define the broad objectives of the organisation.

Flexible budgets

KEY TERM

A **flexible budget** is a budget which, by recognising different cost behaviour patterns, is designed to change as volumes of output change.

1.3 Flexible budgets may be used in one of two ways.

(a) **At the planning stage**. For example, suppose that a company expects to sell 10,000 units of output during the next year. A master budget (the fixed budget) would be prepared on the basis of these expected volumes. However, if the company thinks that output and sales might be as low as 8,000 units or as high as 12,000 units, it may prepare **contingency flexible budgets**, at volumes of, say 8,000, 9,000, 11,000 and 12,000 units and then assess the possible outcomes.

(b) **Retrospectively**. At the end of each month (control period) or year, the results that should have been achieved given the actual circumstances (the flexible budget) can be compared with the actual results. As we shall see, flexible budgets are an essential factor in **budgetary control**.

1.4 Before we look at how flexible budgets are used for budgetary control purposes, we need to see how they are prepared. **Flexible budgeting uses the principles of marginal costing**. In estimating future costs it is often necessary to begin by looking at cost behaviour in the

past. For costs which are wholly fixed or wholly variable no problem arises. But costs which have behaved in the past as mixed costs are more difficult to deal with. A technique for estimating the level of such costs is called the **high-low method**.

Knowledge brought forward from earlier studies

The high-low method

- Review records of costs in previous periods and select the period with the highest activity level and the period with the lowest activity level.
- If necessary, adjust costs to the same level by means of a price index.
- Total cost of high activity level minus total cost of low activity level = variable cost of difference in activity levels.
- Determine the fixed cost by substitution.

Question 1

Rice and Faull Ltd has recorded the following total costs during the last five years.

Year	*Output volume*	*Total cost*	*Average price level index*
	Units	£	
20X0	65,000	145,000	100
20X1	80,000	179,000	112
20X2	90,000	209,100	123
20X3	60,000	201,600	144
20X4	75,000	248,000	160

Required

Calculate the expected costs in 20X5 if output is 85,000 units and the average price level index is 180. (In other words do not ignore inflation!)

Answer

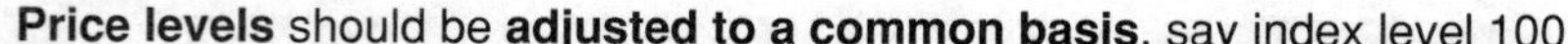

Price levels should be **adjusted to a common basis**, say index level 100.

(a)

	Output	*Total cost*	*Cost at price level index = 100*
		£	£
High level	90,000 units	209,100 × (100/123)	= 170,000
Low level	60,000 units	201,600 × (100/144)	= 140,000
Variable cost	30,000 units		= 30,000

The **variable cost** is therefore £1 per unit.

(b) **Use the variable cost to determine the fixed cost.**

	£
Total cost of 90,000 units (Index 100)	170,000
Variable cost of 90,000 units (× £1)	90,000
Fixed costs (Index 100)	80,000

(c) **Costs in 20X5 for 85,000 units will be as follows.**

	£
Variable costs (Index 100)	85,000
Fixed costs (Index 100)	80,000
Total costs (Index 100)	165,000

At 20X5 price levels (Index 180) = £165,000 ×(180/100) = £297,000

1.5 We can now look at a full example of preparing a flexible budget.

1.6 EXAMPLE: PREPARING A FLEXIBLE BUDGET

(a) Prepare a budget for 20X6 for the direct labour costs and overhead expenses of a production department at the activity levels of 80%, 90% and 100%, using the information listed below and ignoring inflation.

(i) The direct labour hourly rate is expected to be £3.75.

(ii) 100% activity represents 60,000 direct labour hours.

(iii)

Variable indirect labour cost	£0.75 per direct labour hour
Variable consumable supplies cost	£0.375 per direct labour hour
Variable canteen cost	6% of direct and indirect labour costs

(iv) Semi-variable costs are expected to relate to the direct labour hours in the same manner as for the last five years.

Year	*Direct labour hours*	*Semi-variable costs*
		£
20X1	64,000	20,800
20X2	59,000	19,800
20X3	53,000	18,600
20X4	49,000	17,800
20X5	40,000 (estimate)	16,000 (estimate)

(v) *Fixed costs*

	£
Depreciation	18,000
Maintenance	10,000
Insurance	4,000
Rates	15,000
Management salaries	25,000

(b) Calculate the **budget cost allowance (ie expected expenditure)** or **flexed budget** for 20X6 assuming that 57,000 direct labour hours are worked.

1.7 SOLUTION

(a)

	80% level *48,000 hrs*	*90% level* *54,000 hrs*	*100% level* *60,000 hrs*
	£'000	£'000	£'000
Direct labour	180.00	202.50	225.0
Other variable costs			
Indirect labour	36.00	40.50	45.0
Consumable supplies	18.00	20.25	22.5
Canteen etc	12.96	14.58	16.2
Total variable costs (£5.145 per hour)	246.96	277.83	308.7
Semi-variable costs (W)	17.60	18.80	20.0
Fixed costs			
Depreciation	18.00	18.00	18.0
Maintenance	10.00	10.00	10.0
Insurance	4.00	4.00	4.0
Rates	15.00	15.00	15.0
Management salaries	25.00	25.00	25.0
Budgeted costs	336.56	368.63	400.7

Working

Using the **high/low method:**

	£
Total cost of 64,000 hours	20,800
Total cost of 40,000 hours	16,000
Variable cost of 24,000 hours	4,800
Variable cost per hour (£4,800/24,000)	£0.20

	£
Total cost of 64,000 hours	20,800
Variable cost of 64,000 hours (× £0.20)	12,800
Fixed costs	8,000

Semi-variable costs are calculated as follows.

			£
60,000 hours	(60,000 × £0.20) + £8,000	=	20,000
54,000 hours	(54,000 × £0.20) + £8,000	=	18,800
48,000 hours	(48,000 × £0.20) + £8,000	=	17,600

(b) The **budget cost allowance** for 57,000 direct labour hours of work would be as follows.

		£
Variable costs	(57,000 × £5.145)	293,265
Semi-variable costs	(£8,000 + (57,000 × £0.20))	19,400
Fixed costs		72,000
		384,665

2 FLEXIBLE BUDGETS AND BUDGETARY CONTROL

KEY TERM

Budgetary control involves drawing up budgets for the areas of responsibility for individual managers (for example production managers, purchasing managers and so on) and of regularly comparing actual results against expected results. The differences between actual results and expected results are called **variances** and these are used to provide a guideline for control action by individual managers.

2.1 Note that individual managers are held responsible for investigating differences between budgeted and actual results, and are then expected to take corrective action or amend the plan in the light of actual events.

2.2 The wrong approach to budgetary control is to compare actual results against a fixed budget. Suppose that Windy Ltd manufactures a single product, the cloud. Budgeted results and actual results for June 20X2 are shown below.

	Budget	*Actual results*	*Variance*
Production and sales of the cloud (units)	2,000	3,000	
	£	£	£
Sales revenue (a)	20,000	30,000	10,000 (F)
Direct materials	6,000	8,500	2,500 (A)
Direct labour	4,000	4,500	500 (A)
Maintenance	1,000	1,400	400 (A)
Depreciation	2,000	2,200	200 (A)
Rent and rates	1,500	1,600	100 (A)
Other costs	3,600	5,000	1,400 (A)
Total costs (b)	18,100	23,200	5,100
Profit (a) – (b)	1,900	6,800	4,900 (F)

2.3 (a) Here the variances are meaningless for control purposes. Costs were higher than budget because the output volume was also higher; variable costs would be expected to increase above the costs budgeted in the fixed budget. There is no information to show whether control action is needed for any aspect of costs or revenue.

(b) For control purposes, it is necessary to know the following.

(i) Were actual costs higher than they should have been to produce and sell 3,000 clouds?
(ii) Was actual revenue satisfactory from the sale of 3,000 clouds?

2.4 The **correct approach to budgetary control** is as follows.

- **Identify fixed and variable costs**
- **Produce a flexible budget using marginal costing techniques**

2.5 Let's suppose that we have the following estimates of cost behaviour for Windy Ltd.

(a) Direct materials, direct labour and maintenance costs are variable.
(b) Rent and rates and depreciation are fixed costs.
(c) Other costs consist of fixed costs of £1,600 plus a variable cost of £1 per unit made and sold.

2.6 Now that the cost behaviour patterns are known, a **budget cost allowance** can be calculated for each item of expenditure. This allowance is shown in a flexible budget as the expected expenditure on each item for the relevant level of activity. The budget cost allowances are calculated as follows.

(a) Variable cost allowances = original budgets × (3,000 units/2,000 units)
eg material cost allowance = £6,000 × $^3/_2$ = £9,000

(b) Fixed cost allowances = as original budget

(c) Semi-fixed cost allowances = original budgeted fixed costs + (3,000 units × variable cost per unit)

eg other cost allowances = £1,600 + (3,000 × £1) = £4,600

2.7 The budgetary control analysis should be as follows.

	Fixed budget (a)	*Flexible budget (b)*	*Actual results (c)*	*Budget variance (b) - (c)*
Production and sales (units)	2,000	3,000	3,000	
	£	£	£	£
Sales revenue	20,000	30,000	30,000	0
Variable costs				
Direct materials	6,000	9,000	8,500	500 (F)
Direct labour	4,000	6,000	4,500	1,500 (F)
Maintenance	1,000	1,500	1,400	100 (F)
Semi-variable costs				
Other costs	3,600	4,600	5,000	400 (A)
Fixed costs				
Depreciation	2,000	2,000	2,200	200 (A)
Rent and rates	1,500	1,500	1,600	100 (A)
Total costs	18,100	24,600	23,200	1,400 (F)
Profit	1,900	5,400	6,800	1,400 (F)

Note. **(F) denotes a favourable variance** and **(A) an adverse or unfavourable variance.**

2.8 We can **analyse** the above as follows.

(a) In selling 3,000 units the expected profit should have been, not the fixed budget profit of £1,900, but the flexible budget profit of £5,400. Instead, actual profit was £6,800 ie £1,400 more than we should have expected. One of the reasons for the improvement is that, **given output and sales** of 3,000 units, **costs were lower than expected** (and sales revenue exactly as expected).

	£
Direct materials cost variance	500 (F)
Direct labour cost variance	1,500 (F)
Maintenance cost variance	100 (F)
Other costs variance	400 (A)
Fixed cost variances	
Depreciation	200 (A)
Rent and rates	100 (A)
	1,400 (F)

(b) Another reason for the improvement in profit above the fixed budget profit is the **sales volume**. Windy Ltd sold 3,000 clouds instead of 2,000 clouds.

	£	£
Sales revenue increased by		10,000
Variable costs increased by:		
direct materials	3,000	
direct labour	2,000	
Maintenance	500	
variable element of other costs	1,000	
Fixed costs are unchanged		6,500
Profit increased by		3,500

Profit was therefore increased by £3,500 because sales volumes increased.

(c) A full variance analysis statement would be as follows.

	£	£
Fixed budget profit		1,900
Variances		
Sales volume	3,500 (F)	
Direct materials cost	500 (F)	
Direct labour cost	1,500 (F)	
Maintenance cost	100 (F)	
Other costs	400 (A)	
Depreciation	200 (A)	
Rent and rates	100 (A)	
		4,900 (F)
Actual profit		6,800

2.9 If management believes that any of these variances are large enough to justify it, they will investigate the reasons for them to see whether any corrective action is necessary or whether the plan needs amending in the light of actual events.

Question 2

The budgeted and actual results of Crunch Ltd for September were as follows. The company uses a marginal costing system. There were no opening or closing stocks.

Sales and production	*Fixed budget* 1,000 units		*Actual* 700 units	
	£	£	£	£
Sales		20,000		14,200
Variable cost of sales				
Direct materials	8,000		5,200	
Direct labour	4,000		3,100	
Variable overhead	2,000		1,500	
		14,000		9,800
Contribution		6,000		4,400
Fixed costs		5,000		5,400
Profit/(loss)		1,000		(1,000)

Required

Prepare a budget that will be useful for management control purposes.

Answer

We need to prepare a **flexible budget for 700 units.**

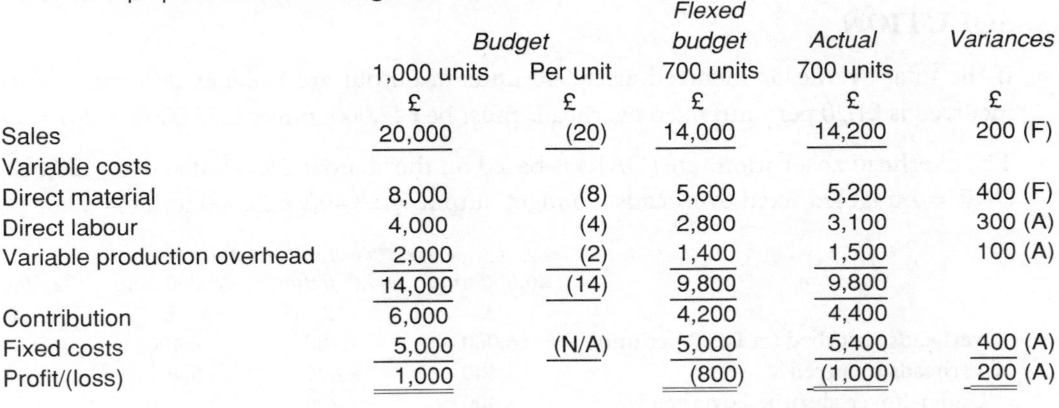

	Budget 1,000 units	Per unit	*Flexed budget* 700 units	*Actual* 700 units	*Variances*
	£	£	£	£	£
Sales	20,000	(20)	14,000	14,200	200 (F)
Variable costs					
Direct material	8,000	(8)	5,600	5,200	400 (F)
Direct labour	4,000	(4)	2,800	3,100	300 (A)
Variable production overhead	2,000	(2)	1,400	1,500	100 (A)
	14,000	(14)	9,800	9,800	
Contribution	6,000		4,200	4,400	
Fixed costs	5,000	(N/A)	5,000	5,400	400 (A)
Profit/(loss)	1,000		(800)	(1,000)	200 (A)

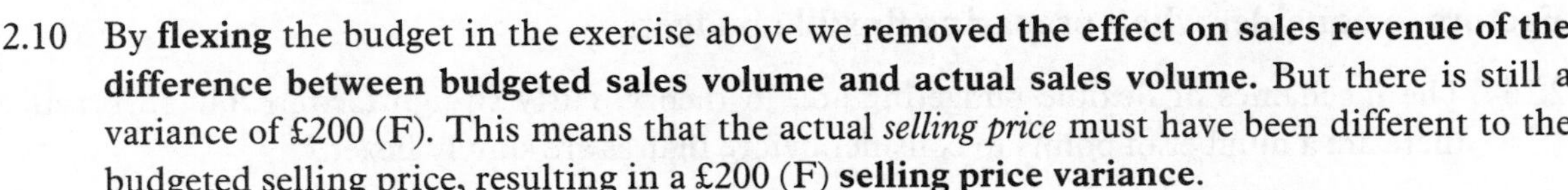

2.10 By **flexing** the budget in the exercise above we **removed the effect on sales revenue of the difference between budgeted sales volume and actual sales volume.** But there is still a variance of £200 (F). This means that the actual *selling price* must have been different to the budgeted selling price, resulting in a £200 (F) **selling price variance.**

Preparing a flexible budget - absorption costing

2.11 Flexible budgeting allows you to see what total costs should be at differing levels of output. Since fixed costs are the same at all levels of output (within a normal or relevant range of activity), only variable costs vary with increases or decreases in the level of activity.

2.12 Although **fixed costs *incurred* do not change as the level of activity increases or decreases,** if an organisation uses absorption costing the **amount of fixed costs absorbed will vary.** This is because the fixed overhead **absorption rate** is predetermined at the start of the budget period, and is **based on the expected level of activity in the *fixed* budget.**

2.13 Suppose that a company which has an absorption costing system budgets for fixed production overhead of £4,000 and output of 1,000 units. The overhead absorption rate will therefore be £4 per unit. If the company decides to prepare a fixed master budget and also flexible budgets at output levels of 900 units and 1,100 units, the overhead costs in the budget would be as follows.

	Flexible budget 900 units	*Fixed budget 1,000 units*	*Flexible budget 1,100 units*
	£	£	£
Overhead cost of production			
(× £4 per unit) - absorbed	3,600	4,000	4,400
(Under-)/over-absorbed overhead	(400)	-	400
Overhead incurred	4,000	4,000	4,000

2.14 EXAMPLE: FLEXIBLE BUDGETS AND ABSORPTION COSTING

An organisation's management requires a flexible overhead budget for levels of output of 20,000, 24,000 and 32,000 units respectively. The standard of activity has been set at 28,000 units. Total overhead incurred at this level would be £42,000 of which variable overhead would be £1.20 per unit.

Task

Calculate the under-/over-absorbed fixed overheads at each level of activity.

2.15 SOLUTION

If the total overheads incurred at 28,000 units of output are £42,000, and variable overhead incurred is £1.20 per unit, fixed overheads must be £42,000 minus £(28,000 × 1.20) = £8,400.

The overhead absorption rate (OAR) is based on the standard level of activity, 28,000 units. OAR = budgeted fixed overheads ÷ budget output = £8,400 ÷ 28,000 units = £0.30 per unit

	Level of output and sales			
	20,000 units	*24,000 units*	*28,000 units*	*32,000 units*
	£	£	£	£
Overheads absorbed (at £0.30 per unit)	6,000	7,200	8,400	9,600
Overheads incurred	8,400	8,400	8,400	8,400
(Under-)/over-absorbed overheads	(2,400)	(1,200)	0	1,200

Factors to consider when preparing flexible budgets

2.16 The mechanics of flexible budgeting are, in theory, fairly straightforward but in practice there are a number of points to consider before figures are simply flexed.

(a) Splitting mixed costs is not always straightforward.

(b) Fixed costs may behave in a step-line fashion as activity levels increase/decrease.

(c) Account must be taken of the assumptions upon which the original fixed budget was based. Such assumptions might include the constraint posed by limiting factors, the rate of inflation, judgements about future uncertainty, the demand for the organisation's products and so on.

(d) 'Flexing ... can incorporate changes for any factor which differs from what applied when the budget was prepared, for example different states of the economy. In this way, flexing is saying "If I knew then what I know now what budget would I set?" It is a useful concept but can lead to some concern, if taken to extremes, because managers can be confused and frustrated if faced throughout the year with a possibly moving target.'

(Mike Tayles, *ACCA Students Newsletter*, December 1998)

3 BEHAVIOURAL IMPLICATIONS OF BUDGETING

3.1 The purpose of a budgetary control system is to assist management in planning and controlling the resources of their organisation by providing appropriate control information. The information will only be valuable, however, if it is interpreted correctly and used purposefully by managers *and* employees.

3.2 The correct use of control information therefore depends not only on the content of the information itself, but also on the behaviour of its recipients. This is because control in business is exercised by people. Their attitude to control information will colour their views on what they should do with it and a number of behavioural problems can arise.

(a) The **managers who set the budget** or standards are **often not the managers** who are then made **responsible for achieving budget targets.**

(b) The **goals of the organisation as a whole**, as expressed in a budget, **may not coincide with the personal aspirations of individual managers**.

(c) **Control is applied at different stages by different people**. A supervisor might get weekly control reports, and act on them; his superior might get monthly control reports, and decide to take different control action. Different managers can get in each others' way, and resent the interference from others.

Motivation

3.3 Motivation is what makes people behave in the way that they do. It comes from individual attitudes, or group attitudes. Individuals will be motivated by personal desires and interests. These may be in line with the objectives of the organisation, and some people 'live for their jobs'. Other individuals see their job as a chore, and their motivations will be unrelated to the objectives of the organisation they work for.

3.4 It is therefore vital that the goals of management and the employees harmonise with the goals of the organisation as a whole. This is known as goal congruence. Although obtaining goal congruence is essentially a behavioural problem, **it is possible to design and run a budgetary control system which will go some way towards ensuring that goal congruence is achieved**. Managers and employees must therefore be favourably disposed towards the budgetary control system so that it can operate efficiently.

3.5 The management accountant should therefore try to ensure that employees have positive attitudes towards **setting budgets, implementing budgets** (that is, putting the organisation's plans into practice) and feedback of results (**control information**).

Poor attitudes when setting budgets

3.6 But poor attitudes or hostile behaviour towards the budgetary control system can begin at the **planning stage. If managers are involved in preparing a budget** the following may happen.

(a) Managers may **complain that they are too busy** to spend much time on budgeting.

(b) They may **build 'slack' into their expenditure estimates**.

(c) They may argue that **formalising a budget plan on paper is too restricting** and that managers should be allowed flexibility in the decisions they take.

(d) They may set budgets for their budget centre and **not coordinate** their own plans with those of other budget centres.

(e) They may **base future plans on past results**, instead of using the opportunity for formalised planning to look at alternative options and new ideas.

3.7 On the other hand, **managers may not be involved in the budgeting process**. Organisational goals may not be communicated to them and they might have their budget decided for them by senior management or administrative decision. It is **hard for people to be motivated to achieve targets set by someone else.**

Poor attitudes when putting plans into action

3.8 Poor attitudes also arise **when a budget is implemented.**

(a) Managers might **put in only just enough effort** to achieve budget targets, without trying to beat targets.

(b) A formal budget might **encourage rigidity and discourage flexibility.**

(c) **Short-term planning** in a budget **can draw attention away from the longer-term consequences** of decisions.

(d) There might be **minimal cooperation and communication** between managers.

(e) Managers will often try to make sure that they **spend up to their full budget allowance, and do not overspend,** so that they will not be accused of having asked for too much spending allowance in the first place.

Poor attitudes and the use of control information

3.9 The **attitude of managers towards the accounting control information** they receive **might reduce the information's effectiveness.**

(a) Management accounting control reports could well be seen as having a relatively **low priority** in the list of management tasks. Managers might take the view that they have more pressing jobs on hand than looking at routine control reports.

(b) Managers might **resent control information**; they may see it as **part of a system of trying to find fault with their work.** This resentment is likely to be particularly strong when budgets or standards are imposed on managers without allowing them to participate in the budget-setting process.

(c) If budgets are seen as **pressure devices** to push managers into doing better, control reports will be resented.

(d) Managers **may not understand the information** in the control reports, because they are unfamiliar with accounting terminology or principles.

(e) Managers might have a **false sense of what their objectives should be.** A production manager might consider it more important to maintain quality standards regardless of cost. He would then dismiss adverse expenditure variances as inevitable and unavoidable.

(f) **If there are flaws in the system of recording actual costs,** managers will dismiss control information as unreliable.

(g) **Control information** might be **received weeks after the end of the** period to which it relates, in which case managers might regard it as out-of-date and no longer useful.

(h) Managers might be **held responsible for variances outside their control.**

3.10 It is therefore obvious that accountants and senior management should try to implement systems that are acceptable to budget holders and which produce positive effects.

Pay as a motivator

3.11 Many researchers agree that **pay can be an important motivator,** when there is a formal link between higher pay (or other rewards, such as promotion) and achieving budget targets. Individuals are likely to work harder to achieve budget if they know that they will be rewarded for their successful efforts. There are, however, problems with using pay as an incentive.

(a) A serious problem that can arise is that **formal reward and performance evaluation systems can encourage dysfunctional behaviour**. Many investigations have noted the tendency of managers to pad their budgets either in anticipation of cuts by superiors or to make the subsequent variances more favourable. And there are numerous examples of managers making decisions in response to performance indices, even though the decisions are contrary to the wider purposes of the organisation.

(b) The targets must be challenging but fair, otherwise individuals will become dissatisfied. **Pay can be a demotivator as well as a motivator**!

4 PARTICIPATION AND PERFORMANCE EVALUATION

Participation

4.1 It has been argued that **participation** in the budgeting process **will improve motivation** and so will improve the quality of budget decisions and the efforts of individuals to achieve their budget targets (although obviously this will depend on the personality of the individual, the nature of the task (narrowly defined or flexible) and the organisational culture).

4.2 There are basically two ways in which a budget can be set: from the **top down** (imposed budget) or from the **bottom up** (participatory budget).

Imposed style of budgeting

4.3 In this approach to budgeting, **top management prepare a budget with little or no input from operating personnel** which is then imposed upon the employees who have to work to the budgeted figures.

4.4 The times when imposed budgets are effective are as follows.

- In newly-formed organisations
- In very small businesses
- During periods of economic hardship
- When operational managers lack budgeting skills
- When the organisation's different units require precise coordination

4.5 They are, of course, advantages and disadvantages to this style of setting budgets.

(a) **Advantages**

- Strategic plans are likely to be incorporated into planned activities.
- They enhance the coordination between the plans and objectives of divisions.
- They use senior management's awareness of total resource availability.
- They decrease the input from inexperienced or uninformed lower-level employees.
- They decrease the period of time taken to draw up the budgets.

(b) **Disadvantages**

- Dissatisfaction, defensiveness and low morale amongst employees.
- The feeling of team spirit may disappear.
- The acceptance of organisational goals and objectives could be limited
- The feeling of the budget as a punitive device could arise.
- Unachievable budgets for overseas divisions could result if consideration is not given to local operating and political environments.
- Lower-level management initiative may be stifled.

Participative style of budgeting

4.6 In this approach to budgeting, **budgets are developed by lower-level managers who then submit the budgets to their superiors**. The budgets are based on the lower-level managers' perceptions of what is achievable and the associated necessary resources.

4.7 **Participative budgets** are effective in the following circumstances.

- In well-established organisations
- In very large businesses
- During periods of economic affluence
- When operational managers have strong budgeting skills
- When the organisation's different units act autonomously

4.8 The **advantages** of participative budgets are as follows.

- They are based on information from employees most familiar with the department.
- Knowledge spread among several levels of management is pulled together.
- Morale and motivation is improved.
- They increase operational managers' commitment to organisational objectives.
- In general they are more realistic.
- Co-ordination between units is improved.
- Specific resource requirements are included.
- Senior managers' overview is mixed with operational level details.

4.9 There are, on the other hand, a number of **disadvantages** of participative budgets.

- They consume more time.
- Changes implemented by senior management may cause dissatisfaction.
- Budgets may be unachievable if managers' are not qualified to participate.
- They may cause managers to introduce budgetary slack.
- They can support 'empire building' by subordinates.
- An earlier start to the budgeting process could be required.

Negotiated style of budgeting

4.10 At the two extremes, budgets can be dictated from above or simply emerge from below but, in practice, different levels of management often agree budgets by a process of negotiation. In the imposed budget approach, operational managers will try to negotiate with senior managers the budget targets which they consider to be unreasonable or unrealistic. Likewise senior management usually review and revise budgets presented to them under a participative approach through a process of negotiation with lower level managers. **Final budgets are therefore most likely to lie between what top management would really like**

and what junior managers believe is feasible. The budgeting process is hence a **bargaining process** and it is this bargaining which is of vital importance, **determining whether the budget is an effective management tool or simply a clerical device**.

Performance evaluation

4.11 A very important **source of motivation to perform well** (to achieve budget targets, perhaps, or to eliminate variances) is, not surprisingly, being **kept informed about how actual results are progressing, and how actual results compare with target**. Individuals should not be kept in the dark about their performance.

The information fed back about actual results should have the qualities of good information.

(a) Reports should be clear and comprehensive.

(b) Significant variances should be highlighted for investigation.

(c) Reports should be timely, which means they must be produced in good time to allow the individual to take control action before any adverse results get much worse.

4.12 Surprisingly research evidence suggests that **all too often accounting performance measures lead to a lack of goal congruence**. Managers seek to improve their performance on the basis of the indicator used, even if this is not in the best interests of the organisation as a whole. For example, a production manager may be encouraged to achieve and maintain high production levels and to reduce costs, particularly if his or her bonus is linked to these factors. Such a manager is likely to be highly motivated. But the need to maintain high production levels could lead to high levels of slow-moving stock, resulting in an adverse effect on the company's cash flow.

4.13 The **impact of an accounting system on managerial performance** depends ultimately on how the information is used. Research by Hopwood has shown that there are three distinct ways of using budgetary information to evaluate managerial performance.

(a) **A budget constrained style of evaluation.** 'The manager's performance is primarily evaluated upon the basis of his ability to continually meet the budget on a short-term basis. This criterion of performance is stressed at the expense of other valued and important criteria and the manager will receive unfavourable feedback from his superior if, for instance, his actual costs exceed the budgeted costs, regardless of other considerations.'

(b) **A profit conscious style of evaluation.** 'The manager's performance is evaluated on the basis of his ability to increase the general effectiveness of his unit's operations in relation to the long-term purposes of the organisation. For instance, at the cost centre level one important aspect of this ability concerns the attention which he devotes to reducing long-run costs. For this purpose, however, the budgetary information has to be used with great care in a rather flexible manner.'

(c) **A non-accounting style of evaluation.** 'The budgetary information plays a relatively unimportant part in the superior's evaluation of the manager's performance.'

4.14 A summary of the effects of the three styles of evaluation is as follows.

	Style of evaluation		
	Budget constrained	*Profit conscious*	*Non-accounting*
Involvement with costs	HIGH	HIGH	LOW
Job-related tension	HIGH	MEDIUM	MEDIUM
Manipulation of the accounting reports	EXTENSIVE	LITTLE	LITTLE
Relations with the supervisor	POOR	GOOD	GOOD
Relations with colleagues	POOR	GOOD	GOOD

Research has shown no clear preference for one style over another.

Budgetary slack

KEY TERM

Budgetary slack is the difference between the minimum necessary costs and the costs built into the budget or actually incurred.

4.15 In the process of preparing budgets, managers might **deliberately overestimate costs and underestimate sales**, so that they will not be blamed in the future for overspending and poor results.

In controlling actual operations, managers must then **ensure that their spending rises to meet their budget**, otherwise they will be 'blamed' for careless budgeting.

4.16 A typical situation is for a manager to waste money on non-essential expenses so that he uses all his budget allowances. The reason behind his action is the fear that unless the allowance is fully spent it will be reduced in future periods thus making his job more difficult as the future reduced budgets will not be so easy to attain. Because inefficiency and slack are allowed for in budgets, achieving a budget target means only that costs have remained within the accepted levels of inefficient spending.

4.17 Conversely, it has been noted that, after a run of mediocre results, some managers deliberately overstate revenues and understate cost estimates, no doubt feeling the need to make an immediate favourable impact by promising better performance in the future. They may merely delay problems, however, as the managers may well be censured when they fail to hit these optimistic targets.

5 THE USE OF BUDGETS AS TARGETS

5.1 Once decided budgets become targets. As targets, they can motivate managers to achieve a high level of performance. But **how difficult should targets be**? And how might people react to targets of differing degrees of difficulty in achievement?

(a) There is likely to be a **demotivating** effect where an **ideal standard** of performance is set, because adverse efficiency variances will always be reported.

(b) A **low standard of efficiency** is also **demotivating**, because there is no sense of achievement in attaining the required standards.

(c) A **budgeted level of attainment** could be 'normal': that is, the **same as the level that has been achieved in the past**. Arguably, this level will be **too low**. It might **encourage budgetary slack**.

5.2 It has been argued that **each individual has a personal 'aspiration level'**. This is a level of performance in a task with which the individual is familiar, which the individual undertakes for himself to reach. This aspiration level might be quite challenging and if individuals in a work group all have similar aspiration levels it should be possible to incorporate these levels within the official operating standards.

5.3 Some care should be taken, however, in applying this.

(a) If a manager's **tendency to achieve success is stronger than the tendency to avoid failure**, budgets with **targets of intermediate levels of difficulty** are the most **motivating**, and stimulate a manager to better performance levels. Budgets which are either too easy to achieve or too difficult are de-motivating, and managers given such targets achieve relatively low levels of performance.

(b) A manager's **tendency to avoid failure might be stronger than the tendency to achieve success**. (This is likely in an organisation in which the budget is used as a pressure device on subordinates by senior managers). Managers might then be discouraged from trying to achieve budgets of intermediate difficulty and tend to avoid taking on such tasks, resulting in poor levels of performance, worse than if budget targets were either easy or very difficult to achieve.

5.4 It has therefore been suggested that in a situation where budget targets of an intermediate difficulty *are* motivating, such targets ought to be set if the purpose of budgets is to motivate; however, although budgets which are set for **motivational purposes** need to be stated in terms of **aspirations rather than expectations**, budgets for planning and decision purposes need to be stated in terms of the best available estimate of expected actual performance. The **solution** might therefore be to have **two budgets**.

(a) A **budget for planning and decision making based on reasonable expectations**.

(b) A second **budget for motivational purposes**, with **more difficult targets of performance** (that is, targets of an intermediate level of difficulty).

These two budgets might be called an '**expectations budget**' and an '**aspirations budget**' respectively.

6 THE MANAGEMENT ACCOUNTANT AND MOTIVATION

6.1 As we have seen, budgets serve many purposes, but in some instances their purposes can conflict and have an effect on management behaviour. Management and the management accountant therefore require strategies and methods for dealing with the resulting tensions and conflict. For example, should targets be adjusted for uncontrollable and unforeseeable environmental influence? But what is then the effect on motivation if employees view performance standards as changeable?

6.2 Can performance measures and the related budgetary control system ever motivate managers towards achieving the organisation's goals?

(a) Accounting measures of performance **can't provide a comprehensive assessment** of what a person has achieved for the organisation.

(b) It is usually **impossible to segregate controllable and uncontrollable components of performance**. This can lead to unfairness in evaluating performance.

(c) Accounting **reports tend to concentrate on short-term achievements**, to the exclusion of the long-term effects.

(d) Many accounting **reports try to serve several different purposes**, and in trying to satisfy several needs actually satisfy none properly.

6.3 The management accountant does not have the authority to do much on his or her own to improve hostile or apathetic attitudes to control information. There has to be support, either from senior management or from cost and profit centre managers. However, the management accountant can do quite a lot to improve and then maintain the standard of a budgetary control reporting system.

(a) **Senior management can offer support** by doing the following.

- Making sure that a **system of responsibility accounting is adopted**.
- Allowing **managers to have a say in formulating their budgets**.
- Offering **incentives** to managers who meet budget targets.
- **Not regarding budgetary control information as a way of apportioning blame.**

(b) **Cost centre/profit centre managers should accept their responsibilities**. In-house training courses could be held to encourage a collective, cooperative and positive attitude amongst managers.

(c) The **management accountant should improve** (or maintain) the **quality of the budgetary control system** by doing the following.

(i) **Developing a working relationship with operational managers**, going out to meet them and discussing the control reports.

(ii) **Explaining the meaning of budgets and control reports.**

(iii) **Keeping accounting jargon in these reports to a minimum.**

(iv) Making **reports clear and to the point**, for example using the principle of reporting by exception.

(v) Providing control information with a **minimum of delay.**

(vi) **Making control information as useful as possible**, by distinguishing between directly attributable costs over which a manager should have influence and apportioned or fixed costs which are unavoidable or uncontrollable.

(vii) Trying to make sure that **actual costs are recorded accurately**.

(viii) Trying to ensure that **budgets are up-to-date**, either by having a system of rolling budgets, or else by updating budgets or standards as necessary, and ensuring that standards are 'fair' so that control information is realistic.

Exam focus point

There are no ideal solutions to the conflicts caused by the operation of a budgetary control system. Management and the management accountant have to develop their own ways of dealing with them, taking into account their organisation, their business and the personalities involved. You should think about how the budgetary control system operates in your organisation and the conflicts, if there are any, caused by it. How are the conflicts dealt with? Real life examples can be usefully incorporated into solutions in the exam.

Question 3

Discuss the behavioural aspects of participation in the budgeting process and any difficulties you might envisage.

Answer

The level of participation in the budgeting process can vary from zero participation to a process of group decision making. There are a number of behavioural aspects of participation to consider.

(a) **Communication**. Managers cannot be expected to achieve targets if they do not know what those targets are. Communication of targets is made easier if managers have participated in the budgetary process from the beginning.

(b) **Motivation**. Managers are likely to be better motivated to achieve a budget if they have been involved in compiling it, rather than having a dictatorial budget imposed on them.

(c) **Realistic targets**. A target must be achievable and accepted as realistic if it is to be a motivating factor. A manager who has been involved in setting targets is more likely to accept them as realistic. In addition, managers who are close to the operation of their departments may be more aware of the costs and potential savings in running it.

(d) **Goal congruence**. One of the best ways of achieving goal congruence is to involve managers in the preparation of their own budgets, so that their personal goals can be taken into account in setting targets.

Although participative budgeting has many advantages, difficulties might also arise.

(a) **Pseudo-participation**. Participation may not be genuine, but merely a pretence at involving managers in the preparation of their budgets. Managers may feel that their contribution is being ignored, or that the participation consists of merely obtaining their agreement to a budget which has already been decided. If this is the case then managers are likely to be more demotivated than if there is no participation at all.

(b) **Coordination**. If participative budgeting is well managed it can improve the coordination of the preparation of the various budgets. There is, however, a danger that too many managers will become involved so that communication becomes difficult and the process become complex.

(c) **Training**. Some managers may not possess the necessary skill to make an effective contribution to the preparation of their budgets. Additional training may be necessary, with the consequent investment of money and time. It may also be necessary to train managers to understand the purposes and advantages of participation.

(d) **Slack**. If budgets are used in a punitive fashion for control purposes then managers will be tempted to build in extra expenditure to provide a 'cushion' against overspending. It is easier for them to build in slack in a participative system.

Chapter roundup

- **Fixed budgets** remain unchanged regardless of the level of activity; **flexible budgets** are designed to flex with the level of activity. Comparison of a fixed budget with the actual results for a different level of activity is of little use for control purposes. Flexible budgets should be used to show what cost and revenues should have been for the actual level of activity. The differences between the components of the fixed budget and the actual results are known as **budget variances**.
- Used correctly a budgetary control system can **motivate** but it can also produce undesirable **negative reactions**.
- There are basically two ways in which a budget can be set: from the top down (imposed budget) or from the **bottom up** (**participatory** budget). Many writers refer to a third style (negotiated).
- There are three ways of using budgetary information to evaluate managerial performance (**budget constrained style**, **profit conscious style**, **non-accounting style**).
- **Budgetary slack** is the difference between the minimum necessary costs and the costs built into the budget or actually incurred.
- In certain situations it is useful to prepare an **expectations budget** and an **aspirations budget**.
- Management and the management accountant require strategies and methods for dealing with the **tensions** and **conflict** resulting from the **conflicting purposes** of budget.

Quick quiz

1 *Fill in the gaps.*

A flexible budget is a budget which, by recognising ...., is designed to .... as the level of activity changes.

2 An extract of the costs incurred at two different activity levels is shown. Classify the costs according to their behaviour patterns and show the budget cost allowance for an activity of 1,500 units.

	1,000 units	*2,000 units*	*Type of cost*	*Budget cost allowance for 1,500 units*
	£	£		£
Fuel	3,000	6,000	....	....
Photocopying	9,500	11,000	....	....
Heating	2,400	2,400	....	....
Direct wages	6,000	8,000	....	....

3 *Choose the appropriate words from those highlighted.*

A fixed budget is based on output of 500 units.

- A flexible budget for 550 units is produced. This will show overheads as being **under/over** absorbed.
- A flexible budget is also produced for 450 units. This will show overheads as being **under/over** absorbed.

4 *Match the descriptions to the budgeting style.*

Description

(a) Budget allowances are set without the involvement of the budget holder

(b) All budget holders are involved in setting their own budgets

(c) Budget allowances are set on the basis of discussions between budget holders and those to whom they report

Budgeting style

Negotiated budgeting
Participative budgeting
Imposed budgeting

5 Budgetary slack is necessary to ensure that managers are able to meet their targets. True or false?

6 *Fill in the gaps.*

An expectations budget would be most useful for the purposes of ...., whereas an aspirations budget is more appropriate for ....

7 Which of the following actions could be used by a management accountant to improve/maintain the quality of the budgetary control system?

(a) Ensure that relationships are not built up with operational managers.

(b) Ensure that control reports use the appropriate technical vocabulary understood by accounting personnel only.

(c) Do not provide control information too soon after a period end as operational managers need time to reflect on events before being inundated with volumes of control information.

(d) Do not distinguish between controllable and uncontrollable costs as this will give operational managers the opportunity to abdicate responsibility for everything.

(e) Do not change the budget once it has been set at the beginning of the year.

Answers to quick quiz

1 cost behaviour patterns
flex or change

2 Variable £4,500
Semi-variable £10,250
Fixed £2,400
Semi-variable £7,000

3 The budget for 550 units will show over absorption, the other under absorption.

4 (a) Imposed budgeting
(b) Participative budgeting
(c) Negotiated budgeting

5 False. Budgets should be reviewed to ensure that operational managers have not included slack.

6 (a) planning and decision making based on reasonable expectations
(b) improving motivation by setting targets of an intermediate level of difficulty

7 None of the suggestions should be used.

(a) A working relationship with operational managers should be developed.

(b) Accounting jargon in reports should be kept to a minimum so that they are easily understood.

(c) Control information should be provided with a minimum of delay. Beware of information overload.

(d) Managers should only be responsible for costs over which they have control.

(e) Budgets should be kept as up to date as possible.

Now try the questions below from the Exam Question Bank

Question to try	Level	Marks	Time
14	Exam	25	45 mins
15	Exam	25	45 mins

Chapter 12

ALTERNATIVE BUDGET SYSTEMS

	Topic list	Syllabus reference
1	Incremental budgeting and zero based budgeting	9(b)
2	The main features of zero based budgeting systems	9(b)
3	Using zero based budgeting	9(b)
4	Continuous budgets	9(b)
5	Activity based budgeting	9(b)
6	The future of budgeting	9(b)

Introduction

The system of budgeting which we have looked at so far in this Study Text may not always be appropriate for certain organisations or for certain types of cost and revenue. **Zero based budgeting** and **continuous budgets** are alternative budget systems which can be applied in certain circumstances and situations. **Activity based budgets** may use bases other than volume of output for flexing budgets. This chapter looks in detail at these systems.

In the next chapter we will look at quantitative aids to budgeting.

Study guide

Section 25 – Budget planning and control III

- Describe and evaluate the main features of zero based budgeting systems
- Describe the areas/organisations in which zero based budgeting may be applied
- Describe and evaluate incremental budgeting and discuss the differences with zero based budgeting
- Describe and evaluate periodic and continuous budgeting systems

Exam guide

The topics covered in this chapter are likely to be examined in conjunction with other topics in both Section A and Section B.

1 INCREMENTAL BUDGETING AND ZERO BASED BUDGETING

KEY TERM

Incremental budgeting is the traditional approach to budgeting and involves basing next year's budget on the current year's results plus an extra amount for estimated growth or inflation next year.

1.1 **Incremental budgeting** is so called because it is concerned mainly with the increments in costs and revenues which will occur in the coming period.

1.2 Incremental budgeting is a reasonable procedure if current operations are as effective, efficient and economical as they can be. It is also appropriate for budgeting for costs such as staff salaries, which may be estimated on the basis of current salaries plus an increment for inflation and are hence administratively fairly easy to prepare.

1.3 In general, however, it is an **inefficient form of budgeting** as it **encourages slack** and **wasteful spending** to creep into budgets. Past inefficiencies are perpetuated because cost levels are rarely subjected to close scrutiny.

1.4 To ensure that inefficiencies are not concealed, however, alternative approaches to budgeting have been developed. One such approach is **zero based budgeting (ZBB)**.

Question 1

Can incremental budgeting be used to budget for rent? What about for advertising expenditure?

Answer

Incremental budgeting is appropriate for budgeting for rent, which may be estimated on the basis of current rent plus an increment for the annual rent increase. Advertising expenditure, on the other hand, is not so easily quantifiable and is more discretionary in nature. Using incremental budgeting for advertising expenditure could allow slack and wasteful spending to creep into the budget.

2 THE MAIN FEATURES OF ZERO BASED BUDGETING SYSTEMS

The principles of zero based budgeting (ZBB)

2.1 ZBB rejects the assumption inherent in incremental budgeting that this year's activities will continue at the same level or volume next year, and that next year's budget can be based on this year's costs plus an extra amount, perhaps for expansion and inflation.

KEY TERM

Zero based budgeting involves preparing a budget for each cost centre from a zero base. Every item of expenditure has then to be justified in its entirety in order to be included in the next year's budget.

2.2 In reality, however, managers do not have to budget from zero, but can **start from their current level of expenditure and work downwards,** asking what would happen if any particular aspect of current expenditure and current operations were removed from the budget. In this way, every aspect of the budget is examined in terms of its cost and the benefits it provides and the selection of better alternatives is encouraged.

Implementing zero based budgeting

2.3 The implementation of ZBB involves a number of steps but of greater importance is the **development of a questioning attitude** by all those involved in the budgetary process. Existing practices and expenditures must be challenged and searching questions asked.

- Does the activity need to be carried out?

- What would be the consequences if the activity was not carried out?
- Is the current level of provision current?
- Are there alternative ways of providing the function?
- How much should the activity cost?
- Is the expenditure worth the benefits achieved?

2.4 The basic approach of ZBB has three steps.

Step 1. **Define decision packages,** comprehensive **descriptions of specific organisational activities which management can use to evaluate the activities and rank them in order of priority against other activities.** There are two types.

(a) **Mutually exclusive packages** contain **alternative methods of getting the same job done**. The best option among the packages must be selected by comparing costs and benefits and the other packages are then discarded.

(b) **Incremental packages divide one aspect of an activity into different levels of effort.** The 'base' package will describe the minimum amount of work that must be done to carry out the activity and the other packages describe what additional work could be done, at what cost and for what benefits.

Suppose that a cost centre manager is preparing a budget for maintenance costs. He might first consider two mutually exclusive packages. Package A might be to keep a maintenance team of two men per shift for two shifts each day at a cost of £60,000 per annum, whereas package B might be to obtain a maintenance service from an outside contractor at a cost of £50,000. A cost-benefit analysis will be conducted because the quicker repairs obtainable from an in-house maintenance service might justify its extra cost. If we now suppose that package A is preferred, the budget analysis must be completed by describing the incremental variations in this chosen alternative.

(a) The 'base' package would describe the minimum requirement for the maintenance work. This might be to pay for one man per shift for two shifts each day at a cost of £30,000.

(b) Incremental package 1 might be to pay for two men on the early shift and one man on the late shift, at a cost of £45,000. The extra cost of £15,000 would need to be justified, for example by savings in lost production time, or by more efficient machinery.

(c) Incremental package 2 might be the original preference, for two men on each shift at a cost of £60,000. The cost-benefit analysis would compare its advantages, if any, over incremental package 1; and so on.

Question 2

What might the base and incremental packages for a personnel department cover?

Answer

The base package might cover the recruitment and dismissal of staff. Incremental packages might cover training, pension administration, trade union liaison, staff welfare and so on.

Step 2. **Evaluate and rank each activity (decision package)** on the basis of its benefit to the organisation. This can be a lengthy process. Minimum work requirements (those that are essential to get a job done) will be given high priority and so too will work which meets legal obligations. In the accounting department these would be minimum requirements to operate the payroll, purchase ledger and sales ledger systems, and to maintain and publish a set of accounts.

Step 3. **Allocate resources** in the budget according to the funds available and the evaluation and ranking of the competing packages.

The advantages and limitations of implementing ZBB

2.5 The **advantages** of zero based budgeting are as follows.

- It is possible to identify and **remove inefficient or obsolete operations.**
- It forces employees to **avoid wasteful expenditure**.
- It can **increase motivation.**
- It **responds to changes** in the business environment.
- **ZBB documentation provides** an in-depth **appraisal of an organisation's operations.**
- It **challenges the status quo.**
- In summary, ZBB should result in a **more efficient allocation of resources.**

2.6 The major **disadvantage** of zero based budgeting is the **volume of extra paperwork** created. The assumptions about costs and benefits in each package must be continually updated and new packages developed as soon as new activities emerge. The following problems might also occur.

(a) **Short-term benefits** might be **emphasised** to the detriment of long-term benefits.

(b) It might give the impression **that all decisions have to be made in the budget**. Management must be able to meet unforeseen opportunities and threats at all times, however, and must not feel restricted from carrying out new ideas simply because they were not approved by a decision package, cost benefit analysis and the ranking process.

(c) It may **call for management skills** both in constructing decision packages and in the ranking process **which the organisation does not possess**. Managers may have to be trained in ZBB techniques.

(d) The organisation's **information systems may not be capable of providing suitable information.**

(e) **The ranking process can be difficult**. Managers face three common problems.

(i) A large number of packages may have to be ranked.

(ii) It can be difficult to rank packages which appear to be equally vital, for legal or operational reasons.

(iii) It is difficult to rank activities which have qualitative rather than quantitative benefits - such as spending on staff welfare and working conditions.

2.7 In summary, perhaps the **most serious drawback to ZBB is that it requires a lot of management time and paperwork**. One way of obtaining the benefits of ZBB but of overcoming the drawbacks is to apply it selectively on a rolling basis throughout the organisation. This year finance, next year marketing, the year after personnel and so on. In this way all activities will be thoroughly scrutinised over a period of time.

3 USING ZERO BASED BUDGETING

3.1 ZBB is not particularly suitable for direct manufacturing costs, which are usually budgeted using standard costing, work study and other management planning and control techniques. It is best applied to **support expenses**, that is expenditure incurred in

departments which exist to support the essential production function. These support areas include marketing, finance, quality control, personnel, data processing, sales and distribution. In many organisations, these expenses make up a large proportion of the total expenditure. These activities are less easily quantifiable by conventional methods and are more **discretionary** in nature.

3.2 ZBB can also be successfully applied to **service industries** and **non-profit-making organisations** such as local and central government departments, educational establishments, hospitals and so on, and in any organisation where alternative levels of provision for each activity are possible and where the costs and benefits are separately identifiable.

3.3 ZBB can also be used to make rationalisation decisions. 'Rationalisation' is a euphemism for cutting back on production and activity levels, and cutting costs. The need for service departments to operate above a minimum service level or the need for having a particular department at all can be questioned, and ZBB can be used to make rationalisation decisions when an organisation is forced to make spending cuts.

4 CONTINUOUS BUDGETS

Dynamic conditions

4.1 **Actual conditions may differ from those anticipated when the budget was drawn up** for a number of reasons.

(a) **Organisational changes** may occur.

(i) A change in structure, from a functional basis, say, to a process-based one

(ii) New agreements with the workforce about flexible working or safety procedures

(iii) The reallocation of responsibilities following, say, the removal of tiers of middle management and the 'empowerment' of workers further down the line

(b) Action may be needed to **combat an initiative by a competitor.**

(c) **New technology** may be introduced to improve productivity, reduce labour requirements or enhance quality.

(d) **Environmental conditions** may change: there may be a general boom or a recession, an event affecting supply or demand, or a change in government or government policy.

(e) The level of **inflation** may be higher or lower than that anticipated.

(f) The **level of activities** may be different from the levels planned.

4.2 Any of these changes **may make the original budget quite inappropriate,** either in terms of the numbers expected, or the way in which responsibility for achieving them is divided, or both.

Exam focus point

Dynamic conditions and rolling/continuous budgets are key syllabus areas.

4.3 If management need the chance to revise their plans, they may decide to introduce a system of **continuous budgets** (also called **rolling budgets).**

KEY TERM

A **continuous** or **rolling budget** is a budget which is continuously updated by adding a further accounting period (a month or quarter) when the earlier accounting period has expired.

4.4 Continuous budgets are an attempt to prepare targets and plans which are **more realistic and certain**, particularly with a regard to price levels, by **shortening the period between preparing budgets.**

4.5 Instead of preparing a **periodic budget** annually for the full budget period, there would be **budgets every one, two, three or four months** (three to six, or even twelve budgets each year). **Each of these budgets would plan for the next twelve months** so that the current budget is extended by an extra period as the current period ends: hence the name rolling budgets.

4.6 Suppose, for example, that a continuous budget is prepared every three months. The first three months of the budget period would be planned in great detail, and the remaining nine months in lesser detail, because of the greater uncertainty about the longer-term future. If a first continuous budget is prepared for January to March in detail and April to December in less detail, a new budget will be prepared towards the end of March, planning April to June in detail and July to March in less detail. Four rolling budgets would be prepared every 12 months on this 3 and 9 month basis, requiring, inevitably, greater administrative effort.

The advantages and disadvantages of continuous budgets

4.7 The **advantages** are as follows.

(a) They **reduce the element of uncertainty** in budgeting because they concentrate detailed planning and control on short-term prospects where the degree of uncertainty is much smaller.

(b) They force managers to reassess the budget regularly, and to **produce budgets** which are **up to date in the light of current events and expectations.**

(c) **Planning and control will be based on a recent plan** which is likely to be far more realistic than a fixed annual budget made many months ago.

(d) Realistic budgets are likely to have a **better motivational influence** on managers.

(e) There is **always a budget which extends for several months ahead**. For example, if rolling budgets are prepared quarterly there will always be a budget extending for the next 9 to 12 months. This is not the case when fixed annual budgets are used.

4.8 The **disadvantages** of continuous budgets can be a deterrent to using them.

(a) They involve **more time, effort and money** in budget preparation.

(b) Frequent budgeting might have an **off-putting effect on managers** who doubt the value of preparing one budget after another at regular intervals.

(c) Revisions to the budget might involve revisions to standard costs too, which in turn would involve revisions to stock valuations. This could replace a large **administrative effort** from the accounts department every time a rolling budget is prepared.

Continuous budgets or updated annual budgets

4.9 If the expected changes are not likely to be continuous there is a strong argument that routine updating of the budget is unnecessary. **Instead the annual budget could be updated whenever changes become foreseeable,** so that a budget might be updated once or twice, and perhaps more often, during the course of the year.

4.10 When a fixed budget is updated, a 'rolling' budget would probably not be prepared. If a budget is updated in month 8 of the year, the updated budget would relate to months 8 - 12. It would not be extended to month 7 of the following year.

5 ACTIVITY BASED BUDGETING

KEY TERM

At its simplest, **activity based budgeting (ABB)** is merely the use of costs determined using ABC as a basis for preparing budgets.

More formally ABB involves defining the activities that underlie the financial figures in each function and using the level of activity to decide how much resource should be allocated, how well it is being managed and to explain variances from budget.

5.1 Implementing ABC leads to the realisation that the **business as a whole** needs to be **managed** with far more reference to the behaviour of activities and cost drivers identified. For example, traditional budgeting may make managers 'responsible' for activities which are driven by factors beyond their control: the cost of setting-up new personnel records and of induction training would traditionally be the responsibility of the personnel manager even though such costs are driven by the number of new employees required by managers other than the personnel manager.

5.2 **Claimed results of using ABB**

(a) Different activity levels will provide a foundation for the base package and incremental packages of ZBB.

(b) The organisation's overall strategy and any actual or likely changes in that strategy will be taken into account because ABB attempts to manage the business as the sum of its interrelated parts.

(c) Critical success factors (an activity in which a business must perform well if it is to succeed) will be identified and performance measures devised to monitor progress towards them.

(d) The focus is on the whole of an activity, not just its separate parts, and so there is more likelihood of getting it right first time. For example, what is the use of being able to produce goods in time for their despatch date if the budget provides insufficient resources for the distribution manager who has to deliver them.

Flexing budgets using cost drivers

5.3 There may be a considerable **case for flexing budgets on the basis of differences between budgeted and actual cost-driving activities**. For example, if inspection costs are driven by the number of inspections that take place (rather than varying in relation to production volume, which is the normal basis for flexing), then the budget should be flexed on this basis.

	Budget		*Actual*		*Variance*	
	No	£'000	No	£	No	£'000
Inspections/inspection costs	1,000	140	1,100	165	100	25

5.4 The adverse variance of £25,000 may be analysed as an activity level variance of (100 × £140) = £14,000 and an expenditure variance of (1,100 × £(150 – 140)) = £11,000.

5.5 This kind of analysis simply requires you to be more flexible (if you will forgive the pun) in your application of basic techniques.

Exam focus point

Although ABB is not mentioned in the Study Guide, it is specifically mentioned in the syllabus and so you would be advised to have an awareness of the topic and to recognise how it offers an alternative approach to flexing budgets.

6 THE FUTURE OF BUDGETING

6.1 **Recent research** shows that **80%** of companies are **dissatisfied** with their planning and budgeting processes.

6.2 **Criticisms of traditional budgeting**

- Time consuming and costly
- Major barrier to responsiveness, flexibility and change
- Adds little value given the amount of management time required
- Rarely strategically focused
- Makes people feel undervalued
- Reinforces departmental barriers rather than encouraging knowledge sharing
- Based on unsupported assumptions and guesswork as opposed to sound, well-constructed performance data
- Developed and updated infrequently

6.3 **Ways in which companies are adapting planning and budgeting processes**

- Use of rolling forecasts
- Separation of the forecasting process from the budget to increase speed and accuracy and reduce management time
- Focus on the future rather than past performance
- Use of the balanced scorecard

6.4 Some companies such as the Swedish bank Svenska Handelsbanken (now one of Europe's most successful banks) have abandoned budgeting completely.

Chapter roundup

- The traditional approach to budgeting, known as **incremental budgeting**, bases the budget on the current year's results plus an extra amount for estimated growth or inflation next year. It encourages slack and wasteful spending to creep into budgets.
- The principle behind **zero based budgeting (ZBB)** is that the budget for each cost centre should be made from 'scratch' or zero. Every item of expenditure must be justified in its entirety in order to be included in the next year's budget.
- There is a three-step approach to ZBB.
  - Define decision units
  - Evaluate and rank packages
  - Allocate resources
- ZBB is particularly useful for budgeting for discretionary costs and for rationalisation purposes.
- **Continuous budgets** (**rolling budgets**) are budgets which are continuously updated by adding a further period (say a month or a quarter) and deducting the earliest period.
- At its simplest, **activity based budgeting (ABB)** is merely the use of costs determined using ABC for preparing budgets. More formally, it involves defining the activities that underlie the financial figures in each function and using the level of activity to decide how much resource should be allocated, how well it is being managed and to explain variances from budget.

Quick quiz

1 Incremental budgeting is widely used and is a particularly efficient form of budgeting.

True ☐

False ☐

2 What are the three steps of ZBB?

Step 1 ....

Step 2 ....

Step 3 ....

3 To which of the following can ZBB be usefully applied?

	Use ZBB	*Do not use ZBB*
Personnel		
Social services department of local government		
Direct material costs		
Sales department		
Schools		
An inefficient production department		
An efficient production department		

4 *Choose the appropriate word from those highlighted.*

A continuous budget is also known as a **periodic/rolling** budget.

5 If a system of a ABB is in use, how might the cost of scheduling production be flexed?

A Number of items produced
B Number of set-ups
C Number of direct labour hours
D Number of parts used in production

Answers to quick quiz

1 False. Incremental budgeting is inefficient.

2 *Step 1.* Define decision packages
Step 2. Evaluate and rank activities (decision package)
Step 3. Allocate resources

3

	Use ZBB	*Do not use ZBB*
Personnel	✓	
Social services department of local government	✓	
Direct material costs		✓
Sales department	✓	
Schools	✓	
An inefficient production department	✓	
An efficient production department		✓

4 It is also known as a rolling budget.

5 B

Now try the question below from the Exam Question Bank

Question to try	Level	Marks	Time
16	Introductory	-	-

Chapter 13

QUANTITATIVE AIDS IN BUDGETING

Topic list		Syllabus reference
1	Forecasting using historical data	9(e)
2	Linear regression analysis	9(e)
3	Scatter diagrams and correlation	9(e)
4	Sales forecasting	9(e)
5	Regression and forecasting	9(e)
6	The components of time series	9(e)
7	Finding the trend	9(e)
8	Finding the seasonal variations	9(e)
9	Time series analysis and forecasting	9(e)
10	Forecasting problems	9(e)
11	Using spreadsheet packages to build business models	9(e)

Introduction

We have seen how to prepare budgets but we have not yet looked at where the figures which go into the budgets come from. As we will see in this chapter, to produce a budget calls for the **preparation of forecasts of costs and revenues.** Various quantitative techniques can assist with these **'number-crunching' aspects of budgeting.** This chapter aims to provide an understanding of those techniques. Note that the techniques will be described within their budgetary context.

It has been said that **budgeting is more a test of forecasting skill than anything else** and there is a certain amount of truth in such a comment. Forecasts need to be made of sales volumes and prices, wage rates and earnings, material availability and prices, rates of inflation, the cost of bought-in services and the cost of overhead items such as power. However, it is not sufficient to simply add a percentage to last year's budget in the hope of achieving a realistic forecast.

A **forecast** is an estimate of what might happen in the future. It is a **best estimate**, based on certain assumptions about the conditions that are expected to apply. A **budget**, in contrast, is a **plan** of what the organisation is aiming to achieve and what it has set as a target. A budget should be **realistic** and so it will be based to some extent on forecasts prepared. In formulating a budget, however, management will be trying to establish some control over the conditions that will apply in the future.

Study guide

Section 26 – Quantitative aids to budgeting

- Describe and apply the following techniques
  - Least squares regression
  - Scatter diagrams and correlation
  - Forecasting with least squares regression
  - Time series to identify trends and seasonality
  - Forecasting with time series
- Evaluate the results of quantitative aids

Exam guide

Budget techniques and quantitative aims are a key area of the syllabus. You might be required to employ one or more of the techniques in either a Section A or a Section B question. Alternatively you may face an entire Section B question on, say, time series analysis.

1 FORECASTING USING HISTORICAL DATA

1.1 Numerous techniques have been developed for using past costs incurred as the basis for forecasting future values. These techniques range from simple arithmetic and visual methods to advanced computer-based statistical systems. With all techniques, however, there is the **presumption that the past will provide guidance to the future**. Before using any extrapolation techniques, the **past data** must therefore be critically examined to **assess their appropriateness for the intended purpose**. The following checks should be made.

(a) The **time period** should be long enough to include any periodically paid costs but short enough to ensure that averaging of variations in the level of activity has not occurred.

(b) The **data** should be examined to ensure that any non-activity level factors affecting costs were roughly the same in the past as those forecast for the future. Such factors might include changes in technology, changes in efficiency, changes in production methods, changes in resource costs, strikes, weather conditions and so on. Changes to the past data are frequently necessary.

(c) The **methods of data collection** and the accounting policies used should not introduce bias. Examples might include depreciation policies and the treatment of by-products.

(d) Appropriate choices of **dependent** and **independent variables** must be made.

1.2 The two forecasting methods which we are going to look at (the scatter diagram method and linear regression analysis) are based on the assumption that a **linear relationship** links levels of cost and levels of activity.

Knowledge brought forward from earlier studies

Linear relationships

- A **linear relationship** can be expressed in the form of an equation which has the general form $y = a + bx$

  where y is the **dependent** variable, depending for its value on the value of x

  x is the **independent** variable, whose value helps to determine the corresponding value of y

  a is a **constant**, a fixed amount

  b is a constant, being the **coefficient of x** (that is, the number by which the value of x should be multiplied to derive the value of y)

- If there is a linear relationship between total costs and level of activity, y = total costs, x = level of activity, a = fixed cost (the cost when there is no activity level) and b = variable cost per unit.

- The graph of a linear equation is a **straight line** and is determined by two things, the **gradient** (or slope) of the straight line and the point at which the straight line crosses the y axis (the **intercept**).

  - Gradient = b in the equation $y = a + bx = (y_2 - y_1)/(x_2 - x_1)$ where (x_1, y_1), (x_2, y_2) are two points on the straight line
  - Intercept = a in the equation $y = a + bx$

2 LINEAR REGRESSION ANALYSIS

2.1 **Linear regression analysis,** also known as the **'least squares technique'**, is a **statistical method** of estimating costs using historical data from a number of previous accounting periods.

2.2 Linear regression analysis is used to derive a **line of best fit which has the general form**

y = a + bx where

y, the dependent variable = total cost
x, the independent variable = the level of activity
a, the intercept of the line on the y axis = the fixed cost
b, the gradient of the line = the variable cost per unit of activity.

2.3 Historical data is collected from previous periods and adjusted to a common price level to remove inflationary differences. This provides a number of readings for activity levels (x) and their associated costs (y). Then, by substituting these readings into the formulae below for a and b, estimates of the fixed cost and variable cost per unit are provided.

EXAM FORMULA

If $y = a + bx$, $b = \dfrac{n\Sigma xy - \Sigma x\Sigma y}{n\Sigma x^2 - (\Sigma x)^2}$ and $a = \dfrac{\Sigma y}{n} - \dfrac{b\Sigma x}{n}$

where n is the number of pair of data for x and y.

Exam focus point

Note that you don't need to learn this formula, or the one in Section 3, as they are provided in the exam. But it would be very easy to make a mistake when copying them down so always double check back to the exam paper.

2.4 EXAMPLE: LEAST SQUARES METHOD

The transport department of Norwest Council operates a large fleet of vehicles. These vehicles are used by the various departments of the Council. Each month a statement is prepared for the transport department comparing actual results with budget. One of the items in the transport department's monthly statement is the cost of vehicle maintenance. This maintenance is carried out by the employees of the department. To facilitate control, the transport manager has asked that future statements should show vehicle maintenance costs analysed into fixed and variable costs.

Data from the six months from January to June inclusive are given below.

	Vehicle maintenance cost	*Vehicle running hours*
	£	
January	13,600	2,100
February	15,800	2,800
March	14,500	2,200
April	16,200	3,000
May	14,900	2,600
June	15,000	2,500

Required

Analyse the vehicle maintenance costs into fixed and variable costs, based on the data given, utilising the least squares method.

2.5 SOLUTION

If y = a + bx, where y represent costs and x represents running hours (since costs depend on running hours) then $b = (n\Sigma xy - \Sigma x\Sigma y)/(n\Sigma x^2 - (\Sigma x)^2)$, when n is the number of pairs of data, which is 6 in this problem.

x	*y*	*xy*	x^2
'000 hrs	£'000		
2.1	13.6	28.56	4.41
2.8	15.8	44.24	7.84
2.2	14.5	31.90	4.84
3.0	16.2	48.60	9.00
2.6	14.9	38.74	6.76
2.5	15.0	37.50	6.25
15.2	90.0	229.54	39.10

Variable cost per hour, b $= (6(229.54) - (15.2)(90.00))/(6(39.1) - (15.2)^2)$

$= (1{,}377.24 - 1{,}368)/(234.6 - 231.04) = 9.24/3.56 = £2.60$

Fixed costs (in £'000), a $= (\Sigma y/n) - (b\Sigma x/n) = (90/6) - (2.6(15.2)/6) = 8.41$ approx, say £8,400

Question 1

You are given the following data for output at a factory and costs of production over the past five months.

Month	*Output* '000 units x	*Costs* £'000 y
1	20	82
2	16	70
3	24	90
4	22	85
5	18	73

Required

(a) Calculate an equation to determine the expected cost level for any given output volume.

(b) Prepare a budget for total costs if output is 22,000 units.

Answer

(a) *Workings*

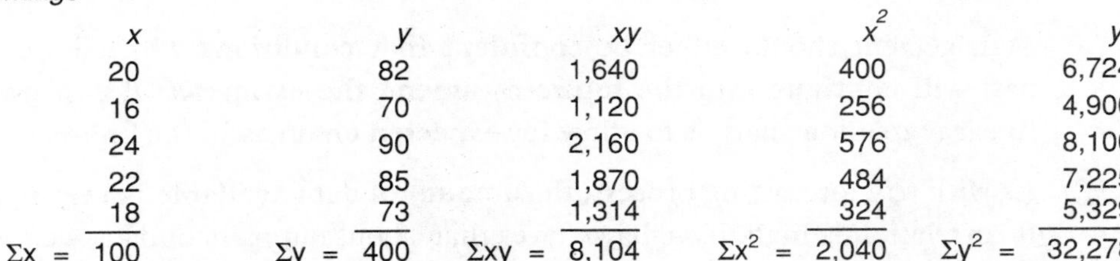

x	y	xy	x^2	y^2
20	82	1,640	400	6,724
16	70	1,120	256	4,900
24	90	2,160	576	8,100
22	85	1,870	484	7,225
18	73	1,314	324	5,329
Σx = 100	Σy = 400	Σxy = 8,104	Σx^2 = 2,040	Σy^2 = 32,278

n = 5 (There are five pairs of data for x and y values)

b $= (n\Sigma xy - \Sigma x\Sigma y)/(n\Sigma x^2 - (\Sigma x)^2) = ((5 \times 8{,}104) - (100 \times 400))/((5 \times 2{,}040) - 100^2)$

$= (40{,}520 - 40{,}000)/(10{,}200 - 10{,}000) = 520/200 = 2.6$

a $= \bar{y} - b\bar{x} = (400/5) - (2.6 \div (100/5)) = 28$

y = 28 + 2.6x

where y = total cost, in thousands of pounds and x = output, in thousands of units.

(b) If the output is 22,000 units, we would expect costs to be 28+ 2.6 × 22 = 85.2 = £85,200.

The conditions suited to the use of linear regression analysis

2.6 The conditions which should apply if linear regression analysis is to be used to estimate costs are as follows.

(a) A **linear cost function should be assumed.** This assumption can be tested by measures of reliability, such as the correlation coefficient and the coefficient of determination (which ought to be reasonably close to 1). We will be looking at these concepts later in the chapter.

(b) When calculating a line of best fit, there will be a range of values for x. In Question 1, the line y = 28 + 2.6x was predicted from data with output values ranging from x = 16 to x = 24. Depending on the degree of correlation between x and y, we might safely use the estimated line of best fit to forecast values for y, provided that the value of x remains within the range 16 to 24. We would be on less safe ground if we used the equation to predict a value for y when x = 10, or 30, or any other value outside the range 16 to 24, because we would **have to assume that costs behave in the same way outside the range of x values used to establish the line in the first place.**

KEY TERMS

- **Interpolation** means using a line of best fit to predict a value within the two extreme points of the observed range.
- **Extrapolation** means using a line of best fit to predict a value outside the two extreme points.

(c) The **historical data** for cost and output should be **adjusted to a common price level** (to overcome cost differences caused by inflation) and the historical data should also be **representative of current technology, current efficiency levels and current operations** (products made).

(d) As far as possible, **historical data should be accurately recorded** so that variable costs are properly matched against the items produced or sold, and fixed costs are properly matched against the time period to which they relate. For example, if a factory rental is £120,000 per annum, and if data is gathered monthly, these costs should be charged £10,000 to each month instead of £120,000 in full to a single month.

(e) Management should either be **confident that conditions** which have existed in the past **will continue into the future or amend the estimates** of cost produced by the linear regression analysis to **allow for expected changes** in the future.

(f) As with any forecasting process, the **amount of data available is very important**. Even if correlation is high, if we have fewer than about ten pairs of data, we must regard any forecast as being somewhat unreliable.

(g) It must be assumed that the **value of one variable, y, can be predicted or estimated from the value of one other variable, x.**

Question 2

The relationship between total operating cost and quantity produced (in a manufacturing company) is given by the linear regression model TC = 5,000 + 500Q, where TC = total operating cost (in £) per annum and Q = quantity produced per annum (kg).

What reservations might you have about relying on the above model for decision-making purposes?

Answer

(a) The reliability of the model is unknown if we do **not know the correlation coefficient**. A low correlation would suggest that the model may be unreliable.

(b) The model is probably **valid only over a certain range** of quantity produced. Outside this range, the relationship between the two variables may be very different.

(c) The model is **based on past data**, and assumes that what has happened in the past will happen in the future.

(d) The model **assumes that a linear relationship exists** between the quantity produced per annum and the total operating costs per annum. It is possible that a non-linear relationship may exist.

(e) The **fixed costs** of £5,000 per annum may be **misleading** if they include an element of allocated costs.

3 SCATTER DIAGRAMS AND CORRELATION

The scatter diagram method of forecasting

3.1 By this method of cost estimation, cost and activity data are plotted on a graph. A **'line of best fit'** is then drawn. This line should be drawn through the middle of the plotted points as closely as possible so that the distance of points above the line are equal to distances below the line. Where necessary costs should be adjusted to the same indexed price level to allow for inflation.

Scatter diagram method of estimating costs

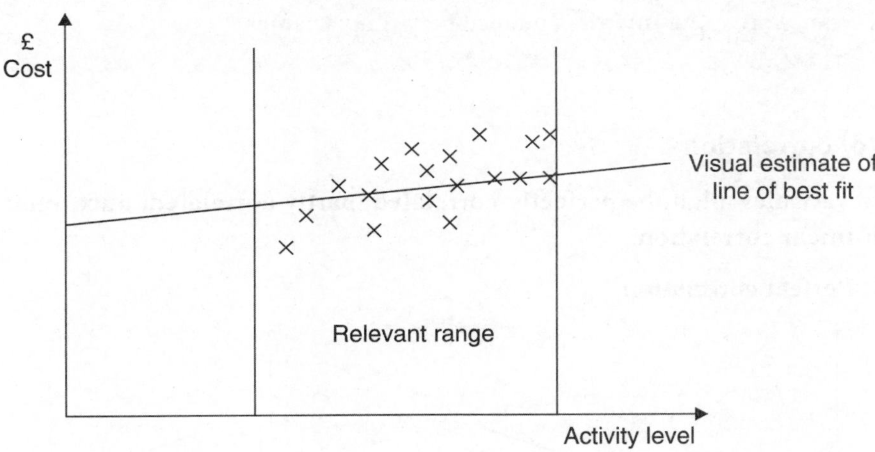

3.2 The fixed cost is the intercept of the line of best fit on the vertical axis. Suppose the fixed cost is £500 and that one of the plotted points (which is very close to the line or actually on it) represents output of 100 units and total cost of £550. The variable cost of 100 units is therefore calculated as £(550 – 500) = £50 and so the variable cost per unit is £0.50. The equation of the line of best fit is therefore *approximately* y = 500 + 0.5x.

3.3 If the company to which this data relate wanted to forecast total costs when output is 90 units, a forecast based on the equation would be 500 + (0.5 × 90) = £545. Alternatively the **forecast could be read directly from the graph using the line of best fit.**

3.4 The disadvantage of the scatter diagram method is that the cost line is drawn by visual judgement and so is a **subjective approximation.**

Correlation

3.5 (a)

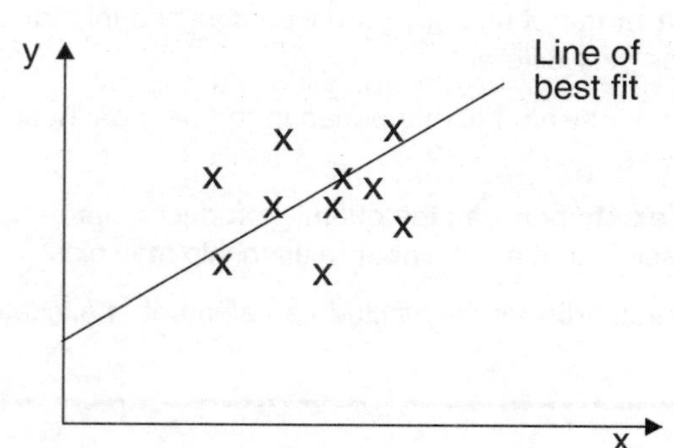

(b)

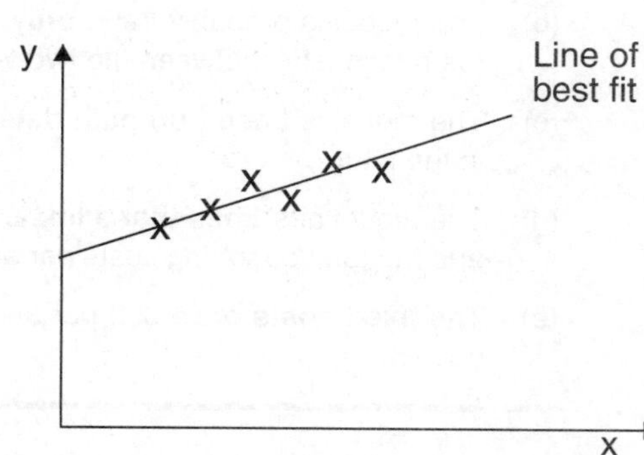

In the scatter diagrams above, you should agree that a line of best fit is more likely to reflect the 'real' relationship between x and y in (b) than in (a). In (b), the pairs of data are all close to the line of best fit, whereas in (a), there is much more scatter around the line.

In the situation represented in scatter diagram (b), forecasting the value of y from a given value for x would be more likely to be accurate than in the situation represented in (a). This is because there would be greater correlation between x and y in (b) than in (a).

KEY TERM

Correlation is the degree to which change in one variable is related to change in another - in other words, the interdependence between variables.

Degrees of correlation

3.6 Two variables might be **perfectly correlated, partly correlated, uncorrelated** or subject to **non-linear correlation.**

(a) **Perfect correlation**

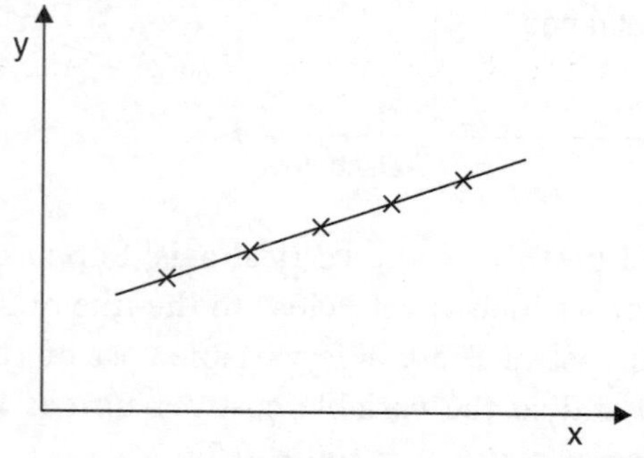

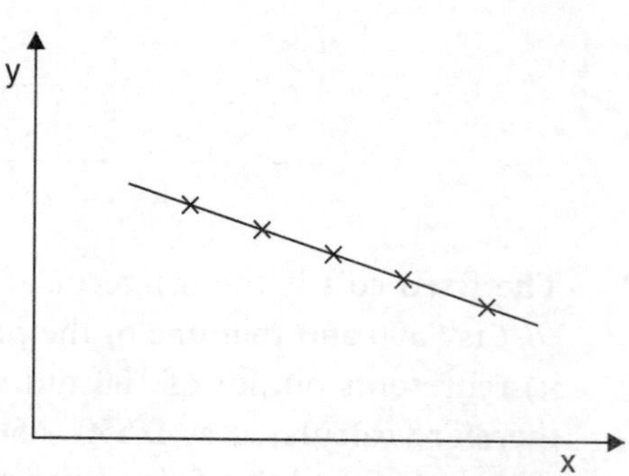

All the pairs of values lie on a straight line. An **exact linear relationship** exists between the two variables.

(b) **Partial correlation**

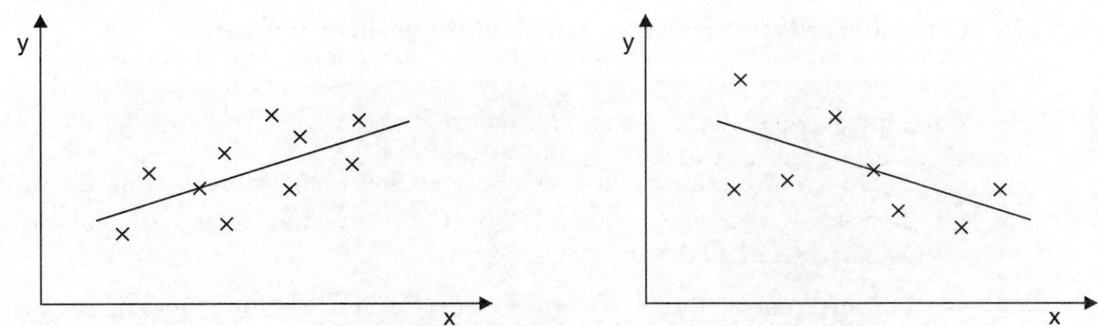

In the left hand diagram, although there is no exact relationship, **low values of x tend to be associated with low values of y, and high values of x with high values of y.**

In the right hand diagram, there is no exact relationship, but **low values of x tend to be associated with high values of y and vice versa.**

(c) **No correlation**

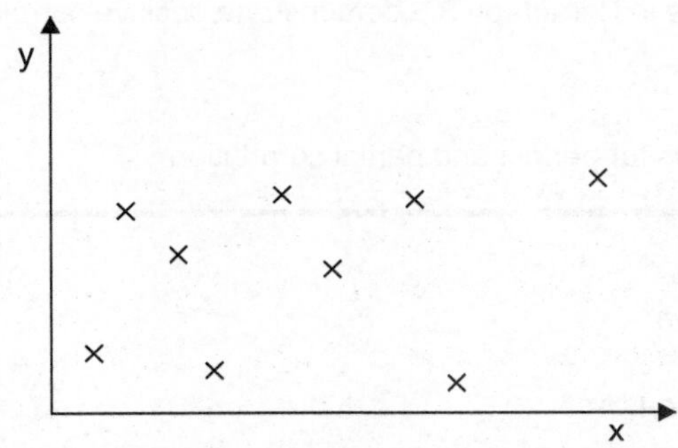

The values of these two variables are not correlated with each other.

(d) **Non-linear or curvilinear correlation**

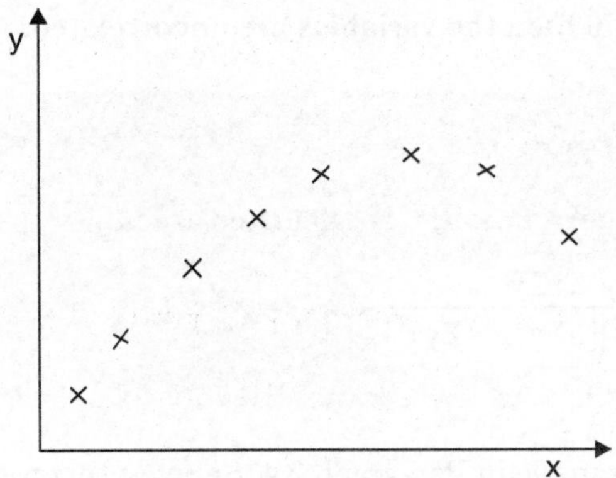

There is a relationship between x and y since the points are on an obvious curve but it is not a linear relationship.

Positive and negative correlation

3.7 Correlation, whether perfect or partial, can be **positive** or **negative**.

KEY TERMS

- **Positive correlation** is the type of correlation where low values of one variable are associated with low values of the other, and high values of one variable are associated with high values of the other.
- **Negative correlation** is the type of correlation where low values of one variable are associated with high values of the other, and high values of one variable with low values of the other.

Question 3

Which of the diagrams in Paragraph 3.6 demonstrate positive correlation?

Answer

The left hand diagrams for perfect and partial correlation.

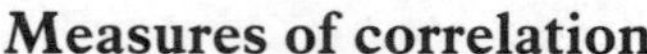

Measures of correlation

The coefficient of correlation, r

3.8 The **degree of correlation between two variables** can be measured using the **Pearsonian coefficient of correlation** (also called the **product moment correlation coefficient**).

r has a value between –1 (perfect negative correlation) and +1 (perfect positive correlation). If r = 0 then the variables are uncorrelated.

EXAM FORMULA

The **coefficient of correlation,** r, is calculated as follows.

$$r = \frac{n\Sigma xy - \Sigma x\Sigma y}{\sqrt{[n\Sigma x^2 - (\Sigma x)^2][n\Sigma y^2 - (\Sigma y)^2]}}$$

3.9 Look back at the example in Paragraph 2.4. Suppose that we wanted to know the correlation between vehicle maintenance costs and vehicle running hours. We can use a lot of the calculation in Paragraph 2.5 to determine r.

$$r = \frac{6(229.54) - (15.2)(90.0)}{\sqrt{[6(39.1) - (15.2)^2][6\Sigma y^2 - (90.0)^2]}} = \frac{1{,}377.24 - 1{,}368}{\sqrt{[(234.6 - 231.04)(6\Sigma y^2 - 8{,}100)]}}$$

All we need to calculate is Σy^2.

							Total
y (£'000)	13.60	15.80	14.50	16.20	14.90	15.00	90.00
y^2	184.96	249.64	210.25	262.44	222.01	225.00	1,354.30

$$r = \frac{9.24}{\sqrt{(3.56)(6 \times (1{,}354.30) - 8{,}100)}} = 0.96$$

3.10 A **fairly high degree of positive correlation** between x (vehicle running hours) and y (vehicle maintenance cost) is indicated here **because r is quite close to +1**.

The coefficient of determination, r^2

KEY TERM

The **coefficient of determination** is a measure of the proportion of the change in the value of one variable that can be explained by variations in the value of the other variable.

3.11 In our example, $r^2 = (0.96)^2 = 0.9216$, and so 92% of variation in the value of y (cost) can be explained by a linear relationship with x (running hours). This leaves only 8% of variations in y to be predicted from other factors. It is therefore **likely that vehicle** running hours could be used with a high degree of confidence to predict costs during a period.

Correlation and causation

3.12 If two variables are well correlated this may be due to pure chance or there may be a reason for it. The **larger the number of pairs of data**, the **less likely it is that the correlation is due to chance**, though that possibility should never be ignored.

3.13 **If there is a reason, it may not be causal.** Monthly net income is well correlated with monthly credit to a person's bank account, for the logical (rather than causal) reason that for most people the one equals the other. **Even if there is a causal explanation** for a correlation, it **does not follow that variations in the value of one variable cause variations in the value of the other**. Sales of ice cream and of sunglasses are well correlated, not because of a direct causal link but because the weather influences both variables.

3.14 Having said this, it is of course possible that where two variables are correlated, there is a direct causal link to be found.

The interactions of r^2 and r with linear regression

3.15 The successful application of linear regression models depends on x and y being closely linearly related. r measures the strength of the linear relationship between two variables but **what numerical value of r is suggestive of sufficient linearity in data to allow one to proceed with linear regression?** The lower the value of r, the less chance of forecasts made using linear regression being adequate.

3.16 If there is a perfect linear relationship between the two variables ($r = \pm 1$), we can predict y from any given value of x with great confidence. If correlation is high (for example $r = 0.9$), the actual values will all be quite close to the regression line and so predictions should not be far out. If correlation is below about 0.7, predictions will only give a very rough guide to the likely value of y.

3.17 If $r = 0.75$, say, you may feel that the linear relationship between the two variables is fairly strong. But $r^2 = 56.25\%$ indicates that only just over half of the variations in the dependent variable can be explained by a linear relationship with the independent variable. The low figure could be because a non-linear relationship is a better model for the data or because extraneous factors need to be considered (and hence multiple regression analysis should be used). It is a **common rule of thumb that $r^2 \geq 80\%$ indicates that linear regression may be applied for the purpose of forecasting.**

4 SALES FORECASTING

4.1 The sales budget is frequently the first budget prepared since **sales is usually the principal budget factor**, but before the sales budget can be prepared a sales forecast has to be made. Sales forecasting is complex *and* difficult and involves the consideration of a number of factors detailed in Chapter 10.

4.2 As well as bearing in mind those factors, management can use a number of forecasting methods, often combining them to reduce the level of uncertainty.

(a) **Sales personnel** can be asked to provide estimates.

(b) **Market research** can be used (especially for new products or services).

(c) **Mathematical** models can be set up so that repetitive computer simulations can be run which permit managers to review the results that would be obtained in various circumstances.

(d) Various **mathematical techniques** can be used to estimate sales levels. We will cover these in the remainder of the chapter.

5 REGRESSION AND FORECASTING

5.1 The same regression techniques as those considered earlier in the chapter can be used to **calculate a regression line (a trend line) for a time series.** A time series is simply a series of figures or values recorded over time (such as total annual costs for the last ten years). The determination of a trend line is particularly useful in forecasting. (We will be looking at time series and trend lines in more detail in the next section.)

5.2 The **years (or days or months) become the x variables in the regression formulae** by **numbering them from 0 upwards.**

5.3 EXAMPLE: REGRESSION AND FORECASTING

Sales of product B over the seven year period from 20X1 to 20X7 were as follows.

Year	*20X1*	*20X2*	*20X3*	*20X4*	*20X5*	*20X6*	*20X7*
Sales of B ('000 units)	22	25	24	26	29	28	30

There is high correlation between time and the volume of sales.

Required

Calculate the trend line of sales, and forecast sales in 20X8 and 20X9.

5.4 SOLUTION

Workings

Year	*x*	*y*	*xy*	x^2
20X1	0	22	0	0
20X2	1	25	25	1
20X3	2	24	48	4
20X4	3	26	78	9
20X5	4	29	116	16
20X6	5	28	140	25
20X7	6	30	180	36
	$\Sigma x = 21$	$\Sigma y = 184$	$\Sigma xy = 587$	$\Sigma x^2 = 91$

n = 7

Where y = a + bx

b = ((7 × 587) – (21 × 184))/((7 × 91) – (21 × 21)) = 245/196 = 1.25

a = (184/7) – ((1.25 × 21)/7) = 22.5357, say 22.5

y = 22.5 + 1.25x where x = 0 in 20X1, x = 1 in 20X2 and so on.

Using this trend line, predicted sales in 20X8 (year 7) would be 22.5 + 1.25 × 7 = 31.25 = 31,250 units.

Similarly, for 20X9 (year 8) predicted sales would be 22.5 + 1.25 × 8 = 32.50 = 32,500 units.

6 THE COMPONENTS OF TIME SERIES

KEY TERM

A **time series** is a series of figures or values recorded over time.

6.1 The following are examples of time series.

- Output at a factory each day for the last month
- Monthly sales over the last two years
- The Retail Prices Index each month for the last ten years

KEY TERM

A graph of a time series is called a **historigram**.

6.2 (Note the letters 'ri'; this is not the same as a histogram.) For example, consider the following time series.

Year	*20X0*	*20X1*	*20X2*	*20X3*	*20X4*	*20X5*	*20X6*
Sales (£'000)	20	21	24	23	27	30	28

The historigram is as follows.

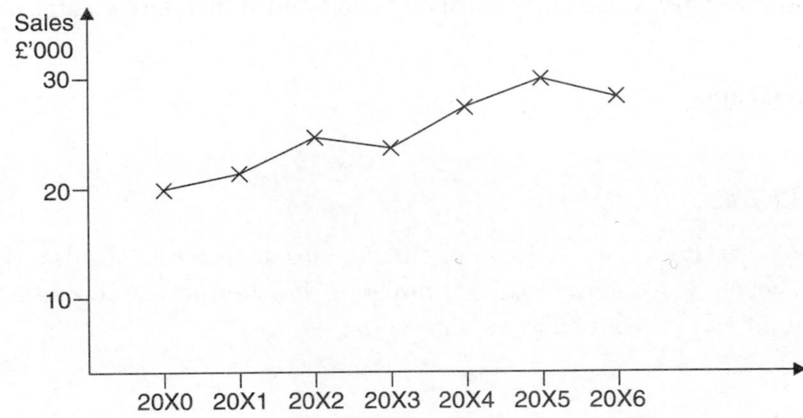

The horizontal axis is always chosen to represent time, and the vertical axis represents the values of the data recorded.

6.3 There are several **components of a time series** which it may be necessary to identify.

(a) A **trend**

(b) **Seasonal variations** or fluctuations

(c) Cycles, or **cyclical variations**

(d) Non-recurring, **random variations**. These may be caused by unforeseen circumstances such as a change in government, a war, technological change or a fire.

The trend

KEY TERM

The **trend** is the underlying long-term movement over time in values of data recorded.

6.4 In the following examples of time series, there are three types of trend.

	Output per labour hour	*Cost per unit*	*Number of employees*
	Units	£	
20X4	30	1.00	100
20X5	24	1.08	103
20X6	26	1.20	96
20X7	22	1.15	102
20X8	21	1.18	103
20X9	17	1.25	98
	(A)	(B)	(C)

(a) In time series **(A)** there is a **downward trend** in the output per labour hour. Output per labour hour did not fall every year, because it went up between 20X5 and 20X6, but the long-term movement is clearly a downward one.

(b) In time series **(B)** there is an **upward trend** in the cost per unit. Although unit costs went down in 20X7 from a higher level in 20X6, the basic movement over time is one of rising costs.

(c) In time series **(C)** there is **no clear movement** up or down, and the number of employees remained fairly constant. The trend is therefore a static, or level one.

Seasonal variations

KEY TERM

Seasonal variations are short-term fluctuations in recorded values, due to different circumstances which affect results at different times of the year, on different days of the week, at different times of day, or whatever.

6.5 Here are two examples of seasonal variations.

(a) Sales of ice cream will be higher in summer than in winter.

(b) The telephone network may be heavily used at certain times of the day (such as mid-morning and mid-afternoon) and much less used at other times (such as in the middle of the night).

6.6 'Seasonal' is a term which may appear to refer to the seasons of the year, but its meaning in time series analysis is somewhat broader, as the examples given above show.

6.7 EXAMPLE: A TREND AND SEASONAL VARIATIONS

The number of customers served by a company of travel agents over the past four years is shown in the following historigram.

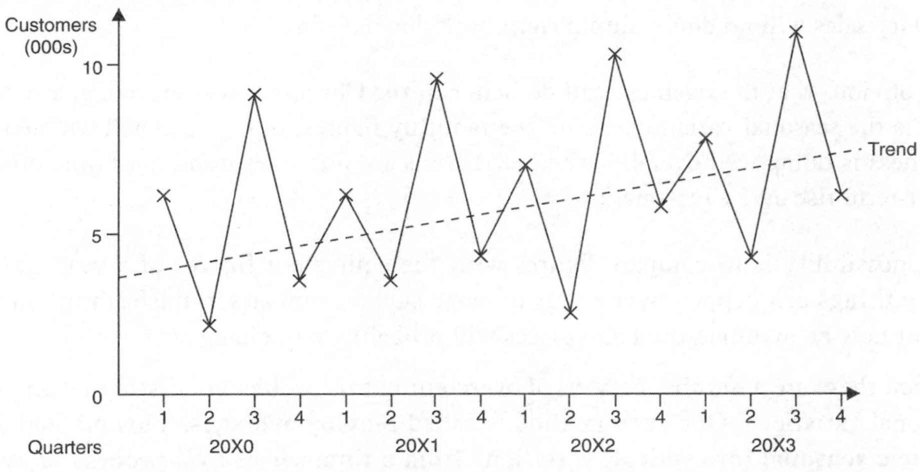

In this example, there would appear to be large seasonal fluctuations in demand, but there is also a basic upward trend.

Cyclical variations

6.8 Cyclical variations are **medium-term changes in results caused by circumstances which repeat in cycles.** In business, cyclical variations are commonly associated with economic cycles, successive booms and slumps in the economy. Economic cycles may last a few years. Cyclical variations are longer term than seasonal variations.

Summarising the components

6.9 In practice a time series could incorporate all of the four features we have been looking at and, to make reasonably accurate forecasts, the four features often have to be isolated. We can begin the process of isolating each feature by summarising the components of a time series as follows.

The **actual time series, Y = T + S + C + R**

where **Y = the actual time series**
T = the trend series
S = the seasonal component
C = the cyclical component
R = the random component

6.10 Though you should be aware of the cyclical component, it is unlikely that you will be expected to carry out any calculation connected with isolating it. The mathematical model which we will use, the **additive model**, therefore excludes any reference to C and is **Y = T + S + R.**

KEY TERM

The **additive model** expresses a time series as Y = T + S + R.

We will begin by looking at how to find the trend in a time series.

7 FINDING THE TREND

7.1 Look at these monthly sales figures.

	August	*September*	*October*	*November*	*December*
Sales (£'000)	0.02	0.04	0.04	3.20	14.60

7.2 It looks as though the business is expanding rapidly - and so it is, in a way. But when you know that the business is a Christmas card manufacturer, then you see immediately that the January sales will no doubt slump right back down again.

7.3 It is obvious that the business will do better in the Christmas season than at any other time - that is the seasonal variation. Using the monthly figures, how can he tell whether or not the business is doing well overall - whether there is a rising sales trend over time other than the short-term rise over Christmas?

7.4 One possibility is to compare figures with the equivalent figures of a year ago. However, many things can happen over a year to make such a comparison misleading - new products might now be manufactured and prices will probably have changed.

7.5 In fact, there are a number of ways of overcoming this problem of distinguishing trend from seasonal variations. One such method is called **moving averages**. This method attempts to **remove seasonal (or cyclical) variations from a time series by a process of averaging so as to leave a set of figures representing the trend.**

7.6 A **moving average** is an average of the results of a fixed number of periods. Since it is an average of several time periods, it is **related to the mid-point of the overall period.**

7.7 EXAMPLE: MOVING AVERAGES

Year	*Sales*
	Units
20X0	390
20X1	380
20X2	460
20X3	450
20X4	470
20X5	440
20X6	500

Required

Take a moving average of the annual sales over a period of three years.

7.8 SOLUTION

(a) Average sales in the three year period 20X0 – 20X2 were (390 + 380 + 460)/3 = 1,230/3 = 410. This average relates to the middle year of the period, 20X1.

(b) Similarly, average sales in the three year period 20X1 – 20X3 were (380 + 460 + 450)/3 = 1,290/3 = 430. This average relates to the middle year of the period, 20X2.

(c) The average sales can also be found for the periods 20X2 - 20X4, 20X3 - 20X5 and 20X4 - 20X6, to give the following.

Year	*Sales*	*Moving total of 3 years sales*	*Moving average of 3 years sales (÷ 3)*
20X0	390		
20X1	380	1,230	410
20X2	460	1,290	430
20X3	450	1,380	460
20X4	470	1,360	453
20X5	440	1,410	470
20X6	500		

Note the following points.

(i) The **moving average series has five figures** relating to the years 20X1 to 20X5. The **original series had seven figures** for the years from 20X0 to 20X6.

(ii) There is an upward trend in sales, which is more noticeable from the series of moving averages than from the original series of actual sales each year.

7.9 The above example averaged over a three-year period. Over what period should a moving average be taken? The answer to this question is that the **moving average which is most appropriate will depend on the circumstances and the nature of the time series.**

(a) A moving average which takes an **average of the results in many time periods will represent results over a longer term** than a moving average of two or three periods.

(b) On the other hand, with a moving average of results in many time periods, the **last figure in the series will be out of date by several periods.** In our example, the most recent average related to 20X5. With a moving average of five years' results, the final figure in the series would relate to 20X4.

(c) When there is a **known cycle** over which seasonal variations occur, such as all the days in the week or all the seasons in the year, the **most suitable moving average would be one which covers one full cycle.**

Moving averages of an even number of results

7.10 In the previous example, **moving averages were taken of the results in an *odd* number of time periods,** and the **average then related to the mid-point of the overall period.**

7.11 If a **moving average** were taken of results in an **even number of time periods,** the basic technique would be the same, but the mid-point of the overall period would not relate to a single period. For example, suppose an average were taken of the following four results.

Spring	120	
Summer	90	Average 115
Autumn	180	
Winter	70	

The average would relate to the mid-point of the period, between summer and autumn.

7.12 The trend line average figures need to relate to a particular time period; otherwise, seasonal variations cannot be calculated. To overcome this difficulty, we take a **moving average of the moving average.** An example will illustrate this technique.

7.13 EXAMPLE: MOVING AVERAGES OVER AN EVEN NUMBER OF PERIODS

Calculate a moving average trend line of the following results of Linden Ltd.

Year	*Quarter*	*Volume of sales* '000 units
20X5	1	600
	2	840
	3	420
	4	720
20X6	1	640
	2	860
	3	420
	4	740

7.14 SOLUTION

A moving average of four will be used, since the volume of sales would appear to depend on the season of the year, and each year has four quarterly results. The moving average of four does not relate to any specific period of time; therefore a second moving average of two will be calculated on the first moving averages.

Year	*Quarter*	*Actual volume of sales* '000 units (A)	*Moving total of 4 quarters' sales* '000 units (B)	*Moving average of 4 quarters' sales* '000 units (B ÷ 4)	*Mid-point of 2 moving averages Trend line* '000 units (C)
20X5	1	600			
	2	840			
			2,580	645.0	
	3	420			650.00
			2,620	655.0	
	4	720			657.50
			2,640	660.0	
20X6	1	640			660.00
			2,640	660.0	
	2	860			662.50
			2,660	665.0	
	3	420			
	4	740			

7.15 By taking a mid point (a moving average of two) of the original moving averages, we can relate the results to specific quarters (from the third quarter of 20X5 to the second quarter of 20X6).

8 FINDING THE SEASONAL VARIATIONS

8.1 Once a trend has been established we can find the seasonal variations. As we saw earlier, the additive model for time series analysis is Y = T + S + R. We can therefore write Y – T = S + R. In other words, if we deduct the trend series from the actual series, we will be left with the seasonal and residual components of the time series. If we assume that the random component is relatively small, and hence negligible, the **seasonal component can be found as S = Y – T,** the **de-trended series.**

8.2 The actual and trend sales for Linden Ltd (as calculated in Paragraph 7.14) are set out below. The **difference between the actual results for any one quarter (Y) and the trend figure for that quarter (T)** will be the seasonal variation for that quarter.

Year	*Quarter*	*Actual*	*Trend*	*Seasonal variation*
20X5	1	600		
	2	840		
	3	420	650.00	–230.00
	4	720	657.50	62.50
20X6	1	640	660.00	–20.00
	2	860	662.50	197.50
	3	420		
	4	740		

8.3 Suppose that seasonal variations for the third and fourth quarters of 20X6 and the first and second quarters of 20X7 are –248.75, 62.50, –13.75 and 212.50 respectively. The variation between the actual result for a particular quarter and the trend line average is not the same from year to year, but an **average of these variations can be taken.**

	Q_1	Q_2	Q_3	Q_4
20X5			–230.00	62.50
20X6	–20.00	197.50	–248.75	62.50
20X7	–13.75	212.50		
Total	–33.75	410.00	–478.75	125.00
Average (÷ 2)	–16.875	205.00	–239.375	62.50

8.4 Variations around the basic trend line should cancel each other out, and add up to zero. At the moment, they do not. We therefore **spread the total of the variations** (11.25) **across the four quarters** (11.25 ÷ 4) **so that the final total of the variations sum to zero.**

	Q_1	Q_2	Q_3	Q_4	*Total*
Estimated quarterly variations	– 16.8750	205.0000	–239.3750	62.5000	11.250
Adjustment to reduce variations to 0	–2.8125	–2.8125	–2.8125	–2.8125	–11.250
Final estimates of quarterly variations	–19.6875	202.1875	–242.1875	59.6875	0
These might be rounded as follows	Ql: –20,	Q2: 202,	Q3:-242,	Q4: 60,	Total: 0

Seasonal variations using the proportional model

8.5 The method of estimating the seasonal variations in the above example was to use the differences between the trend and actual data. This model **assumes that the components of the series are independent** of each other, so that an increasing trend does not affect the seasonal variations and make them increase as well, for example.

The alternative is to use the **proportional model** whereby each actual figure is expressed as a proportion of the trend. Sometimes this method is called the **multiplicative model.**

KEY TERM

The **proportional (multiplicative) model** summarises a time series as Y = T × S × R.

8.6 The **trend component** will be the **same whichever model is used** but the values of the **seasonal and random components** will **vary according to the model being applied.**

8.7 The example on Linden Ltd can be reworked on this alternative basis. The trend is calculated in exactly the same way as before but we need a different approach for the seasonal variations. The proportional model is Y = T × S × R and, just as we calculated S = Y – T for the additive model above we can calculate **S = Y/T** for the proportional model.

Year	Quarter	Actual (Y)	Trend (T)	Seasonal percentage (Y/T)
20X5	1	600		
	2	840		
	3	420	650.00	0.646
	4	720	657.50	1.095
20X6	1	640	660.00	0.970
	2	860	662.50	1.298
	3	420		
	4	740		

8.8 Suppose that seasonal variations for the next four quarters are 0.628, 1.092, 0.980 and 1.309 respectively. The summary of the seasonal variations expressed in proportional terms is therefore as follows.

	Q_1	Q_2	Q_3	Q_4
	%	%	%	%
20X5			0.646	1.095
20X6	0.970	1.298	0.628	1.092
20X7	0.980	1.309		
Total	1.950	2.607	1.274	2.187
Average	0.975	1.3035	0.637	1.0935

8.9 **Instead of summing to zero, as with the additive approach, the averages should sum (in this case) to 4.0, 1.0 for each of the four quarters.** They actually sum to 4.009 so 0.00225 has to be deducted from each one.

	Q_1	Q_2	Q_3	Q_4
Average	0.97500	1.30350	0.63700	1.09350
Adjustment	–0.00225	–0.00225	–0.00225	–0.00225
Final estimate	0.97275	1.30125	0.63475	1.09125
Rounded	0.97	1.30	0.64	1.09

8.10 Note that the **proportional model is better than the additive model when the trend is increasing or decreasing over time.** In such circumstances, seasonal variations are likely to be increasing or decreasing too. The additive model simply adds absolute and unchanging seasonal variations to the trend figures whereas the proportional model, by multiplying increasing or decreasing trend values by a constant seasonal variation factor, takes account of changing seasonal variations.

9 TIME SERIES ANALYSIS AND FORECASTING

9.1 By extrapolating a trend and then adjusting for seasonal variations, forecasts of future values can be made.

9.2 Forecasts of future values should be made as follows.

(a) **Find a trend line using moving averages or using linear regression analysis (see Section 5).**

(b) **Use the trend line to forecast future trend line values.**

(c) **Adjust these values by the average seasonal variation applicable to the future period, to determine the forecast for that period.** With the additive model, add (or subtract for negative variations) the variation. With the multiplicative model, multiply the trend value by the variation proportion.

9.3 Extending a trend line outside the range of known data, in this case forecasting the future from a trend line based on historical data, is known as **extrapolation.**

9.4 EXAMPLE: FORECASTING

The sales (in £'000) of swimwear by a large department store for each period of three months and trend values found using moving averages are as follows.

Quarter	*20X4*		*20X5*		*20X6*		*20X7*	
	Actual £'000	*Trend* £'000	*Actual* £'000	*Trend* £'000	*Actual* £'000	*Trend* £'000	*Actual* £'000	*Trend* £'000
First			8		20	40	40	57
Second			30	30	50	45	62	
Third			60	31	80	50	92	
Fourth	24		20	35	40	54		

Using the additive model, seasonal variations have been determined as follows.

Quarter 1	*Quarter 2*	*Quarter 3*	*Quarter 4*
–£18,250	+£2,750	+£29,750	–£14,250

Required

Predict sales for the last quarter of 20X7 and the first quarter of 20X8, stating any assumptions.

9.5 SOLUTION

We might guess that the trend line is rising steadily, by (57 – 40)/4 = 4.25 per quarter in the period 1st quarter 20X6 to 1st quarter 20X7 (57 being the prediction in 1st quarter 20X7 and 40 the prediction in 1st quarter 20X6). Since the trend may be levelling off a little, a quarterly increase of +4 in the trend will be assumed.

		Trend	*Seasonal variation*	*Forecast*
1st quarter	20X7	57		
4th quarter	20X7 (+ (3 × 4))	69	–14.25	54.75
1st quarter	20X8 (+ (4 × 4))	73	–18.25	54.75

Rounding to the nearest thousand pounds, the forecast sales are £55,000 for each of the two quarters.

9.6 Note that you could actually plot the trend line figures on a graph, extrapolate the trend line into the future and read off forecasts from the graph using the extrapolated trend line.

9.7 If we had been using the proportional model, with an average variation for (for example) quarter 4 of 0.8, our prediction for the fourth quarter of 20X7 would have been 69 × 0.8 = 55.2, say £55,000.

Question 4

The trend in a company's sales figures can be described by the linear regression equation y = 780 + 4x, where x is the month number (with January 20X3 as month 0) and y is sales in thousands of pounds. The average seasonal variation for March is 106%.

Required

Forecast the sales for March 20X5.

Answer

x = 26

Forecast = 1.06 × [780 + (4 × 26)] = 937.04 = £937,040 or about £937,000.

10 FORECASTING PROBLEMS

10.1 All forecasts are subject to error, but the likely errors vary from case to case.

- The **further into the future** the forecast is for, the **more unreliable** it is likely to be.
- The **less data** available on which to base the forecast, the **less reliable** the forecast.
- The **pattern** of trend and seasonal variations **may not continue** in the future.
- **Random variations** may upset the pattern of trend and seasonal variation.

10.2 There are a number of changes that also may make it difficult to forecast future events.

Type of change	Examples
Political and economic changes	Changes in interest rates, exchange rates or inflation can mean that future sales and costs are difficult to forecast.
Environmental changes	The opening of high-speed rail links might have a considerable impact on some companies' markets.
Technological changes	These may mean that the past is not a reliable indication of likely future events. For example new faster machinery may make it difficult to use current output levels as the basis for forecasting future production output.
Technological advances	Advanced manufacturing technology is changing the cost structure of many firms. Direct labour costs are reducing in significance and fixed manufacturing costs are increasing. This causes forecasting difficulties because of the resulting changes in cost behaviour patterns, breakeven points and so on.
Social changes	Alterations in taste, fashion and the social acceptability of products can cause forecasting difficulties.

11 USING SPREADSHEET PACKAGES TO BUILD BUSINESS MODELS

11.1 A spreadsheet is a type of general purpose software package with **many business applications,** not just accounting ones. It **can be used to build a model,** in which data is presented in these **rows and columns,** and it is up to the model builder to determine what data or information should be presented in it, how it should be presented and how the data should be manipulated by the spreadsheet program. The most widely used spreadsheet packages are Lotus 1-2-3 and Excel.

11.2 The idea behind a spreadsheet is that the model builder should **construct a model as follows.**

(a) Identify what data goes into each row and column and by **inserting text** (for example, column headings and row identifications).

(b) **Specify how the numerical data in the model should be derived.** Numerical data might be derived using one of the following methods.

- **Insertion into the model via keyboard input.**

- **Calculation from other data in the model** by means of a formula specified within the model itself. The model builder must insert these formulae into the spreadsheet model when it is first constructed.
- **Retrieval from data on a disk file** from another computer application program or module.

The advantages of spreadsheets

11.3 The uses of spreadsheets are really only limited by your imagination, and by the number of rows and columns in the spreadsheet, but some of the more **common accounting applications** are listed below.

- Balance sheets
- Cash flow analysis/forecasting
- General ledger
- Inventory records
- Job cost estimates
- Market share analysis and planning
- Profit projections
- Profit statements
- Project budgeting and control
- Sales projections and records
- Tax estimation

11.4 The great value of spreadsheets derives from their **simple format** of rows, columns and worksheets of data, and the ability of the data **users to have direct access themselves** to their spreadsheet model via their own PC. For example, an accountant can construct a cash flow model with a spreadsheet package on the PC on his desk: he can **create** the model, **input** the data, **manipulate** the data and **read or print the output** direct. He will also have fairly **instant access** to the model whenever it is needed, in just the time it takes to load the model into his PC. Spreadsheets therefore bring computer modelling within the everyday reach of data users.

The disadvantages of spreadsheets

11.5 Spreadsheets have disadvantages if they are not properly used.

(a) A **minor error in the design** of a model at any point can **affect the validity of data** throughout the spreadsheet. Such errors can be very difficult to trace.

(b) Even if it is properly designed in the first place, it is very **easy to corrupt** a model by accidentally changing a cell or inputting data in the wrong place.

(c) It is possible to **become over-dependent on them**, so that simple one-off tasks that can be done in seconds with a pen and paper are done on a spreadsheet instead.

(d) The possibility for experimentation with data is so great that it is possible to **lose sight of the original intention** of the spreadsheet.

(e) Spreadsheets **cannot take account of qualitative factors** since they are invariably difficult to quantify. Decisions should not be made on the basis of quantitative information alone.

In summary, spreadsheets should be seen as a **tool in planning and decision making**. The user must make the decision.

'What if' analysis

11.6 Once a model has been constructed the consequences of changes in any of the variables may be tested by asking **'what if' questions, a form of sensitivity analysis**. For example, a spreadsheet may be used to develop a cash flow model, such as that shown below.

	A	B	C	D
1		Month 1	Month 2	Month 3
2	Sales	1,000	1,200	1,440
3	Cost of sales	(650)	(780)	(936)
4	Gross profit	350	420	504
5				
6	Receipts:			
7	Current month	600	720	864
8	Previous month	-	400	480
9				-
10		600	1,120	1,344
11	Payments	(650)	(780)	(936)
12		(50)	340	408
13	Balance b/f	-	(50)	290
14	Balance c/f	(50)	290	698

11.7 **Typical 'what if' questions for sensitivity analysis**

(a) What if the cost of sales is 68% of sales revenue, not 65%?

(b) What if payment from debtors is received 40% in the month of sale, 50% one month in arrears and 10% two months in arrears, instead of 60% in the month of sale and 40% one month in arrears?

(c) What if sales growth is only 15% per month, instead of 20% per month?

11.8 Using the spreadsheet model, the answers to such questions can be obtained simply and quickly, using the editing facility in the program. The information obtained should **provide management with a better understanding of what the cash flow position in the future might be, and what factors are critical to ensuring that the cash position remains reasonable.** For example, it might be found that the cost of sales must remain less than 67% of sales value to achieve a satisfactory cash position.

Chapter roundup

- This chapter has considered the quantitative methods the management accountant can use to obtain information for inclusion in budgets.
- **Linear regression analysis** (least squares technique) involves determining a **line of best fit.**
- **Scatter diagrams** can be used to estimate the fixed and variable components of costs.
- **Correlation** describes the extent to which the values of two variables are related. Two variables might be **perfectly** correlated, **partly** correlated or **uncorrelated**. The correlation may be **positive** or **negative**. The degree of correlation between two variables can be measured using the **Pearsonian coefficient of correlation, r**. The **coefficient of determination** indicates the variations in the dependent variable that can be explained by variations in the independent variable.
- A **time series** is a series of figures or values recorded over time. A time series has four components: a **trend**, **seasonal variations**, **cyclical variations** and **random variations**. **Trend** values can be determined by a process of **moving averages**. **Seasonal variations** can be estimated using the **additive** model or the **proportional** (**multiplicative**) model.
- **Forecasts** can be made by calculating a **trend line** (using moving averages or linear regression), using the trend line to forecast future trend line values, and adjusting these values by the **average seasonal variation** applicable to the future period.
- **Spreadsheet packages** can be used to build business **models** to assist the forecasting and planning process.
- Management should have reasonable **confidence** in their estimates and forecasts. The assumptions on which the forecasts/estimates are based should be properly understood and the methods used to make a forecast or estimate should be in keeping with the nature, quantity and reliability of the data on which the forecast or estimate will be based. There is no point in using a 'sophisticated' technique with unreliable data; on the other hand, if there is a lot of accurate data about historical costs, it would be a waste of the data to use the scatter diagram method for cost estimating.

Quick quiz

1 If the relationship between production costs and output is connected by the linear relationship y = 75x + 47,000, what is 47,000?

A The number of units produced
B Total production costs
C The production cost if 75 units are produced
D The fixed production costs

2 *Fill in the missing words.*

Extrapolation involves using a .... of best .... to predict a value .... the two extreme points of the observed range.

3 Between sales of suntan cream and sales of cold drinks, one would expect (assuming spending money to be unlimited)

A positive, but spurious, correlation
B negative, but spurious, correlation
C positive correlation indicating direct causation
D negative correlation indicating direct causation

4 Which of the following statements is/are true of the coefficient of determination?

(a) It is the square of the Pearsonian coefficient of correlation
(b) It can never quite equal 1
(c) If it is high, this proves that variations in one variable cause variations in the other

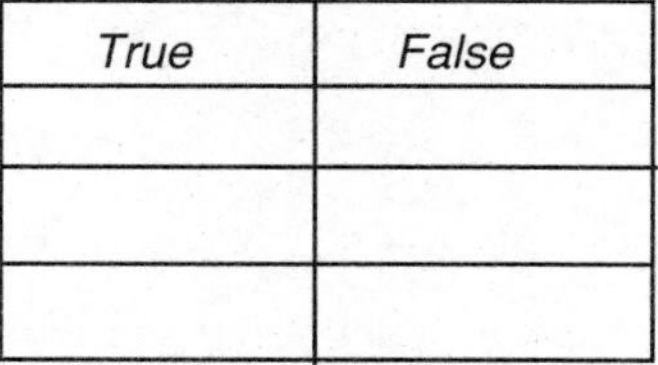

True	False

5 What variable is used to signify 'time' in the regression equation y = a + bx when regression analysis is used for forecasting?

A x
B a
C b
D y

6 Which of the four components of a time series is missing from the list below?

Trend
Seasonal variations
Random variations

7 *Fill in the gaps with the appropriate mathematical symbols.*

Additive model of time series	Y = T .... S .... R
Seasonal component, S	S = Y .... T
Proportional model of time series	Y = T .... S .... R
Seasonal component, S	S = Y .... T

Answers to quick quiz

1 D

2 line
fit
outside

3 A. When cold drinks sell well, so will suntan cream. Neither sales level causes the other; both are caused by the weather.

4 Statement (a) is true. The coefficient of determination is r^2.
Statement (b) is false. r can reach 1 or –1, so r^2 can reach 1.
Statement (c) is false. Correlation does not prove a causal link.

5 A The correct answer is x.

6 Cyclical variations

7

Additive model of time series	=	T + S + R
Seasonal component, S	=	Y – T
Proportional model of time series	=	T x S x R
Seasonal component, S	=	Y ÷ T

Now try the question below from the Exam Question Bank

Question to try	Level	Marks	Time
17	Exam	25	45 mins

Part D
Decision making

Chapter 14

DECISION MAKING

	Topic list	Syllabus reference
1	**Relevant and non-relevant costs**	**6(f)**
2	**The assumptions in relevant costing**	**6(f)**
3	**Limiting factor analysis**	**6(f)**
4	**Make or buy decisions**	**6(f)**
5	**Shutdown problems**	**6(f)**
6	**Extra shift decisions and overtime**	**6(f)**
7	**Accepting or rejecting orders**	**6(f)**
8	**Cost-volume-profit analysis**	**6(f)**
9	**Joint product decisions**	**6(f)**
10	**Pricing decisions**	**6(e), 6(f)**
11	**Qualitative factors in decision making**	**6 (f)**

Introduction

Although **decision making** in general runs throughout the *Financial Management and Control* syllabus (for example, in relation to setting budgets and standards in the chapters you have already covered), we are going to look at the topic in some detail in this chapter.

A management accountant may make decisions, but the principal **role of the management accountant** will be to **provide management information,** to **present that information** to the decision makers to help them to reach their decisions, and to **make recommendations** and **give advice** and **suggestions** to the decision maker. The provision of this management information is a complex task, decision-making information being unlike the accounting information recorded in the financial accounts and/or conventional cost accounts. It is not, however, a difficult task (once you have read this Study Text). It **relies on the application of the principles of marginal costing** (which you have covered in this Study Text), a **knowledge of cost behaviour** (covered in earlier studies) and **relevant costing**, which we will look at in this chapter.

Study guide

Section 27 – Costs and decision making

- Describe and distinguish between relevant and non-relevant costs
- Apply and evaluate limiting factor analysis
- Evaluate make or buy problems, shutdown decisions, additional shift decisions and overtime, accepting or rejecting special orders, and further processing
- Describe and apply cost-volume-profit analysis
- Describe and evaluate different product pricing approaches

Exam guide

Section B questions could well centre on the decision-making techniques covered here. You may also need to apply them as part of a Section A question.

The issues covered in this chapter are useful background to the Oxford Brookes Degree Research and Analysis Project Topic 10, which requires you to analyse how management accounting techniques are used to support decision-making in organisations.

1 RELEVANT AND NON-RELEVANT COSTS

1.1 The **costs which should be used for decision making** are often referred to as **relevant costs.**

KEY TERM

A **relevant cost** is a future cash flow arising as a direct consequence of a decision.

1.2 (a) **Relevant costs are future costs.**

(i) A decision is about the future; it cannot alter what has been done already. A cost that has been incurred in the past is totally irrelevant to any decision that is being made 'now'.

(ii) Costs that have been incurred include not only costs that have already been paid, but also **costs that are the subject of legally binding contracts**, even if payments due under the contract have not yet been made. (These are known as **committed costs**.)

(b) **Relevant costs are cash flows.**

Costs or charges which do not reflect additional cash spending should be **ignored** for the purpose of decision making. These include the following.

(i) **Depreciation,** as a fixed overhead incurred.

(ii) **Notional rent or interest,** as a fixed overhead incurred.

(iii) **All overheads absorbed**. Fixed overhead absorption is always irrelevant since it is overheads to be incurred which affect decisions.

(c) **Relevant costs are incremental costs.**

A relevant cost is one which **arises as a direct consequence of a decision**. Thus, only costs which will differ under some or all of the available opportunities should be considered; relevant costs are therefore sometimes referred to as incremental costs.

Relevant costs are therefore future, incremental cash flows.

1.3 Other terms can be used to describe relevant costs.

KEY TERM

Avoidable costs are costs which would not be incurred if the activity to which they relate did not exist.

One of the situations in which it is necessary to identify the avoidable costs is in deciding whether or not to discontinue a product. The only costs which would be saved are the avoidable costs, which are usually the variable costs and sometimes some specific fixed costs. Costs which would be incurred whether or not the product is discontinued are known as unavoidable costs.

KEY TERM

Opportunity cost is the benefit which could have been earned, but which has been given up, by choosing one option instead of another.

Suppose for example that there are three mutually exclusive options, A, B and C. The net profit from each would be £80, £100 and £70 respectively. Since only one option can be selected option B would be chosen because it offers the biggest benefit.

	£
Profit from option B	100
Less opportunity cost (ie the benefit from the most profitable alternative, A)	80
Differential benefit of option B	20

The decision to choose option B would not be taken simply because it offers a profit of £100, but because it offers a differential profit of £20 in excess of the next best alternative.

Exam focus point

Having read the paragraph above, could you now explain what is meant by opportunity cost? If candidates in the December 2001 exam were able to, they were awarded two marks.

Non-relevant costs

1.4 A number of terms are used to describe costs that are **irrelevant for decision making** because they are either not future cash flows or they are costs which will be incurred anyway, regardless of the decision that is taken.

KEY TERM

A **sunk cost** is a cost which has already been incurred and hence should not be taken account of in decision making.

An **example** of this type of cost is **depreciation**. If the fixed asset has been purchased, depreciation may be charged for several years but the cost is a sunk cost, about which nothing can now be done.

KEY TERM

A **committed cost** is a future cash outflow that will be incurred anyway, whatever decision is taken now about alternative opportunities.

Committed costs may exist because of contracts already entered into by the organisation, which it cannot get out of.

KEY TERM

A **notional cost** or **imputed cost** is a hypothetical accounting cost to reflect the use of a benefit for which no actual cash expense is incurred.

Examples in cost accounting systems include **notional rent** (such as that charged to a subsidiary of an organisation for the use of accommodation which the organisation owns) or **notional interest** charges on capital employed (sometimes made against a profit centre or cost centre).

Although **historical costs** are irrelevant for decision making, historical cost data will often provide the best available basis for predicting future costs.

Fixed and variable costs

1.5 Unless you are given an indication to the contrary, you should assume the following.

(a) Variable costs will be relevant costs.
(b) Fixed costs are irrelevant to a decision.

This need not be the case, however, and you should analyse variable and fixed cost data carefully. Do not forget that 'fixed' costs may only be fixed in the short term.

1.6 There might, however, be occasions when a variable cost is in fact a sunk cost. For example, suppose that a company has some units of raw material in stock. They have been paid for already, and originally cost £2,000. They are now obsolete and are no longer used in regular production, and they have no scrap value. However, they could be used in a special job which the company is trying to decide whether to undertake. The special job is a 'one-off' customer order, and would use up all these materials in stock.

In deciding whether the job should be undertaken, the relevant cost of the materials to the special job is nil. Their original cost of £2,000 is a sunk cost, and should be ignored in the decision.

However, if the materials did have a scrap value of, say, £300, then their relevant cost to the job would be the opportunity cost of being unable to sell them for scrap, ie £300.

Attributable fixed costs

1.7 There might be occasions when a fixed cost is a relevant cost.

(a) **Directly attributable fixed costs** are those costs which, although fixed within a relevant range of activity level, or regarded as fixed because management has set a budgeted expenditure level (for example advertising costs are often treated as fixed), would, in fact, do one of two things.

   (i) **Increase if certain extra activities were undertaken**

   (ii) **Decrease/be eliminated entirely if a decision were taken either to reduce the scale of operations or shut down entirely**

(b) **General fixed overheads** are those fixed overheads which will be **unaffected** by **decisions to increase or decrease the scale of operations**. An apportioned share of head office charges is an example.

1.8 You should appreciate that whereas **directly attributable fixed costs will be relevant** to a decision in hand, **general fixed overheads will not be.**

1.9 EXAMPLE: RELEVANT COSTS

A company has been making a machine to order for a customer, but the customer has since gone into liquidation, and there is no prospect that any money will be obtained from the winding up of the company. Costs incurred to date in manufacturing the machine are £50,000 and progress payments of £15,000 had been received from the customer prior to the liquidation. The sales department has found another company willing to buy the machine for £34,000 once it has been completed. To complete the work, the following costs would be incurred.

(a) Materials: these have been bought at a cost of £6,000. They have no other use, and if the machine is not finished, they would be sold for scrap for £2,000.

(b) Further labour costs would be £8,000. Labour is in short supply, and if the machine is not finished, the work force would be switched to another job, which would earn £30,000 in revenue, and incur direct costs of £12,000 and absorbed (fixed) overhead of £8,000.

(c) Consultancy fees £4,000. If the work is not completed, the consultant's contract would be cancelled at a cost of £1,500.

(d) General overheads of £8,000 would be added to the cost of the additional work.

Required

Assess whether the new customer's offer should be accepted.

1.10 SOLUTION

(a) **Costs incurred in the past, or revenue received in the past are not relevant** because they cannot affect a decision about what is best for the future. Costs incurred to date of £50,000 and revenue received of £15,000 should therefore be ignored.

(b) Similarly, the price paid in the past for the materials is irrelevant. The only relevant cost of materials affecting the decision is the **opportunity cost** of the revenue from scrap which would be forgone - £2,000.

(c)

	£
Labour costs required to complete work	8,000
Opportunity costs: contribution forgone by losing other work £(30,000 – 12,000)	18,000
Relevant cost of labour	26,000

(d) The **incremental** cost of consultancy from completing the work is the difference between the cost of completing the work and the cost of cancelling the contract (£(4,000 – 1,500) = £2,500).

(e) **Absorbed overhead** is a notional accounting cost and should be **ignored.** Actual overhead incurred is the only overhead cost to consider. General overhead costs (and the absorbed overhead of the alternative work for the labour force) should be ignored.

(f) **Relevant costs** may be summarised as follows.

		£	£
Revenue from completing work			34,000
Relevant costs			
Materials:	opportunity cost	2,000	
Labour:	basic pay	8,000	
	opportunity cost	18,000	
Incremental cost of consultant		2,500	
			30,500
Extra profit to be earned by accepting the completion order			3,500

Exam focus point

A relevant costing question requiring a similar approach to that used in the example above appeared in the December 2001 paper. If you understand the example above then you would have had no problem in picking up the 11 marks available in the exam.

Identifying relevant costs

The relevant cost of materials

1.11 The relevant cost of raw materials is generally their **current replacement cost** unless the **materials have already been purchased but will not be replaced.** The relevant cost of using them will then be the **higher** of the following.

- Their **current resale value**

- The **value they would obtain if they were put to an alternative use**

If the materials have no resale value and no other possible use, then the relevant cost of using them for the opportunity under consideration would be nil.

1.12 The flowchart below shows how the relevant costs of materials can be identified, **provided that** the materials are **not in short supply** and so have **no internal opportunity cost**.

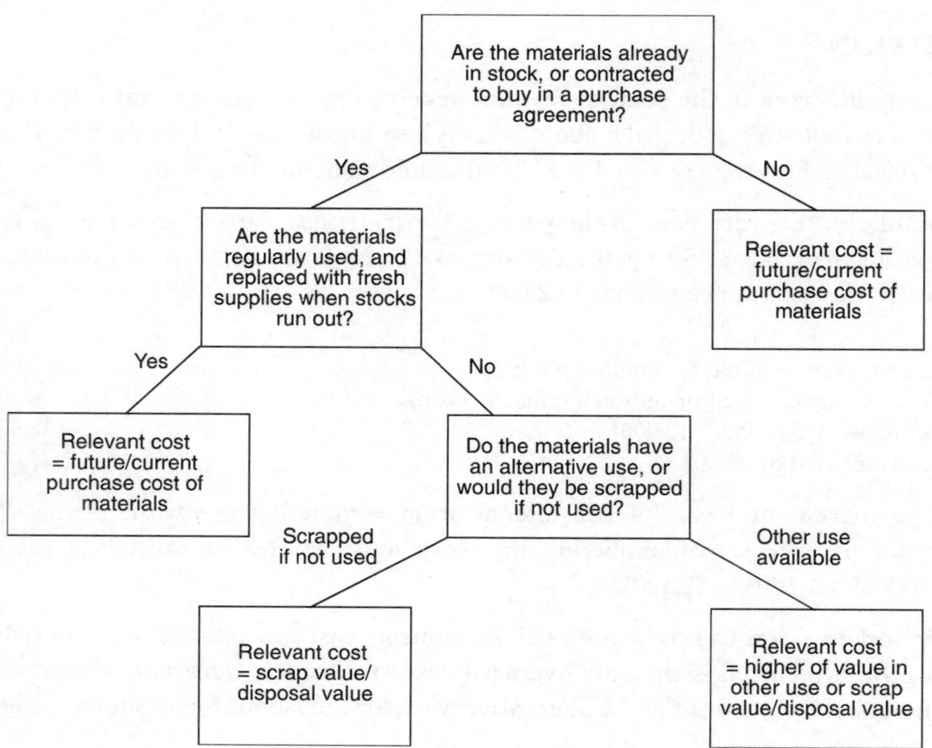

1.13 You should test your knowledge of the relevant cost of materials by attempting the following question.

Question 1

Darwin Ltd has been approached by a customer who would like a special job to be done for him, and who is willing to pay £22,000 for it. The job would require the following materials.

Material	*Total units required*	*Units already in stock*	*Book value of units in stock* £/unit	*Realisable value* £/unit	*Replacement cost* £/unit
A	1,000	0	-	-	6.00
B	1,000	600	2.00	2.50	5.00
C	1,000	700	3.00	2.50	4.00
D	200	200	4.00	6.00	9.00

Material B is used regularly by Darwin Ltd, and if units of B are required for this job, they would need to be replaced to meet other production demand.

Materials C and D are in stock as the result of previous over buying, and they have a restricted use. No other use could be found for material C, but the units of material D could be used in another job as substitute for 300 units of material E, which currently costs £5 per unit (and of which the company has no units in stock at the moment).

Required

Calculate the relevant costs of material for deciding whether or not to accept the contract.

Answer

(a) **Material A** is not yet owned. It would have to be bought in full at the replacement cost of £6 per unit.

(b) **Material B** is used regularly by the company. There are existing stocks (600 units) but if these are used on the contract under review a further 600 units would be bought to replace them. Relevant costs are therefore 1,000 units at the replacement cost of £5 per unit.

(c) 1,000 units of **material C** are needed and 700 are already in stock. If used for the contract, a further 300 units must be bought at £4 each. The existing stocks of 700 will not be replaced. If they are used for the contract, they could not be sold at £2.50 each. The realisable value of these 700 units is an opportunity cost of sales revenue forgone.

(d) The required units of **material D** are already in stock and will not be replaced. There is an opportunity cost of using D in the contract because there are alternative opportunities either to sell the existing stocks for £6 per unit (£1,200 in total) or avoid other purchases (of material E), which would cost 300 × £5 = £1,500. Since substitution for E is more beneficial, £1,500 is the opportunity cost.

(e) **Summary of relevant costs**

	£
Material A (1,000 × £6)	6,000
Material B (1,000 × £5)	5,000
Material C (300 × £4) plus (700 × £2.50)	2,950
Material D	1,500
Total	15,450

The relevant cost of using machines

1.14 Once a machine has been bought its cost is a **sunk** cost. **Depreciation** is not a relevant cost, because it is not a cash flow. However, **using** machinery may involve some incremental costs. These costs might be referred to as **user costs** and they include hire charges and any fall in resale value of owned assets, through use.

1.15 EXAMPLE: THE RELEVANT COST OF USING MACHINES

Sydney Ltd is considering whether to undertake some contract work for a customer. The machinery required for the contract would be as follows.

(a) A special cutting machine will have to be hired for three months for the work (the length of the contract). Hire charges for this machine are £75 per month, with a minimum hire charge of £300.

(b) All other machinery required in the production for the contract has already been purchased by the organisation on hire purchase terms. The monthly hire purchase payments for this machinery are £500. This consists of £450 for capital repayment and £50 as an interest charge. The last hire purchase payment is to be made in two months' time. The cash price of this machinery was £9,000 two years ago. It is being depreciated on a straight line basis at the rate of £200 per month. However, it still has a useful life which will enable it to be operated for another 36 months.

The machinery is highly specialised and is unlikely to be required for other, more profitable jobs over the period during which the contract work would be carried out. Although there is no immediate market for selling this machine, it is expected that a customer might be found in the future. It is further estimated that the machine would lose £200 in its eventual sale value if it is used for the contract work.

Required

Calculate the relevant cost of machinery for the contract.

1.16 SOLUTION

(a) The cutting machine will incur an incremental cost of £300, the minimum hire charge.

(b) The historical cost of the other machinery is irrelevant as a past cost; depreciation is irrelevant as a non-cash cost; and future hire purchase repayments are irrelevant because they are committed costs. The only relevant cost is the loss of resale value of the machinery, estimated at £200 through use. This user cost will not arise until the machinery is eventually resold and the £200 should be discounted to allow for the time value of money. However, discounting is ignored here.

(c) **Summary of relevant costs**

	£
Incremental hire costs	300
User cost of other machinery	200
	500

Question 2

A machine which originally cost £12,000 has an estimated life of ten years and is depreciated at the rate of £1,200 a year. It has been unused for some time, however, as expected production orders did not materialise.

A special order has now been received which would require the use of the machine for two months.

The current net realisable value of the machine is £8,000. If it is used for the job, its value is expected to fall to £7,500. The net book value of the machine is £8,400.

Routine maintenance of the machine currently costs £40 a month. With use, the cost of maintenance and repairs would increase to £60 a month.

Ignore the time value of money.

Required

Calculate the relevant cost of using the machine for the order.

Answer

	£
Loss in net realisable value of the machine through using it on the order £(8,000 – 7,500)	500
Costs in excess of existing routine maintenance costs £(120 – 80)	40
Total marginal user cost	540

Relevant cost of labour

1.17 **Often** the labour force will be paid irrespective of the decision made and the costs are therefore **not incremental**. Take care, however, if the labour force could be put to an **alternative use**, in which case the relevant costs are the **variable costs** of the labour and associated variable overheads **plus** the **contribution forgone** from not being able to put it to its alternative use.

2 THE ASSUMPTIONS IN RELEVANT COSTING

2.1 If you make an assumption in answering an examination question and you are not sure that the examiner or marker will appreciate or recognise the assumption you are making, you should explain it in narrative in your solution.

2.2 Some of the **assumptions** that are typically made in relevant costing are as follows.

(a) **Cost behaviour patterns are known**; if a department closes down, for example, the attributable fixed cost savings would be known.

(b) The **amount** of fixed costs, unit variable costs, sales price and sales demand are **known with certainty**.

(c) The objective of decision making in the short run is to **maximise 'satisfaction'**, which is often regarded as '**short-term profit**'.

(d) The **information** on which a decision is based is **complete and reliable**.

3 LIMITING FACTOR ANALYSIS

3.1 One of the more common decision-making problems is a budgeting decision in a situation where there are not enough resources to meet the potential sales demand, and so a decision has to be made about using what resources there are as effectively as possible.

KEY TERM

A **key factor** or **limiting factor** is a scarce resource which limits the activity of an organisation.

3.2 There might be just one limiting factor (other than maximum sales demand) but there might also be several scarce resources, with two or more of them putting an effective limit on the level of activity that can be achieved. We shall concentrate on single limiting factor problems and a technique for resolving these.

3.3 A limiting factor could be sales if there is a limit to sales demand but any one of the organisation's resources (labour, materials, manufacturing capacity, financial resources and so on) may be insufficient to meet the level of production demanded.

(a) If **sales demand** is the factor which **restricts greater production output, profit will be maximised by making exactly the amount required for sales** (and no more) **provided that each product sold earns a positive contribution.**

(b) If **labour supply, materials availability, machine capacity or cash availability limits production** to less than the volume which could be sold, management is faced with the **problem of deciding what to produce** and what should not be produced because there are insufficient resources to make everything.

3.4 **It is assumed in limiting factor accounting that management wishes to maximise profit and that profit will be maximised when contribution is maximised** (given no change in fixed cost expenditure incurred). In other words, marginal costing ideas are applied.

Contribution will be maximised by earning the biggest possible contribution per unit of limiting factor. Thus if grade A labour is the limiting factor, contribution will be maximised by earning the biggest contribution per hour of grade A labour worked.

The **limiting factor decision** therefore **involves the determination of the contribution earned by each different product per unit of limiting factor.** In limiting factor decisions, we generally **assume that fixed costs are the same whatever production mix is selected,** so that the **only relevant costs are variable costs.**

3.5 EXAMPLE: LIMITING FACTOR

D Ltd makes two products, the B and the S. Unit variable costs are as follows.

	B	*S*
	£	£
Direct materials	1	3
Direct labour (£3 per hour)	6	3
Variable overhead	1	1
	8	7

The sales price per unit is £14 per B and £11 per S. During July the available direct labour is limited to 8,000 hours. Sales demand in July is expected to be 3,000 units for B and 5,000 units for S.

Required

Determine the profit-maximising production levels, assuming that monthly fixed costs are £20,000, and that opening stocks of finished goods and work in progress are nil.

3.6 SOLUTION

Step 1. **Confirm that the limiting factor is something other than sales demand.**

	B	*S*	*Total*
Labour hours per unit	2 hrs	1 hr	
Sales demand	3,000 units	5,000 units	
Labour hours needed	6,000 hrs	5,000 hrs	11,000 hrs
Labour hours available			8,000 hrs
Shortfall			3,000 hrs

Labour is the limiting factor on production.

Step 2. **Identify the contribution earned by each product per unit of scarce resource,** that is per labour hour worked.

	B	*S*
	£	£
Sales price	14	11
Variable cost	8	7
Unit contribution	6	4
Labour hours per unit	2 hrs	1 hr
Contribution per labour hour (= unit of limiting factor)	£3	£4

Although Bs have a higher unit contribution than Ss, two Ss can be made in the time it takes to make one B. Because labour is in short supply it is more profitable to make Ss than Bs.

Step 3. **Work out the budgeted production and sales.** Sufficient Ss will be made to meet the full sales demand, and the remaining labour hours available will then be used to make Bs.

(a)

Product	*Demand*	*Hours Required*	*Hours available*	*Priority of manufacture*
S	5,000	5,000	5,000	1st
B	3,000	6,000	3,000 (bal)	2nd
		11,000	8,000	

(b)

Product	Units	Hours Needed	Contribution per unit	Total
			£	£
S	5,000	5,000	4	20,000
B	1,500	3,000	6	9,000
		8,000		29,000
Less fixed costs				20,000
Profit				9,000

Note that it is *not* more profitable to begin by making as many units as possible of the product with the bigger unit contribution. We could make 3,000 units of B in 6,000 hours and 2,000 units of S in the remaining 2,000 hours but profit would be only £6,000. Unit contribution is not the correct way to decide priorities, because it takes two hours to earn £6 from a B and one hour to earn £4 from a S. Ss make more profitable use of the scarce resource, labour hours.

Question 3

Twickers Ltd makes two products, widgets and splodgets, for which there is unlimited demand at the budgeted selling prices. A widget takes three hours to make, and has a variable cost of £18 and a selling price of £30. A splodget takes two hours to make, and has a variable cost of £10 and a selling price of £20. Both products use the same type of labour, which is in short supply.

Required

Determine the product which should be made to maximise profits, and describe the other considerations which might alter your decision.

Answer

We must **rank** the products in order of **contribution earning capability per labour hour**.

	Widgets per unit	Splodgets per unit
	£	£
Sales price	30	20
Variable costs	18	10
Contribution	12	10
Hours per unit	3	2
Contribution per labour hour	£4	£5

Although widgets have the higher unit contribution, splodgets are more profitable because they make a greater contribution per labour hour. Three splodgets (worth 3 × £10 = £30) can be made in the same time as two widgets (worth only 2 × £12 = £24).

A profit-maximising decision would therefore be to produce splodgets only, given the assumptions made. It is important to remember, however, that **other considerations**, so far excluded from the problem, might alter the decision.

(a) Can the selling price of either product be raised, thereby increasing unit contribution, and the contribution per labour hour, and also reducing demand? Since demand is apparently unlimited, it would be reasonable to suspect that both products are underpriced.

(b) Would a decision to make and sell only splodgets have a harmful effect on customer loyalty and demand? To what extent are sales of each product interdependent? For example, a manufacturer of knives and forks could not expect to cease production of knives without affecting demand for forks.

(c) Would a decision to cease production of widgets have no effect on fixed costs? The assumption that fixed costs are unaffected by limiting factor decisions is not always valid, and closure of either the widgets or the splodgets production line might result in fixed cost savings. These savings would need to be considered when making the product mix decision.

(d) Will the decision affect the long-term plans of the company as well as the short term? If widgets are not produced, it is likely that competitors will take over the markets vacated by Twickers Ltd. Labour skilled in the manufacture of widgets will be lost, and a decision at a later date to re-open manufacture of widgets might not be possible.

Limiting factor analysis and restricted freedom of action

3.7 In certain circumstances an organisation faced with a limiting factor on production and sales **might not be able to produce the profit-maximising product mix** because the mix and/or volume of products that can be produced and sold is also restricted by a factor other than a scarce resource.

(a) The organisation might have **contracted to supply a certain number of products** to a customer.

(b) The organisation might have to produce and sell a minimum quantity of one or more of its products to **provide a complete product range and/or to maintain customer goodwill.**

(c) The organisation might need to **maintain a certain market share** of one or more of its products.

3.8 In each of these cases, the organisation might have to **produce more of a particular product or products than the level established by ranking** according to contribution per unit of limiting factor.

3.9 The basic approach to dealing with such situations is to **rank the products in the normal way** but the **optimum production plan must take into account the minimum production requirements. The remaining resource must then be allocated according to the ranking.**

3.10 Work carefully through the following example which illustrates this approach.

3.11 EXAMPLE: RESTRICTED FREEDOM OF ACTION

Harvey Ltd is currently preparing its budget for the year ending 30 September 20X2. The company manufactures and sells three products, Beta, Delta and Gamma.

The unit selling price and cost structure of each product is budgeted as follows.

	Beta	*Delta*	*Gamma*
	£	£	£
Selling price	100	124	32
Variable costs:			
Labour	24	48	6
Materials	26	7	8
Overhead	10	5	6
	60	60	20
Contribution per unit	40	64	12

Direct labour rate is budgeted at £6 per hour, and fixed costs at £1,300,000 per annum. The company has a maximum production capacity of 228,000 direct labour hours.

A meeting of the board of directors has been convened to discuss the budget and to resolve the problem as to the quantity of each product which should be made and sold. The sales director presented the results of a recent market survey which reveals that market demand for the company's products will be as follows.

Product	*Units*
Beta	24,000
Delta	12,000
Gamma	60,000

The production director proposes that since Gamma only contributes £12 per unit, the product should no longer be produced, and the surplus capacity transferred to produce additional quantities of Beta and Delta. The sales director does not agree with the proposal. Gamma is considered necessary to complement the product range and to maintain customer goodwill. If Gamma is not offered, the sales director believes that sales of Beta and Delta will be seriously affected. After further discussion the board decided that a minimum of 10,000 units of each product should be produced. The remaining production capacity would then be allocated so as to achieve the maximum profit possible.

Required

Prepare a budget statement which clearly shows the maximum profit which could be achieved in the year ending 30 September 20X2.

3.12 SOLUTION

Step 1. **Ascertain whether labour hours are a scarce resource.**

	Units demanded	*Labour hours per unit*	*Total labour hours*
Beta	24,000	4 (£24/£6)	96,000
Delta	12,000	8 (£48/£6)	96,000
Gamma	60,000	1 (£6/£6)	60,000
			252,000

Step 2. **Rank the products.**

Since only 228,000 hours are available we need to establish which product earns the greatest contribution per labour hour.

	Beta	*Delta*	*Gamma*
Contribution	40	64	12
Labour hours	4	8	1
Contribution per labour hour	£10	£8	£12
Ranking	2nd	3rd	1st

Step 3. **Determine a production plan.**

The optimum production plan must take into account the requirement that 10,000 units of each product are produced, and then allocate the remaining hours according to the above ranking.

		Hours
Beta	10,000 units × 4 hours	40,000
Delta	10,000 units × 8 hours	80,000
Gamma	10,000 units × 1 hour	10,000
		130,000
Gamma	50,000 units × 1 hour (full demand)	50,000
Beta	12,000 units × 4 hours (balance)	48,000
		228,000

Step 4. **Draw up a budget.**

BUDGET STATEMENT

Contribution	£
Beta (22,000 units × £40)	880,000
Delta (10,000 units × £64)	640,000
Gamma (60,000 units × £12)	720,000
	2,240,000
Fixed costs	1,300,000
Profit	940,000

Question 4

Jam Ltd makes two products, the K and the L. The K sells for £50 per unit, the L for £70 per unit. The variable cost per unit of the K is £35, that of the L £40. Each unit of K uses 2 kgs of raw material. Each unit of L uses 3 kgs of material.

In the forthcoming period the availability of raw material is limited to 2,000 kgs. Jam Ltd is contracted to supply 500 units of K. Maximum demand for the L is 250 units. Demand for the K is unlimited.

What is the profit-maximising product mix?

Answer

	K	*L*
Contribution per unit	£15	£30
Contribution per unit of limiting factor	£15/2 = £7.50	£30/3 = £10
Ranking	2	1

Production plan	*Raw material used*
	kg
Contracted supply of K (500 x 2 kg)	1,000
Meet demand for L (250 x 3 kg)	750
Remainder of resource for K (125 x 2 kg)	250
	2,000

∴ Produce 250 units of L and 625 units of K.

Limiting factors and shadow prices

3.13 Whenever there are limiting factors, there will be **opportunity costs.** For example, suppose that a company manufactures two items X and Y, which earn a contribution of £24 and £18 per unit respectively. Product X requires 4 machine hours per unit, and product Y 2 hours. Only 5,000 machine hours are available, and potential sales demand is for 1,000 units each of X and Y.

3.14 Machine hours would be a limiting factor, and with X earning £6 per hour and Y earning £9 per hour, the profit-maximising decision would be as follows.

	Units	Hours	*Contribution* £
Y	1,000	2,000	18,000
X (balance)	750	3,000	18,000
		5,000	36,000

Priority is given to Y because the **opportunity cost** of making Y instead of more units of X is £6 per hour (X's contribution per machine hour), and since Y earns £9 per hour, the incremental benefit of making Y instead of X would be £3 per hour.

3.15 If extra machine hours could be made available, more units of X (up to 1,000) would be made, and an extra contribution of £6 per hour could be earned. Similarly, if fewer machine hours were available, the decision would be to make fewer units of X and to keep production of Y at 1,000 units, and so the loss of machine hours would cost the company £6 per hour in lost contribution. This £6 per hour, the **marginal contribution-earning potential of the limiting factor at the profit-maximising output level,** is referred to as the **shadow price** (or **dual price**) of the limiting factor.

> **KEY TERM**
>
> A **shadow price** is the increase in value obtainable from having available one additional unit of a limiting resource at the original cost.

Note that the shadow price only applies while the extra unit of resource can be obtained at its normal variable cost. The shadow price also indicates the amount by which contribution could fall if an organisation is deprived of one unit of the resource.

3.16 The shadow price of a resource is its **internal opportunity cost.** This is the marginal contribution towards fixed costs and profit that can be earned for each unit of the limiting factor that is available. A knowledge of the shadow price of a resource will help managers to decide how much it is worth paying to acquire another unit of the resource.

Using limiting factor analysis

3.17 Limiting factor analysis provides us with a profit-maximising product mix, within the assumptions made. It is important to remember, however, that other considerations might entirely alter the decision reached.

Qualitative factors

3.18 When a decision is being made, qualitative factors should also be borne in mind.

Factor	Examples
Demand	Will the decision reached (perhaps to make and sell just one product rather than two) have a harmful effect on customer loyalty and sales demand? For example, a manufacturer of knives and forks could not expect to cease production of knives without affecting sales demand for the forks.
Long-term effects	Is the decision going to affect the long-term as well as the short-term plans of the organisation? If a particular product is not produced, or produced at a level below sales demand, is it likely that competitors will take over vacated markets? Labour skilled in the manufacture of the product may be lost and a decision to reopen or expand production of the product in the future may not be possible.
Labour	If labour is a limiting factor, is it because the skills required are difficult to obtain, perhaps because the organisation is using very old-fashioned production methods, or is the organisation a high-tech newcomer in a low-tech area? Or perhaps the conditions of work are so unappealing the people simply do not want to work for the organisation.
Other limiting factors	The same sort of questions should be asked whatever the limiting factor. If machine hours are in short supply is this because more machines are needed, or newer, more reliable and efficient machines? If materials are in short supply, what are competitors doing? Have they found an equivalent or better substitute? Is it time to redesign the product?

Assumptions in limiting factor analysis

3.19 In the examples we have been looking at, certain assumptions have been made. If any of the assumptions are not valid, then the profit-maximising decision might be different. These assumptions are as follows.

(a) **Fixed costs will be the same** regardless of the decision that is taken, and so the profit-maximising and contribution-maximising output level will be the same.

This will not necessarily be true, since some fixed costs might be directly attributable to a product or service. A decision to reduce or cease altogether activity on a product or service might therefore result in some fixed cost savings, which would have to be taken into account.

(b) **The unit variable cost is constant,** regardless of the output quantity of a product or service. This implies the following.

(i) The price of resources will be unchanged regardless of quantity; for example, there will be no bulk purchase discount of raw materials.

(ii) Efficiency and productivity levels will be unchanged; regardless of output quantity the direct labour productivity, the machine time per unit, and the materials consumption per unit will remain the same.

(c) **The estimates of sales demand** for each product, and the **resources required** to make each product, **are known with certainty.**

In the example in Paragraph 3.5, there were estimates of the maximum sales demand for the two products, and these estimates were used to establish the profit-maximising product mix. Suppose the estimates were wrong? The product mix finally chosen would then either mean that some sales demand of the most profitable item would be unsatisfied, or that production would exceed sales demand, leaving some stock unsold. Clearly, once a profit-maximising output decision is reached, management will have to keep their decision under continual review, and adjust their decision as appropriate in the light of actual results.

(d) **Units of output are divisible,** and a profit-maximising solution might include fractions of units as the optimum output level.

Where fractional answers are not realistic, some rounding of the figures will be necessary.

Exam focus point

An examination problem might present you with a situation in which there is a limiting factor, without specifically stating that this is so, and you will have the task of recognising what the situation is. You may be given a hint with the wording of the question.

(a) 'It is possible that the main raw material used in manufacturing the products will be difficult to obtain in the next year.'

(b) 'The company employs a fixed number of employees who work a maximum overtime of eight hours on top of the basic 36 hour week. The company has also agreed that no more staff will be recruited next year.'

In (a) there is a hint that raw materials might be a limiting factor. In (b), perhaps less obviously, a maximum limit is placed on the available labour hours, and so the possibility should occur to you that perhaps labour is a limiting factor.

If you suspect the existence of a limiting factor, some quick computations should confirm your suspicions.

(a) Calculate the amount of the scarce resource (material quantities, labour hours, machine hours and so on) needed to meet the potential sales demand.

(b) Calculate the amount of the scarce resource available (for example number of employees multiplied by maximum working hours per employee).

4 MAKE OR BUY DECISIONS

4.1 A make or buy problem involves a decision by an organisation about whether it should make a product or carry out an activity with its own internal resources, or whether it should pay another organisation to make the product or carry out the activity. Examples include

whether a company should manufacture its own components, or else buy the components from an outside supplier.

4.2 The 'make' option should give management **more direct control** over the work, but the **'buy' option** often has the benefit that the external organisation has a **specialist skill and expertise** in the work. Make or buy decisions should certainly not be based exclusively on cost considerations.

4.3 If an organisation has the freedom of choice about whether to make internally or buy externally and has no scarce resources that put a restriction on what it can do itself, the **relevant costs** for the decision will be the **differential costs between the two options.**

4.4 EXAMPLE: MAKE OR BUY

Shellfish Ltd makes four components, W, X, Y and Z, for which costs in the forthcoming year are expected to be as follows.

	W	*X*	*Y*	*Z*
Production (units)	1,000	2,000	4,000	3,000
Unit marginal costs	£	£	£	£
Direct materials	4	5	2	4
Direct labour	8	9	4	6
Variable production overheads	2	3	1	2
	14	17	7	12

Directly attributable fixed costs per annum and committed fixed costs are as follows.

	£
Incurred as a direct consequence of making W	1,000
Incurred as a direct consequence of making X	5,000
Incurred as a direct consequence of making Y	6,000
Incurred as a direct consequence of making Z	8,000
Other fixed costs (committed)	30,000
	50,000

A subcontractor can supply units of W, X, Y and Z for £12, £21, £10 and £14 respectively.

Required

Decide whether Shellfish Ltd should make or buy the components.

4.5 SOLUTION AND DISCUSSION

(a) The **relevant costs** are the **differential costs between making and buying,** and they consist of **differences in unit variable costs plus differences in directly attributable fixed costs.** Subcontracting will result in some fixed cost savings.

	W	*X*	*Y*	*Z*
	£	£	£	£
Unit variable cost of making	14	17	7	12
Unit variable cost of buying	12	21	10	14
	£(2)	£4	£3	£2
Annual requirements (units)	1,000	2,000	4,000	3,000

	W	*X*	*Y*	*Z*
	£	£	£	£
Extra variable cost of buying (per annum)	(2,000)	8,000	12,000	6,000
Fixed costs saved by buying	1,000	5,000	6,000	8,000
Extra total cost of buying	(3,000)	3,000	6,000	(2,000)

(b) The company would save £3,000 pa by subcontracting component W (where the purchase cost would be less than the marginal cost per unit to make internally) and would save £2,000 pa by subcontracting component Z (because of the saving in fixed costs of £8,000).

(c) Important **further considerations** would be as follows.

(i) If components W and Z are subcontracted, the company will have spare capacity. How should that **spare capacity be profitably used**? Are there **hidden benefits** to be obtained from subcontracting? Would the company's workforce resent the loss of work to an outside subcontractor, and might such a decision cause an **industrial dispute**?

(ii) Would the subcontractor be **reliable with delivery times,** and would he supply components of the same **quality** as those manufactured internally?

(iii) Does the company wish to be **flexible** and **maintain better control** over operations by making everything itself?

(iv) Are the **estimates** of fixed cost savings **reliable**? In the case of Product W, buying is clearly cheaper than making in-house. In the case of product Z, the decision to buy rather than make would only be financially beneficial if the fixed cost savings of £8,000 could really be 'delivered' by management.

Exam focus point

In the exam you are unlikely to be asked to make a decision based solely on numerical analysis. The examiner could well ask you to discuss non-quantitative issues such as those covered in (c) above. This was the case in the December 2001 exam, when a proposal had to be evaluated (numerically) for five marks, but commentary on the basis of the decision was worth an additional two marks.

Make or buy decisions and scarce resources

4.6 A company might **want to do more things than it has the resources for,** and so its alternatives would be as follows.

(a) Make the best use of the available resources and ignore the opportunities to buy help from outside

(b) Combine internal resources with buying externally so as to do more and increase profitability

4.7 Buying help from outside is justifiable if it adds to profits. A further decision is then required on how to split the work between internal and external effort. What parts of the work should be given to suppliers or sub-contractors so as to maximise profitability?

4.8 In a situation where a company must **sub-contract work to make up a shortfall in its own in-house capabilities,** its **total costs will be minimised** if those **units bought have the lowest extra variable cost of buying per unit of scarce resource saved.**

This basic principle can be illustrated with a simple example.

4.9 EXAMPLE: MAKE OR BUY DECISION WITH SCARCE RESOURCES

Seaman Ltd manufactures three components, S, A and T using the same machines for each. The budget for the next year calls for the production and assembly of 4,000 of each component. The variable production cost per unit of the final product is as follows.

	Machine hours	Variable cost
		£
1 unit of S	3	20
1 unit of A	2	36
1 unit of T	4	24
Assembly		20
		100

Only 24,000 hours of machine time will be available during the year, and a sub-contractor has quoted the following unit prices for supplying components: S £29; A £40; T £34.

Required

Advise Seaman Ltd.

4.10 SOLUTION

The company's budget calls for 36,000 hours of machine time, if all the components are to be produced in-house. Only 24,000 hours are available, and so there is a shortfall of 12,000 hours of machine time, which is therefore a limiting factor. The shortage can be overcome by subcontracting the equivalent of 12,000 machine hours' output to the subcontractor.

The assembly costs are not relevant costs because they are unaffected by the decision.

The decision rule is to **minimise the extra variable costs of sub-contracting per unit of scarce resource saved** (that is, per machine hour saved).

	S	*A*	*T*
	£	£	£
Variable cost of making	20	36	24
Variable cost of buying	29	40	34
Extra variable cost of buying	9	4	10
Machine hours saved by buying	3 hrs	2 hrs	4 hrs
Extra variable cost of buying per hour saved	£3	£2	£2.50

This analysis shows that it is **cheaper to buy A than to buy T** and it is **most expensive to buy S**. The **priority for making** the components in-house will be in the **reverse order**: S, then T, then A. There are enough machine hours to make all 4,000 units of S (12,000 hours) and to produce 3,000 units of T (another 12,000 hours). 12,000 hours' production of T and A must be sub-contracted.

The cost-minimising and so profit-maximising make and buy schedule is as follows.

	Component	*Machine hours used/saved*	*Number of units*	*Unit variable cost*	*Total variable cost*
				£	£
Make:	S	12,000	4,000	20	80,000
	T	12,000	3,000	24	72,000
		24,000			152,000
Buy:	T	4,000	1,000	34	34,000
	A	8,000	4,000	40	160,000
		12,000			
Total variable cost of components, excluding assembly costs					346,000

Question 5

TW Ltd manufactures two products, the D and the E, using the same material for each. Annual demand for the D is 9,000 units, while demand for the E is 12,000 units.

The variable production cost per unit of the D is £10, that of the E £15. The D requires 3.5 kgs of raw material per unit, the E requires 8 kgs of raw material per unit.

Supply of raw material will be limited to 87,500 kgs during the year.

A sub contractor has quoted prices of £17 per unit for the D and £25 per unit for the E to supply the product.

How many of each product should TW Ltd manufacture in order to maximise profits?

Answer

	D	*E*
	£ per unit	£ per unit
Variable cost of making	10	15
Variable cost of buying	17	25
Extra variable cost of buying	7	10
Raw material saved by buying	3.5 kgs	8 kgs
Extra variable cost of buying per kg saved	£2	£1.25
Priority for internal manufacture	1	2

Production plan			*Material used*
			kgs
∴ Make	D	(9,000 x 3.5 kgs)	31,500
	E	(7,000 x 8 kgs)	56,000
			87,500

The remaining 5,000 units of E should be purchased from the contractor.

9,000 units of D and 7,000 units of E should be manufactured.

5 SHUTDOWN PROBLEMS

5.1 Shutdown problems involve the following type of decisions.

(a) **Whether or not to close down** a factory, department, product line or other activity, either because it is making losses or because it is too expensive to run

(b) If the decision is to shut down, **whether the closure should be permanent or temporary**

5.2 Although in practice shutdown decisions will involve longer-term considerations (such as savings in annual operating costs for a number of years), and capital expenditures and revenues (sales of fixed assets and redundancy payments), it is possible for **shutdown problems to be simplified into short-run decisions,** by assuming that either fixed asset sales and redundancy costs would be negligible or that income from fixed asset sales would match redundancy costs and so these **capital items would be self-cancelling.** In such circumstances the financial aspect of shutdown decisions would be based on short-run relevant costs.

5.3 EXAMPLE: ADDING OR DELETING PRODUCTS

A company manufactures three products, Pawns, Rooks and Bishops. The present net annual income from these is as follows.

	Pawns	*Rooks*	*Bishops*	*Total*
	£	£	£	£
Sales	50,000	40,000	60,000	150,000
Variable costs	30,000	25,000	35,000	90,000
Contribution	20,000	15,000	25,000	60,000
Fixed costs	17,000	18,000	20,000	55,000
Profit/loss	3,000	(3,000)	5,000	5,000

The company is concerned about its poor profit performance, and is considering whether or not to cease selling Rooks. It is felt that selling prices cannot be raised or lowered without adversely affecting net income. £5,000 of the fixed costs of Rooks are direct fixed costs which would be saved if production ceased. All other fixed costs, it is considered, would remain the same.

By **stopping production of Rooks**, the consequences would be a **£10,000 fall in profits.**

	£
Loss of contribution	(15,000)
Savings in fixed costs	5,000
Incremental loss	(10,000)

Suppose, however, it were possible to use the resources realised by stopping production of Rooks and **switch to producing a new item,** Crowners, which would sell for £50,000 and incur variable costs of £30,000 and extra direct fixed costs of £6,000. A new decision is now required.

	Rooks	*Crowners*
	£	£
Sales	40,000	50,000
Less variable costs	25,000	30,000
	15,000	20,000
Less direct fixed costs	5,000	6,000
Contribution to shared fixed costs and profit	10,000	14,000

It would be more profitable to shut down production of Rooks and switch resources to making Crowners, in order to boost profits by £4,000 to £9,000.

Relative profitability

5.4 The relative profitability of products can be judged by **calculation** of their contribution to sales **(C/S) ratios**. Suppose an organisation produces three products A, B and C, and that production capacity is limited. If product A has a C/S ratio of 22%, product B a C/S ratio of 27% and product C a C/S ratio of 25%, given unlimited demand for the three products the organisation should concentrate on producing product B.

Temporary closure

5.5 The decision whether to shut down temporarily should take into account the following factors.

- The **impact on the organisation's other products** and the product in question
- Problems of **recruitment** of skilled labour when production begins again
- Possibility of **plant obsolescence**
- Problems of closing down and **restarting production** in some industries
- Expenditure on disconnection of services, start up costs and so on

If contribution is only just covering fixed costs but improved trading conditions in the future seem likely it may be worth continuing the business.

Other considerations in such decisions

5.6 (a) A product may be retained if it is providing a contribution, albeit a small one. Retaining a wide range of **low volume/low contribution products** would add to the **complexity** and hence costs of manufacture, however, but very little to overall profit. Low volume/low contribution products should therefore be examined on a regular basis.

(b) The **effect on demand for other products** if a particular product is no longer produced should be taken into account.

(c) The extent to which demand for **other products** (existing or new) can expand to **use** the **capacity** vacated by the product being deleted is an issue.

(d) **Pricing policy**. Is the product a **loss leader?** Is the product in the introductory stage of its **life cycle** and consequently priced low to help it to become accepted and hence maximise its long-term market share (**penetration pricing**).

Exam focus point

Be very careful when setting out any relevant cost evaluation. **Do not** incorporate in the same analysis both the incremental costs and revenues that would apply if the decision proceeded (such as continuing with a product) *and* the avoidable costs if it did not (deleting the product). This is a mistake candidates often make. You should consider first a decision to continue with the product and then compare it with a decision to delete the product.

Idle production capacity

5.7 If an organisation does decide to shut down a factory, department, product line or other activity, it may well be faced with a decision about what to do with the resulting idle production capacity.

(a) **Marketing strategies** could be used to increase demand for existing products.

(b) **Idle plant and machinery could be moved to another department** or factory, thereby reducing expenditure on new plant and machinery and/or interest charges.

(c) **Special orders could be accepted,** providing that the contribution generated is either greater than any reduction in fixed overheads which would occur if the idle capacity was not used or greater than any increase in fixed overheads if the idle capacity were to be used.

(d) **Space could be sub-let** to a third party.

Such considerations are particularly important if the closure is only temporary.

6 EXTRA SHIFT DECISIONS AND OVERTIME

6.1 Extra shift decisions are another type of decision problem. They are concerned with whether or not it is worth opening up an extra shift for operations.

6.2 **Qualitative factors** in extra shift decisions include the following.

(a) **Would the work force be willing** to work the shift hours, and if so, what overtime or shift work premium over their basic pay might they expect to receive?

(b) **Do extra hours have to be worked just to remain competitive**? Banks might decide to open on Saturdays just to match what competitors are doing and so keep customers.

(c) Would extra hours result in **more sales revenue, or would there merely be a change in the demand pattern**? For example, if a shop were trying to decide whether to open on Sundays, one consideration would be whether the customers it would get on Sunday would simply be customers who would otherwise have done their shopping on another day of the week instead, or whether they would be additional customers.

6.3 When a business expands, the management is often faced with the problems of whether to acquire larger premises and more plant and machinery and whether to persuade existing personnel to work longer hours (on an overtime basis) or to engage extra staff who would use the existing equipment but at a different time (on a shift basis).

6.4 If the management decide to **incur additional expenditure on premises** and plant, that expenditure is a **fixed cost**. It will therefore be necessary to determine how much additional contribution will be required from the anticipated increased production to cover the extra fixed cost.

If it is decided to use the existing fixed assets, but for a longer period each day, the choice of shift working or overtime will also involve a marginal costing consideration.

(a) If **overtime** is selected, the **direct wages cost per unit produced will be increased** because the wages paid to workers on overtime are a basic rate plus an overtime bonus.

(b) If the management opt for **shift working** the shift premium may not be as expensive as the overtime premium so the **direct wages cost may be relatively lower**. On the other hand, there may be **an increase in fixed (or semi-fixed) costs** such as lighting, heating and canteen facilities.

7 ACCEPTING OR REJECTING ORDERS

7.1 In general terms, an order will probably be accepted if it increases contribution and profit, and rejected if it reduces profit.

If an organisation has **spare capacity** (which means that it would *not* have to turn away existing business), a 'special' (one-off) order (which is normally (in the exam) at a price below the normal price of the product), should be **accepted if the price offered makes some contribution to fixed costs and profit**. In other words, the variable cost of the order needs to be less than the price offered. Fixed costs are irrelevant to such a decision since they will be incurred regardless of whether or not the order is accepted. Additional fixed costs incurred as a result of accepting the order must be taken into account, however.

If an organisation **does not have sufficient spare capacity, existing business should only be turned away if the contribution from the order is greater than the contribution from the business which must be sacrificed.**

7.2 EXAMPLE: ACCEPTING OR REJECTING ORDERS

Holdup Ltd makes a single product which sells for £20, and for which there is great demand. It has a variable cost of £12, made up as follows.

	£
Direct material	4
Direct labour (2 hrs)	6
Variable overhead	2
	12

The labour force is currently working at full capacity producing a product that earns a contribution of £4 per labour hour. A customer has approached the company with a request for the manufacture of a special order for which he is willing to pay £5,500. The costs of the order would be £2,000 for direct materials, and 500 labour hours will be required.

Required

Decide whether the order should be accepted.

7.3 SOLUTION

(a) **Labour is a limiting factor.** By accepting the order, work would have to be diverted away from the standard product, and contribution will be lost, that is, there is an opportunity cost of accepting the new order, which is the contribution forgone by being unable to make the standard product.

(b) Direct labour pay costs £3 per hour, but it is also usually assumed that variable production overhead varies with hours worked, and must therefore be spent in addition to the wages cost of the 500 hours.

(c)

	£	£
Value of order		5,500
Cost of order		
Direct materials	2,000	
Direct labour (500 hrs × £3)	1,500	
Variable overhead (500 hrs × £1)	500	
Opportunity cost (500 hrs × £4) (Contribution forgone)	2,000	
Relevant cost of the order		6,000
Loss incurred by accepting the order		(500)

Although accepting the order would earn a contribution of £1,500 (£5,500 – £4,000), the lost production of the standard product would reduce contribution earned elsewhere by £2,000 and so the order should not be accepted.

Other considerations must also be taken into account, however.

(a) Will **relationships with existing customers,** or prices that can be commanded in the market, be affected if the order is accepted?

(b) As a loss leader, could it **create further business opportunities**?

(c) Should existing business be turned away in order to fulfil a one-off enquiry or could a **long-term contract** be established?

8 COST-VOLUME-PROFIT ANALYSIS

Knowledge brought forward from earlier studies

Cost-volume-profit (breakeven) analysis

- Contribution per unit = unit selling price – unit variable costs
- Profit = (sales volume × contribution per unit) – fixed costs
- Breakeven point = activity level at which there is neither profit nor loss

$$= \frac{\text{total fixed costs}}{\text{contribution per unit}} = \frac{\text{Contribution required to breakeven}}{\text{Contribution per unit}}$$

- Contribution/sales (C/S) ratio = profit/volume (P/V) ratio = (contribution/sales) × 100%
- Sales revenue at breakeven point = fixed costs ÷ C/S ratio
- Margin of safety (in units) = budgeted sales units – breakeven sales units
- Margin of safety (as %) $= \frac{\text{budgeted sales} - \text{breakeven sales}}{\text{budgeted sales}} \times 100\%$
- Sales volume to achieve a target profit $= \frac{\text{fixed cost} + \text{target profit}}{\text{contribution per unit}}$
- Breakeven chart
- Contribution (contribution breakeven) chart

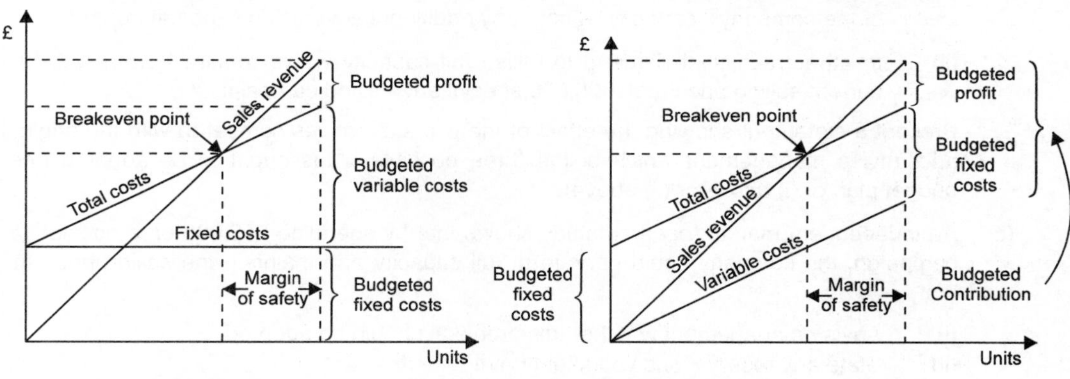

- Profit/volume (P/V) chart
- Multiproduct chart

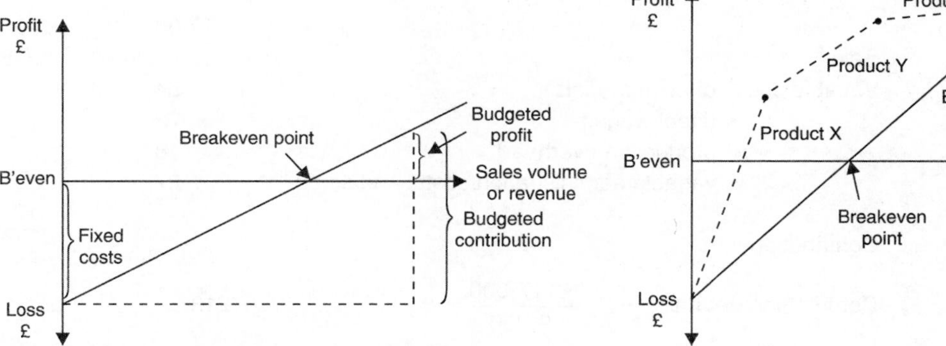

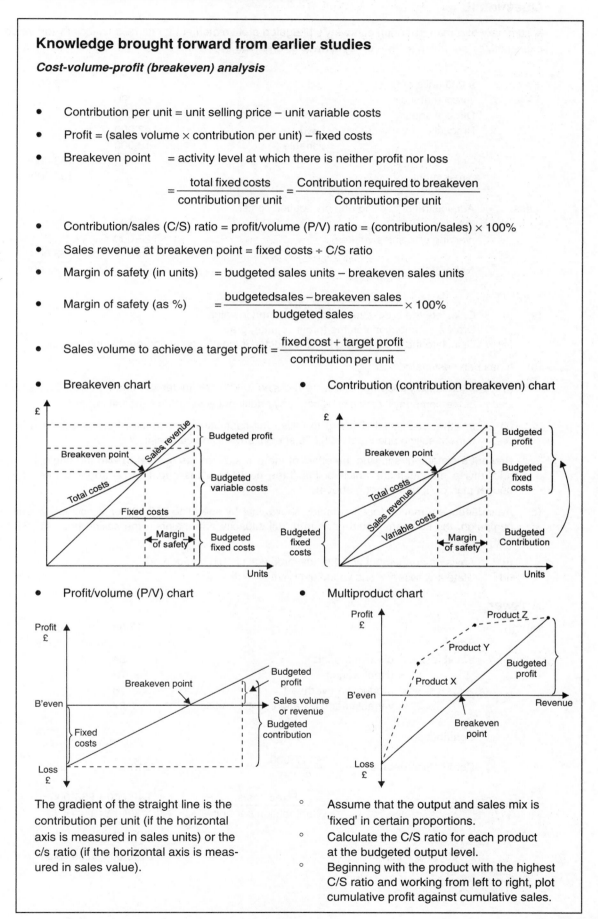

The gradient of the straight line is the contribution per unit (if the horizontal axis is measured in sales units) or the c/s ratio (if the horizontal axis is measured in sales value).

- Assume that the output and sales mix is 'fixed' in certain proportions.
- Calculate the C/S ratio for each product at the budgeted output level.
- Beginning with the product with the highest C/S ratio and working from left to right, plot cumulative profit against cumulative sales.

Question 6

A summary of a manufacturing company's budgeted profit statement for its next financial year, when it expects to be operating at 75% of capacity, is given below.

			£	£
Sales	9,000 units at £32			288,000
Less:	Direct materials		54,000	
	Direct wages		72,000	
	Production overhead:	fixed	42,000	
		variable	18,000	
				186,000
	Gross profit			102,000
Less:	Administration, selling and distribution costs:			
	fixed		36,000	
	varying with sales volume		27,000	
				63,000
	Net profit			39,000

Required

(a) (i) Calculate the breakeven point in units and in value.
(ii) Draw a contribution volume (profit volume) graph.
(iii) Calculate the profit that could be expected if the company operated at full capacity.

(b) It has been estimated that:

(i) if the selling price per unit were reduced to £28, the increased demand would utilise 90% of the company's capacity without any additional advertising expenditure; and

(ii) to attract sufficient demand to utilise full capacity would require a 15% reduction in the current selling price and a £5,000 special advertising campaign.

Present a statement showing the effect of the two alternatives compared with the original budget and advise management which of the three possible plans ought to be adopted (the original budget plan or (i) above or (ii) above).

(c) An independent market research study shows that by spending £15,000 on a special advertising campaign, the company could operate at full capacity and maintain the selling price at £32 per unit.

(i) Advise management whether this proposal should be adopted.
(ii) State any reservations you might have.

Answer

(a) (i)

		£'000	£'000
Sales			288
Variable costs:	direct materials	54	
	direct wages	72	
	production overhead	18	
	variable administration costs, and so on	27	
			171
Contribution			117

$$\text{Contribution per unit} = \frac{£117{,}000}{9{,}000} = £13$$

$$\text{Breakeven point} = \frac{\text{Fixed costs}}{\text{Contribution per unit}} = \frac{£42{,}000 + £36{,}000}{£13}$$

$= 6{,}000$ units

$6{,}000 \text{ units} \times £32 = £192{,}000$ sales value

(ii)

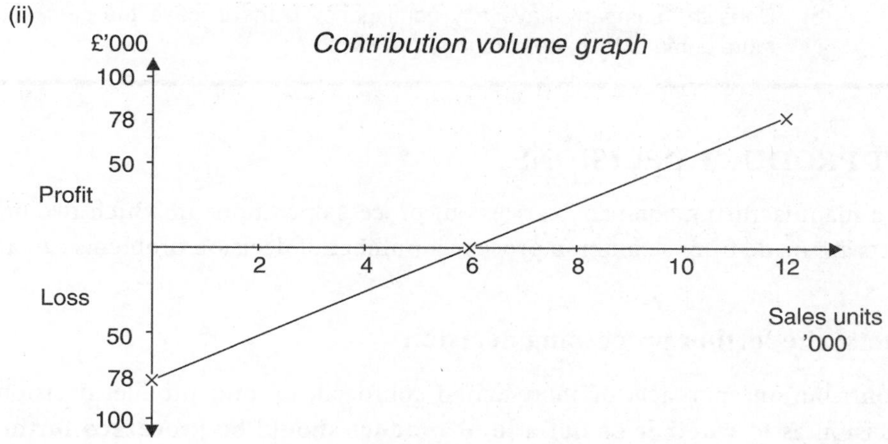

(iii) Assuming that cost behaviour patterns remain the same if activity increases to 100% capacity, a profit of £78,000 can be expected.

	£'000
Contribution (12,000 × £13)	156
Less: fixed production overhead	42
fixed administration costs, and so on	36
Profit	78

(b) *Alternative (i)*

	£'000
Sales (£28 × 10,800 units)	302.4
Variable costs (£171,000 × $\frac{90}{75}$)	205.2
Contribution	97.2
Fixed costs	78.0
Profit	19.2

Alternative (ii)

	£'000	£'000
Sales (£27.20 × 12,000 units)		326.4
Variable costs (£171,000 × $\frac{100}{75}$)		228.0
Contribution		98.4
Fixed costs - budgeted	78.0	
- special advertising	5.0	
		83.0
Profit		15.4

A unit price of £32, as suggested in the original budget plan, should be adopted, as it produces the highest profit of £39,000.

(c) (i)

	£'000	£'000
Sales (£32 × 12,000 units)		384
Variable costs (as (b)(ii))		228
Contribution		156
Fixed costs: budgeted	78	
advertising	15	
		93
Profit		63

The proposed advertising campaign generates a considerable increase in profit and should be adopted.

(ii) Reservations about the recommendation are as follows.

(1) The advertising expenditure has to be incurred before results are known. This increases the risk involved and raises the breakeven point.

(2) How reliable is the market research information?

(3) Does the company have any contingency plans in case the campaign generates more demand than the company can satisfy?

9 JOINT PRODUCT DECISIONS

9.1 When a manufacturing company carries out process operations in which two or more joint products are made from a common process, a number of decision problems can arise.

Joint products: the further processing decision

9.2 The contribution approach, or incremental approach, to joint product decisions concerns the decision as to **whether or not a joint product should be processed further after the point of separation, or whether it should be sold without further processing.** Note that **joint (pre-separation) costs** are incurred regardless of the decision and are therefore **irrelevant.**

9.3 EXAMPLE: FURTHER PROCESSING

The Poison Chemical Company produces two joint products, Alash and Pottum from the same process. Joint processing costs of £150,000 are incurred up to split-off point, when 100,000 units of Alash and 50,000 units of Pottum are produced. The selling prices at split-off point are £1.25 per unit for Alash and £2.00 per unit for Pottum.

The units of Alash could be processed further to produce 60,000 units of a new chemical, Alashplus, but at an extra fixed cost of £20,000 and variable cost of 30p per unit of input. The selling price of Alashplus would be £3.25 per unit.

Required

Ascertain whether the company should sell Alash or Alashplus.

9.4 SOLUTION

The only **relevant costs/incomes** are those which **compare selling Alash against selling Alashplus.** Every other cost is irrelevant: they will be incurred regardless of what the decision is.

	Alash			*Alashplus*
Selling price per unit	£1.25			£3.25
	£		£	£
Total sales	125,000			195,000
		Fixed	20,000	
		Variable	30,000	
Post-separation processing costs	-			50,000
Sales minus post-separation (further processing) costs	125,000			145,000

It is £20,000 more profitable to convert Alash into Alashplus.

Question 7

Ruffage Ltd manufactures two products, T42 and 24T. These products are made jointly in process A, and then processed further, separately, with the manufacture of T42 completed in process B and 24T in process C. Costs and revenues for September were as follows.

2,000 tonnes of material (costing £36,000) were input to process A, 500 tonnes (costing £5,000) were added in process B and 1,000 tonnes (costing £8,000) were added in process C. Labour and overhead were £24,000 in process A, £20,000 in process B and £25,000 in process C.

Output from process A was 1,000 tonnes of part-finished T42 and 1,000 tonnes of part-finished 24T. At this stage in processing the sales value of T42 is £26 per tonne and of 24T is £39 per tonne. All completed output of T42 (1,500 tonnes) was sold in the month for £66,000 and all completed output of 24T (2,000 tonnes) was sold for £66,000.

Required

(a) Calculate the profitability of each product in the month, assuming that joint costs in process A are apportioned using the following methods.

(i) On a physical units basis

(ii) On the basis of sales value at the point of separation

(b) Comment on what these figures suggest about the following.

(i) Whether either product makes losses and ought not to be manufactured

(ii) Whether either product should be sold partially-finished as output from process A, instead of processed further in process B or C

Answer

(a) (i) **Units basis of apportionment**

	Product T42	*Product 24T*	*Total*
	£	£	£
Process A costs (apportioned 1:1)	30,000	30,000	60,000
Process B costs	25,000	-	25,000
Process C costs		33,000	33,000
Total costs	55,000	63,000	118,000
Revenue	66,000	66,000	132,000
Profit	11,000	3,000	14,000

(ii) **Sales revenue basis of apportionment**

	Product T42	*Product 24T*	*Total*
	£	£	£
Process A costs (apportioned 26:39)	24,000	36,000	60,000
Process B costs	25,000	-	25,000
Process C costs	-	33,000	33,000
Total costs	49,000	69,000	118,000
Revenue	66,000	66,000	132,000
Profit	17,000	(3,000)	14,000

(b) Product 24T makes a loss when the sales revenue basis of apportionment is used, but not when the units basis of apportionment is used. The difference between profit and loss is due simply to how the common costs in Process A are shared between the two products.

Although product 24T **makes a loss by one method**, it would be **wrong to conclude that it should not be made at all.** If the company continues to make T42, it has got to make 24T as well, at least in process A, since the products are output jointly from a common process. And if product 24T does **make some contribution** towards covering fixed overheads, it is **worth making and selling**, if no better alternative exists.

In this situation, there is some **choice.** Product 24T can either be sold as part-finished output from process A, for £39 per tonne, or processed further in process C. The **relevant analysis** of this decision would be:

	£
Revenue from process C output	66,000
Revenue obtainable from sale of process A output (1,000 × 39)	39,000
Extra revenue from further processing	27,000
Costs of process C	33,000
Possible loss in process C	(6,000)

Not all of the £33,000 of process C costs might be **avoidable**. If there are some fixed and unavoidable costs charged to process C, there would be a smaller loss incurred by operating process C instead of selling part-finished product 24T. It might even be profitable to run process C, for example if avoidable costs were only £25,000, say, out of the £33,000 total costs for process C.

Even so, the possibility ought to be drawn to management's attention that it **might be more profitable to close down process C and sell product 24T in its part-complete form**. Neither method of cost apportionment that we used brings out this information for management's attention, and so both methods of costing are **inadequate** in this respect.

10 PRICING DECISIONS

10.1 Although, in general, the price charged for a product must exceed its cost, cost is only one of the **factors to bear in mind** when making a price-setting decision.

(a) **The organisation's objectives**. Although we generally assume that an organisation's objective is to maximise profit, it could be that increased market share, to be known as a supplier of luxury goods or to provide a service to the community is the objective towards which an organisation is working and around it should base its pricing policy.

(b) **The market in which the organisation operates**. If the organisation is operating under conditions of perfect competition, neither producer nor user has any market power and both must accept the prevailing market price. If the organisation is in the position of a monopolist, it can use its market power to set a profit-maximising price. However, most of British industry can be described as an oligopoly. Whilst each large firm has the ability to influence market prices, the unpredictable reaction from the other giants makes the final industry price difficult to determine.

(c) **Demand**. The volume of demand for a good in the market as a whole is influenced by variables such as the following.

(i) Price of the good
(ii) Price of other goods
(iii) Size and distribution of household income
(iv) Tastes and fashion
(v) Expectations
(vi) Obsolescence

(d) The volume of demand for one organisation's goods rather than another's is influenced by three principal factors: product life cycle (covered in Chapter 3), quality and marketing.

(i) **Quality**. One firm's product may be perceived to be better quality than another's, and may in some cases actually be so, if it goes faster or does whatever it is meant to do in a 'better' way. Other things being equal, the better quality good will be more in demand than other versions.

(ii) **Marketing**. You may be familiar with the 'four Ps' of the marketing mix, all of which influence demand for a firm's goods.

(1) Price
(2) Product
(3) Place
(4) Promotion

(e) **Price elasticity of demand**. The price an organisation charges will be affected by whether demand for an item is *elastic* (a small change in the price produces a large change in the quantity demanded) or *inelastic* (a small change in the price produces only a small change in the quantity demanded).

(f) **Costs**. An organisation has to decide whether a price should be based on fully absorbed cost or marginal cost.

(g) **Competition**. When competitors sell exactly the same product in the same market, price differences are likely to have a significant effect on demand. For example, the price of petrol at filling stations in a local area will be much the same. If it was not, customers would go to the cheapest place. When organisations sell similar products which are not exactly identical, or where the geographical location of the sales point is of some significance, there is more scope for charging different prices.

(h) **Inflation**. An organisation should recognise the effects of inflation on its pricing decisions.

(i) **Legislation**. Certain organisations have their prices controlled by legislation or regulatory bodies.

(j) **Availability of substitutes**. When an organisation is making a pricing decision it must take into account products/services that customers could switch to if they were not happy with the price set. For example, coach transport organisations have to consider the ability of customers to switch to travelling by rail.

(k) **Newness**. If a product is the first of its kind, there will be no competition and the company, for a time at least, will be able to set a price at which it is thought profits can be maximised. If the new product being launched is following a competitor's product onto the market, however, the price that can be charged will be constrained by what the competitor is already doing.

  (i) Low prices may be charged when a product is first launched (**market penetration pricing**) to obtain penetration of the market.

  (ii) Alternatively high prices can be charged (**market skimming pricing**) in conjunction with heavy spending on advertising and sales promotion to obtain sales, with the aim of gaining high unit profits early in the product's life.

Approaches to pricing

Full cost plus pricing

10.2 This is a traditional approach to pricing, whereby the sales price is determined by **calculating the full cost of the product and adding a percentage mark-up for profit**.

10.3 A business might decide on an average profit mark-up as a general guideline for pricing decisions. This would be particularly useful for businesses that carry out a large amount of **contract work or jobbing work**, for which individual job or contract prices must be quoted regularly to prospective customers. However, the **percentage profit mark-up** does not have to be fixed, but **can be varied** to suit the circumstances. In particular, the percentage mark-up can be varied to suit demand conditions in the market.

10.4 The full cost plus approach to pricing is commonly used in practice, but varying the size of the profit mark-up gives the pricing decisions much-needed flexibility so as to adapt to demand conditions.

10.5 The **advantages** of full cost plus pricing are as follows.

(a) Since the size of the profit margin can be varied at management's discretion, a decision based on a price in excess of full cost should ensure that a company working at normal capacity will cover all its fixed costs and make a profit. This will be beneficial if:

  (i) They carry out large contracts which must make a sufficient profit margin to cover a fair share of fixed costs

(ii) They must justify their prices to potential customers (for example for government contracts)

(iii) They find it difficult to estimate expected demand at different sales prices

(b) It is a simple, quick and cheap method of pricing which can be delegated to junior managers. This may be particularly important with jobbing work where many prices must be decided and quoted each day.

Marginal cost plus pricing

10.6 Instead of pricing products or services by adding a profit margin on to *full* cost, a business might **add a profit margin on to marginal cost** (either the marginal cost of production or else the marginal cost of sales). This is sometimes called **mark-up pricing**.

10.7 The **advantages** of a marginal cost plus approach to pricing are as follows.

(a) The mark-up can be varied, and so provided that a rigid mark-up is not used, mark-up pricing can be adjusted to reflect demand conditions.

(b) It draws management attention to contribution and the effects of higher or lower sales volumes on profit. In this way, it helps to create a better awareness of the concepts and implications of marginal costing and breakeven analysis. For example, if a product costs £10 a unit and a mark-up of 150% is added to reach a price of £25 a unit, management should be clearly aware that every additional £1 of sales revenue would add 60p to contribution and profit.

(c) Mark-up pricing is convenient where there is a readily identifiable basic variable cost. Retail industries are the most obvious example, and it is quite common for the prices of goods in shops to be fixed by adding a mark-up (20% or 33¹/₃%, say) to the purchase cost.

10.8 One of the **drawbacks** to marginal cost plus pricing is that it ignores fixed overheads in the pricing decision, but the price must be high enough to ensure that a profit is made after covering fixed costs.

Minimum pricing

10.9 A minimum price is the price that would have to be charged so that the **following costs are just covered.**

- **The incremental costs of producing and selling the item**
- **The opportunity costs of the resources consumed in making and selling the item**

A minimum price **would leave the business no better or worse off in financial terms than if it did not sell the item.**

10.10 Two essential points about a minimum price are as follows.

(a) It is based on relevant costs.

(b) It is **unlikely that a minimum price would actually be charged** because if it were, it would not provide the business with any incremental profit. However, the minimum price for an item **shows** the following.

(i) **An absolute minimum below which the price should not be set.**

(ii) **The incremental profit that would be obtained from any price that is actually charged in excess of the minimum.**

10.11 If there are **no scarce resources and a company has spare capacity, the minimum price of a product is the incremental cost of making it**. Any price in excess of this minimum would provide an incremental contribution towards profit. **If there are scarce resources and a company makes more than one product**, minimum prices **must include an allowance for the opportunity cost** of using the scarce resources to make and sell the product (instead of using the resources on the next most profitable product).

11 QUALITATIVE FACTORS IN DECISION MAKING

11.1 Qualitative factors in decision making are factors which might influence the eventual decisions but which have not been quantified in terms of relevant income or costs. They may stem from non-financial objectives and from factors which might be quantifiable in money terms, but which have not been quantified, perhaps because there is insufficient information to make reliable estimates.

11.2 Qualitative factors in decision making will vary with the circumstances and nature of the opportunity being considered. Here are some examples.

Qualitative factor	Detail
Availability of cash	There must be sufficient cash to finance any purchases of equipment and build-up of working capital. If cash is not available, new sources of funds (for example an overdraft or loan) must be sought.
Inflation	If the income from an opportunity is fixed by contract, but the costs might increase with inflation, the contract's profitability would be over-stated unless inflation is taken into account.
Employees	Any decision involving the shutdown of a plant or changes in work procedures or location will require acceptance by employees, and ought to have regard to employee welfare.
Customers	Decisions about new products, the quality of output or after-sales service will inevitably affect customer loyalty and customer demand. Remember that a decision involving one product may have repercussions on customer attitudes towards a range of products.
Competitors	In a competitive market, some decisions may stimulate a response from rival companies. The decision to reduce selling prices to raise demand may fail if all competitors take similar action.
Timing factors	There might be a choice in deciding when to take up an opportunity. There might also be choice about whether a shutdown should be permanent or temporary. Temporary closure may be a viable proposition during a period of slack demand. And if a decision is taken to sell goods at a low price where the contribution earned will be relatively small, it is important to consider the duration of the low price promotion. If it is a long-term feature of selling, and if demand for the product increases, the company's total contribution may sink to a level where it fails even to cover fixed costs.
Suppliers	Long-term goodwill may be damaged by a decision to close a product line temporarily. Decisions to change the specifications for purchased components, or change stockholding policies so as to create patchy, uneven demand might also put a strain on suppliers.

Qualitative factor	Detail
Feasibility	A proposal may look feasible, but technical experts or managers may have reservations about their ability to carry it out.
Flexibility and internal control	Decisions to subcontract work, or to enter into a long-term contract, have the disadvantages of inflexibility and lack of controllability.
Unquantified opportunity costs	Even where no opportunity costs are specified, it is probable that other opportunities would be available for using the resources to earn profit.
Political pressures	Some large companies may suffer political pressures applied by the government to influence their investment or disinvestment decisions.
Legal constraints	A decision might occasionally be rejected because of questions about the legality of the proposed action.

Exam focus point

It is not sufficient to learn these qualitative factors by heart. You must be able to apply them to the circumstances of the question. For example, there is little point talking about the effect of the decision on employees if the question concerns a one-man organisation.

Chapter roundup

- In making decisions, the only costs which are **relevant** are those which will be affected by the decision. Such costs will be **future, incremental cash flows**.
- **Opportunity costs** are relevant costs. An opportunity cost is the benefit which could have been earned, but which has been given up by choosing one option instead of another.
- **Non-relevant costs** include sunk costs, committed costs, notional costs and historic costs.
- **Fixed costs** which are affected by a decision are called directly attributable fixed costs.
- In a **limiting factor** situation, contribution will be maximised by earning the **biggest possible contribution per unit of limiting factor.**
- If an organisation has to **produce more of a particular product** or products than the level established by ranking according to contribution per unit of limiting factor, the products should be ranked in the normal way but the optimum production plan must **first** take into account the **minimum production requirements.** The **remaining resource** must then be **allocated** according to the **ranking.**
- The **shadow price** or **dual price** of a limiting factor is the increase in value which would be created by having one additional unit of the limiting factor at the original cost.
- In a **make or buy situation with no limiting factors**, the relevant costs for the decision maker are the **differential costs** between the two options.
- In a situation where an organisation must **subcontract work to make up a shortfall in its own in-house capacity**, its total **costs** will be **minimised** if the **units bought** have the **lowest extra variable cost of buying per unit of scarce resource saved by buying.**
- The decision to work an **extra shift** should be taken on the basis of whether the costs of the shift are exceeded by the benefits to be obtained.
- If an organisation has **spare capacity** (which means that it would *not* have to turn away existing business), an order should be **accepted if the price offered makes some contribution to fixed costs and profit**. If an organisation **does not have sufficient spare capacity, existing business should only be turned away if the contribution from the order is greater than the contribution from the business which must be sacrificed.**
- Decisions about whether to **process a joint product further** or sell at the split-off point take no account of the joint costs, which are irrelevant to the decision. The decision is made on the basis of a **comparison between additional costs and additional revenues**.
- **Cost-volume-profit (CVP) analysis** looks at the relationships between volumes of output and the associated costs, revenues and profits. Make sure that you can calculate the following

  - **Breakeven point**
  - **CIS ratio**
  - **Margin of safety**

  You should also be able to sketch a number of **charts**.

  - Breakeven chart
  - Contribution chart
  - P/V chart
  - Multiproduct chart

- **Cost** is only one of the factors to be considered in a pricing decision.
- Pricing approaches include **full cost plus**, **marginal cost plus** and **minimum pricing.**
- **Qualitative factors** can affect decisions and should therefore be taken into account.

Quick quiz

1 *Classify the following costs as relevant or non-relevant.*

	Relevant	*Non-relevant*
Depreciation		
Avoidable costs		
Sunk cost		
Imputed cost		
Variable costs		
Absorbed overheads		
Opportunity cost		
Directly attributable fixed cost		
General fixed overheads		

2 *Fill in the blanks.*

In a limiting factor situation, contribution will be .... by earning the biggest possible contribution per unit of ....

3 When deciding, purely on financial grounds, whether or not to process a joint product further, what information is required.

I Value of the common process costs
II Method of apportioning the common costs
III Sales value of the joint product at the separation point
IV Final sales value of the joint product
V Further processing costs

A I, II and III
B III, IV and V
C IV and V
D I, II, IV and V
E All of them

4 *Use the terms in the list to fill in the blanks in the formulae below.*

Breakeven point = ... ÷ ....

P/V ratio = (................. ÷ ....) × 100%

Margin of safety = ((................. − ....) ÷ ....) × 100%

Sales volume to achieve target profit = (................. + ...) ÷ ....

Missing terms

- Contribution
- Budgeted sales
- Fixed cost
- Total fixed costs
- Breakeven sales
- Contribution per unit
- Sales
- Budgeted sales
- Target profit
- Contribution per unit

5 *Label the chart with the terms below.*

- Total costs
- Breakeven point
- Budgeted variable costs
- Margin of safety
- Budgeted fixed costs
- Budgeted profit
- Sales revenue
- Fixed costs
- £
- Units

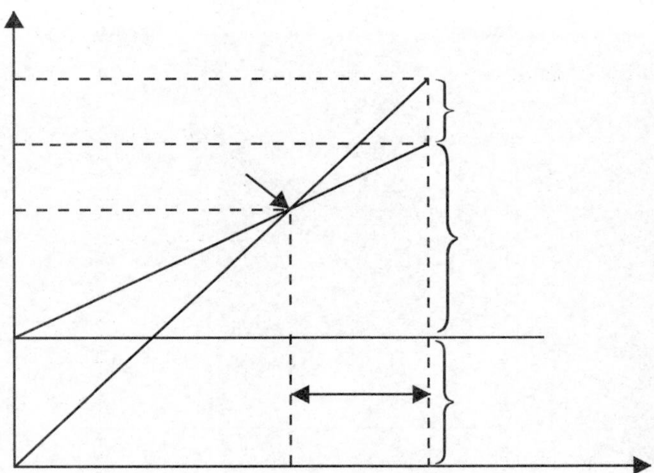

6 Sketch and label a P/V chart.

7 *Choose the four phases of the product life cycle from the following list.*

Birth	Demise	Growth
Peak period	Maturity	Decline
Rejuvination	Introduction	Death
Contraction	Swell	Expansion
Middle age	Youth	Infancy

8 Elastic demand means that a small change in price produces a large change in demand.

True ☐ False ☐

9 Full cost plus pricing is also known as mark-up pricing.

True ☐ False ☐

Answers to quick quiz

1

	Relevant	*Non-relevant*
Depreciation		✓
Avoidable costs	✓	
Sunk cost		✓
Imputed cost		✓
Variable costs	✓	
Absorbed overheads		✓
Opportunity cost	✓	
Directly attributable fixed cost	✓	
General fixed overheads		✓

2 maximised
limiting factor

3 B

4 Breakeven point = total fixed costs ÷ contribution per unit

P/V ratio = (contribution ÷ sales) ×100%

Margin of safety = ((budgeted sales – breakeven sales) ÷ budgeted sales) ×100%

Sales volume to achieve target profit = (fixed cost + target profit) ÷ contribution per unit

5

6

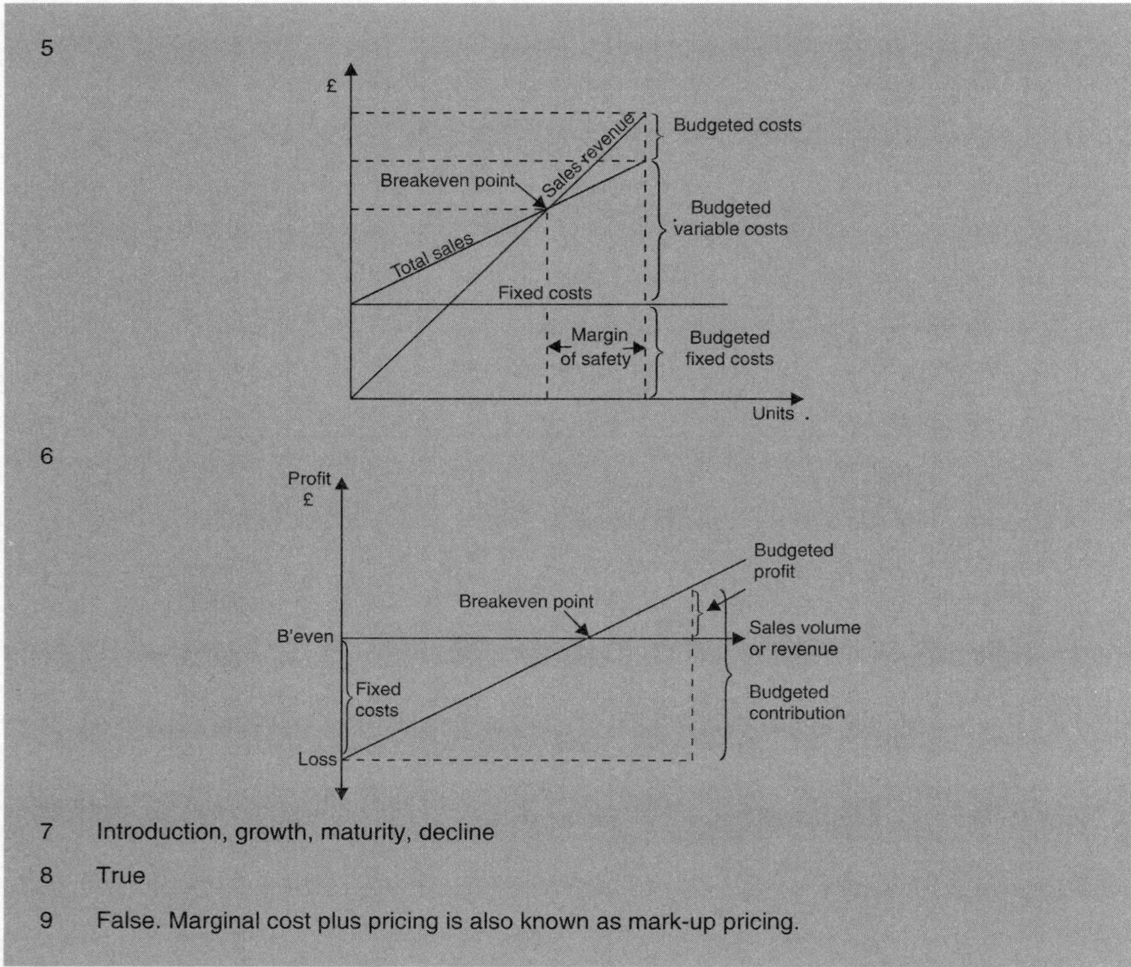

7 Introduction, growth, maturity, decline

8 True

9 False. Marginal cost plus pricing is also known as mark-up pricing.

Now try the questions below from the Exam Question Bank

Question to try	Level	Marks	Time
18	Exam	25	45 mins
19	Exam	25	45 mins

Part E

The framework of financial management

Chapter 15

FINANCIAL MANAGEMENT AND FINANCIAL OBJECTIVES

Topic list		Syllabus reference
1	The scope of financial management	1(a), (b)
2	Objectives of private sector companies	1(c)
3	Non-financial objectives	1(c)
4	Stakeholders in a company	1(d)
5	Bodies which are not purely commercial	1(e)
6	Measuring performance	1(a)
7	Performance measurement in the public sector	1(e)

Introduction

Starting with this chapter and in the remaining chapters of this Text, we examine the work of the financial manager and the framework within which the financial manager operates. After introducing the **scope of financial management**, we consider the **objectives** of organisations. We go on to examine **performance indicators** for both business enterprises and non-commercial organisations.

In later chapters, we will be studying the **resources** available for an organisation to meet objectives and the methods available for doing so.

Study guide

Section 3 – The nature and scope of financial management

- Broadly describe the relationship between financial management, management accounting and financial accounting
- Discuss the nature and scope of financial objectives for private sector companies in the context of organisational objectives
- Discuss the role of social and non-financial objectives in private sector companies and identify their financial implications
- Identify objectives (financial and otherwise) in not-for-profit organisations and identify the extent to which they differ from private sector companies
- Discuss the problems of multiple stakeholders in financial management and the consequent multiple objectives and scope for conflict

Exam guide

In the exam you may be asked to explain the role and purpose of financial management. You may be tested on the objectives of stakeholders other than shareholders, and non-profit making organisations, so do not neglect these areas. When assessing the desirability of undertaking an investment project you may need to discuss non-financial objectives. The Oxford Brookes Degree Research and Analysis Project Topic 8 requires you to analyse a financial situation of your choice.

Exam focus point

As we begin coverage of the financial management part of the syllabus, bear in mind the format of the paper (as set out in the Introduction to this Study Text). You cannot pass Paper 2.4 without knowing the financial management areas thoroughly. It is not possible to scrape through largely on management accounting knowledge without paying much attention to financial management.

1 THE SCOPE OF FINANCIAL MANAGEMENT

What is financial management?

1.1 **Financial management** can be defined as the management of the finances of an organisation in order to achieve the financial objectives of the organisation. The usual assumption in financial management for the private sector is that the objective of the company is to **maximise shareholders' wealth**. Broadly, there are two aspects of financial management: **financial planning** and **financial control**.

Financial planning

1.2 The financial manager will need to **plan** to ensure that enough funding is available at the right time to meet the needs of the organisation for short, medium and long-term capital.

(a) In the short term, funds may be needed to pay for purchases of stocks, or to smooth out changes in debtors, creditors and cash: the financial manager is here ensuring that **working capital requirements** are met.

(b) In the medium or long term, the organisation may have planned purchases of **fixed assets** such as plant and equipment, for which the financial manager must ensure that **funding** is available.

1.3 The financial manager contributes to decisions on the uses of funds raised by **analysing financial data** to **determine uses** which meet the **organisation's financial objectives.** Is project A to be preferred to Project B? Should a new asset be bought or leased?

Financial control

1.4 The **control** function of the financial manager becomes relevant for funding which has been raised. Are the various activities of the organisation meeting its objectives? Are assets being used efficiently? To answer these questions, the financial manager may **compare data** on **actual performance** with **forecast performance**. Forecast data will have been prepared in the light of past performance (historical data) modified to reflect expected future changes. Future changes may include the effects of economic development, for example an economic recovery leading to a forecast upturn in revenues.

Financial management decisions

1.5 The financial manager makes decisions relating to **investment, financing** and **dividends**.

1.6 Investments in assets must be **financed** somehow. Financial management is also concerned with the **management of short-term funds** and with how funds can be raised over the long term, for example by the following methods.

- Taking more credit
- Retention of profits for reinvestment in the business

- The issue of new shares to raise capital
- Borrowing, from banks or other lenders
- Leasing of assets, as an alternative to outright purchase

1.7 Retention of profits was mentioned above as a financing decision. The other side of this decision is that if profits are retained, there is less to pay out to shareholders as dividends, which might deter investors. An appropriate balance needs to be struck in addressing the **dividend decision**: how much of its profits should the company pay out as dividends and how much should it retain for investment to provide for future growth and new investment opportunities?

1.8 We shall be looking at various aspects of the investment, financing and dividend decisions of financial management over the remaining chapters of this Study Text.

Examples of different types of investment decision	
Decisions **internal** to the business enterprise	• Whether to undertake new projects • Whether to invest in new plant and machinery • Research and development decisions • Investment in a marketing or advertising campaign
Decisions involving **external parties**	• Whether to carry out a takeover or a merger involving another business • Whether to engage in a joint venture with another enterprise
Disinvestment decisions	• Whether to sell off unprofitable segments of the business • Whether to sell old or surplus plant and machinery • The sale of subsidiary companies

Question 1

'The financial manager should identify surplus assets and dispose of them'. Why?

Answer

A surplus asset earns no return for the business. The business is likely to be paying the 'cost of capital' in respect of the money tied up in the asset, ie the money which it can realise by selling it.

If surplus assets are sold, the business may be able to invest the cash released in more productive ways, or alternatively it may use the cash to cut its liabilities. Either way, it will enhance the return on capital employed for the business as a whole.

Although selling surplus assets yields short-term benefits, the business should not jeopardise its activities in the medium or long term by disposing of productive capacity until the likelihood of it being required in the future has been fully assessed.

Management accounting, financial accounting and financial management

1.9 Of course, it is not just people *within* an organisation who require information. Those external to the organisation such as banks, shareholders, the Inland Revenue, creditors and government agencies all desire information too.

1.10 **Management accountants provide internally-used information. The financial accounting function provides externally-used information.** The management accountant is not concerned with the calculation of earnings per share and the financial accountant is not concerned with the variances between budgeted and actual labour expenditure.

1.11 **Management information provides a common source from which are prepared financial accounts and management accounts.** The **differences** between the two types of accounts **arise in the manner in which the common source of data is analysed.**

Financial accounts	Management accounts
Financial accounts **detail the performance of an organisation over a defined period and the state of affairs at the end of that period.**	Management accounts are **used to aid management record, plan** and **control activities and to help the decision-making process.**
Limited companies must, **by law,** prepare financial accounts.	There is **no legal requirement** to prepare management accounts.
The **format** of published financial accounts is **determined by law,** by SSAPs and by FRSs. In principle the accounts of different organisations can therefore be easily compared.	The **format** of management accounts is entirely at management discretion: **no strict rules** govern the way they are prepared or presented.
Financial accounts **concentrate on the business as a whole,** aggregating revenues and costs from different operations, and are an end in themselves.	Management accounts can **focus on specific areas** of an organisation's activities. Information may aid a decision rather than be an end product of a decision.
Most financial accounting information is of a **monetary** nature.	Management accounts incorporate **non-monetary** measures.
Financial accounts present an essentially **historic** picture of **past** operations.	Management accounts are both a **historical** record and a **future** planning tool.

1.12 As we have seen financial management is **the management of finance.** Finance is used by an organisation just as, for example, labour is used by an organisation. Finance therefore needs management in a similar way to labour. The management accounting function provides information to ensure the effective management of labour and, in the same way, the financial management function provides information on, for example, projected cash flows to aid the effective management of finance.

2 OBJECTIVES OF PRIVATE SECTOR COMPANIES

2.1 In much of economic theory, it is assumed that the firm behaves in such a way as to maximise **profits,** where profit is viewed in an economist's sense. Unlike the accountant's concept of cost, total costs by this economist's definition includes an element of reward for the risk-taking of the entrepreneur, called 'normal profit'.

Profit maximisation

2.2 Where the entrepreneur is in full managerial control of the firm, as in the case of a small owner-managed company or partnership, the **economist's assumption of profit maximisation** would seem to be very reasonable.

2.3 Even in companies owned by shareholders but run by non-shareholding managers, if the manager is serving the company's (ie the shareholders') interests, we might expect that the profit maximisation assumption should be close to the truth.

Other objectives

2.4 Managers are paid to make the decisions about prices and output, but it is the shareholders who expect to benefit from the profits. Managers, it is argued, will not necessarily make pricing decisions that will maximise profits.

(a) They have **no personal interests** at stake in the size of profits earned, except in so far as they are accountable to the shareholders for the profits they make.

(b) There is **no competitive pressure** in the market to be efficient, minimise costs and maximise profits.

2.5 Given the **divorce of management from ownership**, price and output decisions may be taken by managers with a **managerial aim** rather than the **aim of profit maximisation.** However there is the constraint that managers must take some account of shareholders' interests because they are formally responsible for them and so are accountable to shareholders for their decisions.

(a) One 'managerial model' of the firm, Baumol's **sales maximisation model,** assumes that the firm acts to maximise sales revenue rather than profits, in order to maintain or increase its market share, to ensure survival and to discourage competition. Managers benefit personally because of the prestige of running a large and successful company, and also because salaries and other perks are likely to be higher in bigger companies than smaller ones.

(b) Another managerial model, Williamson's **management discretion model,** assumes that managers act to **further their own interests** and so **maximise their own utility,** subject to a **minimum profit** requirement. The model states that utility, which a manager aims to maximise, is a function of several different things.

(i) The manager's own salary

(ii) Expenditure on his or her staff (prestige and influence depend on the numbers and pay levels of subordinate staff)

(iii) The amount of perquisites (luxurious office, personal secretary, company car, expense account etc)

(iv) The authority to make 'discretionary investments' (ie new investments other than straightforward replacement decisions)

2.6 The profit aimed for will not be maximum profit, because of management's wishes for expenditure on themselves, their staff and the perquisites of management.

2.7 Cyert and March's **consensus theory** suggested that a firm is an **organisational coalition** of shareholders, managers, employees and customers, with each group having different goals. Thus there is a need for **political compromise** in establishing the goals of the firm. Each group must settle for less than it would ideally want to have - shareholders must settle for less than maximum profit, and managers for less than maximum utility, and so on.

2.8 The assumptions of economic theory and various theories of the firm all contain an element of truth. However, they do not provide the financial manager with an easy yardstick with which to work.

2.9 In the theory of company finance, such a yardstick is provided in the assumption that the financial manager's job is to **maximise the market value** of the company. Specifically, the main financial objective of a company should be to maximise the wealth of its ordinary shareholders. Within this context, the financial manager seeks to ensure that investments earn a **return**, for the benefit of shareholders.

How are the wealth of shareholders and the value of a company measured?

2.10 If the financial objective of a company is to maximise the value of the company, and in particular the value of its ordinary shares, we need to be able to put values on a company and its shares. How do we do it?

2.11 Three possible methods for the valuation of a company might occur to us.

(a) **Balance sheet valuation**

Here assets will be valued on a **going concern basis.** Certainly, investors will look at a company's balance sheet. If retained profits rise every year, the company will be a profitable one. Balance sheet values are not a measure of 'market value', although retained profits might give some indication of what the company could pay as dividends to shareholders.

(b) **Break-up basis**

This method of valuing a business is only of interest when the business is threatened with **liquidation**, or when its management is thinking about selling off individual assets to raise cash.

(c) **Market values**

The market value is the price at which buyers and sellers will trade stocks and shares in a company. This is the method of valuation which is most relevant to the financial objectives of a company.

(i) When shares are traded on a recognised stock market, such as the Stock Exchange, the market value of a company can be measured by the **price** at which shares are currently being traded.

(ii) When shares are in a private company, and are not traded on any stock market, there is no easy way to measure their market value. Even so, the financial objective of these companies should be to **maximise** the **wealth** of their **ordinary shareholders**.

2.12 The wealth of the shareholders in a company comes from:

- **Dividends** received
- **Market value** of the shares

2.13 A shareholder's **return** on investment is obtained in the form of:

- **Dividends** received
- **Capital gains** from increases in the market value of his or her shares

How is the value of a business increased?

2.14 If a company's shares are traded on a stock market, the wealth of shareholders is increased when the share price goes up. The price of a company's shares will go up when the company makes attractive profits, which it pays out as **dividends** or **re-invests** in the business to achieve future profit growth and dividend growth. However, to increase the share price the company should achieve its attractive profits without taking business risks and financial risks which worry shareholders.

2.15 If there is an increase in earnings and dividends, management can hope for an increase in the share price too, so that shareholders benefit from both **higher revenue** (dividends) and also **capital gains** (higher share prices). Management should set targets for factors which they can influence directly, such as profits and dividend growth. A financial objective might be expressed as the aim of increasing profits, earnings per share and dividend per share by, say, 10% a year for each of the next five years.

Other financial targets

2.16 In addition to targets for earnings, EPS, and dividend per share, a company might set **other financial targets**, such as:

(a) A restriction on the company's level of **gearing**, or debt. For example, a company's management might decide:

   (i) The ratio of long-term debt capital to equity capital should never exceed, say, 1:1.

   (ii) The cost of interest payments should never be higher than, say, 25% of total profits before interest and tax.

(b) A target for **profit retentions**. For example, management might set a target that dividend cover (the ratio of distributable profits to dividends actually distributed) should not be less than, say, 2.5 times.

(c) A target for **operating profitability**. For example, management might set a target for the profit/sales ratio (say, a minimum of 10%) or for a return on capital employed (say, a minimum ROCE of 20%).

2.17 These financial targets are not primary financial objectives, but they can act as subsidiary targets or constraints which should help a company to achieve its main financial objective without incurring excessive risks. They are usually measured over a year rather than over the long term.

2.18 Remember however that short-term measures of return can encourage a company to pursue **short-term** objectives at the expense of **long-term** ones, for example by deferring new capital investments, or spending only small amounts on research and development and on training.

2.19 A major problem with setting a number of different financial targets, either primary targets or supporting secondary targets, is that they might not all be consistent with each other. When this happens, some compromises will have to be accepted.

2.20 EXAMPLE: FINANCIAL TARGETS

Lion Grange Ltd has recently introduced a formal scheme of long range planning. Sales in the current year reached £10,000,000, and forecasts for the next five years are £10,600,000, £11,400,000, £12,400,000, £13,600,000 and £15,000,000. The ratio of net profit after tax to sales is 10%, and this is expected to continue throughout the planning period. Net asset turnover, currently 0.8 times, will remain more or less constant.

It was suggested at a recent board meeting that:

(a) If profits rise, dividends should rise by at least the same percentage

(b) An earnings retention rate of 50% should be maintained

(c) The ratio of long-term borrowing to long-term funds (debt plus equity) is limited (by the market) to 30%, which happens also to be the current gearing level of the company

You are required to prepare a financial analysis of the draft long range plan.

2.21 SOLUTION

The draft financial plan, for profits, dividends, assets required and funding, can be drawn up in a table, as follows.

	Current Year £m	*Year 1* £m	*Year 2* £m	*Year 3* £m	*Year 4* £m	*Year 5* £m
Sales	10.00	10.60	11.40	12.40	13.60	15.00
Net profit after tax	1.00	1.06	1.14	1.24	1.36	1.50
Dividends (50% of profit after tax)	0.50	0.53	0.57	0.62	0.68	0.75
Net assets (125% of sales)	12.50	13.25	14.25	15.50	17.00	18.75
Equity (increased by retained earnings)	8.75**	9.28	9.85	10.47	11.15	11.90
Maximum debt (30% of assets)	3.75	3.97	4.28	4.65	5.10	5.63
Funds available	12.50	13.25	14.13	15.12	16.25	17.53
(Shortfalls) in funds *	0	0	(0.12)	(0.38)	(0.75)	(1.22)

* Given maximum gearing of 30% and no new issue of shares = funds available minus net assets required.

**The current year equity figure is a balancing figure, equal to the difference between net assets and long-term debt, which is currently at the maximum level of 30% of net assets.

Question 2

Suggest policies on dividends, retained earnings and gearing for Lion Grange Limited, using the data above.

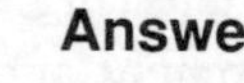

Answer

The financial objectives of the company are not compatible with each other. Adjustments will have to be made.

(a) Given the assumptions about sales, profits, dividends and net assets required, there will be an increasing shortfall of funds from year 2 onwards, unless new shares are issued or the gearing level rises above 30%.

(b) In years 2 and 3, the shortfall can be eliminated by retaining a greater percentage of profits, but this may have a serious adverse effect on the share price. In year 4 and year 5, the shortfall in funds cannot be removed even if dividend payments are reduced to nothing.

(c) The net asset turnover appears to be low. The situation would be eased if investments were able to generate a higher volume of sales, so that fewer fixed assets and less working capital would be required to support the projected level of sales.

(d) If asset turnover cannot be improved, it may be possible to increase the profit to sales ratio by reducing costs or increasing selling prices.

(e) If a new issue of shares is proposed to make up the shortfall in funds, the amount of funds required must be considered very carefully. Total dividends would have to be increased in order to pay dividends on the new shares. The company seems unable to offer prospects of suitable dividend payments, and so raising new equity might be difficult.

(f) It is conceivable that extra funds could be raised by issuing new debt capital, so that the level of gearing would be over 30%. It is uncertain whether investors would be prepared to lend money so as to increase gearing. If more funds were borrowed, profits after interest and tax would fall so that the share price might also be reduced.

---

3 NON-FINANCIAL OBJECTIVES 12/01

3.1 A company may have important **non-financial objectives**, which will limit the achievement of financial objectives. Examples of non-financial objectives are as follows.

(a) **The welfare of employees**

A company might try to provide **good wages and salaries**, comfortable and safe working conditions, good training and career development, and good pensions. If redundancies are necessary, many companies will provide generous redundancy payments, or spend money trying to find alternative employment for redundant staff.

(b) **The welfare of management**

Managers will often take decisions to improve their **own circumstances**, even though their decisions will incur expenditure and so reduce profits. High salaries, company cars and other perks are all examples of managers promoting their own interests.

(c) **The provision of a service**

The major objectives of some companies will include fulfilment of a responsibility to **provide a service** to the public. Examples are the privatised British Telecom and British Gas. Providing a service is of course a key responsibility of government departments and local authorities.

(d) **The fulfilment of responsibilities towards customers**

Responsibilities towards **customers** include providing in good time a product or service of a **quality** that customers expect, and dealing **honestly and fairly** with customers. **Reliable supply arrangements,** also **after-sales service arrangements,** are important.

(e) **The fulfilment of responsibilities towards suppliers**

Responsibilities towards **suppliers** are expressed mainly in terms of **trading relationships**. A company's size could give it considerable power as a buyer. The company should not use its power unscrupulously. Suppliers might rely on getting prompt payment, in accordance with the agreed terms of trade.

(f) **The welfare of society as a whole**

The management of some companies is aware of the role that their company has to play in exercising **corporate social responsibility**. This includes **compliance with applicable laws and regulations** but is wider than that. Companies may be aware of their responsibility to minimise pollution and other harmful 'externalities' (such as excessive traffic) which their activities generate. In delivering 'green' environmental policies, a company may improve its corporate image as well as reducing harmful externality effects. Companies also may consider their '**positive**' **responsibilities,** for example to make a contribution to the community by local sponsorship.

Other non-financial objectives are **growth, diversification** and **leadership in research and development**.

Exam focus point

12 marks were available in December 2001 for a general discussion of organisations' non-financial objectives.

Financial and non-financial objectives

3.2 Non-financial objectives do not negate financial objectives, but they do suggest that the simple theory of company finance, that the objective of a firm is to maximise the wealth of ordinary shareholders, is too simplistic. Financial objectives may have to be compromised in order to satisfy non-financial objectives.

4 STAKEHOLDERS IN A COMPANY

KEY TERM

There is a variety of different groups or individuals whose interests are directly affected by the activities of a firm. These groups or individuals are referred to as **stakeholders** in the firms.

4.1 The various stakeholder groups in a firm can be classified as follows.

Stakeholder groups	
Internal	Employees and pensioners Managers
Connected	Shareholders Debtholders Customers Bankers Suppliers Competitors
External	Government Pressure groups Local and national communities Professional and regulatory bodies

Objectives of stakeholder groups

4.2 The various groups of stakeholders in a firm will have different goals which will depend in part on the particular situation of the enterprise. Some of the more important aspects of these different goals are as follows.

(a) **Ordinary (equity) shareholders**

Ordinary (equity) shareholders are the providers of the risk capital of a company. Usually their goal will be to **maximise the wealth which they have** as a result of the ownership of the shares in the company.

(b) **Trade creditors**

Trade creditors have supplied goods or services to the firm. Trade creditors will generally be profit-maximising firms themselves and have the objective of **being paid the full amount due by the date agreed**. On the other hand, they usually wish to ensure that they continue their trading relationship with the firm and may sometimes be prepared to accept later payment to avoid jeopardising that relationship.

(c) **Long-term creditors**

Long-term creditors, which will often be banks, have the objective of **receiving payments of interest and capital** on the loan by the due date for the repayments. Where the loan is secured on assets of the company, the creditor will be able to appoint a receiver to dispose of the company's assets if the company defaults on the repayments. To avoid the possibility that this may result in a loss to the lender if the assets are not sufficient to cover the loan, the lender will wish to **minimise the risk of default** and will not wish to lend more than is prudent.

(d) **Employees**

Employees will usually want to **maximise their rewards** paid to them in salaries and benefits, according to the particular skills and the rewards available in alternative employment. Most employees will also want **continuity of employment**.

(e) **Government**

Government has objectives which can be formulated in political terms. Government agencies impinge on the firm's activities in different ways including through taxation of the firm's profits, the provision of grants, health and safety legislation, training initiatives and so on. Government policies will often be related to macroeconomic objectives such as **sustained economic growth** and **high levels of employment**.

(f) **Management**

Management has, like other employees (and managers who are not directors will normally be employees), the objective of **maximising** their **own rewards**. Directors and the managers to whom they delegate responsibilities must manage the company for the benefit of shareholders. The objective of reward maximisation might conflict with the exercise of this duty.

Stakeholder groups and strategy

4.3 The actions of stakeholder groups in pursuit of their various goals can exert influence on strategy. The greater the power of the stakeholder, the greater his influence will be. Each stakeholder group will have different expectations about what it wants, and the **expectations of the various groups may conflict**. Each group, however, will influence strategic decision-making.

Shareholders and management

4.4 Although ordinary shareholders (equity shareholders) are the owners of the company to whom the board of directors are accountable, the actual powers of shareholders tend to be restricted, except in companies where the shareholders are also the directors. The **day-to-day** running of a company is the responsibility of **management.** Although the company's results are submitted for shareholders' approval at the annual general meeting (AGM), there is often apathy and acquiescence in directors' recommendations.

4.5 **Shareholders** are often ignorant about their company's current situation and future prospects. They have no right to inspect the books of account, and their forecasts of future prospects are gleaned from the annual report and accounts, stockbrokers, investment journals and daily newspapers. The relationship between management and shareholders is sometimes referred to as an **agency relationship**, in which managers act as agents for the shareholders.

KEY TERM

Agency relationship: a description of the relationship between management and shareholders expressing the idea that managers act as agents for the shareholder, using delegated powers to run the company in the shareholders' best interests.

4.6 However, if managers hold none or very few of the equity shares of the company they work for, what is to stop them from working inefficiently? or not bothering to look for profitable new investment opportunities? **or** giving themselves high salaries and perks?

4.7 One power that shareholders possess is the right to **remove** the **directors** from office. But shareholders have to take the initiative to do this, and in many companies, the shareholders lack the energy and organisation to take such a step. Even so, directors will want the company's report and accounts, and the proposed final dividend, to meet with shareholders' approval at the AGM.

4.8 Another reason why managers might do their best to improve the financial performance of their company is that managers' pay is often related to the size or profitability of the company. Managers in very big companies, or in very profitable companies, will normally expect to earn higher salaries than managers in smaller or less successful companies. There is also an argument for giving managers some **profit-related pay**, or providing incentives which are related to profits or share price.

4.9 The **advantages** of having a **wide range of shareholders** include the following.

(a) There is likely to be **greater activity** in the market in the firm's shares.

(b) There is less likelihood of one shareholder having a **controlling interest**.

(c) Since shareholdings are smaller on average, there is likely to be **less effect** on the **share price** if one shareholder sells his holding.

(d) There is a **greater likelihood** of a **takeover** bid being **frustrated**.

Disadvantages of a large number of shareholders include the following.

(a) **Administrative costs** will be **high**. These include the costs of sending out copies of the annual report and accounts, counting proxy votes, registering new shareholders and paying dividends.

(b) Shareholders will have **differing tax positions** and **objectives** in holding the firm's shares, which makes a dividend/retention policy more difficult for the management to decide upon.

Shareholders, managers and the company's long-term creditors

4.10 The relationship between long-term creditors of a company, the management and the shareholders of a company encompasses the following factors.

(a) Management may decide to raise finance for a company by taking out long-term or medium-term loans. They might well be taking **risky investment decisions** using outsiders' money to finance them.

(b) Investors who provide debt finance will rely on the company's management to generate enough net cash inflows to make **interest payments on time**, and eventually to repay loans.

However, long-term creditors will often take **security** for their loan, perhaps in the form of a fixed charge over an asset (such as a mortgage on a building). Debentures are also often subject to certain restrictive covenants, which restrict the company's rights to borrow more money until the debentures have been repaid.

If a company is unable to pay what it owes its creditors, the creditors may decide to **exercise their security** or to apply for the company to be **wound up**.

(c) The money that is provided by long-term creditors will be invested to earn profits, and the profits (in excess of what is needed to pay interest on the borrowing) will provide **extra dividends** or retained profits for the shareholders of the company. In other words, shareholders will expect to increase their wealth using creditors' money.

Shareholders, managers and government

4.11 The government does not have a direct interest in companies (except for those in which it actually holds shares). However, the government does often have a strong indirect interest in companies' affairs.

(a) **Taxation**

The government raises taxes on sales and profits and on shareholders' dividends. It also expects companies to act as tax collectors for income tax and VAT. The **tax structure** might influence investors' preferences for either dividends or capital growth.

(b) **Encouraging new investments**

The government might provide **funds** towards the cost of some investment projects. It might also encourage private investment by offering **tax incentives.**

(c) **Encouraging a wider spread of share ownership**

In the UK, the government has made some attempts to encourage more private individuals to become company shareholders, by means of **attractive privatisation issues** (such as in the electricity, gas and telecommunications industries) and tax incentives, such as PEPs (personal equity plans) to encourage individuals to invest in shares.

(d) **Legislation**

The government also influences **companies**, and the **relationships** between shareholders, creditors, management, employees and the general public, through legislation, including the Companies Acts, legislation on employment, health and safety regulations, legislation on consumer protection and consumer rights and environmental legislation.

(e) **Economic policy**

A government's economic policy will affect business activity. For example, **exchange rate policy** will have implications for the revenues of exporting firms and for the purchase costs of importing firms. Policies on **economic growth, inflation, employment, interest rates** and so on are all relevant to business activities.

5 BODIES WHICH ARE NOT PURELY COMMERCIAL

Nationalised industries

5.1 Following the privatisation programme of the 1980s and early 1990s, the UK's nationalised industries are much fewer in number than they were. The largest nationalised industries remaining is the Post Office. London Transport is another.

Strategic objectives for the nationalised industries

5.2 Nationalised industries are financed by government loans, and some borrowing from the capital markets. They do not have equity capital, and there is no stock exchange to give a day-by-day valuation of the business.

5.3 The financial objective cannot be to maximise the wealth of its owners, the government or the general public, because this is not a concept which can be applied in practice. Financial objectives will generally be subordinated to a number of political and social considerations.

(a) A nationalised industry may be expected to provide a certain **standard of service** to all customers, regardless of the fact that some individuals will receive a service at a charge well below its cost. For example, the postal service must deliver letters to remote locations for the price of an ordinary first or second class stamp.

(b) The need to provide a service may be of such overriding social and political importance that the government is prepared to **subsidise** the industry. For example transport can be viewed as a social necessity and a certain level of service must be provided, with losses made up by government subsidies.

Investment plans and investment appraisal in nationalised industries

5.4 Nationalised industries in the UK have generally been expected to aim at a **rate of return** (before interest and tax) on their new investment programmes of **5% in real terms**. This is required so that the industries do not divert resources away from those areas where they could be used to best effect.

Corporate plans, targets and aims for nationalised industries

5.5 Each nationalised industry has **financial targets** and a series of **performance aims**. These targets and performance aims are set for a period of three to five years ahead, and may be included within a broader corporate plan.

External financing limits (EFLs) for nationalised industries

5.6 **External financing limits (EFLs)** control the flow of finance to and from nationalised industries. They set a limit on the amount of finance the industry can obtain from the government, and in the case of very profitable industries, they set requirements for the net repayment of finance to the government.

Not-for-profit organisations

5.7 Some organisations, such as **charities,** are set up with a prime objective which is not related to making profits. These organisations exist to pursue non-financial aims, such as providing a service to the community. However, there will be financial constraints which limit what any such organisation can do.

(a) A not-for-profit organisation **needs finance** to pay for its operations, and the major financial constraint is the amount of funds that it can obtain.

(b) Having obtained funds, a not-for-profit organisation should seek to get **value for money** from use of the funds:

(i) **Economy**: not spending £2 when the same thing can be bought for £1
(ii) **Efficiency**: getting the best use out of what money is spent on
(iii) **Effectiveness**: spending funds so as to achieve the organisation's objectives

5.8 The nature of financial objectives in a not-for-profit organisation can be explained in more detail, using **government departments** in the UK as an illustration.

5.9 Since managing government is different from managing a company, a different framework is needed for **planning and control**. This is achieved by

- Setting **objectives** for each
- **Careful planning** of public expenditure proposals
- Emphasis on getting **value for money**

5.10 A development in recent years has been the creation of agencies to carry out specific functions (such as vehicle licensing). These **executive agencies** are answerable to the government for providing a certain level of service, but are independently managed on business principles.

6 MEASURING PERFORMANCE

Measuring financial performance

6.1 As part of the system of financial control in an organisation, it will be necessary to have ways of measuring the progress of the enterprise, so that managers know how well the company is doing. A common means of doing this is through ratio analysis, which is concerned with comparing and quantifying relationships between financial variables, such as those variables found in the balance sheet and profit and loss account of the enterprise.

Exam focus point

The examiner has said, more than once, that knowledge of how to calculate and interpret key ratios is a weak point for many candidates. Make sure that it is one of your strong points. In reviewing ratio analysis below, we are in part revising material included in previous units.

The broad categories of ratios

6.2 Ratios can be grouped into the following four categories: **profitability and return; debt and gearing; liquidity**: control of cash and other working capital items; **shareholders' investment ratios** ('stock market ratios').

6.3 The key to obtaining meaningful information from ratio analysis is **comparison**: comparing ratios **over a number of periods** within the same business to establish whether the business is improving or declining, and **comparing ratios between similar businesses** to see whether the company you are analysing is better or worse than average within its own business sector.

Pyramids

The Du Pont system of ratio analysis involves constructing a pyramid of interrelated ratios like that below.

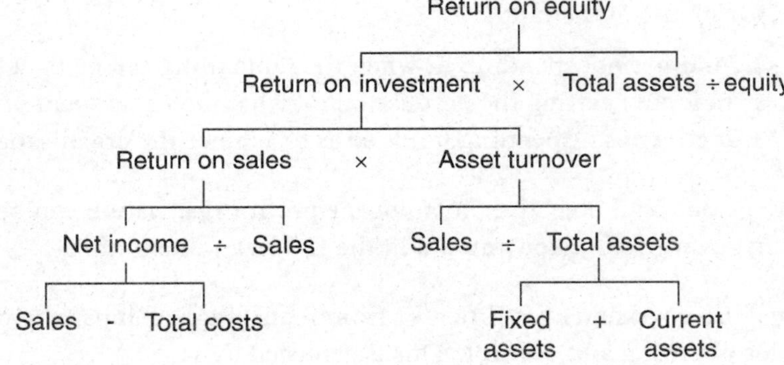

6.5 Such ratio pyramids help in providing for an overall management plan to achieve profitability, and allow the interrelationships between ratios to be checked.

Profitability

6.6 A company ought of course to be profitable if it is to maximise shareholder wealth, and obvious checks on profitability are:

(a) Whether the company has made a profit or a loss on its ordinary activities
(b) By how much this year's profit or loss is bigger or smaller than last year's profit or loss

6.7 **Profit before taxation** is generally thought to be a better figure to use than profit after taxation, because there might be unusual variations in the tax charge from year to year which would not affect the underlying profitability of the company's operations

6.8 Another profit figure that should be considered is **profit before interest and tax (PBIT)**. This is the amount of profit which the company earned before having to pay interest to the providers of loan capital. By providers of loan capital, we usually mean **longer term** loan capital, such as debentures and medium-term bank loans.

Profitability and return: the return on investment (ROI)

6.9 You cannot assess profits or profit growth properly without relating them to the amount of funds (the capital) employed in making the profits. The most important profitability ratio is therefore **return on capital employed (ROCE),** also called **return on investment (ROI),** which states the profit as a percentage of the amount of capital employed.

KEY TERMS

Return on Capital Employed = $\frac{\text{PBIT}}{\text{Capital employed}}$

Capital employed = Shareholders' funds *plus* 'creditors: amounts falling due after more than one year' *plus* any long-term provisions for liabilities and charges.

Evaluating the ROCE

6.10 What does a company's ROCE tell us? What should we be looking for? There are three comparisons that can be made.

(a) The **change** in ROCE from one year to the next

(b) The ROCE being **earned** by **other companies**, if this information is available

(c) A comparison of the ROCE with **current market borrowing rates**

(i) What would be the **cost of extra borrowing** to the company if it needed more loans, and is it earning a ROCE that suggests it could make high enough profits to make such borrowing worthwhile?

(ii) Is the company making a ROCE which suggests that it is making **profitable use** of its **current borrowing**?

Secondary ratios

6.11 We may analyse the ROCE by looking at the kinds of interrelationships between ratios used in ratio pyramids, which we mentioned earlier. We can thus find out why the ROCE is high or low, or better or worse than last year. Profit margin and asset turnover together explain the ROCE, and if the ROCE is the primary profitability ratio, these other two are the secondary ratios. The relationship between the three ratios is as follows.

Profit margin × asset turnover = ROCE

$$\frac{\text{PBIT}}{\text{Sales}} \times \frac{\text{Sales}}{\text{Capital employed}} = \frac{\text{PBIT}}{\text{Capital employed}}$$

6.12 It is also worth commenting on the **change in turnover** from one year to the next. Strong sales growth will usually indicate volume growth as well as turnover increases due to price rises, and volume growth is one sign of a prosperous company.

Gross profit margin, the net profit margin and profit analysis

6.13 Depending on the format of the profit and loss account, you may be able to calculate the **gross profit margin** as well as the **net profit margin**. Looking at the two together can be quite informative.

6.14 EXAMPLE: PROFIT MARGINS

A company has the following summarised profit and loss accounts for two consecutive years.

	Year 1	*Year 2*
	£	£
Turnover	70,000	100,000
Less cost of sales	42,000	55,000
Gross profit	28,000	45,000
Less expenses	21,000	35,000
Net profit	7,000	10,000

Although the net profit margin is the same for both years at 10%, the gross profit margin is not.

In year 1 it is: $\frac{28{,}000}{70{,}000} = 40\%$ and in year 2 it is: $\frac{45{,}000}{100{,}000} = 45\%$

6.15 Is this good or bad for the business? An increased profit margin must be good because this indicates a wider gap between selling price and cost of sales. However, given that the net profit ratio has stayed the same in the second year, expenses must be rising. In year 1 expenses were 30% of turnover, whereas in year 2 they were 35% of turnover. This indicates that administration or selling and distribution expenses may require tighter control.

6.16 A percentage analysis of profit between year 1 and year 2 is as follows.

	Year 1	*Year 2*
	%	%
Cost of sales as a % of sales	60	55
Gross profit as a % of sales	40	45
	100	100
Expenses as a % of sales	30	35
Net profit as a % of sales	10	10
Gross profit as a % of sales	40	45

Debt and gearing ratios

6.17 Debt ratios are concerned with how much the company owes in relation to its size and whether it is getting into heavier debt or improving its situation.

(a) When a company is heavily in debt, and seems to be getting even more heavily into debt, banks and other would-be lenders are very soon likely to **refuse further borrowing** and the company might well find itself in trouble.

(b) When a company is earning only a modest profit before interest and tax, and has a heavy debt burden, there will be **very little profit** left over for shareholders after the interest charges have been paid.

6.18 These are the two main reasons why companies should keep their debt burden under control. Three ratios that are particularly worth looking at are the debt ratio, the gearing ratio and the interest cover.

The debt ratio

6.19 The **debt ratio** is the ratio of a **company's total debts** to its **total assets.**

(a) Assets consist of fixed assets at their **balance sheet value**, plus **current assets.**

(b) Debts consist of **all creditors,** whether amounts falling due within one year or after more than one year, but not long-term provisions.

6.20 Gearing measures the relationships between shareholders' capital plus reserves, and either prior charge capital or borrowings or both.

KEY TERM

Prior charge capital is capital which has:

- A right to payment of interest or preference dividend before there can be any earnings for ordinary shareholders
- A prior claim on the company's assets in the event of a winding up

6.21 Although there is no single definition of prior charge capital, it is usual to regard it as consisting of:

(a) Any preference share capital

(b) Interest-bearing long-term capital

(c) Interest-bearing short-term debt capital with less than 12 months to maturity, including any bank overdraft

However, (c) might be excluded.

6.22 Commonly used measures of gearing are based on the balance sheet values of the fixed interest and equity capital. They include:

$$\frac{\text{Prior charge capital}}{\text{Equity capital (including reserves)}}$$

and

$$\frac{\text{Prior charge capital}}{\text{Total capital employed}}$$

Interest cover

6.23 The **interest cover** ratio shows whether a company is earning enough profits before interest and tax to pay its interest costs comfortably, or whether its interest costs are high in relation to the size of its profits, so that a fall in PBIT would then have a significant effect on profits available for ordinary shareholders.

KEY TERM

$$\textbf{Interest cover} = \frac{\text{Profit before interest and tax}}{\text{Interest charges}}$$

6.24 Interest payments should be taken gross, from the note to the accounts, and not net of interest receipts, as shown in the profit and loss account.

6.25 An interest cover of 2 times or less would be low, and it should really exceed 3 times before the company's interest costs can be considered to be within acceptable limits.

Liquidity ratios: cash and working capital

6.26 Profitability is of course an important aspect of a company's performance, and debt or gearing is another. Neither, however, addresses directly the key issue of **liquidity**. A company needs liquid assets so that it can meet its debts when they fall due. The main liquidity ratios will be described later in this text.

Shareholders' investment ratios

6.27 A further set of ratios of importance to the financial manager are the ratios which help equity shareholders and other investors to assess the value and quality of an investment in the ordinary shares of a company. These ratios will be described later in this text.

Environmental reporting

6.28 As well as tracking financial performance, managers of organisations need to understand the impact of the operations of the organisation on the environment. This is important not just because of external pressures, but also so that organisations can gain from opportunities and avoid necessary penalties or costs. It has been argued that environmental reports should become a part of the regular process of financial reporting. Norsk Hydro was a pioneer in this field when it produced an environmental report in 1990.

6.29 Environmental reporting has become fairly widespread, with the majority of large UK companies now mentioning the environment in their annual report and accounts. In other countries, Dow Chemicals, Danish Steelworks, Kunert and BSO Origin are among those that have experimented with green reporting. Many companies include statements of **environmental policy** in their annual reports. A smaller number include quantified **indicators** of **environmental performance**.

6.30 For example, ICI plc includes statements reporting progress against targets, one of which relates to the reduction of hazardous wastes. However, environmental reporting is relatively rare among smaller companies.

6.31 The development of environmental reporting occurred in a period of increasing regulatory requirements in the UK and in the rest of the EU to report more specific data on environmental matters. Over the same period, many large companies sought ways of promoting their corporate image as well as their individual products. Provided the data presents the company's efforts in a positive light, reporting of environmental data should help to enhance people's perception of a company's qualities.

7 PERFORMANCE MEASUREMENT IN THE PUBLIC SECTOR

7.1 In public sector organisations, an increasing volume of information on performance and 'value for money' is produced for internal and external use. The ways in which performance can be measured depends very much upon which organisation is involved.

(a) The first question which would need to be asked is 'what are the **aims** and **objectives** of the organisation?' For example, the objective of Companies House is to maintain and make available records of company reports.

(b) The next question to ask is 'How can we tell if the organisation is **meeting** the objectives?' Quantified information - ie information in the form of numbers - will be useful, and this will consist mainly of output and performance measures and indicators. For these, targets can be set. Any individual organisational unit should have no more than a handful of key targets.

7.2 Individual targets are likely to fall under the headings:

- **Financial performance targets**
- **Volume of output targets**
- **Quality of service targets**
- **Efficiency targets**

Performance measurement in central government

7.3 Over recent years, much of the work of central government has been reorganised into semi-autonomous **executive agencies**, which we mentioned earlier in the chapter.

7.4 The following are examples of targets related to **financial performance** in executive agencies.

(a) **Full cost recovery** (Civil Service College, Central Office of Information and others), plus unit cost targets

(b) **Commercial revenue** to offset costs (Met Office)

(c) **Non-Exchequer income** as a **percentage** of **total income** (National Engineering Laboratory)

7.5 Targets related to **output** can be difficult to set. In many cases the output of executive agencies is not tangible. For example, the Historic Royal Palaces Agency not only deals with visitors, whose numbers can be counted, but is also responsible for maintaining the fabric of royal palaces - an output which is more difficult to measure. In such cases, performance will be best measured by appraising the **progress** of the **project** as a whole.

7.6 Example of **quality** targets set for executive agencies include the following.

(a) **Timeliness**

- Time to handle applications
- Car driving tests to be reduced to 6 weeks nationally (Driving Standards Agency)
- All cheques to be banked within 35 hours (Accounts Services Agency)

(b) **Quality of product**

- Number of print orders delivered without fault (HMSO)
- 95% business complaints handled within 5 days
- 85% overall customer satisfaction rating

7.7 Efficiency improvements may come through reducing the cost of inputs without reducing the quality of outputs. Alternatively, areas of activity affecting total costs may be reduced. Targets related to **efficiency** include the following.

- **Percentage reduction** in **price paid** for purchases of stationery and paper
- Reduction in the ratio of **cost of support services** to **total cost**
- 8.7% **efficiency increase** in the use of **accommodation**

Performance measurement in local government

7.8 The performance measures chosen by local authorities usually consist of **comparative statistics** and **unit costs.** Reporting on comparative statistics was recommended by the Department of the Environment in its code of practice *Local authority Annual Reports* (1982).

7.9 The following list illustrates the types of comparative statistics suggested in the code of practice.

PERFORMANCE MEASURES IN LOCAL GOVERNMENT

For the authority's total expenditure and for each function	Net cost per 1,000 population Manpower per 1,000 population
Primary education, secondary education	Pupil/teacher ratio Cost per pupil
School meals	Revenue/cost ratio Pupils receiving free meals as a proportion of school roll
Home helps	Contract hours per 1,000 population over 65
Police	Population per police officer Serious offences per 1,000 population
Fire	Proportion of area at high risk
Public transport	Passenger journeys per week per 1,000 population
Highways	Maintenance cost per kilometre

Chapter roundup

- Financial management decisions cover **investment** decisions **financing** and **dividend** decisions.
- Financial targets may include targets for: **earnings; earnings per share; dividend per share; gearing level; profit retention; operating profitability**.
- Non-financial objectives may include: **employee welfare; management welfare; the welfare of society; service provision objectives; fulfilment of responsibilities to customers and suppliers**.
- **Stakeholders** are individuals or groups who are affected by the activities of the firm. They can be classified as **internal** (employees and managers), **connected** (shareholders, customers and suppliers) and **external** (local communities, pressure groups, government).
- The usual assumption in financial management for the private sector is that the primary financial objective of the company is to **maximise shareholders' wealth.**
- **Performance measurement** is a part of the system of financial control of an enterprise as well as being important to investors.

Quick quiz

1 Give a definition of financial management.

2 What three broad types of decision does financial management involve?

3 What main financial objective does the theory of company finance assume that a business organisation has?

4 If earnings per share fall from one year to the next, so will the level of dividends.

☐ True

☐ False

5 Tick which are stakeholder groups for a company.

Employees ☐
Ordinary shareholders ☐
The Board of Directors ☐
Trade creditors ☐

6 Complete the 'Three Es' of value for money.

'Doing things well': E ....

'Doing thing cheaply': E ....

'Doing the right things': E ....

7 Which of the following are examples of financial objectives that a company might choose to pursue?

A Provision of good wages and salaries
B Restricting the level of gearing to below a specified target level
C Dealing honestly and fairly with customers on all occasions
D Producing environmentally friendly products

8 Which of the following decisions is not an investment decision?

A Whether to go ahead with an advertising campaign
B Whether to retain more profits for reinvestment in the business
C Whether to carry out a takeover of another company
D Whether to initiate a new research project

Answers to quick quiz

1 The management of the finances of an organisation in order to achieve the financial objectives of the organisation.

2 Investment decisions, financing decisions, dividend decisions.

3 To maximise the wealth of the company's ordinary shareholders.

4 False. Dividends may still be maintained from payments out of profits retained in earlier periods.

5 You should have ticked all four boxes.

6 Doing things well: Efficiency. Doing things cheaply: Economy. Doing the right things: Effectiveness.

7 B This is a financial objective that relates to the level of risk that the company accepts.

8 B This is the correct answer. Decisions on the level of retentions are financing decisions, not investment decisions.

A This is a decision that will involve the expenditure of funds in anticipation of earning additional profits. It is therefore an investment decision.

C A takeover would involve the outlay of additional funds with the aim of increasing group profits. It is therefore an investment decision.

D The research project would involve the outlay of funds now with the aim of increasing future company profits. It is therefore an investment decision.

Now try the question below from the Exam Question Bank

Question to try	Level	Marks	Time
20	Introductory	n/a	20 mins

Chapter 16

THE FINANCIAL MANAGEMENT FRAMEWORK

Topic list		Syllabus reference
1	Financial intermediation and credit creation	2(a)
2	Commercial banks as providers of funds	2(b)
3	Money markets and capital markets	2(b)
4	The efficient market hypothesis	2(c)
5	Rates of interest and rates of return	2(d)
6	The separation theorem	5(a)(i)
7	International money and capital markets	2(b)

Introduction

Having discussed the scope of financial management and the objectives of firms and other organisations in Chapter 15, we now introduce the framework of **markets** and **institutions** through which the financing of a business takes place. We also look at some theoretical aspects of how this framework operates including the **efficient market hypothesis**, which tries to account for why share prices behave as they do.

Study guide

Section 4 – The financial management framework

- Identify the general role of financial intermediaries
- Explain the role of commercial banks as providers of funds (including the creation of credit)
- Discuss the risk/return trade-off
- Identify the international money and capital markets and outline their operation
- Explain the functions of a stock market and corporate bond market
- Explain the key features of different types of security in terms of the risk/return trade-off
- Outline the Efficient Markets Hypothesis and assess its broad implications for corporate policy and financial management
- Explain the Separation Theorem
- Explain the functions of, and identify the links between, the money and capital markets

Exam guide

You would not get a complete question on the topics covered in this chapter. You might however be asked a part question that relates to the circumstances of a particular company, for instance how an AIM listing can benefit it.

1 FINANCIAL INTERMEDIATION AND CREDIT CREATION

KEY TERM

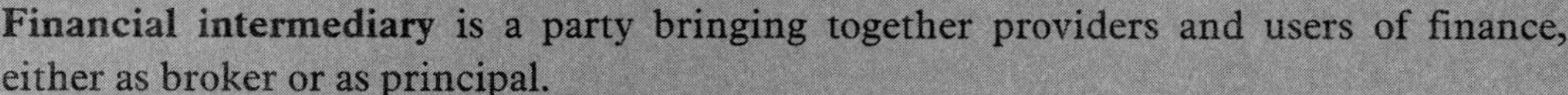

Financial intermediary is a party bringing together providers and users of finance, either as broker or as principal.

1.1 A **financial intermediary** is an institution which links lenders with borrowers, by obtaining deposits from lenders and then re-lending them to borrowers.

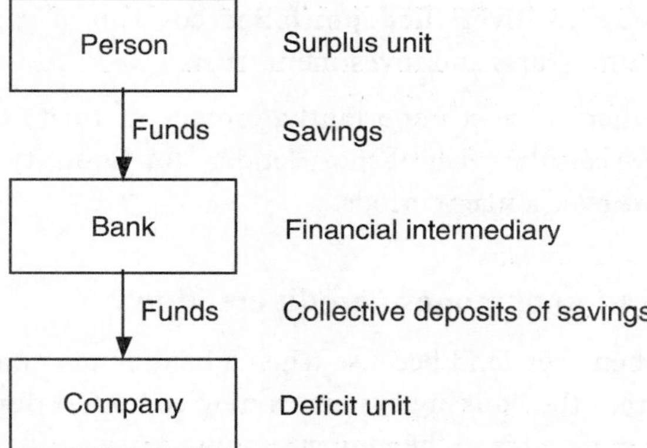

1.2 Not all intermediation takes place between savers and investors. Some institutions (such as the discount houses which intermediate between the Bank of England and the commercial banks) act mainly as **intermediaries** between **other institutions**. Financial intermediaries may also lend abroad or borrow from abroad.

Exam focus point

Bear in mind that *financial markets* and *institutions* are topic areas on which the examiner is not expected to set full questions. These topics could, however, be examined in subsections of a question.

1.3 **Examples of financial intermediaries**

- Commercial banks
- Finance houses
- Building societies
- Government's National Savings department
- Institutional investors eg pension funds and investment trusts

The benefits of financial intermediation

1.4 Financial intermediaries perform the following functions.

(a) They provide obvious and **convenient** ways in which a lender can save money. Instead of having to find a suitable borrower for his money, the lender can deposit his money with a financial intermediary. All the lender has to do is decide for **how long** he might want to lend the money, and **what sort of return** he requires, and he can then choose a financial intermediary that offers a **financial instrument** to suit his requirements.

(b) Financial intermediaries also provide a **ready source of funds** for **borrowers**. Even when money is in short supply, a borrower will usually find a financial intermediary prepared to lend some.

(c) They can **aggregate** or **'package'** the amounts lent by savers and lend on to borrowers in different amounts.

(d) **Risk** for individual lenders is reduced by **pooling**. Since financial intermediaries lend to a large number of individuals and organisations, any losses suffered through default by borrowers or capital losses are effectively pooled and **borne** as **costs** by the intermediary. Such losses are **shared among lenders in general**.

(e) By pooling the funds of large numbers of people, some financial institutions are able to give investors access to **diversified portfolios** covering a varied range of different securities, such as unit trusts and investment trusts.

(f) Financial intermediaries, most importantly, provide **maturity transformation**; ie they bridge the gap between the wish of most lenders for **liquidity** and the desire of most borrowers for **loans** over longer periods.

Bank deposits and the creation of money ('credit creation')

1.5 Banks create money when they lend because when a bank lends money, most of the money will find its way back into the banking system as **new customer deposits**. This means that the amount lent by the bank adds to the money supply.

1.6 Suppose, for example, that in a country with a single bank, a customer C deposits £100,000. The bank, we will assume, re-lends all these deposits to another customer D. This customer D uses the money he has borrowed to buy goods and services from firm Y. If firm Y, after receiving payment, then puts the money into its own account with the bank, the bank's deposits will have doubled.

Liabilities of the bank		*Assets of the bank*	
	£		£
Deposit of customer C	100,000	Loan to customer D	100,000
Deposit of firm Y	100,000		
	200,000		

1.7 This will enable the bank to re-lend more money (another £100,000), to bring its assets up to £200,000 and this in turn will create even more bank deposits. This cycle could go on and on, with the bank making more and more loans, and the people who are paid for goods and services bought with the loans putting all their receipts back into the bank as extra deposits. In short, **'every loan creates a deposit'**.

1.8 Extra bank lending (and building society lending) therefore has a dual effect. It **increases the money supply**. It **provides credit** which borrowers use to increase their amount of spending. Lending adds to spending in the economy.

KEY TERM

Credit creation is the process whereby banks and other deposit-taking and lending institutions can, on the basis of an increase in reserve assets, expand the volume of lending and deposit liabilities by more than the initial increase in reserves.

2 COMMERCIAL BANKS AS PROVIDERS OF FUNDS

2.1 An important grouping of financial intermediaries is the **commercial banks,** which include:

(a) The retail banks, which include the well known 'High Street' banks

(b) The wholesale banks, which offer services mainly to larger customers, including large companies (The wholesale banks include merchant banks and overseas banks.)

The functions of the commercial banks

2.2 The functions of the commercial banks include the following.

(a) They provide a **payments mechanism** - a way in which individuals, firms and government can make payments to each other. The '**clearing system**' of the clearing banks enables individuals and firms to make payments by cheque.

(b) The banks are also a source from which individuals and firms can **obtain notes and coin.**

(c) They provide a place for individuals, firms and government to **store their wealth.** Banks compete with other financial institutions to attract the funds of individuals and firms.

(d) They act as **providers of funds** by lending money in the form of loans or overdrafts.

Bank borrowing

2.3 Borrowings from banks are an important source of finance to companies as well as to unincorporated businesses. Bank lending is still mainly short-term although medium-term lending has grown considerably in recent years.

2.4 Short-term borrowing may take various forms.

(a) An **overdraft,** which a company should keep within a limit set by the bank. Interest is charged (at a variable rate) on the amount by which the company is overdrawn from day to day.

(b) A **short-term loan.** This may last for up to three years.

(c) **Medium-term loans.** These are loans for a period of from three to ten years.

2.5 The rate of interest charged on medium-term bank lending to large companies will typically be a set margin above the **London Inter-Bank Offered Rate (LIBOR),** with the size of the margin depending on the **credit standing** and **riskiness** of the borrower.

2.6 Lending to **smaller companies** will typically be at a margin **above the bank's base rate** and at either a variable or a fixed rate of interest.

2.7 Lending on **overdraft** is always at a **variable rate.**

2.8 A loan at a variable rate of interest is sometimes referred to as a **floating rate loan.**

2.9 **Longer term bank loans** will sometimes be available, usually for the purchase of property, where the loan takes the form of a mortgage.

3 MONEY MARKETS AND CAPITAL MARKETS

3.1 The **capital markets,** being markets for long-term capital, are distinguished from the **money markets,** which are markets for:

- Trading short-term financial instruments
- Short-term lending and borrowing

KEY TERMS

Short-term capital is capital that is lent or borrowed for a period which might range from as short as overnight up to about one year, and sometimes longer.

Long-term capital is capital invested or lent and borrowed for a period of five years or more.

3.2 There is a 'grey area' between long-term and short-term capital, which is lending and borrowing for a period from about a year up to about five years, which may be referred to as **medium-term capital**.

The money markets

3.3 The money markets are **operated** by the **banks** and other **financial institutions**. Although the money markets largely involve borrowing and lending by banks, some large companies and nationalised industries, as well as the government, are involved in money market operations. The building societies have also become major participants in the money markets since liberalisation of the building societies has allowed them to raise wholesale funds.

3.4 The primary market is known as the **official market**, the other markets as the **parallel** or **wholesale markets**.

Types of market	
Primary market	Approved institutions deal in financial instruments with Bank of England (UK Central bank) Bank of England uses trading to control short-term interest rates
Interbank market	Banks lend short-term funds to each other
Eurocurrency market	Banks lend and borrow in foreign currencies
Certificate of deposit market	Market for trading in Certificates of Deposit (negotiable instruments acknowledging deposits)
Local authority market	Local authorities borrow short-term funds by issuing and selling short-term debt instruments
Finance house market	Dealing in short-term loans raised from money markets by finance houses
Inter-company market	Direct short-term lending between treasury departments of large companies

The capital markets

3.5 Capital markets are markets for trading in long-term finance, in the form of long-term financial instruments such as equities and debentures. In the UK, the principal capital markets are:

(a) The Stock Exchange '**main market**' (for companies with a full Stock Exchange listing)
(b) The more loosely regulated 'second tier' **Alternative Investment Market (AIM)**

3.6 The Stock Exchange is also the market for dealings in **government securities**.

3.7 Firms obtain long-term or medium-term capital in one of the following ways.

(a) They may raise **share capital**. Most new issues of share capital are in the form of ordinary share capital. Firms that issue ordinary share capital are inviting investors to take an **equity stake** in the business, or to increase their existing equity stake.

(b) They may raise **loan capital**. Long-term loan capital might be raised in the form of a mortgage or debenture.

3.8 The stock markets serve two main purposes.

(a) As **primary markets** they enable organisations to **raise new finance,** by issuing new shares or new debentures. In the UK, a company must **have public company status** (be a plc) to be allowed to raise finance from the public on a capital market.

(b) As **secondary markets** they enable existing investors to **sell their investments,** should they wish to do so. A shareholder in a 'listed' company can sell his shares whenever he wants to on the Stock Exchange. The marketability of securities is a very important feature of the capital markets, because investors are more willing to buy stocks and shares if they know that they could sell them easily, should they wish to.

3.9 These are the main functions of a stock market, but we can add two more important ones.

(a) When a company comes to the stock market for the first time, and 'floats' its shares on the market, the owners of the company can **realise** some of the **value of their shares** in cash, because they will offer a proportion of their personally-held shares for sale to new investors.

(b) When one company wants to **take over** another, it is common to do so by issuing shares to finance the takeover. Takeovers by means of a share exchange are only feasible if the shares that are offered can be readily traded on a stock market, and so have an identifiable market value.

Question 1

Get hold of a copy of the Companies and Markets section of the weekday Financial Times, and look out for points relevant to your studies. Note the various London Money Rates in the Money Markets section, the parts covering the London Stock Exchange, and the share prices quotations on the London Share Service pages. This may help to put some of the topics covered here into context.

The Alternative Investment Market (AIM)

3.10 The London Stock Exchange launched the AIM in 1995 as a market for smaller, growing, companies that cannot qualify for or do not wish to join the Official List (or 'main market').

3.11 AIM companies might be new business 'start-ups' or well established family businesses, from high technology firms to traditional manufacturers. The AIM is designed to attract companies which wish to **cut the cost** of a **stock market** quotation.

3.12 The main advantages of an **AIM listing** are:

- Wider access to capital
- Enhanced credibility among financial institutions
- A higher public profile

OFEX

3.13 An unquoted company might choose to seek finance from investors, including members of the general public, through **OFEX**, a facility allowing trading in the securities of unquoted companies. OFEX is not a regulated market; it is a mechanism whereby stock exchange member firms in effect match business 'off exchange'; in the securities of certain unquoted companies.

Institutional investors

3.14 **Institutional investors** are institutions which have large amounts of funds which they want to invest, and they will invest in stocks and shares or any other assets which offer satisfactory returns and security or lend money to companies directly. The institutional investors are now the biggest investors on the stock market.

3.15 The major institutional investors in the UK are **pension funds, insurance companies, investment trusts, unit trusts** and **venture capital organisations.** Of these, pension funds and insurance companies have the largest amounts of funds to invest.

Capital market participants

3.16 The various participants in the capital markets are summarised in the diagram below.

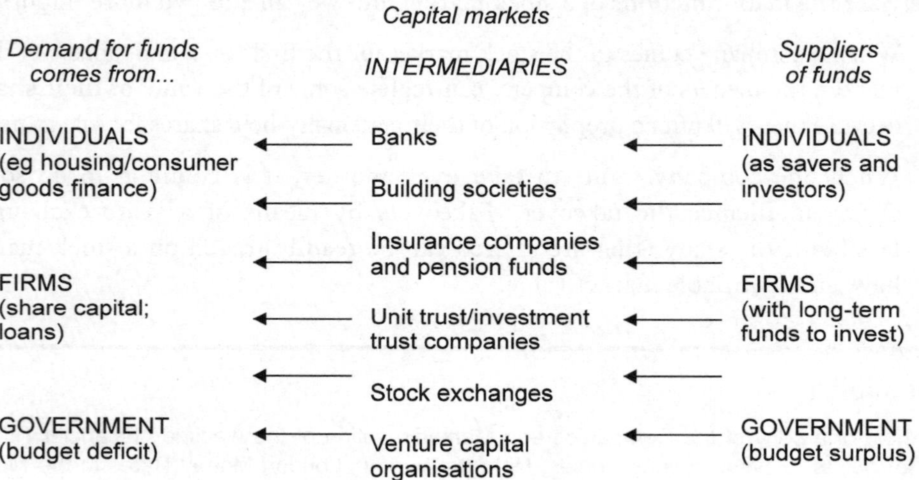

4 THE EFFICIENT MARKET HYPOTHESIS

4.1 The UK and US stock markets are perhaps efficient capital markets. An 'efficient capital market' in this context is one in which:

(a) The prices of securities bought and sold **reflect all** the **relevant information** which is available to the buyers and sellers - in other words, share prices change quickly to reflect all new information about future prospects.

(b) **No individual dominates** the market.

(c) **Transaction costs** of buying and selling are **not so high** as to discourage trading significantly.

4.2 If the stock market is efficient, share prices should vary in a rational way.

(a) If a company makes a **profitable investment,** shareholders will get to know about it, and the **market price** of its shares will **rise** in anticipation of future dividend increases.

(b) If a company makes a **bad investment** shareholders will find out and so the **price** of its shares will **fall.**

(c) If **interest rates rise**, shareholders will want a **higher return** from their investments, so **market prices** will **fall.**

4.3 An efficient market is one in which the market prices of all the securities traded on it reflect all the available information. In such a market, there would be no possibility of 'speculative bubbles' in which share prices are pushed up or down by speculative pressure to unrealistically high or low levels.

Varying degrees of efficiency

4.4 There are three main degrees or 'forms' of 'information processing' efficiency.

- Weak form
- Semi-strong form
- Strong form

4.5 Under the **weak form** hypothesis of **market efficiency**, current share prices **reflect all information available from past changes in the price.**

4.6 Research to prove that the stock market displays weak form efficiency has been based on the principle that:

- If share price changes are random, and
- If there is no connection between past price movements and new share price changes,

then it should be possible to prove statistically that there is no correlation between successive changes in the price of a share, that is, that **trends** in prices **cannot be detected**. Proofs of the absence of trends have been claimed in the work of various writers.

4.7 **Semi-strong form** tests attempt to show that the stock market displays semi-strong efficiency, by which we mean that current share prices reflect both:

- All **relevant information** about **past price movements** and their implications, and
- All **knowledge** which is **available publicly**

4.8 Research in both the UK and the USA has suggested that market prices anticipate mergers several months before they are formally announced, and the conclusion drawn is that the stock markets in these countries *do* exhibit semi-strong efficiency.

4.9 **Strong form** efficiency means that share prices reflect all information available:

- From past price changes
- From public knowledge or anticipation, and
- From insider knowledge available to experts such as investment managers

4.10 If strong form efficiency applies, management should concentrate simply on **maximising** the **net present value** of its **investments.** It need not worry, for example, about the effect on share prices of financial results in the published accounts. Investors will make allowances for low profits or dividends in the current year if higher profits or dividends are expected in the future.

The implications of the efficient market hypothesis

4.11 If the strong form of the efficient market hypothesis is correct, a company's **real financial position** will be **reflected in its share price**. Its real financial position includes both its **current position** and its expected **future profitability**.

4.12 The implication for an investor is that if the market shows **strong form** or **semi-strong form** efficiency, he can **rarely spot shares** at a **bargain price** that will soon rise sharply in value. This is because the market will already have anticipated future developments, and will have reflected these in the share price. All an investor can do, instead of looking for share bargains, is to concentrate on building up a **good spread of shares** (a portfolio) in order to achieve a satisfactory balance between **risk and return.**

Question 2

In the share price crash of October 1987, share prices on the world's stock markets fell suddenly by 20% to 40%. Why does this raise a question about the validity of the efficient market hypothesis?

Answer

The question is: if EMH is correct, how can shares that were valued at one level on one day suddenly be worth 40% less the next day, without any change in expectations of corporate profits and dividends? It would appear that speculation must have caused share prices to rise to levels which were unsustainable in the longer term.

5 RATES OF INTEREST AND RATES OF RETURN

5.1 **Interest rates** are effectively the 'prices' governing lending and borrowing. The borrower pays interest to the lender at a certain percentage of the capital sum, as the price for the use of the funds borrowed. As with other prices, supply and demand effects apply. For example, the higher the rates of interest that are charged, the lower will be the demand for funds from borrowers.

The pattern of interest rates

5.2 The pattern of interest rates refers to the variety of interest rates on different financial assets, and the margin between interest rates on lending and deposits that are set by banks. Note that the **pattern of interest rates** is a different thing from the **general level of interest rates.**

5.3 Why are there such a large number of interest rates? In other words, how is the **pattern** of interest rates to be explained? The answer to this question relates to several factors.

(a) **Risk**

There is a trade-off between risk and return. Higher-risk borrowers must pay higher yields on their borrowing, to compensate lenders for the greater risk involved. Banks will assess the creditworthiness of the borrower, and set a rate of interest on its loan at a certain mark-up above its base rate or the LIBOR.

(b) **Need to make a profit on re-lending**

Financial intermediaries make their profits from re-lending at a higher rate of interest than the cost of their borrowing. For example, the interest rate charged on bank loans exceeds the rate paid on deposits and the mortgage rate charged by building societies exceeds the interest rate paid on deposits.

(c) **Duration of the lending**

The term of the loan or asset will affect the rate of interest charged on it. In general, longer-dated assets will earn a higher yield than similar short-dated assets but this is not always the case. The differences are referred to as the **term structure** of interest rates.

(d) **Size of the loan or deposit**

The yield on assets might vary with the size of the loan or deposit. Administrative cost savings help to allow **lower rates of interest** to be charged by banks **on larger loans** and **higher rates of interest** to be paid on **larger time deposits.**

(e) **Different types of financial asset**

Different types of financial asset attract **different rates of interest**. This is partly because different types of asset attract different sorts of lender/investor. For example, bank deposits attract individuals and companies, whereas long-dated government securities are particularly attractive to various institutional investors.

5.4 The rates of interest paid on government borrowing (the **Treasury bill rate** for short-term borrowing and the **gilt-edged rate** for long-dated government stocks) provide benchmarks for other interest rates. For example:

(a) Clearing banks might set the three months inter-bank rate (LIBOR) at about 1% above the Treasury bill rate.

(b) Banks in turn lend (wholesale) at a rate higher than LIBOR.

The term structure of interest rates: the yield curve

5.5 In addition interest rates depend on the term to maturity of the asset. For example, government stock might be short-dated, medium-dated, or long-dated. The **term structure of interest rates** refers to the way in which the yield on a security varies according to the term of the borrowing, that is the length of time until the debt will be repaid as shown by the **yield curve**. Normally, the longer the term of an asset to maturity, the higher the rate of interest paid on the asset.

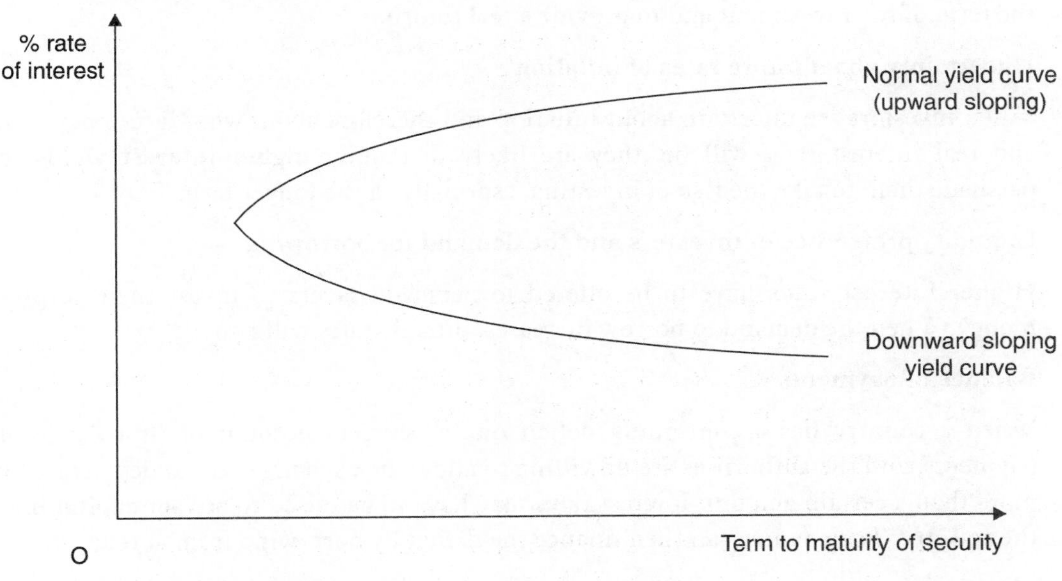

5.6 The reasons why, in theory, the yield curve will normally be upward sloping, so that long-term financial assets offer a higher yield than short-term assets, are as follows.

(a) The investor must be **compensated** for **tying up** his **money** in the asset for a **longer period of time**.

(b) There is a **greater risk** in lending long-term than in lending short-term. To compensate investors for this risk, they might require a higher yield on longer dated investments.

5.7 So why might a yield curve slope downwards, with short-term rates higher than longer-term rates?

(a) **Expectations** about the way that interest rates will move in the future affect the term structure of interest rates. When interest rates are expected to fall, short-term rates might be higher than long-term rates, and the yield curve would be downward sloping.

(b) **Government policy** on interest rates might be significant too. A policy of keeping interest rates relatively high might therefore have the effect of forcing short-term interest rates higher than long-term rates.

(c) The **market segmentation theory** of interest rates suggests that the slope of the yield curve will reflect conditions in **different segments** of the market. This theory holds that the major investors are confined to a particular segment of the market and will not switch segment even if the forecast of likely future interests rates changes.

The general level of interest rates

5.8 Interest rates on any one type of financial asset will vary over time. In other words, the general level of interest rates might go up or down. The general level of interest rates is affected by several factors.

(a) **Need for a real return**

Investors normally want to **earn a 'real' rate of return** on their investment. The appropriate 'real' rate of return will depend on factors such as investment risk.

(b) **Inflation**

Nominal rates of interest should be sufficient to **cover expected rates of inflation** over the term of the investment and to provide a real return.

(c) **Uncertainty about future rates of inflation**

When investors are uncertain about inflation and therefore about what future nominal and real interest rates will be, they are likely to require **higher interest yields** to persuade them to take the risk of investing, especially in the longer term.

(d) **Liquidity preference of investors and the demand for borrowing**

Higher interest rates have to be offered to persuade savers to invest their surplus money. When the demand to borrow increases, interest rates will rise.

(e) **Balance of payments**

When a country has a continuing deficit on the current account of its balance of payments, and the authorities are unwilling to allow the exchange rate to depreciate by more than a certain amount, interest rates may have to be raised to **attract capital** into the country. The country can then finance the deficit by borrowing from abroad.

(f) **Monetary policy**

From mid-1997, decisions over UK interest rate policy have been made by the Monetary Policy Committee of the Bank of England. The Bank of England influences very short-term money market rates by means of **open market operations**. Usually longer term money market rates, and then banks' base rates, will respond to the authorities' wish for interest rate changes.

(g) **Interest rates abroad**

The rate of interest in one country will be influenced by **external factors,** such as interest rates in other countries and expectations about the exchange rate. When interest rates in overseas countries are high, interest rates on domestic currency investments must also be comparably high, to avoid capital transfers abroad and a fall in the exchange rate of the domestic currency.

The risk-return trade-off

5.9 We have explained how rates of interest, and therefore rates of return to lenders, will be affected by the risk involved in lending. The idea of a risk-return trade-off can, however, be extended beyond a consideration of interest rates.

5.10 An investor has the choice between different forms of investment. The investor may earn interest by depositing funds with a financial intermediary who will lend on to, say, a company, or it may invest in loan stock of a company. Alternatively, the investor may invest directly in a company by purchasing shares in it.

5.11 The current market price of a security is found by discounting the future expected earnings stream at a rate suitably adjusted for risk. This means that investments carrying a higher degree of risk will demand a higher rate of return. This rate of return or yield has two components:

- **Annual income** (dividend or interest)
- **Expected capital gain**

In general, the higher the risk of the security, the more important is the capital gain component of the expected yield.

5.12 Some of the main forms of investment are listed below in ascending order of risk.

(a) **Government stock**

The risk of default is negligible. Hence this tends to form the **base level** for returns in the market. The only uncertainty concerns the movement of interest rates over time, and hence longer dated stocks will tend to carry a higher rate of interest.

(b) **Company loan stock**

Although there is some risk of default on company loan stock (also called corporate bonds), the stock is usually **secured** against corporate assets.

(c) **Preference shares**

These are generally riskier than loan stock since they rank behind debt in the event of a liquidation, although they rank ahead of **ordinary shares**. The return takes the form of a **fixed percentage dividend** based on the par value of the share.

(d) **Ordinary shares**

Ordinary shares carry a high level of risk. Dividends are paid out of distributable profits after all other liabilities have been paid and can be subject to **large fluctuations** from year to year. However, there is the potential for significant **capital appreciation** in times of growth. In general, the level of risk will vary with the operational and financial **gearing** of the company and the nature of the markets in which it operates.

The reverse yield gap

5.13 Because debt involves lower risk than equity investment, we might expect yields on debt to be lower than yields on shares. More usually, however, the opposite applies and the yields on shares are lower than on low-risk debt; this situation is known as a **reverse yield gap**. A reverse yield gap can occur because shareholders may be willing to accept lower returns on their investment in the short term, in anticipation that they will make capital gains in the future.

Interest rates and shareholders' required rates of return

5.14 Given that equity shares and interest-earning investments stand as alternatives from the investor's point of view, changes in the general level of interest rates can be expected to have an effect on the rates of return which shareholders will expect.

5.15 If the return expected by an investor from an equity investment (ie an investment in shares) is 11% and the dividend paid on the shares is 15 pence, the market value of one share will be 15 pence / 11% = £1.36.

5.16 Suppose that interest rates then fall. Because the option of putting the funds on deposit has become less attractive, the shareholders' required return will fall, to say, 9%. Then the market value of one share will increase to 15 pence / 9% = £1.67.

5.17 You can see from this that an **increase** in the shareholders' **required rate of return** (perhaps resulting from an increase in the general level of interest rates) will lead to a **fall** in the **market value** of the share.

6 THE SEPARATION THEOREM

6.1 The essence of the separation theorem is that **financial decisions of investors** are made **independently of companies' decisions to invest in assets.**

6.2 To illustrate why this is so, we need to consider how investors use the capital market.

6.3 When investing, investors must choose a portfolio which gives them a satisfactory **balance** between the **expected returns** from the portfolio and the **risk** that actual returns from the portfolio will be higher or lower than expected. Some portfolios will be more risky than others.

6.4 Traditional investment theory suggests that rational investors wish to maximise return and minimise risk. Thus if two portfolios have the same element of risk, the investor will choose the one yielding the higher return. Similarly, if two portfolios offer the same return the investor will select the portfolio with the lesser risk. This is illustrated by Figure 1.

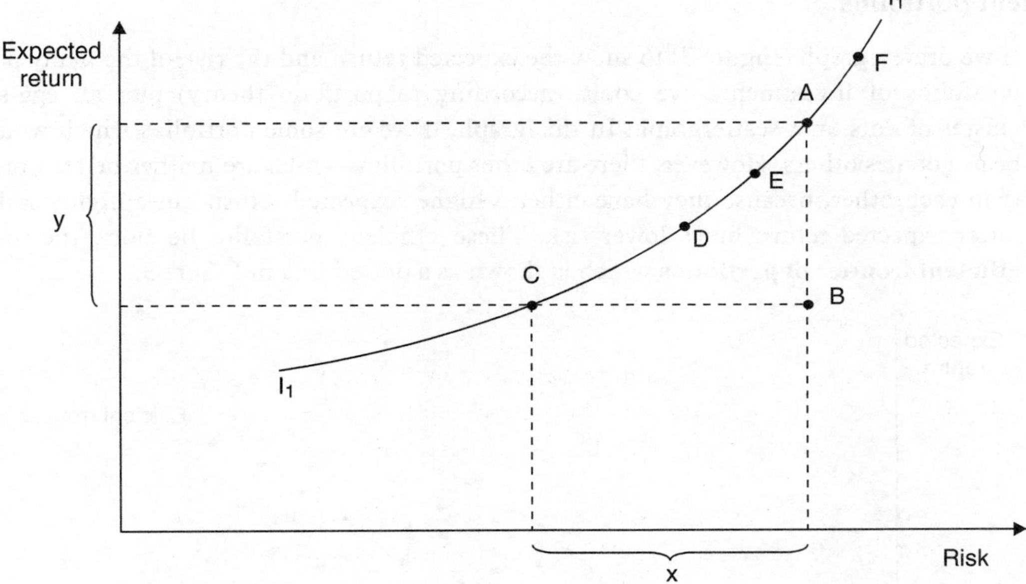

Figure 1 An investor's indifference curve

6.5 Portfolio A will be preferred to portfolio B because it offers a higher expected return for the same level of risk. Similarly, portfolio C will be preferred to portfolio B because it offers the same expected return for lower risk. But whether an investor chooses portfolio A or portfolio C will depend on the individual's attitude to risk, whether he wishes to accept a greater risk for a greater expected return.

6.6 The curve I_1 is an investor's indifference curve. The investor will have no preference between any portfolios which give a mix of risk and expected return which lies on the curve, since he derives equal **utility** from each of them. Thus, to the investor the portfolios A, C, D, E and F are all just as good as each other, and all of them are better than portfolio B.

6.7 An investor would prefer combinations of return and risk on **indifference curve** A to those on curve B (Figure 2) because curve A offers higher returns for the same degree of risk (and less risk for the same expected returns). For example, for the same amount of risk x, the expected return on curve A is y_1, whereas on curve B it is only y_2.

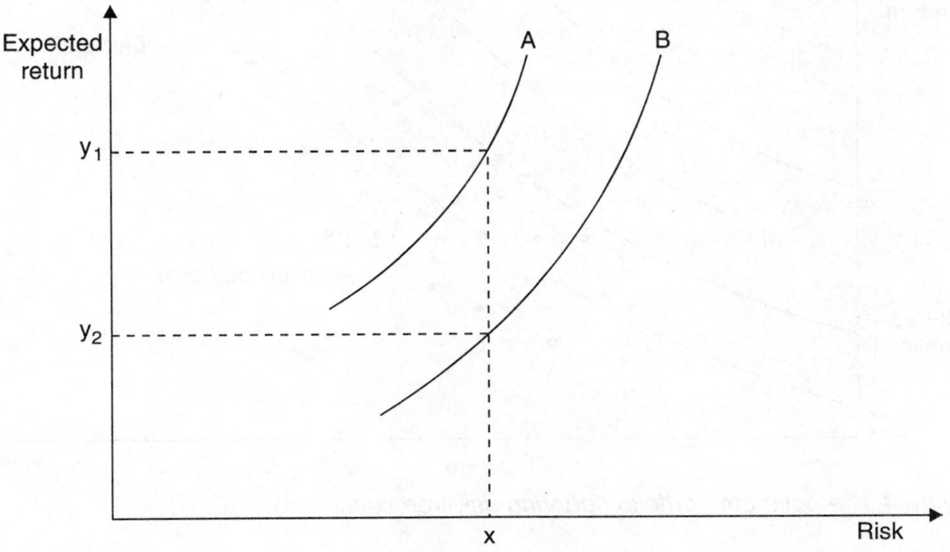

Figure 2 Indifference curves compared

Efficient portfolios

6.8 If we drew a graph (Figure 3) to show the expected return and the risk of the many possible portfolios of investments, we could (according to portfolio theory) plot an egg-shaped cluster of dots on a scattergraph. In this graph, there are some portfolios which would not be as good as others. However, there are other portfolios which are neither better nor worse than each other, because they have either a higher expected return but a higher risk, or a lower expected return but a lower risk. These 'efficient' portfolios lie along the so-called **efficient frontier of portfolios** which is shown as a dotted line in Figure 3.

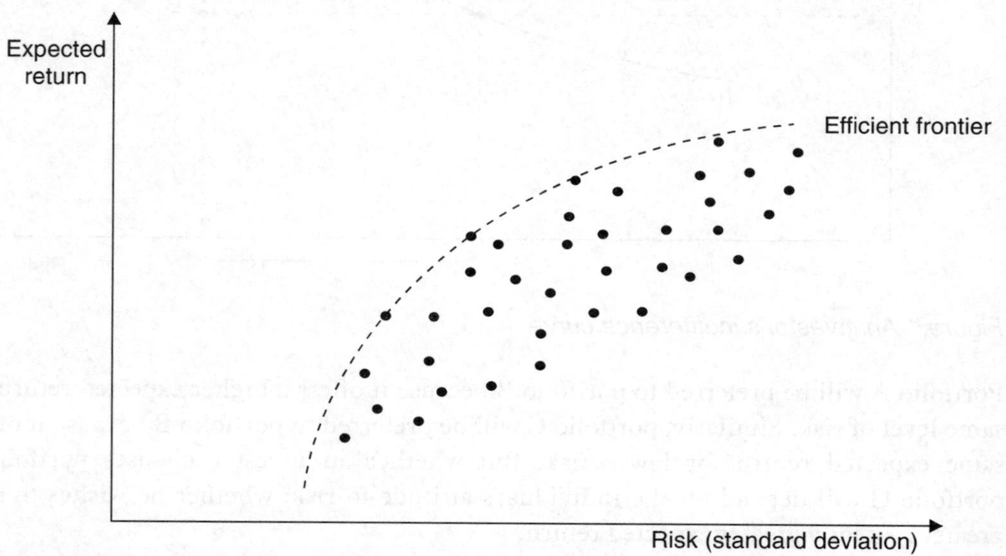

Figure 3 The efficient frontier of available investment portfolios

6.9 We can now place an investor's indifference curves on the same graph as the possible portfolios of investments (the **egg-shaped scatter graph**), as in Figure 4. An investor would prefer a portfolio of investments on indifference curve A to a portfolio on curve B, which in turn is preferable to a portfolio on curve C which in turn is preferable to curve D. No portfolio exists, however, which is on curve A or curve B.

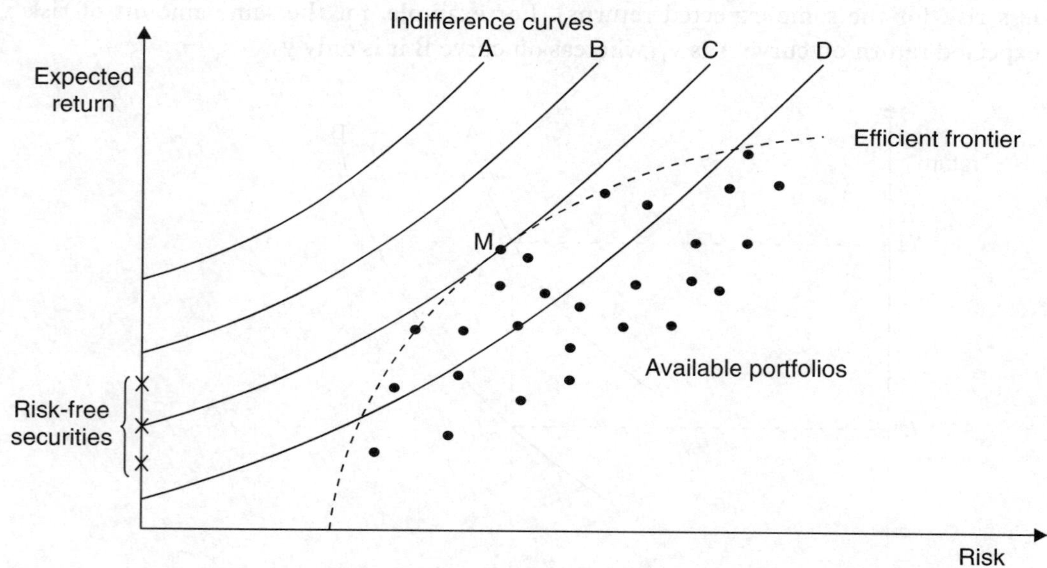

Figure 4 The optimum portfolio (ignoring risk-free securities)

6.10 The optimum portfolio (or portfolios) to select is one where an indifference curve touches the efficient frontier of portfolios at a tangent. In Figure 4, this is the portfolio marked M,

where indifference curve C touches the efficient frontier at a tangent. Any portfolio on an indifference curve to the right of curve C, such as one on curve D, would be worse than M.

Risk-free investments

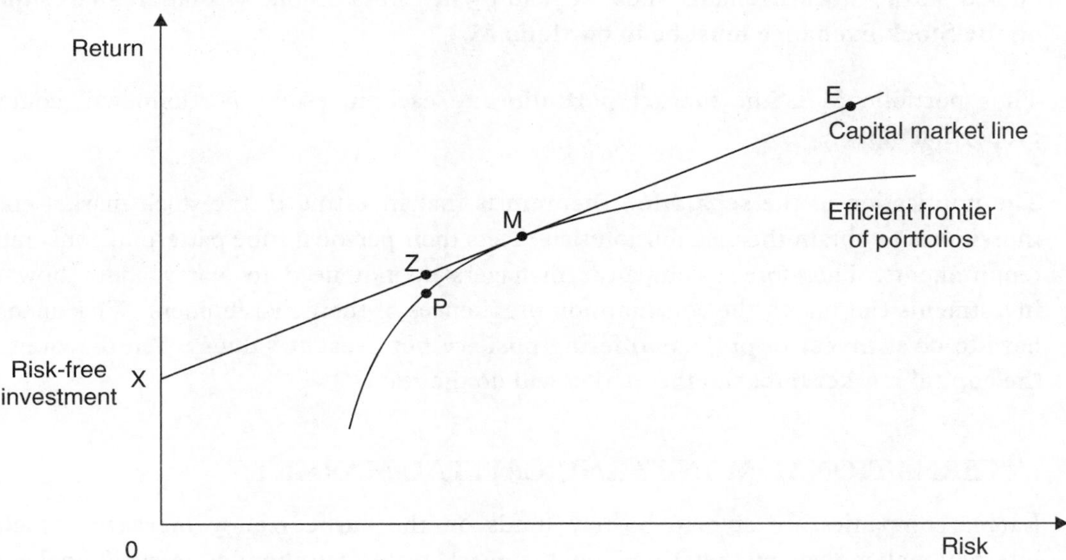

Figure 5 The capital market line

6.11 The efficient frontier is a curved line, not a straight line. This is because the additional return for accepting a greater level of risk will not be constant. The curve eventually levels off because a point will be reached where no more return can be offered to an investor for accepting more risk.

6.12 All the portfolios under consideration carry some degree of risk. But some investments are risk-free. It is extremely unlikely that the British Government would default on any payment of interest and capital on its stocks. Thus government stocks can be taken to be risk-free investments. If we introduce a **risk-free investment** into the analysis we can see that the old efficient frontier is superseded (Figure 5).

6.13 The straight line XZME is drawn at a tangent to the efficient frontier and cuts the y axis at the point of the risk-free investment's return. The line (known as the **capital market line** (CML)) becomes the new efficient frontier.

6.14 Portfolio M is the same as in Figure 4. It is the efficient portfolio which will appeal to the investor most, ignoring risk-free investments. Portfolio Z is a mixture of the investments in portfolio M and risk-free investments. Investors will prefer portfolio Z (a mixture of risky portfolio M and the risk-free investment) to portfolio P because a higher return is obtained for the same level of risk. The only portfolio consisting entirely of **risky investments** a rational investor should want to hold is portfolio M. All other risky portfolios are inefficient (because they are below the CML).

6.15 As with the curvilinear frontier, one portfolio on the capital market line is as attractive as another to a rational investor. One investor may wish to hold portfolio Z, which lies 2/3 of the way along the CML between risk-free investment X and portfolio M (that is, a holding comprising 2/3 portfolio M and 1/3 risk-free securities). Another investor may wish to hold portfolio E, which entails putting all his funds in portfolio M and borrowing money at the risk-free rate to acquire more of portfolio M.

6.16 We have said that investors will only want to hold one portfolio of risky investments: portfolio M. This may be held in conjunction with a holding of the risk-free investment (as with portfolio Z). Alternatively, an investor may borrow funds to augment his holding of M (as with portfolio E). Therefore, since all investors wish to hold portfolio M, and all shares quoted on the Stock Exchange must be held by investors, it follows that **all shares quoted on the Stock Exchange must be in portfolio M**.

6.17 Thus portfolio M is the **market portfolio** and each investor's portfolio will contain a proportion of it.

6.18 The implication of the **separation theorem** is that investing in the stock market enables individuals to obtain the distribution that meets their personal time pattern of consumption requirements. Therefore a company's managers do not need to worry about how their investments can match the consumption preferences of their shareholders. What managers have to do is **invest in projects offering positive net present values** when **discounted at the capital market rate**, and the market will do the rest.

7 INTERNATIONAL MONEY AND CAPITAL MARKETS

7.1 Larger companies are able to borrow funds on the **eurocurrency markets** (which are international money markets) and on the markets for **eurobonds** (international capital markets).

Exam focus point

Don't suggest these international markets as possible sources of finance for a *smaller* business in an exam answer.

Eurocurrency markets

7.2 A UK company might borrow money from a bank or from the investing public, in sterling. But it might also borrow in a foreign currency, especially if it trades abroad, or if it already has assets or liabilities abroad denominated in a foreign currency.

7.3 When a company borrows in a foreign currency, the loan is known as a **eurocurrency loan.**

KEY TERM

Eurocurrency is currency which is held by individuals and institutions outside the country of issue of that currency.

7.4 For example, if a UK company borrows US $50,000 from its bank, the loan will be a 'eurodollar' loan. London is a major centre for eurocurrency lending and companies with foreign trade interests might choose to borrow from their bank in another currency.

7.5 The **eurocurrency markets** involve the depositing of funds with a bank outside the country of the currency in which the funds are denominated and re-lending these funds for a fairly short term, typically three months. Most eurocurrency transactions in fact takes place between banks of different countries and take the form of negotiable certificates of deposit.

International capital markets

7.6 Large companies may arrange borrowing facilities from their bank, in the form of bank loans or bank overdrafts. Instead, however, they might prefer to borrow from private investors. In other words, instead of obtaining a £10,000,000 bank loan, a company might issue 'bonds', or 'paper' in order to borrow directly from investors, with:

(a) The bank merely **arranging the transaction**, finding investors who will take up the bonds or paper that the borrowing company issues

(b) **Interest** being payable to the **investors themselves**, not to a bank

7.7 In recent years, a strong international market has built up which allows very large companies to borrow in this way, long-term or short-term. As well as eurobonds, there is also a less highly developed market in international equity share issues ('**euro-equity**').

KEY TERM

A **eurobond** is a bond denominated in a currency which often differs from that of the country of issue.

7.8 **Eurobonds** are long-term loans raised by international companies or other institutions and sold to investors in several countries at the same time. Such bonds can be sold by one holder to another. The term of a eurobond issue is typically ten to 15 years.

7.9 Eurobonds may be the most suitable source of finance for a large organisation with an excellent credit rating, such as a large successful multinational company, which:

(a) Requires a **long-term loan** to **finance a big capital expansion** programme. The loan may be for at least five and up to 20 years.

(b) Requires **borrowing** which is **not subject to the national exchange** controls of any government.

In addition, domestic capital issues may be regulated by the government or central bank, with an orderly queue for issues. In contrast, eurobond issues can be made whenever market conditions seem favourable.

7.10 A borrower who is contemplating a eurobond issue must consider the **exchange risk** of a long-term foreign currency loan. If the money is to be used to purchase assets which will earn revenue in a currency **different to that of the bond issue**, the borrower will run the risk of exchange losses.

7.11 If the money is to be used to purchase assets which will earn revenue in the **same currency,** the borrower can match these revenues with payments on the bond, and so remove or reduce the exchange risk.

7.12 An **investor** subscribing to a bond issue will be concerned about the following factors.

(a) **Security**

The borrower must be of **high quality**.

(b) **Marketability**

Investors will wish to have a **ready market** in which bonds can be bought and sold. If the borrower is of high quality the bonds or notes will be readily negotiable.

(c) **Anonymity**

Investors in eurobonds tend to be attracted to the **anonymity** of this type of issue, as the bonds are generally issued to bearer.

(d) The **return on the investment**

This is paid tax-free.

Chapter roundup

- In this chapter, we have covered some important aspects of the **markets** and **institutions** which are relevant to the practice of financial management.
- A **financial intermediary** links those with surplus funds (eg **lenders**) to those with funds deficits (eg potential **borrowers**) thus providing **aggregation** and **economies of scale**, **risk pooling** and **maturity transformation**.
- The **capital markets** and **money markets** are markets for long-term and short-term capital respectively.
- A stock market (in the UK: the **main market** plus the **AIM**) acts as a **primary market** for raising finance, and as a **secondary market** for the trading of existing securities (ie stocks and shares).
- The **efficient market hypothesis** suggests that **share prices reflect** the **type of information** which is available to investors.
- The **pattern of interest rates** on financial assets is influenced by the **risk** of the assets, the **duration** of the lending, and the **size** of the loan.
- There is a **trade-off** between **risk and return**. Investors in riskier assets expect to be compensated for the risk. In the case of ordinary shares, investors hope to achieve their return in the form of an increase in the share price (a capital gain) as well as from dividends.
- **International money and capital markets** are available for larger companies wishing to raise larger amounts of finance.
- The **separation theorem** implies that companies should concentrate on **maximisation of present value**, since the stock market will enable individuals to obtain the income pattern from their investments that corresponds to their consumption requirements.

Quick quiz

1 For short-term borrowing, a company will go to the **money markets/capital markets**? (Which?)

2 (a) From which does the **demand** for capital markets funds come: Individuals/Firms/Government? (Delete any that do not apply).

(b) From which does the **supply** of capital market funds come: Individuals/Firms/Government? (Delete any that do not apply).

3 Identify five types of capital market intermediaries.

4 Is the Stock Exchange a money market?

5 Which of the following is not a function of the London Stock Exchange?

A Enabling organisations to raise new finance

B Enabling shareholders to realise the value of their shares

C Enabling companies to become public companies

D Enabling takeovers by share exchanges

6 The semi-strong form of the hypothesis implies that share prices will reflect information such as earning forecasts and announcements of acquisitions.

☐ True

☐ False

7 Which of the following statements is true of the Alternative Investment market (AIM)?

A AIM shares are treated as quoted for tax purposes.

B Companies wishing to have their shares traded on AIM must meet eligibility criteria in terms of size and profitability.

C There are more obligations to issue shareholder circulars than on the main market.

D There are no Stock Exchange requirements for the percentage of shares in public hands.

8 What is meant by efficiency in the context of the efficient market hypothesis?

Answers to quick quiz

1 Money markets.

2 (a) and (b): You should have deleted none.

3 Any five of: banks; building societies; insurance companies; pension funds; unit trust companies; investment trusts; Stock Exchanges; venture capital organisations.

4 No. The Stock Exchange is a capital market, not a money market.

5 C Not every public company is listed on the London Stock Exchange.

6 True.

7 D This is the correct answer. There are no minimum requirements, although if too few shares are freely available there will be no realistic market price.

A AIM shares are treated as unquoted for tax purposes, meaning that a number of reliefs are available to investors.

B There are no eligibility criteria for new entrants.

C This is incorrect; public announcements will generally be sufficient.

8 Efficiency in processing information in the pricing of stocks and shares.

Now try the question below from the Exam Question Bank

Question to try	Level	Marks	Time
21	Introductory	n/a	30 mins

Chapter 17

MACROECONOMIC POLICY

Topic list		Syllabus reference
1	**Outline of macroeconomic policy**	**2(e)**
2	**Fiscal policy**	**2(e)**
3	**Monetary and interest rate policy**	**2(d), (e)**
4	**Exchange rates**	**2(e)**
5	**Inflation**	**2(e)**

Introduction

In Chapters 17 and 18 we shall be concerned with the economic policies pursued by governments.

Study guide

Section 1 – The economic environment I

Macroeconomic objectives

- Identify and explain the main macro-economic policy targets
- Explain how government economic policy may affect planning and decision-making in business
- Define and explain the role of fiscal, monetary, interest rate and exchange rate policy

Fiscal policy

- Identify the main tools of fiscal policy
- Explain how public expenditure is financed and the meaning of PSBR
- Explain how PSBR and taxation policy interact with other economic indicators
- Identify the implications of fiscal policy for business

Section 2 – The economic environment II

- Identify the main tools of monetary policy
- Identify the factors which influence inflation and exchange rates, including the impact of interest rates
- Identify the implications of monetary, inflation and exchange rate policy for business

Exam guide

The emphasis in the exam will be discussing how economic conditions or policies affect particular businesses, for example the impact of a change in interest rates.

1 OUTLINE OF MACROECONOMIC POLICY

Exam focus point

Topics in economics will be tested in parts of longer questions only. But the economics in the paper should not be neglected – examiners often criticise students' lack of knowledge of economics.

Microeconomics, macroeconomics and economic policy

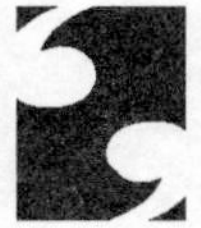

KEY TERMS

Microeconomics is concerned with the behaviour of individual firms and consumers or households. **Macroeconomics** is concerned with the economy at large, and with the behaviour of large aggregates such as the national income, the money supply and the level of employment.

1.1 A government will of course be concerned with how the economy is behaving as a whole, and therefore with **macroeconomic variables.**

1.2 Macroeconomic policy can affect planning and decision making in various ways, for example via interest rate changes, which affect borrowing costs and required rates of return, as we saw earlier.

1.3 Note also that a government might adopt policies which try to exert influence at the **microeconomic** level. Examples include policies to remove regulations which restrict competition in particular labour markets or goods markets and policies to bring state-owned businesses into private ownership.

Economic policies and objectives

1.4 The policies pursued by a government may serve various objectives.

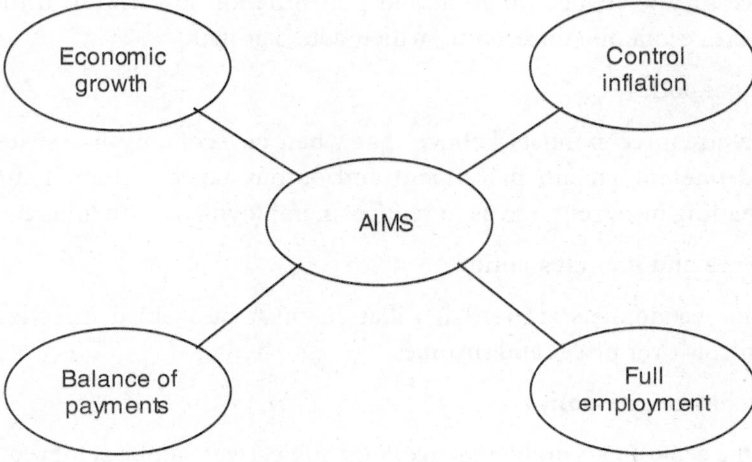

(a) **Economic growth**

'Growth' implies an increase in national income in 'real' terms - ie increases caused by price inflation are not real increases at all.

(b) **Control price inflation**

This means achieving **stable prices**. This has become a central objective of UK economic policy in recent years.

(c) **Full employment**

Full employment does not mean that everyone who wants a job has one all the time, but it does mean that unemployment levels are low, and involuntary unemployment is short-term.

(d) **Balance of payments**

The wealth of a country relative to others, a country's creditworthiness as a borrower, and the goodwill between countries in international relations might all depend on the achievement of an external trade balance over time. Deficits in external trade, with imports exceeding exports, might also be damaging for the prospects of economic growth.

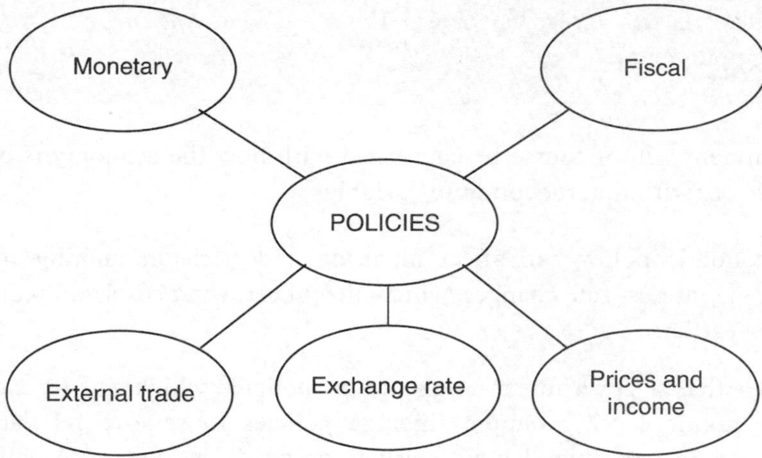

1.5 To try to achieve its intermediate and overall objectives, a government will use a number of different policy tools or policy instruments. These include the following.

(a) **Monetary policy**

Monetarist economists believe that control over the growth of the money supply is necessary to reduce inflation and that inflation is harmful to the economy because it creates economic uncertainty which deters growth.

(b) **Fiscal policy**

Keynesian economists believe that when an economy has spare production capacity and unemployment, investment and output can be stimulated (through government spending or tax cuts) so as to reduce unemployment without creating more inflation.

(c) **Prices and incomes policy**

Some economists argue that inflation must be tackled directly through government controls over prices and incomes.

(d) **Exchange rate policy**

Some economists argue that economic objectives can be achieved through management of the exchange rate by the government. The strength or weakness of sterling's value, for example, will influence the volume of UK imports and exports, the balance of payments and interest rates.

(e) **External trade policy**

A government might have a policy for promoting economic growth by stimulating exports. Another argument is that there should be import controls to provide some form of protection for domestic manufacturing industries by making the cost of imports higher and the volume of imports lower. Protection could encourage domestic output to rise, stimulating the domestic economy.

1.6 These **policy tools** are not mutually exclusive and a government might adopt a policy mix of monetary policy, fiscal policy and exchange rate policy in an attempt to achieve its intermediate and ultimate economic objectives.

Conflicts in policy objectives and instruments

1.7 Macroeconomic policy aims cannot necessarily all be sustained together for a long period of time; attempts to achieve one objective will often have adverse effects on others, sooner or later.

(a) There may be a **conflict** between **steady balanced growth** in the economy and **full employment**. Although a growing economy should be able to provide more jobs, there is some concern that since an economy must be modernised to grow and modern technology is labour-saving, it might be possible to achieve growth without creating many more jobs, and so keeping unemployment at a high level.

(b) In the UK, **problems** with **creating more employment** and a **steady growth** in the economy have been the balance of payments, the foreign exchange value of sterling, inflation and the money supply. The objectives of lower unemployment and economic growth have been difficult to achieve because of the problems and conflicts with secondary objectives.

(i) To create jobs and growth, there must be an **increase in aggregate demand**. When demand picks up there will be a surge in imports, with foreign goods bought by UK manufacturers (eg raw materials) and consumers.

(ii) The high rate of imports creates a **deficit in the balance of payments**, which in turn will weaken sterling and raise the cost of imports, thus giving some impetus to price rises.

(iii) To maintain the value of sterling, **interest rates** in the UK might need to be kept **high**, and high interest rates appear to **deter** companies from **investing**.

1.8 In practice, achieving the best mix of economic policies also involves a number of problems, such as the following.

- Inadequate **information**
- **Time lags** between use of policy and effects being noticeable
- **Political pressures** for short-term solutions
- Unpredictable **side-effects** of policies
- The influence of **other countries**
- **Conflict** between policy instruments

Effects of economic policy on business enterprises

1.9 Economic policy affects business enterprises in both service and manufacturing industries in various ways, for example as follows.

(a) By influencing the level of **aggregate demand (AD)** for goods and services in the economy, macroeconomic policy **affects** the **environment** for business. Business planning should take account of the likely effect of changes in AD for sales growth. Business planning will be easier if government policy is relatively stable.

(b) Tax changes brought about by **fiscal policy** affect businesses. For example, labour costs will be affected by changes in **employer's national insurance contributions**. If indirect taxes such as VAT or excise duty rise, either the additional cost will have to be absorbed or the rise will have to be passed on to consumers in higher prices.

(c) **Interest rate changes** brought about by government policy affect the borrowing costs of business.

(d) **Inflation**, perhaps induced by policies to boost demand, can **create uncertainty** for business as well as consumers. Businesses will be affected variously, depending on the relative price inflation on its input prices and output prices. A manufacturing industry may indeed make gains from increasing selling prices on stocks it has built up when its purchase prices were lower.

(e) Membership of an **exchange rate system** may reduce uncertainties for businesses involved in international trade because exchange rate fluctuations will be reduced. A service industry is less likely to be affected because it is less likely to be involved in substantial international trade.

2 FISCAL POLICY

Fiscal policy, national income and demand management

KEY TERM

Fiscal policy is action by the government to spend money, or to collect money in taxes, with the purpose of influencing the condition of the national economy.

2.1 A government might intervene in the economy by:

(a) **Spending more money** and **financing this expenditure** by **borrowing**

(b) **Collecting more in taxes without increasing public spending**

(c) **Collecting more in taxes** in order to **increase public spending**, thus diverting income from one part of the economy to another

2.2 Government spending is an '**injection**' into the economy, adding to aggregate demand and therefore national income, whereas taxes are a 'withdrawal' from the economy. Fiscal policy can thus be used as an instrument of demand management.

Three elements of public finance

2.3 Broadly, there are three elements in public finance.

(a) **Expenditure**

Expenditure by the government (public expenditure), at a national and local level

(b) **Income**

Expenditure must be financed, and the government must have income.

(i) Most government income comes from taxation.

(ii) Some income is obtained from direct charges to users of government services.

(c) **Borrowing**

To the extent that a government's expenditure exceeds its income, it must borrow to make up the difference. The amount that the government must borrow each year is the **public sector borrowing requirement** or PSBR.

(i) The government may borrow from the non-bank sector by issuing relatively illiquid forms of debt (eg national savings certificates and long-term government debt). This is known as **'funding' the debt**.

(ii) The government can issue relatively liquid debt such as Treasury bills to the bank sector. This is known as **'unfunded' debt**.

(iii) **Funding policy** refers to the balance between funded and unfunded debt, which differ in the effects they have on the economy. The issuing of funded debt by government may 'crowd out' other borrowers from the market. An increase in **'unfunded' debt** will increase the liquid assets held by the banking system, enabling the banks to create more credit. The resulting increase in the money supply may be inflationary.

Budget surplus; budget deficit; balanced budget

2.4 When a government's income exceeds its expenditure, and there is a negative PSBR - ie a public sector debt repayment or 'PSDR' - we say that the government is running a **budget surplus.** When a government's expenditure exceeds its income, so that it must borrow to make up the difference, there is a PSBR and we say that the government is running a **budget deficit**. When a government's expenditure and income are the same, so that the PSBR is nil, there is a **balanced budget**.

The broad aims of fiscal policy

KEY TERM

Demand management is an approach to economic policy which seeks to control the level of aggregate demand through fiscal policy and/or monetary policy.

2.5 Fiscal policy appears to offer a method of managing aggregate demand in the economy.

(a) If the government spends more - for example, on public works such as hospitals, roads and sewers - without raising more money in taxation (ie by borrowing more) it will **increase expenditure** in the economy, and so **raise demand**.

(b) If the government kept its own spending at the same level, but **reduced** the levels of taxation, it would **also stimulate demand** in the economy because firms and households would have more of their own money after tax for consumption or saving/investing.

(c) In the same way, a government can **reduce demand** in the economy by **raising taxes** or **reducing its expenditure**.

2.6 The Keynesian (**demand management**) view is that a depressed economy can be **revived by increases in public expenditure** (ie through fiscal policy). Increasing investment, an initial stimulus to expenditure, will result in an even bigger increase in national income.

2.7 Monetarists disagree. They believe that a depressed economy cannot be successfully revived by an increase in public expenditure. Any increase in expenditure will normally have to be financed by increased borrowing which will further depress the economy through a '**crowding out' effect**, and higher interest rates; and it will increase the money supply and will cause more inflation.

The UK Labour government's fiscal policy approach

2.8 The UK Labour government elected in 1997 set out five principles which were to lie at the heart of its fixed policy framework.

(a) **Transparency** in the setting of fiscal policy objectives, the implementation of fiscal policy and in the presentation of the public accounts

(b) **Stability** in the fiscal policy-making process and in the way fiscal policy impacts on the economy

(c) **Responsibility** in the management of the public finances

(d) **Fairness,** including between generations

(e) **Efficiency** in the design and implementation of fiscal policy and in managing both sides of the public sector balance sheet

2.9 Fiscal policy is said to be based on the following two fiscal rules announced in the July 1997 Budget.

(a) The **golden rule**: over the economic cycle, the government will borrow only to invest and not to fund current spending, and

(b) **Public debt** as a proportion of national income will be held over the economic cycle at a **stable and prudent level**

The Private Finance Initiative (PFI)

2.10 Under the UK's **Private Finance Initiative,** launched in 1992, no public expenditure is approved without private sector options being explored first.

2.11 The PFI is intended to promote the use of private sector finance for public projects, so as to **transfer some of the risks** associated with the projects to the private sector, and to **make use of the skills**, experience and risk management expertise of the private sector.

2.12 The PFI applies to various types of public expenditure, from relatively simple catering or cleaning contracts to complex contracts such as a new train system or roadway involving design, construction and long-term operation and maintenance.

2.13 From its launch in 1992 up to October 1997, the total of PFI signed deals was £7.5 billion. Over this period, this total is not very large. The new Labour Government has reviewed the Initiative during 1997, and has introduced simplified procedures in an attempt to improve the level of take-up.

3 MONETARY AND INTEREST RATE POLICY

3.1 Money is important because:

(a) It '**oils the wheels**' of **economic activity,** providing an easy method for exchanging goods and services (ie buying and selling).

(b) The total amount of money in a national economy may have a **significant influence** on **economic activity and inflation.**

The role and aims of monetary policy

KEY TERM

Monetary policy is the regulation of the economy through control of the monetary system by operating on such variables as the money supply, the level of interest rates and the conditions for availability of credit.

3.2 The **effectiveness** of monetary policy will depend on:

(a) Whether the **targets** of **monetary policy** are **achieved successfully**

(b) Whether the **success** of **monetary policy** leads on to the **successful achievement** of the **intermediate target** (eg lower inflation), and

(c) Whether the **successful achievement** of the **intermediate target** (eg lower inflation) leads on to the **successful achievement** of the **overall objective** (eg strong economic growth)

Targets of monetary policy

3.3 Targets of monetary policy are likely to relate to the volume of national income and expenditure.

- Growth in the size of the money stock (money supply)
- The level of interest rates
- The volume of credit or growth in the volume of credit
- The exchange rate against other currencies
- The volume of expenditure in the economy (ie national income or GNP itself)

Monetary aggregates figures

3.4 To give you some idea of the relative 'sizes' of the main definitions of money, UK money stock figures for a particular month are shown below.

			£bn
M0	=	notes and coin in circulation outside the Bank of England	21.3
	+	banks' operational deposits with the Bank of England	0.1
			21.4
M2	=	non-bank sector holdings of notes and coin	18.1
	+	non bank private sector's retail sterling deposits with UK banks and building societies	384.6
			402.7

			£bn
M4	=	non-bank private sector holdings of:	
		notes and coin	18.3
	+	banks' retail deposits	182.4
	+	building societies' shares and deposits	202.0
	+	other interest bearing deposits	158.0
			560.7

The monetarist viewpoint

3.5 Monetarists argue that since money is a direct substitute for all other assets, an increase in the money supply, given a fairly stable velocity of circulation, will have a direct effect on demand for other assets because there will be more money to spend on those assets. If the total output of the economy is fixed, then an increase in the money supply will lead directly to higher prices.

The money stock as a target of monetary policy

3.6 To monetarist economists, the money stock is a possible intermediate target of economic policy. This is because they claim that an increase in the money supply will raise prices and money incomes, and this in turn will raise the demand for money to spend.

The growth in the volume of credit as a target for monetary policy

3.7 The government might decide to restrict credit lending (impose a 'credit squeeze') and so set targets for limited growth of credit in the economy. An increase in bank lending (ie in the volume of credit) is likely to lead to a rise in the level of expenditure in the economy because people borrow money in order to spend it. Higher bank lending is also likely to result in higher bank deposits and thus an increase in the money stock.

Fiscal policy as an instrument of monetary policy

3.8 Fiscal policy can work in co-operation with monetary policy. For example, a fiscal policy of reducing government expenditure and cutting the PSBR will have the effect of reducing the growth in M4.

Reserve requirements on banks as a means of controlling the money supply

3.9 As another technique for controlling money supply growth, the government might impose reserve requirements on banks.

(a) One type of reserve requirement is a compulsory **minimum cash reserve ratio** (ie the ratio of cash to total assets).

(b) Another form of reserve requirement is that banks should have a minimum ratio of **reserve assets** to total deposits. Reserve assets are types of short-term liquid assets.

Direct controls as a technique of monetary control

3.10 Yet another way of controlling the growth of the money supply is to impose direct controls on bank lending. Direct controls may be either quantitative or qualitative.

(a) **Quantitative controls** might be imposed on either **bank lending** (assets) or **bank deposits** (liabilities).

(b) **Qualitative controls** might be used to alter the **type of lending** by banks. For government (via the Bank) can ask the banks to limit their lending to the pers

Exchange rate control as an instrument or target of monetary policy

3.11 The **exchange rates** between the domestic currencies and other currencies, a exchange rates, have implications for the **balance of payments, inflation,** and **economic growth**. The government might seek to achieve a target exchange rate for its currency.

Interest rates as a target for monetary policy

3.12 The authorities may decide that interest rates themselves should be a target of monetary policy. This would be appropriate if it is considered that there is a direct relationship between interest rates and the level of expenditure in the economy.

3.13 It certainly seems logical that interest rates should have a strong influence on economic activity.

(a) However firms choose to raise funds, their **cost of capital** will be determined by interest rates. Corporate borrowing rates are normally linked to bank base rate. The exact rate will depend upon the risk element involved.

(b) We shall see later in this text how the cost of capital matters when determining the **viability of commercial investments.**

3.14 However although empirical evidence suggests there is some connection between interest rates and investment (by companies) and consumer expenditure, the connection is not a stable and predictable one. Some economists argue that the key element affecting investment is **business confidence** rather than the level of interest rates. Interest rate changes are only likely to affect the level of expenditure after a considerable time lag.

3.15 In 1997 the new Labour Government of the UK gave responsibility for setting short-term interest rates to the central bank, the Bank of England. The Bank now sets rates at a level which it considers appropriate, given the inflation rate target set by the Government. The purpose of having the central bank setting interest rates is to remove the risk of **political influence** over the decisions. If the UK joins **European monetary union** and therefore adopts the **Euro** as its currency, the interest rates that prevail will effectively be set at the European level.

Question 1

Outline the effects on the economy of a policy of high interest rates to dampen demand and inflation.

Answer

An increase in interest rates is thought to reduce the money supply in the economy and thereby to reduce the level of effective demand which will, in turn, decrease inflation and improve the balance of payments (the latter by decreasing the demand for imports, and freeing more domestic output for sale abroad). Aggregate expenditure in the economy will decrease, for various reasons.

(a) A higher interest rate encourages savings at the expense of consumer expenditure.

(b) Higher interest rates will increase mortgage payments and will thus reduce the amount of disposable income in the hands of home buyers for discretionary spending.

(c) The higher cost of consumer credit will deter borrowing and spending on consumer durables.

(d) Higher prices of goods due to higher borrowing costs for industry will also reduce some consumer expenditure in the economy.

Investment expenditure may also decline for two reasons.

(a) Higher interest rates deter some investment due to increased borrowing costs.

(b) Higher interest rates may make the corporate sector pessimistic about future business prospects and confidence in the economy. This may further reduce investment in the economy.

To the extent that higher domestic interest rates lead to an appreciation of the exchange rate, this should reduce inflation by lowering the cost of imported items. Exporters will experience pressure on their costs as the result of the more competitive price conditions they face, and may be less willing to concede high wage demands, and thus wage inflation may be constrained. The desired outcomes of the authorities' interest rate policy noted above may be negated by the following effects of higher interest rates.

(a) Higher interest results in greater interest income for savers, who may increase their spending due to this interest windfall.

(b) Since mortgage payments are the single largest constituent of the Retail Prices Index (RPI), any increase in them will be reflected immediately in RPI increases. This could lead to higher wage demands in the economy, and may result in a wage-price spiral.

(c) By encouraging capital inflows, higher interest rates will tend to lead to an appreciation of the currency's exchange rate. This makes exports less competitive and imports more attractive.

(d) A reduction in investment may decrease the pressure of demand in the economy but at the same time it will set in motion a process which in the future could reduce the economy's potential for production.

(e) To the extent that higher interest rates do squeeze demand in the economy, they will reduce employment, decreasing the proceeds of taxation and increasing the government expenditure on the unemployed.

---

4 EXCHANGE RATES

KEY TERM

An **exchange rate** is the rate at which one country's currency can be traded in exchange for another country's currency.

4.1 Dealers in foreign exchange - ie banks - make their profit by buying currency at one exchange rate, and selling it at a different rate. This means that there is a selling rate and a buying rate for a currency.

Factors influencing the exchange rate for a currency

4.2 The exchange rate between two currencies is determined primarily by supply and demand in the foreign exchange markets. Demand comes from individuals, firms and governments who want to buy a currency and supply comes from those who want to sell it.

4.3 Supply and demand in turn are subject to a number of influences.

- The rate of inflation, compared with the rate of inflation in other countries
- Interest rates, compared with interest rates in other countries
- The balance of payments
- Speculation
- Government policy on intervention to influence the exchange rate

4.4 Other factors influence the exchange rate through their relationship with the items identified above.

(a) **Total income and expenditure** (demand) in the **domestic economy** detern demand for goods. This includes imported goods and demand for goods prc the country which would otherwise be exported if demand for them did not ex home markets.

(b) **Output capacity** and the **level of employment** in the domestic economy might influence the balance of payments, because if the domestic economy has full employment already, it will be unable to increase its volume of production for exports.

(c) The **growth** in the **money supply** influences interest rates and domestic inflation.

Inflation and the exchange rate

4.5 **If the rate of inflation is higher in one country than in another country, the value of its currency will tend to weaken against the other country's currency.**

4.6 **Purchasing power parity theory** attempts to explain changes in the exchange rate exclusively by the rate of inflation in different countries. The theory predicts that the exchange value of a foreign currency depends on the **relative purchasing power** of each currency in its own country. As a simple example, suppose that there is only one commodity, which costs £110 in the UK and 880 kroners in Denmark. The exchange rate would be £1 = 8 kroners. If, as a result of inflation, the cost of the commodity in the UK rises to £120, the exchange rate would adjust to:

$$8 \times \frac{110}{120} \times £1 = 7.33 \text{ kroners.}$$

4.7 If the exchange rate remained at £1 = 8 kroners, it would be cheaper to import more of the commodity from Denmark for £110 and the UK would have a balance of trade deficit. This would only be corrected by an alteration in the exchange rate, with the pound weakening against the kroner.

4.8 Purchasing power parity theory states that an exchange rate varies according to relative price changes, so that:

$$\text{'Old' exchange rate} \times \frac{\text{Price level in country A}}{\text{Price level in country B}} = \text{'New' exchange rate}$$

4.9 The theory has been found to be inadequate to explain movements in exchange rates **in the short term,** mainly because it ignores payments between countries (ie demand and supply transactions) and the influence of supply and demand for currency on exchange rates.

4.10 Purchasing power parity theory is more likely to have some validity in the long run, and it is certainly true that the currency of a country which has a much higher rate of inflation than other countries will weaken on the foreign exchange market. In other words, the rate of inflation relative to other countries is certainly a factor which influences the exchange rate.

4.11 Although this influence is obvious, it is not predominant. This is apparent from the fact that if exchange rates did respond to demand and supply for current account items, then the balance of payments on the current account of all countries would tend towards equilibrium. This is not so, and **in practice other factors influence exchange rates more strongly**.

4.12 Demand for currency to invest in overseas capital investments and supply of currency from firms disinvesting in an overseas currency have more influence on the exchange rate, in the short term at least, than the demand and supply of goods and services.

4.13 If a country has a persistent deficit in its balance of payments current account, international confidence in that country's currency will eventually be eroded, and in the long term, its exchange rate will fall as capital inflows are no longer sufficient to counterbalance the country's trade deficit.

Question 2

Demand for imports in a country is inelastic in response to price changes and demand for the country's exports is also inelastic. The country's government raises interest rates substantially, and interest rates in other countries remain unchanged. What will be the effect of the rise in interest rates on the level of imports and on the level of exports?

Answer

Higher interest rates should attract more investments from abroad into the country, and so there will be *capital inflows* into the country. The capital inflows should cause an *appreciation in the currency,* because foreign investors must buy the currency to pay for their investments in the country. With an appreciation in the currency, imports become cheaper to buy and exports become more expensive to foreign buyers. With inelastic demand, this means that total spending on imports will fall. The volume of exports will fall, and so total revenue from exports in the exporter's *domestic currency* will fall too. (Total spending by foreign buyers on exports will rise, but only in their own currency.)

Consequences of an exchange rate policy

4.14 **Reasons for a policy of controlling the exchange rate**

(a) To **rectify a balance of trade deficit,** by trying to bring about a fall in the exchange rate.

(b) To **prevent a balance of trade surplus** from getting too large, by trying to bring about a limited rise in the exchange rate.

(c) To **emulate economic conditions** in other countries. The UK's membership of the ERM (from October 1990 until suspended in 1992) had as one of its aims that of emulating the conditions of lower inflation which exist in other ERM member countries.

(d) To **stabilise the exchange rate** of its currency. Exporters and importers will then face less risk of exchange rate movements wiping out their profits. A stable currency increases confidence in the currency and promotes international trade.

Fixed exchange rates

4.15 A government might try to keep the exchange rate at its fixed level, but if it cannot control inflation, the **real value** of its currency would not remain fixed. If one country's rate of inflation is higher than others, its export prices would become uncompetitive in overseas markets and the country's trade deficit would grow. Devaluation of the currency would be necessary for a recovery.

4.16 If exchange rates are fixed, any changes in **(real) interest rates** in one country will create pressure for the **movement of capital** into or out of the country. Capital movements would put pressure on the country's exchange rate to change. It follows that if exchange rates are fixed and capital is allowed to move freely between countries (ie there are not exchange controls) all countries must have consistent policies on interest rates.

Floating exchange rates

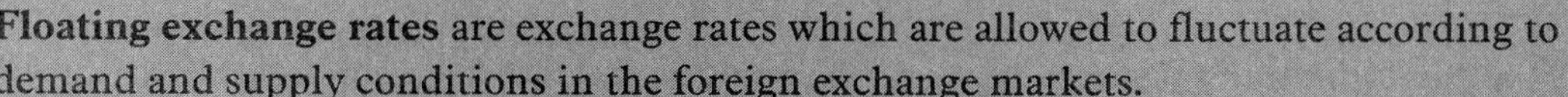

KEY TERM

Floating exchange rates are exchange rates which are allowed to fluctuate according to demand and supply conditions in the foreign exchange markets.

4.17 Floating exchange rates are at the opposite end of the spectrum to fixed rates. At this extreme, exchange rates are completely left to the free play of demand and supply market forces, and there is no official financing at all. The ruling exchange rate is, therefore, at equilibrium by definition.

4.18 In practice, many governments seek to combine the advantages of exchange rate stability with flexibility and to avoid the disadvantages of both rigidly fixed exchange rates and free floating. **Managed** (or dirty) **floating** refers to a system whereby exchange rates are allowed to float, but from time to time the authorities will intervene in the foreign exchange market:

- To use their official reserves of foreign currencies to buy their own domestic currency
- To sell their domestic currency to buy more foreign currency for the official reserves

4.19 Buying and selling in this way would be intended to influence the exchange rate of the domestic currency. Governments do not have official reserves large enough to dictate exchange rates to the market, and can only try to 'influence' market rates with intervention.

4.20 **Speculation** in the capital markets often has a much bigger impact short-term than changes in supply and demand. While exchange rates remain volatile, international trading companies can do a number of things to reduce their risk of suffering losses on foreign exchange transactions, including the following.

(a) Many companies buy currencies **'forward'** at a fixed and known price.

(b) **Dealing in a 'hard' currency** may lessen the risks attached to volatile currencies.

(c) **Operations can be managed** so that the proportion of sales in one currency are matched by an equal proportion of purchases in that currency.

(d) **Invoicing can be in the domestic currency**. This means that the customer bears all the foreign exchange risk, however, and, in industries where customers have high bargaining power, this may be an unacceptable arrangement. Furthermore there is the risk that sales will be adversely affected by high prices, reducing demand.

(e) **Outsource activities** to the local market. Many of the Japanese car firms which have invested in the UK in recent years have made efforts to obtain many of their inputs, subject to quality limits, from local suppliers. Promotional activities can also be sourced locally.

(f) Firms can aim at **segments** in the market which are not particularly price sensitive. For example, many German car marques such as Mercedes have been marketed in the US on the basis of quality and exclusivity. This is a type of strategy based on differentiation focus.

Consequences of membership of an exchange rate system

4.21 Exchange rate stability within an exchange rate regime may **help dampen inflation** by preventing a government from allowing the currency to drift downwards in value to compensate for price inflation.

4.22 At the same time, it means that **interest rate policy** must be **consistent** with keeping the currency stable.

4.23 Other possible consequences of stabilisation within an exchange rate system are that there may be effects on **people's expectations** and on the **perceived risk of exchange rate** movements between member currencies. As well as allowing firms to **plan and forecast** with **greater certainty**, exchange rate stability ought to make a currency **less risky** to hold.

European Economic and Monetary Union

4.24 There are three main aspects to the proposed European monetary union.

(a) **A common currency** (the euro).

(b) **A European central bank**. The European central bank has several roles.

- Issuing the common currency
- Conducting monetary policy on behalf of the central government authorities
- Acting as lender of last resort to all European banks
- Managing the exchange rate for the common currency

(c) A **centralised monetary policy** would apply across all the countries within the union. This would involve the surrender of control over aspects of economic policy and therefore surrender of some political sovereignty by the government of each member state to the central government body of the union.

The EMU timetable

4.25 EMU is a topical issue. Italy, France, Ireland, Germany, Belgium, Luxembourg, the Netherlands, Finland, Greece, Spain, Portugal and Austria have signed up for EMU and replaced their own currencies with the euro on 1 January 2002. The UK decided to opt out but retains the right to join at a later stage.

For and against EMU

4.26 The arguments for and against EMU can be summarised as follows, with particular reference to the UK's position.

For	**Against**
Economic policy stability	**Loss of national control over economic policy**
• EMU members will be required to keep to strict economic criteria • Politicians in member countries will be less able to pursue short-term economic policies, for example just before an election, to gain political advantage	• Under EMU, monetary policy would largely be in the hands of the new European central bank • Individual countries' fiscal policies would also need to stay in line with European policy criteria • The European economic policy framework would put great emphasis on price stability

For	Against
	• Restrictive monetary policies could result in disproportionate unemployment and output effects
Facilitation of trade	**Compensate for weaker economies**
• Will eliminate risk of currency fluctuations affecting trade and investment between EMU member countries • Will eliminate need to 'hedge' against such risks • Will be savings in foreign exchange transaction costs for companies, as well as tourists • Will enhance ease of trade with non EU countries	• For the UK, the possible benefits of being economically linked to stronger European economies are reduced and possibly even outweighed by the need to compensate for weaker economies • Stronger economies would be under pressure to 'bail out' member countries which borrow too much in order to hold the system together
Lower interest rates	**Confusion in the transition to EMU**
• Will remove risk of inflation and depreciating currencies, reducing interest rates • Will stabilise interest rates at a level closer to that of Germany, reducing interest costs for businesses and government	• Introduction of a new currency and coinage would cause confusion to businesses and consumers • Firms might use it as an opportunity to push through price rises
Preservation of the City's position	**Loss of national pride**
• If the UK opts out of EMU, the City's position as one of the major European financial capitals will be threatened • In turn, the City's role as a leading global financial market would also be jeopardised • Inward investment from the rest of the EU would also be likely to diminish	• Sterling is a symbol of national cohesion • EMU puts its members on the road to a federal Europe, it is suggested, making the UK parliament into little more than a regional town hall within Europe, with no more power than local government. Such a move might dent national pride and adversely affect economic confidence
Seigneurage	
• Seigneurage is the benefits accruing from the right to issue currency. If the euro becomes a global reserve currency, non-EU nations will buy it to hold rather than for purposes of trade. This will support the exchange rate and allow interests rate to be lower	• The proposal to have national variants of euro coins and notes is merely a cosmetic attempt to preserve national identities

4.27 The ultimate impact of the Euro cannot be assessed until all European Union members are also members of the common currency. However the single currency is already having a number of impacts upon business.

(a) UK companies that have an **overseas parent company** may be asked to issue invoices in Euros. Therefore UK companies may have to make payments in Euros to domestic suppliers and thus face **potential foreign exchange exposure.**

(b) The introduction of the Euro may **increase competition**. Prices from suppliers in all countries that use the Euro will be quoted in the same currency and hence it will be easier for customers to compare prices between different suppliers.

5 INFLATION

Why is inflation a problem?

5.1 An economic policy objective which now has a central place in the policy approaches of the governments of many developed countries is that of stable prices. Why is a high rate of price inflation harmful and undesirable?

Redistribution of income and wealth

5.2 Inflation leads to a redistribution of income and wealth in ways which may be undesirable. Redistribution of wealth might take place from creditors to debtors. This is because debts lose real value with inflation. For example, if you owed £1,000, and prices then doubled, you would still owe £1,000, but the **real value of your debt** would have been halved.

5.3 In general, in times of inflation those with **economic power** tend to gain at the expense of others, particularly those on fixed incomes.

Balance of payments effects

5.4 If a country has a higher rate of inflation than its major trading partners, its exports will become relatively expensive and imports relatively cheap. As a result, the **balance of trade** will **suffer**, affecting employment in exporting industries and in industries producing import-substitutes.

Uncertainty of the value of money and prices

5.5 If the rate of inflation is imperfectly anticipated, no one has certain knowledge of the true rate of inflation. As a result, no one has certain knowledge of the **value of money** or of the **real meaning of prices**. As prices convey less information, the process of resource allocation is less efficient and rational decision-making is almost impossible.

Resource costs of changing prices

5.6 In times of high inflation **substantial labour time** is spent on planning and implementing price changes. **Customers** may also have to **spend more** time making price comparisons if they seek to buy from the lowest cost source.

Economic growth and investment

5.7 It is sometimes claimed that inflation is harmful to a country's economic growth and level of investment. A study by *Robert Barro* (*Bank of England Quarterly Bulletin*, May 1995) examines whether the evidence available supports this view. Barro found from data covering over 100 countries from 1960 to 1990 that, on average, an increase in inflation of ten percentage points per year reduced the growth rate of real GDP per capita by 0.2 to 0.3 percentage points per year, and lowered the ratio of investment to GDP by 0.4 to 0.6 percentage points.

Measuring inflation

5.8 We have already referred to the way in which inflation erodes the real value of money. In order to measure changes in the real value of money as a single figure, we need to group all goods and services into a single price index.

Consumer price indices

5.9 A consumer price index is based on a chosen 'basket' of items which consumers purchase. A weighting is decided for each according to the average spending on the item by consumers.

5.10 The **UK Retail Prices Index** (RPI) is intended to measure the change from month to month in the cost of goods and services of the sort bought by a typical household. The relative importance attached to each of the various goods and services is revised each year using the latest available results of the Family Expenditure Survey. Unlike the general consumer price indices of many other countries, the UK RPI includes mortgage repayment costs.

The causes of inflation

5.11 The causes of inflation are complex, because there will be several factors operating simultaneously, each having some effect on price levels. The relative strength or influence of each of these factors at any given time may be difficult to assess.

Demand-pull inflation

5.12 **Demand-pull inflation** occurs when the economy is buoyant and there is a high aggregate demand which is **in excess of the economy's ability to supply.**

(a) Because aggregate demand exceeds supply, prices rise.

(b) Since supply needs to be raised to meet the higher demand, there will be an increase in demand for factors of production, and so factor rewards (wages, interest rates, and so on) will also rise.

Cost-push inflation

5.13 **Cost-push inflation** occurs where the costs of factors of production rise regardless of whether or not they are in short supply. This appears to be particularly the case with **wages**: workers anticipate inflation rates and demand wage increases to compensate. Interest rate rises can also add to the rate of inflation, because mortgage costs will rise.

5.14 **Import cost-push inflation** occurs when the cost of essential imports rise regardless of whether or not they are in short supply. This has occurred in the past with the oil price rises of the 1970s. Additionally, a fall in the value of a country's currency will have import cost-push effects since a weakening currency increases the price of imports.

Expectational inflation

5.15 A further problem is that once the rate of inflation has begun to increase, a serious danger of **expectational inflation** will occur.

(a) This means, regardless of whether the factors that have caused inflation are still persistent or not, there will arise a generally held view of what inflation is likely to be.

(b) To protect future income, **wages and prices** will be **raised** now by the **expected amount** of future inflation. This can lead to the vicious circle known as the **wage-price spiral,** in which inflation becomes a relatively permanent feature because of people's expectations that it will occur.

Question 3

(a) A government can help to counter demand-pull inflation by reducing interest rates. True or false?

(b) A government can help to counter demand-pull inflation by increasing value added tax. True or false?

(c) A government can help to counter cost-push inflation by increasing income tax rates. True or false?

(d) A government can help to counter cost-push inflation by linking wage increases to productivity improvements. True or false?

Answer

(a) *False.* On the contrary, this would increase consumer borrowing and hence stimulate demand-pull inflation.

(b) *True.* This might increase total spending on goods and services *inclusive* of the tax, but spending *net* of tax will probably fall.

(c) *False.* Increasing direct taxation will reduce consumers' disposable income, and is therefore a measure aimed at countering demand-pull inflation, not cost-push inflation.

(d) *True.* This will reduce the unit costs of production.

Control of inflation: various approaches

5.16 The best way of controlling inflation will depend on the causes of it. In practice, it may be difficult to know which cause is most significant. The table on the next page sets out various policies designed to control inflation.

ANTI-INFLATION POLICIES

Perceived cause of inflation	*Policy to control inflation*
• Demand-pull (high consumer demand)	• Take steps to reduce demand in the economy, perhaps by ° Higher taxation, to cut consumer spending ° Lower government expenditure (and lower government borrowing to finance its expenditure) ° Higher interest rates
• Cost-push factors (higher wage costs and other costs working through to higher prices)	• Take steps to reduce production costs and price rises ° De-regulate labour markets ° Encourage greater productivity in industry ° Apply controls over wage and price rises (prices and incomes policy)
• Import cost-push factors	• Take steps to reduce the quantities or the price of imports. Such a policy might involve trying to achieve either an appreciation or depreciation of the domestic currency
• Excessively fast growth in the money supply	• Take steps to try to reduce the rate of money supply growth, perhaps by ° Cutting the Public Sector Borrowing Requirement ° Funding the PSBR by borrowing from the non-bank private sector ° Trying to control or reduce bank lending ° Trying to achieve a balance of trade surplus ° Maintaining interest rates at a level that might deter money supply growth
• Expectations of inflation	• Pursue clear policies which indicate the government's determination to reduce the rate of inflation

Chapter roundup

- Macroeconomic policy involves
  - Policy **objectives** - the ultimate aims of economic policy
  - Policy **targets** - quantified levels or ranges which policy is intended to achieve
  - Policy **instruments** - the tools used to achieve objectives
- Achievement of **economic growth, low inflation, full employment** and a **trade balance** are policy objectives.
- Policy targets might be set for **money supply growth** or the **rate of inflation**, for example.
- **Fiscal policy** seeks to influence the economy by managing the amounts which the government spends and the amounts it collects through taxation. Fiscal policy can be used as an instrument of **demand management**.
- A government may use **monetary policies** to pursue its economic aims. Tools for implementing monetary policy include:
  - Influence over interest rates
  - Fiscal policy
  - Exchange rate policy
  - The regulation of banks and other financial institutions
- **Inflation** is a sustained increase in the general level of prices over time.
- Inflation is a problem for individuals and firms, for example **lenders** and those on **fixed incomes**. It could also **affect economic growth, investment, international competitiveness** and the **evaluation of companies' performance.**
- A country can **rectify** a **balance of payments deficit** in three ways.
  - Allowing its currency to depreciate or **devalue** in foreign exchange value
  - Imposing **protectionist measures** or exchange control regulations
  - **Deflationary** economic measures in the domestic economy
- Exchange rates are determined by **supply and demand**, even under fixed exchange rate systems.
- Governments can intervene to influence the exchange rate by, for example, **adjusting interest rates**. Government policies on exchange rates might be **fixed or floating exchange rates** as two extreme policies, but 'in-between' schemes have been more common.

Quick quiz

1. What is the difference between fiscal policy and monetary policy?
2. What effect does a high interest rate have on the exchange rate?
3. How do deflationary measures help to eliminate a balance of payments deficit?
4. What causes inflation?

   Match the characteristics with the types.

   (i) Demand – pull
   (ii) Cost – push
   (iii) Expectational
   (iv) Money supply growth

   A It leads to the wage-price spiral
   B The economy is buoyant and there is pressure on its ability to supply
   C Keynesians argue that this is a symptom rather than a cause
   D Factor rewards rise whether or not they are in short supply

5. *Fill in the blank.*

   .... involves the study of the economy at large, in particular the behaviour of aggregates such as national income, money supply and levels of employment.

6 Name five factors that can influence the level of exchange rates.

7 What are likely to be the main aims of a government's economy policy?

8 What is the wage-price spiral?

Answers to quick quiz

1 A government's fiscal policy is concerned with taxation, borrowing and spending and their effects upon the economy. Monetary policy is concerned with money, the money supply, interest rates, inflation and the exchange rate.

2 It attracts foreign investment, thus increasing the demand for the currency. The exchange rate rises as a result.

3 Domestic deflation cuts demand, including demand for imports. Industry is thus encouraged to switch to export markets.

4 (i) B Aggregate demand exceeds the output capacity of the economy. Keynesians saw this as the main cause of inflation and predicted it could only occur when unemployment was low.

(ii) D Particularly by rises in wages.

(iii) A The expectation of inflation will cause it to persist even when the underlying causes have been removed, since higher wages will be demanded.

(iv) C However, monetarists argue that expansion of the money supply beyond the rate of real growth will be inflationary.

5 Macroeconomics

6 (a) Comparative inflation rates

(b) Comparative interest rates

(c) Balance of payments

(d) Speculation

(e) Government policy

7 Main objectives include:

(a) Sustainable growth

(b) Control of price inflation

(c) Full employment

(d) Balance between imports and exports

8 The wage-price spiral is where businesses and employees expect prices to rise and thus seek to increase their prices and wages. The result is that expectations of price rises become self-fulfilling.

Now try the question below from the Exam Question Bank

Question to try	Level	Marks	Time
22	Introductory	n/a	35 mins

Chapter 18

GOVERNMENT INTERVENTION

	Topic list	Syllabus reference
1	Competition policy	2(f)
2	Official aid schemes	2(f)
3	Supply side policies	2(f)
4	Environmental ('green') policies	2(f)
5	Corporate governance	2(f)

Introduction

This chapter is the last in the book to deal with the broader economic environment within which organisations operate.

Study guide

Section 2 – The economic environment II

Aspects of government intervention and regulation

- Explain the requirement for and the role of competition policy
- Explain the requirement for and the role of official aid intervention
- Explain the requirement for and the role of Green policies
- Identify examples of government intervention and regulation

Exam guide

Again these topics are most likely to be tested in part of a question. If for example the company described in the question is considering taking over another company, the question may ask you to discuss when the government might intervene.

1 COMPETITION POLICY

Regulation and market failure

KEY TERM

Market failure is said to occur when the market mechanism fails to result in economic efficiency, and therefore the outcome is sub-optimal.

1.1 An important role of the government is the regulation of private markets where these fail to bring about an efficient use of resources. In response to the existence of market failure, and as an alternative to taxation and public provision of production, the state often resorts to regulating economic activity in a variety of ways. Of the various forms of market failure, the following are the cases where regulation of markets can often be the most appropriate policy response.

(a) **Imperfect competition**

Where one company's large share or complete domination of the market is leading to **inefficiency** or **excessive profits**, the state may intervene, for example through controls on prices or profits, in order to try to reduce the effects of this power.

(b) **Social costs**

A possible means of dealing with the problem of social costs or **externalities** is *via* some form of regulation. Regulations might include, for example, controls on emissions of pollutants, restrictions on car use in urban areas, the banning of smoking in public buildings, or compulsory car insurance.

(c) **Imperfect information**

Regulation is often the best form of government action whenever informational inadequacies are undermining the efficient operation of private markets. This is particularly so when consumer choice is being distorted.

(d) **Equity**

The government may also resort to regulation to **improve social justice**.

Types of regulation

1.2 **Regulation** can be defined as any form of state interference with the operation of the free market. This could involve regulating demand, supply, price, profit, quantity, quality, entry, exit, information, technology, or any other aspect of production and consumption in the market.

1.3 In many markets the participants (especially the firms) may decide to maintain a system of voluntary **self-regulation,** possibly in order to try to avert the imposition of government controls. Areas where self-regulation often exists include the professions (eg the Law Society, the British Medical Association and other professional bodies).

Competition policy in the UK

1.4 Overall responsibility for the conduct of policy lies with the Secretary of State for Trade and Industry. However, day to day supervision is carried out by the Office of Fair Trading (OFT), headed by its Director General (DG). The OFT may refer companies to the **Competition Commission** (formerly called the Monopolies and Mergers Commission) or the Restrictive Practices Court for investigation.

Monopolies and mergers

KEY TERM

In a pure **monopoly**, there is only one firm, the sole producer of a good, which has no closely competing substitutes.

1.5 In practice government policy is concerned not just with situations where one firm has a 100% market share, but other situations where an organisation has a significant market share.

1.6 The Competition Commission can also be asked to investigate what could be called **'oligopoly situations'** involving explicit or implicit collusion between firms.

1.7 The investigation is not automatic. Once the case has been referred, the Commission must decide whether or not the monopoly is acting **'against the public interest'**.

1.8 In its report, the Competition Commission will say if a monopoly situation has been found to exist and, if so, will make recommendations to deal with it. These may involve various measures.

- Price cuts
- Price and profit controls
- Removal of entry barriers
- The breaking up of the firm (rarely).

Case example

In October 2000 the Competition Commission published a report into the supply of groceries by multiple stores, considering whether these stores were making excessive profits. The report concluded that because of industry changes, in particular the entry of Wal-Mart into the industry, that there was sufficient competition, and that excessive prices were not being charged, nor excessive profits being earned.

The Commission did however identify three areas of concern.

(a) The relationship between supermarket chains and their suppliers including farmers. The Commission recommended that a compulsory Code of Practice should be introduced for the largest chains (ASDA, Safeway, Sainsbury, Somerfield and Tesco) including provisions about standard terms, prompt payment and appropriate compensation.

(b) There were some instances of persistent selling below cost, and price flexing (varying prices in different geographical areas in the light of local competition.) The Commission considered a number of remedies including a ban on below cost selling and requiring supermarkets to put their prices on the Internet. However in the end it concluded that no action should be taken because the remedies would themselves have adverse effects.

(c) The Commission expressed concern about the limited choice of supermarkets in certain areas and recommended that consumer choice be increased by new store openings wherever possible.

1.9 A prospective **merger** between two or more companies may be referred to the Competition Commission for investigation if either of the following two criteria are satisfied.

(a) The merger will create a firm with **monopoly power**, ie one that has 25% or more market share.

(b) The merger involves the **transfer** of at least **£30 million** of assets.

1.10 Again, referral to the Competition Commission is not automatic, and since the legislation was first introduced, only a small proportion of all merger proposals have been referred.

1.11 If a potential merger is investigated, the Commission has again to determine whether or not the merger would be against the public interest. As with monopolies, it will assess the relative benefits and costs in order to arrive at a decision.

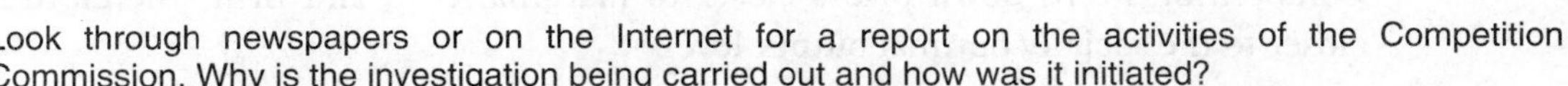

Question

Look through newspapers or on the Internet for a report on the activities of the Competition Commission. Why is the investigation being carried out and how was it initiated?

Restrictive practices

1.12 The other strand of competition policy is concerned with preventing the development of anti-competitive practices such as **price-fixing agreements** (cartels). Under the legislation, all agreements between firms must be notified to the OFT and the DG will then decide if the agreement should be examined by the Restrictive Practices Court. The presumption of the Court is that the agreement will be declared illegal, unless it can be shown to satisfy one of the 'gateways' as defined in the Restrictive Practices Act 1976.

1.13 These gateways (ie reasons for allowing the agreement) include the following.

- To protect employment in a particular area
- To protect the public against injury
- To protect exports
- To counter measures taken by other firms which restrict competition

European Union competition policy

1.14 As a member of the European Union (EU), the UK is also now subject to EU competition policy. This is enshrined in Articles 85 (dealing with restrictive practices) and 86 (concerned with monopoly) of the Treaty of Rome.

Deregulation

1.15 Deregulation or 'liberalisation' is, in general, the opposite of regulation. Deregulation can be defined as the removal or weakening of any form of statutory (or voluntary) regulation of free **market activity**. Deregulation allows **free market forces** more scope to determine the outcome.

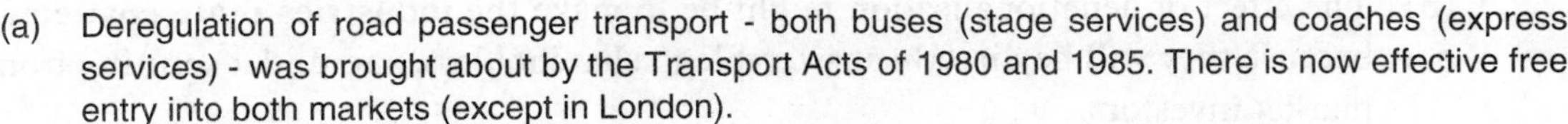

Case examples

Here are some examples of deregulation in the UK over recent years.

(a) Deregulation of road passenger transport - both buses (stage services) and coaches (express services) - was brought about by the Transport Acts of 1980 and 1985. There is now effective free entry into both markets (except in London).

(b) The monopoly position enjoyed by some professions has been removed, for example in opticians' supply of spectacles and solicitors' monopoly over house conveyancing. In addition, the controls on advertising by professionals have been loosened.

1.16 Deregulation, whose main aim is to introduce more competition into an industry by removing statutory or other entry barriers, has the following potential benefits.

(a) **Improved incentives for internal/cost efficiency**

Greater competition compels managers to try harder to keep down costs.

(b) **Improved allocative efficiency**

Competition keeps down prices closer to marginal cost, and firms therefore produce closer to the socially optimal output level.

1.17 In some industries it could have certain disadvantages, including the following.

(a) **Loss of economies of scale**

If increased competition means that each firm produces less output on a smaller scale, unit costs will be higher.

(b) **Lower quality or quantity of service**

The need to reduce costs may lead firms to reduce quality or eliminate unprofitable but socially valuable services.

(c) **Need to protect competition**

It may be necessary to implement a regulatory regime to protect competition where inherent forces have a tendency to eliminate it, for example if there is a dominant firm already in the industry, as in the case of British Telecom. In this type of situation, effective 'regulation for competition' will be required, ie regulatory measures aimed at maintaining competitive pressures, whether existing or potential.

Privatisation and denationalisation

1.18 **Privatisation** takes three broad forms.

(a) The **deregulation of industries,** to allow private firms to compete against state-owned businesses where they were not allowed to compete before (for example, deregulation of bus and coach services; deregulation of postal services)

(b) **Contracting out work** to **private firms,** where the work was previously done by government employees - for example, refuse collection or hospital laundry work

(c) **Transferring the ownership** of **assets from** the **state to private shareholders** - for example, the denationalisation of British Gas and British Telecom (now called BT)

1.19 Privatisation can improve efficiency, in one of two ways.

(a) If the effect of privatisation is to **increase competition**, the effect might be to reduce or eliminate allocative inefficiency.

(b) The effect of denationalisation might be to make the **industries more cost-conscious,** because they will be directly answerable to shareholders, and under scrutiny from stock market investors.

1.20 There are other possible advantages of privatisation.

(a) Denationalisation provides an **immediate source of money** for the government.

(b) Privatisation reduces **bureaucratic and political meddling** in the industries concerned.

(c) It encourages **wider share ownership**. Denationalisation is one method of creating wider share ownership, as the sale of BT, British Gas and some other nationalised industries have shown in the UK.

1.21 There are arguments against privatisation too.

(a) State-owned industries are more likely to respond to the **public interest**, ahead of the profit motive. For example, state-owned industries are more likely to cross-subsidise unprofitable operations from profitable ones; for example the Post Office will continue to deliver letters to the isles of Scotland even though the service might be very unprofitable.

(b) Encouraging private competition to state-run industries might be **inadvisable** where significant economies of scale can be achieved by monopoly operations.

2 OFFICIAL AID SCHEMES

2.1 The government provides finance to companies in cash grants and other forms of official direct assistance, as part of its policy of helping to develop the national economy, especially in high technology industries and in areas of high unemployment.

2.2 Government incentives might be offered on:

(a) A **regional basis**, giving help to firms that invest in an economically depressed area of the country

(b) A **selective national basis**, giving help to firms that invest in an industry that the government would like to see developing more quickly, for example robotics or fibre optics

2.3 In Europe, such assistance is increasingly limited by European Union policies designed to prevent the distortion of free market competition. The UK government's powers to grant aid for modernisation and development are now severely restricted.

The Enterprise Initiative

2.4 The Enterprise Initiative is a package of measures offered by the Department of Trade and Industry (DTI) to businesses in the UK. It includes regional selective grant assistance. A network of 'Business Links', which are local business advice centres, is also provided.

2.5 **Regional selective assistance** is available for investment projects undertaken by firms in **Assisted Areas**. The project must be commercially viable, create or safeguard employment, demonstrate a need for assistance and offer a distinct regional and national benefit. The amount of grant will be negotiated as the minimum necessary to ensure the project goes ahead.

3 SUPPLY SIDE POLICIES

3.1 Supply side economists, focus policy upon the **conditions of aggregate supply**, taking the view that the availability, quality, and cost of resources are the long-term determinants of national income and prices. They argue that by putting resources to work an economy will **automatically** generate the additional income necessary to purchase the higher outputs, ie **supply creates its own demand.**

3.2 Supply side economists advise against state involvement in the economy at both the microeconomic and macroeconomic levels.

3.3 **Microeconomic involvement** is disliked for the following reasons.

(a) Price regulation **distorts** the **signalling function** essential for markets to reach optimal equilibrium.

(b) Wage regulation **distorts** the labour market's **ability to ensure full employment**.

(c) Public ownership **blunts** the **incentive effects** of the profit motive and leads to inefficiency.

(d) Government grants and subsidies **encourage inefficient** and lame-duck **industries**.

(e) Public provision of services may not **encourage efficiency** and can **limit** the **discipline** of consumer choice.

(f) Employment legislation, such as employment protection, **limits market flexibility** by discouraging recruitment and encouraging over-manning.

3.4 **Macroeconomic intervention** by government is regarded as harmful for several reasons.

(a) **Demand management** will be **inflationary** in the long run.

(b) **High taxes** will act as a **disincentive**.

(c) The **possibility** of **politically motivated policy changes** will create damaging uncertainty in the economy. This will discourage long-term investment.

4 ENVIRONMENTAL ('GREEN') POLICIES

4.1 The environment is increasingly seen as an important issue facing managers in both the public and private sectors. The problems of pollution and the environment appear to call for international co-operation between governments. Pollutants expelled into the atmosphere in the UK are said to cause 'acid rain' to fall in Scandinavia, for example.

Pollution policy

KEY TERM

Externalities: positive or negative effects on third parties resulting from production and consumption activities

4.2 **Pollution,** for example from exhaust gas emissions or the dumping of waste, is often discussed in relation to environmental policy. If polluters take little or no account of their actions on others, this generally results in the output of polluting industries being greater than is optimal.

4.3 One solution is to levy a tax on polluters equal to the cost of removing the effect of the externality they generate: the **polluter pays principle.** This will encourage firms to cut emissions and provides an incentive for them to research ways of permanently reducing pollution.

4.4 Apart from the imposition of a tax, there are a number of other measures open to the government in attempting to reduce pollution. One of the main measures available is the application of **subsidies** which may be used either to persuade polluters to reduce output and hence pollution, or to assist with expenditure on production processes, such as new machinery and air cleaning equipment, which reduce levels of pollution.

Case example

One subsidy in the UK is that given to householders for loft insulation: this reduces energy consumption, in turn reducing emissions of pollutants.

Legislation

4.5 An alternative approach used in the UK is to impose **legislation** laying down regulations governing waste disposal and atmospheric emissions. Waste may only be disposed of with prior consent and if none is given, or it is exceeded, the polluter is fined. There may also be attempts with this type of approach to specify standards of, for example, air and water quality with appropriate penalties for not conforming to the required standards.

Exam focus point

The UK Chancellor of the Exchequer Gordon Brown has asserted that the environment would be put 'at the core of the government's objectives for the tax system'. This statement makes green taxes a topical issue, and therefore perhaps more likely to be examined.

Advantages of 'environmentally friendly policies' for a firm

4.6 There may be various reasons why a firm may gain from adopting a policy of strict compliance with environmental regulations, or of going further and taking voluntary initiatives to protect aspects of the environment.

(a) If potential customers perceive the firm to be environmentally friendly, some may be **more inclined** to **buy its products**.

(b) A corporate image which embraces environmentally friendly policies may **enhance relationships** with the **public in general** or with local communities.

(c) People may prefer to work for an **environmentally friendly firm**.

(d) **'Ethical' investment funds** may be more likely to buy the firm's shares.

5 CORPORATE GOVERNANCE

KEY TERM

Corporate governance is 'the system by which companies are directed and controlled'.

Cadbury report

5.1 The first major development during the 1990s in corporate governance was the Cadbury committee.

Corporate governance

5.2 The Cadbury committee reported in December 1992. Its report went beyond purely financial matters and made recommendations about corporate governance in general.

Code of Best Practice

5.3 This was aimed at the directors of all UK plcs, but the directors of all companies were encouraged to use the Code for guidance.

Board of directors

5.4 The report stressed the importance of the board of directors meeting on a **regular basis**, retaining **full control** over the company and monitoring executive management. Certain matters such as major acquisitions or disposals of assets, should be **referred** automatically to the **board**. There should be a **clear division of responsibilities** at the head of a company. Generally this would mean the posts of chairman and chief executive being held by different people; if they were held by the same person there should be a **strong independent element** on the board.

Accounts

5.5 The Cadbury committee stressed the importance of the board presenting a **balanced** and **understandable assessment** of the company's position. The directors should **explain** their **responsibilities** for preparing accounts. Statements should also be made about the company's ability to continue as a **going concern**, and the effectiveness of its **internal controls**.

Greenbury report

5.6 In July 1995 the Greenbury committee's report on directors' remuneration was published. The report developed a number of recommendations of the Cadbury committee. Greenbury stressed the importance of the role of the **remuneration committee**, which the report recommended should consist entirely of non-executive directors.

The remuneration committee

5.7 The most important recommendation was that the board should set up a remuneration committee of non-executive directors to **determine** the company's **general policy** on the **remuneration** of **executive directors and** specific remuneration packages for each director.

The Hampel report

5.8 The Hampel committee was set up in 1996 to **conduct a review** of the Cadbury code and its implementation to ensure that the original purpose is being achieved, proposing amendments to and deletions from the code as necessary.

5.9 The Hampel committee produced a final report in January 1998. The introduction to the report pointed out that the primary duty of directors is to shareholders, to **enhance** the **value** of **shareholders' investment** over time. Relationships with other stakeholders were important, but making the directors responsible to other stakeholders would mean there was no clear yardstick for judging directors' performance.

Directors

5.10 The committee stressed that executive and non-executive directors should continue to have the same duties under the law. The committee stated that the roles of **chairman** and **chief executive** should generally be **separate**, but whether or not the roles of chairman and chief executive are combined, a **senior non-executive director** should be **identified**. The report also stressed the importance of monitoring director performance with all directors submitting themselves for **re-election at least once every three years**, and boards assessing the performance of individual directors and collective board performance.

Directors' remuneration

5.11 In common with the Cadbury and Greenbury reports, the Hampel committee saw the remuneration committee as the key mechanism for setting the pay of executive directors. Remuneration committees should develop policy on remuneration and devise reasonable remuneration packages for individual executive directors.

Stock Exchange requirements

5.12 Hampel proposed combining the various best practices, principles and codes of Cadbury, Greenbury and Hampel into one single 'supercode'. The Stock Exchange has issued a **Combined Code** on corporate governance, which was derived from the recommendations of the Cadbury, Greenbury and Hampel reports. In June 1998 the Stock Exchange Listing Rules were amended to make compliance with the new code obligatory for listed companies for accounting periods ending after 31 December 1998.

5.13 The Combined Code requires listed companies to include in their accounts:

(a) A narrative statement of how they **applied** the **principles** set out in the Combined Code. This should provide explanations which enable their shareholders to assess how the principles have been applied.

(b) A statement as to whether or not they **complied throughout** the **accounting period** with the provisions set out in the Combined Code. Listed companies that did not comply throughout the accounting period with all the provisions must specify the provisions with which they did not comply, and give **reasons** for **non-compliance**.

Chapter roundup

- The government influences markets in various ways, one of which is through direct **regulation** (eg the **Competition Commission).**
- **Privatisation** is a policy of introducing private enterprise into industries which were previously stated-owned or state-operated.
- The freedom of European governments to offer cash **grants** and other forms of direct assistance to business is limited by European Union policies designed to prevent the distortion of free market competition.
- The **supply side economics** of the monetarists is directed at deregulation of markets and reduction in the role of government.
- There are a number of policy approaches to **pollution**, such as **polluter pays policies, subsidies** and direct **legislation**.

Quick quiz

1 Give four reasons for government intervention in markets.

2 *Fill in the blanks.*

Privatisation has three forms

..Deregulation.......... of industries

Contracting.......................... to private firms

Transferring .... from .... to ....

3 According to the theories of supply-side economists, what will happen if the market is freed from government intervention?

4 What is the situation called when there is only one firm, the sole producer of a good, which has no closely competing substitutes?

A Duopoly

B Oligopoly

C Monopoly

D Totopoly

5 *Fill in the blank.*

.... are positive or negative effects on third parties resulting from production and consumption activities.

6 What is corporate governance?

7 What according to supply side economists determine national income and prices?

8 Which of the following measures can be used to deal with monopolies?

A Price controls ✓

B Profit controls ✓

C Removal of entry barriers ✓

D Breaking the firm up ✓

Answers to quick quiz

1 (a) Imperfect competition
(b) Social costs/externalities
(c) Imperfect information
(d) Equity

2 Deregulation of industries

Contracting out to private firms

Transferring ownership of assets from the state to private shareholders

3 The free market will automatically generate the highest level of national income and employment available to the economy.

4 C Monopoly

5 Externalities

6 The system by which companies are directed and controlled

7 The availability, quality and cost of resources

8 All of them

Now try the question below from the Exam Question Bank

Question to try	Level	Marks	Time
23	Exam	25	45 mins

Part F
Working capital management

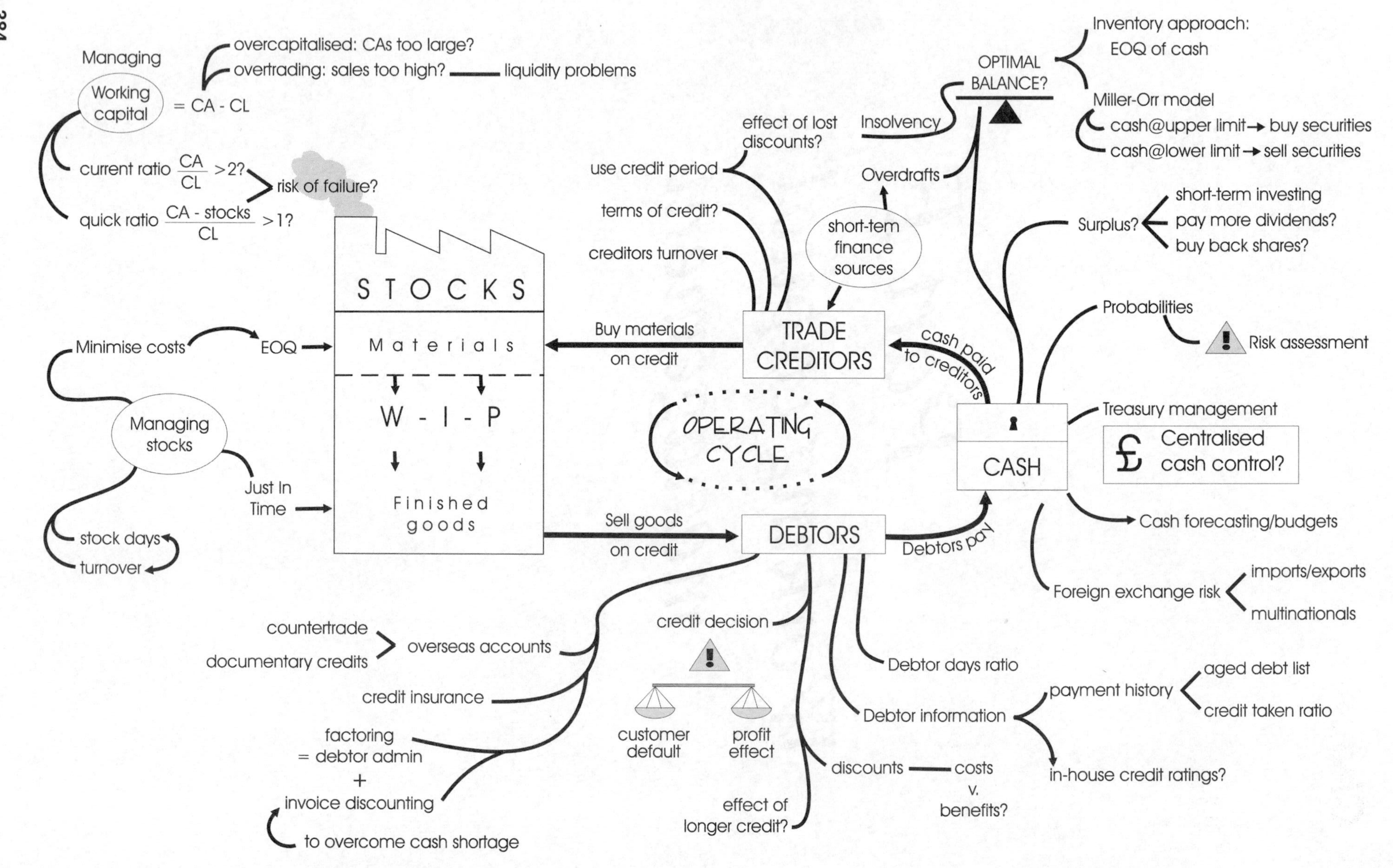

Managing
Working capital
= CA - CL
overcapitalised: CAs too large?
overtrading: sales too high? — liquidity problems
current ratio CA/CL >2?
quick ratio (CA - stocks)/CL >1?
risk of failure?
STOCKS
Materials
W - I - P
Finished goods
Minimise costs
EOQ
Managing stocks
Just In Time
stock days
turnover
Buy materials on credit
TRADE CREDITORS
use credit period
effect of lost discounts?
terms of credit?
creditors turnover
short-tem finance sources
Overdrafts
Insolvency
OPTIMAL BALANCE?
Inventory approach:
EOQ of cash
Miller-Orr model
cash@upper limit → buy securities
cash@lower limit → sell securities
Surplus?
short-term investing
pay more dividends?
buy back shares?
Probabilities
Risk assessment
cash paid to creditors
OPERATING CYCLE
CASH
Treasury management
Centralised cash control?
Cash forecasting/budgets
Foreign exchange risk
imports/exports
multinationals
Sell goods on credit
DEBTORS
Debtors pay
countertrade
documentary credits
overseas accounts
credit insurance
factoring
= debtor admin
+
invoice discounting
to overcome cash shortage
credit decision
customer default
profit effect
effect of longer credit?
discounts — costs v. benefits?
Debtor days ratio
Debtor information
payment history
aged debt list
credit taken ratio
in-house credit ratings?

Chapter 19

MANAGEMENT OF WORKING CAPITAL

Topic list		Syllabus reference
1	Working capital and its management	3
2	Working capital and cash flow	3

Introduction

The framework of **financial management** was described in Chapter 15. In Chapters 16 to 18, we have studied the **macroeconomic environment** within which all organisations and their financial managers must work. In this chapter, we return to consider functions of the financial manager relating to the **management of working capital** in general terms.

In Chapter 20 to 21, we shall be looking at specific aspects of the management of **cash**, **stocks** (inventories), **debtors** and **creditors**.

Study guide

Section 5 – Management of working capital I

General issues

- Explain the nature and scope of working capital management
- Distinguish between cash flow and profits
- Explain the requirement for effective working capital management
- Explain the relationship between working capital management and business solvency
- Distinguish the working capital needs of different types of business

Exam guide

Working capital is a key topic in this paper so the next four chapters are very important. You need to be able to discuss the elements of working capital, assess the significance of different levels of working capital and explain how poor working capital management can lead to over-capitalisation, or overtrading (and possibly insolvency). The Oxford Brookes degree Research and Analysis Project Topic 15 requires you to analyse the role of working capital on the profitability and/or efficiency of an organisation of your choice.

1 WORKING CAPITAL AND ITS MANAGEMENT

Importance of working capital management

KEY TERM

Net working capital of a business is its current assets less its current liabilities.

KEY CURRENT ASSETS AND LIABILITIES	
Current assets	**Current liabilities**
Cash	Trade creditors
Stock of raw materials	Taxation payable
Work in progress	Dividend payments due
Finished goods	Short-term loans
Amounts receivable from debtors	Long-term loans maturing within one year
Marketable securities	

1.1 Every business needs adequate **liquid resources** to maintain day-to-day cash flow. It needs enough to pay wages and salaries as they fall due and enough to pay creditors if it is to keep its workforce and ensure its supplies.

1.2 Maintaining adequate working capital is **not just important** in the **short term**. Sufficient liquidity must be maintained in order to ensure the survival of the business in the long term as well. Even a profitable company may fail if it does not have adequate cash flow to meet its liabilities as they fall due.

1.3 On the other hand, an excessively conservative approach to working capital management resulting in high levels of cash holdings will harm profits because the opportunity to make a return on the assets tied up as cash will have been missed.

Exam focus point

Some aspect of working capital management is likely to be included in each paper.

KEY TERM

Working capital cycle is the period of time which elapses between the point at which cash begins to be expended on the production of a product and the collection of cash from a purchaser.

1.4 The connection between investment in working capital and cash flow may be illustrated by means of the **working capital cycle** (also called the **cash cycle, operating cycle** or **trading cycle**).

1.5 The working capital cycle in a manufacturing business equals:

The average time that raw materials remain in stock
Less the period of credit taken from suppliers
Plus the time taken to produce the goods
Plus the time taken by customers to pay for the goods

1.6 If the turnover periods for stocks and debtors lengthen, or the payment period to creditors shortens, then the operating cycle will lengthen and the investment in working capital will increase.

Working capital (liquidity) ratios

The current ratio and the quick ratio

1.7 The **current ratio** is the standard test of liquidity.

KEY TERM

Current ratio $= \dfrac{\text{Current assets}}{\text{Current liabilities}}$

1.8 A company should have enough current assets that give a promise of 'cash to come' to meet its commitments to pay its current liabilities. Obviously, a ratio in **excess of 1** should be expected. In practice, a ratio comfortably in excess of 1 should be expected, but what is 'comfortable' varies between different types of businesses.

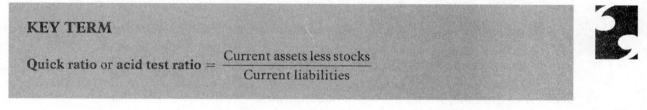

The quick ratio

KEY TERM

Quick ratio or **acid test ratio** $= \dfrac{\text{Current assets less stocks}}{\text{Current liabilities}}$

1.9 Companies are not able to convert all their current assets into cash very quickly. In some businesses, where stock turnover is slow, most stocks are not very liquid assets, because the cash cycle is so long. For these reasons, we calculate an additional liquidity ratio, known as the quick ratio or acid test ratio.

1.10 This ratio should ideally be at least 1 for companies with a slow stock turnover. For companies with a fast stock turnover, a quick ratio can be less than 1 without suggesting that the company is in cash flow difficulties.

The debtors' payment period

KEY TERM

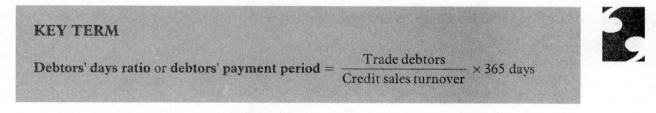

Debtors' days ratio or **debtors' payment period** $= \dfrac{\text{Trade debtors}}{\text{Credit sales turnover}} \times 365 \text{ days}$

1.11 This is a rough measure of the average length of time it takes for a company's debtors to pay what they owe.

1.12 The trade debtors are not the *total* figure for debtors in the balance sheet, which includes prepayments and non-trade debtors. The trade debtors figure will be itemised in an analysis of the total debtors, in a note to the accounts.

1.13 The estimate of debtor days is only approximate.

(a) The **balance sheet value** of debtors might be **abnormally high** or low compared with the 'normal' level the company usually has. This may apply especially to smaller companies, where the size of year-end debtors may largely depend on whether a few or even a single large debtor pay just before or just after the year-end.

(b) Turnover in the profit and loss account excludes value added tax (VAT), but the debtors' figure in the balance sheet includes VAT. We are not strictly comparing like with like.

The stock turnover period

KEY TERMS

$$\textbf{Stock days} = \frac{\text{Average stock}}{\text{Cost of sales}} \times 365 \text{ days}$$

$$\textbf{Stock turnover} = \frac{\text{Cost of sales}}{\text{Average stock}}$$

1.14 This is another estimated figure, which indicates the average number of days that items of stock are held for. As with the average debt collection period, it is only an approximate figure, but one which should be reliable enough for finding changes over time.

1.15 A lengthening stock turnover period indicates:

(a) A **slowdown** in **trading**, or

(b) A **build-up** in **stock levels**, perhaps suggesting that the investment in stocks is becoming excessive

1.16 If we add together the stock days and the debtor days, this should give us an indication of how soon stock is convertible into cash, thereby giving a further indication of the **company's liquidity**.

The creditors' turnover period

KEY TERM

$$\textbf{Creditors' payment period} = \frac{\text{Average trade creditors}}{\text{Purchases or Cost of sales}} \times 365 \text{ days}$$

1.17 The creditors' turnover ratio often helps to assess a company's liquidity; an increase in creditor days is often a sign of lack of long-term finance or poor management of current assets, resulting in the use of extended credit from suppliers, increased bank overdraft and so on.

The need for funds for investment in current assets

1.18 These liquidity ratios are a guide to the risk of cash flow problems and insolvency. If a company suddenly finds that it is **unable to renew** its **short-term liabilities** (for example, if the bank suspends its overdraft facilities, there will be a **danger of insolvency** unless the company is able to turn enough of its current assets into cash quickly.

1.19 Current liabilities are often a cheap method of finance (trade creditors do not usually carry an interest cost). Companies may therefore consider that, in the interest of higher profits, it is worth accepting some risk of insolvency by increasing current liabilities, taking the maximum credit possible from suppliers.

Working capital needs of different types of business

1.20 Different industries have different optimum working capital profiles, reflecting their methods of doing business and what they are selling.

(a) Businesses with a lot of **cash sales** and few credit sales should have **minimal debtors**.

(b) Businesses that exist solely to trade will only have **finished goods in stock**, whereas **manufacturers** will have **raw materials** and **work in progress** as well. Also some finished goods, notably foodstuffs, have to be sold within a few days because of their perishable nature.

(c) **Large companies** may be able to use their strength as customers to obtain **extended credit periods** from their suppliers. By contrast small companies, particularly those that have recently commenced trading, may be required to pay their suppliers immediately.

(d) Some businesses will be receiving **most of their monies** at **certain times** of the year, whilst incurring expenses throughout the year. Examples include travel agents who will have peaks reflecting demand for holidays during the summer and at Christmas.

Over-capitalisation and working capital

1.21 If there are excessive stocks, debtors and cash, and very few creditors, there will be an over-investment by the company in current assets. Working capital will be excessive and the company will be in this respect over-capitalised.

Indicators of over-capitalisation	
Sales/working capital	Compare with previous years or, similar companies
Liquidity ratios	Current ratio > 2:1 Quick ratio > 1:1 indicate over-investment
Turnover periods	Long turnover periods for stock and debtors or short credit period from suppliers may be unnecessary

1.22 EXAMPLE: WORKING CAPITAL RATIOS

Calculate liquidity and working capital ratios from the following accounts of a manufacturer of products for the construction industry, and comment on the ratios.

	20X8	*20X7*
	£m	£m
Turnover	2,065.0	1,788.7
Cost of sales	1,478.6	1,304.0
Gross profit	586.4	484.7
Current assets		
Stocks	119.0	109.0
Debtors (note 1)	400.9	347.4
Short-term investments	4.2	18.8
Cash at bank and in hand	48.2	48.0
	572.3	523.2

	20X8 £m	20X7 £m
Creditors: amounts falling due within one year		
Loans and overdrafts	49.1	35.3
Corporation taxes	62.0	46.7
Dividend	19.2	14.3
Creditors (note 2)	370.7	324.0
	501.0	420.3
Net current assets	71.3	102.9

Notes

		20X8 £m	20X7 £m
1	Trade debtors	329.8	285.4
2	Trade creditors	236.2	210.8

1.23 SOLUTION

	20X8		20X7	
Current ratio	$\frac{572.3}{501.0}$	= 1.14	$\frac{523.2}{420.3}$	= 1.24
Quick ratio	$\frac{453.3}{501.0}$	= 0.90	$\frac{414.2}{420.3}$	= 0.99
Debtors' payment period	$\frac{329.8}{2,065.0}$	× 365 = 58 days	$\frac{285.4}{1,788.7}$	× 365 = 58 days
Stock turnover period	$\frac{119.0}{1,478.6}$	× 365 = 29 days	$\frac{109.0}{1,304.0}$	× 365 = 31 days
Creditors' turnover period	$\frac{236.2}{1,478.6}$	× 365 = 58 days	$\frac{210.8}{1,304.0}$	× 365 = 59 days

(a) The company is a manufacturing group serving the construction industry, and so would be expected to have a comparatively lengthy debtors' turnover period, because of the relatively poor cash flow in the construction industry.

(b) The company compensates for this by ensuring that they do not pay for raw materials and other costs before they have sold their stocks of finished goods (hence the similarity of debtors' and creditors' turnover periods).

(c) The company's current ratio is a little lower than average but its quick ratio is better than average and very little less than the current ratio. This suggests that stock levels are strictly controlled, which is reinforced by the low stock turnover period.

It would seem that working capital is tightly managed, to avoid the poor liquidity which could be caused by a high debtors' turnover period and comparatively high creditors.

Overtrading

1.24 In contrast with over-capitalisation, overtrading happens when a business tries to **do too much too quickly** with **too little long-term capital,** so that it is trying to support too large a volume of trade with the capital resources at its disposal.

1.25 Even if an overtrading business operates at a profit, it could easily run into serious trouble because it is **short of money**. Such liquidity troubles stem from the fact that it does not have enough capital to provide the cash to pay its debts as they fall due.

1.26 Symptoms of overtrading are as follows.

(a) There is a **rapid increase** in **turnover**.

(b) There is a **rapid increase** in the **volume of current assets** and possibly also fixed assets. Stock turnover and debtors turnover might slow down, in which case the rate of increase in stocks and debtors would be even greater than the rate of increase in sales.

(c) There is only a **small increase** in **proprietors' capital** (perhaps through retained profits). Most of the increase in assets is financed by credit, especially:

   (i) **Trade creditors** - the payment period to creditors is likely to lengthen

   (ii) A **bank overdraft**, which often reaches or even exceeds the limit of the facilities agreed by the bank

(d) Some **debt ratios** and **liquidity ratios** alter dramatically.

   (i) The **proportion** of **total assets** financed by proprietors' capital falls, and the proportion financed by credit rises.

   (ii) The **current ratio** and the **quick ratio** fall.

   (iii) The business might have a **liquid deficit**, that is, an excess of current liabilities over current assets.

Exam focus point

This list of signs is important; you must be aware of why businesses run into financial difficulties. In the exam you might be expected to diagnose overtrading from information given about a company.

1.27 EXAMPLE: OVERTRADING

Great Ambition Ltd appoints a new managing director who has great plans to expand the company. He wants to increase turnover by 100% within two years, and to do this he employs extra sales staff. He recognises that customers do not want to have to wait for deliveries, and so he decides that the company must build up its stock levels. There is a substantial increase in the company's stocks. These are held in additional warehouse space which is now rented. The company also buys new cars for its extra sales representatives.

The managing director's policies are immediately successful in boosting sales, which double in just over one year. Stock levels are now much higher, but the company takes longer credit from its suppliers, even though some suppliers have expressed their annoyance at the length of time they must wait for payment. Credit terms for debtors are unchanged, and so the volume of debtors, like the volume of sales, rises by 100%.

In spite of taking longer credit, the company still needs to increase its overdraft facilities with the bank, which are raised from a limit of £40,000 to one of £80,000. The company is profitable, and retains some profits in the business, but profit margins have fallen. **Gross profit margins** are lower because some prices have been reduced to obtain extra sales. **Net profit margins** are lower because overhead costs are higher. These include sales representatives' wages, car expenses and depreciation on cars, warehouse rent and additional losses from having to write off out-of-date and slow-moving stock items.

1.28 The balance sheet of the company might change over time from (A) to (B).

	Balance sheet (A)			Balance sheet (B)		
	£	£	£	£	£	£
Fixed assets			160,000			210,000
Current assets						
Stock		60,000			150,000	
Debtors		64,000			135,000	
Cash		1,000			-	
		125,000			285,000	
Current liabilities						
Bank	25,000			80,000		
Creditors	50,000			200,000		
		75,000			280,000	
			50,000			5,000
			210,000			215,000
Share capital			10,000			10,000
Profit and loss account			200,000			205,000
			210,000			215,000
Sales			£1,000,000			£2,000,000
Gross profit			£200,000			£300,000
Net profit			£50,000			£20,000

1.29 In situation (B), the company has **reached** its **overdraft** limit and has **four times** as many **creditors** as in situation (A) but with only **twice the sales turnover. Stock levels** are much **higher**, and **stock turnover** is **lower.**

1.30 The company is overtrading. If it had to pay its next trade creditor, or salaries and wages, before it received any income, it could not do so without the bank allowing it to exceed its overdraft limit. The company is profitable, although profit margins have fallen, and it ought to expect a prosperous future. But if it does not sort out its cash flow and liquidity, it will not survive to enjoy future profits.

1.31 Suitable solutions to the problem would be measures to reduce the degree of overtrading.

(a) **New capital** from the shareholders could be injected.

(b) **Better control** could be applied to stocks and debtors. The company could **abandon ambitious plans** for increased sales and more fixed asset purchases until the business has had time to consolidate its position, and build up its capital base with retained profits.

1.32 A business seeking to increase its turnover too rapidly without an adequate capital base is not the only **cause of overtrading. Other causes** are as follows.

(a) When a business repays a loan, it often replaces the old loan with a new one. However a business might **repay a loan without replacing it,** with the consequence that it has **less long-term capital** to finance its current level of operations.

(b) A business might be profitable, but in a period of **inflation,** its **retained profits** might be **insufficient** to pay for **replacement** fixed assets and stocks, which now cost more because of inflation.

The working capital requirement

1.33 **Computing the working capital requirement** is a matter of calculating the value of current assets less current liabilities, perhaps by taking averages over a one year period.

1.34 EXAMPLE: WORKING CAPITAL REQUIREMENTS

The following data relate to Corn Ltd, a manufacturing company.

Turnover for the year	£1,500,000
Costs as percentages of sales	%
Direct materials	30
Direct labour	25
Variable overheads	10
Fixed overheads	15
Selling and distribution	5

On average:

(a) Debtors take 2.5 months before payment
(b) Raw materials are in stock for three months
(c) Work-in-progress represents two months worth of half produced goods
(d) Finished goods represents one month's production
(e) Credit is taken as follows:

(i)	Direct materials	2 months
(ii)	Direct labour	1 week
(iii)	Variable overheads	1 month
(iv)	Fixed overheads	1 month
(v)	Selling and distribution	0.5 months

Work-in-progress and finished goods are valued at material, labour and variable expense cost.

Compute the working capital requirement of Corn Ltd assuming the labour force is paid for 50 working weeks a year.

1.35 SOLUTION

(a) The annual costs incurred will be as follows.

		£
Direct materials	30% of £1,500,000	450,000
Direct labour	25% of £1,500,000	375,000
Variable overheads	10% of £1,500,000	150,000
Fixed overheads	15% of £1,500,000	225,000
Selling and distribution	5% of £1,500,000	75,000

(b) The average value of current assets will be as follows.

		£	£
Raw materials	3/12 × £450,000		112,500
Work-in-progress			
Materials (50% complete)	1/12 × £450,000	37,500	
Labour (50% complete)	1/12 × £375,000	31,250	
Variable overheads (50% complete)	1/12 × £150,000	12,500	
			81,250
Finished goods			
Materials	1/12 × £450,000	37,500	
Labour	1/12 × £375,000	31,250	
Variable overheads	1/12 × £150,000	12,500	
			81,250
Debtors	2.5/12 × £1,500,000		312,500
			587,500

(c) Average value of current liabilities will be as follows.

Materials	2/12 × £450,000	75,000
Labour	1/50 × £375,000	7,500
Variable overheads	1/12 × £150,000	12,500
Fixed overheads	1/12 × £225,000	18,750
Selling and distribution	0.5/12 × £75,000	3,125
		116,875

(d) Working capital required is (£(587,500 – 116,875)) = 470,625

It has been assumed that all the direct materials are allocated to work-in-progress when production starts.

Exam focus point

In the exam you may be asked to calculate the working capital requirement in £ using the method described above. Alternatively (as was the case in the December 2001 exam) you may be asked to calculate the requirement in terms of time, in which case the answer would be the length of the **working capital cycle** (see earlier in this chapter).

Predicting business failure

1.36 Investors will wish to know whether additional funds could be lent to the company with reasonable safety, and whether the company would fail without additional funds.

1.37 One method of predicting business failure is the use of **liquidity ratios** (the current ratio and the quick ratio). A company with a current ratio well below 2:1 or a quick ratio well below 1:1 might be considered illiquid and in danger of failure.

Z scores

1.38 E I Altman researched into the simultaneous analysis of several financial ratios as a combined predictor of business failure. Altman analysed 22 accounting and non-accounting variables for a selection of failed and non-failed firms in the USA and from these, five key indicators emerged. These five indicators were then used to derive a **Z score**. Firms with a Z score above a certain level would be predicted to be financially sound, and firms with a Z score below a certain level would be categorised as probable failures.

1.39 Altman's Z score model (derived in 1968) emerged as:

$$Z = 1.2X_1 + 1.4X_2 + 3.3X_3 + 0.6X_4 + 1.0X_5$$

where

X_1 = working capital/total assets
X_2 = retained earnings/total assets
X_3 = earnings before interest and tax/total assets
X_4 = market value of equity/book value of total debt (a form of gearing ratio)
X_5 = sales/total assets

2 WORKING CAPITAL AND CASH FLOW

Cash flow planning

2.1 Since a company must have adequate cash inflows to survive, management should plan and control cash flows as well as profitability. **Cash budgeting** is an important element in short-term cash flow planning. If a budget reveals that a short-term cash shortage can be expected,

steps will be taken to meet the problem (perhaps by arranging a bigger bank overdraft facility).

2.2 Cash budgets and cash flow forecasts on their own do not give full protection against a cash shortage and enforced liquidation of the business by creditors. There may be **unexpected changes** in cash flow patterns.

Question

Give examples of unforeseen changes which may affect cash flow patterns.

Answer

Your list probably included some of the following.

(a) A change in the general economic environment. An economic recession will cause a slump in trade.

(b) A new product, launched by a competitor, which takes business away from a company's traditional and established product lines.

(c) New cost-saving product technology, which forces the company to invest in the new technology to remain competitive.

(d) Moves by competitors which have to be countered (for example a price reduction or a sales promotion).

(e) Changes in consumer preferences, resulting in a fall in demand.

(f) Government action against certain trade practices or against trade with a country that a company has dealings with.

(g) Strikes or other industrial action.

(h) Natural disasters, such as floods or fire damage, which curtail an organisation's activities.

Strategic fund management

2.3 **Strategic fund management** is an extension of cash flow planning, which takes into consideration the ability of a business to overcome unforeseen problems with cash flows. It recognises that the assets of a business can be divided into three categories.

(a) Assets which are needed to carry out the 'core' activities of the business.

(b) **Assets** which are **not essential** for carrying out the main activities of the business, and which could be **sold off** at **fairly short notice**. These assets will consist mainly of short-term marketable investments.

(c) **Assets** which are **not essential** for carrying out the main activities of the business, and which could be sold off to raise cash, although it would probably take **time to arrange** the sale, and the amount of **cash obtainable** from the sale might be **uncertain**. These assets would include:

(i) Long-term investments (for example, substantial shareholdings in other companies)

(ii) Subsidiary companies engaged in 'peripheral' activities, which might be sold off to another company or in a management buyout

(iii) Land and buildings

2.4 If an unexpected event takes place which threatens a company's cash position, the company could meet the threat by:

(a) **Working capital management** to improve cash flows by reducing stocks and debtors, taking more credit, or negotiating a higher bank overdraft facility

(b) **Changes to dividend policy**

(c) Arranging to **sell off non-essential assets**

Chapter roundup

- The amount tied up in **working capital** is equal to the value of raw materials, work-in-progress, finished stocks and debtors less creditors. The size of this net figure has a direct effect on the **liquidity** of an organisation.
- **Liquidity ratios** may help to indicate whether a company is **over-capitalised**, with excessive working capital, or if a business is likely to fail. A business which is trying to do too much too quickly with too little long-term capital is **overtrading**.

Quick quiz

1 Which of the following is the most likely to be a symptom of overtrading?

A Static levels of stock turnover

B Rapid increase in profits

C Increase in the level of the current ratio

D Rapid increase in sales

2 The operating cycle is:

	A The time	
Less	B The time	
Plus	C The time	
Plus	D The time	

Fill in the blanks.

3 Fill in the blanks with the following:

Current liabilities; current assets; stocks; 2; 1.

Quick ratio = $\dfrac{\text{............ less ....}}{\text{..................................}}$ (This should be at least ....)

4 Which of the following describes *overcapitalisation* and which describes *overtrading*?

A A company with excessive investment in working capital
B A company trying to support too large a volume of trade with the capital resources at its disposal

5 Which of the following statements best defines the current ratio?

A The ratio of current assets to current liabilities.
For the majority of businesses it should be at least 2.

B The ratio of current assets to current liabilities.
For the majority of businesses it should be at least 1.

C The ratio of current assets excluding stock to current liabilities.
For the majority of businesses it should be at least 1.

D The ratio of current assets excluding stock to current liabilities.
For the majority of businesses it should be at least 2.

6 The debtors' payment period is a calculation of the time taken to pay by all debtors.

☐ True

☐ False

7 What are the two most likely reasons for a lengthening stock turnover period?

8 What is the working capital requirement of a company with the following average figures over a year?

	£
Stock	3,750
Trade debtors	1,500
Cash and bank balances	500
Trade creditors	1,800

Answers to quick quiz

1 D Rapid increase in sales

2 A The time raw materials remain in stock
B The time period of credit taken from suppliers
C The time taken to produce goods
D The time taken by customers to pay for goods

3 Quick ratio = $\frac{\text{Current assets less stocks}}{\text{Current liabilities}}$ (This should be at least 1)

4 A Overcapitalisation
B Overtrading

5 A Current assets to current liabilities: 2

6 False; the calculation normally only includes trade debtors.

7 (a) A slowdown in trading
(b) A build-up of stock levels

8 Working capital requirement = current assets less current liabilities
= 3,750 + 1,500 + 500 – 1,800
= £3,950

Now try the question below from the Exam Question Bank

Question to try	Level	Marks	Time
24	Exam	25	45 mins

Chapter 20

THE MANAGEMENT OF DEBTORS AND CREDITORS

Topic list		Syllabus reference
1	**Total credit**	3
2	**The management of debtors**	3
3	**Using debtor information**	3
4	**Foreign trade and debt management**	3
5	**The management of creditors and short-term finance**	3

Introduction

This chapter deals with specific techniques in the management of debtors, creditors and short-term finance.

Study guide

Section 6 – Management of working capital II

Management of debtors

- Explain the role of debtors in the working capital cycle
- Explain how the credit-worthiness of customers may be assessed
- Evaluate the balance of risks and costs of customer default against the profitability of marginal business
- Explain the role of factoring and invoice discounting
- Explain the role of settlement discounts
- Discuss the particular problems of managing overseas accounts receivable
- Calculate and interpret debtor ratios
- Apply the tools and techniques of debtor management
- Analyse and evaluate the results of debtor management techniques

Management of creditors

- Explain the role of creditors in the working capital cycle
- Explain the availability of credit and the role of the guarantee
- Identify the risks of taking increased credit and buying under extended credit terms
- Explain how methods of paying suppliers may influence cash flows of both parties
- Discuss the particular problems of managing overseas accounts payable
- Calculate and interpret creditor ratios
- Apply the tools and techniques of creditor management
- Analyse and evaluate the results of creditor management technique

Exam guide

Debtor management is a key aspect of working capital management. Expect to be asked to calculate the financial effects of different policies. You may also be asked to discuss the benefits and drawbacks of trade credit as a source of finance.

1 TOTAL CREDIT

1.1 Finding a **total level of credit** which can be offered is a matter of finding the least costly balance between enticing customers, whose use of credit entails considerable costs, and refusing opportunities for profitable sales. Firstly it helps to see what debtors, which often account for 30% of the total assets of a business, actually represent.

Measuring total debtors

1.2 There are three methods of assessing how many days sales are represented by debtors.

(a) The days sales in debtors ratio, sometimes called **debtors turnover** as evidenced in analysis of financial statements. This can be calculated as an annual figure. It represents the length of the credit period taken by customers.

$$\frac{\text{Total debtors} \times 365}{\text{Sales in 365 days}} = \text{Days sales}$$

For example, in 20X4 X plc made sales of £700,000 and at 31 December 20X4, debtors stood at £90,000. The comparable figures for 20X3 were £600,000 (annual sales) and £70,000 (debtors at 31.12.X3).

	20X4		*20X3*	
Debtors represent	$\frac{£90,000 \times 365}{£700,000}$	= 47 days	$\frac{£70,000 \times 365}{£600,000}$	= 43 days

In 20X4, the company is taking longer to collect its debts.

(b) **Count-back method**. Rather than annualising, this simply assumes that the majority of debtors are most current.

Let us take an example. Assume that at the end of March total debtors stood at £1m. Sales in March were £500,000; in February, £450,000 and in January £500,000.

	£
Total debtors at the end of March	1,000,000
Less March sales	500,000
	500,000
Less February sales	450,000
	50,000
Less January sales, unpaid portion	50,000
	-

We can calculate the days outstanding as follows.

	Days
March: entire turnover	31
February: entire turnover	28
January: $\frac{50,000}{500,000} \times 31$ days	3
	62 days

(c) The **partial month method** analyses each month's sales and the unpaid portion. These are then aggregated together. Assume that at the end of June, total debtors are £1.5m. Data related to the previous months are as follows.

	Sales (a)	Unpaid (b)	Days (c)	$\frac{b}{a} \times c$
	£	£		Days
June	500,000	500,000	30	30.00
May	450,000	400,000	31	27.50
April	500,000	300,000	30	18.00
March	600,000	150,000	31	7.75
February	400,000	50,000	28	3.50
January	500,000	100,000	31	6.20
Before January	None	None	N/A	N/A
Total	2,950,000	1,500,000	N/A	92.95
		(ie Debtors)		

1.3 The **partial month method** not only provides an overall debtors ageing figure but, as importantly, it also enables an analysis broken down by month. However the **days sales outstanding** (DSO) ratio is calculated, we can examine the effect of this on profitability and cash flow.

Effect on profit of extending credit

1.4 The main cost of offering credit is the interest expense. How can we assess the effect on profit?

1.5 Let us assume that the Zygo Company sells widgets for £1,000, which enables it to earn a profit, after all other expenses except interest, of £100 (ie a 10% margin).

(a) Aibee buys a widget for £1,000 on 1 January 20X1, but does not pay until 31 December 20X1. Zygo relies on overdraft finance, which costs it 10% pa. The effect is:

	£
Net profit on sale of widget	100
Overdraft cost £1,000 × 10% pa	(100)
Actual profit after 12 months credit	Nil

In other words, the entire profit margin has been wiped out in 12 months.

(b) If Aibee had paid after six months, the effect would be:

	£
Net profit	100
Overdraft cost £1,000 × 10% pa × $^6/_{12}$ months	(50)
	50

Half the profit has been wiped out. (*Tutorial note.* The interest cost might be worked out in a more complex way to give a more accurate figure.)

(c) If the cost of borrowing had been 18%, then the profit would have been absorbed before seven months had elapsed. If the net profit were 5% and borrowing costs were 15%, the interest expense would exceed the net profit after four months.

1.6 A second general point is the relation of **total credit to bad debts**. Burt Edwards argues that there is a law of 10-to-1: 'Experience in different industries shows that the annual interest expense of borrowings to support overdue debts, ie those in excess of agreed payment terms, is at least ten times the total lost in bad debts'. This is not a 'law', but has been observed to be the case over a variety of UK businesses.

Question 1

Winterson Tools Ltd has an average level of debtors of £2m at any time representing 60 days outstanding. (Their terms are thirty days.) The firm borrows money at 10% a year. The managing director is proud of the credit control: 'I only had to write off £10,000 in bad debts last year,' she says proudly. Is she right to be proud?

Answer

At the moment, Winterson Tools Ltd is paying 10% × £1m (ie $^{30}/_{60}$ days × £2m) = £100,000 in interest caused by customers taking the extra month to pay.

1.7 The level of total credit can then have a significant effect on **profitability**. That said, if credit considerations are included in pricing calculations, extending credit can, in fact, increase profitability. If offering credit generates extra sales, then those extra sales will have additional repercussions on:

(a) The amount of stock maintained in the warehouse, to ensure that the extra demand must be satisfied

(b) The amount of money the company owes to its creditors (as it will be increasing its supply of raw materials)

2 THE MANAGEMENT OF DEBTORS

2.1 Several factors should be considered by management when a policy for **credit control** is formulated. These include:

(a) The administrative costs of **debt collection**

(b) The procedures for **controlling credit** to individual customers and for debt collection

(c) The amount of **extra capital required** to finance an extension of total credit - there might be an increase in debtors, stocks and creditors, and the net increase in working capital must be financed

(d) The cost of the **additional finance** required for any increase in the volume of debtors (or the savings from a reduction in debtors) - this cost might be bank overdraft interest, or the cost of long-term funds (such as loan stock or equity)

(e) Any **savings or additional expenses** in operating the credit policy (for example the extra work involved in pursuing slow payers)

(f) The **ways** in which the credit policy could be **implemented** - for example:

(i) Credit could be eased by giving debtors a longer period in which to settle their accounts - the cost would be the resulting increase in debtors

(ii) A discount could be offered for early payment - the cost would be the amount of the discounts taken

(g) The **effects of easing credit,** which might be to encourage a higher proportion of bad debts, and an increase in sales volume. Provided that the extra gross contribution from the increase in sales exceeds the increase in fixed cost expenses, bad debts, discounts and the finance cost of an increase in working capital, a policy to relax credit terms would be profitable

The debt collection policy

2.2 The overall **debt collection policy** of the firm should be such that the administrative costs and other costs incurred in debt collection do not exceed the benefits from incurring those

costs. Beyond a certain level of spending, however, additional expenditure on debt collection would not have enough effect on bad debts or on the average collection period to justify the extra administrative costs.

Assessing creditworthiness

2.3 **Credit control** involves the initial investigation of potential credit customers and the continuing control of outstanding accounts. The main points to note are as follows.

(a) New customers should give two **good references,** including one from a bank, before being granted credit.

(b) **Credit ratings** might be **checked** through a credit rating agency.

(c) A **new customer's credit limit** should be **fixed** at a **low level** and only increased if his payment record subsequently warrants it.

(d) For large value customers, a **file** should be **maintained** of any available financial information about the customer. This file should be reviewed regularly. Information is available from:

(i) An analysis of the company's annual report and accounts

(ii) Extel cards (sheets of accounting information about public companies in the UK, and also major overseas companies, produced by Extel)

(e) The **Department of Trade and Industry** and the Export Credit Guarantee Department will both be able to advise on overseas companies.

(f) **Press comments** may give information about what a company is currently doing (as opposed to the historical results in Extel cards or published accounts which only show what the company has done in the past).

(g) The company could send a member of staff to **visit** the company concerned, to get a first-hand impression of the company and its prospects. This would be advisable in the case of a prospective major customer.

(h) **Aged lists of debts** should be produced and reviewed at regular intervals. Credit control monitoring should be an integral part of monitoring total working capital.

(i) The **credit limit** for an existing customer should be periodically **reviewed,** but it should only be raised if the customer's credit standing is good.

(j) Procedures should be in place to ensure that **further orders** are **not accepted** from nor goods sent to a customer who is in difficulties. If a customer has exceeded his credit limit, or has not paid debts despite several reminders, or is otherwise known to be in difficulties, sales staff and warehouse staff must be notified immediately (and not, for example, at the end of the week, by which time more goods might have been supplied).

2.4 An organisation might devise a **credit-rating system** for new individual customers that is based on characteristics of the customer (such as whether the customer is a home owner, and the customer's age and occupation). Points would be awarded according to the characteristics of the customer, and the amount of credit that is offered would depend on his or her credit score.

Extension of credit

2.5 To determine whether it would be profitable to extend the level of total credit, it is necessary to assess:

- The **extra sales** that a **more generous credit policy** would stimulate
- The **profitability** of the **extra sales**

- The **extra length** of the **average debt collection period**
- The **required rate of return** on the investment in additional debtors

2.6 EXAMPLE: DEBTOR MANAGEMENT (1)

Russian Beard Ltd is considering a change of credit policy which will result in an increase in the average collection period from one to two months. The relaxation in credit is expected to produce an increase in sales in each year amounting to 25% of the current sales volume.

Selling price per unit	£10
Variable cost per unit	£8.50
Current annual sales	£2,400,000

The required rate of return on investments is 20%. Assume that the 25% increase in sales would result in additional stocks of £100,000 and additional creditors of £20,000.

Advise the company on whether or not to extend the credit period offered to customers, if:

(a) All customers take the longer credit of two months

(b) Existing customers do not change their payment habits, and only the new customers take a full two months credit

2.7 SOLUTION

The change in credit policy is justifiable if the rate of return on the additional investment in working capital would exceed 20%.

Extra profit	
Contribution/sales ratio	15%
Increase in sales revenue	£600,000
Increase in contribution and profit	£90,000

(a) *Extra investment, if all debtors take two months credit*

	£
Average debtors after the sales increase (2/12 × £3,000,000)	500,000
Less current average debtors (1/12 × £2,400,000)	200,000
Increase in debtors	300,000
Increase in stocks	100,000
	400,000
Less increase in creditors	20,000
Net increase in working capital investment	380,000

$$\text{Return on extra investment } \frac{\pounds 90,000}{\pounds 380,000} = 23.7\%$$

(b) *Extra investment, if only the new debtors take two months credit*

	£
Increase in debtors (2/12 of £600,000)	100,000
Increase in stocks	100,000
	200,000
Less increase in creditors	20,000
Net increase in working capital investment	180,000

$$\text{Return on extra investment } \frac{\pounds 90,000}{\pounds 180,000} = 50\%$$

In both case (a) and case (b) the new credit policy appears to be worthwhile.

Settlement discounts

2.8 To see whether the offer of a **settlement discount** (for early payment) is financially worthwhile we must compare the cost of the discount with the benefit of a reduced investment in debtors.

2.9 Varying the discount allowed for early payment of debts affects the **average collection period** and affects the **volume of demand** (and possibly, therefore, indirectly affects bad debt losses). We shall begin with examples where the offer of a discount for early payment does not affect the volume of demand.

2.10 EXAMPLE: DEBTOR MANAGEMENT (2)

Lowe and Price Ltd has annual credit sales of £12,000,000, and three months are allowed for payment. The company decides to offer a 2% discount for payments made within ten days of the invoice being sent, and to reduce the maximum time allowed for payment to two months. It is estimated that 50% of customers will take the discount. If the company requires a 20% return on investments, what will be the effect of the discount? Assume that the volume of sales will be unaffected by the discount.

2.11 SOLUTION

Our approach is to calculate:

(a) The profits forgone by offering the discount

(b) The interest charges saved or incurred as a result of the changes in the cash flows of the company

Thus:

(a) The volume of debtors, if the company policy remains unchanged, would be:

$3/12 \times £12{,}000{,}000 = £3{,}000{,}000$.

(b) If the policy is changed the volume of debtors would be:

$$\left(\frac{10}{365} \times 50\% \times £12{,}000{,}000\right) + \left(\frac{2}{12} \times 50\% \times £12{,}000{,}000\right)$$

$$= £164{,}384 + £1{,}000{,}000 = £1{,}164{,}384.$$

(c) There will be a reduction in debtors of £1,835,616.

(d) Since the company can invest at 20% a year, the value of a reduction in debtors (a source of funds) is 20% of £1,835,616 each year in perpetuity, that is, £367,123 a year.

(e) *Summary*

	£
Value of reduction in debtors each year	367,123
Less discounts allowed each year (2% × 50% × £12,000,000)	120,000
Net benefit of new discount policy each year	247,123

2.12 An extension of the payment period allowed to debtors may be introduced in order to increase sales volume.

Question 2

Enticement Ltd currently expects sales of £50,000 a month. Variable costs of sales are £40,000 a month (all payable in the month of sale). It is estimated that if the credit period allowed to debtors were to be increased from 30 days to 60 days, sales volume would increase by 20%. All customers would be expected to take advantage of the extended credit. If the cost of capital is $12\frac{1}{2}$% a year (or approximately 1% a month), is the extension of the credit period justifiable in financial terms?

Answer

	£
Current debtors (1 month)	50,000
Debtors after implementing the proposal (2 months)	120,000
Increase in debtors	70,000
Financing cost (× 12½%)	8,750
Annual contribution from additional sales	
(12 months × 20% × £10,000)	24,000
Annual net benefit from extending credit period	15,250

The percentage cost of an early settlement discount to the company giving it can be estimated by the formula:

FORMULA TO LEARN

$$\left[\frac{d}{(100-d)} \times \frac{365}{t}\right]\%$$

where:

d is the discount offered (5% = 5, etc)

t is the reduction in the payment period in days that is necessary to obtain the early payment discount

Bad debt risk

2.13 Different credit policies are likely to have differing levels of bad debt risk. The higher turnover resulting from easier credit terms should be sufficiently profitable to exceed the cost of:

- Bad debts, and
- The additional investment necessary to achieve the higher sales

2.14 EXAMPLE: DEBTOR MANAGEMENT (3)

Grabbit Quick Ltd achieves current annual sales of £1,800,000. The cost of sales is 80% of this amount, but bad debts average 1% of total sales, and the annual profit is as follows.

	£
Sales	1,800,000
Less cost of sales	1,440,000
	360,000
Less bad debts	18,000
Profit	342,000

The current debt collection period is one month, and the management consider that if credit terms were eased (option A), the effects would be as follows.

	Present policy	*Option A*
Additional sales (%)	–	25%
Average collection period	1 month	2 months
Bad debts (% of sales)	1%	3%

The company requires a 20% return on its investments. The costs of sales are 75% variable and 25% fixed. Assume there would be no increase in fixed costs from the extra turnover; and that there would be no increase in average stocks or creditors. Which is the preferable policy, Option A or the present one?

2.15 SOLUTION

The increase in profit before the cost of additional finance for Option A can be found as follows.

(a)

	£
Increase in contribution from additional sales	
25% × £1,800,000 × 40%*	180,000
Less increase in bad debts	
(3% × £2,250,000) – £18,000	49,500
Increase in annual profit	130,500

* The C/S ratio is 100% – (75% × 80%) = 40%

(b)

	£
Proposed investment in debtors	
£2,250,000 × 1/6	375,000
Less current investment in debtors	
£1,800,000 × 1/12	150,000
Additional investment required	225,000
Cost of additional finance at 20%	£45,000

(c) As the increase in profit exceeds the cost of additional finance, Option A should be adopted.

Credit insurance

2.16 Companies might be able to obtain credit insurance against certain approved debts going bad through a specialist credit insurance firm. A company cannot insure against all its bad debt losses, but may be able to insure against losses above the normal level.

2.17 When a company arranges **credit insurance,** it must submit specific proposals for credit to the insurance company, stating the name of each customer to which it wants to give credit and the amount of credit it wants to give. The insurance company will accept, amend or refuse these proposals, depending on its assessment of each of these customers.

Factoring 12/01

2.18 A **factor** is defined as 'a doer or transactor of business for another', but a factoring organisation specialises in trade debts, and manages the debts owed to a client (a business customer) on the client's behalf.

KEY TERM

Factoring is an arrangement to have debts collected by a factor company, which advances a proportion of the money it is due to collect.

2.19 **The main aspects of factoring** include the following.

(a) **Administration** of the client's invoicing, sales accounting and debt collection service

(b) **Credit protection** for the client's debts, whereby the factor takes over the risk of loss from bad debts and so 'insures' the client against such losses

(c) Making **payments** to the client **in advance** of collecting the debts. This is sometimes referred to as 'factor finance' because the factor is providing cash to the client against outstanding debts.)

Benefits of factoring

2.20 The **benefits of factoring** for a business customer include the following.

(a) The business can **pay** its **suppliers promptly**, and so be able to take advantage of any early payment discounts that are available.

(b) **Optimum stock levels** can be **maintained**, because the business will have enough cash to pay for the stocks it needs.

(c) **Growth** can be **financed** through **sales** rather than by injecting fresh external capital.

(d) The business gets **finance linked** to its **volume of sales**. In contrast, overdraft limits tend to be determined by historical balance sheets.

(e) The **managers** of the business **do not** have to **spend** their **time** on the problems of **slow paying debtors.**

(f) The business does **not incur** the **costs** of **running** its own **sales ledger department,** and can use the **expertise** of debtor management that the factor has.

2.21 An important **disadvantage** is that debtors will be making payments direct to the factor, which is likely to present a negative picture of the firm.

2.22 EXAMPLE: FACTORING

A company makes annual credit sales of £1,500,000. Credit terms are 30 days, but its debt administration has been poor and the average collection period has been 45 days with 0.5% of sales resulting in bad debts which are written off.

A factor would take on the task of debt administration and credit checking, at an annual fee of 2.5% of credit sales. The company would save £30,000 a year in administration costs. The payment period would be 30 days.

The factor would also provide an advance of 80% of invoiced debts at an interest rate of 14% (3% over the current base rate). The company can obtain an overdraft facility to finance its debtors at a rate of 2.5% over base rate.

Should the factor's services be accepted? Assume a constant monthly turnover.

2.23 SOLUTION

It is assumed that the factor would advance an amount equal to 80% of the invoiced debts, and the balance 30 days later.

(a) The current situation is as follows, using the company's debt collection staff and a bank overdraft to finance all debts.

Credit sales	£1,500,000 pa
Average credit period	45 days

The annual cost is as follows:

	£
$\frac{45}{365} \times £1{,}500{,}000 \times 13.5\%$	24,966
Bad debts: 0.5% × £1,500,000	7,500
Total cost	32,466

(b) *The cost of the factor.* 80% of credit sales financed by the factor would be 80% of £1,500,000 = £1,200,000. For a consistent comparison, we must assume that 20% of credit sales would be financed by a bank overdraft. The average credit period would be only 30 days. The annual cost would be as follows.

			£
Factor's finance:	$\frac{30}{365}$	× £1,200,000 × 14%	13,808
Overdraft:	$\frac{30}{365}$	× £300,000 × 13.5%	3,329
			17,137
Cost of factor's services: 2.5% × £1,500,000			37,500
Less savings in company's administration costs			(30,000)
Net cost of the factor			24,637

(c) *Conclusion.* The factor is cheaper. In this case, the factor's fees exactly equal the savings in bad debts (£7,500) and administration costs (£30,000). The factor is then cheaper overall because it will be more efficient at collecting debts. The advance of 80% of debts is not needed, however, if the company has sufficient overdraft facility because the factor's finance charge of 14% is higher than the company's overdraft rate of 13.5%.

Exam focus point

Points to look out for in questions about factoring are who bears the risk of bad debts, and company administration costs that may be saved by using a factor.

Invoice discounting

KEY TERM

Invoice discounting is the purchase (by the provider of the discounting service) of trade debts at a discount. Invoice discounting enables the company from which the debts are purchased to raise working capital.

2.24 **Invoice discounting** is related to factoring and many factors will provide an invoice discounting service. It is the purchase of a selection of invoices, at a discount. The invoice discounter does not take over the administration of the client's sales ledger. Therefore the finance is proved **without recourse** to the client company.

2.25 A client should only want to have some invoices discounted when he has a temporary cash shortage, and so invoice discounting tends to consist of one-off deals. **Confidential invoice discounting** is an arrangement whereby a debt is confidentially assigned to the factor, and the client's customer will only become aware of the arrangement if he does not pay his debt to the client.

2.26 If a client needs to generate cash, he can approach a factor or invoice discounter, who will offer to purchase selected invoices and advance up to 75% of their value. At the end of each month, the factor will pay over the balance of the purchase price, less charges, on the invoices that have been settled in the month.

3 USING DEBTOR INFORMATION

Payment record of individual debtors

3.1 **Debtors' payment records** must be **monitored** continually. This depends on successful sales ledger administration.

(a) **Invoices** must be posted at the right time.

(b) **Receipts** should be posted when they arrive, and allocated specifically to the invoices to which they relate.

(c) Any **queries** (eg customers debiting their own credit balance with a debit note as 'notification' to the supplier) need to be dealt with quickly.

(d) Orders should *always* be **vetted against credit limits**: this indicates the importance of prompt updating, as above.

(e) A **customer history analysis** can be prepared: this is like a statement, but with:

(i) Total annual sales, on a rolling twelve month basis
(ii) Outstanding amounts owed
(iii) Days sales outstanding at each month end

The advantage of this is that trends in the account can be monitored, as can also the ageing of the debtor balance.

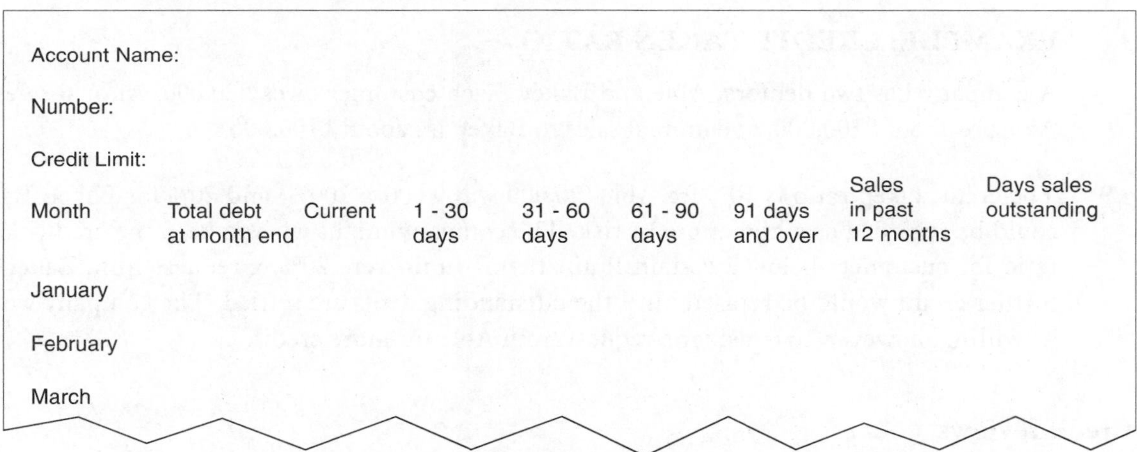

Account Name:

Number:

Credit Limit:

Month	Total debt at month end	Current	1 - 30 days	31 - 60 days	61 - 90 days	91 days and over	Sales in past 12 months	Days sales outstanding
January								
February								
March								

3.2 With this information it should be possible to develop in-house credit ratings.

In-house credit ratings

3.3 Credit monitoring can be simplified by a system of **in-house credit ratings**. For example, a company could have five credit-risk categories for its customers. These credit categories or ratings could be used to decide either individual credit limits for customers within that category or the frequency of the credit review. Guidelines could be provided to help credit controllers decide into which category a customer belongs.

3.4 Over time, the payment habits of a customer can be assessed, and the customer's credit rating (and credit limits) can be set accordingly. Any deterioration in a customer's payment record could raise concerns about the customer's creditworthiness.

3.5 EXAMPLE: CATEGORISATION OF CREDIT CUSTOMERS

A company categorises its credit customers into the following four groups.

1 Prompt payers
2 Those who pay within 30 days of the due date
3 Those who pay between 40 and 60 days of the due date
4 Those who pay over 60 days late

The recent payment record of a regular customer, Victor, is as follows.

Invoice number	*Date of invoice*	*Date payable*	*Payment received*	*Days overdue*
3257	7 March	7 April	28 April	21
3816	26 June	26 July	1 September	37
3942	19 July	19 August	1 September	13
4185	3 September	3 October	5 November	33
				104

Average days overdue = 26 days (104 ÷ 4)

3.6 Victor would be rated in credit category 2 by the company. A review of the payment record suggests that Victor delays payment until around the end of the month following the due date. This is quite typical business practice, and although Victor is not a good payer, there is a discernible payment pattern that could persuade the company to treat Victor as an average credit risk.

3.7 A **credit taken ratio** can be used to monitor the credit limits of customers. This compares the amount currently owed by a customer with the annual sales turnover in his account.

3.8 EXAMPLE: CREDIT TAKEN RATIO

A company has two debtors, Able and Baker. Each customer owes £20,000. Annual sales to Able are about £200,000, and annual sales to Baker are about £100,000.

3.9 The credit taken ratio is 10% for Able (20,000 ÷ 200,000 × 100%) and 20% for Baker. Baker could be regarded as a higher credit risk. The company might wish to keep the credit-taken ratio for customers below a certain limit. If this limit were 20%, a request from Baker for further credit would be refused until the outstanding debts are settled. The company would be willing, however, to consider a request from Able for more credit.

Credit reviews

3.10 A **customer's payment record** and the **debtors aged analysis** should be examined regularly, as a matter of course. Breaches of the credit limit, or attempted breaches of it, should be brought immediately to the attention of the credit controller.

3.11 Otherwise, the credit controller will not have the time to examine *each* customer's account thoroughly every month. The credit controller's efforts will be expended on customers thought to be higher risk, or where there are other special factors (a debt that has gone bad). The credit situation will be reviewed more frequently, and a decision taken as to whether the credit should be extended. Illustrative internal weightings, review periods and credit offered are indicated below.

Rating	Payment record	Financial indicators	Frequency of credit reviews	Credit limit (as % of customer's annual purchases)
A Very high risk	Accounts overdue by 60 + days	Low profits Poor liquidity Highly indebted		Cash only (payment with order)
B High risk	Accounts overdue by 30 - 60 days	Deteriorating profitability, liquidity, or gearing High credit taken ratio	Monthly	Reduce to 10% of annual purchases
C Average risk	Accounts overdue up to 30 days	Stable position	Quarterly	15% of annual purchases
D Below average risk	Accounts paid on time	Stable or improving position	Six-monthly	25% of annual purchases
E Low risk	Accounts paid early Public sector customers	Strong financial position, or public sector ownership	Annually	For negotiation with the customer

Debtors age analysis

3.12 An **aged debtors listing** will probably look very much like the schedule illustrated below. The analysis splits up the total balance on the account of each customer across different columns according to the dates of the transactions which make up the total balance. Thus, the amount of an invoice which was raised 14 days ago will form part of the figure in the column headed 'up to 30 days', while an invoice which was raised 36 days ago will form part of the figure in the column headed 'up to 60 days'. (In the schedule below, 'up to 60 days' is used as shorthand for 'more than 30 days but less than 60 days'.)

HEATH LIMITED

AGE ANALYSIS OF DEBTORS AS AT 31.1.X2

Account number	*Customer name*	*Balance*	*Up to 30 days*	*Up to 60 days*	*Up to 90 days*	*Over 90 days*
B004	Brilliant Ltd	804.95	649.90	121.00	0.00	34.05
E008	Easimat Ltd	272.10	192.90	72.40	6.80	0.00
H002	Hampstead Ltd	1,818.42	0.00	0.00	724.24	1,094.18
M024	Martlesham Ltd	284.45	192.21	92.24	0.00	0.00
N030	Nyfen Ltd	1,217.54	1,008.24	124.50	0.00	84.80
T002	Todmorden College	914.50	842.00	0.00	72.50	0.00
T004	Tricorn Ltd	94.80	0.00	0.00	0.00	94.80
V010	Volux Ltd	997.06	413.66	342.15	241.25	0.00
Y020	Yardsley Smith & Co	341.77	321.17	20.60	0.00	0.00
Totals		6,745.59	3,620.08	772.89	1,044.79	1,307.83
Percentage		100%	53.6%	11.5%	15.5%	19.4%

3.13 The age analysis of debtors may be used to help decide what action to take about older debts. Going down each column in turn starting from the column furthest to the right and working across, we can see that there are some rather old debts which ought to be investigated.

3.14 A number of **refinements** can be suggested to the aged debtors listing to make it easier to use.

(a) A report can be printed in which **overdue accounts** are seen first: this highlights attention on these items.

(b) It can help to aggregate data by **class of customer**. In this case, a report would be printed containing, for debtors aggregated into regions, type of customer, industry sectors etc:

(i) Sales revenue
(ii) Outstanding amount owed, broken down into age
(iii) Days' sales outstanding

(c) There is no reason why this should not apply to individual debtor accounts as below. You could also include the date of the last transaction on the account (eg last invoice, last payment).

Account number	*Customer name*	*Balance*	*Up to 30 days*	*Up to 60 days*	*Up to 90 days*	*Over 90 days*	*Sales revenue in last 12 months*	*Days sales outstanding*
B004	Brilliant Ltd	804.95	649.90	121.00	0.00	34.05	6,789.00	43

3.15 We can see from the age analysis of Heath Ltd's debtors given earlier that the relatively high proportion of debts over 90 days (19.4%) is largely due to the debts of Hampstead Ltd. Other customers with debts of this age are Brilliant Ltd, Nyfen Ltd and Tricorn Ltd.

Debtors' ageing and liquidity

3.16 Also of interest to the credit controller is the *total* percentage figure calculated at the bottom of each column. In practice the credit controller will be concerned to look at this figure first of all, in order to keep the ageing figures consistent. Why might a credit controller be worried by an increase in the ageing? If the credit controller knows the customers are going to pay, should it matter?

3.17 The answer is that any reduction in the inflow caused by an overall increase in the debtors period affects the company's ability to pay its debts and increases its use of overdraft finance: unauthorised overdrafts carry a hefty fee as well as interest.

3.18 **Additional ratios** which might be useful in debtor management, in addition to day's sales outstanding, are as follows.

(a) **Overdues as a percentage of total debt**. For example, assume that if Heath Limited (Paragraph 1.2) offers credit on 30 day terms. Brilliant Ltd's debt could be analysed as:

$$\frac{£121.00 + £34.05}{£804.95} = 19.3\% \text{ overdue}$$

(b) **If debts are disputed**, it is helpful to see what a proportion these are of the total debtors and the total overdue. If, of Heath's total debtors of £6,745.59, an amount of £973.06 related to disputed items, the ratio of disputed debts to total outstanding would be:

$$\frac{£973.06}{£6,745.59} = 14.4\%$$

As a percentage of total items *over* 30 days old:

$$\frac{£973.06}{£6,745.59 - £3,620.08} = 31\%$$

An increasing disputes ratio can indicate:

(i) Invoicing problems
(ii) Operational problems

Debtor quality and liquidity

3.19 The **quality** of debtors has an important impact on a firm's overall liquidity. Debtor quality is determined by their age and risk.

3.20 Some **industries** have a higher level of risk than others, in other words, there is a higher probability that customers will fail to pay. Some markets are riskier than others, which is why export credit insurance premiums are higher for some countries than others. Selling goods to a country with possible payment difficulties is riskier than selling them in the home market.

Policing total credit

3.21 The total amount of credit offered, as well as individual accounts, should be policed to ensure that the senior management policy with regard to the total credit limits is maintained. A **credit utilisation report** can indicate the extent to which total limits are being utilised. An example is given below.

Customer	*Limit*	*Utilisation*	
	£'000	£'000	%
Alpha	100	90	90
Beta	50	35	70
Gamma	35	21	60
Delta	250	125	50
	435	271	
		62.2%	

This might also contain other information, such as days sales outstanding and so on.

3.22 Reviewed in aggregate, this can reveal the following.

(a) The **number of customers** who might **want more credit**

(b) The **extent** to which the **company is exposed to debtors**

(c) The '**tightness**' of the policy (It might be possible to increase profitable sales by offering credit. On the other hand, perhaps the firm offers credit too easily.)

3.23 It is possible to design credit utilisation reports to highlight other trends.

(a) The **degree of exposure** to **different countries**

(b) The **degree of exposure** to **different industries** (Some countries or industries may be worthy of more credit; others may be too risky.)

3.24 Credit utilisation can also be analysed by industry within country or by country within industry. It is also useful to relate credit utilisation to total sales.

4 FOREIGN TRADE AND DEBT MANAGEMENT

4.1 **Foreign debts** raise the following special problems.

(a) When goods are sold abroad, the customer might ask for credit. Exports take time to arrange, and there might be complex paperwork. Transporting the goods can be slow, if they are sent by sea. These **delays** in **foreign trade** mean that exporters often build up large investments in stocks and debtors. These working capital investments have to be financed somehow.

(b) The **risk of bad debts** can be **greater** with foreign trade than with domestic trade. If a foreign debtor refuses to pay a debt, the exporter must pursue the debt in the debtor's own country, where procedures will be subject to the laws of that country.

There are several measures available to exporters to overcome these problems.

Reducing the investment in foreign debtors

4.2 A company can reduce its investment in foreign debtors by insisting on **earlier payment** for goods. Another approach is for an exporter to arrange for a bank to give **cash for a foreign debt**, sooner than the exporter would receive payment in the normal course of events. There are several ways in which this might be done.

(a) **Advances against collections**. Where the exporter asks his bank to handle the collection of payment (of a bill of exchange or a cheque) on his behalf, the bank may be prepared to make an advance to the exporter against the collection. The amount of the advance might be 80% to 90% of the value of the collection.

(b) **Negotiation of bills or cheques**. This is similar to an advance against collection, but would be used where the bill or cheque is payable outside the exporter's country (for example in the foreign buyer's country).

(c) **Documentary credits**. These are described below.

Reducing the bad debt risk

4.3 Methods of minimising bad debt risks are broadly similar to those for domestic trade. An exporting company should vet the creditworthiness of each customer, and grant credit terms accordingly.

Export factoring

4.4 The functions performed by an **overseas factor** or **export factor** are essentially the same as with the factoring of domestic trade debts, which was described earlier in this chapter.

4.5 The charges levied by an overseas factor may turn out to be cheaper than using alternative methods such as letters of credit, which are discussed below.

Documentary credits

4.6 **Documentary credits** provide a method of payment in international trade, which gives the exporter a secure risk-free method of obtaining payment. At the same time, documentary credits are a method of obtaining short-term finance from a bank, for working capital. This is because a bank might agree to discount or negotiate a bill of exchange, and so the exporter receives immediate payment of the amount due to him, less the discount, instead of having to wait for payment until the end of the credit period allowed to the buyer. The buyer is able to get a period of credit before having to pay for the imports.

4.7 The buyer (a foreign buyer, or a UK importer) and the seller (a UK exporter or a foreign supplier) first of all agree a contract for the sale of the goods, which provides for payment through a documentary credit. The *buyer* then requests a bank in his country to issue a **letter of credit** in favour of the exporter. The issuing bank, by issuing its letter of credit, guarantees payment to the beneficiary.

4.8 A documentary credit arrangement must be made between the exporter, the buyer and participating banks **before the export sale takes place**. Documentary credits are slow to arrange, and administratively cumbersome; however, they might be considered essential where the risk of non-payment is high.

Countertrade

4.9 **Countertrade** is a means of financing trade in which goods are exchanged for other goods. Three parties might be involved in a 'triangular' deal. Countertrade is thus a form of **barter**. It accounts for around 10% - 15% of total international trade according to one estimate.

Export credit insurance

KEY TERM

Export credit insurance is insurance against the risk of non-payment by foreign customers for export debts.

4.10 You might be wondering why export credit insurance should be necessary, when exporters can pursue **non-paying customers** through the courts in order to obtain payment. The answer is that:

(a) If a credit customer defaults on payment, the task of pursuing the case through the courts will be lengthy, and it might be a long time before payment is eventually obtained.

(b) There are various reasons why non-payment might happen (Export credit insurance provides insurance against non-payment for a variety of risks in addition to the buyer's failure to pay on time.)

4.11 Not all exporters take out export credit insurance because premiums are very high and the benefits are sometimes not fully appreciated. If they do, they will obtain an insurance policy from a private insurance company that deals in export credit insurance.

Overseas debtors; general policies

4.12 There are also a number of general credit control policies that can be particularly important when dealing with overseas customers.

(a) Prior to the sale, the customer's **credit rating** should be **checked**, and the terms of the contract specified. One key term may be demanding the use of an **irrevocable letter of credit** as a term of release of goods. The terms of the **remittance** and the bank to be used should be specified.

(b) The **paperwork** relating to the sales should be carefully completed and checked, in particular the shipping and delivery documentation.

(c) Goods should only be released if payment has been made, or is sufficiently certain, either because of the customer's **previous record** or because the customer has issued a **promissory note.**

(d) Receipts should be **rapidly processed** and late **payments chased.**

5 THE MANAGEMENT OF CREDITORS AND SHORT-TERM FINANCE

Exam focus point

It may seem an obvious point, but take care not to confuse debtors and creditors, as many students do under exam pressure.

Management of trade creditors

5.1 The management of trade creditors involves:

- Attempting to obtain **satisfactory credit** from suppliers
- Attempting to **extend credit** during periods of cash shortage
- Maintaining **good relations** with regular and important suppliers

5.2 If a supplier offers a discount for the early payment of debts, the evaluation of the decision whether or not to **accept the discount** is similar to the **evaluation of the decision** whether or not to **offer a discount**. One problem is the mirror image of the other. The methods of evaluating the offer of a discount to customers were described earlier.

Sources of short-term finance

5.3 Taking trade credit from suppliers is one way in which a company can obtain some **short-term finance**, in addition to its longer term sources. Short-term finance can also be obtained:

(a) With a **bank overdraft**

(b) By **raising finance** from a bank or other organisation against the **security of trade debtors,** for example through factoring or invoice discounting (both described earlier in this chapter)

(c) For larger companies, by issuing **short-term debt instruments**, such as 'commercial paper'

Trade credit

5.4 **Taking credit** from suppliers is a normal feature of business. Nearly every company has some trade creditors waiting for payment. Trade credit is a source of short-term finance because it helps to keep working capital down. It is usually a cheap source of finance, since suppliers rarely charge interest. However, trade credit *will* have a cost, whenever a company is offered a discount for early payment, but opts instead to take longer credit.

Trade credit and the cost of lost early payment discounts

5.5 Trade credit from suppliers is a major source of finance. It is particularly important to small and fast growing firms. The costs of making maximum use of trade credit include the loss of suppliers' goodwill, and the loss of any available cash discounts for the early payment of debts.

5.6 The cost of lost cash discounts can be estimated by the formula:

$$\left[\frac{d}{(100-d)} \times \frac{365}{t}\right]\%$$

where d is the % discount, d = 5 for 5%.

t is the reduction in the payment period in days which would be necessary to obtain the early payment discount, final date to obtain discount – final date for payment

This is the same formula that was used for debtors.

5.7 EXAMPLE: TRADE CREDIT

X Ltd has been offered credit terms from its major supplier of 2/10, net 45. That is, a cash discount of 2% will be given if payment is made within ten days of the invoice, and payments must be made within 45 days of the invoice. The company has the choice of paying 98p per £1 on day 10 (to pay before day 10 would be unnecessary), or to invest the 98p for an additional 35 days and eventually pay the supplier £1 per £1. The decision as to whether the discount should be accepted depends on the opportunity cost of investing 98p for 35 days. What should the company do?

5.8 SOLUTION

If the company refuses the cash discount, and pays in full after 45 days, the implied cost in interest per annum would be approximately:

$$\frac{2}{100-2} \times \frac{365}{35} = 21.3\%$$

Suppose that X Ltd can invest cash to obtain an annual return of 25%, and that there is an invoice from the supplier for £1,000. The two alternatives are as follows.

	Refuse discount	*Accept discount*
	£	£
Payment to supplier	1,000.0	980
Return from investing £980 between day 10 and day 45:		
$£980 \times \frac{35}{365} \times 25\%$	23.5	—
Net cost	976.5	980

It is cheaper to refuse the discount because the investment rate of return on cash retained, in this example, exceeds the saving from the discount.

5.9 Although a company may delay payment beyond the final due date, thereby obtaining even longer credit from its suppliers, such a policy would generally be inadvisable. Unacceptable delays in payment will **worsen the company's credit rating**, and additional credit may become difficult to obtain.

Bills of exchange

5.10 **Bills of exchange** are a form of trade credit. When A sells goods to B, the settlement of the debt might be arranged by means of a **bill of exchange** (called a **trade bill** as B is a trader).

Step 1. A draws bill on B

B will pay certain sum of money on certain date

Step 2. B accepts the bill by signing it, acknowledging B's debt to A and giving a promise to pay

B will pay certain sum of money on certain date. Signed: B

Step 3. After term of bill expired, B pays A.

B =£££⇒ A

Trade bills and obtaining finance against the security of debtors

5.11 When a company obtains payment from its customers through **trade bills**, it can arrange to obtain finance from its bank against the security of the bill.

5.12 If A Ltd sells goods to B Ltd for £50,000, the terms of payment might be agreed so that A Ltd draws a 90 day bill of exchange on B Ltd for £50,000, which B Ltd 'accepts'. A Ltd can then ask its bank to discount the bill, and A Ltd will receive payment (less discount) now from the bank instead of in 90 days from B Ltd. After 90 days, B Ltd must pay the bank or other holder of the bill.

5.13 The rate of discount on the bill, which is the cost to A Ltd of discounting, will depend on the '**quality**' of the bill. A **higher discount** applies to **trade bills** (bills drawn on and accepted by companies such as B Ltd) than to **bank bills** (bills drawn on and accepted by a bank). A lower discount is called a 'finer' discount.

Acceptance credits

5.14 **Acceptance credits** (also known as **bank bills**) are a source of finance from banks for large companies, which are an alternative to bank overdrafts. Acceptance credits have much in common with bills of exchange, but they are different.

(a) A bank and a large corporate customer **agree a facility** which allows the customer to **draw bills of exchange** on the bank, which the bank will accept. The bills are normally payable after 60 or 90 days, but might have a term as long as 180 days. They can be denominated in sterling or in a foreign currency.

(b) The **accepted bills** are then **sold** (discounted) by the bank in the discount market on behalf of the customer, and the money obtained from the sale, minus the bank's acceptance commission, is made available to the customer. Because of the bank's standing and reputation, bills accepted by it can be sold in the market at a low rate of discount.

(c) When a bill matures, the **company** will **pay the bank** the **value** of the bill and the bank will use the money in turn to pay the bill holder.

5.15 Acceptance credits are attractive to customers for the following reasons.

(a) They provide companies with **alternative finance** to a bank overdraft, with the money being obtained from a source outside the bank (the purchaser of the discounted bills).

(b) The amount of credit is promised to the customer for a **stated period of time**.

(c) There may be a **cost advantage** to the customer, because the rate of discount on bank bills in the discount market might be lower than the interest rate on a bank loan, or overdraft, which is related to the bank base rate or LIBOR. The reason for this is mainly that the interest rate on a discounted bill is fixed for the life of the bill (typically 90 days). Overdraft rates are going up, it would be more costly to maintain an overdraft than to have an acceptance credit facility.

(d) The company can **assess** the **cost of its credit facility** with **more certainty**, because costs are fixed over the life of a bill.

Assessment of creditors

5.16 How long a company takes to pay its trade creditors is measured by the creditors' turnover.

KEY TERM

Creditors' turnover $= \dfrac{\text{Average creditors}}{\text{Purchases}} \times 365 \text{ days}$

Cost of sales may be used as an alternative to purchases.

5.17 The creditors' turnover ratio often helps to assess a company's liquidity. An increase in creditors days is often a sign of **lack** of **long-term finance** or **poor management** of **current assets.**

Chapter roundup

- In managing **debtors**, the **creditworthiness** of customers needs to be assessed. The risks and costs of a customer defaulting will need to be balanced against the profitability of the business provided by that customer.
- **Settlement discounts** may be employed to shorten average credit periods, and to reduce the investment in debtors and therefore **interest costs**. The benefit in interest cost saved should exceed the cost of the discounts allowed.
- Some companies use **factoring** and **invoice discounting** to help short-term liquidity or to reduce administration costs. **Insurance**, particularly of overseas debts, can also help reduce the risk of bad debts.
- Regular monitoring of debtors is very important. Individual debtors can be assessed using a **customer history analysis** and a **credit rating system**. The overall level of debtors can be monitored using an **aged debtors listing** and **credit utilisation report**, as well as reports on the level of bad debts.
- Effective management of **trade creditors** involves seeking satisfactory credit terms from supplier, getting credit extended during periods of cash shortage, and maintaining good relations with suppliers.

Quick quiz

1 How can we calculate the number of days sales represented by debtors?

2 List typical column headings that you would expect to see in an aged analysis of debtors.

3 What service involves collecting debts of a business, advancing a proportion of the money it is due to collect?

4 What service involves advancing a proportion of a selection of invoices, without administration of the sales ledger of the business?

5 Cost of lost discount = $\left(\frac{d}{(100-d)} \times \frac{365}{t}\right)\%$. What do d and t represent?

6 Which of the following does not determine the amount of credit offered by a supplier?

A The credit terms the supplier obtains from its own suppliers

B The ease with which the buyer can go elsewhere

C The supplier's total risk exposure

D The number of purchases made by the buyer each year

7 If a customer decided to pass up the chance of a cash discount of 1% in return for reducing her average payment period from 70 to 30 days, what would be the implied cost in interest per annum?

A 9.13%

B 9.22%

C 12.17%

D 12.29%

8 Which of the following is a **disadvantage** to a company of using a factor for its debtors?

A It is easier to finance growth through sales

B Managers spend less time on slow paying debtors

C Debtors pay direct to the factor

D It is easier to pay suppliers promptly to obtain discounts

Answers to quick quiz

1 $\frac{\text{Total debtors}}{\text{Annual sales}} \times 365 = \text{Days sales}$

2
- Account number
- Customer name
- Total balance
- Up to 30 days
- Up to 60 days
- Up to 90 days
- Over 90 days

3 Factoring.

4 Invoice discounting.

5 d is the percentage discount given, t is the reduction in payment to obtain the discount (in days).

6 D The number of purchases. (Although the amount of annual purchases may well be a factor)

7 B Cost $= \left[\frac{d}{(100-d)} \times \frac{365}{t}\right]\%$

$= \frac{1}{100-1} \times \frac{365}{70-30}$

$= 9.22\%$

8 C This may present a negative picture of the company to customers.

Now try the question below from the Exam Question Bank

Question to try	Level	Marks	Time
25	Introductory	n/a	30 mins

Chapter 21

THE MANAGEMENT OF STOCKS AND CASH

	Topic list	Syllabus reference
1	**The management of stocks**	3
2	**The management of cash**	3
3	**Foreign exchange risk**	3
4	**Treasury management**	3

Introduction

This chapter concludes our study of working capital management methods by considering how stock and cash are managed. We also cover in outline how some companies can reduce risks from fluctuating exchange rates, a topic that will be very important when you come to study Paper 3.7.

Study guide

Section 5 – Management of working capital I

Management of stock

- Calculate and interpret stock ratios
- Explain the role of stock in the working capital cycle
- Apply the tools and techniques of stock management
- Analyse and evaluate the results of stock management techniques

Section 7 – Management of working capital II

Management of cash

- Explain the role of cash in the working capital cycle
- Calculate optimal cash balances
- Describe the functions of and evaluate the benefits from centralised cash control and Treasury Management
- Calculate and interpret cash ratios
- Apply the tools and techniques of cash management
- Analyse and evaluate the results of cash management techniques

Exam guide

You may be asked to make calculations of economic holding quantities, or discuss different management policies (for example different ways of managing the treasury function).

1 THE MANAGEMENT OF STOCKS

1.1 Almost every company carries stocks of some sort, even if they are only stocks of consumables such as stationery. For a manufacturing business, stocks (sometimes called inventories), in the form of **raw materials**, **work in progress** and **finished goods**, may amount to a substantial proportion of the total assets of the business.

1.2 Some businesses attempt to control stocks on a scientific basis by balancing the costs of stock shortages against those of stock holding. The 'scientific' control of stocks may be analysed into three parts.

(a) The **economic order quantity (EOQ) model** can be used to decide the optimum order size for stocks which will minimise the costs of ordering stocks plus stockholding costs.

(b) If **discounts for bulk purchases** are available, it may be cheaper to buy stocks in large order sizes so as to obtain the discounts.

(c) Uncertainty in the demand for stocks and/or the supply lead time may lead a company to decide to hold **buffer stocks** in order to reduce or eliminate the risk of 'stock-outs' (running out of stock).

STOCK COSTS

Holding costs	The cost of capital Warehousing and handling costs Deterioration Obsolescence Insurance Pilferage
Procuring costs	Ordering costs Delivery costs
Shortage costs	Contribution from lost sales Extra cost of emergency stock Cost of lost production and sales in a stock-out
Cost of stock	Relevant particularly when calculating discounts

The basic EOQ formula

KEY TERM

The **economic order quantity (EOQ)** is the optimal ordering quantity for an item of stock which will minimise costs.

1.3 Let D = usage in units for one period (the demand)

P = purchase price per item

Co = cost of placing one order

C_H = holding cost per unit of stock for one period

Q = reorder quantity

(Co and C_H: relevant costs only)

Assume that demand is constant, the lead time is constant or zero and purchase costs per unit are constant (ie no bulk discounts).

The total annual cost of having stock is:

(a) Holding costs + ordering costs

$$\frac{Q \times C_H}{2} + \frac{Co \times D}{Q}$$

(b) The objective is to minimise $T = \frac{Q \times C_H}{2} + \frac{Co \times D}{Q}$

1.4 The order quantity, EOQ, which will minimise these total costs is:

EXAM FORMULA

$$EOQ = \sqrt{\frac{2CoD}{C_H}}$$

Exam focus point

The EOQ formula may be given in the exam question, but you should learn it just in case it isn't given.

1.5 EXAMPLE: ECONOMIC ORDER QUANTITY

The demand for a commodity is 40,000 units a year, at a steady rate. It costs £20 to place an order, and 40p to hold a unit for a year. Find the order size to minimise stock costs, the number of orders placed each year, and the length of the stock cycle.

1.6 SOLUTION

$Q = \sqrt{\frac{2CoD}{C_H}} = \sqrt{\frac{2 \times 20 \times 40{,}000}{0.4}}$ = 2,000 units. This means that there will be $\frac{40{,}000}{2{,}000}$ = 20 orders placed each year, so that the stock cycle is once every 52 ÷ 20 = 2.6 weeks. Total costs will be $(20 \times £20) + (\frac{2{,}000}{2} \times 40p) = £800$ a year.

Uncertainties in demand and lead times: a re-order level system

KEY TERM

Reorder level = maximum usage × maximum lead time.

It is the measure of stock at which a replenishment order should be placed. Use of the above formula builds in a measure of safety stock and minimises the possibility of the organisation running out of stock, a **stock-out**.

1.7 When the volume of demand is uncertain, or the supply lead time is variable, there are problems in deciding what the re-order level should be. By holding a **safety stock**, a company can reduce the likelihood that stocks run out during the re-order period (due to high demand or a long lead time before the new supply is delivered). The **average annual** cost of such a safety stock would be:

Quantity of safety stock (in units)	×	Stock holding cost per unit per annum

1.8 The diagram below shows how the stock levels might fluctuate with this system. Points marked 'X' show the re-order level at which a new order is placed. The number of units ordered each time is the EOQ. Actual stock levels sometimes fall below the safety stock level, and sometimes the re-supply arrives before stocks have fallen to the safety level, but on average, extra stock holding amounts to the volume of safety stock. The size of the safety stock will depend on whether stock-outs (running out of stock) are allowed.

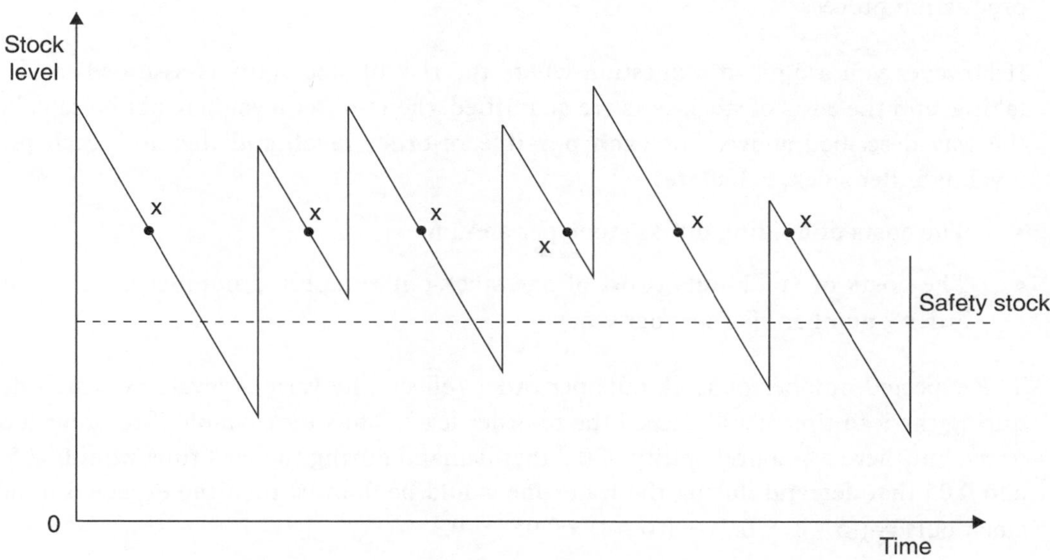

1.9 Instead of being constant the demand may have a normal or Poisson distribution, in which case you would need to know the **average weekly demand**, the **standard deviation** and the **risk** that the organisation was prepared to take of **running out of stock**.

Maximum and minimum stock levels

> **KEY TERM**
>
> **Maximum stock level** = reorder level + reorder quantity – (minimum usage × minimum lead time)

1.10 The maximum level acts as a warning signal to management that stocks are reaching a potentially wasteful level.

> **KEY TERM**
>
> **Minimum stock level** or **safety stock** = reorder level – (average usage × average lead time)

1.11 The minimum level acts as a warning to management that stocks are approaching a dangerously low level and that stockouts are possible.

KEY TERM

Average stock = Minimum level × $\frac{\text{reorder level}}{2}$

1.12 This formula assumes that stock levels fluctuate evenly between the minimum (or safety) stock level and the highest possible stock level (the amount of stock immediately after an order is received, safety stock and reorder quantity).

1.13 This approach assumes that a business wants to minimise the risk of stock-outs at all costs. In the modern manufacturing environment stock-outs can have a disastrous effect on the production process.

1.14 If however you are given a question where the risk of stock-outs is assumed to be worth taking, and the costs of stock-outs are quantified, the re-order level may not be calculated in the way described above. For **each possible re-order level**, and therefore each **possible level** of buffer stock, **calculate**:

- The **costs of holding buffer stock** per annum
- The **costs of stock-outs** (Cost of one stock-out × expected number of stock-outs per order × number of orders per year)

1.15 The expected number of stock-outs per order reflects the various levels by which demand during the lead time could exceed the re-order level. Thus for example if re-order level is 4 units, but there was a probability of 0.2 that demand during the lead time would be 5 units, and 0.05 that demand during the lead time would be 6 units, then the expected number of stock-outs = ((5 – 4) × 0.2) + ((6 – 4) × 0.05) = 0.3.

The effect of discounts

1.16 The solution obtained from using the simple EOQ formula may need to be modified if bulk discounts (also called quantity discounts) are available. To decide mathematically whether it would be worthwhile taking a discount and ordering larger quantities, it is necessary to minimise:

Total purchasing costs + Ordering costs + Stockholding costs.

1.17 The total cost will be minimised:

- At the pre-discount EOQ level, so that a discount is not worthwhile, or
- At the minimum order size necessary to earn the discount

1.18 EXAMPLE: BULK DISCOUNTS

The annual demand for an item of stock is 45 units. The item costs £200 a unit to purchase, the holding cost for one unit for one year is 15% of the unit cost and ordering costs are £300 an order. The supplier offers a 3% discount for orders of 60 units or more, and a discount of 5% for orders of 90 units or more. What is the cost-minimising order size?

1.19 SOLUTION

(a) The EOQ ignoring discounts is:

$$\sqrt{\frac{2 \times 300 \times 45}{15\% \text{ of } 200}} = 30 \text{ units}$$

	£
Purchases (no discount) 45 × £200	9,000
Holding costs 15 units × £30	450
Ordering costs 1.5 orders × £300	450
Total annual costs	9,900

(b) With a discount of 3% and an order quantity of 60 units costs are as follows.

	£
Purchases £9,000 × 97%	8,730
Holding costs 30 units × 15% of 97% of £200	873
Ordering costs 0.75 orders × £300	225
Total annual costs	9,828

(c) With a discount of 5% and an order quantity of 90 units costs are as follows.

	£
Purchases £9,000 × 95%	8,550.0
Holding costs 45 units × 15% of 95% of £200	1,282.5
Ordering costs 0.5 orders × £300	150.0
Total annual costs	9,982.5

The cheapest option is to order 60 units at a time.

Question 1

A company uses an item of stock as follows.

Purchase price:	£96 per unit
Annual demand:	4,000 units
Ordering cost:	£300
Annual holding cost:	10% of purchase price
Economic order quantity:	500 units

Should the company order 1,000 units at a time in order to secure an 8% discount?

Answer

The total annual cost at the economic order quantity of 500 units is as follows.

	£
Purchases 4,000 × £96	384,000
Ordering costs £300 × (4,000/500)	2,400
Holding costs £96 × 10% × (500/2)	2,400
	388,800

The total annual cost at an order quantity of 1,000 units would be as follows.

	£
Purchases £384,000 × 92%	353,280
Ordering costs £300 × (4,000/1,000)	1,200
Holding costs £96 × 92% × 10% × (1,000/2)	4,416
	358,896

The company should order the item 1,000 units at a time, saving £(388,800 - 358,896) = £29,904 a year.

Just-in-time (JIT) procurement

1.20 Some manufacturing companies have sought to reduce their inventories of raw materials and components to as low a level as possible. **Just-in-time procurement** and **stockless production** are terms which describe a policy of obtaining goods from suppliers at the latest possible time (ie when they are needed) and so avoiding the need to carry any materials or components stock.

1.21 Introducing JIT might bring the following potential benefits.

- Reduction in stock holding costs
- Reduced manufacturing lead times
- Improved labour productivity
- Reduced scrap/rework/warranty cost
- Price reductions on purchased materials
- Reduction in the number of accounting transactions

Reduced stock levels mean that a lower level of investment in working capital will be required.

1.22 JIT will not be appropriate in some cases. For example, a restaurant might find it preferable to use the traditional economic order quantity approach for staple non-perishable food stocks but adopt JIT for perishable and 'exotic' items. In a hospital, a stock-out could quite literally be fatal and so JIT would be quite unsuitable.

Exam focus point

You may be required to evaluate the benefits of introducing a JIT arrangement, given certain assumptions about the costs and benefits.

Stock ratios

KEY TERMS

$$\textbf{Stock days} = \frac{\text{Average stock}}{\text{Cost of sales}} \times 365 \text{ days}$$

$$\textbf{Stock turnover} = \frac{\text{Cost of sales}}{\text{Average stock}}$$

1.23 The optimum period of **stock days** will vary industry by industry, and may vary for different lines held by the same firm.

1.24 A high stock days or low stock turnover figure may arise for various reasons. It may be that the firm is being excessively **prudent** in its stockholding policies, or it may be due to **obsolete** or **slow-moving** stock.

1.25 An excessively low figure for **stock days** or **high turnover** figure may also give cause for concern. It may indicate **supply difficulties**, and that there is a significant chance that the company will run out of stock and hence lose sales.

2 THE MANAGEMENT OF CASH

Why organisations hold cash

2.1 The economist John Maynard Keynes identified three reasons for holding cash.

(a) Firstly, a business needs cash to meet its **regular commitments** of paying its creditors, its employees' wages, its taxes, its annual dividends to shareholders and so on. This reason for holding cash is what Keynes called the **transactions motive**.

(b) Keynes identified the **precautionary motive** as a second motive for holding cash. This means that there is a need to maintain a 'buffer' of cash for **unforeseen contingencies**. In the context of a business, this buffer may be provided by an **overdraft facility**, which has the advantage that it will cost nothing until it is actually used.

(c) Keynes identified a third motive for holding cash - the **speculative motive**. Some businesses hold surplus cash as a speculative asset in the hope that interest rates will rise. However many businesses would regard large long-term holdings of cash as not prudent.

2.2 How much cash should a company keep on hand or 'on short call' at a bank? The more cash which is on hand, the easier it will be for the company to meet its bills as they fall due and to take advantage of discounts.

2.3 However, holding cash or near equivalents to cash has a cost - the **loss of earning** which would otherwise have been obtained by using the funds in another way. The financial manager must try to balance liquidity with profitability.

Cash flow problems

2.4 Cash flow problems can arise in various ways.

(a) **Making losses**

If a business is continually making losses, it will eventually have cash flow problems. If the loss is due to a large depreciation charge, the cash flow troubles might only begin when the business needs to replace fixed assets.

(b) **Inflation**

In a period of inflation, a business needs **ever-increasing amounts** of cash just to replace used-up and worn-out assets. A business can be making a profit in historical cost accounting terms, but still not be receiving enough cash to buy the replacement assets it needs.

(c) **Growth**

When a business is growing, it needs to **acquire more fixed assets**, and to **support higher amounts of stocks and debtors**. These additional assets must be paid for somehow (or financed by creditors).

(d) **Seasonal business**

When a business has seasonal or cyclical sales, it may have cash flow difficulties at certain times of the year, when

(i) Cash inflows are low, but

(ii) Cash outflows are high, perhaps because the business is building up its stocks for the next period of high sales

(e) **One-off items of expenditure**

A single non-recurring item of expenditure may create a cash flow problem. Examples include the repayment of loan capital on maturity of the debt or the purchase of an exceptionally expensive item, such as a freehold property.

Methods of easing cash shortages

2.5 The steps that are usually taken by a company when a need for cash arises, and when it cannot obtain resources from any other source such as a loan or an increased overdraft, are as follows.

(a) **Postponing capital expenditure**

Some new fixed assets might be needed for the **development and growth of the business**, but some capital expenditures might be postponable without serious consequences. If a company's policy is to replace company cars every two years, but the company is facing a cash shortage, it might decide to replace cars every three years.

(b) **Accelerating cash inflows which would otherwise be expected in a later period**

One way would be to press debtors for earlier payment. Often, this policy will result in a **loss of goodwill** and problems with customers. It might be possible to encourage debtors to pay more quickly by offering discounts for earlier payment.

(c) **Reversing past investment decisions by selling assets previously acquired**

Some assets are less crucial to a business than others. If cash flow problems are severe, the option of selling investments or property might have to be considered.

(d) **Negotiating a reduction in cash outflows, to postpone or reduce payments**

There are several ways in which this could be done.

(i) **Longer credit** might be taken from suppliers. Such an extension of credit would have to be negotiated carefully: there would be a risk of having further supplies refused.

(ii) **Loan repayments** could be rescheduled by agreement with a bank.

(iii) A **deferral** of the payment of **corporation tax** might be agreed with the Inland Revenue. The Inland Revenue will charge interest on the outstanding amount of tax.

(iv) **Dividend payments** could be **reduced**. Dividend payments are discretionary cash outflows, although a company's directors might be constrained by shareholders' expectations, so that they feel obliged to pay dividends even when there is a cash shortage.

Deviations from expected cash flows

2.6 **Cash budgets**, whether prepared on an annual, monthly, weekly or even a daily basis, can only be estimates of cash flows. Even the best estimates will not be exactly correct, so deviations from the cash budget are inevitable.

2.7 A cash budget model could be constructed, using a PC and a spreadsheet package, and the **sensitivity** of cash flow forecasts to changes in estimates of sales, costs and so on could be analysed. By planning for different eventualities, management should be able to prepare **contingency measures** in advance and also **appreciate** the **key factors** in the cash budget.

2.8 A knowledge of the **probability distribution** of possible outcomes for the cash position will allow a **more accurate estimate** to be made of the minimum cash balances, or the borrowing power necessary, to provide a satisfactory margin of safety. Unforeseen deficits can be hard to finance at short notice, and advance planning is desirable.

Float

2.9 The term **float** is sometimes used to describe the amount of money tied up between **the time when a payment is initiated** (for example when a debtor sends a cheque in payment, probably by post), and **the time when the funds become available for use** in the recipient's bank account.

2.10 There are three reasons why there might be a lengthy float.

(a) **Transmission delay**

When payment is sent through the post, it will take a day or longer for the payment to reach the payee.

(b) **Delay in banking the payments received**

The payee, on receipt of a cheque or cash, might **delay presenting** the **cheque** or the cash to his bank. The length of this (lodgement) delay will depend on administrative procedures in the payee's organisation.

(c) **The time needed for a bank to clear a cheque**

A payment is not available for use in the payee's bank account until the **cheque** has been **cleared.** This will usually take two or three days for cheques payable in the UK. For cheques payable abroad, the delay is much longer.

2.11 There are several measures that could be taken to reduce the float.

(a) The payee should ensure that the lodgement delay is kept to a minimum. **Cheques** received should be presented to the bank on the day of receipt.

(b) The payee might, in some local cases, arrange to **collect cheques** from the payer's premises.

(c) The payer might be asked to pay through his own branch of a bank, using the **bank giro system.**

(d) **BACS** (Bankers' Automated Clearing Services Ltd) is a banking system which provides for the computerised transfer of funds between banks. In addition, BACS is available to **corporate customers** of banks for **making payments**.

(e) For regular payments, **standing orders** or **direct debits** might be used.

(f) **CHAPS** (Clearing House Automated Payments System) is a computerised system for banks to make **same-day clearances** (that is, immediate payment) between each other.

Inefficient cash management

2.12 A lengthy float suggests inefficient cash management. But there are other types of delay in receiving payment from debtors, which might also suggest inefficient cash management.

(a) There is the delay created by the **length of credit** given to customers. There is often a 'normal' credit period for an industry, and companies might be unable to grant less time for payment than this.

(b) There are avoidable delays caused by **poor administration** (in addition to lodgement delay), such as:

(i) **Failure to notify** the **invoicing department** that goods have been despatched, so that invoices are not sent promptly

(ii) **Cheques from debtors** being **made out incorrectly**, to the wrong company perhaps, because invoices do not contain clear instructions

2.13 EXAMPLE: CASH MANAGEMENT

Ryan Coates owns a chain of seven clothes shops in the London area. Takings at each shop are remitted once a week on Thursday evening to the head office, and are then banked at the start of business on Friday morning. As business is expanding, Ryan Coates has hired an accountant to help him. The accountant gave him the following advice.

'Turnover at the seven shops totalled £1,950,000 last year, at a constant daily rate, but you were paying bank overdraft charges at a rate of 11%. You could have reduced your overdraft costs by banking the shop takings each day, except for Saturday's takings. Saturday takings could have been banked on Mondays.'

Comment on the significance of this statement, stating your assumptions. The shops are closed on Sundays.

2.14 SOLUTION

(a) A bank overdraft rate of 11% a year is approximately 11/365 = 0.03% a day.

(b) Annual takings of £1,950,000 would be an average of £1,950,000/312 = £6,250 a day for the seven shops in total, on the assumption that they opened for a 52 week year of six days a week (312 days).

(c) Using the approximate overdraft cost of 0.03% a day, the cost of holding £6,250 for one day instead of banking it is 0.03% × £6,250 = £1.875.

(d) Banking all takings up to Thursday evening of each week on Friday morning involves an unnecessary delay in paying cash into the bank. The cost of this delay would be **either** the opportunity cost of investment capital for the business **or** the cost of avoidable bank overdraft charges.

It is assumed here that the overdraft cost is higher and is therefore more appropriate to use. It is also assumed that, for interest purposes, funds are credited when banked.

Takings on	*Could be banked on*	*Number of days delay incurred by Friday banking*
Monday	Tuesday	3
Tuesday	Wednesday	2
Wednesday	Thursday	1
Thursday	Friday	0
Friday	Saturday	6
Saturday	Monday	4
		16

In one week, the total number of days delay incurred by Friday banking is 16. At a cost of £1.875 a day, the weekly cost of Friday banking was £1.875 × 16 = £30.00, and the annual cost of Friday banking was £30.00 × 52 = £1,560.

(e) *Conclusion*. The company could have saved about £1,560 a year in bank overdraft charges last year. If the overdraft rate remains at 11% and turnover continues to increase, the saving from daily banking would be even higher next year.

Inventory approach to cash management

2.15 A number of different cash management models indicate the **optimum amount of cash** that a company should hold. One such model is based on the idea that deciding on optimum cash balances is like deciding on optimum stock levels.

2.16 We can distinguish two types of cost which are involved in obtaining cash:

(a) The **fixed cost** represented, for example, by the issue cost of equity finance or the cost of negotiating an overdraft

(b) The **variable cost** (opportunity cost) of keeping the money in the form of cash

2.17 The inventory approach uses an equation of the same form as the EOQ formula for stock management which we looked at earlier. The average total cost incurred for period in holding a certain average level of cash (C) is:

$$\frac{Qi}{2} + \frac{FS}{Q}$$

Where S = the amount of cash to be used in each time period
F = the fixed cost of obtaining new funds
i = the interest cost of holding cash or near cash equivalents
Q = the total amount to be raised to provide for S

Similarly to the EOQ, C is minimised when:

$$Q = \sqrt{\frac{2FS}{i}}$$

2.18 EXAMPLE: INVENTORY APPROACH TO CASH MANAGEMENT

Finder Limited faces a fixed cost of £4,000 to obtain new funds. There is a requirement for £24,000 of cash over each period of one year for the foreseeable future. The interest cost of new funds is 12% per annum; the interest rate earned on short-term securities is 9% per annum. How much finance should Finder Limited raise at a time?

2.19 SOLUTION

The cost of holding cash is 12% – 9% = 3%

The optimum level of Q (the 'reorder quantity') is:

$$\sqrt{\frac{2 \times 4{,}000 \times 24{,}000}{0.03}} = £80{,}000$$

The optimum amount of new funds to raise is £80,000. This amount is raised every 80,000 ÷ 24,000 = $3^1/_3$ years.

Drawbacks of the inventory approach

2.20 The inventory approach illustrated above has the following drawbacks.

(a) In reality, it is unlikely to be **possible** to **predict amounts required** over future periods with much certainty.

(b) No **buffer stock** of cash is allowed for. There may be costs associated with running out of cash.

(c) There may be other **normal costs** of holding cash which increase with the average amount held.

The Miller-Orr model

2.21 In an attempt to produce a more realistic approach to cash management, various models more complicated than the inventory approach have been developed. One of these, the

Miller-Orr model, manages to achieve a reasonable degree of realism while not being too elaborate.

2.22 We can begin looking at the Miller-Orr model by asking what will happen if there is no attempt to manage cash balances. Clearly, the cash balance is likely to 'meander' upwards or downwards. The Miller-Orr model imposes limits to this meandering.

2.23 If the cash balance reaches an **upper limit** (point A in Figure 2) the firm **buys sufficient securities** to return the cash balance to a normal level (called the 'return point'). When the cash balance reaches a lower limit (point B in Figure 2), the firm sells securities to bring the balance back to the return point.

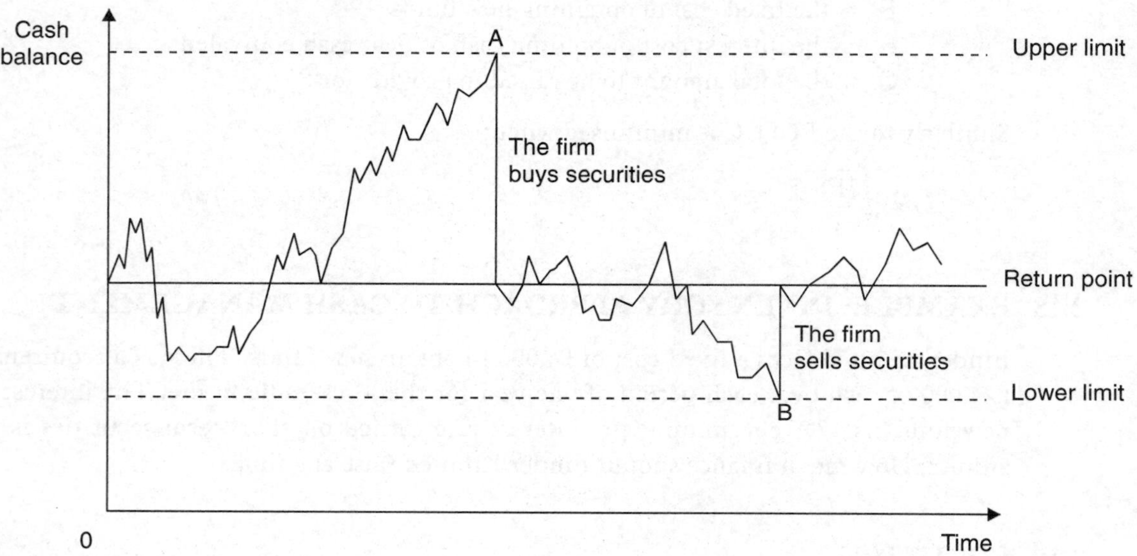

Figure 2 Miller-Orr model

2.24 How are the upper and lower limits and the return point set? Miller and Orr showed that the answer to this question depends on the **variance of cash flows, transaction costs** and **interest rates**. If the day-to-day variability of cash flows is high or the transaction cost in buying or selling securities is high, then wider limits should be set. If interest rates are high, the limits should be closer together.

2.25 To keep the interest costs of holding cash down, the return point is set at one-third of the distance (or 'spread') between the lower and the upper limit.

$$\text{Return point} = \text{Lower limit} + {}^{1}/_{3} \times \text{spread}$$

2.26 The formula for the spread is:

$$\text{Spread} = 3\left(\frac{3}{4} \times \frac{\text{transaction cost} \times \text{variance of cash flows}}{\text{interest rate}}\right)^{\frac{1}{3}}$$

2.27 To use the Miller-Orr model, it is necessary to follow the steps below.

Step 1. Set the **lower limit** for the **cash balance**. This may be zero, or it may be set at some minimum safety margin above zero.

Step 2. **Estimate** the **variance** of **cash flows**, for example from sample observations over a 100-day period.

Step 3. **Note the interest rate** and the **transaction cost** for each sale or purchase of securities (the latter is assumed to be fixed).

Step 4. **Compute the upper limit** and the **return point** from the model and implement the limits strategy.

You may be given the information to help you through the early steps, as in the question below.

Question 2

The following data applies to a company.

Step 1. The minimum cash balance is £8,000.

Step 2. The variance of daily cash flows is 4,000,000, equivalent to a standard deviation of £2,000 per day.

Step 3. The transaction cost for buying or selling securities is £50. The interest rate is 0.025 per cent per day.

You are required to formulate a decision rule using the Miller-Orr model.

Answer

Step 4. The spread between the upper and the lower cash balance limits is calculated as follows.

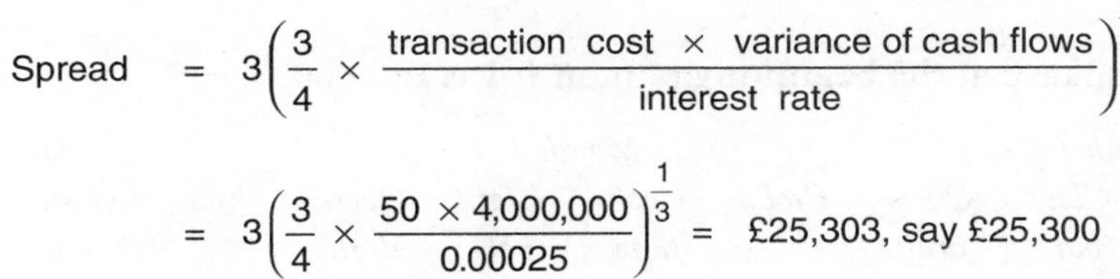

$$\text{Spread} = 3\left(\frac{3}{4} \times \frac{\text{transaction cost} \times \text{variance of cash flows}}{\text{interest rate}}\right)^{\frac{1}{3}}$$

$$= 3\left(\frac{3}{4} \times \frac{50 \times 4{,}000{,}000}{0.00025}\right)^{\frac{1}{3}} = £25{,}303, \text{ say } £25{,}300$$

The upper limit and return point are now calculated.

Upper limit = Lower limit + £25,300 = £8,000 + £25,300 = £33,300

Return point = lower limit + $^1/_3$ × spread = £8,000 + $^1/_3$ × £25,300 = £16,433, say £16,400

The decision rule is as follows. If the cash balance reaches £33,300, buy £16,900 (= 33,300 – 16,400) in marketable securities. If the cash balance falls to £8,000, sell £8,400 of marketable securities for cash.

2.28 The **usefulness of the Miller-Orr model** is limited by the assumptions on which it is based. In practice, cash inflows and outflows are unlikely to be entirely **unpredictable** as the model assumes: for example, for a retailer, seasonal factors are likely to affect cash inflows.

2.29 However, the Miller-Orr model may save management time which might otherwise be spent in responding to those cash inflows and outflows which cannot be predicted.

Applying probabilities in cash management problems

2.30 Probabilities can be applied to cash management problems.

2.31 EXAMPLE: PROBABILITIES IN CASH MANAGEMENT

Sinkos Wim Ltd has an overdraft facility of £100,000, and currently has an overdraft balance at the bank of £34,000. The company maintains a cash float of £10,000 for transactions and precautionary purposes. It is unclear whether a long awaited economic recovery will take place, and the company has prepared cash budgets as set out below for the next three months using two different assumptions about economic events. The cash flow in months 2 and 3 depend on the cash flows in the previous month.

Estimated net cash flows

Month 1		*Month 2*		*Month 3*	
Probability	*Cash flow* £'000	*Probability*	*Cash flow* £'000	*Probability*	*Cash flow* £'000
		0.8	25	0.5	30
0.7	(40)			0.5	20
		0.2	10	0.5	10
				0.5	0
		0.8	0	0.5	(10)
0.3	(60)			0.5	(20)
		0.2	(10)	0.5	(40)
				0.5	(50)

If the company intends to maintain a cash float of £10,000 at the end of each month, what is the probability that this will be possible at the end of each of months 1, 2 and 3 given the current overdraft limit?

2.32 SOLUTION

The opening balance at the beginning of month 1 is £10,000.

Month 1				*Month 2*				*Month 3*			
Prob.	*Cash flow* £'000	*Clos. bal.* £'000	*Over-draft* £'000	*Prob.*	*Cash flow* £'000	*Clos. bal.* £'000	*Over-draft* £'000	*Prob.*	*Cash flow* £'000	*Clos. bal.* £'000	*Over-draft* £'000
								0.28	30	10	19
				0.56	25	10	49	0.28	20	10	29
0.7	(40)	10	74								
								0.07	10	10	54
				0.14	10	10	64	0.07	0	10	64
								0.12	(10)	6	100
				0.24	0	10	94	0.12	(20)	(4)	100
0.3	(60)	10	94								
								0.03	(40)	(34)	100
				0.06	(10)	6	100	0.03	(50)	(44)	100

The probabilities that the cash float of £10,000 can be maintained at the end of each month are as follows.

Month 1: $0.7 + 0.3 = 1.0$
Month 2: $0.56 + 0.14 + 0.24 = 0.94$
Month 3: $0.28 + 0.28 + 0.07 + 0.07 = 0.7$

Question 3

Using the figures in the above example, state the probabilities that the company completely runs out of cash at the end of each month.

Answer

Under none of the projected outcomes for months 1 and 2 does the company run out of cash.
For month 3, the probability of the company running out of cash is:
$0.12 + 0.03 + 0.03 = 0.18$

Investing surplus cash

2.33 Companies and other organisations sometimes have a **surplus of cash** and become 'cash rich'. A cash surplus is likely to be temporary, but while it exists the company should seek to obtain a good return by investing or depositing the cash, without the risk of a capital loss (or at least, without the risk of an excessive capital loss).

2.34 Three possible reasons for a cash surplus are:

(a) Profitability from trading operations

(b) Low capital expenditure, perhaps because of an absence of profitable new investment opportunities

(c) Receipts from selling parts of the business

2.35 A company might keep surplus cash in liquid form to **benefit from high interest rates** that might be available from bank deposits, when returns on re-investment in the company appear to be lower; or to have cash available should a **strategic opportunity** arise, perhaps for the takeover of another company for which a cash consideration might be needed.

2.36 If a company has no plans to grow or to invest, then surplus cash not required for transactions or precautionary purposes should normally be **returned** to **shareholders.**

2.37 Surplus cash may be returned to shareholders by:

(a) Increasing the usual level of the annual **dividends** which are paid

(b) Making a one-off **special dividend payment** (For example, National Power plc and BT plc have made such payments in recent years.)

(c) Using the money to **buy back its own shares** from some of its shareholders. This will reduce the total number of shares in issue, and should therefore raise the level of **earnings per share**

Short-term investments

2.38 Temporary cash surpluses are likely to be:

(a) **Deposited** with a **bank** or similar financial institution

(b) Invested in **short-term debt instruments** (Debt instruments are debt securities which can be traded.)

(c) Invested in **longer term debt instruments,** which can be sold on the stock market when the company eventually needs the cash

(d) Invested in **shares of listed companies,** which can be sold on the stock market when the company eventually needs the cash

Short-term deposits

2.39 Cash can of course be put into a **bank deposit** to **earn interest**. The rate of interest obtainable depends on the size of the deposit, and varies from bank to bank.

2.40 There are other types of deposit.

(a) **Money market lending**

There is a very large money market in the UK for inter-bank lending. The interest rates in the market are related to the London Interbank Offer Rate (LIBOR) and the London Interbank Bid Rate (LIBID).

(i) A large company will be able to lend surplus cash **directly** to a **borrowing bank** in the market.

(ii) A smaller company with a fairly large cash surplus will usually be able to **arrange** to **lend money** on the **interbank market**, but through its bank, and possibly on condition that the money can only be withdrawn at three months notice.

(b) **Local authority deposits**

Local authorities often need **short-term cash,** and investors can deposit funds with them for periods ranging from overnight up to one year or more.

(c) **Finance house deposits**

These are **time deposits** with finance houses (usually subsidiaries of banks).

Short-term debt instruments

2.41 There are a number of **short-term debt instruments** which an investor can re-sell before the debt matures and is repaid. These debt instruments include **certificates of deposit** (CDs) and **Treasury bills.**

Certificates of deposit (CDs)

2.42 A **CD** is a security that is issued by a bank, acknowledging that a certain amount of money has been deposited with it for a certain period of time (usually, a short term). The CD is issued to the **depositor,** and attracts a **stated amount of interest.** The **depositor** will be another bank or a large commercial organisation.

2.43 CDs are negotiable and traded on the CD market (a money market), so if a CD holder wishes to obtain immediate cash, he can sell the CD on the market at any time. This second-hand market in CDs makes them attractive, flexible investments for organisations with excess cash.

Treasury bills

2.44 **Treasury bills** are issued weekly by the government to finance short-term cash deficiencies in the government's expenditure programme. They are **IOUs** issued by the government, giving a promise to pay a certain amount to their holder on maturity. Treasury bills have a term of **91 days to maturity,** after which the holder is paid the full value of the bill.

3 FOREIGN EXCHANGE RISK

Exam focus point

If any calculations are required relating to exchange rate risk in Paper 2.4, they will only be simple calculations.

3.1 A company may become exposed to risk from movements in exchange rates in a number of ways, as an exporter of goods or services or through being a member of an international group.

3.2 Perhaps the most important aspect of **managing overseas debtors** is the problem that **exchange rates** may **change** before payment is received. Hedging involves measures to reduce exposure to such **foreign exchange risk.**

Transaction exposure

3.3 Much international trade involves credit. An importer will take credit often for **several months** and **sometimes longer**, and an exporter will **grant credit**. One consequence of taking and granting credit is that international traders will know in advance about the receipts and payments arising from their trade.

3.4 **Importers and exporters** alike will be concerned about the profit they can expect to make from trade.

(a) An exporter who invoices a foreign buyer in the buyer's currency will expect to be able to exchange his foreign currency proceeds from the buyer for his domestic currency and earn **enough domestic currency** to **cover his costs** and **make a profit**.

(b) Similarly, an importer might buy goods from abroad for which he is invoiced in foreign currency. If he plans to sell the imports, he will produce a price list for his customers, or agree prices to earn **enough domestic currency** from selling the goods to **pay** the **foreign supplier** in foreign currency, and make a profit.

3.5 The great danger to profit margins is the movement in exchange rates. The risk faces:

- Exporters who invoice in a foreign currency, and
- Importers who pay in a foreign currency

Matching receipts and payments

3.6 A company can reduce or eliminate its foreign exchange transaction exposure by matching receipts and payments. Wherever possible, a company that expects to make payments and have receipts in the same foreign currency should plan to **offset** its **payments** against its **receipts** in the currency.

3.7 Since the company will be setting off foreign currency receipts against foreign currency payments, it does not matter whether the currency strengthens or weakens against the company's 'domestic' currency because there will be no purchase or sale of the currency.

3.8 The process of matching is made simpler by having **foreign currency accounts** with a bank. UK residents are allowed to have bank accounts in any foreign currency. Receipts of foreign currency can be credited to the account pending subsequent payments in the currency.

3.9 Since a company is unlikely to have exactly the same amount of receipts in a currency as it makes payments, it will still be exposed to the extent of the surplus of income, and so the company may wish to avoid exposure on this surplus by arranging forward exchange cover.

3.10 **Offsetting** (matching payments against receipts) will be cheaper than arranging a forward contract to buy currency and another forward contract to sell the currency, provided that:

- **Receipts occur before payments**, and
- The **time difference** between receipts and payments in the currency is **not too long**

Leads and lags

3.11 Companies might try to use:

- **Lead payments**: payments in advance, or
- **Lagged payments**: delaying payments beyond their due date

in order to take advantage of foreign exchange rate movements.

3.12 With a lead payment, paying in advance of the due date, there is a finance cost to consider. This is the interest cost on the money used to make the payment.

Currency of invoice

3.13 One way of avoiding exchange rate risk is for an exporter to **invoice** his foreign customer in his **domestic currency**, or for an importer to **arrange** with his **foreign supplier** to be **invoiced** in his **domestic currency**. However, although either the exporter or the importer can avoid any exchange risk in this way, only one of them can deal in his domestic currency. The other must accept the exchange risk, since there will be a period of time elapsing between agreeing a contract and paying for the goods (unless payment is made with the order).

Forward exchange contracts

3.14 Forward exchange contracts allow a trader who knows that he will have to buy or sell foreign currency at a date in the future, to make the purchase or sale at a predetermined rate of exchange. The trader will therefore know in advance either how much **local currency** he will **receive** (if he is selling foreign currency to the bank) or how much local currency he must **pay** (if he is buying foreign currency from the bank).

KEY TERM

A **forward exchange contract** is:

(a) An immediately firm and binding contract between a bank and its customer

(b) For the purchase or sale of a specified quantity of a stated foreign currency

(c) At a rate of exchange fixed at the time the contract is made

(d) For performance (delivery of the currency and payment for it) at a future time which is agreed upon when making the contract. This future time will be either a specified date, or any time between two specified dates.

Forward rates and future exchange rate movements

3.15 A forward price is the **spot price** ruling on the day a forward exchange contract is made plus or minus the **interest differential** for the period of the contract.

3.16 The forward rate is not a forecast of what the spot rate will be on a given date in the future; it will be a coincidence if the forward rate turns out to be the same as the spot rate on that future date.

3.17 It is however likely that the spot rate will move in the direction **indicated** by the **forward** rate. Currencies with **high interest rates** are likely to **depreciate in value** against currencies with **lower interest rates**. The attraction of higher interest persuades investors to hold amounts of a currency that is expected to depreciate.

3.18 EXAMPLE: MOVEMENT OF SPOT RATES

For example, suppose that a spot rate on 1 June is US$1.7430 - 1.7440 to £1, and the three months forward rate (for 1 September) is US$1.7380 - 1.7395 to £1. It is likely that between 1 June and 1 September, sterling will weaken slightly against the dollar. In this example, interest rates in the UK on 1 June would be higher than interest rates in the USA, which accounts for the forward rates for dollars against sterling being lower than the spot rates on 1 June.

Fixed and option contracts

3.19 A forward exchange contract may be either **fixed** or **option.**

(a) '**Fixed**' means that **performance** of the contract will **take place** on a **specified date** in the **future**. For example, a two months forward fixed contract taken out on 1 September will require performance on 1 November.

(b) '**Option**' means that performance of the contract may take place, at the **option** of the **customer**:

(i) **At any date** from the contract being made up to and including a specified final date for performance

(ii) **At any date** between **two specified dates.**

The contract must be performed at some time; the customer cannot avoid performance altogether.

Premiums and discounts: quoting a forward rate

3.20 A forward exchange rate might be higher or lower than the spot rate. If it is higher, the quoted currency will be cheaper forward than spot. For example, if in the case of Swiss francs against sterling (i) the spot rate is 2.156 – 2.166 and (ii) the three months forward rate is 2.207 – 2.222:

(a) A bank would sell 2,000 francs:

(i) At the spot rate, now, for £927.64 $\left(\frac{2,000}{2.156}\right)$

(ii) In three months time, under a forward contract, for £906.21 $\left(\frac{2,000}{2.207}\right)$

(b) A bank would buy 2,000 francs:

(i) At the spot rate, now, for £923.36 $\left(\frac{2,000}{2.166}\right)$

(ii) In three months time, under a forward contract, for £900.09 $\left(\frac{2,000}{2.222}\right)$

3.21 In both cases, the quoted currency (Francs) would be worth less against sterling in a forward contract than at the current spot rate. This is because it is quoted **forward cheaper**, or 'at a discount', against sterling.

3.22 If the **forward exchange rate** is **lower** than the spot rate, the **quoted currency** will be **more expensive forward** than spot. For example, if the spot rate for Euros against sterling is 1.60 - 1.61, and the one month forward rate is 1.57 – 1.58, then Euros are more expensive (quoted 'at a premium') forward than spot.

(a) If the **forward rate** for a currency is **cheaper** than the spot rate, it is at a **forward discount** to the spot rate. The **forward rate** will be **higher** than the **spot rate** by the **amount** of the **discount**.

(b) If the **forward rate** for a currency is **more expensive** than the spot rate, it is at a **forward premium** to the spot rate. The forward rate will be lower than the spot rate by the amount of the premium.

3.23 A **discount** is therefore **added** to the spot rate, and a **premium** is therefore **subtracted** from the spot rate. It might help you to think of the mnemonic 'ADDIS'. This may help you to remember that we ADD DIScounts and so subtract premiums.

3.24 EXAMPLE: FORWARD EXCHANGE CONTRACTS

A UK importer knows on 1 April that he must pay a foreign seller 26,500 Swiss francs in one month's time, on 1 May. He can arrange a forward exchange contract with his bank on 1 April, whereby the bank undertakes to sell the importer 26,500 Swiss francs on 1 May, at a fixed rate of say 2.64.

The UK importer can be certain that whatever the spot rate is between Swiss francs and sterling on 1 May, he will have to pay on that date, at this forward rate:

$$\frac{26{,}500}{2.64} = £10{,}037.88.$$

(a) If the spot rate is lower than 2.64, the importer would have **successfully protected himself** against a weakening of sterling, and would have avoided paying more sterling to obtain the Swiss francs.

(b) If the spot rate is higher than 2.64, sterling's value against the Swiss franc would mean that the **importer** would **pay more** under the forward exchange contract than he would have had to pay if he had obtained the francs at the spot rate on 1 May. He cannot avoid this extra cost, because a forward contract is binding.

Option forward exchange contracts

3.25 **Option contracts** are normally used to cover whole months straddling the likely payment date, where the customer is not sure of the exact date on which he will want to buy or sell currency.

3.26 Option contracts can also be used bit by bit. For example, if a customer makes an option forward contract to sell 100,000 Euros at any time between 3 July and 3 August, he might sell €20,000 on 5 July, €50,000 on 15 July and €30,000 on 1 August.

3.27 When a customer makes an option forward exchange contract with his bank, the bank will quote the rate which is **most favourable to itself** out of the forward rates for all dates within the option period. The customer has the option to call for performance of the contract on any date within the period, and the bank will try to ensure that the customer does not obtain a favourable rate at the bank's expense.

Money market hedges

3.28 An exporter who invoices foreign customers in a foreign currency can hedge against the exchange risk by:

- **Borrowing** an amount in the foreign currency **immediately**
- **Converting** the **foreign currency** into **domestic currency** at the **spot rate**

- **Repaying the loan** with **interest** out of the eventual foreign currency receipts

3.29 Similarly, if a company has to make a foreign currency payment in the future, it can **buy the currency now** at the spot rate and **put it on deposit**, using the principal and the interest earned to make the foreign currency payment when it falls due.

Choosing between the forward exchange market and the money market

3.30 When a company expects to receive or pay a sum of foreign currency in the next few months, it can choose between using the forward exchange market and the money market to hedge against the foreign exchange risk.

3.31 EXAMPLE: CHOOSING THE CHEAPEST METHOD

Trumpton plc has bought goods from a US supplier, and must pay $4,000,000 for them in three months time. The company's finance director wishes to hedge against the foreign exchange risk, and the company wishes to consider either using forward exchange contracts or using money market borrowing or lending.

The following annual interest rates and exchange rates are currently available.

	US dollar		*Sterling*	
	Deposit rate	*Borrowing rate*	*Deposit rate*	*Borrowing rate*
	%	%	%	%
1 month	7	10.25	10.75	14.00
3 months	7	10.75	11.00	14.25

	$/£ exchange rate ($ = £1)
Spot	1.8625 - 1.8635
1 month forward	0.60c - 0.58c pm
3 months forward	1.80c - 1.75c pm

Which is the cheapest method for Trumpton plc? Ignore commission costs (the bank charges for arranging a forward contract or a loan).

3.32 SOLUTION

The two methods must be compared on a similar basis, which means working out the cost of each to Trumpton either now or in three months time. Here the cost to Trumpton now will be determined.

Choice 1: the forward exchange market

Trumpton must buy dollars in order to pay the US supplier. The exchange rate in a forward exchange contract to buy $4,000,000 in three months time (bank sells) is:

	$
Spot rate	1.8625
Less 3 months premium	0.0180
Forward rate	1.8445

The cost of the $4,000,000 to Trumpton in three months time will be:

$$\frac{\$4{,}000{,}000}{\$1.8445} = £2{,}168{,}609.38$$

This is the cost in three months. To work out the cost now, we could say that by deferring payment for three months, the company is:

(a) Saving having to borrow money now at 14.25% a year to make the payment now, or
(b) Avoiding the loss of interest on cash on deposit, earning 11% a year

The choice between (a) and (b) depends on whether Trumpton plc needs to borrow to make any current payment (a) or is cash rich (b). Here, assumption (a) is selected, but (b) might in fact apply.

At an annual interest rate of 14.25% the rate for three months is approximately 14.25/4 = 3.5625%. The 'present cost' of £2,168,609.38 in three months time is:

$$\frac{£2{,}168{,}609.38}{1.035625} = £2{,}094{,}010.27$$

Choice 2: the money markets

Using the money markets involves **borrowing in the foreign currency**, if the company will eventually receive the currency, or **lending in the foreign currency**, if the company will eventually pay the currency.

Here, Trumpton will pay $4,000,000 and so it would lend US dollars. It would lend enough US dollars for three months, so that the principal repaid in three months time plus interest will amount to the payment due of $4,000,000.

(a) Since the US dollar deposit rate is 7%, the rate for three months is approximately 7/4 = 1.75%.

(b) To earn $4,000,000 in three months time at 1.75% interest, Trumpton would have to lend now:

$$\frac{\$4{,}000{,}000}{1.0175} = \$3{,}931{,}203.93$$

These dollars would have to be purchased now at the spot rate of (bank sells) $1.8625. The cost would be:

$$\frac{\$3{,}931{,}203.93}{\$1.8625} = £2{,}110{,}713.52$$

By lending US dollars for three months, Trumpton is matching eventual receipts and payments in US dollars, and so has hedged against foreign exchange risk.

4 TREASURY MANAGEMENT

KEY TERM

Treasury management can be defined as: 'The corporate handing of all financial matters, the generation of external and internal funds for business, the management of currencies and cash flows, and the complex strategies, policies and procedures of corporate finance.' (Association of Corporate Treasurers)

4.1 Large companies rely heavily on the financial and currency markets. These markets are volatile, with interest rates and foreign exchange rates changing continually and by significant amounts. To manage cash (funds) and currency efficiently, many large companies have set up a separate treasury department.

4.2 A treasury department, even in a large organisation, is likely to be quite small, with perhaps a staff of three to six qualified accountants, bankers or corporate treasurers working under the treasurer.

Centralisation of the treasury department

4.3 The following are advantages of having a specialist **centralised treasury department.**

(a) **Centralised liquidity management**

(i) Avoids having a mix of cash surpluses and overdrafts in different localised bank accounts

(ii) Facilitates bulk cash flows, so that lower bank charges can be negotiated

(b) Larger volumes of cash are available to invest, giving better **short-term investment opportunities** (for example money markets, high-interest accounts and CDs).

(c) Any **borrowing** can be **arranged in bulk**, at lower interest rates than for smaller borrowings, and perhaps on the eurocurrency or eurobond markets.

(d) **Foreign exchange risk management** is likely to be improved in a group of companies. A central treasury department can **match foreign currency income** earned by one subsidiary with **expenditure** in the same currency by another subsidiary. In this way, the risk of losses on adverse exchange rate movements can be avoided with out the expense of forward exchange contracts or other hedging methods.

(e) A specialist treasury department can employ **experts** with knowledge of dealing in forward contracts, futures, options, eurocurrency markets, swaps and so on. Localised departments could not have such expertise.

(f) The centralised pool of **funds required for precautionary purposes** will be **smaller** than the sum of separate precautionary balances which would need to be held under decentralised treasury arrangements.

(g) Through having a separate **profit centre**, attention will be focused on the contribution to group profit performance that can be achieved by good cash, funding, investment and foreign currency management.

4.4 Possible advantages of **decentralised** cash management are as follows.

(a) Sources of finance can be **diversified** and can match **local assets.**

(b) **Greater autonomy** can be given to **subsidiaries** and divisions because of the closer relationships they will have with the decentralised cash management function.

(c) A decentralised treasury function may be **more responsive** to the needs of individual operating units.

(d) Since cash balances will not be aggregated at group level, there will be **more limited opportunities** to invest such balances on a short-term basis.

Chapter roundup

- An **economic order quantity** can be calculated as a guide to minimising costs in managing **stock** levels. **Bulk discounts** can however mean that a different order quantity minimises stock costs.
- **Uncertainties** in demand and lead times taken to fulfil orders mean that stock will be ordered once it reaches a re-order level (maximum usage x maximum lead time).
- Optimal **cash** holding levels can be calculated from formal models, such as the **inventory approach** and the **Miller-Orr model**.
- **Cash shortages** can be eased by postponing capital expenditure, selling assets, taking longer to pay creditors and pressing debtors for earlier payment.
- **Temporary surpluses** of cash can be invested in a variety of financial instruments. Longer-term surpluses should be returned to shareholders if there is a lack of investment opportunities.
- The use of **forward exchange contracts** in which a future rate of exchange is fixed in advance, is one of the most important ways in reducing foreign exchange risk. Other means include **matching receipts and payments, leads and lags, invoicing in the domestic currency** and **money market hedging.**
- **Treasury management** in a modern enterprise covers various areas, and in a large business may be a centralised function.

Quick quiz

1 The basic EOQ formula for stock indicates whether bulk discounts should be taken advantage of

☐ True

☐ False

2 Identify the potential benefits of JIT manufacturing.

3 Possible reasons for a lengthy float are:

(a) .... delay

(b) .... delay

(c) .... delay

4 In the Miller-Orr cash management model

Return point = Lower limit + ... × spread

5 Why might a treasurer choose *not* to 'hedge' against the risk of a foreign exchange movement?

6 PB Ltd uses 2,500 units of component X per year. The company has calculated that the cost of placing and processing a purchase order for component X is £185, and the cost of holding one unit of component X for a year is £25.

What is the economic order quantity (EOQ) for component X, and assuming a 52-week year, what is the average frequency at which purchase orders should be placed?

7 The economic order quantity model can be used to determine:

Order quantity	*Buffer stock*	*Re-order level*
Yes/No	Yes/No	Yes/No

8 Which of the following is most likely to reduce a firm's working capital?

A Adopting the Miller-Orr model of cash management

B Lengthening the period of credit given to debtors

C Buying new machinery

D Adopting just-in-time procurement and lean manufacturing

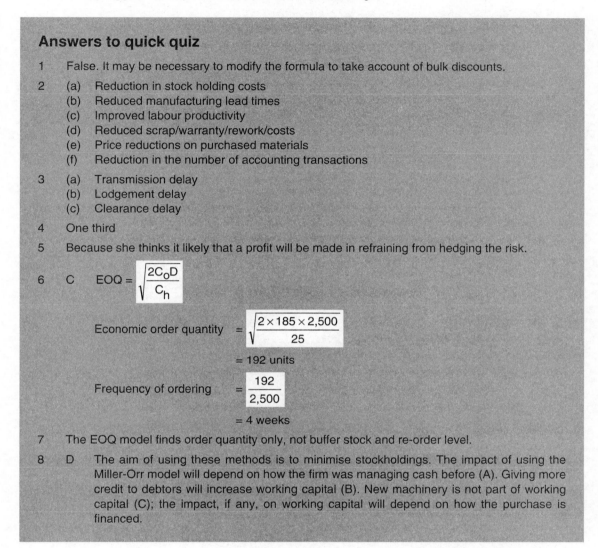

Answers to quick quiz

1 False. It may be necessary to modify the formula to take account of bulk discounts.

2 (a) Reduction in stock holding costs
(b) Reduced manufacturing lead times
(c) Improved labour productivity
(d) Reduced scrap/warranty/rework/costs
(e) Price reductions on purchased materials
(f) Reduction in the number of accounting transactions

3 (a) Transmission delay
(b) Lodgement delay
(c) Clearance delay

4 One third

5 Because she thinks it likely that a profit will be made in refraining from hedging the risk.

6 C $\text{EOQ} = \sqrt{\frac{2C_oD}{C_h}}$

Economic order quantity $= \sqrt{\frac{2 \times 185 \times 2{,}500}{25}}$

= 192 units

Frequency of ordering $= \frac{192}{2{,}500}$

= 4 weeks

7 The EOQ model finds order quantity only, not buffer stock and re-order level.

8 D The aim of using these methods is to minimise stockholdings. The impact of using the Miller-Orr model will depend on how the firm was managing cash before (A). Giving more credit to debtors will increase working capital (B). New machinery is not part of working capital (C); the impact, if any, on working capital will depend on how the purchase is financed.

Now try the question below from the Exam Question Bank

Question to try	Level	Marks	Time
26	Exam	25	45 mins

Part G
Finance and investment appraisal

Chapter 22

EQUITY FINANCING

Topic list		Syllabus reference
1	Sources of equity funds	4(a), (b), (e)
2	Equity shares and markets	4(a), (b), (e)
3	Rights issues and vendor placings	4(a), (b), (e)
4	Scrip dividends, scrip issues and stock splits	4(a), (b), (e)
5	Stock market ratios	4(a), (b), (e)
6	Dividend policy	4(a), (b), (e)

Introduction

In the case of long-term finance (covered in this chapter and Chapter 23), the main choice is between **equity** and **debt** finance.

Study guide

Section 9 – Sources of finance II: Equity financing

- Describe ways in which a company may obtain a stock market listing
- Describe how stock markets operate, including AIM
- Explain the requirements of stock market investors in terms of returns of investment
- Calculate, analyse and evaluate appropriate financial ratios (eg EPS, PE, yield, etc.)
- Outline and apply the dividend valuation model, including the growth adjustment
- Explain the importance of internally generated funds
- Describe the advantages and disadvantages of rights issues
- Calculate the price of rights
- Explain the purpose and impact of a bonus issue, scrip dividends and stock splits

Exam guide

Sources of finance are a major topic. You may be asked to describe appropriate sources of finance for a particular company, and also discuss in general terms when different sources of finance should be utilised and when they are likely to be available. Dividend policy is also important for all types of company.

1 SOURCES OF EQUITY FUNDS

Different sources of funds

1.1 A company might raise new funds from the following sources.

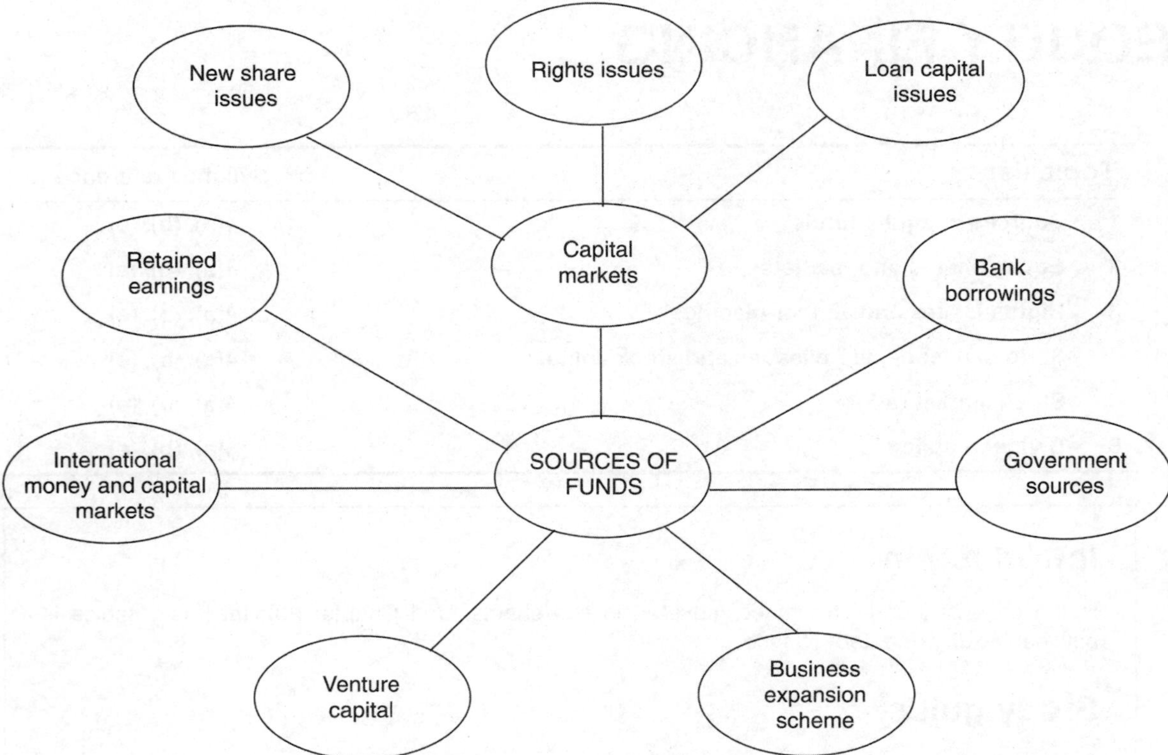

1.2 In practice retained earnings will be the most important source of funds. Simply retaining profits offers an important simple low-cost source of finance, although this method may not provide enough funds, for example if the firm is seeking to grow.

2 EQUITY SHARES AND MARKETS

Ordinary (equity) shares

2.1 **Ordinary shares** are issued to the owners of a company. The ordinary shares of UK companies have a nominal or 'face' value, typically £1 or 50p, but shares with a nominal value of 1p, 2p or 25p are not uncommon.

2.2 You should understand that the **market value** of a quoted company's shares bears **no relationship** to their nominal value, except that when ordinary shares are issued for cash, the issue price must be equal to or (more usually) more than the nominal value of the shares. Outside the UK it is not uncommon for a company's shares to have no nominal value.

2.3 **Deferred ordinary (equity) shares** are a form of ordinary shares, which are entitled to a dividend only after a certain date or only if profits rise above a certain amount. Voting rights might also differ from those attached to other ordinary shares.

2.4 A new issue of shares might be made in a variety of different circumstances.

(a) The company might want to raise more cash, for example for expansion of its operations. If, for example, a company with 200,000 ordinary shares in issue decides to issue 50,000 new shares to raise cash, should it offer the **new shares** to **existing shareholders**, or should it **sell them** to **new shareholders** instead?

(i) If a company sells the new shares to existing shareholders in proportion to their existing shareholding in the company, we have a **rights issue**.

(ii) If the **number of new shares** is **small** compared to the number of shares already in issue, it might be decided instead to sell them to **new shareholders**, since ownership of the company would only be minimally affected.

(b) The company might want to issue new shares partly to raise cash but more importantly to **'float' its shares** on a stock market. When a UK company is floated, it must make available a **minimum proportion** of its shares to the general investing public.

(c) The company might issue **new shares** to the shareholders of another company, in order to take it over.

2.5 A public company that wishes to obtain additional equity funds may do so either on:

(a) The **Alternative Investment Market**, or

(b) **Recognised Investment Exchanges** which provide **full listings.** The most important of these is the London **Stock Exchange.**

Reason for seeking a stock market listing

2.6 The following are reasons why a company may seek a stock market listing.

(a) **Access to a wider pool of finance**

A stock market listing widens the number of potential investors. It may also improve the company's credit rating, making debt finance easier and cheaper to obtain.

(b) **Improved marketability of shares**

Shares that are traded on the stock market can be bought and sold in relatively small quantities at any time. Existing investors can easily realise a part of their holding.

(c) **Transfer of capital to other uses**

Founder owners may wish to liquidate the major part of their holding either for personal reasons or for investment in other new business opportunities.

(d) **Enhancement of the company image**

Quoted companies are commonly believed to be more financially stable. Listing may improve the image of the company with its customers and suppliers, allowing it to gain additional business and to improve its buying power.

(e) **Facilitation of growth by acquisition**

A listed company is in a better position to make a paper offer for a target company than an unlisted one.

2.7 However, the owners of a private company which becomes a listed 'plc' (public company) must accept that the change is likely to involve a significant **loss of control** to a wider circle of investors. The **risk** of the company being **taken over** will also **increase** following listing.

2.8 In order to issue shares on a recognised investment exchange, a company has to obtain:

- Admission to listing from the Financial Services Authority
- Admission to trading from the recognised investment exchange

Issues of shares

2.9 Shares can be issued on the London Stock Exchange by means of an **offer for sale**, a **prospectus issue**, a **placing** or an **introduction.** Of these an offer for sale or a placing are the most common.

Offers for sale

2.10 An **offer for sale** is a means of selling the shares of a company to the public at large.

(a) When companies 'go public' for the first time, a **large issue** will probably take the form of an offer for sale. A smaller issue is more likely to be a placing, since the amount to be raised can be obtained more cheaply if the issuing house or other sponsoring firm approaches selected institutional investors privately.

(b) A new issue by an already quoted company is likely to be a placing or a rights issue, which are described later.

The issue price and offers for sale

2.11 The offer price must be advertised a short time in advance, so it is fixed **without certain knowledge** of the condition of the market at the time applications are invited. To ensure the success of an issue, share prices are often set at a low level. An issuing house normally tries to ensure that a share price rises to a premium above its issue price soon after trading begins. A target premium of 20% above the issue price would be fairly typical.

2.12 Companies will be keen to avoid over-pricing an issue, so that the issue is **undersubscribed,** leaving underwriters with the unwelcome task of having to buy up the unsold shares. On the other hand, if the issue price is too low then the issue will be **oversubscribed** and the company would have been able to raise the required capital by issuing fewer shares.

2.13 The share price of an issue is usually advertised as being based on a certain **P/E ratio,** the ratio of the price to the company's most recent earnings per share figure in its audited accounts. The issue's P/E ratio can then be compared by investors with the P/E ratios of similar quoted companies.

Offers for sale by tender

2.14 One way of trying to ensure that the issue price reflects the value of the shares as perceived by the market is to make an **offer for sale by tender.** A **minimum price** will be fixed and subscribers will be invited to tender for shares at prices equal to or above the minimum. The shares will be **allotted at the highest price** at which they will **all be taken up**. This is known as the **striking price**.

2.15 Offers by tender are less common than offers for sale for the following reasons.

(a) The decision to make an **offer by tender reflects** badly on the **issuing house's ability** to determine the issue price.

(b) The use of tenders may leave the **determination of prices** to the **public** rather than the City 'experts'. However, in practice the major influence on the striking price will be the tenders of the institutional investors.

(c) An offer for sale is **more certain** in the amount of finance that will be raised.

(d) Some potential investors may be deterred from applying for shares as they do **not wish** to **have to decide** on a price.

2.16 An increase in the use of offers for sale by tender might follow a **general increase** in **share values**. The striking price in an offer for sale by tender is likely to be higher than the issue price set by the issuing company itself, since the issue price would have to be sufficiently low to make reasonably certain that the issue would be fully subscribed by investors.

2.17 EXAMPLE: OFFER FOR SALE BY TENDER

Byte Henderson plc is a new company that is making its first public issue of shares. It has decided to make the issue by means of an offer for sale by tender. The intention is to issue up to 4,000,000 shares (the full amount of authorised share capital) at a minimum price of 300 pence. The money raised, net of issue costs of £1,000,000, would be invested in projects which would earn benefits with a present value equal to 130% of the net amount invested.

The following tenders have been received. (Each applicant has made only one offer.)

Price tendered per share	*Number of shares applied for at this price*
£	
6.00	50,000
5.50	100,000
5.00	300,000
4.50	450,000
4.00	1,100,000
3.50	1,500,000
3.00	2,500,000

(a) How many shares would be issued, and how much in total would be raised, if Byte Henderson plc chooses:

(i) To maximise the total amount raised?

(ii) To issue exactly 4,000,000 shares?

(b) Harvey Goldfinger, a private investor, has applied for 12,000 shares at a price of £5.50 and has sent a cheque for £66,000 to the issuing house that is handling the issue. In both cases (a)(i) and (ii), how many shares would be issued to Mr Goldfinger, assuming that any partial acceptance of offers would mean allotting shares to each accepted applicant in proportion to the number of shares applied for? How much will Mr Goldfinger receive back out of the £66,000 he has paid?

(c) Estimate the likely market value of shares in the company after the issue, assuming that the market price fully reflects the investment information given above and that exactly 4,000,000 shares are issued.

2.18 SOLUTION

(a) We begin by looking at the cumulative tenders.

Price	*Cumulative number of shares applied for*	*Amount raised if price is selected, before deducting issue costs*
£		£
6.00	50,000	300,000
5.50	150,000	825,000
5.00	450,000	2,250,000
4.50	900,000	4,050,000
4.00	2,000,000	8,000,000
3.50	3,500,000	12,250,000
3.00	6,000,000	12,000,000

(i) To maximise the total amount raised, the issue price should be £3.50. The total raised before deducting issue costs would be £12,250,000.

(ii) To issue exactly 4,000,000 shares, the issue price must be £3.00. The total raised would be £12,000,000, before deducting issue costs.

(b) (i) Harvey Goldfinger would be allotted 12,000 shares at £3.50 per share. He would receive a refund of 12,000 × £2 = £24,000 out of the £66,000 he has paid.

(ii) If 4,000,000 shares are issued, applicants would receive two thirds of the shares they tendered for. Harvey Goldfinger would be allotted 8,000 shares at £3 per share and would receive a refund of £42,000 out of the £66,000 he has paid.

(c) The net amount raised would be £12,000,000 minus issue costs of £1,000,000, £11,000,000.

The present value of the benefits from investment would be 130% of £11,000,000, £14,300,000. If the market price reflects this information, the price per share would rise to $\frac{£14{,}300{,}000}{4{,}000{,}000}$ = £3.575 per share.

A placing

2.19 A **placing** is an arrangement whereby the shares are not all offered to the public. Instead, the sponsoring market maker arranges for most of the issue to be bought by a **small number of investors**, usually institutional investors such as pension funds and insurance companies.

The choice between an offer for sale and a placing

2.20 When a company is planning a flotation on to the AIM, or a full Stock Exchange listing, is it likely to prefer an offer for sale of its shares, or a placing? **Placings are much cheaper**, although most of the shares will be placed with a relatively small number of (institutional) shareholders, which means that most of the shares are unlikely to be available for trading after the flotation. This is a particular problem for smaller companies.

A prospectus issue

2.21 In a **prospectus issue**, or public issue, a company offers its **own shares** to the general public. An issuing house or merchant bank may act as an agent, but not as an underwriter. This type of issue is therefore risky, and is rare. Well known companies making a large new issue may use this method, and the company would almost certainly already have a quotation on the Stock Exchange.

A Stock Exchange introduction

2.22 By this method of obtaining a quotation, no shares are made available to the market, neither existing nor newly created shares; nevertheless, the Stock Exchange grants a quotation. This will only happen where shares in a large company are already widely held, so that a market can be seen to exist. A company might want an **introduction** to obtain:

- Greater marketability for the shares
- A known share valuation for inheritance tax purposes
- Easier access in the future to additional capital

Underwriting

2.23 A company about to issue new securities in order to raise finance might decide to have the issue underwritten. **Underwriters** are financial institutions which agree (in exchange for a fixed fee, perhaps 2% of the finance to be raised) to **buy** at the **issue price** any securities which are not subscribed for by the investing public.

2.24 Underwriters **remove the** risk of a share issue's being **under-subscribed,** but at a cost to the company issuing the shares. It is not compulsory to have an issue underwritten.

2.25 As an alternative to underwriting an issue, a company could choose to issue its share at a **deep discount**, that is, at a price well below the current market price, to ensure the success of the issue. A major disadvantage of issuing shares at a deep discount is that, the total amount required for dividends in future years will be that **much higher**, since more shares would have to be issued at the low price to raise the amount of finance required.

2.26 Because of the costs of underwriting, many companies now use a '**bought deal**', whereby an investment bank buys the whole of a new issue at a small discount to the market.

Pricing shares for a stock market launch

2.27 The following factors will be taken into account.

(a) Are there **similar companies already quoted**, whose P/E ratios can be used for comparison? The chosen P/E ratio can be multiplied by the company's most recent EPS, as shown in the prospectus, to arrive at a draft share price. This price can be negotiated with the company's current owners.

A company which is coming to the AIM will obtain a lower P/E ratio than a similar company on the main market.

(b) What are **current market conditions**?

(c) With what **accuracy** can the company's **future trading prospects** be forecast?

(d) Companies normally set a price which gives an **immediate premium** when the launch takes place. A sponsor will usually try to ensure that the market price rises to a premium of about 20% over the launch price on the day that the launch takes place.

(e) A **steady growth** in the share price year by year should be achievable.

The timing and costs of new equity issues

2.28 New equity issues in general will be more common when share prices are high than when share prices are low.

(a) When **share price are high,** investors' confidence will probably be high, and investors will be more willing to put money into companies with the potential for growth.

(b) By issuing shares at a high price, a company will **reduce** the **number of shares** it **needs** to issue to raise the amount of capital it wants. This will **reduce** the **dilution of earnings** for existing shareholders.

(c) Following on from (b), the company's **total dividend commitment** on the new shares, to meet shareholders' expectations, will be **lower**.

(d) If **share prices are low, business confidence** is likely to be **low** too. Companies may not want to raise capital for new investments until expectations begin to improve.

2.29 Typical **costs** of a share issue include:

- Underwriting costs
- The Stock Exchange listing fee (the initial charge) for the new securities

- Fees of the issuing house, solicitors, auditors, and public relations consultants
- Charges for printing and distributing the prospectus
- Advertising, which must be done in national newspapers

3 RIGHTS ISSUES AND VENDOR PLACINGS

KEY TERM

A **rights issue** is an offer to existing shareholders enabling them to buy more shares, usually at a price lower than the current market price.

3.1 Existing shareholders have **pre-emption rights** when new shares are issued. So that existing shareholders' rights are not diluted by the issue of new shares, section 89 of Companies Act 1985 requires that before any equity shares are allotted for cash they must first be offered to existing shareholders.

3.2 A **rights issue** provides a way of raising new share capital by means of an offer to existing shareholders, inviting them to subscribe cash for new shares in proportion to their existing holdings.

3.3 For example, a rights issue on a one for four basis at 280p per share would mean that a company is inviting its existing shareholders to subscribe for one new share for every four shares they hold, at a price of 280p per new share. A rights issue may be made by any type of company. The analysis below, however, applies primarily to listed companies.

3.4 The major advantages of a rights issue are as follows.

(a) Rights issues are **cheaper** than **offers for sale** to the general public. This is partly because **no prospectus** is not normally required, partly because the administration is simpler and partly because the cost of underwriting will be less.

(b) Rights issues are **more beneficial** to **existing shareholders** than issues to the general public. New shares are issued at a discount to the current market price, to make them attractive to investors. A rights issue **secures** the **discount** on the market price for existing shareholders, who may either keep the shares or sell them if they wish.

(c) **Relative voting** rights are **unaffected** if shareholders all take up their rights.

(d) The finance raised may be used to **reduce gearing** in book value terms by increasing share capital and/or to pay off long-term debt which will reduce gearing in market value terms.

Deciding the issue price for a rights issue

3.5 The **offer price** in a rights issue will be lower than the current market price of existing shares. The size of the discount will vary, and will be larger for difficult issues. The offer price must however be at or above the **nominal value** of the shares, so as not to contravene company law.

3.6 A company making a rights issue must set a price which is **low enough** to **secure** the **acceptance** of shareholders, who are being asked to provide extra funds, but not too low, so as to avoid excessive dilution of the earnings per share.

Exam focus point

A question could ask for discussion on the effect of a rights issue, as well as calculations, eg of the effect on EPS.

3.7 EXAMPLE: RIGHTS ISSUE (1)

Seagull plc can achieve a profit after tax of 20% on the capital employed. At present its capital structure is as follows.

	£
200,000 ordinary shares of £1 each	200,000
Retained earnings	100,000
	300,000

The directors propose to raise an additional £126,000 from a rights issue. The current market price is £1.80.

Required

(a) Calculate the number of shares that must be issued if the rights price is: £1.60; £1.50; £1.40; £1.20.

(b) Calculate the dilution in earnings per share in each case.

3.8 SOLUTION

The earnings at present are 20% of £300,000 = £60,000. This gives earnings per share of 30p. The earnings after the rights issue will be 20% of £426,000 = £85,200.

Rights price	*No of new share (£126,000 ÷ rights price)*	*EPS (£85,200 ÷ total no of shares)*	*Dilution*
£		Pence	Pence
1.60	78,750	30.6	+ 0.6
1.50	84,000	30.0	–
1.40	90,000	29.4	– 0.6
1.20	105,000	27.9	– 2.1

3.9 Note that at a high rights price the earnings per share are increased, not diluted. The breakeven point (zero dilution) occurs when the rights price is equal to the capital employed per share: £300,000 ÷ 200,000 = £1.50.

The market price of shares after a rights issue: the theoretical ex rights price

3.10 When a rights issue is announced, all existing shareholders have the right to subscribe for new shares, and so there are rights attached to the existing shares. The shares are therefore described as being '**cum rights**' (with rights attached) and are traded cum rights. On the first day of dealings in the newly issued shares, the rights no longer exist and the old shares are now '**ex rights**' (without rights attached).

3.11 After the announcement of a rights issue, share prices normally **fall**. The extent and duration of the fall may depend on the number of shareholders and the size of their holdings. This temporary fall is due to **uncertainty** in the market about the consequences of the issue, with respect to future profits, earnings and dividends.

3.12 After the issue has actually been made, the market price per share will normally fall, because there are more shares in issue and the new shares were issued at a discount price.

3.13 In theory, the new market price will be the consequence of an adjustment to allow for the discount price of the new issue, and a theoretical ex rights price can be calculated.

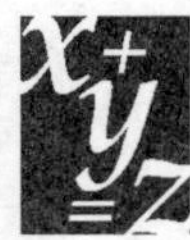

FORMULA TO LEARN

Theoretical ex-rights price $= \frac{1}{N+1}((N \times \text{cum rights price}) + \text{issue price})$

where N = number of shares required to buy one new share.

3.14 EXAMPLE: RIGHTS ISSUE (2)

Fundraiser plc has 1,000,000 ordinary shares of £1 in issue, which have a market price on 1 September of £2.10 per share. The company decides to make a rights issue, and offers its shareholders the right to subscribe for one new share at £1.50 each for every four shares already held. After the announcement of the issue, the share price fell to £1.95, but by the time just prior to the issue being made, it had recovered to £2 per share. This market value just before the issue is known as the cum rights price. What is the theoretical ex rights price?

3.15 SOLUTION

The theoretical ex rights price $= \frac{1}{4+1}((4 \times £2) + £1.50) = \frac{£9.50}{5} = £1.90$

The value of rights

3.16 The value of rights is the theoretical gain a shareholder would make by exercising his rights.

(a) Using the above example, if the price offered in the rights issue is £1.50 per share, and the market price after the issue is expected to be £1.90, the value attaching to a right is £1.90 – £1.50 = £0.40. A shareholder would therefore be expected to gain 40 pence for each new share he buys.

If he does not have enough money to buy the share himself, he could sell the right to subscribe for a new share to another investor, and receive 40 pence from the sale. This other investor would then buy the new share for £1.50, so that his total outlay to acquire the share would be £0.40 + £1.50 = £1.90, the theoretical ex rights price.

(b) The value of rights attaching to existing shares is calculated in the same way. If the value of rights on a new share is 40 pence, and there is a one for four rights issue, the value of the rights attaching to each existing share is 40 ÷ 4 = 10 pence.

The theoretical gain or loss to shareholders

3.17 The possible courses of action open to shareholders are:

(a) To **'take up' or 'exercise' the rights**, that is, to buy the new shares at the rights price. Shareholders who do this will maintain their percentage holdings in the company by subscribing for the new shares.

(b) To **'renounce' the rights** and sell them on the market. Shareholders who do this will have lower percentage holdings of the company's equity after the issue than before the issue, and the total value of their shares will be less.

(c) To **renounce part of the rights and take up the remainder**. For example, a shareholder may sell enough of his rights to enable him to buy the remaining rights shares he is entitled to with the sale proceeds, and so keep the total market value of his shareholding in the company unchanged.

(d) To **do nothing**. Shareholders may be protected from the consequences of their inaction because rights not taken up are sold on a shareholder's behalf by the company. The Stock Exchange rules state that if new securities are not taken up, they should be sold by the company to new subscribers for the benefit of the shareholders who were entitled to the rights.

Question 1

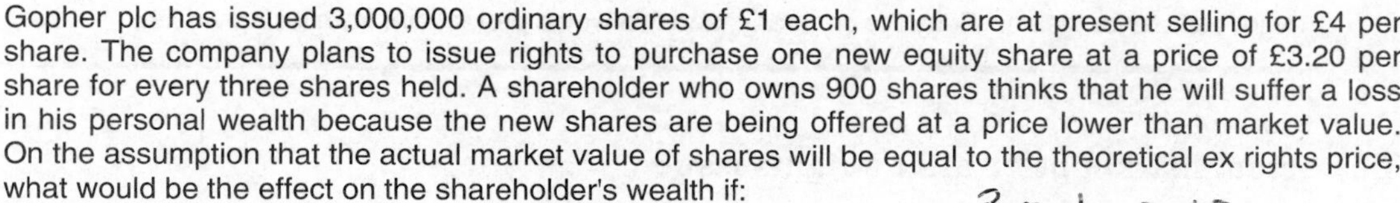

Gopher plc has issued 3,000,000 ordinary shares of £1 each, which are at present selling for £4 per share. The company plans to issue rights to purchase one new equity share at a price of £3.20 per share for every three shares held. A shareholder who owns 900 shares thinks that he will suffer a loss in his personal wealth because the new shares are being offered at a price lower than market value. On the assumption that the actual market value of shares will be equal to the theoretical ex rights price, what would be the effect on the shareholder's wealth if:

(a) He sells all the rights
(b) He exercises half of the rights and sells the other half
(c) He does nothing at all?

Answer

The theoretical ex rights price $= \frac{1}{3+1}((3 \times 4) + 3.20)$

$= £3.80$

	£
Theoretical ex rights price	3.80
Price per new share	3.20
Value of rights per new share	0.60

The value of the rights attached to each existing share is $\frac{£0.60}{3} = £0.20$.

We will assume that a shareholder is able to sell his rights for £0.20 per existing share held.

(a) If the shareholder sells all his rights:

	£
Sale value of rights (900 × £0.20)	180
Market value of his 900 shares, ex rights × £3.80)	3,420
Total wealth	3,600
Total value of 900 shares cum rights (× £4)	£3,600

The shareholder would neither gain nor lose wealth. He would not be required to provide any additional funds to the company, but his shareholding as a proportion of the total equity of the company will be lower.

(b) If the shareholder exercises half of the rights (buys 450/3 = 150 shares at £3.20) and sells the other half:

	£
Sale value of rights (450 × £0.20)	90
Market value of his 1,050 shares, ex rights (× £3.80)	3,990
	4,080
Total value of 900 shares cum rights (× £4)	3,600
Additional investment (150 × £3.20)	480
	4,080

The shareholder would neither gain nor lose wealth, although he will have increased his investment in the company by £480.

(c) If the shareholder does nothing, but all other shareholders either exercise their rights or sell them, he would lose wealth as follows.

	£
Market value of 900 shares cum rights (× £4)	3,600
Market value of 900 shares ex rights (× £3.80)	3,420
Loss in wealth	180

It follows that the shareholder, to protect his existing investment, should either exercise his rights or sell them to another investor. If he does not exercise his rights, the new securities he was entitled to subscribe for might be sold for his benefit by the company, and this would protect him from losing wealth.

The actual market price after a rights issue

3.18 The actual market price of a share after a rights issue may differ from the theoretical ex rights price. This will occur when:

Expected yield from new funds raised ≠ Earnings yield from existing funds

3.19 The market will take a view of how profitably the new funds will be invested, and will value the shares accordingly. An example will illustrate this point.

3.20 EXAMPLE: RIGHTS ISSUE (3)

Musk plc currently has 4,000,000 ordinary shares in issue, valued at £2 each, and the company has annual earnings equal to 20% of the market value of the shares. A one for four rights issue is proposed, at an issue price of £1.50. If the market continues to value the shares on a price/earnings ratio of 5, what would be the value per share if the new funds are expected to earn, as a percentage of the money raised:

(a) 15%?
(b) 20%?
(c) 25%?

How do these values in (a), (b) and (c) compare with the theoretical ex rights price? Ignore issue costs.

3.21 SOLUTION

The theoretical ex rights price will be calculated first.

	£
Four shares have a current value (× £2) of	8.00
One new share will be issued for	1.50
Five shares would have a theoretical value of	9.50

$$\text{Theoretical ex rights price} = \frac{1}{4+1}((4 \times 2) + 1.50)$$

$$= £1.90$$

3.22 The new funds will raise 1,000,000 × £1.50 = £1,500,000.

Earnings as a % of Money raised	*Additional earnings*	*Current earnings*	*Total earnings after the issue*
	£	£	£
15%	225,000	1,600,000	1,825,000
20%	300,000	1,600,000	1,900,000
25%	375,000	1,600,000	1,975,000

3.23 If the market values shares on a P/E ratio of 5, the total market value of equity and the market price per share would be as follows.

Total earnings	*Market value*	*Price per share (5,000,000 shares)*
£	£	£
1,825,000	9,125,000	1.825
1,900,000	9,500,000	1.900
1,975,000	9,875,000	1.975

3.24 (a) If the additional funds raised are expected to generate earnings at the **same rate** as existing funds, the **actual market value** will probably be the **same** as the theoretical ex rights price.

(b) If the new funds are expected to generate earnings at a **lower rate**, the **market value** will **fall** below the theoretical ex rights price. If this happens, **shareholders** will **lose**.

(c) If the new funds are expected to earn at a **higher rate** than current funds, the **market value** should **rise** above the theoretical ex rights price. If this happens, shareholders will profit by taking up their rights.

3.25 The decision by individual shareholders as to whether they take up the offer will therefore depend on:

- The **expected rate of return** on the investment (and the risk associated with it)
- The **return obtainable from other investments** (allowing for the associated risk)

Rights issues or issuing shares for cash to new investors?

3.26 When shares are issued for cash to outside buyers, existing shareholders forfeit their **pre-emption rights** to shares. Companies can issue shares for cash without obtaining prior approval from shareholders for each such share issue, provided that they have obtained approval from shareholders within the past 12 months to make new issues of shares for cash which are not rights issues. (This shareholder approval could be obtained at the company's AGM.)

3.27 Companies can thus issue shares for cash without having to bear the high costs of a rights issue, for example by placing shares for cash at a higher price than they might have been able to obtain from a rights issue.

Vendor placings

3.28 A vendor placing occurs when there is an issue of shares by one company to take over another. The shares are then sold in a placing to raise cash to pay to the shareholders in the target company, who are selling their shares in the takeover.

Other instances of issuing shares

3.29 There are some other methods of issuing shares on the Stock Exchange. These are as follows.

(a) **Open offer**

This is an offer to existing shareholders to subscribe for new shares in the company but, unlike a rights issue:

(i) The offer is **not** necessarily **pro rata** to existing shareholdings

(ii) The offer is not allotted on **renounceable documents** (With rights issues the offer to subscribe for new shares must be given on a renounceable letter, so that the shareholder can sell his rights if he so wishes)

(b) **Capitalisation issue**

This is a '**scrip issue**' of shares which does not raise any new funds (see later in this chapter). It is made to 'capitalise' reserves of the company: in effect, to change some reserves into share capital. Shareholders receive new shares **pro rata** to their existing shareholdings.

(c) **Vendor consideration issue**

This is an issue of shares whereby one company acquires the shares of another in a takeover or merger. For example, if A plc wishes to take over B plc, A might make a 'paper' offer to B's shareholders, try to buy the shares of B by offering B's shareholders newly issued shares of A. This is now a common form of share issue, because mergers and takeovers are fairly frequent events.

(d) **Employee share option schemes**

These are schemes for awarding shares to employees. A company awards its employees share options, which are rights to subscribe for new shares at a later date at a **predetermined price** (commonly, the market price of the shares when the options are awarded, or the market price less a discount). When and if the options are eventually exercised, the employees will receive the newly issued shares at a price that ought by then to be below the market price.

4 SCRIP DIVIDENDS, SCRIP ISSUES AND STOCK SPLITS

4.1 Scrip dividends, scrip issues and stock splits are not methods of raising new equity funds, but they

- Alter the share capital structure of a company
- Increasing the issued share capital of the company (scrip dividends and scrip issues)

Scrip dividends

KEY TERM

A **scrip dividend** is a dividend payment which takes the form of new shares instead of cash.

4.2 Effectively, it converts profit and loss reserves into issued share capital. When the directors of a company would prefer to retain funds within the business but consider that they must pay at least a certain amount of dividend, they might offer equity shareholders the choice of a **cash dividend** or a **scrip dividend**. Each shareholder would decide separately which to take.

4.3 Recently **enhanced scrip dividends** have been offered by a number of companies. With enhanced scrip dividends, the value of the shares offered is much greater than the cash alternative, giving investors an incentive to choose the shares.

Scrip issues

KEY TERM

A **scrip issue** (or **bonus issue**) is an issue of new shares to existing shareholders, by converting equity reserves into issued share capital.

4.4 For example, if a company with issued share capital of 100,000 ordinary shares of £1 each made a one for five scrip issue, 20,000 new shares would be issued to existing shareholders, one new share for every five old shares held. Issued share capital would be increased by £20,000, and reserves (probably share premium account, if there is one) reduced by this amount.

4.5 By creating more shares in this way, a scrip issue does not raise new funds, but does have the advantage of making **shares cheaper** and therefore (perhaps) more easily marketable on the Stock Exchange.

Stock splits

4.6 The advantage of a scrip issue mentioned above is also the reason for a **stock split**. A stock split occurs where, for example, each ordinary share of £1 each is split into two shares of 50p each, thus creating cheaper shares with greater marketability. Investors also normally should expect a company which splits its shares in this way to be planning for substantial earnings growth and dividend growth in the future. As a consequence, the market price of shares may benefit.

4.7 The difference between a stock split and a scrip issue is that a scrip issue converts equity reserves into share capital, whereas a stock split leaves reserves unaffected.

5 STOCK MARKET RATIOS

5.1 A company will only be able to raise finance if investors think that the returns they can expect are satisfactory in view of the risks they are taking. We must therefore consider how investors appraise companies. We will concentrate on quoted companies.

5.2 Information that is relevant to market prices and returns is available from published stock market information, and in particular from certain **stock market ratios**.

The dividend yield

KEY TERM

$$\textbf{Dividend yield} = \frac{\text{Gross dividend per share}}{\text{Market price per share}} \times 100\%$$

5.3 The gross dividend is the dividend paid plus the appropriate tax credit. The gross dividend yield is used in preference to a net dividend yield, so that investors can make a direct comparison with (gross) interest yields from loan stock and gilts.

5.4 EXAMPLE: DIVIDEND YIELD

A company pays a dividend of 15p (net) per share. The market price is 240p. What is the dividend yield if the rate of tax credit is 10%?

$$\text{Gross dividend per share} = 15\text{p} \times \frac{100}{(100-10)} = 16.67\text{p}$$

$$\text{Dividend yield} = \frac{16.67\text{p}}{240\text{p}} \times 100\% = 6.95\%$$

Interest yield

KEY TERM

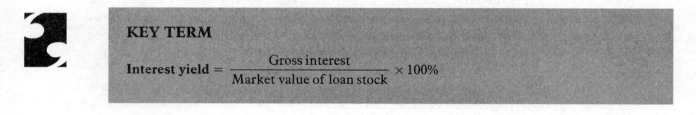

$$\textbf{Interest yield} = \frac{\text{Gross interest}}{\text{Market value of loan stock}} \times 100\%$$

5.5 EXAMPLE: INTEREST YIELD

An investment buys £1,000 (nominal value) of a bond with a coupon of 8% for the current market value of £750.

$$\text{Interest yield} = \frac{1{,}000 \times 8\%}{750} \times 100\% = 10.67\%$$

Exam focus point

The interest yield, which is the investor's rate of return, is different from the coupon rate of 8%. Many students confuse these in their exam answers.

Dividend yield and interest yield

5.6 In practice, the dividend yield on shares of quoted companies is less than the interest yield on debentures and loan stock. The share price often rises each year, giving shareholders capital gains. In the long run, shareholders will want the **return** on their **shares**, in terms of dividends received plus capital gains, to **exceed** the **return** that investors get from **fixed interest securities**.

Earnings per share (EPS)

> **KEY TERM**
>
> **Earnings per share** (is the result of) dividing the net profit or loss for the period attributable to ordinary shareholders with the weighted average number of ordinary shares outstanding during the period. For the purpose of calculating basic earnings per share, the net profit or loss for the period attributable to ordinary shareholders should be the net profit or loss for the period after deducting dividends and other appropriations in respect of non-equity shares. *(Financial Reporting Standard 14, 9 and 10)*

5.7 **Earnings per share (EPS)** is widely used as a measure of a company's performance and is of particular importance in comparing results over a period of several years. A company must be able to sustain its earnings in order to pay dividends and re-invest in the business so as to achieve future growth. Investors also look for **growth** in the EPS from one year to the next.

5.8 EPS on its own does not tell us anything. It must be seen in the context of several other matters.

(a) EPS is used for **comparing results** of a company over time. Is its EPS growing? What is the rate of growth? Is the rate of growth increasing or decreasing?

(b) Is there likely to be a **significant dilution** of EPS in the future, perhaps due to the exercise of share options or warrants, or the conversion of convertible loan stock into equity?

(c) EPS should **not be used blindly** to compare the earnings of one company with another. For example, if A plc has an EPS of 12p for its 10,000,000 10p shares and B plc has an EPS of 24p for its 50,000,000 25p shares, we must take account of the numbers of shares. When earnings are used to compare one company's shares with another, this is done using the P/E ratio or perhaps the earnings yield.

(d) If EPS is to be a reliable basis for comparing results, it must be **calculated consistently**.

Question 2

Walter Wall Carpets plc made profits before tax in 20X8 of £9,320,000. Tax amounted to £2,800,000.

The company's share capital is as follows.

	£
Ordinary shares (10,000,000 shares of £1)	10,000,000
8% preference shares	2,000,000
	12,000,000

Calculate the EPS for 20X8.

Answer

	£
Profits before tax	9,320,000
Less tax	2,800,000
Profits after tax	6,520,000
Less preference dividend (8% of £2,000,000)	160,000
Earnings	6,360,000
Number of ordinary shares	10,000,000
EPS	63.6p

5.9 Note that:

(a) EPS is a figure based on **past data**, and

(b) It is **easily manipulated** by changes in accounting policies and by mergers or acquisitions

5.10 The use of the measure in calculating management bonuses makes it particularly liable to manipulation. The attention given to EPS as a performance measure by City analysts is arguably disproportionate to its true worth. Investors should be more concerned with future earnings, but of course estimates of these are more difficult to reach than the readily available figure.

5.11 A **fully diluted EPS** (FDEPS) can be measured where the company has issued securities that might be converted into ordinary shares at some future date, such as convertible loan stock, share warrants or share options.

KEY TERM

The **fully diluted earnings per share** measures a hypothetical EPS, based on earnings in the period under review, if the company's ordinary shares were increased to their maximum number by the exercise of all existing share options and warrants, and the conversion of existing convertible loan stock etc. The FDEPS gives investors an appreciation of by how much EPS might be affected if and when the options, warrants or conversion rights are exercised.

5.12 Total earnings are increased by:

(a) The **savings in interest** (net of tax) from the conversion of loan stock into shares

(b) In the case of share options or warrants, the **addition to profits** (net of tax) from investing the cash obtained from their exercise (estimated on the assumption that the cash is invested in $2^1/_2$% Consolidated Stock at their market price on the first) day of the period)

5.13 EXAMPLE: FULLY DILUTED EARNING PER SHARE

Suppose that Walter Wall Carpets plc (see Question 2 above) has in issue £4,000,000 8% convertible unsecured loan stock, convertible in three years' time, with a conversion ratio of 5 shares per £100 of loan stock. The company pays tax at 30%. What is the fully diluted EPS?

5.14 SOLUTION

Undiluted EPS is 63.6 pence, as shown in Question 2.

If all holders of the convertible stock convert their holding to ordinary shares, an additional 200,000 (= 4,000,000/100 × 5) shares will be issued in three years' time.

The interest saving on conversion is:

£4,000,000 × 8% × 0.70 = £224,000.

Therefore:

$$\text{FDEPS} = \frac{6{,}360{,}000 + 224{,}000}{10{,}000{,}000 + 200{,}000} = \frac{6{,}584{,}000}{10{,}200{,}000} = 64.5 \text{ pence}$$

The price earnings ratio

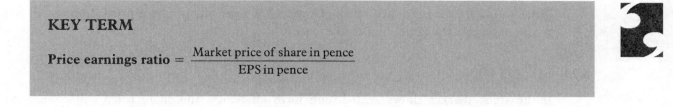

> **KEY TERM**
>
> **Price earnings ratio** = $\frac{\text{Market price of share in pence}}{\text{EPS in pence}}$

5.15 The **price earnings (P/E) ratio** is the most important yardstick for assessing the relative worth of a share.

This is the same as:

$$\frac{\text{Total market value of equity}}{\text{Total earnings}}$$

5.16 The **value of the P/E ratio** reflects the **market's appraisal** of the share's **future prospects**. It is an important ratio because it relates two key considerations for investors, the market price of a share and its earnings capacity.

5.17 EXAMPLE: PRICE EARNINGS RATIO

A company has recently declared a dividend of 12p per share. The share price is £3.72 cum div and earnings for the most recent year were 30p per share. Calculate the P/E ratio.

5.18 SOLUTION

$$\text{P/E ratio} = \frac{\text{MV ex div}}{\text{EPS}} = \frac{£3.60}{30\text{p}} = 12$$

Changes in EPS: the P/E ratio and the share price

5.19 The **dividend valuation** model or fundamental theory of share values is the theory that **share prices are related** to **expected future dividends** on the shares.

5.20 Another approach to assessing what share prices ought to be, which is often used in practice, is a P/E ratio approach.

(a) The relationship between the **EPS** and the **share price** is measured by the **P/E ratio**

(b) The **P/E ratio** does **not vary much** over time

(c) So if the **EPS goes up** or **down**, the **share price** should be expected to **move up or down** too, and the new share price will be the new EPS multiplied by the constant P/E ratio

5.21 For example, if a company had an EPS last year of 30p and a share price of £3.60, its P/E ratio would have been 12. If the current year's EPS is 33p, we might expect that the P/E ratio would remain the same, 12, and so the share price ought to go up to 12 × 33p = £3.96.

5.22 EXAMPLE: EFFECTS OF A RIGHTS ISSUE

Annette Cord Sports Goods plc has 6,000,000 ordinary shares in issue, and the company has been making regular annual profits after tax of £3,000,000 for some years. The share price is £5. A proposal has been made to issue 2,000,000 new shares in a rights issue, at an issue

price of £4.50 per share. The funds would be used to redeem £9,000,000 of 12% debenture stock. The rate of corporation tax is 30%.

What would be the predicted effect of the rights issue on the share price, and would you recommend that the issue should take place?

5.23 SOLUTION

If the stock market shows semi-strong form efficiency, the share price will change on announcement of the rights issue, in anticipation of the change in EPS. The current EPS is 50p per share, and so the current P/E ratio is 10.

	£	£
Current annual earnings		3,000,000
Increase in earnings after rights issue		
Interest saved (12% × £9,000,000)	1,080,000	
Less tax on extra profits (30%)	(324,000)	
		756,000
Anticipated annual earnings		3,756,000
Number of shares (6,000,000 + 2,000,000)		8,000,000
EPS		46.95 pence
Current P/E ratio		10

The anticipated P/E ratio is assumed to be the same.

Anticipated share price	469.5 pence

The proposed share issue is a one for three rights issue, and we can estimate the theoretical ex rights price.

$$\text{Theoretical ex rights price} = \frac{1}{3+1}((3 \times 5) + 4.50)$$

$$= £4.875$$

5.24 The anticipated share price after redeeming the debentures would be 469.5 pence per share, which is less than the theoretical ex rights price. If the rights issue goes ahead and the P/E ratio remains at 10, shareholders should expect a fall in share price below the theoretical ex rights price, which indicates that there would be a **capital loss** on their investment. The rights issue is for this reason not recommended.

Changes in the P/E ratio over time

5.25 Changes in the P/E ratios of companies over time will depend on several factors.

(a) If **interest rates go up**, investors will be attracted away from shares and into debt capital. Share prices will fall, and so P/E ratios will fall. Similarly, if interest rates go down, shares will become relatively more attractive to invest in, so share prices and P/E ratios will go up.

(b) If **prospects** for company **profits improve**, share prices will go up, and P/E ratios will rise.

(c) **Investors' confidence** might be **changed by** a variety of circumstances, such as:

- The prospect of a change in government
- The prospects for greater exchange rate stability between currencies

Dividend cover

KEY TERM

Dividend cover =

$$\frac{\text{Maximum possible equity dividend that could be paid out of current profits}}{\text{Actual dividend for ordinary shareholders}}$$

5.26 The **dividend cover** is the number of times the actual dividend could be paid out of current profits.

The figures for the maximum dividend and the actual dividend may be either **both gross** or **both net**.

5.27 The dividend cover indicates the **proportion** of **distributable profits** for the year that is being **retained** by the company, and the level of risk that the company will not be able to maintain the same dividend payments in future years, should earnings fall. A high dividend cover means that a high proportion of profits are being retained, which might indicate that the company is investing to achieve earnings growth in the future.

Dividend payout ratio

KEY TERM

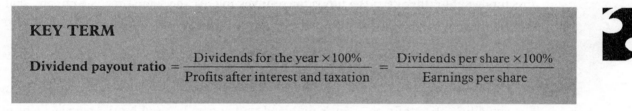

Dividend payout ratio $= \frac{\text{Dividends for the year} \times 100\%}{\text{Profits after interest and taxation}} = \frac{\text{Dividends per share} \times 100\%}{\text{Earnings per share}}$

5.28 The **dividend payout ratio** is closely related to the dividend cover, as it calculates the percentage of post-tax earnings that are distributed as dividends.

5.29 EXAMPLE: DIVIDEND COVER AND DIVIDEND PAYOUT RATIO

The EPS of York plc is 20p. The dividend was 20% on the 25p ordinary shares. Calculate the dividend cover and the dividend payout ratio.

5.30 SOLUTION

$$\text{Dividend cover} = \frac{20\text{p}}{20\% \text{ of } 25\text{p}} = 4$$

A dividend cover of 4 means that the company is retaining 75% of its earnings for reinvestment.

$$\text{Dividend payout ratio} = \frac{20\% \text{ of } 25\text{p}}{20\text{p}} \times 100\% = 25\%$$

6 DIVIDEND POLICY

6.1 For any company, the amount of earnings retained within the business has a direct impact on the amount of dividends. Profit re-invested as retained earnings is profit that could have

been paid as a **dividend**. The major **reasons for using funds from retained earnings** to finance new investments, rather than to pay higher dividends and then raise new equity funds for the new investments, are as follows.

(a) The use of **retained earnings** as a **source of funds** does **not lead** to a **payment** of cash to new providers of finance.

(b) The dividend policy of a company is in practice determined by the directors. From their standpoint, retained earnings are an attractive source of finance because **investment projects** can be undertaken **without involving** either the **shareholders** or any **outsiders**.

(c) The use of retained earnings as opposed to new shares or debentures **avoids issue** costs.

(d) The use of retained earnings **avoids** the possibility of a **change in control** resulting from an issue of new shares.

6.2 Another factor that may be of importance is the **financial and taxation position** of the company's shareholders. If, for example, because of taxation considerations, they would rather make a capital profit (which will only be taxed when the shares are sold) than receive current income, then finance through retained earnings would be preferred to other methods.

6.3 A company must restrict its self-financing through retained profits because shareholders should be paid a **reasonable dividend**, in line with realistic expectations, even if the directors would rather keep the funds for re-investing. At the same time, a company that is looking for extra funds will not be expected by investors (such as banks) to pay generous dividends, nor over-generous salaries to owner-directors.

Signalling effects

6.4 The signalling effect of a company's dividend policy may be used by the management of a company which faces a possible takeover. The dividend level might be increased as a defence against the takeover; investors may take the increased dividend as a signal of improved future prospects, thus **driving** the **share price higher** and making the company more expensive for a potential bidder to take over.

6.5 Investors usually expect a **consistent dividend policy** from the company, with stable dividends each year or, even better, steady dividend growth. Stable dividends or steady dividend growth are usually needed for share price stability. A cut in dividends may be treated by investors as signalling that the future prospects of the company are weak.

Dividends and market values

6.6 What affects the market value of a company's shares? It seems reasonable to suppose that share values will depend upon:

- The **amount in dividends** that a **company pays**
- The **rate of growth** of **dividends**
- The **rate of return** which shareholders require

6.7 The purpose of a company's dividend policy should be to **maximise shareholders' wealth,** which depends on both current dividends and capital gains. Capital gains can be achieved by retaining some earnings for reinvestment and dividend growth in the future.

6.8 The **rate of growth in dividends** is sometimes expressed, theoretically, as:

$$g = bR$$

where g is the annual growth rate in dividends
b is the proportion of profits that are retained
R is the rate of return on new investments

6.9 EXAMPLE: DIVIDEND GROWTH

(a) If a company has a payout ratio of 40%, and retains the rest for investing in projects which yield 15%, the annual rate of growth in dividends could be estimated as 15% × 60% = 9%.

(b) If a company pays out 80% of its profits as dividends, and retains the rest for reinvestment at 15%, the current dividend would be twice as big as in (a), but annual dividend growth would be only 15% × 20% = 3%.

An approach to dividend and retentions policy

6.10 A well established theory of share values is that an equilibrium price for any share (or bond) on a stock market is:

- The **future expected stream of income** from the security
- **Discounted** at a suitable **cost of capital**

Equilibrium market price is thus a **present value** of a **future expected income stream**. The annual income stream for a share is the expected dividend every year in perpetuity.

6.11 The basic dividend-based formula for the market value of shares is expressed in the **dividend valuation model** as follows:

$$\text{MV (ex div)} = \frac{D}{1+r} + \frac{D}{(1+r)^2} + \frac{D}{(1+r)^3} + ... = \frac{D}{r}$$

where MV = ex dividend market value of the shares
D = constant annual dividend
r = shareholders' required rate of return

6.12 Using the **dividend growth model,** we have:

$$P_0 = \frac{D_0(1+g)}{(1+r)} + \frac{D_0(1+g)^2}{(1+r)} + ... = \frac{D_0(1+g)}{(r-g)}$$

where D_0 = Current year's dividend
g = Growth rate in earnings and dividends
$D_0(1+g)$ = Expected dividend in one year's time
P_0 = Market value excluding any dividend currently payable

6.13 EXAMPLE: DIVIDEND GROWTH MODEL

Tantrum plc has achieved earnings of £800,000 this year. The company intends to pursue a policy of financing all its investment opportunities out of retained earnings. There are considerable investment opportunities, which are expected to be available indefinitely. However, if Tantrum plc does not exploit any of the available opportunities, its annual earnings will remain at £800,000 in perpetuity. The following figures are available.

Proportion of earnings retained	*Growth rate in Earnings*	*Required return on all investments by shareholders*
%	%	%
0	0	14
25	5	15
40	7	16

The rate of return required by shareholders would rise if earnings are retained, because of the risk associated with the new investments. What is the optimum retentions policy for Tantrum plc? The full dividend payment for this year will be paid in the near future in any case.

6.14 SOLUTION

Since P_0 (MV ex div) $= \dfrac{D(1+g)}{(r-g)}$

MV cum div $= \dfrac{D(1+g)}{(r-g)} + D$

We are trying to maximise the value of shareholder wealth, which is currently represented by the cum div market value, since a dividend will soon be paid.

(a) If retentions are 0%:

MV cum div $= \dfrac{800{,}000}{0.14} + 800{,}000 = £6{,}514{,}286$

(b) If retentions are 25%, the current dividend will be £600,000 and:

MV cum div $= \dfrac{600{,}000(1.05)}{(0.15-0.05)} + 600{,}000 = £6{,}900{,}000$

(c) If retentions are 40%, the current dividend will be £480,000 and:

MV cum div $= \dfrac{480{,}000(1.07)}{(0.16-0.07)} + 480{,}000 = £6{,}186{,}667$

The best policy (out of the three for which figures are provided) would be to retain 25% of earnings.

6.15 The dividend models are underpinned by a number of assumptions that you should bear in mind.

(a) Investors act **rationally**.

(b) The **estimates** of future dividends and prices used are **reasonable.**

(c) Investors' attitudes to receiving different cash flows at different times can be modelled using **discounted cashflow arithmetic**.

(d) Directors use dividends to **signal** the strength of the company's position (however companies that pay zero dividends do not have zero share values).

(e) Dividends either show **no growth** or **constant growth.**

(f) **Other influences** on share prices are **ignored.**

(g) The company's **earnings** will **increase** sufficiently to maintain dividend growth levels.

(h) The **discount rate** used **exceeds** the **dividend growth rate.**

Dividend policy and shareholders' personal taxation

6.16 The market value of a share has been defined as the sum of all future dividends, discounted at the shareholder's marginal cost of capital. When constant dividends are expected, we have:

$$P_0 = \frac{D}{r}$$

6.17 The cost of capital is generally taken to be a tax-free rate, ignoring the actual rates of personal taxation paid on dividends by different shareholders. To each individual shareholder, however, the dividends are subject to income tax at a rate which depends on his own tax position, and it is possible to re-define his valuation of a share as:

$$P_0 = \frac{D_g(1-t)}{r_t}$$

where D_g = gross dividend (assumed to be constant each year)
t = rate of personal tax on the dividend
r_t = the shareholder's after tax marginal cost of capital

6.18 Presumably, a company should choose between **dividend payout** and **earnings retention** so as to maximise the wealth of its shareholders. However, if not all shareholders have the same tax rates and after tax cost of capital, there might **not** be an **optimum policy** which satisfies all shareholders.

6.19 A further problem occurs when **income from dividends** might be **taxed** either **more or less** heavily than **capital gains**. In the UK, individuals have an annual capital gains exemption which is not available against income, and companies are taxed on capital gains but not on dividend income.

Practical aspects of dividend policy

6.20 So far, we have concentrated on a theoretical approach to establishing an optimal dividend and retentions policy. A practical approach to dividends and retentions should take the following extra factors into consideration.

(a) The need to **remain profitable**. Dividends are paid out of profits, and an unprofitable company cannot for ever go on paying dividends out of retained profits made in the past.

(b) The **law on distributable** profits imposes restrictions.

(c) **Dividend restraints** might be imposed by loan agreements.

(d) The effect of inflation, and the need to retain some profit within the business just to maintain its operating capability unchanged.

(e) The company's **gearing level**. If the company wants extra finance, the sources of funds used should strike a balance between equity and debt finance. Cash from retained earnings is the most readily available source of growth in equity finance.

(f) The company's **liquidity position**. Dividends are a cash payment, and a company must have enough cash to pay the dividends it declares.

(g) Investors usually expect a **consistent dividend policy** from the company, with stable dividends each year or, even better, steady dividend growth.

(h) A large rise or fall in dividends in any year will have a marked effect on the **company's share price**. Stable dividends or steady dividend growth are usually needed for share price stability.

(i) The ease with which the company **could raise extra finance** from sources other than cash from retained earnings. Small companies which find it hard to raise finance might have to rely more heavily on cash generated from retained earnings than large companies.

(j) If a company wants extra finance to invest, cash might be generated through **retention of earnings** can be obtained without incurring transaction costs. Costs of raising new share capital can be high, and even bank borrowings can be quite expensive.

6.21 In practical terms, it is unclear how far dividends play a predominant role in determining share values. At some times, dividends seem to be more important to the market, while at other times, earning figures seem to become predominant.

Question 3

Ochre plc is a company that is still managed by the two individuals who set it up 12 years ago. In the current year, the company acquired plc status and was launched on the Alternative Investment Market (AIM). Previously, all of the shares had been owned by its two founders and certain employees. Now, 40% of the shares are in the hands of the investing public. The company's profit growth and dividend policy are set out below. Will a continuation of the same dividend policy as in the past be suitable now that the company is quoted on the AIM?

	Profits £'000	*Dividend* £'000	*Shares in issue*
4 years ago	176	88	800,000
3 years ago	200	104	800,000
2 years ago	240	120	1,000,000
1 year ago	290	150	1,000,000
Current year	444	222 (proposed)	1,500,000

Answer

	Dividend per share p	*Dividend as % of profit*
4 years ago	11.0	50%
3 years ago	13.0	52%
2 years ago	12.0	50%
1 year ago	15.0	52%
Current year	14.8	50%

The company appears to have pursued a dividend policy of paying out half of after-tax profits in dividend.

This policy is only suitable when a company achieves a stable EPS or steady EPS growth. Investors do not like a fall in dividend from one year to the next, and the fall in dividend per share in the current year is likely to be unpopular, and to result in a fall in the share price.

The company would probably serve its shareholders better by paying a dividend of at least 15p per share, possibly more, in the current year, even though the dividend as a percentage of profit would then be higher.

Exam focus point

Take care not to write in the exam that new investment can be financed by reserves or retained earnings. It is the **cash generated** from retention of earnings which can be used for financing purposes.

Chapter roundup

- A company can obtain a **stock market listing** for its shares through an offer for sale, a prospectus issue, a placing or an introduction.
- A **rights issue** is an offer to existing shareholders for them to buy more shares, usually at lower than the current share price.
- **Scrip dividend schemes** involve shareholders being issued with new shares in lieu of a cash dividend.
- **Bonus** or **scrip issues**, and **stock splits**, are ways of increasing the *number* of shares without raising any extra capital.
- Indicator such as **dividend yield**, **EPS**, **PE ratio** and **dividend cover** can be used to assess investor returns.
- The **dividend valuation model** can be applied with or without dividend growth. The model assumes that a stock market value depends upon the future flow of dividends which can be expected.
- Practical considerations of **dividend policy** suggest that both **dividends** and **earnings** may be important in determining share price.

Quick quiz

1 Identify four reasons why a company may seek a stock market listing.

2 A company's shares have a nominal value of £1 and a market value of £3. In a rights issue, one new share would be issued for every three shares at a price of £2.60. What is the theoretical ex-rights price?

3 A company offers to pay a dividend in the form of new shares which are worth more than the cash alternative which is also offered. What is this dividend in the form of shares called?

4 Match A/B to (i)/(ii), to express the difference between a stock split and a scrip issue.

A A scrip issue .... (i) .... convert equity reserves into share capital

B A stock split .... (ii) .... leaves reserves unaffected

5 Which of the following sources of finance to companies is the most widely used in practice?

A Bank borrowings

B Rights issues

C New share issues

D Retained earnings

6 Which of the following is least likely to be a reason for seeking a stock market flotation?

A Improving the existing owners' control over the business

B Access to a wider pool of finance

C Enhancement of the company's image

D Transfer of capital to other uses

7 A scrip dividend is

A A dividend paid at a fixed percentage rate on the nominal value of the shares

B A dividend paid at a fixed percentage rate on the market value of the shares on the date that the dividend is declared

C A dividend payment that takes the form of new shares instead of cash

D An issue of new shares to existing shareholders by converting equity reserves into issued share capital

8 Which of the following is not true of a rights issue by a listed company?

A Rights issues do not require a prospectus True

B The rights issues price can be at a discount to market price True

C If shareholders do not take up the rights, the rights lapse ✓

D Relative voting rights are unaffected if shareholders exercise their rights True

Answers to quick quiz

1 **Four** of the following **five**: access to a wider pool of finance; improved marketability of shares; transfer of capital to other uses (eg founder members liquidating holdings); enhancement of company image; making growth by acquisition possible.

2 $\frac{1}{3+1}((£3 \times 3) + £2.60)$

= £2.90.

3 An enhanced scrip dividend.

4 A(i); B(ii).

5 D Retained earnings

6 A Flotation is likely to involve a significant loss of control to a wider circle of investors.

7 C A would most commonly be a preference dividend. D is a definition of a scrip issue, not a scrip dividend.

8 C Shareholders have the option of renouncing the rights and selling them on the market.

Now try the question below from the Exam Question Bank

Question to try	Level	Marks	Time
27	Exam	25	45 mins

Chapter 23

DEBT AND NEAR DEBT FINANCING

Topic list		Syllabus reference
1	Preference shares	4(a), (b), (e)
2	Loan stock	4(a), (b), (e)
3	Convertibles and warrants	4(a), (b), (e)

Introduction

In this chapter, we continue with the coverage of the sources of long-term finance begun in Chapter 22, looking first at **preference shares** and **long-term debt** and then at **convertibles** and **warrants**.

When sources of **long-term finance** are used, large sums are usually involved, and so the financial manager needs to consider all the options available with care, looking to the possible effects on the company in the long term.

Study guide

Section 10 – Sources of finance III: Debt and near-debt financing

- Explain the features of different types of preference shares and the reasons for their issue
- Explain the features of different types of long-term straight debt and the reasons for their issue
- Explain the features of convertible debt and warrants and the reasons for their issue
- Broadly describe the reasons for the choice of financing between preference shares, debt and near-debt instruments in terms of the risk/return trade-off
- Assess the effect on EPS of conversion and option rights
- Broadly describe international debt markets and the financing of foreign trade
- Calculate and interpret appropriate ratios

Exam guide

As with equity financing, you should be able to discuss when a company should seek debt finance.

1 PREFERENCE SHARES

KEY TERM

Preference shares are shares which have a fixed percentage dividend, payable in priority to any dividend paid to the ordinary shareholders.

1.1 As with ordinary shares a preference dividend can only be paid if **sufficient distributable profits are available**, although with **cumulative preference shares** the right to an unpaid dividend is carried forward to later years. The arrears of dividend on cumulative preference shares must be paid before any dividend is paid to the ordinary shareholders. The stated dividend (such as 7%) on preference shares is the cash dividend, not grossed up.

Why issue preference shares?

1.2 From the company's point of view, preference shares have some positive features.

(a) **Dividends** do **not** have to be **paid** in a year in which **profits** are **poor**, while this is not the case with interest payments on long-term debt (loans or debentures).

(b) Since they do not normally carry voting rights, preference shares **avoid diluting** the **control** of existing shareholders while an issue of equity shares would not.

(c) Unless they are redeemable, issuing preference shares will **lower** the company's **gearing**. Redeemable preference shares are normally treated as debt when gearing is calculated.

(d) The issue of preference shares does **not restrict** the company's **borrowing power**, at least in the sense that preference share capital is not secured against assets of the business.

(e) The non-payment of dividend does not give the preference shareholders the right to appoint a receiver, a right which is normally given to debenture holders.

1.3 However, **dividend payments on preference shares are not tax deductible** in the way that interest payments on debt are. Furthermore, for preference shares to be attractive to investors, the level of payment needs to be higher than for interest on debt to compensate for the additional risks.

1.4 From the point of view of the investor, preference shares are less attractive than loan stock.

(a) They **cannot be secured** on the company's assets.

(b) The **dividend yield traditionally** offered on preference dividends has been **much too low** to provide an attractive investment compared with the interest yields on loan stock in view of the additional risk involved.

1.5 In recent years preference shares have formed a very small proportion only of new capital issues.

2 LOAN STOCK

KEY TERM

Loan stock is long-term debt capital raised by a company for which interest is paid, usually half yearly and at a fixed rate. Holders of loan stock are therefore long-term creditors of the company.

2.1 Loan stock has a nominal value, which is the debt owed by the company, and interest is paid at a stated '**coupon**' on this amount. For example, if a company issues 10% loan stock, the coupon will be 10% of the nominal value of the stock, so that £100 of stock will receive £10 interest each year. The rate quoted is the gross rate, before tax.

2.2 Unlike shares, debt is often issued **at par**, ie with £100 payable per £100 nominal value. Where the coupon rate is fixed at the time of issue, it will be set according to **prevailing market conditions** given the **credit rating** of the company issuing the debt. Subsequent changes in market (and company) conditions will cause the **market value** of the bond to fluctuate, although the coupon will stay at the fixed percentage of the nominal value.

KEY TERM

Debentures are a form of loan stock, the written acknowledgement of a debt incurred by a company, normally containing provisions about the payment of interest and the eventual repayment of capital.

2.3 A **debenture trust deed** would empower a trustee (such as an insurance company or a bank) to intervene on behalf of debenture holders if the conditions of borrowing under which the debentures were issued are not being fulfilled. This might involve:

(a) **Failure to pay interest** on the due dates

(b) An attempt by the company to **sell off important assets** contrary to the terms of the loan

(c) A company taking out **additional loans** and thereby exceeding previously agreed borrowing limits established either by the articles or by the terms of the debenture trust deed

2.4 **Advantages of debentures over preference shares**

(a) Debentures are a **cheaper form of finance** than preference shares because, unlike preference shares, debenture interest is tax-deductible.

(b) Debentures should be **more attractive** to investors because they will be **secured** on the assets of the company.

(c) Debentureholders **rank above preference shareholders** in the event of a liquidation.

(d) **Issue costs** should be **lower** for debentures than for preference shares.

Debentures with a floating rate of interest

2.5 With these, the issuer can charge the **coupon rate of interest**, in accordance with changes in **market rates of interest**. They may be attractive to both lenders and borrowers when interest rates are volatile, and preferable to fixed interest loan stock or debentures.

(a) **Floating rate debentures protect borrowers** from having to pay high rates of interest on their debentures when market rates of interest have **fallen.** On the other hand, they **allow lenders** to **benefit** from higher rates of interest on their debentures when **market rates** of interest **go up**.

(b) The **market value** of debentures depends on the **coupon rate of interest, relative to market interest rates**. With floating rate debentures the **market value** should be fairly **stable** (and close to par) because interest rates are varied to follow market rate changes. Stable market prices protect the value of the lenders' investment.

2.6 For example, suppose that a company issues 6% fixed rate debentures at par when the market rate of interest is 6%. If interest rates suddenly rise to 12%, the market value of the debentures would fall by half to £50 per cent (£100 nominal value). However, if the debentures had carried a floating rate of interest, the interest rate would have been raised to 12% and the debentures would have retained their market value at par (£100 per cent).

Deep discount bonds

KEY TERM

Deep discount bonds are loan stock issued at a price which is at a large discount to the nominal value of the stock, and which will be redeemable at par (or above par) when they eventually mature.

2.7 For example a company might issue £1,000,000 of loan stock in 20X1, at a price of £50 per £100 of stock, and redeemable at par in the year 20X9. For a company with specific cash flow requirements, the low servicing costs during the currency of the bond may be an attraction, coupled with a high cost of redemption at maturity.

2.8 Investors might be attracted by the **large capital gain** offered by the bonds, which is the difference between the **issue price** and the **redemption value**. However, deep discount bonds will carry a much **lower rate of interest** than other types of loan stock. The only tax advantage is that the gain gets taxed (as **income**) in one lump on maturity or sale, not as amounts of interest each year. The borrower can, however, **deduct notional interest** each year in computing profits.

Zero coupon bonds

KEY TERM

Zero coupon bonds are bonds that are issued at a discount to their redemption value, but no interest is paid on them.

2.9 The investor gains from the difference between the issue price and the redemption value. There is an implied interest rate in the amount of discount at which the bonds are issued (or subsequently re-sold on the market).

(a) The advantage for borrowers is that zero coupon bonds can be used to **raise cash immediately**, and there is **no cash repayment** until redemption date. The cost of redemption is known at the time of issue. The borrower can plan to have funds available to redeem the bonds at maturity.

(b) The **advantage for lenders is restricted,** unless the rate of discount on the bonds offers a high yield. The only way of obtaining cash from the bonds before maturity is to sell them. Their **market value** will depend on the **remaining term** to maturity and **current market interest rates.**

The tax advantage of zero coupon bonds is the same as that for deep discount bonds (see Paragraph 2.8 above).

Security

2.10 Loan stock and debentures will often be secured. **Security** may take the form of either a **fixed charge** or a **floating charge.**

Fixed charge	• Security relates to specific asset/group of assets (land and buildings) • Company can't dispose of assets without providing substitute/consent of lender
Floating charge	• Security in event of default is whatever assets of the class secured (stock/debtors) company then owns • Company can dispose of assets until default takes place • In event of default lenders appoint receiver rather than lay claim to asset

2.11 Not all loan stock is secured. Investors are likely to expect a higher yield with **unsecured loan stock** to compensate them for the extra risk.

The redemption of loan stock

KEY TERM

Redemption is repayment of preference shares and debentures.

2.12 Loan stock and debentures are usually redeemable. They are issued for a term of ten years or more, and perhaps 25 to 30 years. At the end of this period, they will 'mature' and become redeemable (at par or possibly at a value above par).

2.13 Most redeemable stocks have an earliest and a latest redemption date. For example

(a) 12% Debenture Stock 20X7/X9 is redeemable, at any time between the earliest specified date (in 20X7) and the latest date (in 20X9). The **issuing company** can choose the date.

(b) The decision by a company when to redeem a debt will depend on **how much cash is available** to the company to **repay the debt**, and on the nominal rate of interest on the debt.

(c) If the debentures pay 12% nominal interest and current interest rates are lower, say 9%, the company may try to raise a new loan at 9% to redeem debt which costs 12%.

(d) On the other hand, if current interest rates are 14%, the company is unlikely to redeem the debt until the latest date possible, because the debentures would be a cheap source of funds.

2.14 Some loan stock does not have a redemption date, and is '**irredeemable**' or 'undated'. Undated loan stock might be redeemed by a company that wishes to pay off the debt, but there is no obligation on the company to do so.

How will a company finance the redemption of long-term debt?

2.15 There is no guarantee that a company will be able to raise a new loan to pay off a maturing debt. One item you should look for in a company's balance sheet is the **redemption date** of current loans, to establish how much new finance is likely to be needed by the company, and when.

Companies that are unable to repay debt capital

2.16 A company might get into difficulties and be unable to pay its debts. The difficulty could be an inability to repay the debt capital when it is due for redemption or an inability, perhaps temporary, to pay interest on the debt, before the capital is due for redemption.

2.17 When this occurs, the debenture holders or loan stock holders could exercise their right to **appoint a receiver** and to make use of whatever security they have.

2.18 Occasionally, perhaps because the secured assets have fallen in value and would not realise much in a forced sale, or perhaps out of a belief that the company can improve its position soon, unpaid debenture holders might be persuaded to surrender their debentures. In exchange they may get an **equity interest** in the company or **convertible debentures**, paying a lower rate of interest, but carrying the option to convert the debentures into shares at a specified time in the future.

Tax relief on loan interest

2.19 As far as companies are concerned, debt capital is a potentially attractive source of finance because interest charges **reduce the profits** chargeable to corporation tax.

(a) A new issue of loan stock is likely to be preferable to a new issue of preference shares.

(b) Companies might wish to **avoid dilution of shareholdings** and **increase gearing** (the ratio of fixed interest capital to equity capital) in order to improve their earnings per share by benefiting from tax relief on interest payments.

Mortgages

2.20 **Mortgages** are a specific type of secured loan. Companies place the title deeds of freehold or long leasehold property as security with a lender and receive cash on loan, usually repayable over a specified period, with interest payable at a fixed or floating rate. Most organisations owning property which is unencumbered by any charge should be able to obtain a mortgage up to two thirds of the value of the property.

3 CONVERTIBLES AND WARRANTS

Convertible loan stock

KEY TERM

Convertible securities are fixed return securities that may be converted, on pre-determined dates and at the option of the holder, into ordinary shares of the company at a predetermined rate.

3.1 Conversion terms often vary over time. For example, the conversion terms of convertible stock might be that on 1 April 20X2, £2 of stock can be converted into one ordinary share, whereas on 1 April 20X3, the conversion price will be £2.20 of stock for one ordinary share. Once converted, convertible securities cannot be converted back into the original fixed return security.

The conversion value and the conversion premium

3.2 The current market value of ordinary shares into which a unit of stock may be converted is known as the conversion value.

(a) The **conversion value** will be below the value of the stock at the date of issue. It will though be expected to increase as the date for conversion approaches on the assumption that a company's shares ought to increase in market value over time.

(b) The difference between the issue value of the stock and the conversion value as at the date of issue is the implicit **conversion premium.**

Question 1

The 10% convertible loan stock of Starchwhite plc is quoted at £142 per £100 nominal. The earliest date for conversion is in four years time, at the rate of 30 ordinary shares per £100 nominal loan stock. The share price is currently £4.15. Annual interest on the stock has just been paid.

Required

(a) What is the average annual growth rate in the share price that is required for the stockholders to achieve an overall rate of return of 12% a year compound over the next four years, including the proceeds of conversion?

(b) What is the implicit conversion premium on the stock?

Answer

(a)

Year	*Investment*	*Interest*	*Discount factor*	*Terminal value*
	£	£	12%	£
0	(142)		1.000	(142.00)
1		10	0.893	8.93
2		10	0.797	7.97
3		10	0.712	7.12
4		10	0.636	6.36
				(111.62)

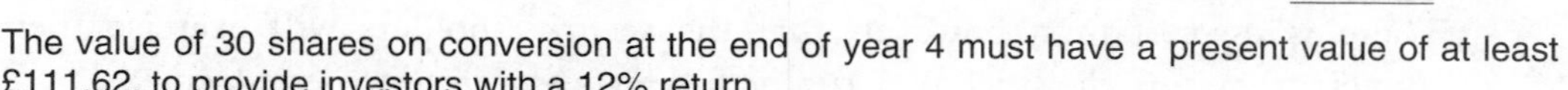

The value of 30 shares on conversion at the end of year 4 must have a present value of at least £111.62, to provide investors with a 12% return.

The money value at the end of year 4 needs to be £111.62 ÷ 0.636 = £175.50.

The current market value of 30 shares is (× £4.15) £124.50.

The growth factor in the share price over four years needs to be:

$$\frac{175.50}{124.50} = 1.4096$$

If the annual rate of growth in the share price, expressed as a proportion, is g, then:

$$(1 + g)^4 = 1.4096$$
$$1 + g = 1.0896$$
$$g = 0.0896, \text{ say } 0.09$$

Conclusion. The rate of growth in the share price needs to be 9% a year (compound).

(b) The conversion premium can be expressed as an amount per share or as a percentage of the current conversion value.

(i) As an amount per share $\frac{£142 - £(30 \times 4.15)}{30} = £0.583$ per share

(ii) As a % of conversion value $\frac{£0.583}{£4.15} \times 100\% = 14\%$

The issue price and the market price of convertible loan stock

3.3 A company will aim to issue loan stock with the **greatest possible conversion premium.** This will mean that, for the amount of capital raised, it will, on conversion, have to issue the **lowest number** of new ordinary shares. The premium that will be accepted by potential investors will depend on the company's **growth potential** and so on prospects for a sizeable increase in the share price.

3.4 Convertible loan stock issued at par normally has a **lower coupon rate of interest** than straight debentures. This lower yield is the price the investor has to pay for the conversion rights. It is, of course, also one of the reasons why the issue of convertible stock is attractive to a company.

3.5 When convertible loan stock is traded on a stock market, its **minimum market price** will be the **price of straight debentures** with the same coupon rate of interest. If the market value falls to this minimum, it follows that the market attaches no value to the conversion rights.

3.6 The actual market price of convertible stock will depend on:

- The **price of straight debt**
- The **current conversion value**
- The **length of time** before conversion may take place
- The **market's expectation** as to future equity returns and the associated risk

If the conversion value rises above the straight debt value then the price of convertible stock will normally reflect this increase.

3.7 Most companies issuing convertible stocks expect them to be converted. They view the stock as **delayed equity**. They are often used either because the company's ordinary share price is considered to be particularly **depressed** at the time of issue or because the issue of equity shares would result in an immediate and significant **drop in earnings per share.** There is no certainty, however, that the security holders will exercise their option to convert; therefore the stock may run its full term and need to be redeemed.

3.8 EXAMPLE: CONVERTIBLE DEBENTURES

CD plc has issued 50,000 units of convertible debentures, each with a nominal value of £100 and a coupon rate of interest of 10% payable yearly. Each £100 of convertible debentures may be converted into 40 ordinary shares of CD plc in three years time. Any stock not converted will be redeemed at 110 (that is, at £110 per £100 nominal value of stock).

Estimate the likely current market price for £100 of the debentures, if investors in the debentures now require a pre-tax return of only 8%, and the expected value of CD plc ordinary shares on the conversion day is:

(a) £2.50 per share
(b) £3.00 per share

3.9 SOLUTION

(a) **Shares are valued at £2.50 each**

If shares are only expected to be worth £2.50 each on conversion day, the value of 40 shares will be £100, and investors in the debentures will presumably therefore redeem their debentures at 110 instead of converting them into shares.

The market value of £100 of the convertible debentures will be the discounted present value of the expected future income stream.

Year		Cash flow	Discount factor	Present value
		£	8%	£
1	Interest	10	0.926	9.26
2	Interest	10	0.857	8.57
3	Interest	10	0.794	7.94
3	Redemption value	110	0.794	87.34
				113.11

The estimated market value is £113.11 per £100 of debentures.

(b) **Shares are valued at £3 each**

If shares are expected to be worth £3 each, the debenture holders will convert their debentures into shares (value per £100 of stock = 40 shares × £3 = £120) rather than redeem their debentures at 110.

Year		Cash flow/value	Discount factor	Present value
		£	8%	£
1	Interest	10	0.926	9.26
2	Interest	10	0.857	8.57
3	Interest	10	0.794	7.94
3	Value of 40 shares	120	0.794	95.28
				121.05

The estimated market value is £121.05 per £100 of debentures.

Question 2

Downon Howett plc is unable to pay the interest on its debt capital, which consists of £5,000,000 of 10% debenture stock. The debenture holders are entitled, under the terms of their trust deed, to appoint a receiver, but the current financial position of Downon Howett plc is so poor that the enforced liquidation of the company would not realise more than a small fraction of the amount owed to the debenture holders. The debenture holders are therefore willing to consider alternatives.

Downon Howett has suggested that either of two options might satisfy them. The debenture holders would surrender their debentures, in exchange for:

(a) 15,000,000 ordinary shares under option 1

(b) £5,000,000 of non-interest-bearing convertible debentures under option 2. The debentures would be convertible into ordinary shares in two years time at the rate of 200 shares per £100 of stock. Alternatively, the debentures (which would not be secured) would be repayable at par after two years.

Estimates of the net realisable value of Downon Howett's assets in two years time are as follows.

Probability	Net realisable value
	£m
0.2	2
0.4	4
0.3	6
0.1	8

If Downon Howett does not go into liquidation, its value as a going concern after two years is estimated to be 150% of the net realisable value of its assets, and the share price will reflect this value. Downon Howett would not be allowed to issue any additional shares, nor pay any dividend, for the next two years. There are currently 10,000,000 shares in issue.

Which option would the debenture holders prefer, on the assumption that they choose the one that maximises the expected value of their wealth?

Answer

(a) If option 1 is selected, the debenture holders would own:

$\frac{15}{10+15}$ = 60% of the shares.

After two years, the EV of these shares would be as follows.

Break up value	*Market value (going concern) 150%*	*Ex debenture holder's share 60%*	*Probability*	*EV*
£m	£m	£m		£m
2	3	1.8	0.2	0.36
4	6	3.6	0.4	1.44
6	9	5.4	0.3	1.62
8	12	7.2	0.1	0.72
				4.14

(b) If option 2 is selected, the debenture holders could choose to demand repayment of the debentures, out of the proceeds of sale of the assets of the company, or to convert the debentures into shares.

They would own $\frac{10}{10+10}$ = 50% of the total number of shares.

Break-up value	*Going concern value*	*Value of convertibles as equity*	*Value of convertibles as debt*	*Convert? *yes or no*	*Value of debenture holders' securities*	*Probability*	
£m	£m	£m	£m		£m		£m
2	3	1.5	2.0	No	2	0.2	0.4
4	6	3.0	4.0	No	4	0.4	1.6
6	9	4.5	5.0	No	5	0.3	1.5
8	12	6.0	5.0	Yes	6	0.1	0.6
							4.1

* The answer is 'no' if the break-up value or the total debt of £5,000,000, whichever is lower, exceeds the value of 50% of the equity of the going concern. The debenture holders will compare the value of their convertibles as debt and as shares, and opt to use them in the form that gives the greater value.

The debenture holders would prefer option 1 to option 2, but only marginally so (with a difference in expected value of only £40,000).

Warrants

KEY TERM

A **warrant** is a right given by a company to an investor, allowing him to subscribe for new shares at a future date at a fixed, pre-determined price (the **exercise price**).

3.10 **Warrants** are usually issued as part of a package with unsecured loan stock: an investor who buys stock will also acquire a certain number of warrants. The purpose of warrants is to make the loan stock more attractive.

3.11 Once issued, warrants are detachable from the stock and can be sold and bought separately before or during the 'exercise period' (the period during which the right to use the warrants to subscribe for shares is allowed). The market value of warrants will depend on expectations of actual share prices in the future.

3.12 During the exercise period, the price of a warrant should not fall below the higher of:

- **Nil**
- The '**theoretical value**', which equals:

(Current share price – Exercise price) × Number of shares obtainable from each warrant

3.13 If, for example, a warrant entitles the holder to purchase two ordinary shares at a price of £3 each, when the current market price of the shares is £3.40.

Minimum market value ('theoretical value') of a warrant = (£3.40 – £3) × 2 = 80p.

3.14 For a company with good growth prospects, the warrant will usually be quoted at a premium above the minimum prior to the exercise period. This premium is known as the **warrant conversion premium.** It is sometimes expressed as a percentage of the current share price.

3.15 EXAMPLE: WARRANT CONVERSION PREMIUM

An investor holds some warrants which can be used to subscribe for ordinary shares on a one for one basis at an exercise price of £2.50 during a specified future period. The current share price is £2.25 and the warrants are quoted at 50p. What is the warrant conversion premium?

3.16 SOLUTION

The easiest way of finding the premium is to deduct the current share price from the cost of acquiring a share using the warrant, treating the warrant as if it were currently exercisable:

	£
Cost of warrant	0.50
Exercise price	2.50
	3.00
Current share price	2.25
Premium	0.75

3.17 In the short run the warrant price and share price normally move fairly closely in line with each other. In the longer term the price of the warrant and hence the premium will depend on:

- The **length of time** before the warrants may be exercised
- The **current price** of the shares compared with the exercise price, and
- The **future prospects** of the company

As the exercise period approaches, the premium will reduce. Towards the end of the exercise period the premium will disappear because, if there were a premium, it would be cheaper to buy the shares directly rather than via the warrant.

3.18 You may be wondering why an investor would prefer to buy warrants at 50p when this means that it will cost him more to get the ordinary shares than if he bought them directly. The attractions of warrants to the investor are:

(a) **Low initial outlay**

The investor only has to spend 50p per share as opposed to £2.25. The investor will be able to buy $4^1/_2$ times as many warrants as shares or, alternatively, invest the remaining £1.75 in other, less risky investments.

(b) **Lower downside potential**

The maximum loss per share is 50p instead of £2.25. Of course the risk of the loss of 50p is much greater than the risk of losing £2.25. The share price of £2.25 is below the exercise price. If it remained at this level until the beginning of the exercise period, the warrants would become worthless as it would not be worthwhile exercising them.

(c) **High potential returns**

Warrants offer the investor the possibility of making a high profit as a percentage of initial cost, as the price of the warrants will tend to move in line with the price of the shares. Thus, if the share price rises by 50p the increase in the value of the warrant will be similar. Using the previous prices, a 50p increase in share price is about 22% but a 50p increase in the warrant price is 100%.

(d) **Capital gains**

As warrants provide no income all profits are in the **form of capital gains** which will be attractive to higher-rate taxpayers who have not used up their annual tax-free allowance.

3.19 The advantages of warrants to the company are as follows.

(a) Warrants themselves do **not involve** the payment of any **interest** or **dividends.** Furthermore, when they are initially attached to loan stock, the interest rate on the loan stock will be lower than for a comparable straight debt.

(b) Warrants make a **loan stock issue more attractive** and may make an issue of unsecured loan stock possible where adequate security is lacking.

(c) Warrants provide a means of **generating additional equity funds** in the future without any immediate dilution in earnings per share.

Chapter roundup

- **Preference shares** carry priority over ordinary equity shares with regard to dividend payments. They do not carry voting rights. They may be attractive to corporate investors, as (unlike interest receipts) dividends received are not subject to corporation tax. However, for the issuing company, dividend payments (unlike interest payments) are not tax-deductible.
- The term **bonds** describes various forms of long-term debt a company may issue, such as **loan stock** or **debentures**, which may be:
  - **Redeemable**
  - **Irredeemable**
- Bonds or loans come in various forms, including:
  - **Floating rate debentures**
  - **Zero coupon bonds**
  - **Convertible loan stock**
- **Convertible securities** give investors the opportunity to turn their stock into shares at a later date if they wish and, because of this, they usually carry a lower rate of interest than a similar non-convertible security. For the companies issuing them, convertibles may be viewed as a delayed form of equity which does not immediately affect EPS.

Quick quiz

1 Debentures are more similar to equity than preference shares.

- [ ] True
- [ ] False

2 Holders of loan stock are long-term debtors of the company.

- [ ] True
- [ ] False

3 A company has 12% debentures in issue, which have a market value of £135 per £100 nominal value. What is:

(a) The coupon rate?

(b) The amount of interest payable per annum per £100 (nominal) of stock?

4 Does an investor have the option of redeeming a company's 11% Debenture Stock 2006/2008 at any date between 1 January 2006 and 31 December 2008 inclusive?

5 Convertible securities are fixed return securities that may be converted into zero coupon bonds/ordinary shares/warrants. (Delete as appropriate.)

6 Which of the following statements about convertible securities is false?

A They are fixed return securities.
B They must be converted into shares before the redemption date.
C The price at which they will be converted into shares is predetermined.
D Issue costs are lower than for equity.

7 Do borrowers benefit from floating rate debentures when interest rates are rising or falling?

8 What is the value of £100 12% debt redeemable in 3 years time at a premium of 20p per £ if the loanholder's required return is 10%?

Answers to quick quiz

1 False. Debentures are a form of loan stock

2 False. They are long-term creditors of the company.

3 (a) 12% (b) £12

4 No. The company will be able to choose the date of redemption.

5 Ordinary shares.

6 B The holder has the option to convert, but he will only convert if it is advantageous for him to do so. If the share price falls, the stock may run its full term and need to be redeemed.

7 Falling

8

Years			*Discount factor 10%*	*Present value*
		£		£
1-3	Interest	12	2.487	29.84
3	Redemption premium	120	0.751	90.12
Value of debt				119.96

Now try the question below from the Exam Question Bank

Question to try	Level	Marks	Time
28	Exam	25	45 mins

Chapter 24

THE CAPITAL STRUCTURE DECISION

Topic list		Syllabus reference
1	**Gearing**	**4(d), (e)**
2	**Factors influencing the level of debt financing**	**4(c), (e)**
3	**Short-term financing and capital structure**	**4(c), (e)**

Introduction

In Chapters 22 and 23, we described different methods by which a company can obtain long-term finance, both in the form of **equity** and in the form of **debt**.

This chapter follows on from Chapter 22 and 23, looking now at the question of what a company's **financial structure** should be. A central question here is: What are the implications of using different proportions of equity and debt finance?

Study guide

Section II – Sources of finance IV: The capital structure decision

- Explain and calculate the level of financial gearing
- Distinguish between operational and financial gearing
- Outline the effects of gearing on the value of shares, company risk and required return
- Explain how a company may determine its capital structure in terms of interest charges, dividends, risk and redemption requirements
- Explain the role of short term financing in the capital structure decision
- Explain the relationship between the management of working capital and the long term capital structure decision
- Calculate and interpret appropriate ratios

Exam guide

You may be asked to explain the implications of different financing decisions on investment opportunities and the company's continued health. Capital structure, particularly of smaller companies, is an important topic in this exam.

1 GEARING

Principles of capital structure

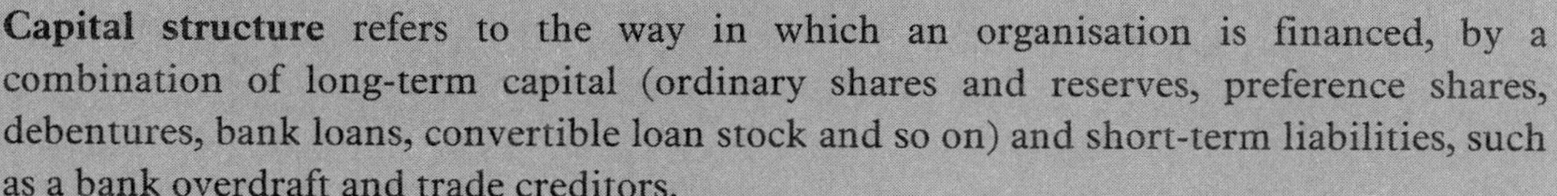

KEY TERM

Capital structure refers to the way in which an organisation is financed, by a combination of long-term capital (ordinary shares and reserves, preference shares, debentures, bank loans, convertible loan stock and so on) and short-term liabilities, such as a bank overdraft and trade creditors.

1.1 The assets of a business must be financed somehow, and when a business is growing, the additional assets must be financed by additional capital.

Matching assets with funds

1.2 As a general rule, **assets which yield profits over a long period of time should be financed** by **long-term funds.**

1.3 In this way, the returns made by the asset will be sufficient to pay either the interest cost of the loans raised to buy it, or dividends on its equity funding.

1.4 If, however a long-term asset is financed by short-term funds, the company cannot be certain that when the loan becomes repayable, it will have enough cash (from profits) to repay it.

1.5 A company would not normally finance all of its short-term assets with short-term liabilities, but instead finance short-term assets partly with short-term funding and partly with long-term funding.

Long-term capital requirements for replacement and growth

1.6 A distinction can be made between long-term capital that is needed to finance the replacement of worn-out assets, and capital that is needed to finance growth.

Aims	Main funding sources
Maintenance of current level of operations	Internal sources
Growth	External finance

Debts and financial risk

1.7 A high level of debt creates financial risk. **Financial risk** can be seen from different points of view.

(a) **The company** as a whole. If a company builds up debts that it cannot pay when they fall due, it will be forced into liquidation.

(b) **Creditors**. If a company cannot pay its debts, the company will go into liquidation owing creditors money that they are unlikely to recover in full.

(c) **Ordinary shareholders**. A company will not make any distributable profits unless it is able to earn enough profit before interest and tax to pay all its interest charges, and then tax. The lower the profits or the higher the interest-bearing debts, the less there will be, if there is anything at all, for shareholders.

The appraisal of capital structures

1.8 The financial risk of a company's capital structure can be measured by a **gearing ratio,** a **debt ratio** or **debt/equity ratio** and by the **interest cover**. A gearing ratio should not be given without stating how it has been defined.

Exam focus point

You need to be able to explain *and calculate* the level of financial gearing using alternative measures.

Gearing ratios

1.9 **Financial gearing** measures the relationship between shareholders' capital plus reserves, and either prior charge capital or borrowings or both.

1.10 As we have seen previously, commonly used measures of financial gearing are based on the balance sheet values of the fixed interest and equity capital. They include:

$$\frac{\text{Prior charge capital}}{\text{Equity capital (including reserves)}}$$

and $$\frac{\text{Prior charge capital}}{\text{Total capital employed}^{\star}}$$

* Either including or excluding minority interests, deferred tax and deferred income.

1.11 With the first definition above, a company is low geared if the gearing ratio is less than 100%, highly geared if the ratio is over 100% and neutrally geared if it is exactly 100%. With the second definition, a company is neutrally geared if the ratio is 50%, low geared below that, and highly geared above that.

Question

From the following balance sheet, compute the company's financial gearing ratio.

	£'000	£'000	£'000
Fixed assets			12,400
Current assets		1,000	
Creditors: amounts falling due within one year			
Loans	120		
Bank overdraft	260		
Trade creditors	430		
Bills of exchange	70		
		880	
Net current assets			120
Total assets less current liabilities			12,520
Creditors: amounts falling due after more than one year			
Debentures		4,700	
Bank loans		500	
			(5,200)
Provisions for liabilities and charges: deferred taxation			(300)
Deferred income			(250)
			6,770

Capital and reserves	£'000
Called up share capital	
Ordinary shares	1,500
Preference shares	500
	2,000
Share premium account	760
Revaluation reserve	1,200
Profit and loss account	2,810
	6,770

Answer

Prior charge capital	£'000
Preference shares	500
Debentures	4,700
Long-term bank loans	500
Prior charge capital, ignoring short-term debt	5,700
Short-term loans	120
Overdraft	260
Prior charge capital, including short-term interest bearing debt	6,080

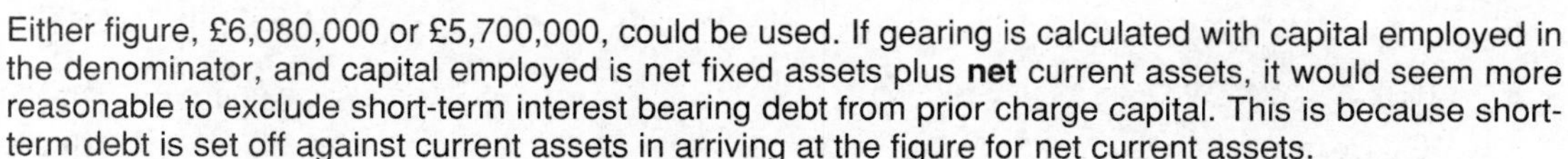
Either figure, £6,080,000 or £5,700,000, could be used. If gearing is calculated with capital employed in the denominator, and capital employed is net fixed assets plus **net** current assets, it would seem more reasonable to exclude short-term interest bearing debt from prior charge capital. This is because short-term debt is set off against current assets in arriving at the figure for net current assets.

Equity = 1,500 + 760 + 1,200 + 2,810 = £6,270,000

The gearing ratio can be calculated in any of the following ways.

(a) $\frac{\text{Prior charge capital}}{\text{Equity}} \times 100\% = \frac{6,080}{6,270} \times 100\% = 97\%$

(b) $\frac{\text{Prior charge capital}}{\text{Equity plus prior charge capital}} \times 100\% = \frac{6,080}{(6,080 + 6,270)} \times 100\% = 49.2\%$

(c) $\frac{\text{Prior charge capital}}{\text{Total capital employed}} \times 100\% = \frac{5,700}{12,520} \times 100\% = 45.5\%$

Gearing ratios based on market values

1.12 An alternative method of calculating a gearing ratio is one based on **market values:**

$$\frac{\text{Market value of debt (including preference shares)}}{\text{Market value of equity + Market value of debt}}$$

1.13 The advantage of this method is that potential investors in a company are able to judge the further debt capacity of the company more clearly by **reference** to **market values** than they could by looking at balance sheet values.

1.14 The disadvantage of a gearing ratio based on market values is that it **disregards** the **value** of the company's **assets,** which might be used to secure further loans. A gearing ratio based on balance sheet values arguably gives a better indication of the security for lenders of fixed interest capital.

The effect of gearing on earnings

1.15 A highly geared company must earn enough profits to **cover** its **interest** charges before anything is available for equity. On the other hand, if borrowed funds are invested in projects which provide returns in excess of the cost of debt capital, then shareholders will enjoy increased returns on their equity.

1.16 Provided that a company can generate returns on capital in excess of the interest payable on debt, introducing financial gearing into the capital structure will enable **earnings per share** to be raised. If the company fails to generate such returns, earnings per share will be reduced, and so gearing increases the **variability of shareholders' earnings**.

1.17 Gearing, however, also **increases** the **probability** of **financial failure** occurring through a company's inability to meet interest payments in poor trading circumstances.

1.18 EXAMPLE: GEARING

Suppose that two companies are identical in every respect except for their gearing. Both have assets of £20,000 and both make the same operating profits (profit before interest and tax: PBIT). The only difference between the two companies is that Nonlever Ltd is all-equity financed and Lever Ltd is partly financed by debt capital, as follows.

	Nonlever Ltd	*Lever Ltd*
	£	£
Assets	20,000	20,000
10% Loan stock	0	(10,000)
	20,000	10,000
Ordinary shares of £1	20,000	10,000

Because Lever Ltd has £10,000 of 10% loan stock it must make a profit before interest of at least £1,000 in order to pay the interest charges. Nonlever Ltd, on the other hand, does not have any minimum PBIT requirement because it has no debt capital. A company which is lower geared is considered less risky than a higher geared company because of the greater likelihood that its PBIT will be high enough to cover interest charges and make a profit for equity shareholders.

Operating gearing

1.19 Financial risk, as we have seen, can be measured by financial gearing. **Business risk** refers to the risk of making only low profits, or even losses, due to the nature of the business that the company is involved in. One way of measuring business risk is by calculating a company's **operating gearing** or 'operational gearing'.

$$\text{Operating gearing} = \frac{\text{Contribution}}{\text{Profit before interest and tax (PBIT)}}$$

Contribution is sales minus variable cost of sales.

1.20 The significance of operating gearing is as follows.

(a) **If contribution is high but PBIT is low**, fixed costs will be high, and only just covered by contribution. Business risk, as measured by operating gearing, will be high.

(b) **If contribution is not much bigger than PBIT**, fixed costs will be low, and fairly easily covered. Business risk, as measured by operating gearing, will be low.

Interest cover

1.21 **Interest cover** is a measure of financial risk which is designed to show the risks in terms of profit rather than in terms of capital values.

$$\text{Interest cover} = \frac{\text{Profit before interest and tax}}{\text{Interest}}$$

1.22 The reciprocal of this, the interest to profit ratio, is also sometimes used. As a general guide, an interest cover of **less than three times** is considered low, indicating that profitability is too low given the gearing of the company.

The debt ratio (debt/equity ratio)

1.23 Another measure of financial risk which we have seen previously is the **debt ratio.**

Debt ratio = Total debts : Total assets

Debt/equity ratio = Debt : Equity

Debt does not include long-term provisions and liabilities such as deferred taxation.

1.24 There is no firm rule on the maximum safe debt ratio, but as a general guide, you might regard 50% as a safe limit to debt.

2 FACTORS INFLUENCING THE LEVEL OF DEBT FINANCING

Limitations and restrictions

2.1 The gearing ratio and the debt/equity ratio indicate whether a company is likely to be successful in raising new funds by means of extra borrowing. Lenders will probably want a higher **interest yield** to compensate them for **higher financial risk** and gearing.

2.2 In addition, ordinary shareholders will probably want a **bigger expected return** from their shares to compensate them for a higher financial risk. The market value of shares will therefore depend on gearing, because of this premium for financial risk that shareholders will want to earn. Directors should bear in mind their responsibility to maximise the value of shares.

2.3 **Business confidence and expectations** of future profits are crucial factors in the determination of how much debt capital investors are prepared to lend. The level of gearing which the market will allow will therefore depend on the **nature** of the company wishing to borrow more funds, and the industry in which it is engaged.

(a) A company which is involved in a **cyclical business,** where profits are subject to periodic ups and downs, should have a relatively **low gearing.**

(b) A company in a business where **profits are stable** should be able to raise a **larger amount of debt**.

2.4 There may be **restrictions on further borrowing** contained in the debenture trust deed for a company's current debenture stock in issue or in the company's articles of association. Potential lenders may want **security** in the form of a legal charge over company assets which the borrowing company is unable to provide.

Inflation, debt capital and interest rates

2.5 The **cost** of any extra finance will reflect investors' expectations about the rate of inflation. Investors will usually want a **real return** on their investment, that is, a return in excess of the rate of inflation.

2.6 Both **inflation** and **uncertainty** about future interest rate changes are reasons why companies are unwilling to borrow long-term at high rates of interest and investors are unwilling to lend long-term when they think that interest yields might go even higher.

2.7 Companies therefore rely quite heavily for borrowed funds on bank borrowing and short-term borrowing (such as money market borrowing). The advantage of short-term borrowing is that the company is **not committed** to paying a high interest rate for a long period.

The idea of an optimal structure; the cost of capital

2.8 When we consider the capital structure decision, the question arises of whether there is an optimal mix of capital and debt which a company should try to achieve.

2.9 One view is that there is an optimal capital mix at which the **average cost of capital**, weighted according to the different forms of capital employed, is **minimised**. As gearing rises, so the return demanded by the ordinary shareholders begins to rise in order to compensate them for the risk resulting from a larger and larger share of profits going to the providers of debt. At very high levels of gearing the holders of debt too will begin to require higher returns as they become exposed to risk of inadequate profits.

2.10 Briefly, the alternative view of **Modigliani and Miller** is that the firm's overall **weighted average cost of capital** is not influenced by changes in its capital structure. Their argument is that the issue of debt causes the cost of equity to rise in such a way that the benefits of debt on returns are exactly offset. Investors themselves adjust their level of personal gearing and thus the level of corporate gearing becomes irrelevant.

2.11 The Modigliani-Miller view however does contain some debatable assumptions. It assumes that investors operate in a **perfect market** where **full information** is **equally available** to all players, and that transaction costs are irrelevant. Further, **companies** can often borrow on better terms than private investors, and importantly the **effects of taxation** are **ignored** in the original Modigliani-Miller theory.

3 SHORT-TERM FINANCING AND CAPITAL STRUCTURE 12/01

3.1 Current and fixed assets can be funded in different ways by employing different capital structures with different proportions of long and short-term sources of funding.

3.2 A distinction is often drawn, when funding of current assets is being discussed, between permanent current assets (many businesses will always have certain minimum levels of stock, debtors, and cash) and fluctuating current assets (the excess of assets held over minimum levels).

3.3 The diagram below illustrates three alternative types of policy A, B and C. The dotted lines A, B and C are the cut-off levels between short-term and long-term financing for each of the policies A, B and C respectively. Assets above the relevant dotted line are financed by short-term funding while assets below the dotted line are financed by long-term funding.

3.4 Fluctuating current assets together with permanent current assets form part of the working capital of the business. This may be financed by either long-term funding (including equity capital) or by current liabilities (short-term funding). This can be seen in terms of policies A, B and C.

(a) Policy A can be characterised as **conservative**. All fixed assets and permanent current assets, as well as part of fluctuating current assets, are financed by long-term funding. The company will only call upon short-term financing at times when fluctuations in current assets push total assets above the level of dotted line A. At times when fluctuating current assets are low and total assets fall below line A, there will be surplus cash which the company will be able to invest in marketable securities.

(b) Policy B is more **aggressive** in its approach to financing working capital. Not only are fluctuating current assets all financed out of short-term sources, but also a part of the permanent current assets. This policy presents an increased risk of liquidity and cash flow problems, although potential returns will be increased if short-term financing can be obtained more cheaply than long-term finance.

(c) A **balance** between risk and return might be best achieved by policy C, in which long-term funds finance permanent assets while short-term funds finance non-permanent assets.

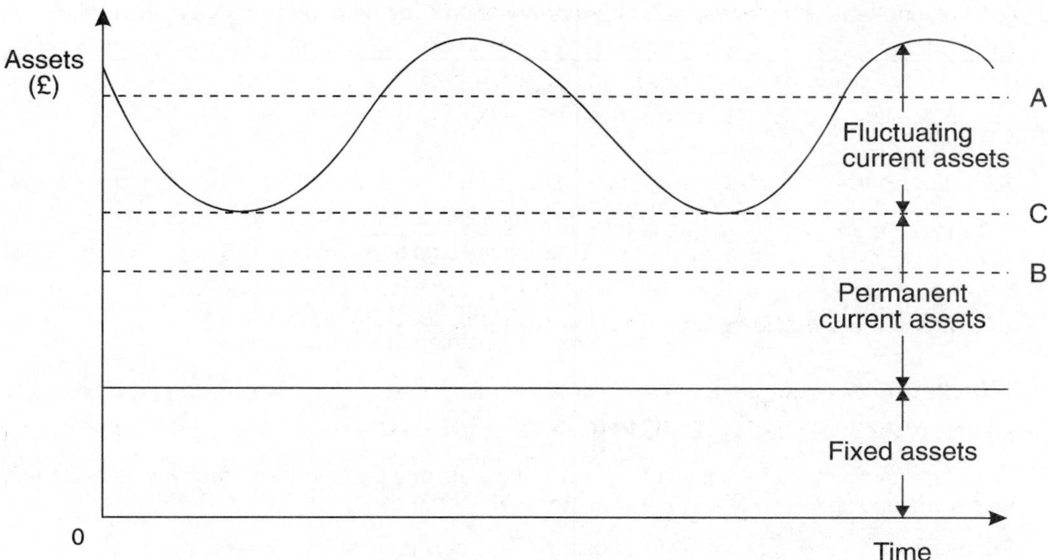

Chapter roundup

- **Gearing** must be considered when deciding how to finance a business.
- **Financial gearing** and **operating** or **operational gearing** need to be distinguished.
    - **Financial gearing** measures the relationship between **shareholders' funds** and **prior charge capital.**
    - **Operating gearing** measures the relationship between **contribution** and **profit before interest and tax.**
- If a company can generate returns on capital in excess of the interest payable on debt, financial gearing will raise the EPS. Gearing will, however, also increase **the variability of returns** for shareholders and increase the chance of corporate **failure**.
- **Gearing** is also limited by the reluctance of lenders to lend to a company which does not have an adequate equity base.
- The way in which a company funds its current and permanent assets through either short-term or long-term finance may be **conservative** at on extreme or **aggressive** at the other.

Quick quiz

1 *Fill in the blanks.*

$$\text{..........................} \text{ gearing} = \frac{\text{Prior charge capital}}{\text{Total capital employed}}$$

$$\text{..........................} \text{ gearing} = \frac{\text{Contribution}}{\text{Profit before interest and tax}}$$

2 *Fill in the blank.*

Interest cover = ...

3 What type of policy is characterised by all fixed assets and permanent current assets being financed by long-term funding?

4 Puppy plc has decided to calculate its gearing ratio according to the formula:

prior charge capital: equity capital (incl reserves)

At what level would it be neutrally geared?

5 Are preference shares prior charge or equity capital?

6 Why should a long-term asset not be financed by short-term loans?

7 What condition has to be fulfilled for increased financial gearing to result in increased earnings per share?

8 What is the debt ratio?

Answers to quick quiz

1 <u>Financial</u> gearing = $\frac{\text{Prior charge capital}}{\text{Total capital employed}}$

<u>Operating</u> gearing = $\frac{\text{Contribution}}{\text{Profit before interest and tax}}$

2 Interest cover = $\frac{\text{Profit before interest and tax}}{\text{Interest}}$

3 Conservative

4 C Gearing is neutral where Debt = Equity, 100% on the basis of this calculation

5 Prior charge capital

6 When the loan becomes repayable, the company cannot be certain that it will have generated enough profits to repay the loan.

7 The returns on capital investment must exceed the interest payable on the extra debt used to finance the investment.

8 Total debt: Total assets

Now try the question below from the Exam Question Bank

Question to try	Level	Marks	Time
29	Exam	25	45 mins

Chapter 25

FINANCING OF SMALL AND MEDIUM-SIZED ENTERPRISES

	Topic list	Syllabus reference
1	**Small and medium-sized enterprises**	4
2	**The problems of financing SME's**	4
3	**Sources of finance for SME's**	4
4	**Government aid for SME's**	4

Introduction

In this chapter we shall be concentrating how small and medium-sized businesses obtain finance. The sources of finance are important but this chapter also discusses why SME's have difficulty raising finance and how they can tackle the obstacles that exist to obtaining finance.

Study guide

Section 8 – Sources of finance I: Small and medium-sized enterprises

- Explain financing in terms of the risk/return trade-off
- Describe the requirements for finance of SME's (purpose, how much, how long)
- Describe the nature of the financing problem for small businesses in terms of the funding gap, the maturity gap and inadequate security
- Identify the role of risk and the lack of information on small companies to help explain the problems of SME financing
- Explain the role of information provision provided by financial statements
- Describe the particular financing problems of low-earning/high growth companies
- Describe the response of government agencies and financial institutions to the SME financing problem
- Explain what other measures may be taken to ease the financial problems of SME's such as trade creditors, factoring, leasing, hire purchase, AIM listing, business angels and venture capital
- Describe how capital structure decisions in SME's may differ from larger organisations
- Describe appropriate sources of finance for SME's
- Calculate and interpret appropriate ratios

Exam guide

Financing of small enterprises is an important topic. You must be able to show in the exam you appreciate the special circumstances of small companies, for example that capital structure may depend solely upon whether funds are available rather than what is optimal in a given situation. The financing of small enterprises was included in the pilot paper *and* the December 2001 exam.

1 SMALL AND MEDIUM-SIZED ENTERPRISES

KEY TERM

Small and medium-sized enterprises (SME's) can be defined as having three characteristics

(a) Firms are likely to be unquoted.

(b) Ownership of the business is restricted to a few individuals, typically a family group

(c) They are not micro businesses that are normally regarded as those very small businesses that act as a medium for self-employment of the owners.

Laney

1.1 The characteristics may alter over time, with the enterprise maybe looking for a listing on the Alternative Investment Market as it expands.

1.2 The SME sector accounts for between a third and a half of sales and employment. The sector is likely to grow over the next few years with the need for businesses to serve niche markets and the shift from the manufacturing to the service sector. If market conditions do change, small businesses may be **more adaptable.**

1.3 There is, however, a significant failure rate amongst small firms. According to a Bank of England survey in 1998, only 47% of new firms still survive five years after commencing trading.

2 THE PROBLEMS OF FINANCING SME'S 12/01

2.1 The money for investment that SME's can obtain comes from the savings individuals make in the economy. Government policy will have a major influence on the level of funds available.

(a) **Tax policy** including concessions given to businesses to invest (capital allowances) and taxes on distributions (higher taxes on dividends mean less income for investors)

(b) **Interest rate policy** with high interest rates working in different ways – borrowing for SME's becomes more expensive, but the supply of funds is also greater as higher rates give greater incentives to investors to save

2.2 SME's however also face **competition** for funds. Investors have opportunities to invest in all sizes of organisation, also overseas and in government debt.

2.3 The main handicap that SME's face in accessing funds is the problem of **uncertainty.**

(a) Whatever the details provided to potential investors, SMEs have **neither** the **business** history **nor larger track record** that larger organisations possess.

(b) Larger enterprises are subject by law to **more public scrutiny**; their accounts have to contain more detail and be audited, they receive more press coverage and so on.

(c) Because of the uncertainties involved, banks often use **credit scoring** systems to **control exposure.**

2.4 Because the information is not available in other ways, SME's will have to provide it when they seek finance. They will need to give a business plan, list of the firm's assets, details of the experience of directors and managers and show how they intend to provide security for sums advanced.

2.5 Prospective lenders, often banks, will then make a decision based on the information provided. The terms of the loan (interest rate, term, security, repayment details) will depend on the **risk** involved, and the lender will also want to monitor their investment.

2.6 A common problem is often that the banks will be **unwilling** to increase **loan funding** without an increase in **security given** (which the owners may be unwilling or unable to give), or an increase in **equity funding** (which may be difficult to obtain). We shall see in the next two sections how mechanisms and policies have been designed to give small firms easier access to equity funding.

Problems of low asset companies

2.7 The problems of uncertainty particularly apply to companies with few tangible assets such as high-technology companies.

Case example

Jim Melton, a significant investor in Internet stocks, has commented that the main three criteria he uses when deciding whether to invest are:

(a) An intuitive factor

(b) The track record of the management

(c) Assessment of the overall market place and whether the business model is actually sustainable in terms of making a profit.

3 SOURCES OF FINANCE FOR SME'S 12/01

3.1 Potential sources of financing for small and medium-sized companies include the following.

- Owner financing
- Overdraft financing
- Bank loans
- Trade credit
- Equity finance
- Business angel financing
- Venture capital
- Leasing (see chapter 31)
- Factoring (see Chapter 20)

3.2 Key sources of finance are discussed in more detail below.

3.3 Surveys have suggested that small firms have problems accessing different sources of finance because managers are insufficiently informed about what is available. However the increased amount of literature and government agencies designed to help small businesses have resulted in a reduction in this difficulty.

Owner financing

3.4 Finance from the owner(s)' personal resources or those of family connections is generally the initial source of finance. At this stage because many assets are intangible, external funding may be difficult to obtain.

Overdraft financing

3.5 Remember this is where payments from a current account exceed income to the account for a temporary period, the bank finances the deficit by means of an **overdraft**. It is very much a form of **short-term lending**, available to both personal and business customers.

3.6 Factors associated with an overdraft are as follows.

(a) **Amount**

The debit amount should not exceed a certain limit agreed between the bank and the borrower, usually with reference to known income.

(b) **Margin**

Interest is charged on the amount overdrawn, usually as a margin over base rate. Interest is calculated on the daily amount overdrawn and is charged to the account quarterly. A fee may also be levied where the bank has agreed a large facility with the customer, even where this facility is not fully used.

(c) **Purpose**

Overdrafts are usually required to cover short-term deficits: for instance, many people run short at the end of each month before their salaries are paid in.

(d) **Repayment**

Overdrafts are technically repayable on demand and it is usual in the facility letter to make this plain to the customer.

(e) **Security**

Depending on the size of the facility open to the customer, security may be required by the bank.

(f) **Benefits**

The customer has a flexible means of short term borrowing; the bank has to accept the fluctuation in the account.

Overdrafts and the operating cycle

3.7 Many SME's require their bank to provide financial assistance for normal trading over the **operating cycle**. To some extent, a business can - and should - put up finance to cover the needs of the operating cycle - ie the need to invest in stocks and debtors; and to some extent, trade creditors will provide financial support by granting credit. However, a bank might also provide financial support by allowing the business an overdraft facility.

3.8 A feature of bank lending to support normal trading finance is that the amount of the overdraft required at any time will depend on the **cash flows of the business**: the timing of receipts and payments, seasonal variations in trade patterns and so on. An overdraft will increase in size if the customer writes more cheques, but will reduce in size when money is paid into the account. There should be times when there will be no overdraft at all, and the account is in credit for a while.

3.9 If the hard core element of the overdraft appears to be becoming a long-term feature of the business, the bank might wish, after discussions with the customer, to convert the hard core of the overdraft into a **medium-term loan**, thus giving formal recognition to its more permanent nature. Otherwise **annual reductions** in the hard core of an overdraft would typically be a requirement of the bank.

Overdrafts and loans compared

3.10 A customer might ask the bank for an overdraft facility when the bank would wish to suggest a loan instead; alternatively, a customer might ask for a loan when an overdraft would be more appropriate.

(a) In most cases, when a customer wants finance to help with **'day to day' trading** and cash flow needs, an overdraft would be the appropriate method of financing. The customer should not be short of cash all the time, and should expect to be in credit in some days, but in need of an overdraft on others.

(b) When a customer wants to borrow from a bank for only a short period of time, even for the purchase of a major fixed asset such as an item of plant or machinery, an overdraft facility might be **more suitable** than a loan, because the customer will stop paying interest as soon as his account goes into credit.

(c) When a customer wants to borrow from a bank, but cannot see his way to repaying the bank except over the course of a few years, the medium-term nature of the financing is best catered for by the provision of a loan rather than an overdraft facility.

3.11 **Advantages of an overdraft over a loan**

(a) The customer **only pays interest when he is overdrawn.**

(b) The bank has the flexibility to **review** the customer's overdraft facility periodically, and perhaps agree to additional facilities, or insist on a reduction in the facility.

(c) An overdraft can do the same job as a **medium-term loan:** a facility can simply be renewed every time it comes up for review.

(d) Being short-term debt, an overdraft will not affect the calculation of a company's **gearing.**

Bear in mind, however, that overdrafts are normally repayable on demand.

3.12 **Advantages of a medium-term loan**

(a) Both the customer and the bank **know exactly** what the repayments of the loan will be and how much interest is payable, and when. This makes planning (budgeting) simpler.

(b) The customer does not have to worry about the bank deciding to reduce or **withdraw** an overdraft facility before he is in a position to repay what is owed. There is an element of 'security' or 'peace of mind' in being able to arrange a loan for an agreed term.

(c) Medium-term loans normally carry a **facility letter** setting out the precise terms of the agreement.

3.13 For purchases of a fixed asset it is important, however, that the term of the loan **should not exceed the economic or useful life** of the asset purchased with the money from the loan. A businessman will often expect to use the revenues earned by the asset to repay the loan, and obviously, an asset can only do this as long as it is in operational use.

3.14 However, a **mix** of overdrafts and loans might be suggested in some cases. Consider a case where a business asks for a loan, perhaps to purchase a shop with stock. The banker **might** wish to suggest a loan to help with the purchase of the shop, but that stock ought to be financed by an overdraft facility. The offer of part-loan part-overdraft is an option that might be well worth considering.

3.15 In practice, although an increasing amount of bank lending is on a fixed-term basis, the time scale may not be all that long. Because of the risk involved, banks are often lending for a period significantly shorter than the life of the investment.

Trade credit

3.16 The use of trade credit finance is discussed in Chapter 20. Undoubtedly trade credit can be a useful source of finance early in a SME's life. Its principal problem is that taking extended credit will mean the **loss of early payment discounts**, and the amounts involved may be significant.

Equity finance

3.17 Other than investment by owners or business angels, businesses with few tangible assets will probably have difficulty obtaining equity finance when they are formed (a problem known as the **equity gap**).

3.18 However, once small firms have become established, they do not necessarily need to seek a market listing to obtain equity financing; shares can be **placed privately**. Letting external shareholders invest does not necessarily mean that the original owners have to cede control, particularly if the shares are held by a number of small investors. However small companies may find it difficult to obtain large sums by this means.

3.19 As noted above, owners will need to invest a certain amount of capital when the business starts up. However subsequently owners can choose whether they withdraw profits from the business or re-invest them.

3.20 Surveys have suggested that the amount of equity invested by owners in a business after startup and retained earnings are relatively low compared with other sources of finance. However the failure of owners to invest limits the assets that can be acquired, and hence the amount of security that can be given for debt capital.

3.21 A major problem with obtaining equity finance can be the inability of the small firm to offer an easy **exit route** for any investors who wish to sell their stake.

(a) The **firm** can **purchase its own shares** back from the shareholders, but this involves the use of cash that could be better employed elsewhere.

(b) The **firm** can obtain a **market listing** but not all small firms do.

Business angel financing

3.22 Business angel financing can be an important initial source of business finance. Business angels are wealthy individuals or groups of individuals who invest directly in small businesses.

3.23 The main problem with business angel financing is that it is informal in terms of a market and can be difficult to set up. However informality can be a strength. There may be less need to provide business angels with detailed information about the company, since business angels generally have prior knowledge of the industry.

3.24 Surveys suggest that business angels are often more patient than providers of other sources of finance. However the money available from individual business angels may be limited, and large sums may only be available from a consortium of business angels.

Venture capital organisations

KEY TERM

Venture capital is risk capital, normally provided in return for an equity stake.

3.25 **Venture capital organisations** have been operating for many years. There are now quite a large number of such organisations.

(a) The British Venture Capital Association is a regulatory body for all the institutions that have joined it as members.

(b) **Investors in Industry plc**, or the **3i group** as it is more commonly known, is the biggest and oldest of the venture capital organisations. It is involved in many venture capital schemes in Europe, Singapore, Japan and the US.

3.26 The supply of venture capital in the UK has grown in recent years, as governments have helped to create an environment which supports entrepreneurial business.

3.27 Like other venture capitalists, the 3i group wants to invest in companies that will be successful. The group's publicity material states that successful investments have certain common characteristics.

- Highly motivated individuals with a strong management team in place
- A well defined strategy
- A clearly defined target market
- Current turnover between £1m and £100m
- A proven ability to outperform your competitors
- Innovation

3.28 The types of venture that the 3i group might invest in include the following.

(a) **Business start-ups**. When a business has been set up by someone who has already put time and money into getting it started, the group may be willing to **provide finance** to enable it to get off the ground.

(b) **Business development**. The group may be willing to **provide development capital** for a company which wants to invest in new products or new markets or to make a business acquisition, and so which needs a major capital injection.

(c) **Management buyouts**. A management buyout is the **purchase** of all or parts of a **business** from its owners by its managers.

(d) Helping a company where one of its owners wants to **realise all or part of his investment**. The 3i group may be prepared to buy some of the company's equity.

Venture capital funds

3.29 Some other organisations are engaged in the creation of **venture capital funds.** In these the organisation raises venture capital funds from investors and invests in management buyouts or expanding companies. The venture capital fund managers usually reward themselves by taking a percentage of the portfolio of the fund's investments.

3.30 **Venture capital trusts** are a special type of fund giving investors tax reliefs.

Finding venture capital

3.31 When a company's directors look for help from a venture capital institution, they must recognise that:

(a) The institution will want an **equity stake** in the company

(b) It will need convincing that the company can be successful (management buyouts of companies which already have a record of **successful trading** have been increasingly favoured by venture capitalists in recent years)

(c) It may want to have a **representative** appointed to the company's board, to look after its interests, or an **independent director** (the 3i group runs an Independent Director Scheme)

3.32 The directors of the company must then contact venture capital organisations, to try to find one or more which would be willing to offer finance. Typically, a venture capitalist will consider offering finance of £500,000 upwards. A venture capital organisation will only give funds to a company that it believes can succeed.

3.33 A survey has indicated that around 75% of requests for venture capital are rejected on an initial screening, and only about 3% of all requests survive both this screening and further investigation and result in actual investments.

3.34 The venture capital organisation ('VC' below) will take account of various factors in deciding whether to not to invest.

Factors in investment decisions	
The nature of the company's **product**	Viability of production and selling potential
Expertise in **production**	Technical ability to produce efficiently
Expertise in **management**	Commitment, skills and experience
The **market and competition**	Threat from rival producers or future new entrants
Future profits	Detailed business plan showing profit prospects that compensate for risks
Board membership	To take account of VC's interests and ensure VC has say in future strategy
Risk borne by existing owners	Owners bear significant risk and invest significant part of their overall wealth

Capital structure

3.35 Significant influences on the capital structure of small firms are:

- The **lack of separation** between **ownership** and **management**
- The **lack of equity finance**

Studies have suggested that the owners' preference and market considerations are also significant. Small firms tend not to have target debt ratios.

3.36 Other studies suggest that the life-cycle of the firm is important. Debt finance is an important early source, its availability depending upon the security available. Longer-term loans may in fact be easier to obtain because they can be secured by mortgages against property.

3.37 As firms mature, however, the reliance on debt declines. There seems to be little evidence of a relationship between gearing, and profitability and risk levels.

4 GOVERNMENT AID FOR SME's

Exam focus point

Availability of government assistance is country-specific. For the exam, at a minimum, you should be aware of the possibilities of such assistance and the major schemes operating in at least one country.

4.1 The UK government has introduced a number of assistance schemes to help businesses, and several of these are designed to encourage lenders and investors to make finance available to small and unquoted businesses. They include the Loan Guarantee Scheme, the Enterprise Initiative, development agencies, the Enterprise Investment Scheme and venture capital trusts.

The Loan Guarantee Scheme

4.2 The **Loan Guarantee Scheme** was introduced by the government in 1981. It is intended to help small businesses to get a loan from the bank, when a bank would otherwise be unwilling to lend because the business cannot offer the security that the bank would want. The borrower's annual turnover must not exceed a limit which depends on the type of business.

4.3 Under the scheme, which was revised in 1993, the bank can lend up to £250,000 without security over **personal** assets or a personal guarantee being required of the borrower. However, all available **business** assets must be used as security if required. The government will guarantee the bulk of the loan, while the borrower must pay an annual premium on the guaranteed part of the loan.

The Enterprise Initiative

4.4 The Enterprise Initiative is a package of measures offered by the Department of Trade and Industry (DTI) to businesses in the UK, including some regional selective grant assistance. Also provided is a network of 'Business Links', which are local business advice centres.

4.5 **Regional selective assistance** is available for investment projects undertaken by firms in **Assisted Areas**. The project must be commercially viable, create or safeguard employment, demonstrate a need for assistance and offer a distinct regional and national benefit. The amount of grant will be negotiated as the minimum necessary to ensure the project goes ahead.

4.6 The **Regional Enterprise Grants** scheme is specially geared to help small firms employing fewer than 25 in one of the Development Areas to expand and diversify. Regional enterprise grants can help finance viable projects for:

(a) Investment - grants of 15% of the cost of fixed assets up to a maximum of £15,000 are available

(b) Innovation - grants of 50% of the agreed project cost up to a maximum grant of £25,000 are available

Development agencies

4.7 The UK government has set up the **Scottish and Welsh Development Agencies** which have been given the task of trying to encourage the development of trade and industry in their areas. The strategy of the agencies has been mainly to encourage the **start-up** and **development of small companies,** although they will also give help to larger companies too.

4.8 The assistance that a development agency might give to a firm could include:

(a) Free factory accommodation, or factory accommodation at a low rent

(b) Financial assistance, in the form of

(i) An interest relief grant for a bank loan (A company developing its business in an area might obtain a bank loan, and the development agency will agree to compensate the bank for providing the loan at a low rate of interest.)

(ii) Direct financial assistance in the form of equity finance or loans

The Enterprise Investment Scheme

4.9 The **Enterprise Investment Scheme (EIS)** is intended to encourage investment in the ordinary shares of unquoted companies. When a qualifying individual subscribes for eligible shares in a qualifying company, the individual saves tax at 20% on the amount subscribed (including any share premium). A **qualifying individual** is one who is not connected with the company at any time in the period from two years before the issue (or from incorporation if later) to five years after the issue. The maximum total investment that can qualify in a tax year is £150,000 per individual. Capital gains generated by individual investors in the EIS are tax-free provided the investment is held for five years.

Venture capital trusts

4.10 Venture capital providers have been around for many years, but in 1993, the UK Government introduced a second measure to encourage equity investment in the form of a new kind of investment trust called a **venture capital trust (VCT)** which came into being in 1995. This followed criticism from banks and small business groups that small companies were too dependent on short-term finance.

4.11 The investment trust must be approved by the Inland Revenue, under rules which require it to invest a large proportion of assets in unquoted companies. Investors gain 20% income tax relief on dividends, provided shares are held in the VCT for three years, and capital gains rollover relief if the gain is invested in a VCT. There is an investment ceiling per person of £100,000.

Chapter roundup

- SME's may **not know about** the sources of finance available.
- Finance may be difficult to obtain because of the **risks** faced by SME's.
- The availability of certain sources of finance will often be conditioned by the **security** that SME's can offer.
- Possible sources of finance for SME's include:
  - Owner financing
  - Overdraft financing
  - Bank loans
  - Trade credit
  - Equity finance
  - Business angel financing
  - Venture capital
  - Leasing
  - Factoring
- **Government aid** for SME's includes the Loan Guarantee Scheme, Enterprise Initiatives and development agencies.

Quick quiz

1 What are the main characteristics of small and medium-sized enterprises defined by Laney?

2 What is business angel financing?

3 What are the key factors involved in the granting of an overdraft?

4 What is the main incentive offered by the Enterprise Investment Scheme?

5 List four factors that a venture capitalist would consider when deciding whether to invest in a company.

6 Which of the following statements about venture capital is correct?

A Venture capital would not be appropriate to finance a management buyout

B Venture capital organisations may provide loan finance as well as equity finance to a company

C Secured medium-term bank loans are a form of venture capital

D Companies with a stock market quotation would have no difficulty raising finance from a venture capital organisation

7 Which of the following business opportunities would be the most attractive to a venture capitalist?

A A consultancy specialising in sustainable development currently employing four consultants that wishes to expand its workforce by 25%

B A manufacturing business that is facing liquidity problems and needs an injection of capital

C A management buyout of a medium sized electrical engineering company

D A carpet manufacturing company that wants to renovate one of its production lines

8 Which of the following sources of funds for business is not commonly offered by commercial banks?

A Overdraft facilities

B Short-term loans

C Medium-term loans

D Long-term loans

Answers to quick quiz

1 (a) Firms are likely to be unquoted.
  (b) Ownership of the business is restricted to a few individuals, typically a family group.
  (c) They are not micro businesses that offer a medium for self-employment of their owners.

2 Direct investment in SME's by individuals or small groups of investors.

3 (a) Amount
  (b) Margin
  (c) Purpose
  (d) Repayment
  (e) Security
  (f) Benefits

4 When a qualifying individual subscribers for eligible shares in a qualifying company, the individual saves tax at 20% on the amounts subscribed.

5 (a) Nature of company's product
  (b) Production expertise
  (c) Management expertise
  (d) Future prospects
  (e) Board membership
  (f) Risk borne by existing owners

6 B Loan finance may be provided.

7 C Venture capital is appropriate for new business ventures or business expansions. It is not appropriate for the day-to-day financing of existing operations, as in B and D. Option A is likely to be too small to attract a venture capital investment.

8 D This is the correct answer. Long-term loans are rarely negotiated with the commercial banks, unless in the form of a mortgage on property.

  A Overdraft facilities are funds that are drawn down as required, up to a pre-determined maximum limit agreed with the bank. They are repayable on demand and are the traditional form of bank finance.

  B Short-term loans with a fixed period of up to three years are another traditional form of bank finance. They carry less risk than the overdraft, but interest will be payable on the full amount, not just the amount in use at any one time.

  C Medium-term loans are for a period of three to ten years. This is a growing form of bank lending, which used to be restricted mainly to short-term financing.

Now try the question below from the Exam Question Bank

Question to try	Level	Marks	Time
30	Exam	25	45 mins

Chapter 26

INVESTMENT DECISIONS

Topic list		Syllabus reference
1	Investment	5(a)
2	Identification of investment opportunities	5(a)
3	The payback period	5(a)
4	The return on capital employed method	5(a)

Introduction

This chapter introduces **investment appraisal** and covers the manner in which investment opportunities are identified and two investment appraisal methods. Chapter 27 will look at investment appraisal using the more sophisticated **DCF** methods.

Study guide

Section 12 – Investment decisions

- Define and distinguish between capital and revenue expenditure
- Compare and contrast fixed asset investment and working capital investment
- Describe the impact of investment projects on financial statements
- Calculate payback and assess its usefulness as a measure of investment worth
- Calculate ROCE and assess its usefulness as a measure of investment worth

Exam guide

As well as using the techniques to assess projects, you may be asked to discuss their drawbacks. The Oxford Brookes degree Research and Analysis Project Topic 14 requires you to investigate recent project decisions by an organisation of your choice.

1 INVESTMENT

1.1 Investment is any expenditure in the expectation of future benefits. We can divide such expenditure into two categories: **capital expenditure**, and **revenue expenditure**.

1.2 Suppose that a business purchases a building for £30,000. It then adds an extension to the building at a cost of £10,000. The building needs to have a few broken windows mended, its floors polished and some missing roof tiles replaced. These cleaning and maintenance jobs cost £900.

1.3 The original purchase (£30,000) and the cost of the extension (£10,000) are **capital expenditure** because they are incurred to **acquire** and then **improve** a fixed asset. The other costs of £900 are **revenue expenditure** because they merely maintain the building and thus the earning capacity of the building.

KEY TERMS

Capital expenditure is expenditure which results in the **acquisition** of fixed assets or an **improvement** in their earning capacity. It is not charged as an expense in the profit and loss account; the expenditure appears as a fixed asset in the balance sheet.

Revenue expenditure is charged to the profit and loss account and is expenditure which is incurred:

(a) For the purpose of the trade of the business - this includes expenditure classified as selling and distribution expenses, administration expenses and finance charges

(b) To maintain the existing earning capacity of fixed assets

Fixed asset investment and working capital investment

1.4 **Investment** can be made in **fixed assets** or **working capital.**

(a) **Investment in fixed assets** involves a significant elapse of time between commitment of funds and recoupment of the investment. Money is paid out to acquire resources which are going to be used on a continuing basis within the organisation.

(b) **Investment in working capital** arises from the need to pay out money for resources (such as raw materials) before it can be recovered from sales of the finished product or service. The funds are therefore only committed for a short period of time.

Investment by the commercial sector

1.5 Investment by commercial organisations might include investment in:

- Plant and machinery
- Research and development
- Advertising
- Warehouse facilities

1.6 The overriding feature of a commercial sector investment is that it is generally **based on financial considerations alone.** The various capital expenditure appraisal techniques that we will be looking at assess the financial aspects of capital investment.

Investment by not-for-profit organisations

1.7 Investment by not-for-profit organisations differs from investment by commercial organisations for several reasons.

(a) Relatively few not-for-profit organisations' capital investments are made with the **intention** of earning a **financial return.**

(b) When there are two or more ways of achieving the same objective (mutually exclusive investment opportunities), a commercial organisation might prefer the option with the **lowest present value of cost.**

Not-for-profit organisations, however, rather than just considering financial cost and financial benefits, will often have regard to the **social costs** and **social benefits** of investments.

(c) The **cost of capital** that is applied to project cash flows by the public sector will not be a 'commercial' rate of return, but one that is **determined** by the **government**. Any targets that a public sector investment has to meet before being accepted will therefore not be based on the same criteria as those in the commercial sector.

2 IDENTIFICATION OF INVESTMENT OPPORTUNITIES

2.1 A company can be offered a number of possible investment projects, each of which might appear attractive in the return it offers as assessed by investment appraisal techniques such as discounted cash flow.

2.2 Igor Ansoff argues, however, that capital investment appraisal is concerned with only the last two steps of a more complex process of strategic decision making. This process has four stages.

- Perception of the need for an investment, or awareness of a potential opportunity
- Formulation of alternative courses of action
- Evaluation of the alternatives
- Choice of one of these alternatives for implementation

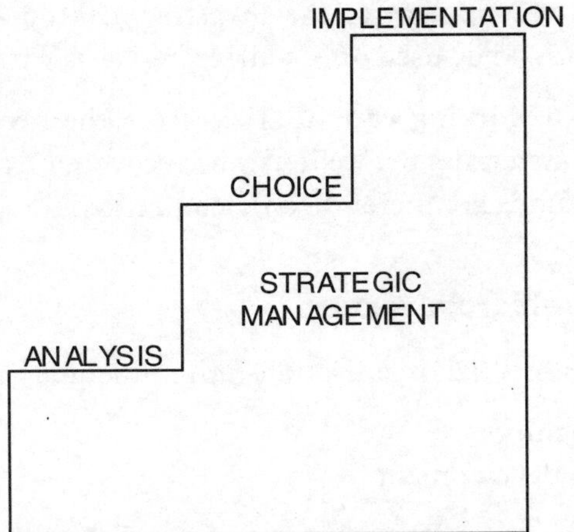

Strategic analysis	
Environmental analysis	Factors in operating environment including political-legal, economic, socio-cultural, technological, competitive
Internal appraisal	Past activities and current resources to see how firm can deal with current environment and environmental change
Mission and objectives	The firm's aims and the requirements of its shareholders
Strategic choice	
Generation of alternative options	Evaluation of alternative options
Selection of a strategy	
Strategic implementation	
Allocation of resources	Design of organisation structure
Direction of organisation's systems and employees	

Corporate appraisal: SWOT analysis

2.3 Environmental analysis and internal assessment are combined, in a process of corporate appraisal known as **SWOT** analysis. This involves a critical assessment of the strengths and weaknesses, opportunities and threats in relation to the internal and environmental factors affecting the organisation.

2.4 A cruciform chart is a table listing the significant strengths and weaknesses and opportunities and threats. It can be used to summarise the major conclusions of a SWOT analysis. In the example below, the development of potential strategies from the analysis is illustrated.

Strengths £10 million of capital available. Production expertise and appropriate marketing skills	**Weaknesses** Heavy reliance on a small number of customers. Limited product range, with no new products and expected market decline. Small marketing organisation.
Threats Major competitor has already entered the new market.	**Opportunities** Government tax incentives for new investment. Growing demand in a new market, although customers so far relatively small in number.

2.5 In this simple example, you can see that the company is in imminent danger of losing its existing markets and must **diversify** its products, or its products and markets. The new market opportunity exists to be exploited. Since the number of customers is currently few, the relatively small size of the existing marketing force would not be an immediate hindrance.

2.6 You can get used to the basic thinking that underlies planning if you try the following short question in SWOT analysis.

Question

Hall Faull Downes Ltd has been in business for 25 years, during which time profits have risen by an average of 3% per annum, although there have been peaks and troughs in profitability due to the ups and downs of trade in the customers' industry. The increase in profits until five years ago was the result of increasing sales in a buoyant market, but more recently, the total market has become somewhat smaller and Hall Faull Downes has only increased sales and profits as a result of improving its market share.

The company produces components for manufacturers in the engineering industry. In recent years, the company has developed many new products and currently has 40 items in its range compared to 24 only five years ago. Over the same five-year period, the number of customers has fallen from 20 to nine, two of whom together account for 60% of the company's sales.

Give your appraisal of the company's future, and suggest what it is probably doing wrong.

Answer

A general interpretation of the facts as given might be sketched as follows.

(a) **Objectives**. The company has no declared objectives. Profits have risen by 3% per annum in the past, therefore failing to keep pace with inflation but this may have been a satisfactory rate of increase in the current conditions of the industry. Even so, stronger growth is indicated in the future.

(b)

Strengths	Weaknesses
Many new products developed. Marketing success in increasing market share.	Products may be reaching the end of their life and entering decline. New product life cycles may be shorter. Reduction in customers. Excessive reliance on a few customers. Doubtful whether profit record is satisfactory.
Threats	**Opportunities**
Possible decline in the end-product. Smaller end-product market will restrict future sales prospects for Hall Faull Downes.	None identified.

(c) **Strengths**. The growth in company sales in the last five years has been as a result of increasing the market share in a declining market. This success may be the result of the following.

(i) Research and development spending
(ii) Good product development programmes
(iii) Extending the product range to suit changing customer needs
(iv) Marketing skills
(v) Long-term supply contracts with customers
(vi) Cheap pricing policy
(vii) Product quality and reliable service

(d) **Weaknesses**

(i) The products may be custom-made for customers so that they provide little or no opportunity for market development.

(ii) Products might have a shorter life cycle than in the past, in view of the declining total market demand.

(iii) Excessive reliance on two major customers leaves the company exposed to the dangers of losing their custom.

(e) **Threats**. There may be a decline in the end-market for the customers' product so that the customer demands for the company's own products will also fall.

(f) **Opportunities**. No opportunities have been identified, but in view of the situation as described, new strategies for the longer term would appear to be essential.

(g) **Conclusions**. The company does not appear to be planning beyond the short term, or is reacting to the business environment in a piecemeal fashion. A strategic planning programme should be introduced.

(h) **Recommendation**. The company must look for new opportunities in the longer term.

(i) In the short term, current strengths must be exploited to continue to increase market share in existing markets and product development programmes should also continue.

(ii) In the longer term, the company must diversify into new markets or into new products and new markets. Diversification opportunities should be sought with a view to exploiting any competitive advantage or synergy that might be achievable.

(iii) The company should use its strengths (whether in R & D, production skills or marketing expertise) in exploiting any identifiable opportunities.

(iv) Objectives need to be quantified in order to assess the extent to which new long-term strategies are required.

Product-market mix

2.7 A firm may be faced with a bewildering variety of options, in relation both to product development and its possible markets. Igor Ansoff developed a tool for analysing these opportunities as follows.

Market penetration	Sell more existing products in existing markets
Market development	Sell existing products in new markets
Product development	Sell new products in existing markets
Diversification	Sell new products in new markets

2.8 In practice, this tool is an oversimplification. New products are often not unrelated to existing ones. They may be a logical development from them (such as a cheesemaker making and selling butter). The new market may have similarities with the existing ones.

Market share, market growth and cash generation: the Boston classification

2.9 The Boston Consulting Group (BCG) have developed the **Boston matrix,** based on empirical research, which classifies a company's products in terms of potential cash generation and cash expenditure requirements.

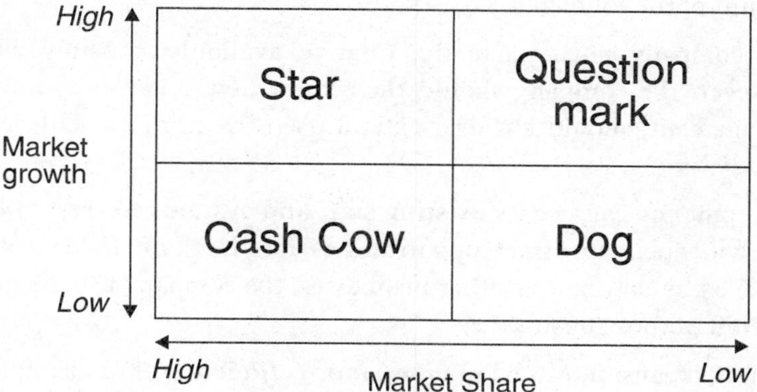

2.10 This **growth/share matrix** is known as the **Boston classification** for product-market strategy.

(a) **Stars**

Stars are products with a **high share** of a **high growth market**. In the short term, these require capital expenditure, in excess of the cash they generate, in order to maintain their market position, but promise high returns in the future.

(b) **Cash cows**

In due course, however, stars will become cash cows, with a high share of a low growth market. **Cash cows** need very little capital expenditure and generate high levels of cash income. The important strategic feature of cash cows is that they are *already* generating high cash returns, which can be used to finance the stars.

(c) **Question marks**

Question marks are products with a **low share** of a **high growth market**. A decision needs to be taken about whether the products justify considerable capital expenditure in the hope of increasing their market share, or whether they should be allowed to 'die' quietly as they are squeezed out of the expanding market by rival products. Question marks will usually be poor cash generators and show a negative cash flow.

(d) **Dogs**

Dogs are products with a **low share** of a **low growth market**. They may be ex-cash cows that have now fallen on hard times. Dogs should be allowed to die, or should be killed off. Although they will show only a modest net cash outflow, or even a modest net cash inflow, they are 'cash traps' which tie up funds and provide a poor return on investment, below the organisation's target rate of return.

There are also **infants** (products in an early stage of development) and **warhorses** (products that have been cash cows in the past, and are still making good sales and earning good profits even now). The idea behind the Boston classification is that a firm should have a mix of cash cows, stars and so on. The cash cows should finance future development.

Organic growth or acquisition?

2.11 A company which is planning to grow must decide on whether to pursue a policy of 'organic' internal growth or a policy of taking over other established businesses, or a mix of the two.

2.12 **Organic growth** requires funding in cash, whereas acquisitions can be made by means of share exchange transactions. A company pursuing a policy of organic growth would need to take account of the following.

(a) The company must make the **finance available**, possibly out of retained profits. However, the company should then know how much it can afford, and with careful management, should not over-extend itself by trying to achieve too much growth too quickly.

(b) The company can use its **existing staff and systems** to create the growth projects, and this will open up career opportunities for the staff. In contrast, when expansion is achieved by taking over other businesses, the company usually acquires and assimilates the staff of those businesses.

(c) Overall expansion can be **planned more efficiently**. For example, if a company wishes to open a new factory or depot, it can site the new development in a place that helps operational efficiency (eg close to other factories, to reduce transport costs). With acquisitions, the company must take on existing sites no matter where they happen to be.

(d) **Economies of scale** can be achieved from more efficient use of central head office functions such as finance, purchasing, personnel and management services. With acquisitions, a company buys the head office functions of other companies and there will either be fewer economies of scale, or more redundancies.

2.13 **Acquisitions** can be made to **enter new product areas**, or to **expand in existing markets**, much **more quickly**. Organic growth takes time. With acquisitions, entire existing operations are assimilated into the company at one fell swoop. Acquisitions can be made without cash, if share exchange transactions are acceptable to both the buyers and sellers of any company which is to be taken over.

2.14 When an acquisition is made to diversify into new product areas, the company will be buying technical expertise, goodwill and customer contracts and so on, which it might take years to develop if it tried to enter the market by growing organically.

Exam focus point

For the exam, you will be expected to have an appreciation of the advantages and disadvantages of internal *versus* external growth.

3 THE PAYBACK PERIOD

3.1 There are a number of ways of evaluating capital projects, two of which we will be examining in this chapter. We will look first at the payback method.

Exam focus point

Exam questions often ask about the pros and cons of the payback method.

KEY TERM

Payback is the time it takes the cash inflows from a capital investment project to equal the cash outflows, usually expressed in years.

3.2 Payback is often used as a 'first screening method'. By this, we mean that when a capital investment project is being considered, the first question to ask is: 'How long will it take to pay back its cost?' The organisation might have a **target payback**, and so it would reject a capital project unless its payback period were less than a certain number of years.

3.3 However, a project should not be evaluated on the basis of payback alone. If a project gets through the payback test, it ought then to be evaluated with a more sophisticated investment appraisal technique.

Why is payback alone an inadequate investment appraisal technique?

3.4 The reason why payback should not be used on its own to evaluate capital investments should seem fairly obvious if you look at the figures below for two mutually exclusive projects (this means that only one of them can be undertaken).

	Project P	*Project Q*
Capital asset	£60,000	£60,000
Profits before depreciation (a rough approximation of cash flows)		
Year 1	£20,000	£50,000
Year 2	£30,000	£20,000
Year 3	£40,000	£5,000
Year 4	£50,000	£5,000
Year 5	£60,000	£5,000

3.5 Project P pays back in year 3 (about one quarter of the way through year 3). Project Q pays back half way through year 2. Using payback alone to judge capital investments, project Q would be preferred.

3.6 However the returns from project P over its life are much higher than the returns from project Q. **Project P** will earn total profits before depreciation of £140,000 on an investment of £60,000. **Project Q** will earn total profits before depreciation of only £25,000 on an investment of £60,000.

Disadvantages of the payback method

3.7 There are a number of serious drawbacks to the payback method.

(a) It **ignores** the **timing** of cash flows within the payback period, the cash flows after the end of payback period and therefore the total project return.

(b) It **ignores the time value of money** (a concept incorporated into more sophisticated appraisal methods). This means that it does not take account of the fact that £1 today is worth more than £1 in one year's time. An investor who has £1 today can either consume it immediately or alternatively can invest it at the prevailing interest rate, say 10%, to get a return of £1.10 in a year's time.

(c) Payback is **unable to distinguish between projects** with the same payback period.

(d) The choice of any **cut-off** payback period by an organisation is **arbitrary**.

(e) It may lead to **excessive investment** in **short-term projects**.

(f) It takes account of the risk of the timing of cash flows but not the **variability** of those cash flows.

Advantages of the payback method

3.8 In spite of its limitations, the payback method continues to be popular, and the following points can be made in its favour.

(a) It is **simple to calculate** and **simple to understand.** This may be important when management resources are limited. It is similarly helpful in communicating information about minimum requirements to managers responsible for submitting projects.

(b) It can be used as a **screening device** as a first stage in eliminating obviously inappropriate projects prior to more detailed evaluation.

(c) The fact that it tends to **bias** in favour of **short-term projects** means that it tends to minimise both financial and business risk.

(d) It can be used when there is a **capital rationing situation** to identify those projects which generate additional cash for investment quickly.

4 THE RETURN ON CAPITAL EMPLOYED METHOD

4.1 The **return on capital employed** method (ROCE) (also called the **accounting rate of return** method or the **return on investment** ROI method) of appraising a capital project is to estimate the accounting rate of return that the project should yield. If it exceeds a target rate of return, the project will be undertaken. In Chapter 15 we discussed how return on capital employed is measured for financial accounting purposes. Here the measure is calculated in relation to investments.

4.2 Unfortunately, there are several different definitions of 'return on investment'. One of the most popular is as follows.

$$\text{ROCE} = \frac{\text{Estimated average profits}}{\text{Estimated average investment}} \times 100\%$$

The others include:

$$\text{ROCE} = \frac{\text{Estimated total profits}}{\text{Estimated initial investment}} \times 100\%$$

$$\text{ROCE} = \frac{\text{Estimated average profits}}{\text{Estimated initial investment}} \times 100\%$$

4.3 There are arguments in favour of each of these definitions. The most important point is, however, that the method selected should be used consistently. For examination purposes we recommend the first definition unless the question clearly indicates that some other one is to be used.

4.4 EXAMPLE: THE RETURN ON CAPITAL EMPLOYED

A company has a target return on capital employed of 20% (using the first definition in Paragraph 4.1 above), and is now considering the following project.

Capital cost of asset	£80,000
Estimated life	4 years
Estimated profit before depreciation	
Year 1	£20,000
Year 2	£25,000
Year 3	£35,000
Year 4	£25,000

The capital asset would be depreciated by 25% of its cost each year, and will have no residual value. You are required to assess whether the project should be undertaken.

4.5 SOLUTION

The annual profits after depreciation, and the mid-year net book value of the asset, would be as follows.

Year	*Profit after depreciation*	*Mid-year net book value*	*ROCE in the year*
	£	£	%
1	0	70,000	0
2	5,000	50,000	10
3	15,000	30,000	50
4	5,000	10,000	50

4.6 As the table shows, the ROCE is low in the early stages of the project, partly because of low profits in Year 1 but mainly because the net book value of the asset is much higher early on in its life.

4.7 The project does not achieve the target ROCE of 20% in its first two years, but exceeds it in years 3 and 4. So should it be undertaken?

4.8 When the ROCE from a project varies from year to year, it makes sense to take an overall or 'average' view of the project's return. In this case, we should look at the return as a whole over the four-year period.

	£
Total profit before depreciation over four years	105,000
Total profit after depreciation over four years	25,000
Average annual profit after depreciation	6,250
Original cost of investment	80,000
Average net book value over the four year period $\frac{(80,000+0)}{2}$	40,000

ROCE = 6,250/40,000 = 15.6%

The project would not be undertaken because it would fail to yield the target return of 20%.

The ROCE and the comparison of mutually exclusive projects

4.9 The ROCE method of capital investment appraisal can also be used to compare two or more projects which are mutually exclusive. The project with the highest ROCE would be selected (provided that the expected ROCE is higher than the company's target ROCE).

4.10 EXAMPLE: THE ROCE AND MUTUALLY EXCLUSIVE PROJECTS

Arrow Ltd wants to buy a new item of equipment which will be used to provide a service to customers of the company. Two models of equipment are available, one with a slightly higher capacity and greater reliability than the other. The expected costs and profits of each item are as follows.

	Equipment item X	*Equipment item Y*
Capital cost	£80,000	£150,000
Life	5 years	5 years
Profits before depreciation	£	£
Year 1	50,000	50,000
Year 2	50,000	50,000
Year 3	30,000	60,000
Year 4	20,000	60,000
Year 5	10,000	60,000
Disposal value	0	0

ROCE is measured as the average annual profit after depreciation, divided by the average net book value of the asset. You are required to decide which item of equipment should be selected, if any, if the company's target ROCE is 30%.

4.11 SOLUTION

	Item X	*Item Y*
	£	£
Total profit over life of equipment		
Before depreciation	160,000	280,000
After depreciation	80,000	130,000
Average annual profit after depreciation	16,000	26,000
(Capital cost + disposal value)/2	40,000	75,000
ROCE	40%	34.7%

Both projects would earn a return in excess of 30%, but since item X would earn a bigger ROCE, it would be preferred to item Y, even though the profits from Y would be higher by an average of £10,000 a year.

The drawbacks to the ROCE method of capital investment appraisal

4.12 The ROCE method of capital investment appraisal has the serious drawback that it does not take account of the **timing** of the **profits from an investment.** Whenever capital is invested in a project, money is tied up until the project begins to earn profits which pay back the investment. Money tied up in one project cannot be invested anywhere else until the profits come in. Management should be aware of the benefits of early repayments from an investment, which will provide the money for other investments.

4.13 There are a number of other disadvantages.

(a) It is based on **accounting profits** and not cash flows. Accounting profits are subject to a number of different accounting treatments.

(b) It is a **relative measure** rather than an absolute measure and hence takes no account of the size of the investment.

(c) It takes **no account** of the **length of the project.**

(d) Like the payback method, it **ignores** the **time value** of money.

4.14 There are, however, advantages to the ROCE method.

(a) It is a **quick and simple calculation.**

(b) It involves a familiar concept of a **percentage return.**

(c) It looks at the **entire project life.**

Chapter roundup

- Investment can be divided into **capital expenditure** and **revenue expenditure** and can be made in **fixed assets** or **working capital**.
- **Strategic analysis** aids the identification of investment opportunities and involves **environmental analysis** and **internal appraisal**, which are combined in **SWOT analysis.**
- The **Boston classification** groups a company's products in terms of potential cash generation and cash expenditure requirements. Products may be stars, cash cows, question marks, dogs, infants or warhorses.
- The **payback method** of investment appraisal and the **ROCE/ARR/ROI** methods of investment appraisal are popular appraisal techniques despite their limitations (of which you should be aware).
  - **Payback** is the amount of time it takes for cash inflows = cash outflows
  - **ROCE** = $\dfrac{\text{Estimated average/total profits}}{\text{Estimated average/initial investment}} \times 100\%$

Quick quiz

1 S
W
O
T
stands for?

2

	Markets	Products
Market penetration		
Market development		
Product development		
Diversification		

Complete the grid using the words 'New' or 'Existing'.

3 *Fill in the blank.*

.... is the time it takes the cash inflows from a capital investment project to equal the cash outflows.

4 Which of the following can be used to calculate the accounting rate of return?

(a) $\dfrac{\text{Estimated average profits}}{\text{Estimated average investment}} \times 100\%$

(b) $\dfrac{\text{Estimated total profits}}{\text{Estimated initial investment}} \times 100\%$

(c) $\dfrac{\text{Estimated average profits}}{\text{Estimated initial investment}} \times 100\%$

5 *Fill in the blanks in these statements about the advantages of the payback method.*

(a) Focus on early payback can enhance ....

(b) Investment risk is ....Increased if payback is longer.

(c) ....Shorter........ term forecasts are likely to be more reliable.

6 The accounting rate of return method of investment appraisal uses accounting profits before depreciation charges.

☐ True

☑ False

7 Complete the Boston classification matrix.

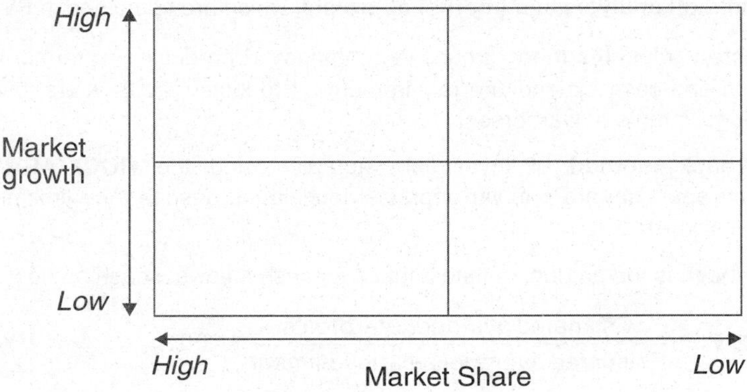

8 Name the four stages of strategic decision making identified by Ansoff.

Answers to quick quiz

1 S trengths

W eaknesses

O pportunities

T hreats

2

	Markets	Products
Market penetration	Existing	Existing
Market development	New	Existing
Product development	Existing	New
Diversification	New	New

3 Payback

4 All three could be used, although (a) $\frac{\text{Estimated average profits}}{\text{Estimated average investment}}$ x 100% is generally best.

5 (a) liquidity
(b) increased
(c) shorter

6 False

7

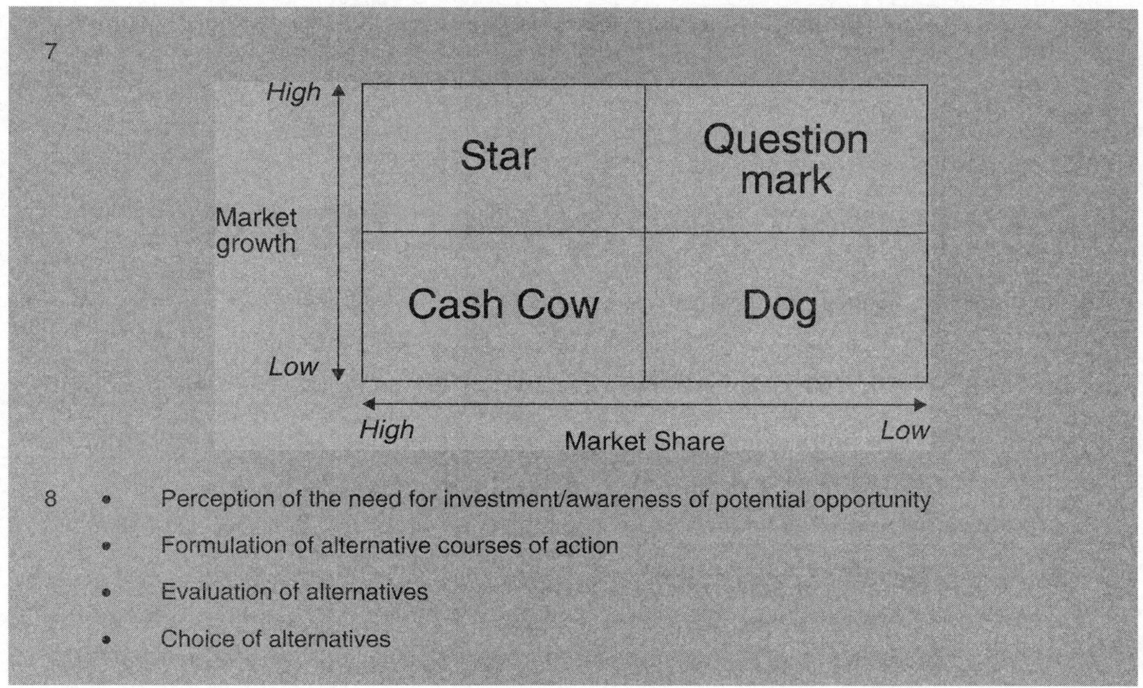

8
- Perception of the need for investment/awareness of potential opportunity
- Formulation of alternative courses of action
- Evaluation of alternatives
- Choice of alternatives

Now try the question below from the Exam Question Bank

Question to try	Level	Marks	Time
31	Exam	25	45 mins

Chapter 27

INVESTMENT APPRAISAL USING DCF METHODS

	Topic list	Syllabus reference
1	Discounted cash flow and the cost of capital	5(a)
2	The net present value method	5(a)
3	The internal rate of return method	5(a)
4	NPV and IRR compared	5(a)
5	The advantages of the DCF method of project appraisal	5(a)
6	Asset replacement decisions	5(a)

Introduction

The **payback** and **ARR** methods of investment appraisal were considered in the previous chapter. This chapter will look at **DCF** methods of investment appraisal. Chapter 28 will look at how **inflation** and **taxation** can be incorporated into appraisal techniques.

Study guide

Section 13 – Investment appraisal using DCF methods

- Explain the importance of the time value of money and the role of the cost of capital in appraising investments
- Identify and evaluate relevant cash flows of potential investments
- Calculate present values to derive the NPV and IRR measures of investment worth
- Explain the superiority of DCF methods over payback and ROCE
- Assess the merits of IRR and NPV
- Apply DCF methods to asset replacement decisions

Exam guide

This chapter and the next few chapters cover topic areas that were central under the old syllabus, and remain key areas under the new syllabus. You may again be asked to discuss the drawbacks of the techniques as well as having to use the techniques themselves. An investment appraisal using the NPV method was part of the compulsory question in December 2001, and is likely to be a regular topic in both sections of the paper in years to come.

1 DISCOUNTED CASH FLOW AND THE COST OF CAPITAL

1.1 **Discounted cash flow**, or **DCF** for short, is an investment appraisal technique which takes into account both the timings of cash flows and also total profitability over a project's life.

1.2 Two important points about DCF are as follows.

(a) DCF looks at the **cash flows** of a project, not the accounting profits. Cash flows are considered because they show the costs and benefits of a project when they actually occur. For example, the capital cost of a project will be the original cash outlay, and not the notional cost of depreciation.

(b) The **timing** of cash flows is taken into account by **discounting them**. The effect of discounting is to give a bigger value per £1 for cash flows that occur earlier: £1 earned after one year will be worth more than £1 earned after two years, which in turn will be worth more than £1 earned after five years, and so on.

Compounding

1.3 Suppose that a company has £10,000 to invest, and wants to earn a return of 10% (compound interest) on its investments. This means that if the £10,000 could be invested at 10%, the value of the investment with interest would build up as follows.

(a)	After 1 year	£10,000 × (1.10)	=	£11,000
(b)	After 2 years	£10,000 × $(1.10)^2$	=	£12,100
(c)	After 3 years	£10,000 × $(1.10)^3$	=	£13,310 and so on.

1.4 This is **compounding.** The formula for the future value of an investment plus accumulated interest after n time periods is:

$$FV = PV\,(1 + r)^n$$

where FV is the future value of the investment with interest
PV is the initial or 'present' value of the investment
r is the compound rate of return per time period, expressed as a proportion (so 10% = 0.10, 5% = 0.05 and so on)
n is the number of time periods.

Discounting

KEY TERM

Present value is the cash equivalent now of a sum of money receivable or payable at a stated future date, discounted at a specified rate of return.

1.5 **Discounting** starts with the future value, and converts a future value to a present value. For example, if a company expects to earn a (compound) rate of return of 10% on its investments, how much would it need to invest now to have the following investments?

(a) £11,000 after 1 year
(b) £12,100 after 2 years
(c) £13,310 after 3 years

1.6 The answer is £10,000 in each case, and we can calculate it by discounting. The discounting formula to calculate the present value of a future sum of money at the end of n time periods is:

$$PV = FV \frac{1}{(1+r)^n}$$

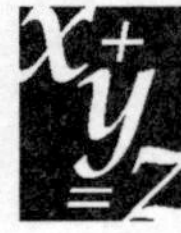

EXAM FORMULA

Present value of 1 = $(1+r)^{-n}$ or $\frac{1}{(1+r)^n}$

(a) After 1 year, $£11{,}000 \times \frac{1}{1.10} = £10{,}000$

(b) After 2 years, $£12{,}100 \times \frac{1}{1.10^2} = £10{,}000$

(c) After 3 years, $£13{,}310 \times \frac{1}{1.10^3} = £10{,}000$

1.7 Discounting can be applied to both money receivable and also to money payable at a future date. By discounting all payments and receipts from a capital investment to a present value, they can be compared on a common basis at a value which takes account of when the various cash flows will take place.

Question 1

Spender Ltd expects the cash inflow from an investment to be £40,000 after 2 years and another £30,000 after 3 years. Its target rate of return is 12%. Calculate the present value of these future returns, and explain what this present value signifies.

Answer

(a)

Year	*Cash flow* £	*Discount factor* 12%	*Present value* £
2	40,000	$\frac{1}{(1.12)^2} = 0.797$	31,880
3	30,000	$\frac{1}{(1.12)^3} = 0.712$	21,360
		Total PV	53,240

(b) The present value of the future returns, discounted at 12%, is £53,240. This means that if Spender Ltd can invest now to earn a return of 12% on its investments, it would have to invest £53,240 now to earn £40,000 after 2 years plus £30,000 after 3 years.

The cost of capital

1.8 The **cost of capital** has two aspects to it.

(a) It is the **cost of funds** that a company raises and uses.

(b) The return that investors expect to be paid for putting funds into the company. It is therefore the **minimum return** that a company should make from its own investments, to earn the cash flows out of which investors can be paid their return.

The cost of capital can therefore be measured by studying the returns required by investors, and used to derive a discount rate for DCF analysis and investment appraisal.

The cost of ordinary share capital

1.9 New funds from equity shareholders are obtained from **new issues of shares**, or as the cash or other funds generated from **retained earnings**.

1.10 Both of these sources of funds have a cost. Shareholders will not be prepared to provide funds for a new issue of shares unless the **return on their investment** is sufficiently attractive. **Retained earnings** also have a cost. This is an **opportunity cost**, the **dividend forgone** by shareholders.

1.11 If we begin by ignoring share issue costs, the cost of equity, both for new issues and retained earnings, can be estimated on the assumption that the **market value** of shares is **directly related** to expected **future dividends** on the shares. Different assumptions can be made about whether dividends are expected to grow in the future.

The cost of debt capital and fixed dividend capital

1.12 The cost of debt capital already issued is, briefly, the **rate of interest** (the internal rate of return) which **equates** the **current market price** with the **discounted future cash receipts** from the security.

Computing a discount rate

1.13 It is possible to compute the costs of individual sources of capital for a company, for example in the form of debt or share capital. But how will this help us to work out the **cost of capital** as a whole, or the **discount rate** to apply in DCF investment appraisals?

1.14 In many cases it will be difficult to associate a particular project with a particular form of finance. A company's funds may be viewed as a pool of resources. Under these circumstances it might seem appropriate to use an average cost of capital as the discount rate. The correct cost of capital to use in investment appraisal is the **marginal cost of the funds raised (or earnings retained)** to finance the investment.

KEY TERM

The **weighted average cost of capital** is the average cost of the company's finance, weighted according to the relative size of each element compared with total capital.

1.15 The **weighted average cost of capital (WACC)** might be considered the most reliable guide to the marginal cost of capital, but only on the assumptions that the company continues to invest:

- In the future
- In projects of a standard level of business risk
- By raising funds in the same proportions as its existing capital structure

Exam focus point

For the Paper 2.4 exam, you will not be required to produce computations of, or to comment on, a WACC: these more advanced skills form part of the Paper 3.7 syllabus. In this paper an exam question will give a discount rate as and where appropriate.

1.16 EXAMPLE: WEIGHTED AVERAGE COST OF CAPITAL

Prudence plc is financed partly by equity and partly by debentures. The equity proportion is always kept at two thirds of the total. The cost of equity is 18% and that of debt 12%. A new project is under consideration which will cost £100,000 and will yield a return before interest of £17,500 a year in perpetuity. Should the project be accepted? Ignore taxation.

1.17 SOLUTION

Since the company will maintain its gearing ratio unchanged, it is reasonable to assume that its marginal cost of funds equals its WACC. The weighted average cost of capital is as follows.

	Proportion	*Cost*		*Cost × proportion*
Equity	$\frac{2}{3}$	18%		12%
Debt	$\frac{1}{3}$	12%		4%
			WACC	16%

1.18 The present value of the future returns in perpetuity can be found using the WACC as the discount rate, as follows.

$$\text{Present value of future cash flows} = \frac{\text{Annual cash flow}}{\text{Discount rate}} = \frac{£17{,}500}{0.16} = £109{,}375$$

The NPV of the investment is £109,375 – £100,000 = £9,375.

Weighting

1.19 In the last example, we simplified the problem of weighting the different costs of capital by giving the proportions of capital. Weights could be based on **market values** (by this method, the cost of retained earnings is implied in the market value of equity). Alternatively, weights could be based on **book values**.

1.20 Although the latter are often easier to obtain they are of doubtful economic significance. It is, therefore, more meaningful to use market values when reliable data is available (which it should be for quoted companies).

1.21 When using market values it is not possible to split the equity value between share capital and reserves and only one **cost of equity** can be **used**. This removes the need to estimate a separate cost of retained earnings.

Arguments for and against using the WACC

1.22 The weighted average cost of capital is **recommended for use in investment appraisal** on the following assumptions.

(a) New investments must be **financed** by **new sources of funds**; retained earnings, new share issues, new loans and so on.

(b) The cost of capital to be applied to project evaluation must reflect the **marginal cost** of new capital.

(c) The weighted average cost of capital reflects the company's **long-term future capital structure**, and capital costs. If this were not so, the current weighted average cost would become irrelevant because eventually it would not relate to any actual cost of capital.

1.23 Thus the **current weighted average cost of capital** should be used to evaluate projects, because a company's capital structure changes only very slowly over time; the marginal cost of new capital should be roughly equal to the weighted average cost of current capital.

1.24 If this view is correct, then by undertaking investments which offer a return in excess of the WACC, a company will increase the market value of its ordinary shares in the long run. This is because the excess returns would provide surplus profits and dividends for the shareholders.

1.25 The following **arguments against using the WACC** as the cost of capital for investment appraisal are based on criticisms of the assumptions that are used to justify use of the WACC.

(a) New investments undertaken by a company might have different **business risk** characteristics from the company's existing operations. As a consequence, the **return required by investors** might go up (or down) if the investments are undertaken, because their business risk is perceived to be higher (or lower).

(b) The finance that is raised to fund a new investment might substantially **change the capital structure** and the perceived **financial risk** of investing in the company. Depending on whether the project is financed by equity or by debt capital, the perceived financial risk of the entire company might change. This must be taken into account when appraising investments.

(c) Many companies raise **floating rate debt capital** as well as fixed interest debt capital. With floating rate debt capital, the interest rate is variable, and is altered every three or six months or so in line with changes in current market interest rates. The cost of debt capital will therefore fluctuate as market conditions vary. Floating rate debt is difficult to incorporate into a WACC computation, and the best that can be done is to substitute an 'equivalent' fixed interest debt capital cost in place of the floating rate debt cost.

Required returns in the public sector

1.26 For private sector projects, the objective in setting required returns will normally be to match or exceed the returns obtainable from comparable investments by those who subscribe capital. In the public sector, the authorities may choose to take account of externalities and the wider social costs and benefits of projects, some of which will not be priced by the market.

1.27 The **social opportunity cost return approach** focuses on the opportunity cost to society of undertaking the project. The discount rate chosen reflects the **rate of return** obtainable from the **next best alternative** use of public funds, including all externalities.

1.28 The **social rate of time preference approach** to adopting a discount rate for public sector projects is based on the argument that society has a longer time horizon than private individuals. To reflect this, a **lower discount rate** is used than would be used for a private sector project.

2 THE NET PRESENT VALUE METHOD 12/01

2.1 There are two methods of using DCF to evaluate capital investments.

- The net present value (**NPV**) method
- The internal rate of return (**IRR**) method, or DCF yield method

KEY TERMS

Net present value or **NPV** is the value obtained by discounting all cash outflows and inflows of a capital investment project by a chosen target rate of return or **cost of capital.**

2.2 The NPV method compares the **present value** of all the **cash inflows** from an investment with the **present value** of all the **cash outflows** from an investment. The NPV is thus calculated as the PV of **cash inflows** minus the PV of **cash outflows.**

NPV	
NPV positive	Return from investment's cash inflows in excess of cost of capital ⇒ undertake project
NPV negative	Return from investment's cash inflows below cost of capital ⇒ don't undertake project
NPV 0	Return from investment's cash inflows same as cost of capital

Note. We assume that the cost of capital is the organisation's target rate of return.

2.3 EXAMPLE: NPV

Slogger Ltd is considering a capital investment, where the estimated cash flows are as follows.

Year	*Cash flow*
	£
0 (ie now)	(100,000)
1	60,000
2	80,000
3	40,000
4	30,000

The company's cost of capital is 15%. You are required to calculate the NPV of the project and to assess whether it should be undertaken.

2.4 SOLUTION

Year	*Cash flow*	*Discount factor*	*Present value*
	£	15%	£
0	(100,000)	1.000	(100,000)
1	60,000	$\frac{1}{(1.15)} = 0.870$	52,200
2	80,000	$\frac{1}{(1.15)^2} = 0.756$	60,480
3	40,000	$\frac{1}{(1.15)^3} = 0.658$	26,320
4	30,000	$\frac{1}{(1.15)^4} = 0.572$	17,160
		NPV =	56,160

(**Note**. The discount factor for any cash flow 'now' (year 0) is always = 1, regardless of what the cost of capital is.) The PV of cash inflows exceeds the PV of cash outflows by £56,160, which means that the project will earn a DCF yield in excess of 15%. It should therefore be undertaken.

Timing of cash flows: conventions used in DCF

2.5 Discounted cash flow applies discounting arithmetic to the relevant costs and benefits of an investment project. Discounting, which reduces the value of future cash flows to a present value equivalent, is clearly concerned with the timing of the cash flows. As a general rule, the following guidelines may be applied.

(a) A cash outlay to be incurred at the beginning of an investment project (**'now'**) occurs in **year 0**. The present value of £1 now, in year 0, is £1 regardless of the value of r.

(b) A cash outlay, saving or inflow which occurs **during the course of a time period** (say, one year) is assumed to occur all at once **at the end of the time period** (at the end of the year). Receipts of £10,000 during year 1 are therefore taken to occur at the end of year 1.

(c) A cash outlay or receipt which occurs **at the beginning of a time period** (say at the beginning of one year) is taken to occur **at the end of the previous year**. Therefore a cash outlay of £5,000 at the beginning of year 2 is taken to occur at the end of year 1.

Discount tables for the PV of £1

2.6 The discount factor that we use in discounting is $\frac{1}{(1+r)^n} = (1+r)^{-n}$

Instead of having to calculate this factor every time we can use tables. Discount tables for the present value of £1, for different values of r and n, are shown in the Appendix to this Study Text. Use these tables to work out your own solution to the following question.

Question 2

LCH Limited manufactures product X which it sells for £5 per unit. Variable costs of production are currently £3 per unit, and fixed costs 50p per unit. A new machine is available which would cost £90,000 but which could be used to make product X for a variable cost of only £2.50 per unit. Fixed costs, however, would increase by £7,500 per annum as a direct result of purchasing the machine. The machine would have an expected life of 4 years and a resale value after that time of £10,000. Sales of product X are estimated to be 75,000 units per annum. LCH Limited expects to earn at least 12% per annum from its investments. Ignore taxation.

You are required to decide whether LCH Limited should purchase the machine.

Answer

Savings are 75,000 × (£3 – £2.50) = £37,500 per annum.

Additional costs are £7,500 per annum.

Net cash savings are therefore £30,000 per annum. (Remember, depreciation is not a cash flow and must be ignored as a 'cost'.)

The first step in calculating an NPV is to establish the relevant costs year by year. All future cash flows arising as a direct consequence of the decision should be taken into account. It is assumed that the machine will be sold for £10,000 at the end of year 4.

Year	*Cash flow*	*PV factor*	*PV of cash flow*
	£	12%	£
0	(90,000)	1.000	(90,000)
1	30,000	0.893	26,790
2	30,000	0.797	23,910
3	30,000	0.712	21,360
4	40,000	0.636	25,440
		NPV =	+7,500

The NPV is positive and so the project is expected to earn more than 12% per annum and is therefore acceptable.

Annuity tables

2.7 In the previous exercise, the calculations could have been simplified for years 1-3 as follows.

$$\begin{aligned} & 30{,}000 \times 0.893 \\ + \; & 30{,}000 \times 0.797 \\ + \; & \underline{30{,}000 \times 0.712} \\ = \; & \underline{\underline{30{,}000 \times 2.402}} \end{aligned}$$

Where there is a constant cash flow from year to year, we can calculate the present value by adding together the discount factors for the individual years.

2.8 These total factors could be described as 'same cash flow per annum' factors, 'cumulative present value' factors or '**annuity**' **factors**. They are shown in the table for cumulative PV of £1 factors which is shown in the Appendix to this Study Text (2.402, for example, is in the column for 12% per annum and the row for year 3.)

EXAM FORMULA

Present value of an annuity of 1 $= \dfrac{1-(1+r)^{-n}}{r}$

Where r = Discount rate
n = Number of periods

Question 3

If you have not used them before, check that you can understand annuity tables by trying the following exercise.

(a) What is the present value of £1,000 in contribution earned each year from years 1-10, when the required return on investment is 11%?

(b) What is the present value of £2,000 costs incurred each year from years 3-6 when the cost of capital is 5%?

Answer

(a) The PV of £1,000 earned each year from year 1-10 when the required earning rate of money is 11% is calculated as follows.

£1,000 × 5.889 = £5,889

(b) The PV of £2,000 in costs each year from years 3-6 when the cost of capital is 5% per annum is calculated as follows.

PV of £1 per annum for years 1 - 6 at 5% =	5.076
Less PV of £1 per annum for years 1 - 2 at 5% =	1.859
PV of £1 per annum for years 3 - 6 =	3.217

PV = £2,000 × 3.217 = £6,434

2.9 EXAMPLE: NPV INCLUDING USE OF ANNUITY TABLES

Elsie Limited is considering the manufacture of a new product which would involve the use of both a new machine (costing £150,000) and an existing machine, which cost £80,000 two years ago and has a current net book value of £60,000. There is sufficient capacity on this machine, which has so far been under-utilised. Annual sales of the product would be 5,000 units, selling at £32 per unit. Unit costs would be as follows.

	£
Direct labour (4 hours at £2 per hour)	8
Direct materials	7
Fixed costs including depreciation	9
	24

The project would have a five-year life, after which the new machine would have a net residual value of £10,000. Because direct labour is continually in short supply, labour resources would have to be diverted from other work which currently earns a contribution of £1.50 per direct labour hour. The fixed overhead absorption rate would be £2.25 per hour (£9 per unit) but actual expenditure on fixed overhead would not alter.

Working capital requirements would be £10,000 in the first year, rising to £15,000 in the second year and remaining at this level until the end of the project, when it will all be recovered. The company's cost of capital is 20%. Ignore taxation.

You are required to assess whether the project is worthwhile.

2.10 SOLUTION

The relevant cash flows are as follows.

(a)	Year 0	Purchase of new machine	£150,000
			£
(b)	Years 1-5	Contribution from new product	
		(5,000 units × £(32 – 15))	85,000
		Less contribution foregone	
		(5,000 × (4 × £1.50))	30,000
			55,000

(c) The project requires £10,000 of working capital at the end of year 1 and a further £5,000 at the start of year 2. **Increases** in working capital **reduce** the **net cash flow** for the period to which they relate. When the working capital tied up in the project is 'recovered' at the end of the project, it will provide an extra cash inflow (for example debtors will eventually pay up).

(d) All other costs, which are past costs, notional accounting costs or costs which would be incurred anyway without the project, are not relevant to the investment decision.

(e) The NPV is calculated as follows.

Year	Equipment	Working capital	Contribution	Net cash flow	Discount factor	PV of net cash flow
	£	£	£	£	20%	£
0	(150,000)	(10,000)		(160,000)	1.000	(160,000)
1		(5,000)		(5,000)	0.833	(4,165)
1-5			55,000	55,000	2.991	164,505
5	10,000	15,000		25,000	0.402	10,050
					NPV =	10,390

The NPV is positive and the project is worthwhile, although there is not much margin for error. Some risk analysis of the project is recommended.

Annual cash flows in perpetuity 12/01

2.11 You need to know how to calculate the cumulative present value of £1 per annum for every year in perpetuity (that is, forever).

FORMULA TO LEARN

When the cost of capital is r, the cumulative PV of £1 per annum in perpetuity is **£1/r**.

2.12 For example, the PV of £1 per annum in perpetuity at a discount rate of 10% would be £1/0.10 = £10.

Similarly, the PV of £1 per annum in perpetuity at a discount rate of 15% would be £1/0.15 = £6.67 and at a discount rate of 20% it would be £1/0.20 = £5.

Question 4

An organisation with a cost of capital of 14% is considering investing in a project costing £500,000 that would yield cash inflows of £100,000 pa in perpetuity.

Required

Assess whether the project should be undertaken.

Answer

Year	*Cash flow*	*Discount factor*	*Present value*
	£	14%	£
0	(500,000)	1.000	(500,000)
1 - ∞	100,000	1/0.14 = 7.143	714,300
		Net present value	214,300

The NPV is positive and so the project should be undertaken.

3 THE INTERNAL RATE OF RETURN METHOD

3.1 Using the **NPV method of discounted cash flow**, present values are calculated by discounting at a target rate of return, or cost of capital, and the difference between the PV of costs and the PV of benefits is the NPV. In contrast, the **internal rate of return (IRR)** method is to calculate the **exact DCF rate of return** which the project is expected to achieve, in other words the rate at which the **NPV is zero**. If the expected rate of return (the IRR or DCF yield) **exceeds** a **target rate** of return, the project would be worth undertaking (ignoring risk and uncertainty factors).

3.2 Without a computer or calculator program, the calculation of the internal rate of return is made using a hit-and-miss technique known as the interpolation method.

Step 1. Calculate a net present value using a rate for the cost of capital that

(a) Is a **whole number**

(b) May give an NPV **close to zero**. As a rough guide try a rate that is about two thirds or three quarters of the accounting return on investment, or accounting rate of return.

Step 2. Having calculated the NPV using the first rate,

(a) If the NPV is **positive**, use a second rate that is **greater** than the first rate
(b) If the NPV is **negative**, use a second rate that is **less** than the first rate

Step 3. Use the two NPV values to **estimate the IRR**. The formula to apply is as follows.

$$IRR \approx a + \left(\left(\frac{A}{A-B} \right) (b-a) \right) \%$$

where a = the lower of the two rates of return used
b = the higher of the two rates of return used
A = the NPV obtained using rate a
B = the NPV obtained using rate b

Note. Ideally A will be a positive value and B will be negative. (If B is negative, then in the equation above you will be subtracting a negative, ie treating it as an added positive).

However do not worry if you have two positive or two negative values, provided they are fairly close to zero. In the exam you will not have time to calculate NPVs using more than two rates.

3.3 EXAMPLE: THE IRR METHOD

A company is trying to decide whether to buy a machine for £80,000 which will save costs of £20,000 per annum for 5 years and which will have a resale value of £10,000 at the end of year 5. If it is the company's policy to undertake projects only if they are expected to yield a DCF return of 10% or more, ascertain whether this project be undertaken.

3.4 SOLUTION

Annual depreciation would be £(80,000 – 10,000)/5 = £14,000.

Step 1. Calculate the first NPV, using a rate that is three quarters of the return on investment.

The return on investment would be:

$$\frac{20{,}000 - \text{depreciation of } 14{,}000}{\frac{1}{2} \text{ of } (80{,}000 + 10{,}000)} = \frac{6{,}000}{45{,}000} = 13.3\%$$

Two thirds of this is 8.9% and so we can start by trying 9%.

The IRR is the rate for the cost of capital at which the NPV = 0.

Year	*Cash flow*	*PV factor*		*PV of cash flow*
	£	9%		£
0	(80,000)	1.000		(80,000)
1-5	20,000	3.890		77,800
5	10,000	0.650		6,500
			NPV	4,300

This is fairly close to zero. It is also **positive**, which means that the actual **rate of return** is **more than 9%.** We can use 9% as one of our two NPVs close to zero.

Step 2. Calculate the second NPV, using a rate that is **greater** than the first rate, as the first rate gave a positive answer.

Suppose we try 12%.

Year	*Cash flow*	*PV factor*		*PV of cash flow*
	£	12%		£
0	(80,000)	1.000		(80,000)
1-5	20,000	3.605		72,100
5	10,000	0.567		5,670
			NPV	(2,230)

This is fairly close to zero and **negative**. The real rate of return is therefore greater than 9% (positive NPV of £4,300) but less than 12% (negative NPV of £2,230).

Step 3. Use the two NPV values to estimate the IRR.

The interpolation method assumes that the NPV rises in linear fashion between the two NPVs close to 0. The real rate of return is therefore assumed to be on a straight line between NPV = £4,300 at 9% and NPV = –£2,230 at 12%.

Using the formula

$$IRR \approx a + \left(\left(\frac{A}{A-B}\right)(b-a)\right)\%$$

$$IRR \approx 9 + \left[\frac{4{,}300}{4{,}300+2{,}230}\times(12-9)\right]\% = 10.98\%\text{, say } 11\%$$

If it is company policy to undertake investments which are expected to yield 10% or more, this project would be undertaken.

3.5 If we were to draw a graph of a 'typical' capital project, with a negative cash flow at the start of the project, and positive net cash flows afterwards up to the end of the project, we could draw a graph of the project's NPV at different costs of capital. It would look like Figure 1.

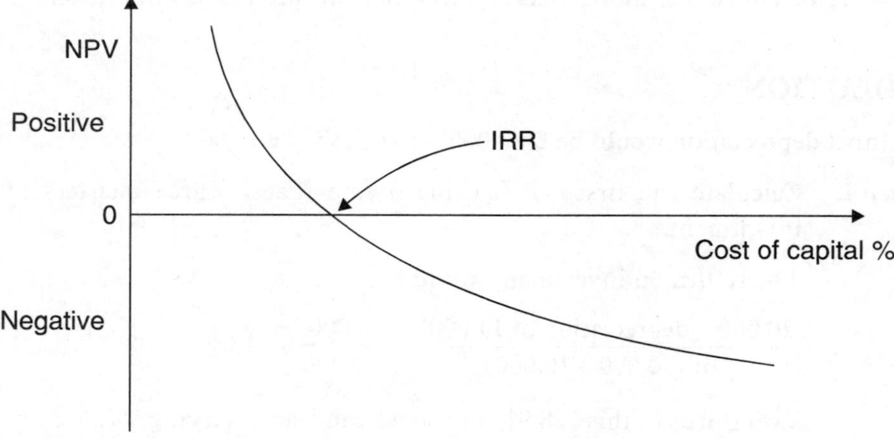

Figure 1

3.6 If we use a cost of capital where the NPV is slightly positive, and use another cost of capital where it is slightly negative, we can estimate the IRR - where the NPV is zero - by drawing a straight line between the two points on the graph that we have calculated.

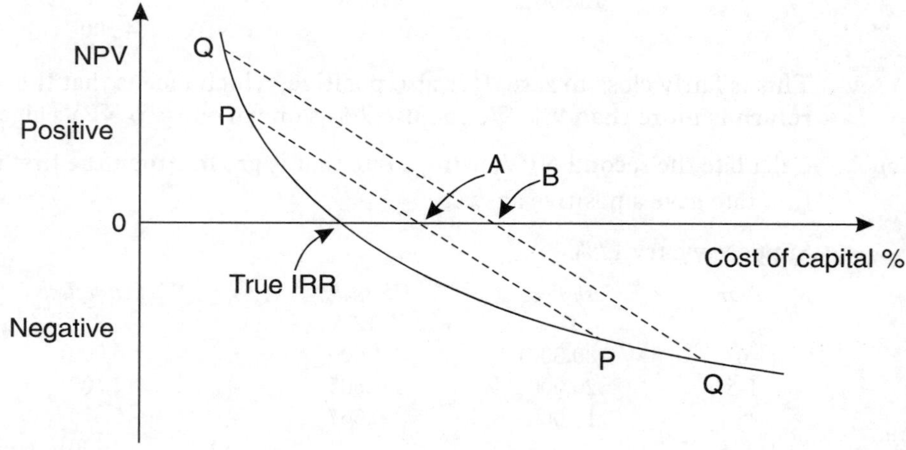

Figure 2

3.7 Consider Figure 2.

(a) If we establish the NPVs at the two points P, we would estimate the IRR to be at point A.

(b) If we establish the NPVs at the two points Q, we would estimate the IRR to be at point B.

The closer our NPVs are to zero, the closer our estimate will be to the true IRR.

Question 5

Find the IRR of the project given below and state whether the project should be accepted if the company requires a minimum return of 17%.

Time		£
0	Investment	(4,000)
1	Receipts	1,200
2	"	1,410
3	"	1,875
4	"	1,150

Answer

The total receipts are £5,635 giving a total profit of £1,635 and average profits of £409. The average investment is £2,000. The ARR is £409 ÷ £2,000 = 20%. Two thirds of the ARR is approximately 14%. The initial estimate of the IRR that we shall try is therefore 14%.

Time	*Cash flow*	*Try 14% Discount factor*	*PV*	*Try 16% Discount factor*	*PV*
	£		£		£
0	(4,000)	1.000	(4,000)	1.000	(4,000)
1	1,200	0.877	1,052	0.862	1,034
2	1,410	0.769	1,084	0.743	1,048
3	1,875	0.675	1,266	0.641	1,202
4	1,150	0.592	681	0.552	635
		NPV	83	NPV	(81)

The IRR must be less than 16%, but higher than 14%. The NPVs at these two costs of capital will be used to estimate the IRR.

Using the interpolation formula:

$$\text{IRR} = 14\% + \left[\frac{83}{83+81} \times (16\% - 14\%)\right] = 15.01\%$$

The IRR is, in fact, exactly 15%. The project should be rejected as the IRR is less than the minimum return demanded.

4 NPV AND IRR COMPARED

4.1 Given that there are two methods of using DCF, the NPV method and the IRR method, the relative merits of each method have to be considered.

Advantages and disadvantages of IRR method

4.2 The main advantage of the IRR method is that the information it provides is **more easily understood** by managers, especially non-financial managers. For example, it is fairly easy to understand the meaning of the following statement.

> 'The project will be expected to have an initial capital outlay of £100,000, and to earn a yield of 25%. This is in excess of the target yield of 15% for investments.'

It is not so easy to understand the meaning of this statement.

> 'The project will cost £100,000 and have an NPV of £30,000 when discounted at the minimum required rate of 15%.'

4.3 However managers may **confuse IRR** and accounting return on capital employed, **ROCE**.

4.4 The IRR method **ignores** the **relative size** of investments. Both the following projects have an IRR of 18%.

	Project A	*Project B*
	£	£
Cost, year 0	350,000	35,000
Annual savings, years 1-6	100,000	10,000

Clearly, project A is bigger (ten times as big) and so more 'profitable' but if the only information on which the projects were judged were to be their IRR of 18%, project B would be made to seem just as beneficial as project A, which is not the case.

Non-conventional cash flows

4.5 The projects we have considered so far have had conventional cash flows (an initial cash outflow followed by a series of inflows). When flows vary from this they are termed non-conventional. The following project has **non-conventional cash flows.**

Year	*Project X*
	£'000
0	(1,900)
1	4,590
2	(2,735)

4.6 Project X would have two IRRs as shown by Figure 3.

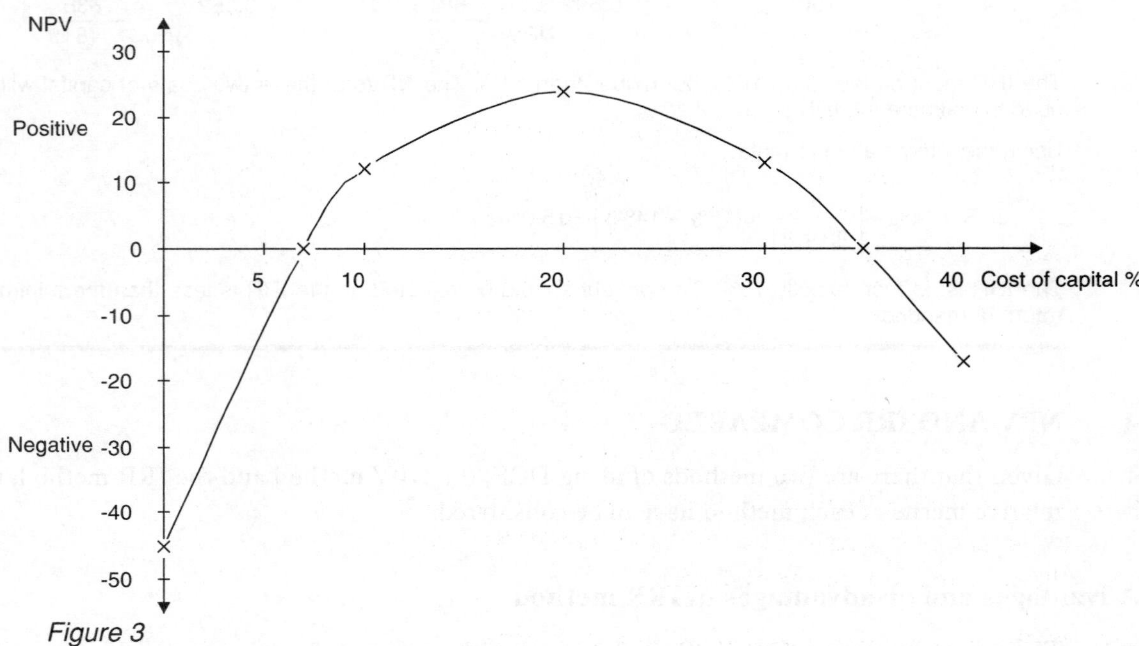

Figure 3

4.7 The NPV rule suggests that the project is acceptable between costs of capital of 7% and 35%.

4.8 Suppose that the required rate on project X is 10% and that the IRR of 7% is used in deciding whether to accept or reject the project. The project would be rejected since it appears that it can only yield 7%.

4.9 The diagram shows, however, that between rates of 7% and 35% the project should be accepted. Using the IRR of 35% would produce the correct decision to accept the project. **Lack of knowledge** of **multiple IRRs** could therefore lead to serious errors in the decision of whether to accept or reject a project.

4.10 In general, if the sign of the net cash flow changes in successive periods, the calculations may produce as many IRRs as there are sign changes. IRR should not normally be used when there are non-conventional cash flows.

Exam focus point

You need to be aware of the possibility of multiple IRRs, but the area is not examinable at a computational level.

Mutually exclusive projects

4.11 Mutually exclusive projects are two or more projects from which only one can be chosen. Examples include the choice of a factory location or the choice of just one of a number of machines. The IRR and NPV methods can, however, give conflicting rankings as to which project should be given priority.

4.12 Let us suppose that a company is considering two mutually exclusive options, option A and option B. The cash flows for each would be as follows.

Year		*Option A*	*Option B*
		£	£
0	Capital outlay	(10,200)	(35,250)
1	Net cash inflow	6,000	18,000
2	Net cash inflow	5,000	15,000
3	Net cash inflow	3,000	15,000

The company's cost of capital is 16%.

4.13 The NPV of each project is calculated below.

		Option A		*Option B*	
Year	*Discount factor*	*Cash flow*	*Present value*	*Cash flow*	*Present value*
		£	£	£	£
0	1.000	(10,200)	(10,200)	(35,250)	(35,250)
1	0.862	6,000	5,172	18,000	15,516
2	0.743	5,000	3,715	15,000	11,145
3	0.641	3,000	1,923	15,000	9,615
		NPV =	+610	NPV =	+1,026

4.14 The DCF yield (IRR) of option A is 20% and the yield of option B is only 18% (workings not shown.) On a comparison of NPVs, option B would be preferred, but on a comparison of IRRs, option A would be preferred.

4.15 If the projects were independent this would be irrelevant since under the NPV rule both would be accepted. With mutually exclusive projects, however, only one project can be accepted. Therefore the ranking is crucial and we cannot be indifferent to the outcomes of the NPV and IRR appraisal methods. The NPV method is preferable.

einvestment assumptions

16 An assumption underlying the NPV method is that any net cash inflows generated during the life of the project will be reinvested at the cost of capital (that is, the **discount rate**). The IRR method, on the other hand, assumes these cash flows can be reinvested to earn a return equal to the IRR of the original project.

4.17 In the example above, the NPV method assumes that the cash inflows of £6,000, £5,000 and £3,000 for option A will be reinvested at the cost of capital of 16% whereas the IRR method assumes they will be reinvested at 20%. In theory, a firm will have accepted all projects which provide a return in excess of the cost of capital. Any other funds which become available can only be reinvested at the cost of capital. This is the assumption implied in the NPV rule.

Summary of NPV and IRR comparison

4.18 (a) When cash flow patterns are conventional both methods gives the **same** accept or reject **decision**.

(b) The IRR method is **more easily understood**.

(c) NPV is **technically superior** to IRR and simpler to calculate.

(d) **IRR** and **accounting ROCE** can be **confused**.

(e) **IRR ignores** the **relative sizes** of investments.

(f) Where cash flow patterns are non-conventional, there may be **several IRRs** which decision makers must be aware of to avoid making the wrong decision.

(g) The **NPV method** is superior for **ranking mutually exclusive projects** in order of attractiveness.

(h) The **reinvestment assumption** underlying the **IRR** method cannot be **substantiated**.

(i) When **discount rates** are **expected to differ** over the life of the project, such **variations** can be incorporated easily into **NPV** calculations, but not into IRR calculations.

(j) Despite the advantages of the NPV method over the IRR method, the **IRR method** is **widely used** in practice.

5 THE ADVANTAGES OF THE DCF METHOD OF PROJECT APPRAISAL

The time value of money

5.1 DCF is a capital appraisal technique that is based on a concept known as the time value of money: the concept that £1 received today is not equal to £1 received in the future. Given the choice between receiving £100 today, and £100 in one year's time, most people would opt to receive £100 today because they could spend it or invest it to earn interest. If the interest rate was 10%, you could invest £100 today and it would be worth (£100 × 1.10) = £110 in one year's time.

5.2 There are, however, other reasons why a present £1 is worth more than a future £1.

(a) **Uncertainty.** Although there might be a promise of money to come in the future, it can never be certain that the money will be received until it has actually been paid.

(b) **Inflation** also means £1 now is worth more than £1 in the future because of inflation. The time value of money concept applies even if there is zero inflation but inflation obviously increases the discrepancy in value between monies received at different times.

5.3 Taking account of the time value of money (by discounting) is one of the principal advantages of the DCF appraisal method. Other advantages are as follows.

- The method uses **all cash flows** relating to the project.
- It allows for the **timing** of the cash flows.
- There are **universally accepted methods** of calculating the NPV and the IRR.

The use of appraisal methods in practice

5.4 A survey of the use of capital investment evaluation methods in the UK carried out by RH Pike in 1992 produced the following results on the frequency of use of different methods by 100 large UK firms.

Capital investment evaluation methods in 100 large UK firms: frequency of use

	Total	*Always*	*Mostly*	*Often*	*Rarely*
Firms using	%	%	%	%	%
Payback	94	62	14	12	6
Accounting rate of return	50	21	5	13	17
Internal rate of return	81	54	7	13	7
Net present value	74	33	14	16	11

(Source: Pike & Neale, *Corporate finance and investment*)

5.5 One reason for the failure of many businesses to use NPV is that its (sometimes long-term) nature may conflict with judgements on a business that are concerned with its (short-term) profits. **Manager's remuneration** may depend upon the level of annual profits, and they may thus be unwilling to risk large initial expenditure on a project that only offers good returns in the significantly uncertain long-term.

5.6 In addition the NPV method is based on the assumption that businesses seek to **maximise** the **wealth of their shareholders**. As discussed previously, this may conflict with the interests of other stakeholders. Public sector organisations will be concerned with the **social opportunity costs.**

5.7 Even when **wealth maximisation** is the key objective, there may be factors that help maximise wealth, but cannot be quantified for NPV purposes, for example investment in a loss-making project for strategic reasons such as obtaining an initial share in an important market.

6 ASSET REPLACEMENT DECISIONS

6.1 As well as assisting with decisions between particular assets, DCF techniques can be used in **asset replacement decisions**, to assess **when** and **how frequently** an asset should be replaced. When an asset is to be replaced by an 'identical' asset, the problem is to decide the optimum interval between replacements. As the asset gets older, it may cost more to maintain and operate, its residual value will decrease, and it may lose some productivity/operating capability.

6.2 There are three basic methods of deciding the optimum replacement cycle.

- The **lowest common multiple method**
- The **finite horizon method**
- The **equivalent annual cost method**

Each method will give the same recommendation, as shown in the paragraphs below.

6.3 All three methods are concerned with the problem that a replacement asset will eventually be replaced itself by an asset which will also in its turn be replaced. Replacements are continuous, and are assumed to occur into the indefinite future.

6.4 **Lowest common multiple method**

Step 1. **Estimate** the **cash flows** over a **period of time** which is the **lowest common multiple** of all the replacement cycles under consideration. Thus for replacement cycles of one, two, three or four years, the lowest common multiple of time is twelve years. In twelve years there would be the following numbers of replacement cycles.

(i) Twelve complete replacement cycles of one year
(ii) Six complete replacement cycles of two years
(iii) Four complete replacement cycles of three years
(iv) Three complete replacement cycles of four years

Step 2. **Discount** these cash flows **over** the **lowest common multiple time period**. The option with the lowest present value of cost will be the optimum replacement cycle.

6.5 EXAMPLE: REPLACEMENT OF AN IDENTICAL ASSET

James Ltd operates a machine which has the following costs and resale values over its four year life.

Purchase cost: £25,000

	Year 1	*Year 2*	*Year 3*	*Year 4*
	£	£	£	£
Running costs (cash expenses)	7,500	10,000	12,500	15,000
Resale value (end of year)	15,000	10,000	7,500	2,500

The organisation's cost of capital is 10%. You are required to assess how frequently the asset should be replaced.

6.6 SOLUTION

Step 1. Calculate the annual cash flows over 12 years.

(a) *Replacement every year*

Year		£	£
0	Purchase		(25,000)
1	Running cost	(7,500)	
	Resale value	15,000	
	New purchase	(25,000)	
			(17,500)
2-11	Same as year 1		(17,500)
12	Running cost	(7,500)	
	Resale value	15,000	
			7,500

The new purchase at the end of year 12 is ignored, because this starts a new 12-year cycle for all four replacement options.

(b) *Replacement every two years*

Year		£	£
0	Purchase		(25,000)
1	Running cost		(7,500)
2	Running cost	(10,000)	
	Resale value	10,000	
	New purchase	(25,000)	
			(25,000)
3,5,7,9,11	Same as year 1		
4,6,8,10	Same as year 2		
12	Running cost	(10,000)	
	Resale value	10,000	
			0

(c) *Replacement every three years*

Year		£	£
0	Purchase		(25,000)
1	Running cost		(7,500)
2	Running cost		(10,000)
3	Running cost	(12,500)	
	Resale value	7,500	
	New purchase	(25,000)	
			(30,000)
4,7,10	Same as year 1		
5,8,11	Same as year 2		
6,9	Same as year 3		
12	Running cost	(12,500)	
	Resale value	7,500	
			(5,000)

(d) *Replacement every four years*

Year		£	£
0	Purchase		(25,000)
1	Running cost		(7,500)
2	Running cost		(10,000)
3	Running cost		(12,500)
4	Running cost	(15,000)	
	Resale value	2,500	
	New purchase	(25,000)	
			(37,500)
5,9	Same as year 1		
6,10	Same as year 2		
7,11	Same as year 3		
8	Same as year 4		
12	Running cost	(15,000)	
	Resale value	2,500	
			(12,500)

Step 2. We can now go on to calculate the PV cost for each replacement cycle, over a 12-year period.

Discount factors are not shown in the figures below.

	Replacement every 2 years		Replacement every 3 years		Replacement every 4 years			
Year	*Cash flow*	*PV at 10%*	*Cash flow*	*PV at 10%*	*Cash flow*	*PV at 10%*	*Cash flow*	*PV at 10%*
	£	£	£	£	£	£	£	£
0	(25,000)	(25,000)	(25,000)	(25,000)	(25,000)	(25,000)	(25,000)	(25,000)
1	(17,500)		(7,500)	(6,818)	(7,500)	(6,818)	(7,500)	(6,818)
2	(17,500)		(25,000)	(20,650)	(10,000)	(8,260)	(10,000)	(8,260)
3	(17,500)		(7,500)	(5,633)	(30,000)	(22,530)	(12,500)	(9,388)
4	(17,500)		(25,000)	(17,075)	(7,500)	(5,123)	(37,500)	(25,613)
5	(17,500)		(7,500)	(4,658)	(10,000)	(6,210)	(7,500)	(4,658)
6	(17,500)	(113,663)	(25,000)	(14,100)	(30,000)	(16,920)	(10,000)	(5,640)
7	(17,500)		(7,500)	(3,848)	(7,500)	(3,848)	(12,500)	(6,413)
8	(17,500)		(25,000)	(11,675)	(10,000)	(4,670)	(37,500)	(17,513)
9	(17,500)		(7,500)	(3,180)	(30,000)	(12,720)	(7,500)	(3,180)
10	(17,500)		(25,000)	(9,650)	(7,500)	(2,895)	(10,000)	(3,860)
11	(17,500)		(7,500)	(2,625)	(10,000)	(3,500)	(12,500)	(4,375)
12	7,500	2,393	0	0	(5,000)	(1,595)	(12,500)	(3,988)
PV of costs		(136,270)		(124,912)		(120,089)		(124,706)

6.7 CONCLUSION

The cheapest replacement policy would be to replace the machine every three years, because this has the lowest total PV of cost.

6.8 The lowest common multiple method becomes a very long and tedious process when the maximum life of the asset is more than about three years. If the maximum life were, say, seven years, there would be seven different replacement options and the lowest common multiple would be 420 years.

The finite horizon method

6.9 The **finite horizon method** is to calculate the present value of costs over a 'significant' time period (perhaps 15 or 20 years). The present values of cash flows beyond this period are unlikely to affect the relative costs of the replacement options.

6.10 In our example, if the PV of costs had been calculated over a finite time period of ten years, the three year replacement option would still have been the cheapest. The finite time horizon method is therefore an approximation method which reduces the figure work needed, in the expectation that in spite of taking a short cut, the result is still the same.

Equivalent annual cost method

6.11 The equivalent annual cost method is the quickest method to use in a period of no inflation.

Step 1. Calculate the **present value of costs** for each **replacement cycle** over **one cycle only.**

These costs are not comparable because they refer to different time periods, whereas replacement is continuous.

Step 2. **Turn the present value** of costs for each replacement cycle into an **equivalent annual cost** (an annuity).

The equivalent annual costs is calculated as follows.

$$\frac{\text{The PV of cost over one replacement cycle}}{\text{The cumulative present value factor for the number of years in the cycle}}$$

For example if there are three years in the cycle, the denominator will be the present value of an annuity for three years at 10% (2.487).

6.12 In our example:

Step 1. Calculate the present value of costs for each replacement cycle over one cycle.

	Replace every year		*Replace every 2 years*		*Replace every 3 years*		*Replace every 4 years*	
Year	*Cash flow*	*PV at 10%*	*Cash flow*	*PV at 10%*	*Cash flow*	*PV at 10%*	*Cash flow*	*PV at 10%*
	£	£	£	£	£	£	£	£
0	(25,000)	(25,000)	(25,000)	(25,000)	(25,000)	(25,000)	(25,000)	(25,000)
1	7,500	6,818	(7,500)	(6,818)	(7,500)	(6,818)	(7,500)	(6,818)
2			0	0	(10,000)	(8,260)	(10,000)	(8,260)
3					(5,000)	(3,755)	(12,500)	(9,388)
4							(12,500)	(8,538)
PV of cost over one replacement cycle		(18,182)		(31,818)		(43,833)		(58,004)

Step 2. Calculate the equivalent annual cost.

We use a discount rate of 10%.

(a) Replacement every year:

$$\text{Equivalent annual cost} = \frac{£(18{,}182)}{0.909} = £(20{,}002)$$

(b) Replacement every two years:

$$\text{Equivalent annual cost} = \frac{£(31{,}818)}{1.736} = £(18{,}328)$$

(c) Replacement every three years:

$$\text{Equivalent annual cost} = \frac{£(43{,}833)}{2.487} = £(17{,}625)$$

(d) Replacement every four years:

$$\text{Equivalent annual cost} = \frac{£(58{,}004)}{3.170} = £(18{,}298)$$

6.13 CONCLUSION

The optimum replacement policy is the one with the lowest equivalent annual cost, every three years. This is the same conclusion reached by the earlier lowest common multiple method.

Exam focus point

The equivalent annual cost method is recommended because it is quicker and less cumbersome than either of the previous two methods described.

Non-identical replacement

6.14 When a machine is to be **replaced by a machine of a different type,** there is a different replacement problem. The decision has to be made as to **when** the existing asset should be replaced rather than how frequently it should be replaced.

6.15 The optimum replacement cycle for the new machine may be calculated by one of the methods described above. This does not resolve the further problem as to whether the old machine should be replaced now, or in one year's time, two year's time, and so on.

6.16 In order to find the optimum date for replacement, we firstly calculate the equivalent annual cost as demonstrated above. Then

Step 1. Calculate the NPV of the **equivalent annual cost in perpetuity** for the new machine, using the formula $\frac{a}{r}$ where r is the cost of capital.

Step 2. Calculate the **total net present value** of the **various options,** taking into account:

(a) The cost in perpetuity of the new machine

(b) The final expenses of the old machine and any residual sales proceeds from the old machine

6.17 EXAMPLE: NON-IDENTICAL REPLACEMENT

Assume James Ltd's machine (in our example above) is a new machine, and will be introduced to replace a non-identical existing machine which is nearing the end of its life and has a maximum remaining life of only three years. The organisation wishes to decide when is the best time to replace the old machine, and estimates of relevant costs have been drawn up as follows.

Year	*Resale value of current machine*	*Extra expenditure and opportunity costs of keeping the existing machine in operation during the year*
	£	£
Now 0	8,500	n/a
1	5,000	9,000
2	2,500	12,000
3	0	15,000

Calculate the best time to replace the existing machine.

6.18 SOLUTION

The costs of the new machine will be those given above, so that the optimum replacement cycle for the new machine will already have been calculated as three years, with an equivalent annual cost in perpetuity of £17,625.

The best time to replace the existing machine will be the option which gives the lowest NPV of **cost in perpetuity**, for both the existing machine and the machine which eventually replaces it.

Step 1. Calculate the NPV of the cost in perpetuity of the new machine using $\frac{a}{r}$.

$$\text{PV of cost} = \frac{£17,625}{0.1} = £176,250$$

The new machine will have a PV of cost in perpetuity of £176,250 from the start of the year when it is eventually purchased. The present value relates to the beginning of the year when the first annual cash flow occurs, so that if replacement occurs now, the first annuity is in year 1, and the PV of cost relates to year 0 values. If replacement occurs at the end of year 1 the first annuity is in year 2, and the PV of cost relates to year 1, and so on.

Step 2. Calculate the present values of each replacement option.

These cash flows show the PV of cost in perpetuity of the new machine, the running costs of the existing machine, and the resale value of the existing machine, at the end of year 0, 1, 2 or 3 as appropriate.

Year	*Replace now*	*Replace in 1 year*	*Replace in 2 years*	*Replace in 3 years*
	£	£	£	£
0	(176,250)	–	–	–
	8,500			
1	–	(176,250)		
		(9,000)	(9,000)	(9,000)
		5,000		
2	–	–	(176,250)	
			(12,000)	(12,000)
			2,500	
3	–	–	–	(176,250)
				(15,000)

The PVs of each replacement option are as follows.

	Year	*Cash flow*	*Discount factor*	*Present value*
		£	10%	£
Replace now	0	(176,250)		
		8,500		
		(167,750)	1.000	(167,750)
Replace in one year	1	(176,250)		
		(9,000)		
		5,000		
		(180,250)	0.909	(163,847)
Replace in two years	1	(9,000)	0.909	(8,181)
	2	(185,750)	0.826	(153,430)
				(161,611)
Replace in three years	1	(9,000)	0.909	(8,181)
	2	(12,000)	0.826	(9,912)
	3	(191,250)	0.751	(143,629)
				(161,722)

6.19 CONCLUSION

The marginally optimum policy would be to replace the existing machine in two years' time, because this has the lowest total PV of cost in perpetuity.

Chapter roundup

- There are two methods of using DCF to evaluate capital investments, the **NPV method** and the **IRR/DCF yield method.**
- The **NPV method** of investment appraisal is to accept projects with a positive NPV. Ensure that you are aware of the three conventions concerning the timings of cash flows.
- An **annuity** is a constant cash flow for a number of years. A **perpetuity** is a constant cash flow forever.
- The **IRR method** of investment appraisal is to accept projects whose IRR (the rate at which the NPV is zero) exceeds a target rate of return. The IRR is calculated using interpolation.
- There are advantages and disadvantages to each appraisal method. Make sure that you can discuss them.
- **DCF methods of appraisal** have a number of **advantages** over other appraisal methods.
    - The time value of money is taken into account.
    - The method takes account of all of a project's cash flows.
    - It allows for the timing of cash flows.
    - There are universally accepted methods of calculating the NPV and IRR.
- DCF techniques can assist **asset replacement decisions.** When an asset is being replaced with an identical asset there are three methods of choosing an **optimum replacement cycle**:
    - The **lowest common multiple method**
    - The **finite horizon method**
    - The **equivalent annual cost method**
- When an asset is being replaced with a **non-identical asset** the decision is one of **when** to replace the asset rather than how frequently.

Quick quiz

1 What is the formula for calculating the future value of an investment plus accumulated interest after n time periods?

2 What is the formula for calculating the present value of a future sum of money out the end of n time periods?

3 List three cash flow timing conventions used in DCF.

4 What is the perpetuity formula? 

5 List three advantages of the DCF method of project appraisal over other appraisal methods.

6 For a certain project, the net present value at a discount rate of 15% is £3,670, and at a rate of 18% the net present value is negative at (£1,390). What is the internal rate of return of the project?

A 15.7%

B 16.5%

C 16.6%

D 17.2%

7 *Tick the correct box to indicate whether or not the following items are included in the cash flows when determining the net present value of a project.*

	Included	*Not included*
(a) The disposal value of equipment at the end of its life		
(b) Depreciation charges for the equipment		
(c) Research costs incurred prior to the appraisal		
(d) Interest payments on the loan to finance the investment		

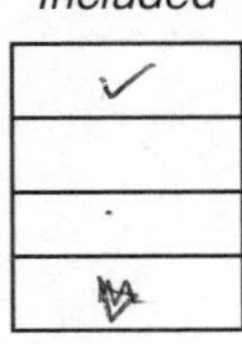
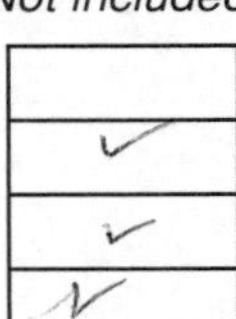

8 The net present value of the costs of operating a machine for the next three years is £10,724 at a cost of capital of 15%. What is the equivalent annual cost of operating the machine?

A £4,697

B £3,575

C £4,111

D £3,109

Answers to quick quiz

1 $FV = PV (1 + r)^n$

2 $PV = FV \frac{1}{(1+r)^n}$

3 (a) A cash outlay to be incurred at the beginning of an investment project occurs in year 0.

(b) A cash outlay, saving or inflow which occurs during the course of a time period is assumed to occur all at once at the end of the time period.

(c) A cash outlay or receipt that occurs at the beginning of a time period is taken to occur at the end of the previous year.

4 Annual cash flow/discount rate.

5 (a) It takes account of the time value of money.
(b) It uses all cash flows relating to a project.
(c) It allows for the timing of cash flows.

6 D 15% + {(3,670/[3,670 + 1,390]) × 3%} = 17.2%

7 (a) Included

(b) Not included (non-cash)

(c) Not included (past cost)

(d) Not usually included, unless the loan incurs a different rate of interest from that which is being used as the discount rate

8 A £10,724/2.283 = £4,697

Now try the question below from the Exam Question Bank

Question to try	Level	Marks	Time
32	Introductory	n/a	45 mins

Chapter 28

ALLOWING FOR INFLATION AND TAXATION

Topic list	Syllabus reference
1 **Allowing for inflation**	**5(a)**
2 **Allowing for taxation**	**5(a)**

Introduction

Having covered the more sophisticated of the investment appraisal techniques which are available in Chapter 27, we will be looking in this chapter at how to incorporate **inflation** and **taxation** into investment decisions. The next chapter will consider how the **risk** associated with a project can be assessed and taken into account.

Study guide

Section 14 – Project appraisal allowing for inflation and taxation

Inflation

- Explain the relationship between inflation and interest rates, distinguishing between real and nominal rates
- Distinguish general inflation from specific price increases and assess their impact on cash flows
- Evaluate capital investment projects on a real terms basis
- Evaluate capital investment projects on a nominal terms basis

Taxation

- Calculate the effect of capital allowances and corporation tax on project cash flows
- Evaluate the profitability of capital investment projects on a post-tax basis

Exam guide

As well as bringing inflation into your DCF calculations, you may be asked to explain the differences between real and nominal rates.

1 ALLOWING FOR INFLATION

1.1 So far we have not considered the effect of **inflation** on the appraisal of capital investment proposals. As the inflation rate increases so will the minimum return required by an investor. For example, you might be happy with a return of 5% in an inflation-free world, but if inflation was running at 15% you would expect a considerably greater yield.

1.2 EXAMPLE: INFLATION (1)

A company is considering investing in a project with the following cash flows.

Time	*Actual cash flows*
	£
0	(15,000)
1	9,000
2	8,000
3	7,000

The company requires a minimum return of 20% under the present and anticipated conditions. Inflation is currently running at 10% a year, and this rate of inflation is expected to continue indefinitely. Should the company go ahead with the project?

1.3 Let us first look at the company's required rate of return. Suppose that it invested £1,000 for one year on 1 January, then on 31 December it would require a minimum return of £200. With the initial investment of £1,000, the total value of the investment by 31 December must therefore increase to £1,200. During the course of the year the purchasing value of the pound would fall due to inflation. We can restate the amount received on 31 December in terms of the purchasing power of the pound at 1 January as follows.

Amount received on 31 December in terms of the value of the pound at 1 January $= \frac{£1,200}{(1.10)^1} = £1,091$

1.4 In terms of the value of the pound at 1 January, the company would make a profit of £91 which represents a rate of return of 9.1% in 'today's money' terms. This is **the real rate of return**. The required rate of 20% is a **money rate of return** (sometimes called a **nominal rate of return**). The **money rate** measures the return in terms of the **pound** which is, of course, falling in value. The **real rate** measures the return in **constant price level** terms.

1.5 The two rates of return and the inflation rate are linked by the equation

FORMULA TO LEARN

(1 + money rate) = (1 + real rate) × (1 + inflation rate)

where all the rates are expressed as proportions.

1.6 In our example,

$$(1 + 0.20) = (1 + 0.091) \times (1 + 0.10) = 1.20$$

Exam focus point

You may be asked in the exam to explain the difference between a real and money terms analysis.

Do we use the real rate or the money rate?

1.7 The rule is as follows.

(a) If the cash flows are expressed in terms of the **actual number of pounds** that will be **received** or **paid** on the **various future dates**, we use the **money rate** for discounting.

(b) If the cash flows are expressed in terms of the **value of the pound at time 0** (that is, in constant price level terms), we use the **real rate.**

1.8 The cash flows given above are expressed in terms of the **actual number** of **pounds** that will be received or paid at the relevant dates. We should, therefore, discount them using the **money rate of return.**

Time	*Cash flow*	*Discount factor*	*PV*
	£	20%	£
0	(15,000)	1.000	(15,000)
1	9,000	0.833	7,497
2	8,000	0.694	5,552
3	7,000	0.579	4,053
			2,102

The project has a positive net present value of £2,102.

1.9 The future cash flows can be re-expressed in terms of the value of the pound at time 0 as follows, given inflation at 10% a year.

Time	*Actual cash flow*		*Cash flow at time 0 price level*
	£		£
0	(15,000)		(15,000)
1	9,000	$9{,}000 \times \frac{1}{1.10}$ =	8,182
2	8,000	$8{,}000 \times \frac{1}{(1.10)^2}$ =	6,612
3	7,000	$7{,}000 \times \frac{1}{(1.10)^3}$ =	5,259

1.10 The cash flows expressed in terms of the value of the pound at time 0 can now be discounted using the real rate of 9.1%.

Time	*Cash flow*	*Discount factor*	*PV*
	£	9.1%	£
0	(15,000)	1.00	(15,000)
1	8,182	$\frac{1}{1.091}$	7,500
2	6,612	$\frac{1}{(1.091)^2}$	5,555
3	5,259	$\frac{1}{(1.091)^3}$	4,050
		NPV	2,105

1.11 The NPV is the same as before (and the present value of the cash flow in each year is the same as before) apart from rounding errors.

The advantages and misuses of real values and a real rate of return

1.12 Although generally companies should discount money values at the money cost of capital, there are some advantages of using real values discounted at a real cost of capital.

(a) When all costs and benefits rise at the same rate of price inflation, **real values** are the **same as current day values,** so that no **further adjustments** need be made to cash flows before discounting. In contrast, when money values are discounted at the money cost of capital, the **prices** in **future years** must be **calculated** before discounting can begin.

(b) The government might prefer to set a **real return** as a target for investments, as being more suitable than a commercial money rate of return.

Costs and benefits which inflate at different rates

1.13 Not all costs and benefits will rise in line with the general level of inflation. In such cases, we can apply the **money rate** to **inflated values** to determine a project's NPV.

1.14 EXAMPLE: INFLATION (2)

Rice Ltd is considering a project which would cost £5,000 now. The annual benefits, for four years, would be a fixed income of £2,500 a year, plus other savings of £500 a year in year 1, rising by 5% each year because of inflation. Running costs will be £1,000 in the first year, but would increase at 10% each year because of inflating labour costs. The general rate of inflation is expected to be 7½% and the company's required money rate of return is 16%. Is the project worthwhile? Ignore taxation.

1.15 SOLUTION

The cash flows at inflated values are as follows.

Year	*Fixed income*	*Other savings*	*Running costs*	*Net cash flow*
	£	£	£	£
1	2,500	500	1,000	2,000
2	2,500	525	1,100	1,925
3	2,500	551	1,210	1,841
4	2,500	579	1,331	1,748

The NPV of the project is as follows.

Year	*Cash flow*	*Discount factor*	*PV*
	£	16%	£
0	(5,000)	1.000	(5,000)
1	2,000	0.862	1,724
2	1,925	0.743	1,430
3	1,841	0.641	1,180
4	1,748	0.552	965
			+ 299

The NPV is positive and the project would seem therefore to be worthwhile.

Variations in the expected rate of inflation

1.16 If the rate of inflation is expected to change, the calculation of the money cost of capital is slightly more complicated.

1.17 EXAMPLE: INFLATION (3)

Mr Gable has just received a dividend of £1,000 on his shareholding in Gonwithy Windmills plc. The market value of the shares is £8,000 ex div. What is the (money) cost of the equity capital, if dividends are expected to rise because of inflation by 10% in years 1, 2 and 3, before levelling off at this year 3 amount?

1.18 SOLUTION

The money cost of capital is the internal rate of return of the following cash flows.

Year	*Cash flow*	*PV factor*	*PV at 15%*	*PV factor*	*PV at 20%*
	£	15%	£	20%	£
0	(8,000)	1.000	(8,000)	1.000	(8,000)
1	1,100	0.870	957	0.833	916
2	1,210	0.756	915	0.694	840
3 - ∞ ⋆	1,331 pa	5.041	6,709	3.472	4,621
			581		(1,623)

The IRR is approximately 15% + $\left[\frac{581}{581--1{,}623}\times(20-15)\right]$ % = 16.3%, say 16%

⋆ The present value factor = Factor 1 - ∞ – Factor yrs 1-2.

For 15%

PV factor $= \frac{1}{0.15} - 1.626$

$= 5.041$

For 20%

PV factor $= \frac{1}{0.2} - 1.528$

$= 3.472$

Expectations of inflation and the effects of inflation

1.19 When managers evaluate a particular project, or when shareholders evaluate their investments, they can only guess at what the rate of inflation is going to be. Their expectations will probably be inaccurate, because it is extremely difficult to forecast the rate of inflation correctly. The only way in which uncertainty about inflation can be allowed for in project evaluation is by **risk** and **uncertainty analysis**. Plans should be made to obtain **'contingency funds'**, for example a higher bank overdraft facility if the rate of inflation exceeds expectations.

1.20 Inflation may be **general,** affecting prices of all kinds, or **specific** to particular prices. Generalised inflation has the following effects.

(a) Since fixed assets and stocks will increase in money value, the same quantities of assets must be financed by **increasing amounts** of capital.

(b) Inflation means higher costs and **higher selling prices**. The effect of higher prices on demand may **not** be **easy to predict**. A company that raises its prices by 10% because the general rate of inflation is running at 10% might suffer a serious fall in demand.

(c) Inflation, because it affects financing needs, is also likely to affect **gearing,** and so the **cost of capital.**

Mid-year and end of year money values

1.21 You might wonder why, in all the examples so far, the cash flows have been inflated to the end of year money prices. Inflation does not usually run at a steady rate.

1.22 In DCF calculations it is more appropriate to use **end of year money values**. This is because by convention, all **cash flows** are assumed to **occur** at the **end of the year**, and a discount factor appropriate to the end of the year is applied.

1.23 In an examination question which introduces inflation into the calculation where **DCF** is **not required** to reach a solution, it may be better to use mid-year prices rather than end of year prices in your figures.

2 ALLOWING FOR TAXATION

2.1 So far, in looking at project appraisal, we have ignored **taxation.** However, payments of tax, or reductions of tax payments, are cash flows and ought to be considered in DCF analysis. Assumptions which may be stated in questions are as follows.

(a) Corporation tax is payable in the year following the one in which the taxable profits are made. Thus, if a project increases taxable profits by £10,000 in year 2, there will be a tax payment, assuming tax at 30%, of £3,000 in year 3.

(b) Net cash flows from a project should be considered as the **taxable profits** arising from the project (unless an indication is given to the contrary).

Exam focus point

Check any question involving tax carefully to see what assumptions about tax rates are made. Also look out for questions which state that tax is payable in the same year as that in which the profits arise.

Capital allowances

2.2 Capital allowances are used to reduce taxable profits, and the consequent reduction in a tax payment should be treated as a **cash saving** arising from the acceptance of a project. Writing down allowances are generally allowed on the cost of **plant and machinery** at the rate of 25% on a **reducing balance** basis.

2.3 Thus if a company purchases plant costing £80,000, the subsequent writing down allowances would be as follows.

Year		*Capital allowance*	*Reducing balance*
		£	£
1	(25% of cost)	20,000	60,000
2	(25% of RB)	15,000	45,000
3	(25% of RB)	11,250	33,750
4	(25% of RB)	8,438	25,312

2.4 When the plant is eventually sold, the difference between the sale price and the reducing balance amount at the time of sale will be treated as a **taxable profit** if the **sale price exceeds** the **reducing balance,** and as a **tax allowable loss** if the **reducing balance exceeds** the **sale price.**

2.5 Examination questions often assume that this loss will be available immediately, though in practice the balance less the sale price continues to be written off at 25% a year as part of a pool balance unless the asset has been de-pooled.

2.6 The cash saving on the capital allowances (or the cash payment for the charge) is calculated by Allowance charge × Corporation tax rate.

2.7 Assumptions about capital allowances could be **simplified** in an **exam question**.

(a) You might be told that capital allowances can be claimed at the rate of 25% of cost on a straight line basis (that is, over four years)

(b) A question might refer to 'tax allowable depreciation', so that the capital allowances equal the depreciation charge.

2.8 There are two possible assumptions about the time when capital allowances start to be claimed.

(a) It can be assumed that the first claim for capital allowances occurs at the **start** of the **project** (at year 0) and so the first tax saving occurs one year later (at year 1).

(b) Alternatively it can be assumed that the **first claim** for **capital allowances** occurs **later** in the **first year,** so the first tax saving occurs one year later, that is, **year 2**.

Examination questions generally will indicate which of the two assumptions is required but you should state your assumptions clearly if you have to make assumptions.

2.9 EXAMPLE: TAXATION

A company is considering whether or not to purchase an item of machinery costing £40,000 in 20X5. It would have a life of four years, after which it would be sold for £5,000. The machinery would create annual cost savings of £14,000.

The machinery would attract writing down allowances of 25% on the reducing balance basis which could be claimed against taxable profits of the current year, which is soon to end. A balancing allowance or charge would arise on disposal. The rate of corporation tax is 30%. Tax is payable one year in arrears. The after-tax cost of capital is 8%. Assume that tax payments occur in the year following the transactions.

Should the machinery be purchased?

2.10 SOLUTION

The first capital allowance is claimed against year 0 profits.

Cost: £40,000

Year	*Allowance*	*Reducing balance (RB)*	
	£	£	
(0) 20X5 (25% of cost)	10,000	30,000	(40,000 – 10,000)
(1) 20X6 (25% of RB)	7,500	22,500	(30,000 – 7,500)
(2) 20X7 (25% of RB)	5,625	16,875	(22,500 – 5,625)
(3) 20X8 (25% of RB)	4,219	12,656	(16,875 – 4,219)
(4) 20X9 (25% of RB)	3,164	9,492	(12,656 – 3,164)

	£
Sale proceeds, end of fourth year	5,000
Less reducing balance, end of fourth year	9,492
Balancing allowance	4,492

2.11 Having calculated the allowances each year, the tax savings can be computed. The year of the cash flow is one year after the year for which the allowance is claimed.

Year of claim	Allowance	Tax saved	Year of tax payment/saving
	£	£	
0	10,000	3,000	1
1	7,500	2,250	2
2	5,625	1,688	3
3	4,219	1,266	4
4	7,656	2,297	5
	35,000 *		

* Net cost £(40,000 – 5,000) = £35,000

These tax savings relate to capital allowances. We must also calculate the extra tax payments on annual savings of £14,000.

2.12 The net cash flows and the NPV are now calculated as follows.

Year	Equipment	Savings	Tax on savings	Tax saved on capital allowances	Net cash flow	Discount factor	Present value of cash flow
	£	£	£	£	£	8%	£
0	(40,000)				(40,000)	1.000	(40,000)
1		14,000		3,000	17,000	0.926	15,742
2		14,000	(4,200)	2,250	12,050	0.857	10,327
3		14,000	(4,200)	1,688	11,488	0.794	9,121
4	5,000	14,000	(4,200)	1,266	16,066	0.735	11,809
5			(4,200)	2,297	(1,903)	0.681	(1,296)
							5,703

The NPV is positive and so the purchase appears to be worthwhile.

An alternative and quicker method of calculating tax payments or savings

2.13 In the above example, the tax computations could have been combined, as follows.

Year	0	1	2	3	4
	£	£	£	£	£
Cost savings	0	14,000	14,000	14,000	14,000
Capital allowance	10,000	7,500	5,625	4,219	7,656
Taxable profits	(10,000)	6,500	8,375	9,781	6,344
Tax at 30%	3,000	(1,950)	(2,512)	(2,934)	(1,903)

2.14 The net cash flows would then be as follows.

Year	Equipment	Savings	Tax	Net cash flow
	£	£	£	£
0	(40,000)			(40,000)
1		14,000	3,000	17,000
2		14,000	(1,950)	12,050
3		14,000	(2,512)	11,488
4	5,000	14,000	(2,934)	16,066
5			(1,903)	(1,903)

The net cash flows are exactly the same as calculated previously.

Taxation and DCF

2.15 The effect of taxation on capital budgeting is theoretically quite simple. Organisations must pay tax, and the effect of undertaking a project will be to increase or decrease tax payments each year. These incremental tax cash flows should be included in the cash flows of the project for discounting to arrive at the project's NPV.

2.16 When **taxation is ignored** in the DCF calculations, the discount rate will reflect the **pre-tax rate of return** required on capital investments. When **taxation is included** in the cash flows, a **post-tax required rate of return** should be used.

Question 1

A company is considering the purchase of an item of equipment, which would earn profits before tax of £25,000 a year. Depreciation charges would be £20,000 a year for six years. Capital allowances would be £30,000 a year for the first four years. Corporation tax is at 30%.

What would be the annual net cash inflows of the project:

(a) For the first four years
(b) For the fifth and sixth years

assuming that tax payments occur in the same year as the profits giving rise to them, and there is no balancing charge or allowance when the machine is scrapped at the end of the sixth year?

Answer

(a)

	Years 1-4	*Years 5-6*
	£	£
Profit before tax	25,000	25,000
Add back depreciation	20,000	20,000
Net cash inflow before tax	45,000	45,000
Less capital allowance	30,000	0
	15,000	45,000
Tax at 30%	4,500	13,500

Years 1 - 4 Net cash inflow after tax £45,000 – £4,500 = £40,500

(b) Years 5 - 6 Net cash inflow after tax = £45,000 – £13,500 = £31,500

Question 2

A company is considering the purchase of a machine for £150,000. It would be sold after four years for an estimated realisable value of £50,000. By this time capital allowances of £120,000 would have been claimed. The rate of corporation tax is 30%.

What are the tax implications of the sale of the machine at the end of four years?

Answer

There will be a balancing charge on the sale of the machine of £(50,000 – (150,000 – 120,000)) = £20,000. This will give rise to a tax payment of 30% × £20,000 = £6,000.

Quarterly accounting for corporation tax

2.17 Under the new UK system, corporation tax is **payable** by companies **quarterly**.

- In the seventh and tenth months of the year in which the profit is earned
- In the first and fourth months of the following year

2.18 This simply means that **half the tax is payable in the year in which the profits are earned** and **half in the following year**.

Exam focus point

This payment timetable is not difficult to remember but details will be given in the exam question anyway.

2.19 EXAMPLE: PAYMENT OF CORPORATION TAX

If a project increases taxable profits by £10,000 in year 2, there will be tax payments of £10,000 × 30% × 50% = £1,500 in both year 2 and in year 3 (assuming a tax rate of 30%). It is these tax payments (that are a direct result of the project) that need to be included in a DCF analysis.

As half the tax on profit is paid in the year to which the profits relate, and half in the following year, the **benefit of the capital or writing down allowance** is also felt **half in the year to which it relates** and **half in the following year.**

2.20 EXAMPLE: TAXATION

A company is considering whether or not to purchase an item of machinery costing £40,000. It would have a life of four years, after which it would be sold for £5,000. The machinery would create annual cost savings of £14,000.

The machinery would attract writing down allowances of 25% on the reducing balance basis. A balancing allowance or charge would arise on disposal. The rate of corporation tax is 30%. Tax is payable quarterly in the seventh and tenth months of the year in which the profit is earned and in the first and fourth months of the following year. The after-tax cost of capital is 8%.

Should the machinery be purchased?

2.21 SOLUTION

Step 1. **WDAs and balancing charges / allowances**

We begin by calculating the WDAs and balancing charge / allowance.

Year		*Reducing balance*
		£
0	Purchase	40,000
1	WDA	(10,000)
	Value at start of year 2	30,000
2	WDA	(7,500)
	Value at start of year 3	22,500
3	WDA	(5,625)
	Value at start of year 4	16,878
4	Sale	(5,000)
	Balancing allowance	11,875

Step 2. **Calculate tax savings / payments**

Having calculated the allowances each year, the **tax savings** can be computed. The tax savings effect two years, the year for which the allowance is claimed and the following year.

Year of claim	*Allowance*	*Tax saved*	*Tax saving*				
	£	£	Yr 1	Yr 2	Yr 3	Yr 4	Yr 5
			£	£	£	£	£
1	10,000	3,000	1,500	1,500			
2	7,500	2,250		1,125	1,125		
3	5,625	1,688			844	844	
4	11,875	3,562				1,781	1,781
	35,000 *		1,500	2,625	1,969	2,625	1,781

* Net cost £(40,000 – 5,000) = £35,000

These tax savings relate to capital allowances. We must also take **the tax effects of the annual savings** of £14,000 into account.

The savings increase taxable profit (costs are lower) and so extra tax must be paid. Each saving of £14,000 will lead to extra tax of £14,000 × 30% × 50% = £2,100 in the year in question and the same amount in the following year.

Step 3. **Calculate NPV**

The **net cash flows and the NPV** are now calculated as follows.

Year	*Equipment*	*Savings*	*Tax on savings*	*Tax saved on capital allowances*	*Net cash flow*	*Discount factor*	*Present value of cash flow*
	£	£	£	£	£	8%	£
0	(40,000)				(40,000)	1.000	(40,000)
1		14,000	(2,100)	1,500	13,400	0.926	12,408
2		14,000	(4,200)	2,625	12,425	0.857	10,648
3		14,000	(4,200)	1,969	11,769	0.794	9,345
4	5,000	14,000	(4,200)	2,625	17,425	0.735	12,807
5			(2,100)	1,781	(319)	0.681	(217)
							4,991

The NPV is positive and so the purchase appears to be worthwhile.

An alternative and quicker method of calculating tax payments or savings

2.22 In the above example, the tax computations could have been combined, as follows.

Year	*1*	*2*	*3*	*4*	*5*
	£	£	£	£	£
Cost savings	14,000	14,000	14,000	14,000	
Capital allowance	10,000	7,500	5,625	11,875	
Taxable profits	4,000	6,500	8,375	2,125	
Tax (paid)/received at 30%	(1,200)	(1,950)	(2,512)	(638)	
Yr of (payment)/saving	(600)	(600)			
		(975)	(975)		
			(1,256)	(1,256)	
				(319)	(319)
(Payment)/saving	(600)	(1,575)	(2,231)	(1,575)	(319)

The net cash flows would then be as follows.

Year	*Equipment*	*Savings*	*Tax*	*Net cash flow*
	£	£	£	£
0	(40,000)			(40,000)
1		14,000	(600)	13,400
2		14,000	(1,575)	12,425
3		14,000	(2,231)	11,769
4	5,000	14,000	(1,575)	17,425
5			(319)	(319)

The net cash flows are exactly the same as calculated previously.

Chapter roundup

- **Inflation** is a feature of all economies, and it must be accommodated in financial planning.
- (1+ money rate of return) = (1 + real rate of return) × (1 + rate of inflation)
- **Real cash flows** (ie adjusted for inflation) should be discounted at a real discount rate.
- **Money cash flows** should be discounted at a money discount rate.
- **Taxation** is a major practical consideration for businesses. It is vital to take it into account in making decisions.
- In investment appraisal, tax is often assumed to be payable **one year in arrears.**
- **Capital allowances** details should be checked in any question you attempt.

Quick quiz

1 What is the relationship between the money rate of return, the real rate of return and the rate of inflation?

2 The money cost of capital is 11%. The expected annual rate of inflation is 5%. What is the real cost of capital? (See below)

3 A company wants a minimum real return of 3% a year on its investments. Inflation is expected to be 8% a year. What is the company's minimum money cost of capital? (See below)

4 Summarise briefly how taxation is taken into consideration in capital budgeting.

5 A company is appraising an investment that will save electricity costs. Electricity prices are expected to rise at a rate of 15% per annum in future, although the general inflation rate will be 10% per annum. The money cost of capital for the company is 20%. What is the appropriate discount rate to apply to the forecast actual money cash flows for electricity?

A 20.0%

B 22.0%

C 26.5%

D 32.0%

6 *Choose the correct words from those highlighted.*

Capital allowances are used to (1) **increase/reduce** taxable profits, and the consequent reduction in a tax payment should be treated as a (2) **cash saving/cash payment** arising from the acceptance of a project.

Writing down allowances are generally allowed on the cost of (3) **materials and labour/plant and machinery** at the rate of (4) **25%/30%** on a (5) **straight line/reducing balance** basis.

When the plant is eventually sold, the difference between the sales price and the reducing balance amount will be treated as a (6) **taxable profit/tax allowable loss** if the sales price exceeds the reducing balance, and as a (7) **taxable profit/tax allowable loss** if the reducing balance exceeds the sales price.

7 If cash flows are expressed in terms of the actual number of pounds that will be received or paid on various future dates, should the money rate or real rate be used for discounting?

8 Red Ltd is considering the purchase of a machine for £2,190,000. It would be sold after four years for an estimated realisable value of £790,000. By this time capital allowances of £1,450,000 would have been claimed. The rate of corporation tax is 30%.

What is the cash flow arising as a result of tax implications on the sale of the machine at the end of four years?

A Inflow of £15,000

B Outflow of £50,000

C Outflow of £459,000

D Outflow of £15,000

Answers to quick quiz

1 (1 + money rate) = (1 + real rate) × (1 + inflation rate)

2 $\frac{1.11}{1.05} = 1.057$. The real cost of capital is 5.7%.

3 1.03 × 1.08 = 1.1124. The money cost of capital is 11.24%.

4 If tax is included in the cash flows, the post-tax rate of required return on capital investments should be used. If tax is ignored, the discount rate should reflect the pre-tax rate of return.

5 A The money rate of 20% is applied to the money cash flows.

6 (1) reduce

(2) cash saving

(3) plant and machinery

(4) 25%

(5) reducing balance

(6) taxable profit

(7) tax allowable loss

7 The money rate

8 D There will be a balancing charge on the sale of the machine of £(790,000 – (2,190,000 – 1,450,000)) = £50,000. This will give rise to a tax payment of 30% × £50,000 = £15,000.

Now try the question below from the Exam Question Bank

Question to try	Level	Marks	Time
33	Exam	25	45 mins

Chapter 29

PROJECT APPRAISAL AND RISK

Topic list		Syllabus reference
1	**What is risk and why does it arise?**	**5(a)**
2	**Sensitivity analysis. Certainty-equivalents**	**5(a)**
3	**Probability analysis**	**5(a)**
4	**Decision tree analysis**	**5(a)**
5	**Simulation models**	**5(a)**
6	**Ways of reducing risk**	**5(a)**

Introduction

This chapter will show some of the different methods of assessing and taking account of the **risk** associated with a project. The last two chapters of this Study Text will consider two further project appraisal topics - **capital rationing** and **leasing**.

Study guide

Section 15 – Project appraisal allowing for risk

- Distinguish between risk and uncertainty
- Identify the sources of risk affecting project profitability
- Evaluate the sensitivity of project NPV to changes in key variables
- Apply the probability approach to calculating expected NPV of a project and the associated standard deviation
- Apply decision tree analysis in project appraisal situations
- Explain the role of simulation in generating a probability distribution for the NPV of a project
- Identify risk reduction strategies for projects
- Evaluate the usefulness of risk assessment methods

Exam guide

Sensitivity calculations are important for exam purposes. 12 marks were available in the compulsory question in December 2001 for sensitivity calculations. The Oxford Brookes degree Research and Analysis Project Topic 14 requires knowledge of how use of different methods of risk and uncertainty analysis might affect investment decisions.

1 WHAT IS RISK AND WHY DOES IT ARISE?

1.1 The terms risk and uncertainty are often used interchangeably but a distinction should be made between them.

Risk	• Several possible outcomes • On basis of past relevant experience, assign probabilities to outcomes
Uncertainty	• Several possible outcomes • Little past experience, thus difficult to assign probabilities to outcomes

1.2 A risky situation is one where we can say that there is a 70% probability that returns from a project will be in excess of £100,000 but a 30% probability that returns will be less than £100,000. If, however, no information can be provided on the returns from the project, we are faced with an uncertain situation.

1.3 In general, risky projects are those whose future cash flows, and hence the project returns, are likely to be variable. The greater the variability is, the greater the risk. The problem of risk is more acute with capital investment decisions than other decisions for the following reasons.

(a) **Estimates** of capital expenditure might be for **several years ahead**, such as for major construction projects. Actual costs may escalate well above budget as the work progresses.

(b) Estimates of **benefits** will be for **several years ahead**, sometimes 10, 15 or 20 years ahead or even longer, and such long-term estimates can at best be approximations.

2 SENSITIVITY ANALYSIS. CERTAINTY-EQUIVALENTS

KEY TERM

Sensitivity analysis is one method of analysing the risk surrounding a capital expenditure project and enables an assessment to be made of how responsive the project's NPV is to changes in the variables that are used to calculate that NPV.

2.1 The NPV could depend on a number of uncertain independent variables.

- Selling price
- Sales volume
- Cost of capital
- Initial cost
- Operating costs
- Benefits

2.2 The basic approach of sensitivity analysis is to **calculate the project's NPV** under **alternative assumptions** to determine how sensitive it is to changing conditions. An indication is thus provided of those variables to which the NPV is most sensitive (**critical variables**) and the **extent** to which those variables **may change** before the investment results in a negative NPV.

2.3 Sensitivity analysis therefore provides an indication of why a project might fail. Management should review critical variables to assess whether or not there is a strong possibility of events occurring which will lead to a negative NPV. Management should also pay particular attention to controlling those variables to which the NPV is particularly sensitive, once the decision has been taken to accept the investment.

2.4 EXAMPLE: SENSITIVITY ANALYSIS

Kenney Ltd is considering a project with the following cash flows.

	Initial investment	*Variable costs*	*Cash inflows*	*Net cash flows*
	£'000	£'000	£'000	£'000
0	7,000			
1		(2,000)	6,500	4,500
2		(2,000)	6,500	4,500

(650,000 units at £10 per unit)

Required

Measure the sensitivity of the project to changes in variables.

2.5 SOLUTION

The PVs of the cash flow are as follows.

Year	*Discount factor*	*PV of initial investment*	*PV of variable costs*	*PV of cash inflows*	*PV of net cash flow*
	8%	£'000	£'000	£'000	£'000
0	1.000	(7,000)			(7,000)
1	0.926		(1,852)	6,019	4,167
2	0.857		(1,714)	5,571	3,857
		(7,000)	(3,566)	11,590	1,024

The project has a positive NPV and would appear to be worthwhile. The changes in cash flows which would need to occur for the project to breakeven (and hence be on the point of being unacceptable) are as follows.

(a) **Initial investment.** The initial investment can rise by £1,024,000 before the investment breaks even. The initial investment may therefore increase by 1,024/7,000 = 15%.

(b) **Sales volume.** The present value of the cash inflows less the present value of the variable costs will have to fall to £7,000,000 for the NPV to be zero.

We need to find the net cash flows in actual values. As the cash flows are equal each year, cumulative discount tables can be used.

(i) The discount factor for 8% and year 2 is 1.783.

(ii) If the discount factor is divided into the required present value of £7,000,000 we get an annual cash flow of £3,925,968.

(iii) Given that the most likely net cash flow is £4,500,000, the net cash flow may decline by approximately £574,032 (4,500,000 – 3,925,968) each year before the NPV becomes zero.

(iv) Total sales revenue may therefore decline by £831,930 (assuming net cash flow is 69% (4,500/6,500) of sales) (therefore sales = 574,032 × 6,500/4,500). At a selling price of £10 per unit this represents 83,193 units.

(v) Alternatively we may state that sales volume may decline by 13% before the NPV becomes negative.

(c) **Selling price.** When sales volume is 650,000 units per annum, total sales revenue can fall to £5,925,968 (£(6,500,000 – 574,032) per annum before the NPV becomes negative. This represents a selling price of £9.12 per unit, which represents a 8.8% reduction in the selling price.

(d) **Variable costs.** The total variable cost can increase by £574,032, or £0.88 per unit. This represents an increase of 28.6%.

(e) **Cost of capital.** We need to calculate the IRR of the project. Let us try discount rates of 15% and 20%.

Year	*Net cash flow*	*Discount factor*	*PV*	*Discount factor*	*PV*
	£'000	15%	£'000	20%	£'000
0	(7,000)	0.870	(6,090)	0.833	(5,831)
1	4,500	0.756	3,402	0.694	3,123
2	4,500	0.658	2,961	0.579	2,606
		NPV =	273	NPV =	(102)

$$\text{IRR} = 0.15 + \left[\frac{273}{273+102} \times (0.20 - 0.15)\right] = 18.64\%$$

The cost of capital can therefore increase by 133% before the NPV becomes negative.

2.6 The elements to which the NPV appears to be most sensitive are the selling price followed by the sales volume. Management should thus pay particular attention to these factors so that they can be carefully monitored.

2.7 EXAMPLE: MORE SENSITIVITY ANALYSIS

Nevers Ure Ltd is considering a project with the following cash flows.

Year	*Purchase of plant*	*Running costs*	*Savings*
	£	£	£
0	(7,000)		
1		2,000	6,000
2		2,500	7,000

The cost of capital is 8%. Measure the sensitivity (in percentages) of the project to changes in the levels of expected costs and savings.

2.8 SOLUTION

The PVs of the cash flows are as follows.

Year	*Discount factors* 8%	*PV of plant cost* £	*PV of Running costs* £	*PV of savings* £	*PV of net cash flow* £
0	1.000	(7,000)			(7,000)
1	0.926		(1,852)	5,556	3,704
2	0.857		(2,143)	5,999	3,856
		(7,000)	(3,995)	11,555	560

2.9 The project has a positive NPV and would appear to be worthwhile. The changes in cash flows which would need to occur for the project to break even (NPV = 0) are as follows.

(a) Plant costs would need to increase by a PV of £560, that is by $\frac{560}{7,000} = 8\%$

(b) Running costs would need to increase by a PV of £560, that is by $\frac{560}{3,995} = 14\%$

(c) Savings would need to fall by a PV of £560, that is by $\frac{560}{11,555} = 4.8\%$

Weaknesses of this approach to sensitivity analysis

2.10 These are as follows.

(a) The method requires that **changes** in each key variable are **isolated.** However management is more interested in the combination of the effects of changes in two or more key variables.

(b) Looking at factors in isolation is unrealistic since they are often **interdependent**.

(c) Sensitivity analysis does not examine the **probability** that any particular variation in costs or revenues might occur.

(d) **Critical factors** may be those over which managers have no control.

(e) In itself it does not provide a decision rule. Parameters defining **acceptability** must be laid down by managers.

The certainty-equivalent approach

2.11 Another method is the **certainty-equivalent approach**. By this method, the expected cash flows of the project are converted to riskless equivalent amounts. The greater the risk of an expected cash flow, the smaller the 'certainty-equivalent' value (for receipts) or the larger the certainty equivalent value (for payments).

2.12 EXAMPLE: CERTAINTY-EQUIVALENT APPROACH

Dark Ages Ltd, whose cost of capital is 10%, is considering a project with the following expected cash flows.

Year	*Cash flow*	*Discount factor*	*Present value*
	£	10%	£
0	(9,000)	1.000	(9,000)
1	7,000	0.909	6,363
2	5,000	0.826	4,130
3	5,000	0.751	3,755
		NPV	+5,248

The project seems to be clearly worthwhile. However, because of the uncertainty about the future cash receipts, the management decides to reduce them to 'certainty-equivalents' by taking only 70%, 60% and 50% of the years 1, 2 and 3 cash flows respectively. (Note that this method of risk adjustment allows for different risk factors in each year of the project.)

On the basis of the information set out above, assess whether the project is worthwhile.

2.13 SOLUTION

The risk-adjusted NPV of the project is as follows.

Year	*Cash flow*	*PV factor*	*PV*
	£		£
0	(9,000)	1.000	(9,000)
1	4,900	0.909	4,454
2	3,000	0.826	2,478
3	2,500	0.751	1,878
		NPV =	– 190

The project is too risky and should be rejected.

2.14 The disadvantage of the 'certainty-equivalent' approach is that the amount of the adjustment to each cash flow is decided **subjectively**.

3 PROBABILITY ANALYSIS

3.1 A **probability distribution** of **'expected cash flows'** can often be estimated, and this may be used to do the following.

Step 1. Calculate an expected value of the NPV

Step 2. Measure risk, for example in the following ways.

(a) By calculating the worst possible outcome and its probability
(b) By calculating the probability that the project will fail to achieve a positive NPV
(c) By calculating the standard deviation of the NPV

3.2 EXAMPLE: PROBABILITY ESTIMATES OF CASH FLOWS

A company is considering a project involving the outlay of £300,000 which it estimates will generate cash flows over its two year life at the probabilities shown in the following table.

Cash flows for project

Year 1

Cash flow	*Probability*
£	
100,000	0.25
200,000	0.50
300,000	0.25
	1.00

Year 2

If cash flow in Year 1 is:	*there is a probability of:*	*that the cash flow in Year 2 will be:*
£		£
100,000	0.25	Nil
	0.50	100,000
	0.25	200,000
	1.00	
200,000	0.25	100,000
	0.50	200,000
	0.25	300,000
	1.00	
300,000	0.25	200,000
	0.50	300,000
	0.25	350,000
	1.00	

The company's investment criterion for this type of project is 10% DCF.

You are required to calculate the expected value (EV) of the project's NPV and the probability that the NPV will be negative.

3.3 SOLUTION

Step 1. Calculate expected value of the NPV.

First we need to draw up a probability distribution of the expected cash flows. We begin by calculating the present values of the cash flows.

Year	*Cash flow*	*Discount factor*	*Present value*
	£'000	10%	£'000
1	100	0.909	90.9
1	200	0.909	181.8
1	300	0.909	272.7
2	100	0.826	82.6
2	200	0.826	165.2
2	300	0.826	247.8
2	350	0.826	289.1

Year 1 PV of cash flow	*Probability*	*Year 2 PV of cash flow*	*Probability*	*Joint probability*	*Total PV of cash inflows*	*EV of PV of cash inflows*
£'000		£'000			£'000	£'000
(a)	(b)	(c)	(d)	(b) × (d)	(a) + (c)	
90.9	0.25	0.0	0.25	0.0625	90.9	5.681
90.9	0.25	82.6	0.50	0.1250	173.5	21.688
90.9	0.25	165.2	0.25	0.0625	256.1	16.006
181.8	0.50	82.6	0.25	0.1250	264.4	33.050
181.8	0.50	165.2	0.50	0.2500	347.0	86.750
181.8	0.50	247.8	0.25	0.1250	429.6	53.700
272.7	0.25	165.2	0.25	0.0625	437.9	27.369
272.7	0.25	247.8	0.50	0.1250	520.5	65.063
272.7	0.25	289.1	0.25	0.0625	561.8	35.113
						344.420

	£
EV of PV of cash inflows	344,420
Less project cost	300,000
EV of NPV	44,420

Step 2. Measure risk.

Since the EV of the NPV is positive, the project should go ahead unless the risk is unacceptably high. The probability that the project will have a negative NPV is the probability that the total PV of cash inflows is less than £300,000. From the column headed 'Total PV of cash inflows', we can establish that this probability is 0.0625 + 0.125 + 0.0625 + 0.125 = 0.375 or 37.5%. This might be considered an unacceptably high risk.

The standard deviation of the NPV

3.4 The disadvantage of using the EV of NPV approach to assess the risk of the project is that the **construction** of the **probability distribution** can become **very complicated.** If we were considering a project over 4 years, each year having five different forecasted cash flows, there would be 625 (5^4) NPVs to calculate. To avoid all of these calculations, an indication of the risk may be obtained by calculating the **standard deviation** of the NPV.

3.5 EXAMPLE: STANDARD DEVIATION OF THE NET PRESENT VALUE

Frame plc is considering which of two mutually exclusive projects, A or B, to undertake. There is some uncertainty about the running costs with each project, and a probability distribution of the NPV for each project has been estimated, as follows.

Project A		*Project B*	
NPV	*Probability*	*NPV*	*Probability*
£'000		£'000	
– 20	0.15	+ 5	0.2
+ 10	0.20	+ 15	0.3
+ 20	0.35	+ 20	0.4
+ 40	0.30	+ 25	0.1

You are required to decide which project should the company choose, if either.

3.6 SOLUTION

We can begin by calculating the EV of the NPV for each project.

Project A			*Project B*		
NPV	*Prob*	*EV*	*NPV*	*Prob*	*EV*
£'000		£'000	£'000		£'000
– 20	0.15	(3.0)	5	0.2	1.0
10	0.20	2.0	15	0.3	4.5
20	0.35	7.0	20	0.4	8.0
40	0.30	12.0	25	0.1	2.5
		18.0			16.0

3.7 Project A has a higher EV of NPV, but what about the risk of variation in the NPV above or below the EV? This can be measured by the standard deviation of the NPV.

3.8 The standard deviation of a project's NPV, s, can be calculated as:

$$s = \sqrt{\Sigma p(x - \overline{x})^2}$$

where $\overline{x}$ is the EV of the NPV.

Project A, $\overline{x}$ = 18				*Project B, $\overline{x}$ = 16*			
x	*p*	*x* – $\overline{x}$	*p(x–* $\overline{x}$ *)*^{2}	*x*	*p*	*x* – $\overline{x}$	*p(x–* $\overline{x}$ *)*^{2}
£'000		£'000		£'000		£'000	
– 20	0.15	– 38	216.6	5	0.2	– 11	24.2
10	0.20	– 8	12.8	15	0.3	– 1	0.3
20	0.35	+ 2	1.4	20	0.4	+ 4	6.4
40	0.30	+ 22	145.2	25	0.1	+ 9	8.1
			376.0				39.0

Project A			*Project B*		
s	=	√376	s	=	√39.0
	=	19.391		=	6.245
	=	£19,391		=	£6,245

3.9 Although Project A has a higher EV of NPV, it also has a higher standard deviation of NPV, and so has greater risk associated with it.

3.10 Which project should be selected? Clearly it depends on the attitude of the company's management to risk.

(a) If management are prepared to take the risk of a **low NPV** in the hope of a high NPV they will opt for project A.

(b) If management are **risk-averse,** they will opt for the less risky project B.

Problems with expected values

3.11 There are the following problems with using expected values in making investment decisions.

- An investment may be **one-off,** and 'expected' NPV may never actually occur.
- **Assigning probabilities** to events is highly **subjective.**
- Expected values **do not evaluate the range** of possible NPV outcomes.

4 DECISION TREE ANALYSIS

Exam focus point

If decision tree analysis comes up in a question, you can expect that it will involve a relatively simple decision tree.

4.1 When appraising a project using the NPV method, it is possible that, of the many variables which affect the NPV, more than one will be **uncertain.** The value of some variables may be dependent on the values of other variables. Many outcomes may therefore be possible and some outcomes may be dependent on previous outcomes. Decision trees are useful tools for clarifying the range of alternative courses of action and their possible outcomes.

4.2 There are two stages in preparing a decision tree.

Step 1. Drawing the tree itself, to show all the choices and outcomes

Step 2. Putting in the numbers: the probabilities, outcome values and EVs

Drawing a decision tree: the basic rules

4.3 Every decision tree starts from a decision point with the decision options that are currently being considered.

(a) You should draw a **line, or branch,** for each option or alternative.

(b) You should **identify** the **decision point,** and any subsequent decision points in the tree, with a symbol. Here, we shall use a square shape.

4.4 It is conventional to draw decision trees from **left to right,** and so a decision tree will start as follows.

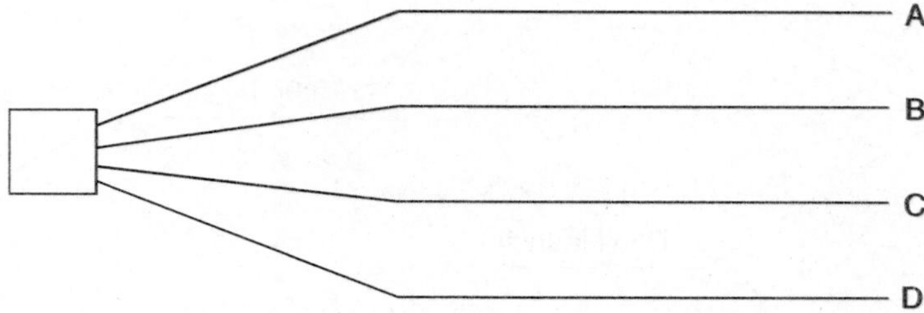

The square is the decision point, and A, B, C and D represent four alternatives from which a choice must be made.

4.5 If the outcome from any choice is certain, the branch of the decision tree for that alternative is complete.

4.6 If, on the other hand, the outcome of a particular choice is uncertain, the various possible outcomes must be shown. We show this on a decision tree by inserting an **outcome point** on the branch of the tree. Each possible outcome is then shown as a subsidiary branch, coming out from the outcome point. The **probability** of each outcome occurring should be written on to the branch of the tree which represents that outcome.

4.7 To distinguish decision points from outcome points, a circle will be used as the symbol for an outcome point.

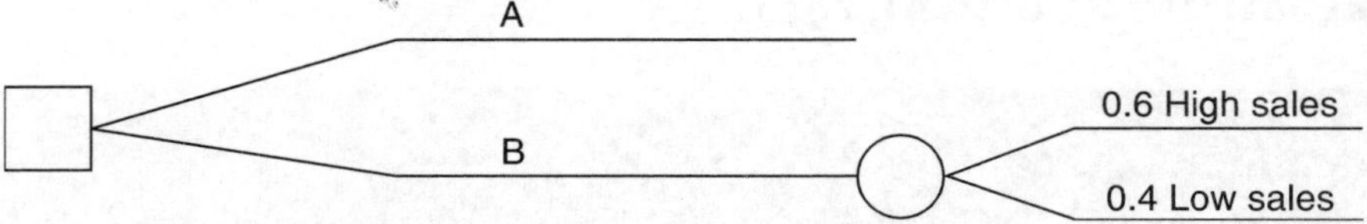

In the example above, there are two choices, A and B. The outcome if A is chosen is known with certainty, but if B is chosen, there are two possible outcomes, high returns (0.6 probability) or low returns (0.4 probability).

4.8 When several outcomes are possible, it is usually simpler to show two or more stages of outcome points on the decision tree.

4.9 EXAMPLE: SEVERAL POSSIBLE OUTCOMES

A company can choose to invest in project XYZ or not. If the investment goes ahead, expected cash inflows and expected costs might be as follows.

Cash inflows	*Probability*	*Costs*	*Probability*
£		£	
10,000	0.8	6,000	0.7
15,000	0.2	8,000	0.3

(a) The decision tree could be drawn as follows.

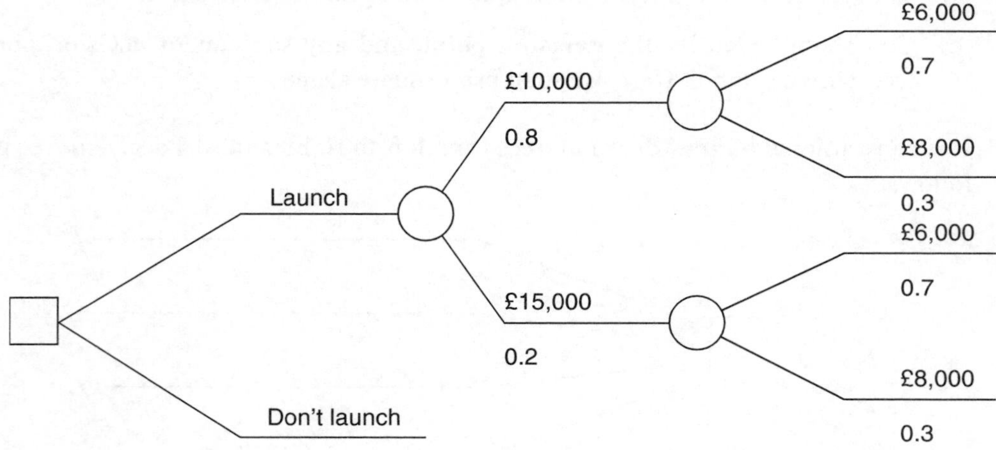

(b) The layout shown above will usually be easier to use than the alternative way of drawing the tree, which is shown below.

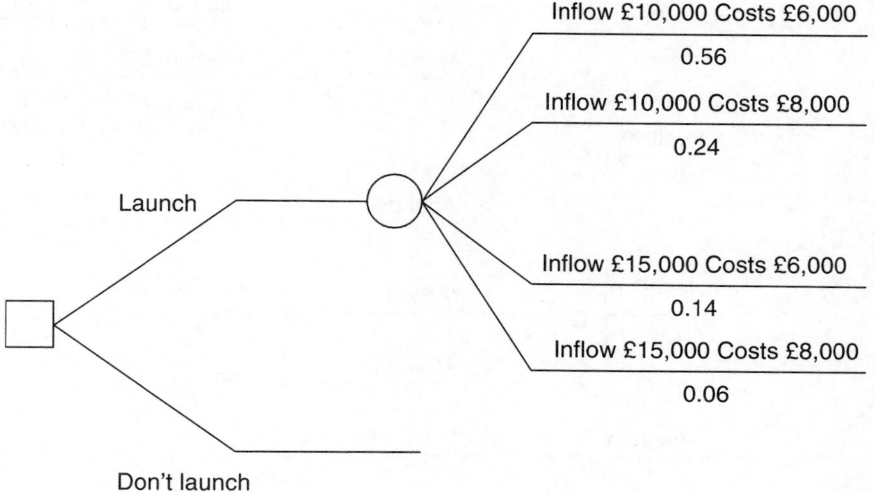

4.10 Sometimes, a decision taken now will lead to other decisions to be taken in the future. When this situation arises, the decision tree can be drawn as a two-stage tree, as follows.

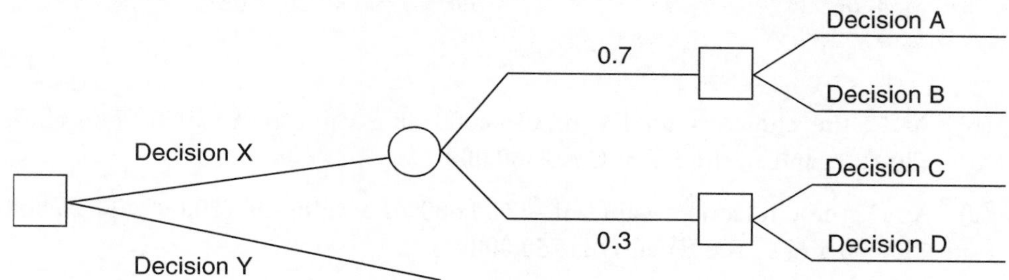

4.11 In this tree, either a choice between A and B or else a choice between C and D will be made, depending on the outcome which occurs after choosing X. The decision tree should be in **chronological order** from left to right.

Evaluating a decision with a decision tree

4.12 The basic rules are as follows.

4.13 We start on the **right hand side** of the tree and **work back** towards the left hand side and the current decision under consideration. Working from right to left, we calculate the EV of revenue, cost, contribution or profit at each outcome point on the tree.

4.14 Consider the decision tree below.

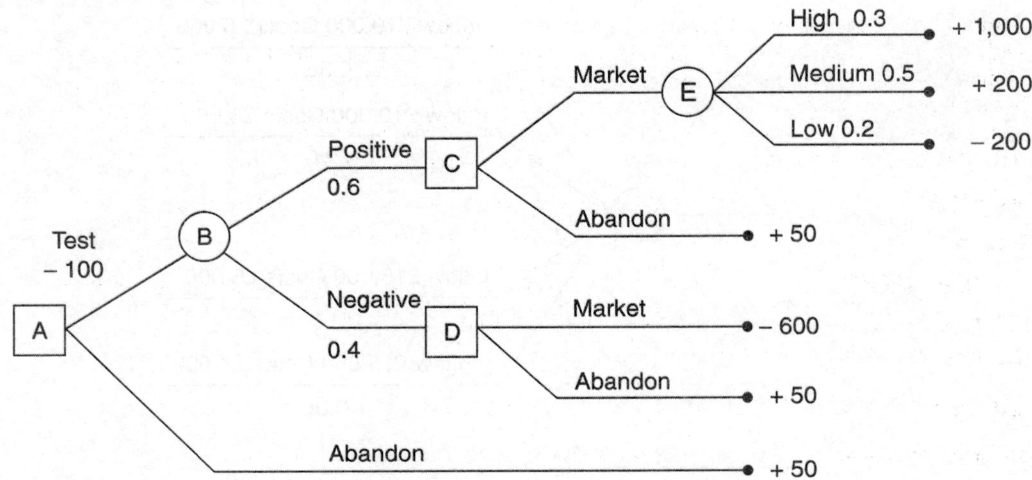

(a) At E the EV is calculated as follows.

	£'000	*Probability*	
	x	*p*	*px*
High	1,000	0.3	300
Medium	200	0.5	100
Low	(200)	0.2	(40)
		EV	360

(b) At C, the choice is an EV of £360,000 or a value of £50,000. The choice would be £360,000 and so the EV at C is **£360,000.**

(c) At D, the choice is a value of –£600,000 or a value of £50,000. The choice would be £50,000 and so the EV at D is **£50,000.**

(d) At B the EV is calculated as follows.

$$EV = (0.6 \times £360{,}000)\ (C) + (0.4 \times £50{,}000)\ (D) = £236{,}000$$

(e) At A the choice is between an EV of £236,000 minus costs of £100,000 or a value of £50,000. The choice would be £136,000 and so the EV at A is £136,000.

4.15 To summarise:

1. At point **A, Test** (EV £136,000)
2. At point **B,** options are
   (a) Test is **positive** (0.6), therefore at point **C, Market** (EV £360,000)
   (b) Test is **negative** (0.4), therefore at point **D, Abandon** (EV £50,000)

Question

Elsewhere Ltd is considering the production of a new consumer item with a five year product lifetime. In order to manufacture this time it would be necessary to build a new plant. After having considered several alternative strategies, management are left with the following three possibilities.

Strategy A: build a large plant at an estimated cost of £600,000. This strategy faces two types of market conditions: high demand with a probability of 0.7 or low demand with a probability of 0.3. If the demand is high the company can expect to receive a net annual cash inflow of £250,000 for each of the next five years. If the demand is low there would be a net annual cash outflow of £50,000.

Strategy B: build a small plant at an estimated cost of £350,000. This strategy also faces two types of market conditions: high demand with a probability of 0.7 or low demand with a probability of 0.3. The net annual cash inflow of the five-year period for the small plant is £25,000 if the demand is low and is £150,000 if the demand is high.

Strategy C: do not build a plant initially. This strategy consists of leaving the decision for one year whilst more information is collected. The resulting information can be positive or negative with

estimated probabilities of 0.8 and 0.2 respectively. At the end of this time management may decide to build either a large plant or a small plant at the same costs as at present providing the information is positive. If the resulting information is negative, management would decide to build no plant at all. Given positive information the probabilities of high and low demand change to 0.9 and 0.1 respectively, regardless of which plant is built. The net annual cash inflows for the remaining four-year period for each type of plant are the same as those given in strategies A and B.

All costs and revenues are given in present value terms and should not be discounted.

Required

(a) Draw a decision tree to represent the alternative courses of action open to the company.

(b) Determine the expected return for each possible course of action and hence decide the best course of action for the management of Elsewhere Ltd.

Answer

(a) **Decision tree for a possible new plant**

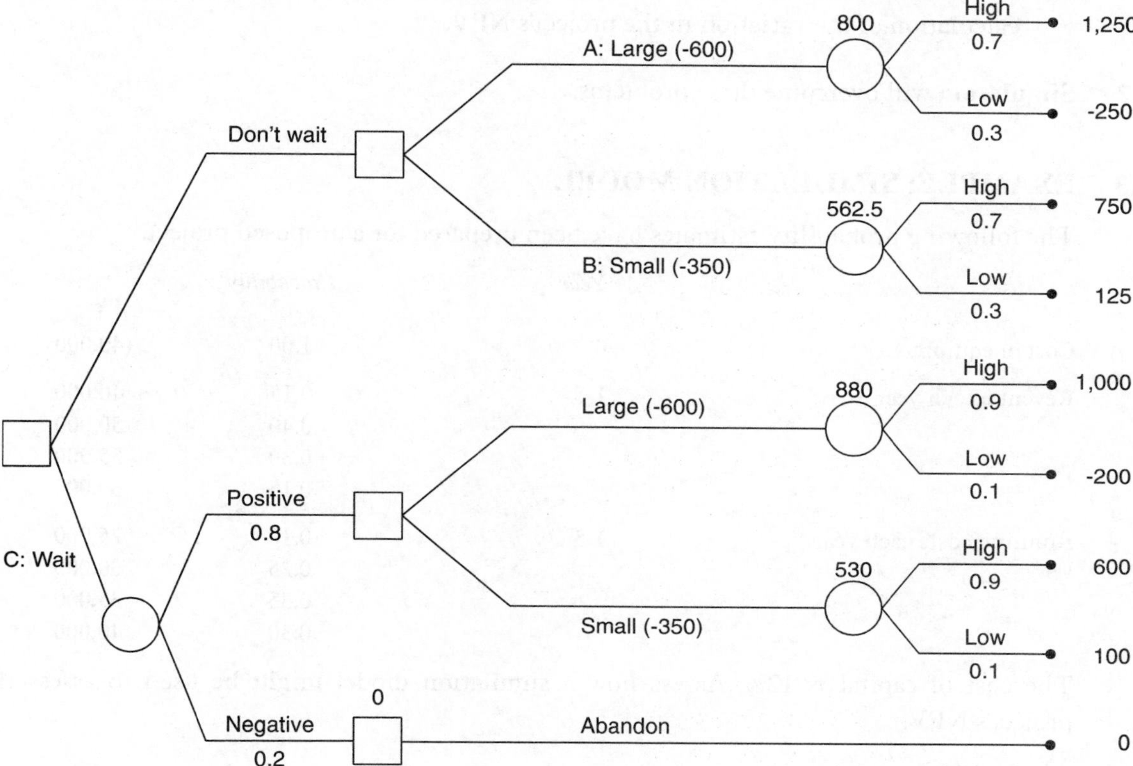

Key

□ Decision point

○ Outcome point

(b) Evaluation of the decision tree (see above) shows that the best course of action is to wait a year, and then build a large plant if positive information is received, but abandon the project if negative information is received.

Expected values (in thousands of pounds) are calculated as follows.

Large plant now (A)	$(0.7 \times 5 \times 250) - (0.3 \times 5 \times 50) - 600$	= 200
Small plant now (B)	$(0.7 \times 5 \times 150) + (0.3 \times 5 \times 25) - 350$	= 212.5
Large plant following positive information		
	$(0.9 \times 4 \times 250) - (0.1 \times 4 \times 50) - 600$	= 280
Small plant following positive information		
	$(0.9 \times 4 \times 150) + (0.1 \times 4 \times 25) - 350$	= 200
Positive information: higher of 280 and 200, ie 280		
Waiting (C)	$(0.8 \times 280) + (0.2 \times 0)$	= 224

224 is higher than either 200 or 212.5, hence the recommendation to wait.

5 SIMULATION MODELS

5.1 A decision tree of a simple project stretching over three years, the net cash flow each year being forecast at five different levels, would have 125 different outcomes.

(a) In practice, you may have to produce separate probabilities for alternative sales revenue outcomes, different items of costs and different possible life spans. A decision tree could therefore have thousands of different branches.

(b) Cash flows may be correlated over time. A new project which is successful in early years is also likely to be successful in later years. When cash flows are correlated over time, the standard deviation calculation (this chapter) will not give a correct calculation of the variation in the project's NPV.

5.2 **Simulation** will overcome these problems.

5.3 EXAMPLE: SIMULATION MODEL

The following probability estimates have been prepared for a proposed project.

	Year	*Probability*	£
Cost of equipment	0	1.00	(40,000)
Revenue each year	1-5	0.15	40,000
		0.40	50,000
		0.30	55,000
		0.15	60,000
Running costs each year	1-5	0.10	25,000
		0.25	30,000
		0.35	35,000
		0.30	40,000

The cost of capital is 12%. Assess how a simulation model might be used to assess the project's NPV.

5.4 SOLUTION

A simulation model could be constructed by assigning a range of random number digits to each possible value for each of the uncertain variables. The random numbers must exactly match their respective probabilities. This is achieved by working upwards cumulatively from the lowest to the highest cash flow values and assigning numbers that will correspond to probability groupings as follows.

Revenue				*Running costs*		
£	*Prob*	*Random numbers*		£	*Prob*	*Random numbers*
40,000	0.15	00 - 14	*	25,000	0.10	00 - 09
50,000	0.40	15 - 54	**	30,000	0.25	10 - 34
55,000	0.30	55 - 84	***	40,000	0.35	35 - 69
60,000	0.15	85 - 99		40,000	0.30	70 - 99

* Probability is 0.15 (15%). Random numbers are 15% of range 00 - 99.

** Probability is 0.40 (40%). Random numbers are 40% of range 00 - 99 but starting at 15.

*** Probability is 0.30 (30%). Random numbers are 30% of range 00 - 99 but starting at 55.

5.5 For revenue, the selection of a random number in the range 00 and 14 has a probability of 0.15. This probability represents revenue of £40,000. Numbers have been assigned to cash flows so that when numbers are selected at random, the cash flows have exactly the same probability of being selected as is indicated in their respective probability distribution above.

5.6 Random numbers would be generated, for example by a computer program, and these would be used to assign values to each of the uncertain variables.

5.7 For example, if random numbers 378420015689 were generated, the values assigned to the variables would be as follows.

Calculation	*Revenue* *Random number*	*Value*	*Costs* *Random number*	*Value*
		£		£
1	37	50,000	84	40,000
2	20	50,000	01	25,000
3	56	55,000	89	40,000

5.8 A computer would calculate the NPV may times over using the values established in this way with more random numbers, and the results would be analysed to provide the following.

(a) An **expected NPV** for the project

(b) A **statistical distribution** pattern for the possible variation in the NPV above or below this average

5.9 The decision whether to go ahead with the project would then be made on the basis of **expected return** and **risk**.

6 WAYS OF REDUCING RISK 12/01

6.1 Only if management know for certainty what is going to happen in the future can they appraise a project in the knowledge that there is no risk. However the future is uncertain by nature. There are, nevertheless, steps that management can take to reduce the riskiness of a project.

(a) A **maximum payback period** can be set to reflect the fact that risk increases the longer the time period under consideration.

(b) A **high discounting rate** can be used so that a cash flow which occurs quite some time in the future will have less effect on the decision.

(c) Projects with **low standard deviations** and **acceptable average predicted outcomes** can be selected. If a business is undertaking a range of projects, it should ensure that some are **low-risk (diversification)**.

(d) **Sensitivity analysis** can be used to determine the critical factors within the decision-making process. Management effort can then be directed to those factors which are critical to the success of a particular decision.

(e) To ensure that future events are no worse than predicted, **prudence, slack** and **overly pessimistic estimates** can be applied.

Chapter roundup

- **Risk** can be applied to a situation where there are several possible outcomes and, on the basis of past relevant experience, probabilities can be assigned to the various outcomes that could prevail.
- **Uncertainty** can be applied to a situation where there are several possible outcomes but there is little past relevant experience to enable the probability of the possible outcomes to be predicted.
- There are a wide range of techniques for incorporating risk into project appraisal.
- **Sensitivity analysis** assesses how responsive the project's NPV is to changes in the variables used to calculate that NPV. One particular approach to sensitivity analysis, the certainty - equivalent approach, involves the conversion of the expected cash flows of the project to riskless equivalent amounts.
- A **probability analysis** of expected cash flows can often be estimated and used both to calculate an expected NPV and to measure risk. The standard deviation of the NPV can be calculated to assess risk when the construction of probability distributions is complicated.
- **Decision tree analysis** clarifies the range of alternative courses of action open and their possible outcomes. Ensure that you know the rules for constructing decision trees and are able to evaluate them.
- **Simulation models** can be used to assess those projects which may have too many outcomes to allow the use of a decision tree or those projects which have correlated cash flows. Simulation models are constructed by assigning a **range of random number digits** to each possible value for each of the uncertain variables. The numbers are assigned to the cash flows so that when numbers are selected at random, the cash flows have exactly the same probability of being selected as is indicated in their particular probability distribution.

Quick quiz

1 Give three examples of uncertain independent variables upon which the NPV of a project may depend.

2 *Fill in the blanks.*

The two key types of point on a decision tree are .... points and .... points.

3 Describe in a sentence each three ways in which managers can reduce risk.

4 Sensitivity analysis allows for uncertainty in project appraisal by assessing the probability of changes in the decision variables.

☐ True

☐ False

5 *Fill in the blanks.*

The .... is where expected cashflows are converted to riskless equivalent amounts.

6 Give three examples of ways that risk can be measured in probability analysis.

7 Expected values can help an accountant evaluate the range of possible Net Present Value outcomes.

☐ True

☐ False

8 In which direction should a decision tree normally be drawn?

A Top of page to bottom of page

B Bottom of page to top of page

C Left of page to right of page

D Right of page to left of page

Answers to quick quiz

1. (a) Selling price
   (b) Sales volume
   (c) Cost of capital
   (d) Initial cost
   (e) Operating costs
   (f) Benefits
2. The two key types of point on a decision tree are **decision** points and **outcome** points.
3. (a) Set maximum payback period.
   (b) Use high discounting rate.
   (c) Select projects with low standard deviations and acceptable average predicted outcomes.
   (d) Use sensitivity analysis to determine the critical factors within the decision-making process.
   (e) Use pessimistic estimates.
4. False
5. Certainty equivalent approach
6. Calculating the worst possible outcome and its probability

   Calculating the probability that the project will fail to achieve a positive NPV

   Calculating the standard deviation of the NPV
7. False
8. C Left of page to right of page

Now try the question below from the Exam Question Bank

Question to try	Level	Marks	Time
34	Introductory	n/a	30 mins

Chapter 30

CAPITAL RATIONING

Topic list		Syllabus reference
1	Causes of a shortage of capital	5(a)
2	Single period capital rationing	5(a)
3	Multi-period capital rationing	5(a)

Introduction

Having looked in Chapters 25 to 29 at the methods available for appraising projects when funds are available, we will now be considering the procedure for assessing projects when capital is a **scarce** resource.

Study guide

Section 16 – Capital rationing

- Distinguish hard and soft capital rationing
- Apply profitability index techniques for single period divisible projects
- Evaluate projects involving single and multi-period capital rationing

Exam guide

As well as being asked to perform the calculations necessary to prioritise different options, you may be asked to discuss why capital rationing arises. Research and Analysis Project Topic 16 in the Oxford Brookes degree requires you to consider the effect of capital rationing on the investment decision.

1 CAUSES OF A SHORTAGE OF CAPITAL

KEY TERM

Capital rationing: a situation in which a company has a limited amount of capital to invest in potential projects, such that the different possible investments need to be compared with one another in order to allocate the capital available most effectively.

Soft capital rationing is brought about by internal factors; **hard capital rationing** is brought about by external factors.

1.1 If an organisation is in a **capital rationing** situation it will not be able to enter into all projects with positive NPVs because there is not enough capital for all of the investments.

Soft and hard capital rationing

1.2 **Soft capital rationing** may arise for one of the following reasons.

(a) Management may be **reluctant** to **issue additional share capital** because of concern that this may lead to **outsiders** gaining control of the business.

(b) **Management** may be **unwilling** to **issue additional share capital** if it will lead to a **dilution of earnings** per share.

(c) Management may **not want to raise additional debt capital** because they do not wish to be committed to **large fixed interest payments.**

(d) Management may wish to **limit investment** to a level that can be financed solely from **retained earnings.**

(e) **Capital expenditure budgets** may restrict spending.

1.3 **Hard capital rationing** may arise for one of the following reasons.

(a) Raising money through the stock market may not be possible if **share prices** are **depressed.**

(b) There may be **restrictions** on **bank lending** due to government control.

(c) Lending institutions may consider an organisation to be **too risky** to be granted further loan facilities.

(d) The **costs** associated with making small **issues** of capital may be too great.

Relaxation of capital constraints

1.4 If an organisation adopts a policy that restricts funds available for investment (soft capital rationing), the policy may be less than optimal. The organisation may reject projects with a positive net present value and forgo opportunities that would have enhanced the market value of the organisation.

1.5 A company may be able to limit the effects of hard capital rationing and exploit new opportunities.

(a) It might **seek joint venture partners** with which to share projects.

(b) As an alternative to direct investment in a project, the company may be able to consider a **licensing** or **franchising agreement** with another enterprise, under which the licensor/franchisor company would receive royalties.

(c) It may be possible to **contract** out parts of a project to reduce the initial capital outlay required.

(d) The company may seek **new** alternative **sources of capital** (subject to any restrictions which apply to it) for example:

- Venture capital
- Debt finance secured on the assets of the project
- Sale and leaseback of property or equipment (see the next chapter)
- Grant aid
- More effective capital management

2 SINGLE PERIOD CAPITAL RATIONING

2.1 We shall begin our analysis by assuming that capital rationing occurs in a single period, and that capital is freely available at all other times.

2.2 The following further assumptions will be made.

(a) If a company does not accept and undertake a project during the period of capital rationing, the **opportunity** to undertake it is **lost**. The project cannot be postponed until a subsequent period when no capital rationing exists.

(b) There is **complete certainty** about the outcome of each project, so that the choice between projects is not affected by considerations of risk.

(c) **Projects** are **divisible**, so that it is possible to undertake, say, half of Project X in order to earn half of the net present value (NPV) of the whole project.

2.3 The basic approach is to rank all investment opportunities so that the NPVs can be maximised from the use of the available funds.

2.4 Ranking in terms of absolute NPVs will normally give incorrect results. This method leads to the **selection of large projects**, each of which has a high individual NPV but which have, in total, a lower NPV than a large number of smaller projects with lower individual NPVs. Ranking is therefore in terms of what is called the **profitability index.**

2.5 This ratio measures the PV of future cash flows per £1 of investment, and so indicates which investments make the best use of the limited resources available.

KEY TERM

Profitability index is the ratio of the present value of the project's future cash flows (not including the capital investment) divided by the present value of the total capital outlays.

2.6 EXAMPLE: CAPITAL RATIONING

Suppose that Hard Times Ltd is considering four projects, W, X, Y and Z. Relevant details are as follows.

Project	*Investment required*	*Present value of cash inflows*	*NPV*	*Profitability index (PI)*	*Ranking as per NPV*	*Ranking as per PI*
	£	£	£			
W	(10,000)	11,240	1,240	1.12	3	1
X	(20,000)	20,991	991	1.05	4	4
Y	(30,000)	32,230	2,230	1.07	2	3
Z	(40,000)	43,801	3,801	1.10	1	2

2.7 Without capital rationing all four projects would be viable investments. Suppose, however, that only £60,000 was available for capital investment. Let us look at the resulting NPV if we select projects in the order of ranking per NPV.

Project	*Priority*	*Outlay*	*NPV*	
		£	£	
Z	1st	40,000	3,801	
Y (balance)*	2nd	20,000	1,487	(2/3 of £2,230)
		60,000	5,288	

* Projects are divisible. By spending the balancing £20,000 on project Y, two thirds of the full investment would be made to earn two thirds of the NPV.

2.8 Suppose, on the other hand, that we adopt the profitability index approach. The selection of projects will be as follows.

Project	*Priority*	*Outlay*	*NPV*	
		£	£	
W	1st	10,000	1,240	
Z	2nd	40,000	3,801	
Y (balance)	3rd	10,000	743	((1/3 of £2,230)
		60,000	5,784	

2.9 By choosing projects according to the PI, the resulting NPV if only £60,000 is available is increased by £496.

2.10 **Problems with the Profitability Index method**

(a) The approach can only be used if **projects** are **divisible**. If the projects are not divisible a decision has to be made by examining the **absolute NPVs** of all possible combinations of complete projects that can be undertaken within the constraints of the capital available. The combination of projects which remains at or under the limit of available capital without any of them being divided, and which maximises the total NPV, should be chosen.

(b) The **selection criterion** is fairly **simplistic**, taking no account of the possible strategic value of individual investments in the context of the overall objectives of the organisation.

(c) The method is of limited use when projects have **differing cash flow patterns**. These patterns may be important to the company since they will affect the timing and availability of funds. With multi-period capital rationing, it is possible that the project with the highest Profitability Index is the slowest in generating returns.

(d) The Profitability Index **ignores** the **absolute size** of individual projects. A project with a high index might be very small and therefore only generate a small NPV.

Question

Bleak House Ltd is experiencing capital rationing in year 0, when only £60,000 of investment finance will be available. No capital rationing is expected in future periods, but none of the three projects under consideration by the company can be postponed. The expected cash flows of the three projects are as follows.

Project	*Year 0*	*Year 1*	*Year 2*	*Year 3*	*Year 4*
	£	£	£	£	£
A	(50,000)	(20,000)	20,000	40,000	40,000
B	(28,000)	(50,000)	40,000	40,000	20,000
C	(30,000)	(30,000)	30,000	40,000	10,000

The cost of capital is 10%. You are required to decide which projects should be undertaken in year 0, in view of the capital rationing, given that projects are divisible.

Answer

The ratio of NPV at 10% to outlay in year 0 (the year of capital rationing) is as follows.

Project	*Outlay in Year 0*	*PV*	*NPV*	*Ratio*	*Ranking*
	£	£	£		
A	50,000	55,700	5,700	1.114	3rd
B	28,000	31,290	3,290	1.118	2nd
C	30,000	34,380	4,380	1.146	1st

The optimal investment policy is as follows.

Ranking	*Project*	*Year 0 outlay*	*NPV*
		£	£
1st	C	30,000	4,380
2nd	B	28,000	3,290
3rd	A (balance)	2,000 (4% of 5,700)	228
NPV from total investment			7,898

Postponing projects

2.11 We have so far assumed that projects cannot be postponed until year 1. If this assumption is removed, the choice of projects in year 0 would be made by reference to the loss of NPV from **postponement**.

2.12 EXAMPLE: POSTPONING PROJECTS

The figures in the previous exercise will be used to illustrate the method. If any project, A, B or C, were delayed by one year, the 'NPV' would now relate to year 1 values, so that in year 0 terms, the NPVs would be as follows.

		NPV in Year 1		*NPV in Year 0 Value*	*Loss in NPV*
		£		£	£
(a)	Project A	5,700 ×	$\frac{1}{1.10}$ =	5,182	518
(b)	Project B	3,290 ×	$\frac{1}{1.10}$ =	2,991	299
(c)	Project C	4,380 ×	$\frac{1}{1.10}$ =	3,982	398

2.13 An index of postponability would be calculated as follows.

Project	*Loss in NPV from one-year postponement*	*Outlay deferred from year 0*	*Postponability index (loss/outlay)*
	£	£	
A	518	50,000	0.0104
B	299	28,000	0.0107
C	398	30,000	0.0133

2.14 The loss in NPV by deferring investment would be greatest for Project C, and least for Project A. It is therefore more profitable to postpone A, rather than B or C, as follows.

Investment in year 0:

Project	*Outlay*		*NPV*
	£		£
C	30,000		4,380
B	28,000		3,290
A (balance)	2,000	(4% of 5,700)	228
	60,000		7,898

Investment in year 1 (balance):

Project A	£48,000	(96% of 5,182)	4,975
Total NPV (as at year 0) of investments in years 0 and 1			12,873

3 MULTI-PERIOD CAPITAL RATIONING

3.1 When capital is expected to be in short supply for more than one period, the selection of an optimal investment programme cannot be made by ranking projects according to a profitability index. Other techniques, notably linear programming, should be used.

Solution by graphical linear programming

3.2 You will have already covered the **graphical approach to linear programming** in your earlier studies. You will be aware that the technique can only be used if there are two variables. The variables in this instance are the **individual investment projects.** This method is confined to dealing with those scenarios concerned with a choice between just two investment projects. We will illustrate this particular approach to multi-period capital rationing with an example.

3.3 EXAMPLE: GRAPHICAL LINEAR PROGRAMMING APPROACH

Finch Ltd has the chance to invest in two projects, A and B, details of which are set out below.

Investment project	*Present value of outlay in period 1*	*Present value of outlay in period 2*	*Present value of outlay in period 3*	*Net present value of investment at time 0*
	£'000	£'000	£'000	£'000
A	30	10	10	56
B	20	4	2	8

Capital investment limits, as set by Finch Ltd's parent company, are as follows.

	£'000
Period 1	36
Period 2	8
Period 3	6

It is assumed that the capital investment limits are absolute and cannot be expanded by project generated cash inflows. Projects are divisible but cannot be repeated more than once. You are required to formulate and solve the linear programming model which will maximise net present value.

3.4 SOLUTION

Step 1. **Define variables**

Let x = the proportion of project A accepted.
Let y = the proportion of project B accepted.

Step 2. **Establish constraints**

$30x + 20y \leq 36$ (period 1 investment)
$10x + 4y \leq 8$ (period 2 investment)
$10x + 2y \leq 6$ (period 3 investment)
$x, y \leq 1$ (proportion must be less than or equal to 1)
$x, y \geq 0$ (proportion must be greater than or equal to 0)

The last two constraints ensure that a project cannot be undertaken more than once but allows for a project to be partially accepted.

Step 3. **Establish objective function**

The objective is to maximise the NPV from the total investment in periods 1, 2 and 3.

Maximise $56x + 8y$.

Step 4. **Graph the model**

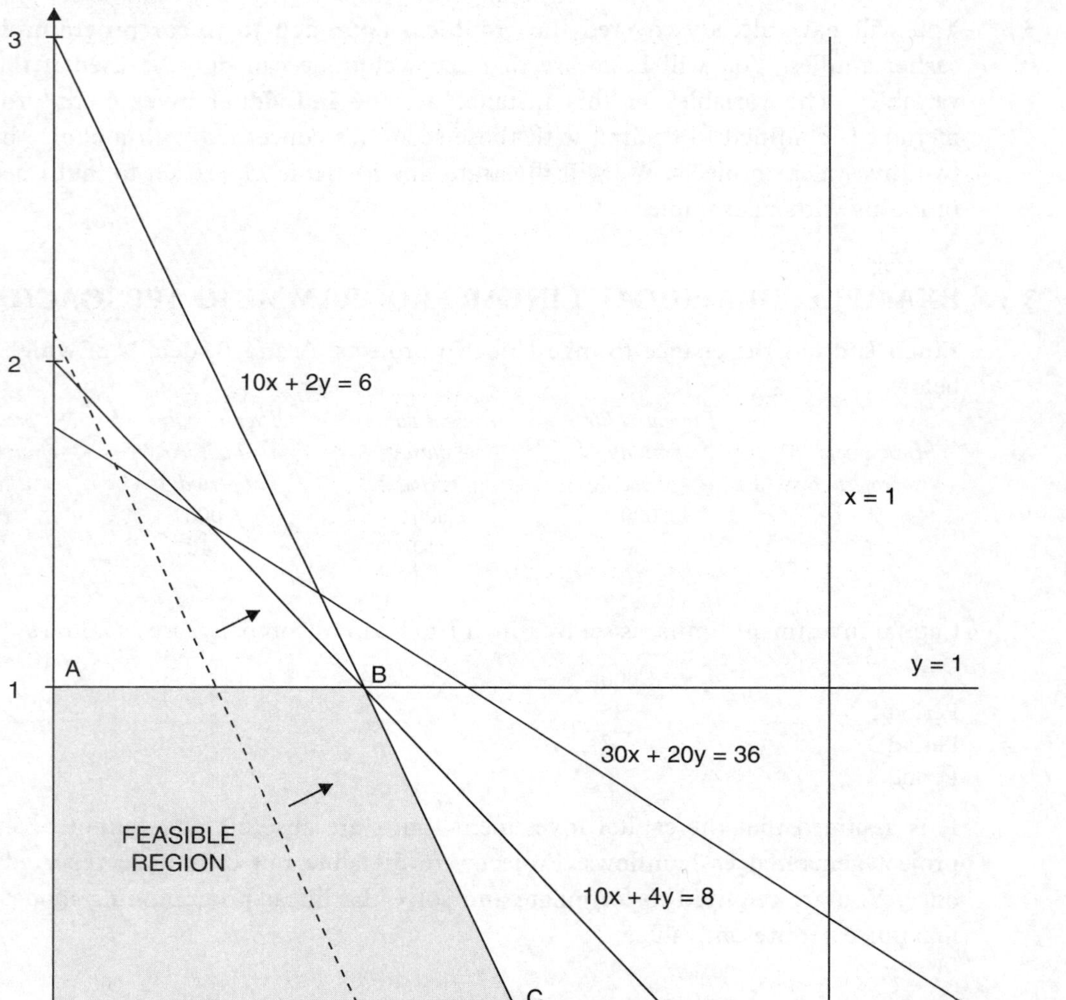

The feasible region is represented by OABC.

Step 5. **Find the best solution**

Using the 'iso-NPV line' plotted on the graph, the optimal solution can be established as at point C (0.6, 0). The optimal solution is therefore to invest in 0.6 of project A and to make no investment in project B.

The total NPV available is therefore 0.6 × £56,000 = £33,600.

More than two investments under consideration

3.5 The graphical approach to linear programming cannot deal with situations where there are more than two investments under consideration.

Exam focus point

A method for solving such linear programming problems is called the simplex method. This is outside the scope of your syllabus.

Limitations of the linear programming approach to capital rationing

3.6 When two constraints apply, the graphical approach to linear programming may be a useful method of selecting projects but there are a number of assumptions and limitations which must be kept in mind if the use of the technique is to be considered.

(a) It assumes that variables are **linearly related.**

(b) It assumes that projects are **divisible** or that scalar multiples of projects are possible.

(c) It assumes that the **returns** of the projects are in **proportion** to the amount invested in each project.

(d) **Uncertainty** is **ignored.** It assumes that all future cash flows and available resources are known with certainty.

(e) It assumes that **all projects** and **constraints** are **independent**.

(f) It is possible that **other investment opportunities** not included in the linear programming model could realise a higher NPV.

(g) Linear programming cannot be used when projects are **mutually exclusive** in multi-period capital rationing situations. Instead integer programming (not part of your syllabus) has to be used.

(h) No account of **risk** attached to the projects or the company's attitude to risk is taken.

Chapter roundup

- **Capital rationing** may occur due to internal factors (soft capital rationing) or external factors (hard capital rationing).
- When capital rationing occurs in a **single period**, projects are ranked in terms of **profitability index**.
- When capital rationing occurs in a **number of periods** and two projects are under consideration, the graphical approach to **linear programming** is used to arrive at an NPV - maximising mix of products.
- Although the graphical approach is a useful technique to use for arriving at optimum project mixes, you should be aware of its limitations.

Quick quiz

1 Profitability index = ... ?

2 Give three assumptions of single period capital rationing.

3 What are the five steps of the graphical linear programming approach to multi-period capital rationing?

4 *Fill in the blanks.*

(1) .... capital rationing is brought about by external factors; (2) .... capital rationing by internal factors.

5 The profitability index method takes into account the absolute size of individual projects.

☐ True

☐ False

6 How many possible investment choices can the graphical linear programming method assess?

7 What is the problem with ranking possible investment projects by size of absolute NPV in a single period capital rationing situation?

8 The profitability index method cannot be used if capital rationing is expected to last for more than one period.

☐ True

☐ False

Answers to quick quiz

1 $\text{Profitability index} = \frac{\text{PV of project's future cash flows (excluding original capital investment)}}{\text{PV of total capital outlays}}$

2 (a) If a project is not accepted and undertaken during the period, the opportunity to undertake it is lost.

(b) There is complete certainty about the outcome of each project.

(c) Projects are divisible.

3 (1) Define variables

(2) Establish constraints

(3) Establish objective function

(4) Graph the model

(5) Find the best solution

4 (1) Hard

(2) Soft

5 False

6 Two

7 This method leads to the selection of large projects, each of which has a high individual NPV, but which have in total lower NPVs than a large number of smaller projects with lower individual NPVs.

8 True

Now try the question below from the Exam Question Bank

Question to try	Level	Marks	Time
35	Exam	25	45 mins

Chapter 31

LEASING DECISIONS

Topic list		Syllabus reference
1	Leasing as a source of finance	5(a)
2	Lease or buy decisions	5(a)

Introduction

In this chapter, we consider the option of **leasing** an asset.

As well as looking at the advantages and disadvantages of different types of lease compared with **other forms of credit finance**, we shall be discussing the tax and cash flow implications of leasing.

Study guide

Section 17 – Leasing decisions

- Distinguish between operating and finance leases
- Apply DCF methods to projects involving buy or lease problems
- Assess the relative advantages and disadvantages of different types of lease
- Describe the impact of leasing on company gearing

Exam guide

You may be asked to calculate the results of different options, and also discuss implications such as differing cash flow patterns.

1 LEASING AS A SOURCE OF FINANCE

The nature of leasing

1.1 Rather than buying an asset outright, using either available cash resources or borrowed funds, a business may lease an asset.

KEY TERMS

Leasing is a contract between a lessor and a lessee for hire of a specific asset selected from a manufacturer or vendor of such assets by the lessee.

The **lessor** has ownership of the asset.

The **lessee** has possession and use of the asset on payment of specified rentals over a period.

1.2 **Examples of lessors**

- Banks
- Insurance companies

1.3 **Types of asset leased**

- Office equipment
- Computers
- Cars
- Commercial vehicles
- Aircraft
- Ships
- Buildings

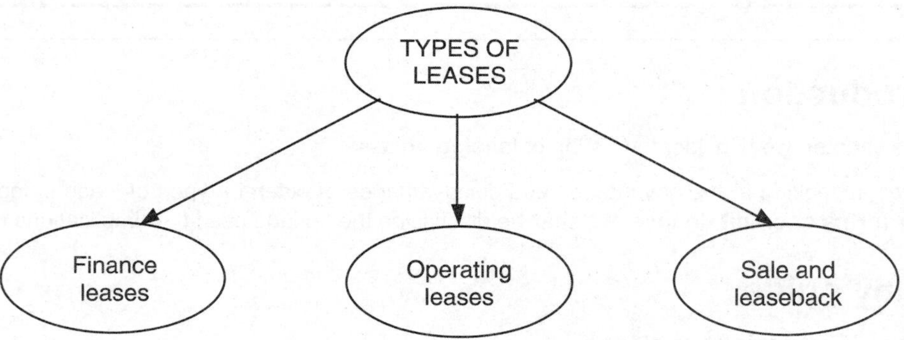

Operating leases

> **KEY TERM**
>
> **Operating lease** is a lease where the lessor retains most of the risks and rewards of ownership.

1.4 **Operating leases** are rental agreements between a lessor and a lessee.

(a) The lessor **supplies** the equipment to the **lessee**.

(b) The **lessor** is **responsible** for **servicing and maintaining** the leased equipment

(c) The **period** of the lease is fairly **short, less** than the expected **economic life** of the asset. At the end of one lease agreement, the lessor can either lease the same equipment to someone else, and obtain a good rent for it, or sell the equipment second-hand

1.5 Much of the growth in the UK leasing business in recent years has been in operating leases.

Finance leases

> **KEY TERM**
>
> A **finance lease** is a lease that transfers substantially all of the risks and rewards of ownership of an asset to the lessee. It is an agreement between the lessee and the lessor for most or all of the asset's expected useful life.

1.6 There are other important characteristics of a finance lease.

(a) The lessee is responsible for the **upkeep, servicing** and **maintenance** of the asset.

(b) The lease has a **primary period** covering all or most of the useful economic life of the asset. At the end of this period, the lessor would not be able to lease the asset to someone else, because the asset would be worn out. The lessor must therefore ensure that the lease payments during the primary period pay for the **full cost** of the asset as well as providing the lessor with a **suitable return** on his investment.

(c) At the end of the primary period the lessee can normally continue to lease the asset for an indefinite secondary period, in return for a very low nominal rent, sometimes called a 'peppercorn rent'. Alternatively, the lessee might be allowed to sell the asset on a lessor's behalf (since the lessor is the owner) and perhaps to keep most of the sale proceeds.

1.7 EXAMPLE: A MOTOR LEASE

The primary period of the lease might be three years, with an agreement by the lessee to make three annual payments of £6,000 each. The lessee will be responsible for repairs and servicing, road tax, insurance and garaging. At the end of the primary period of the lease, the lessee may have the option either to continue leasing the car at a nominal rent (perhaps £250 a year) or to sell the car and pay the lessor 10% of the proceeds.

Sale and leaseback

KEY TERM

Sale and leaseback is when a business that owns an asset agrees to sell the asset to a financial institution and lease it back on terms specified in the agreement.

1.8 The business retains **use** of the asset but has the **funds** from the sale, whilst having to pay rent.

Attractions of leasing

1.9 Attractions include the following.

(a) The supplier of the equipment is **paid** in **full** at the beginning. The equipment is sold to the lessor, and other than guarantees, the supplier has no further financial concern about the asset.

(b) The lessor **invests finance** by purchasing assets from suppliers and makes a **return** out of the lease payments from the lessee. The lessor will also get capital allowances on his purchase of the equipment.

(c) Leasing may have advantages for the lessee:

(i) The lessee may not have enough cash to pay for the asset, and would have difficulty obtaining a bank loan to buy it. If so the lessee has to rent the asset to obtain use of it at all.

(ii) Finance leasing may be cheaper than a bank loan.

(iii) The lessee may find the tax relief available advantageous.

1.10 Operating leases have further advantages.

(a) The leased equipment does not have to be shown in the **lessee's** published **balance sheet,** and so the lessee's balance sheet shows no increase in its gearing ratio.

(b) The equipment is leased for a **shorter period** than its expected useful life. In the case of high-technology equipment, if the equipment becomes out of date before the end of its expected life, the lessee does not have to keep on using it. The lessor will bear the risk of having to sell obsolete equipment secondhand.

1.11 A major growth area in operating leasing in the UK has been in computers and office equipment (such as photocopiers and fax machines) where technology is continually improving.

Hire purchase

1.12 Another form of credit finance with which leasing can be contrasted is **hire purchase,** which is a form of **instalment credit**. There are two basic forms of instalment credit, where an individual or business purchases goods and pays for them by instalments.

(a) **Lender credit** occurs when the buyer borrows money and uses the money to purchase goods outright.

(b) **Vendor credit** occurs when the buyer obtains goods on credit and agrees to pay the vendor by instalments. Hire purchase is an example of vendor credit.

1.13 Hire purchase is similar to leasing, with the exception that ownership of the goods passes to the hire purchase customer on payment of the final credit instalment, whereas a lessee never becomes the owner of the goods.

1.14 Hire purchase agreements nowadays usually involve a finance house.

- The supplier sells the goods to the finance house.
- The supplier delivers the goods to the customer who will eventually purchase them.
- The hire purchase arrangement exists between the finance house and the customer.

1.15 The finance house will nearly always insist that the hirer should pay a **deposit** towards the purchase price, perhaps as low as 10%, or as high as 33%. This is in contrast to a finance lease, where the lessee might not be required to make any large initial payment.

1.16 An industrial or commercial business can use hire purchase as a source of finance. With **industrial hire purchase**, a business customer obtains hire purchase finance from a finance house in order to purchase a fixed asset. Goods bought by businesses on hire purchase include company vehicles, plant and machinery, office equipment and farming machinery. Hire purchase arrangements for fleets of motor cars are quite common.

1.17 When faced with an investment opportunity, an organisation may have to decide whether to

- Purchase the equipment
- Acquire it under a finance lease arrangement
- Acquire it under a hire purchase arrangement

1.18 When a company acquires a capital asset under a hire purchase agreement, it will eventually obtain full legal title to the asset. The HP payments consist of

- 'Capital' payments towards the purchase of the asset
- Interest charges

1.19 For example, if a company buys a car costing £10,000 under an HP agreement, the car supplier might provide HP finance over a three year period at an interest cost of 10%, and the HP payments might be, say, as follows.

	Capital element	*Interest element*	*Total HP payment*
	£	£	£
Year 0: down payment	2,540	0	2,540
Year 1	2,254	746	3,000
Year 2	2,479	521	3,000
Year 3	2,727	273	3,000
Total	10,000	1,540	11,540

1.20 The tax position on a hire purchase arrangement is as follows.

(a) The buyer obtains whatever capital allowances are available, based on the capital element of the cost.

(b) In addition, **interest payments** within the HP payments are an **allowable** expense against tax, spread over the term of the HP agreement.

(c) **Capital payments** within the HP payments, however, are **not allowable** against tax.

2 LEASE OR BUY DECISIONS

2.1 There are several ways of evaluating a decision whether to lease an asset, or to purchase it by another means of finance. The **traditional method** is in two stages.

Step 1. An **acquisition decision** is made on whether the asset is worth having. The present values of operational costs and benefits from using the asset are found to derive a net present value (NPV).

Step 2. A **financing decision** is then made if the acquisition is justified by a positive NPV. This is the decision on whether to **lease or buy**.

2.2 The traditional method is complicated by the need to choose a discount rate for each stage of the decision. In the case of a **non-taxpaying organisation**, the method is applied as follows.

Step 1. The cost of capital that should be applied to the cash flows for the acquisition decision is the cost of capital that the organisation would normally apply to its **project evaluations**.

Step 2. The cost of capital that should be applied to the (differential) cash flows for the financing decision is the **cost of borrowing**.

(i) We assume that if the organisation decided to purchase the equipment, it would finance the purchase by **borrowing funds.**

(ii) We therefore **compare** the **cost of borrowing** with the **cost of leasing** (or hire purchase) by applying this cost of borrowing to the financing cash flows.

2.3 In the case of a tax-paying organisation, taxation should be allowed for in the cash flows, so that the traditional method would recommend:

Step 1. **Discount** the cash flows of the acquisition decision at the firm's **after-tax cost of capital**

Step 2. **Discount** the cash flows of the financing decision at the **after-tax cost of borrowing**

The tax treatment of finance leases in the UK under Finance Act 1991 rules is:

(a) To allow **depreciation** as an expense

(b) To allow the **interest element** of the finance charge as an expense over the period of the lease

2.4 This treatment leads to some complex calculations. The result may not be materially different from that obtained if we assume that the lease payments are allowable for tax in full.

Exam focus point

In the exam, it should be acceptable to make this latter assumption provided that you state it in your answer and provided that the question does not direct otherwise.

2.5 EXAMPLE: LEASE OR BUY DECISIONS (1)

Mallen and Mullins Ltd has decided to install a new milling machine. The machine costs £20,000 and it would have a useful life of five years with a trade-in value of £4,000 at the end of the fifth year. Additional cash profits from the machine would be £8,000 a year for five years. A decision has now to be taken on the method of financing the project. Three methods of finance are being considered.

(a) The company could purchase the machine for cash, using bank loan facilities on which the current rate of interest is 13% before tax.

(b) The company could lease the machine under an agreement which would entail payment of £4,800 at the end of each year for the next five years.

(c) The company could purchase the machine under a hire purchase agreement. This would require an initial deposit of £6,500 and payments of £4,400 per annum at the end of each of the next five years. The interest part of the payments, for tax purposes, would be £2,100 at the end of year 1 and £1,800, £1,400, £1,000 and £700 at the end of each of years 2, 3, 4 and 5 respectively.

The company's weighted average cost of capital, normally used for project evaluating, is 12% after tax. The rate of corporation tax is 30%. If the machine is purchased, the company will be able to claim an annual writing down allowance of 25% of the reducing balance.

Advise the management on whether to acquire the machine, on the most economical method of finance, and on any other matter which should be considered before finally deciding which method of finance should be adopted.

2.6 SOLUTION

The traditional method begins with the **acquisition decision**. The cash flows of the project should be discounted at 12%. The first writing down allowance is assumed to be claimed in the first year resulting in a saving of tax at year 2.

Capital allowances

Year		*Allowance*
		£
1	25% of £20,000	5,000
2	25% of £(20,000 – 5,000)	3,750
3	25% of £(15,000 – 3,750)	2,813
4	25% of £(11,250 – 2,813)	2,109
		13,672
5	£(20,000 – 13,672 – 4,000)	2,328
		16,000

Taxable profits and tax liability

Year	*Cash profits*	*Capital allowance*	*Taxable profits*	*Tax at 30%*
	£	£	£	£
1	8,000	5,000	3,000	900
2	8,000	3,750	4,250	1,275
3	8,000	2,813	5,187	1,556
4	8,000	2,109	5,891	1,767
5	8,000	2,328	5,672	1,702

NPV calculation for the acquisition decision

Year	*Equipment*	*Cash profits*	*Tax*	*Net cash flow*	*Discount factor*	*Present value*
	£	£	£	£	12%	£
0	(20,000)			(20,000)	1.000	(20,000)
1		8,000		8,000	0.893	7,144
2		8,000	(900)	7,100	0.797	5,659
3		8,000	(1,275)	6,725	0.712	4,788
4		8,000	(1,556)	6,444	0.636	4,098
5	4,000	8,000	(1,767)	10,233	0.567	5,802
6			(1,702)	(1,702)	0.507	(863)
					NPV	6,628

2.7 **CONCLUSION**

The net present value (NPV) is positive, and the machine should be acquired, regardless of the method used to finance the acquisition.

2.8 The second stage is the **financing decision**, and cash flows are discounted at the after-tax cost of borrowing, which is at 13% × 70% = 9.1%, say 9%. The only cash flows that we need to consider are those which will be affected by the choice of the method of financing. The operating savings of £8,000 a year, and the tax on these savings, can be ignored.

(a) **The present value (PV) of purchase costs**

Year	*Item*	*Cash flow*	*Discount factor*	*PV*
		£	9%	£
0	Equipment cost	(20,000)	1.000	(20,000)
5	Trade-in value	4,000	0.650	2,600
	Tax savings, from allowances			
2	30% × £5,000	1,500	0.842	1,263
3	30% × £3,750	1,125	0.772	869
4	30% × £2,813	844	0.708	9598
5	30% × £2,109	633	0.650	411
6	30% × £2,328	698	0.596	416
			NPV of purchase	(13,843)

(b) **The PV of leasing costs**

It is assumed that the tax payments are fully tax-allowable.

Year	*Lease payment*	*Savings in tax (30%)*	*Discount factor*	*PV*
	£	£	9%	£
1-5	(4,800) pa		3.890	(18,672)
2-6		1,440 pa	3.569	5,139
			NPV of leasing	(13,533)

(c) **The PV of hire purchase**

Year	*HP payments*	*Capital allowances - tax saved*	*Tax saved due to interest on HP payments at 30%*	*Net cash flow*	*Discount factor at 9%*	*PV*
	£	£		£		£
0	(6,500)			(6,500)	1.000	(6,500)
1	(4,400)			(4,400)	0.917	(4,035)
2	(4,400)	1,500	630	(2,270)	0.842	(1,911)
3	(4,400)	1,125	540	(2,735)	0.772	(2,111)
4	(4,400)	844	420	(3,136)	0.708	(2,220)
5	*(400)*	633	300	533	0.650	346
6		698	210	908	0.596	541
				NPV of hire purchase		(15,890)

* £4,400 less £4,000 trade-in value

2.9 The cheapest option would be to lease the machine. However, other matters should be considered.

(a) **Running expenses**

The calculations assume that the running costs are the same under each alternative. However expenses like maintenance, consumable stores, insurance and so on may differ between the alternatives.

(b) **The effect on cash flow**

Purchasing requires an immediate outflow of £20,000 compared to nothing for leasing. This effect should be considered in relation to the company's liquidity position, which in turn will affect its ability to discharge its debts and to pay dividends.

(c) **Alternative uses of funds**

The proposed outlay of £20,000 for purchase should be considered in relation to alternative investments.

(d) **The trade-in value**

The net present value of purchase is materially affected by the trade-in value of £4,000 in the fifth year. This figure could be very inaccurate.

2.10 A disadvantage of the traditional approach to making a lease or buy decision is that if there is a negative NPV when the operational cash flows of the project are discounted at the firm's cost of capital, the investment will be rejected out of hand. However, the costs of leasing might be so low that the project would be worthwhile provided the leasing option were selected. This suggests that an investment opportunity should not be rejected without first giving some thought to its financing costs.

2.11 **Other methods** of making lease or buy decisions are as follows.

(a) **Make the financing decision first.** Compare the cost of leasing with the cost of purchase, and select the cheaper method of financing; then calculate the NPV of the project on the assumption that the cheaper method of financing is used.

(b) **Combine the acquisition and financing decisions together into a single-stage decision.** Calculate an NPV for the project if the machine is **purchased,** and secondly if the machine is **leased.** Select the method of financing which gives the higher NPV, provided that the project has a positive NPV.

2.12 EXAMPLE: LEASE OR BUY DECISIONS (2)

In the case of Mallen and Mullins Ltd, the NPV with purchase would be + £6,548. This was calculated above. The NPV with leasing would be as follows. A discount rate of 12% is used here.

Year	*Profit less leasing cost*	*Tax at 30%*	*Net cash flow*	*Discount factor*	*PV*
	£	£	£	12%	£
1	3,200		3,200	0.893	2,858
2	3,200	(960)	2,240	0.797	1,785
3	3,200	(960)	2,240	0.712	1,595
4	3,200	(960)	2,240	0.636	1,425
5	3,200	(960)	2,240	0.567	1,270
6		(960)	(960)	0.507	(487)
				NPV	8,446

Using this method, leasing is preferable, because the NPV is £1,898 higher.

2.13 Since **operating leases** are a form of renting, the only cash flows to consider for this type of leasing are the **lease payments** and the **tax saved.** Operating lease payments are allowable expenses for tax purposes.

The position of the lessor

Exam focus point

So far, we have looked at examples of leasing decisions from the viewpoint of the lessee. You may be asked to evaluate a leasing arrangement from the position of the lessor. This is rather like a mirror image of the lessee's position.

2.14 The lessor will receive capital allowances on the expenditure, and the lease payments will be taxable income.

2.15 EXAMPLE: LESSOR'S POSITION

Continuing the same case of Mallen and Mullins Ltd, suppose that the lessor's required rate of return is 12% after tax. The lessor's cash flows will be as follows.

	Cash flow £	*Discount factor* 12%	*PV* £
Purchase costs (see paragraph 2.7)			
Year 0	(20,000)	1.000	(20,000)
Year 5 trade-in	4,000	0.567	2,268
Tax savings			
Year 2	1,500	0.797	1,196
Year 3	1,125	0.712	801
Year 4	844	0.636	537
Year 5	633	0.567	359
Year 6	698	0.507	354
Lease payments: years 1-5	4,800	3.605	17,304
Tax on lease payments: years 2-6	(1,440)	3.218	(4,634)
NPV			(1,815)

Conclusion

The proposed level of leasing payments are not justifiable for the lessor if it seeks a required rate of return of 12%, since the resulting NPV is negative.

Question

The management of a company has decided to acquire Machine X which costs £63,000 and has an operational life of four years. The expected scrap value would be zero. Tax is payable at 30% on operating cash flows one year in arrears. Capital allowances are available at 25% a year on a reducing balance basis.

Suppose that the company has the opportunity either to purchase the machine or to lease it under a finance lease arrangement, at an annual rent of £20,000 for four years, payable at the end of each year. The company can borrow to finance the acquisition at 10%. Should the company lease or buy the machine?

Answer

Working

Capital allowances

Year		£
1	(25% of £63,000)	15,750
2	(75% of £15,750)	11,813
3	(75% of £11,813)	8,859
		36,422
4	(£63,000 - £36,422)	26,578

The financing decision will be appraised by discounting the relevant cash flows at the after-tax cost of borrowing, which is 10% × 70% = 7%.

(a) *Purchase option*

Year	*Item*	*Cash flow* £	*Discount factor* 7%	*Present value* £
0	Cost of machine	(63,000)	1.000	(63,000)
	Tax saved from capital allowances			
2	30% × £15,750	4,725	0.873	4,125
3	30% × £11,813	3,544	0.816	2,892
4	30% × £8,859	2,658	0.763	2,028
5	30% × £26,578	7,973	0.713	5,685
				(48,270)

(b) *Leasing option*

It is assumed that the lease payments are tax-allowable in full.

Year	*Item*	*Cash Flow*	*Discount factor*	*Present value*
		£	7%	£
1-4	Lease costs	(20,000)	3.387	(67,740)
2-5	Tax savings on lease costs (× 30%)	6,000	3.165	18,990
				(48,750)

The purchase option is cheaper, using a cost of capital based on the after-tax cost of borrowing. On the assumption that investors would regard borrowing and leasing as equally risky finance options, the purchase option is recommended.

Chapter roundup

- **Leasing** is a commonly used source of finance.
- We have distinguished three types of leasing:
  - **Operating leases** (**lessor** responsible for maintaining asset)
  - **Finance leases** (**lessee** responsible for maintenance)
  - **Sale and leaseback** arrangements
- The decision whether to **lease or buy** an asset involves two steps.
  - The **acquisition decision:** is the asset worth having? Test by discounting project cash flows at a suitable cost of capital.
  - The **financing decision:** if the asset should be acquired, compare the cash flows of purchasing and leasing or HP arrangements. The cash flows can be discounted at an after-tax cost of borrowing.

Quick quiz

1 Operating leases and finance leases are distinguished for accounting purposes. Which of the following statements is not true of an operating lease?

A The lessor supplies the equipment to the lessee.
B The period of the lease is less than the expected economic life of the asset.
C The lessee is normally responsible for maintaining the leased equipment.
D The lessor retains most of the risks and rewards of ownership.

2 Who is responsible for the servicing of a leased asset in the case of:

(a) An operating lease?
(b) A finance lease?

The lessee	or	The lessor

3 What two steps in a lease or buy decision evaluation may be distinguished?

4 Which discount rate should be used at each stage (delete as applicable)?

	(a)	*Discount rate (b)*
Step 1		Pre-tax/after-tax cost of capital/cost of borrowing
Step 2		Pre-tax/after-tax cost of capital/ cost of borrowing

5 Why should operating leases be popular for users of high technology equipment?

6 Cemstone Plc has decided to acquire a new grinding machine. It cannot afford to purchase the machine outright, and has therefore arranged to pay for it in regular instalments using a finance house. What type of arrangement is this?

A Finance lease
B Operating lease
C Lender credit
D Vendor credit

7 A hire purchase contract is a contract for the hire of an asset that contains a provision giving the hirer an option to acquire legal title to the asset upon the fulfilment of certain conditions stated in the contract.

☐ True
☐ False

8 *Fill in the blank.*

.... credit occurs when the buyer borrows money and uses it to purchase goods outright.

Answers to quick quiz

1 C The lessor is normally responsible for maintaining the equipment.

2 (a) The lessor
(b) The lessee

3/4 ***Step 1***. The acquisition decision - discount at the firm's after-tax cost of capital
Step 2. The financing decision - discount at the after-tax cost of borrowing

5 Because such equipment may soon become obsolete.

6 D Vendor credit. This is also known as hire purchase.

7 True

8 Lender credit

Now try the question below from the Exam Question Bank

Question to try	Level	Marks	Time
36	Exam	25	45 mins

Appendix Mathematical tables

PRESENT VALUE TABLE

Present value of 1 ie $(1+r)^{-n}$

where r = discount rate

n = number of periods until payment

Periods (n)	Discount rates (r) 1%	2%	3%	4%	5%	6%	7%	8%	9%	10%
1	0.990	0.980	0.971	0.962	0.952	0.943	0.935	0.926	0.917	0.909
2	0.980	0.961	0.943	0.925	0.907	0.890	0.873	0.857	0.842	0.826
3	0.971	0.942	0.915	0.889	0.864	0.840	0.816	0.794	0.772	0.751
4	0.961	0.924	0.888	0.855	0.823	0.792	0.763	0.735	0.708	0.683
5	0.951	0.906	0.863	0.822	0.784	0.747	0.713	0.681	0.650	0.621
6	0.942	0.888	0.837	0.790	0.746	0.705	0.666	0.630	0.596	0.564
7	0.933	0.871	0.813	0.760	0.711	0.665	0.623	0.583	0.547	0.513
8	0.923	0.853	0.789	0.731	0.677	0.627	0.582	0.540	0.502	0.467
9	0.914	0.837	0.766	0.703	0.645	0.592	0.544	0.500	0.460	0.424
10	0.905	0.820	0.744	0.676	0.614	0.558	0.508	0.463	0.422	0.386
11	0.896	0.804	0.722	0.650	0.585	0.527	0.475	0.429	0.388	0.350
12	0.887	0.788	0.701	0.625	0.557	0.497	0.444	0.397	0.356	0.319
13	0.879	0.773	0.681	0.601	0.530	0.469	0.415	0.368	0.326	0.290
14	0.870	0.758	0.661	0.577	0.505	0.442	0.388	0.340	0.299	0.263
15	0.861	0.743	0.642	0.555	0.481	0.417	0.362	0.315	0.275	0.239

Periods (n)	11%	12%	13%	14%	15%	16%	17%	18%	19%	20%
1	0.901	0.893	0.885	0.877	0.870	0.862	0.855	0.847	0.840	0.833
2	0.812	0.797	0.783	0.769	0.756	0.743	0.731	0.718	0.706	0.694
3	0.731	0.712	0.693	0.675	0.658	0.641	0.624	0.609	0.593	0.579
4	0.659	0.636	0.613	0.592	0.572	0.552	0.534	0.516	0.499	0.482
5	0.593	0.567	0.543	0.519	0.497	0.476	0.456	0.437	0.419	0.402
6	0.535	0.507	0.480	0.456	0.432	0.410	0.390	0.370	0.352	0.335
7	0.482	0.452	0.425	0.400	0.376	0.354	0.333	0.314	0.296	0.279
8	0.434	0.404	0.376	0.351	0.327	0.305	0.285	0.266	0.249	0.233
9	0.391	0.361	0.333	0.308	0.284	0.263	0.243	0.225	0.209	0.194
10	0.352	0.322	0.295	0.270	0.247	0.227	0.208	0.191	0.176	0.162
11	0.317	0.287	0.261	0.237	0.215	0.195	0.178	0.162	0.148	0.135
12	0.286	0.257	0.231	0.208	0.187	0.168	0.152	0.137	0.124	0.112
13	0.258	0.229	0.204	0.182	0.163	0.145	0.130	0.116	0.104	0.093
14	0.232	0.205	0.181	0.160	0.141	0.125	0.111	0.099	0.088	0.078
15	0.209	0.183	0.160	0.140	0.123	0.108	0.095	0.084	0.074	0.065

ANNUITY TABLE

Present value of annuity of 1, ie presnt value of £1 per annum, receivable or payable at the end of each year for n years $\frac{1-(1+r)^{-n}}{r}$

where r = discount rate

n = number of periods.

Periods (n)	Discount rates (r) 1%	2%	3%	4%	5%	6%	7%	8%	9%	10%
1	0.990	0.980	0.971	0.962	0.952	0.943	0.935	0.926	0.917	0.909
2	1.970	1.942	1.913	1.886	1.859	1.833	1.808	1.783	1.759	1.736
3	2.941	2.884	2.829	2.775	2.723	2.673	2.624	2.577	2.531	2.487
4	3.902	3.808	3.717	3.630	3.546	3.465	3.387	3.312	3.240	3.170
5	4.853	4.713	4.580	4.452	4.329	4.212	4.100	3.993	3.890	3.791
6	5.795	5.601	5.417	5.242	5.076	4.917	4.767	4.623	4.486	4.355
7	6.728	6.472	6.230	6.002	5.786	5.582	5.389	5.206	5.033	4.868
8	7.652	7.325	7.020	6.733	6.463	6.210	5.971	5.747	5.535	5.335
9	8.566	8.162	7.786	7.435	7.108	6.802	6.515	6.247	5.995	5.759
10	9.471	8.983	8.530	8.111	7.722	7.360	7.024	6.710	6.418	6.145
11	10.368	9.787	9.253	8.760	8.306	7.887	7.499	7.139	6.805	6.495
12	11.255	10.575	9.954	9.385	8.863	8.384	7.943	7.536	7.161	6.814
13	12.134	11.348	10.635	9.986	9.394	8.853	8.358	7.904	7.487	7.103
14	13.004	12.106	11.296	10.563	9.899	9.295	8.745	8.244	7.786	7.367
15	13.865	12.849	11.938	11.118	10.380	9.712	9.108	8.559	8.061	7.606

Periods (n)	11%	12%	13%	14%	15%	16%	17%	18%	19%	20%
1	0.901	0.893	0.885	0.877	0.870	0.862	0.855	0.847	0.840	0.833
2	1.713	1.690	1.668	1.647	1.626	1.605	1.585	1.566	1.547	1.528
3	2.444	2.402	2.361	2.322	2.283	2.246	2.210	2.174	2.140	2.106
4	3.102	3.037	2.974	2.914	2.855	2.798	2.743	2.690	2.639	2.589
5	3.696	3.605	3.517	3.433	3.352	3.274	3.199	3.127	3.058	2.991
6	4.231	4.111	3.998	3.889	3.784	3.685	3.589	3.498	3.410	3.326
7	4.712	4.564	4.423	4.288	4.160	4.039	3.922	3.812	3.706	3.605
8	5.146	4.968	4.799	4.639	4.487	4.344	4.207	4.078	3.954	3.837
9	5.537	5.328	5.132	4.946	4.772	4.607	4.451	4.303	4.163	4.031
10	5.889	5.650	5.426	5.216	5.019	4.833	4.659	4.494	4.339	4.192
11	6.207	5.938	5.687	5.453	5.234	5.029	4.836	4.656	4.486	4.327
12	6.492	6.194	5.918	5.660	5.421	5.197	4.988	4.793	4.611	4.439
13	6.750	6.424	6.122	5.842	5.583	5.342	5.118	4.910	4.715	4.533
14	6.982	6.628	6.302	6.002	5.724	5.468	5.229	5.008	4.802	4.611
15	7.191	6.811	6.462	6.142	5.847	5.575	5.324	5.092	4.876	4.675

Exam question bank

1 OVER EMPHASIS (25 marks) *45 mins*

A significant proportion of the management accounting activity within most organisations is concerned with the production and reporting of information for control purposes.

Some commentators have asserted that the control aspect of management accounting is over emphasised. This over emphasis is, they believe, to the detriment of the prime functions of management accounting which are to produce information to assist planning and decision making.

Required

Discuss the above assertion and give your view of its validity.

2 RYMAN COUPLETS LTD (25 marks) *45 mins*

Ryman Couplets Ltd is a newly established company which plans to start operations from the beginning of 20X2. During the first two years, it is considered that there will be some build-up of stocks, so that production volumes will normally exceed demand in the year. Budgeted production and sales for the first two years are as follows.

	20X2			*20X3*		
Product	*X*	*Y*	*Z*	*X*	*Y*	*Z*
Production (000's of units)	20	20	10	20	20	10
Sales (000's of units)	14	16	3	14	12	14

From 20X4 onwards, it is expected that annual production levels will be about the same, but that sales demand will rise to these same levels. The unit sales price and variable costs during 20X2 and 20X3 are expected to be as follows.

Product	*Unit sales price*	*Unit variable costs*
	£	£
X	30	16
Y	35	18
Z	25	12

Fixed production costs will be £560,000 per annum in total.

The products are all manufactured by machine, but some additional direct labour effort is required to finish them. The time required per unit has been measured, by work study techniques, is as follows.

Product	*Machine hours per unit*	*Labour hours per unit*
X	3	2
Y	1	4
Z	2	2

The company's managing director wished to ascertain the expected profitability of each product and the total company profits for 20X2 and 20X3. (You may ignore administration, selling and distribution costs.) His management accountant produced three sets of figures, one using marginal costing and the other two using absorption costing, but each with a different basis of overhead recovery. The managing director was somewhat irate, because each set of figures gave differing results, and he demanded to know which figures were right and which were wrong.

Required

(a) Prepare the three standards of total profit in each of the two years, and the profitability of each product individually. (10 marks)

(b) Compare the resulting figures, and comment on how the absorption costing figures might be improved. Advise the managing director which set of figures is 'correct' and which are 'wrong'. (7 marks)

(c) It is decided to increase production quantities in the first year only by a further 25% in order to build up stocks to a higher level. Calculate the following.

   (i) The annual cost to Ryman Couplets Ltd of the stock increase, if the financial cost of holding stocks is 14% per annum

   (ii) The effect this increase would have on reported profits during 20X2 (only) using each of the three costing methods described (8 marks)

3 SOUTHCOTT LTD

Southcott Ltd is a firm of financial consultants which offers short revision courses on taxation and auditing for professional examinations. The firm has budgeted annual overheads totalling £152,625. Until recently the firm has applied overheads on a volume basis, based on the number of course days offered. The firm has no variable costs and the only direct costs are the consultants' own time which they divide equally between their two courses. The firm is considering the possibility of adopting an activity based costing (ABC) system and has identified the overhead costs as shown below.

Details of overheads

	£
Centre hire	62,500
Enquiries administration	27,125
Brochures	63,000
Total	152,625

The following information relates to the past year and is expected to remain the same for the coming year.

Course	*No of courses sold*	*Duration of course*	*No of enquiries per course*	*No of brochures printed per course*
Auditing	50	2 days	175	300
Taxation	30	3 days	70	200

All courses run with a maximum number of students (30), as it is deemed that beyond this number the learning experience is severely diminished, and the same centre is hired for all courses at a standard daily rate. The firm has the human resources to run only one course at any one time.

Required

(a) Calculate the overhead cost per course for both auditing and taxation using traditional volume based absorption costing.

(b) Recalculate the overhead costs per course using activity based costing and explain your choice of cost driver in your answer.

4 ABC (Pilot paper, 25 marks) *45 mins*

(a) Discuss the conditions under which the introduction of ABC is likely to be most effective, paying particular attention to the following.

(i) Product mix
(ii) The significance of overheads and the ABC method of charging costs
(iii) The availability of information collection procedures and resources
(iv) Other appropriate factors (17 marks)

(b) Explain why ABC might lead to a more accurate assessment of management performance than absorption costing. (8 marks)

5 JOBBING ENGINEERING COMPANY (25 marks) *45 mins*

You have just taken up the position as the first full-time accountant for a jobbing engineering company. Previously the accounting work had been undertaken by the company's auditors who had produced the following summarised profit and loss statement for the financial year which ended on 31 March of this year.

	£	£	£
Sales			2,400,000
Direct material		1,000,000	
Direct labour – Grinding Department	200,000		
Direct labour – Finishing Department	260,000		
		460,000	
Production overhead - Grinding	175,000		
Production overhead - Finishing	208,000		
		383,000	
Administration costs		118,500	
Selling costs		192,000	
			2,153,500
Net profit			246,500

The sales manager is currently negotiating a price for an enquiry for a job which has been allocated number 878 and he has been given the following information by his staff:

Preferred price to obtain a return of $16^{2}/_{3}$% on selling price	£22,656
Lowest acceptable price	£18,880

These prices have been based on the following estimated costs for proposed job 878.

	£	£
Direct material		9,000
Direct labour – Grinding department: 400 hours @ £5	2,000	
Direct labour – Finishing department: 300 hours @ £6	1,800	
		3,800
		12,800
Add 47.5% to cover all other costs		6,080
Total cost		18,880

The sales manager seeks your advice about the validity of the method he is using to quote for Job 878.

The company is currently busy with a fairly full order book but the Confederation of British Industry has forecast that a recession is imminent for the engineering industry.

Required

As the accountant, do the following.

(a) Criticise the method adopted for estimating the costs which are used as the basis for quoting prices for jobs. (7 marks)

(b) Suggest a better method of estimating job costs and calculate a revised job cost and price, based on the information available, to give to the sales manager. (8 marks)

(c) Suggest how you would propose to improve the accounting information to assist with controlling costs and providing information for pricing purposes. (10 marks)

6 FERTILISER

ABC Ltd is a chemical processing company which uses two processes to convert three raw materials W, X and Y into a final product Z which is used as a fertiliser in the farming industry.

At 30 September 20X3 there was work in progress of 8,400 kg in the second process, the cost of which was made up as follows.

	£
Process 1	8,720
Materials	2,000
Labour	3,600
Overhead	7,200
	21,520

The following data relates to October 20X3.

(a) Direct wages incurred

Process 1	£17,160
Process 2	£8,600

(b) Direct materials issued to production

Process 1	10,500 kg of W costing	£4,960
	7,200 kg of X costing	£14,700
Process 2	4,050 kg of Y costing	£15,600

(c) Completed output from the two processes

Process 1	13,100 kg
Process 2	20,545 kg

(d) Closing work in progress (100% complete as to materials but only 50% complete as to conversion cost)

Process 1	2,000 kg
Process 2	1,500 kg

(e) Expected normal losses (caused by evaporation and occurring at the end of processing)

Process 1	15% of throughput
Process 2	10% of throughput

Note. Throughput equals opening work in progress plus materials introduced less closing work in progress.

(f) Production overhead is absorbed using the following absorption rates

Process 1	150% of direct labour cost
Process 2	200% of direct labour cost

Required

Prepare the accounts for each of the two processes for the month of October 20X3.

7 PROCESS COSTING (25 marks) *45 mins*

Process costing, unlike individual job costing, contract costing and batch costing is not specifically related to individual items, but to the volume of 'throughput' during a particular period of time. Define process costing and explain how you would account for incomplete production, process losses and joint accounts.

8 STANDARD COSTING SYSTEM (25 marks) *45 mins*

(a) As a member of your organisation's management accounting team, you are asked to plan the installation and operation of a standard costing system. Describe how you would install this system. Indicate what problems are likely to be encountered and how they could be overcome. (17 marks)

(b) A member of your management accounting team believes that past performance is the best guide to ascertaining standard costs. Discuss this point of view. (8 marks)

9 PAN CO LIMITED (25 marks) *45 mins*

Pan Co Ltd, a manufacturing firm, operates a standard marginal costing system. It makes a number of products including product ZX, which uses a single raw material VW. Standard costs relating to ZX have been calculated as follows.

Standard cost schedule - ZX

	£ per unit
Direct material VW, 10 kg @ £15 per kg	150
Direct labour, 5 hours @ £9 per hour	45
	195
Variable production overhead, 5 hours @ £3 per hour	15
	210

During the week ending 9 November 20X1, 1,000 units of ZX were produced, the relevant information regarding actual performance being as follows.

4,000 kgs of direct material VW were in opening stock, 10,000 kgs were purchased during the week (actual cost being £144,000), and 3,000 kgs were in closing stock. Stocks of the direct material VW are valued at the standard price of £15 per kg. 5,200 direct labour hours were worked during the week, total wages being £48,360. The actual cost of variable production overhead for the week was £16,800.

Required

(a) Compute the cost variances which arose in the week ending 9 November 20X1 under the following headings.

(i) Variable production cost variance
(ii) Direct wages cost variance, and analyse into rate and efficiency
(iii) Direct material cost variance, and analyse into price and usage
(iv) Variable production overhead variance (11 marks)

(b) Prepare a report providing a commentary on the variances for the production manager, indicating any additional information which might prove useful in explaining them. (8 marks)

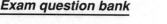

(c) Answer a criticism by the production manager that, given time and usage standards in hours and kgs respectively, he could control the company satisfactorily without the use of any cost standards. (6 marks)

10 RECONCILIATION STATEMENT (25 marks) *45 mins*

The following profit reconciliation statement summarises the performance of one of CL Ltd's products for March 20X7.

			£	
Budgeted profit			4,250	
Sales volume variance			850	A
Standard profit on actual sales			3,400	
Selling price variance			4,000	A
			(600)	
Cost variances	*Adverse*	*Favourable*		
	£	£		
Direct material price		1,000		
Direct material usage	150			
Direct labour rate	200			
Direct labour efficiency	150			
Variable overhead expenditure	600			
Variable overhead efficiency	75			
Fixed overhead expenditure		2,500		
Fixed overhead volume		150		
	1,175	3,650	2,475	F
Actual profit			1,875	

The budget for the same period contained the following data.

Sales volume		1,500 units
Sales revenue	£20,000	
Production volume		1,500 units
Direct materials purchased		750 kgs
Direct materials used		750 kgs
Direct material cost	£4,500	
Direct labour hours		1,125
Direct labour cost	£4,500	
Variable overhead cost	£2,250	
Fixed overhead cost	£4,500	

Additional information

(a) Stocks of raw materials and finished goods are valued at standard cost.
(b) During the month the actual number of units produced was 1,550.
(c) The actual sales revenue was £12,000.
(d) The direct materials purchased were 1,000 kgs.

Required

(a) Calculate the following.

(i) The actual sales volume
(ii) The actual quantity of materials used
(iii) The actual direct material cost
(iv) The actual direct labour hours
(v) The actual direct labour cost
(vi) The actual variable overhead cost
(vii) The actual fixed overhead cost (14 marks)

(b) Explain the possible causes of the direct materials usage variance, direct labour rate variance, and sales volume variance. (6 marks)

(c) Explain why different variances are calculated depending upon the choice of marginal or absorption costing. (5 marks)

11 MIX ETC (Pilot paper, 25 marks) *45 mins*

Pan Ocean Chemicals has one product which requires inputs from three types of material to produce batches of product Synthon. Standard cost details for a single batch are shown below.

	Materials		*Labour*	
Material type	*Standard kgs*	*Standard price per kg*	*Standard hours*	*Standard rate per hour*
		£		£
S1	8	0.3	1	5.00
S2	5	0.5		
S3	3	0.4		

Standard loss of 10% of input is expected. Actual production was 15,408 kgs for the previous week. Details of the materials used are as follows.

Actual material used (kg)

S1	8,284
S2	7,535
S3	3,334

Total labour cost for the week was £6,916 for 1,235 hours worked.

Required

(a) Calculate the following.

(i) Total material mix, yield and usage variances (9 marks)
(ii) Labour rate and efficiency variances (2 marks)

(b) Explain why the sum of the mix variances for materials measured in kg should be zero. (3 marks)

(c) Write a report to management which explains and interprets your results in part (a). The report should pay particular attention to the following.

(i) Explaining what is meant by mix and yield variances in respect of materials
(ii) Possible reasons for all the results you have derived (11 marks)

12 TF PLC (25 marks) *45 mins*

TF plc is considering introducing a computerised responsibility accounting system. You are responsible for the design and implementation of the system, and have shown the managing director a typical report that the system will generate. The managing director has asked the following questions.

- Why does the report highlight controllable cost and profit?
- How does one determine which costs are controllable?
- What is the difference between a cost centre, profit centre and investment centre?
- What benefits are to be gained from a system of responsibility accounting?

Required

Draft a report to the managing director addressing the specific issues he has raised.

13 FREEWHEEL LTD (25 marks) *45 mins*

Freewheel is in the process of preparing its master budget for the six months ending December 20X2. The balance sheet for the year ended 30 June 20X2 is estimated to be as follows.

	Cost	*Deprec prov*	*NBV*
	£	£	£
Fixed assets	140,000	14,000	126,000
Current assets			
Stock	25,000		
Trade debtors	24,600		
Bank	3,000		
Net current liabilities		52,600	
Creditors: Amounts falling due within one year			
Trade creditors	25,000		
Other creditors	9,000		
		34,000	
Net current assets			18,600
Total assets less current liabilities			144,600
Capital and reserves			
Share capital			100,000
Profit and loss account			44,600
			144,600

The budget committee have derived the following trading forecasts for the six months ended 31 December 20X2.

	Sales in units	*Purchases*	*Wages And Salaries*	*Overheads excl. deprec*	*Purchase of fixed assets*	*Issue of 20,000 £1 shares*	*Dividends*
		£	£	£	£	£	£
May	4,000	12,000	8,000	7,000			
June	4,200	13,000	8,000	7,000			
July	4,500	14,000	8,000	7,000			
August	4,600	18,000	10,000	7,000			
September	4,800	16,000	10,000	7,000		20,000	
October	5,000	14,000	10,000	8,000			10,000
November	3,800	12,000	12,000	8,000	30,000		
December	3,000	12,000	12,000	8,000			

You are given the following information.

(a) The selling price in May 20X2 was £6 per unit and this is to be increased to £8 per unit in October. 50% of sales are for cash and 50% on credit to be paid two months later.

(b) Purchases are to be paid for two months after purchase.

(c) Wages and salaries are to be paid 75% in the month incurred and 25% in the following month.

(d) Overheads are to be paid in the month after they are incurred.

(e) The fixed assets are to be paid for in three equal instalments in the three months following purchase.

(f) Dividends are to be paid three months after they are declared and the receipts from the share issue are budgeted to be received in the month of issue.

(g) Fixed assets are depreciated 10% per annum on a straight line basis on those assets owned at 31 December 20X2.

(h) Closing stock at the beginning of the period under review was equal to the previous two months purchases. At 31 December 20X2 it was equal to three months purchases.

Required

(a) Prepare the following budgets for the six months ended 31 December 20X2.

(i) Cash budget (9 marks)
(ii) Budgeted profit and loss account (5 marks)
(iii) Budgeted balance sheet (6 marks)

(b) Comment upon the results, highlighting those areas that you wish to draw to the attention of the budget committee. (5 marks)

14 PRESENTATION (25 marks) *45 mins*

The following statement has been produced for presentation to the general manager of Department X.

	Month ended 31 October 20Y0		
	Original budget	*Actual result*	*Variance*
	£	£	£
Sales	600,000	550,000	(50,000)
Direct materials	150,000	130,000	20,000
Direct labour	200,000	189,000	11,000
Production overhead			
Variable with direct labour	50,000	46,000	4,000
Fixed	25,000	29,000	(4,000)
Variable selling overhead	75,000	72,000	3,000
Fixed selling overhead	50,000	46,000	4,000
Total costs	550,000	512,000	38,000
Profit	50,000	38,000	(12,000)
Direct labour hours	50,000	47,500	
Sales and production units	5,000	4,500	

Note. There are no opening and closing stocks.

The general manager says that this type of statement does not provide much relevant information for him. He also thought that the profit for the month would be well up to budget and was surprised to see a large adverse profit variance.

Required

(a) Re-draft the above statement in a form which would be more relevant for the general manager. (7 marks)

(b) Calculate all sales, material, labour and overhead variances and reconcile to the statement produced in (a). (10 marks)

(c) Produce a short report explaining the principles upon which your re-drafted statement is based and what information it provides. (8 marks)

15 BUDGETS AND PEOPLE (25 marks) *45 mins*

In his study of *The Impact of Budgets on People* Argyris reported inter alia the following comment by a financial controller on the practice of participation in the setting of budgets in his company.

'We bring in the supervisors of budget areas, we tell them that we want their frank opinion but most of them just sit there and nod their heads. We know they're not coming out with exactly how they feel. I guess budgets scare them.'

Required

Suggest reasons why managers may be reluctant to participate fully in setting budgets, and suggest also unwanted side effects which may arise from the imposition of budgets by senior management.

16 ROLLING

The managing director of B Ltd believes that the existing annual budget system is costly to operate and produces unsatisfactory results for a number of reasons.

- Long preparation period
- Business decisions being made throughout the year
- Unpredictable changes in the rate of general inflation
- Sudden changes in the availability and price of raw materials

He has read about rolling budgets and wonders whether these might be more useful for his decision making.

Required

Provide the following.

(a) A brief explanation of rolling budgets
(b) A description of how a rolling budget system would operate
(c) Three significant advantages of a rolling budget system
(d) Three problems likely to be encountered in using a rolling budget system

17 DOMESTIC APPLIANCE (25 marks) *45 mins*

A domestic electrical appliance was introduced on the market in 20X2. At the point of sale customers are offered the chance to purchase an insurance policy to cover repairs and parts for the first five years of operation; these policies cannot be purchased later on, only when the appliance is bought. The table below shows the total industry sales of this appliance for the years 20X2 to 20X8 together with the number of insurance policies sold and a general price index for electrical goods.

	Sales of appliance	*Policy sales*	*Price index for electrical goods*
Year	£'000	*(number)*	*(20X0 = 100)*
20X2	3,600	400	120
20X3	6,250	300	125
20X4	9,170	600	131
20X5	14,000	1,200	140
20X6	21,600	1,700	144
20X7	27,000	2,200	150
20X8	41,600	2,100	160

Required

(a) Explain why it is important to adjust the original appliance sales figures for inflation when identifying the relationship between the sales of the appliance and the number of insurance policies sold. Deflate the appliance sales figures to 20X0 prices. (5 marks)

(b) Calculate the coefficient of determination between the deflated appliance sales figures and the insurance policy sales, and interpret your value. (8 marks)

(c) Calculate the least squares regression equation to predict insurance policy sales from deflated appliance sales. (5 marks)

(d) The total sales of the electrical appliance in 20X9 are estimated at £51,000,000 at 20X9 prices and the price index for electrical goods in the year 20X9 based on 20X0 is predicted to be 170. Use the least squares regression equation to obtain a forecast of insurance policy sales for 20X9. (4 marks)

(e) Comment on the pitfalls of using this type of approach for predicting insurance policy sales in 20X9. (3 marks)

18 PRODUCTION SHORTFALL (25 marks) *45 mins*

(a) A company is preparing its production budget for the year ahead. Two of its processes are concerned with the manufacture of three components which are used in several of the company's products. Capacity (machine hours) in each of these two processes is limited to 2,000 hours. Production costs are as follows.

		Component	
	X	*Y*	*Z*
	£/unit	£/unit	£/unit
Direct materials	15.00	18.50	4.50
Direct labour	12.00	12.50	8.00
Variable overhead	6.00	6.25	4.00
Fixed overhead - Process M	6.00	6.00	4.50
Process N	10.50	10.50	3.50
	49.50	53.75	24.50

The requirement for the following year for component X is 300 units, for component Y 300 units and for component Z 450 units.

Fixed overhead is absorbed on the basis of machine hours at £3.00 per hour in Process M and £3.50 per hour in Process N.

Component X could be obtained from an outside supplier at £44.00 per unit and component Z at £23.00 per unit

Required

(i) Demonstrate that insufficient capacity is available to produce the requirements for components X, Y and Z in the year ahead, and calculate the extent of the shortfall. (5 marks)

(ii) Determine the requirements for bought-in components in order to satisfy the demand for components at minimum cost. (6 marks)

(iii) Consider briefly any other factors which may be relevant to decisions regarding these components in the longer term. (4 marks)

(b) Scarce resources restrict a firm's growth at a particular point of time, which results in management having to take limiting factor decisions in order to achieve maximisation of profit. Examine the various factors that must be taken into account when considering such decisions. (10 marks)

19 SEDGEMAIR PARTNERS (25 marks) *45 mins*

(a) Sedgemair Partners is a medium-sized software consulting and development house. A backlog of software development work has built up due to staff turnover and sickness and the partners have decided it must be cleared. It will require 2,000 software development staff hours to clear the backlog.

Three alternatives have been suggested.

Alternative 1

Cancel a development job which is estimated to need a further 2,500 hours work. It would produce a fee income of £47,000 if completed. There is no cancellation penalty clause in the contract. This action would release sufficient staff to clear the backlog within three months.

Alternative 2

Sub-contract 2,000 hours of development work to another firm at an estimated fee cost of £35,000.

Alternative 3

Employ four extra temporary staff for the next three months.

Set out below is some additional information.

(i) Software development staff are employed at an average salary of £25,000 pa and produce about 2,000 hours work pa each. Employment taxes and employers' pension contributions add a further 25% to salary costs.

(ii) When pricing work for clients Sedgemair usually add 80% to estimated staff costs to cover overheads and profit.

(iii) If the work were to be sub-contracted a senior consultant would need to spend about 80 hours overseeing the contract. Consultants work about 2,000 hours per year at an employment cost of £75,000 pa. Their time is usually charged to clients at £100 per hour.

(iv) Temporary staff would be paid for the hours they work at £15 per hour. No pension contributions would be payable by Sedgemair.

(v) Employment tax is payable in respect of temporary staff at 15% of salary.

(vi) Recruitment costs for the temporary staff (agency fees and interview expenses) are likely to be £750 each.

(vii) Four extra personal computers would be needed at a cost of £2,000 each if temporary staff were employed. Their second-hand value after the work has been completed is expected to be £1,500 each. They would have a four-year life if kept. Alternatively computers could be leased for £750 per quarter each.

(viii) Sedgemair Partners are located in open plan offices on the third and fourth floors of a six-storey office block at a rental cost of £200 per square metre per annum. Each floor comprises 400 square metres. If temporary staff were employed forty square metres of extra space would be needed. This could be obtained by transferring the contents of 20 large filing cabinets to CD ROM at a total cost of £1,300. The cabinets could then be sold for £20 each. An alternative would be to rent a spare office (which has an area of fifty square metres) on the fifth floor of the same building for three months at a rental cost of £1,500 per quarter.

(ix) Heating and lighting costs in the office block average £50 per square metre per annum and are not included in the rent.

(x) Sedgemair have sufficient spare desks and chairs in store for the temporary staff. This furniture was bought in 19X2 at a total cost of £3,000 and now has a second hand value of £1,500. It is partnership policy to depreciate furniture at 10% of cost per annum.

Required

(i) Advise the partners which option is the most cost effective. Show your calculations. (7 marks)

(ii) For each of the 'costs' (i) to (x) above, explain why you decided to include it in or exclude it from your calculations for part (i). (10 marks)

(iii) Describe non-cost factors which would be relevant when considering the three options. (3 marks)

(b) Briefly explain why opportunity costs are important information for decision making and why they are not collected as part of the routine costing system. (5 marks)

20 CORPORATE OBJECTIVES *20 mins*

Discuss whether a quoted company's directors should seek only the maximisation of the company's profit.

21 MARKET EFFICIENCY *30 mins*

Describe the various forms of market efficiency and explain whether it is possible for institutions to out-perform the market.

22 MIXED ECONOMY *35 mins*

In a mixed economy, two of the objectives of a government could be:

(a) To minimise its borrowing requirements, and
(b) To reduce the taxation of incomes.

Required

(a) Identify the general economic effects of these policies on private sector businesses.

(b) Identify the effects that might result from attempts to achieve these objectives by *each* of:

(i) Reductions in public expenditure
(ii) Increases in charges made for the products or services of nationalised industries
(iii) Selling nationalised assets

23 MIDSOUTH ELECTRIC PLC (25 marks) *45 mins*

(a) Among the industries which have been privatised by the UK government in recent years is the electricity supply industry.

Required

Outline the likely objectives of an electricity supply company:

(i) Operating in the public (government-run) sector (4 marks)
(ii) Operating in the private sector (following privatisation) (4 marks)

The information below relates to parts (b) and (c) of the question

Midsouth Electric plc (MSE) is an electricity supply company which was privatised six years ago, in 20X0, having formerly been an authority under government control. On privatisation, the newly issued shares in the company went to an immediate 40% premium on the share market. As a privatised electricity supply company, MSE is now subject to regulatory controls over prices.

The data given below is available. The 20X0 *proforma* figures reflect the company's performance during its last year under government control adjusted to reflect the accounting conventions applying in the private sector.

Midsouth Electric plc
Summarised financial and operational information

	20X0	*20X1*	*20X2*	*20X3*	*20X4*	*20X5*	*20X6*
	Proforma						
	£m	£m	£m	£m	£m	£m	£m
Turnover	760	800	850	880	920	955	995
Profit before taxation	37	49	62	74	88	94	99
Profit after taxation	30	47	52	62	74	77	80
Wages and salaries	110	109	108	108	107	106	106
Directors' emoluments	1.2	1.6	1.8	2.4	3.1	3.4	3.6
Dividends	10*	11	12	14	17	20	24
Net assets	120	126	130	150	165	180	205
Capital spending	25	30	35	50	75	82	90
Price earnings ratio	-	7.4	7.5	8.1	8.5	8.7	9.0
Number of employees	14,500	14,200	14,000	13,700	13,600	13,400	13,200
Output of electricity supplied**	100	102.5	105	107.5	110	113	116

* Notional dividend which would be paid under post-privatisation dividend policy.

** 20X0 = 100

The Retail Prices Index for the years shown is set out below.

	RPI
20X0	100
20X1	102
20X2	103
20X3	105
20X4	106
20X5	107
20X6	109

(b) *Required*

Evaluate whether the privatisation of Midsouth Electric has been a positive step from the point of view of:

(i) Ordinary shareholders (5 marks)
(ii) Employees of the company (4 marks)
(iii) Customers (4 marks)

(c) You read a letter in the press which suggests that electricity supply privatisation has, along with other privatisations, been of great benefit to the economy.

Required

Assess whether Midsouth Electric's privatisation appears to have:

(i) Assisted with attainment of the government's anti-inflation objective (2 marks)
(ii) Been beneficial to growth in the national economy (2 marks)

24 GUSTAFFSON PLC (25 marks) *45 mins*

(a) Define what is meant by the term 'overtrading' and describe some of the typical symptoms. (8 marks)

(b) Gustaffson plc is a toy manufacturing company. It manufactures Polly Playtime, the latest doll craze amongst young girls. The company is now at full production of the doll. The final accounts for 20X9 have just been published and are as follows. 20X8's accounts are also shown for comparison purposes.

PROFIT AND LOSS ACCOUNT Y/E 31 DECEMBER

	20X9	*20X8*
	£'000	£'000
Sales	30,000	20,000
Cost of sales	20,000	11,000
Operating profit	10,000	9,000
Interest	450	400
Profit before tax	9,550	8,600
Tax	2,000	1,200
Profit after tax	7,550	7,400
Dividends	2,500	2,500
Retained profit	5,050	4,900

BALANCE SHEET AS AT 31 DECEMBER

			20X9			*20X8*
	£'000	£'000	£'000	£'000	£'000	£'000
Fixed assets			1,500			1,400
Current assets						
Stock	7,350			3,000		
Debtors	10,000			6,000		
Cash	2,500			4,500		
		19,850			13,500	
Current liabilities						
Overdraft	2,000			–		
Dividends owing	2,500			2,500		
Trade creditors	4,200			2,500		
		(8,700)			(5,000)	
Net current assets			11,150			8,500
8% debentures			(1,200)			(3,500)
Net assets			11,450			6,400
Ordinary shares (25p)			5,000			5,000
Profit and loss a/c			6,450			1,400
			11,450			6,400

(i) By studying the above accounts and using ratio analysis, identify the main problems facing Gustaffson. (13 marks)

(ii) Provide possible solutions to the problems identified in (i). (4 marks)

25 H FINANCE PLC *30 mins*

H Finance plc is prepared to advance 80% of D Ltd's sales invoicing, provided its specialist collection services are used by D Ltd. H Finance plc would charge an additional 0.5% of D Ltd's turnover for this service. D Ltd would avoid administration costs it currently incurs amounting to £80,000 per annum.

The history of D Ltd's debtors' ledgers may be summarised as follows:

	20X8	*20X9*	*20Y0*
Turnover (£'000)	78,147	81,941	98,714
% debtors at year end	17	20	22
% debtors of 90+ days (of turnover)	1.5	2	2.5
Bad debts (£'000)	340	497	615

D Ltd estimates that the aggressive collection procedures adopted by the finance company are likely to result in lost turnover of some 10% of otherwise expected levels.

Currently, each £1 of turnover generates 18 pence additional profit before taxation. D Ltd turns its capital over, on average, three times each year. On receipt by H Finance plc of amounts due from D Ltd's customers, a further 15% of the amounts are to be remitted to D Ltd. The cheapest alternative form of finance would cost 20% per annum.

Required

(a) Calculate whether the factoring of D Ltd's debtors ledger would be worthwhile.
(b) Explain how the factoring of sales invoicing may assist a firm's financial performance.

26 SF (25 marks) *45 mins*

SF Ltd is a family-owned private company with five main shareholders.

SF Ltd has just prepared its cash budget for the year ahead, details of which are shown below. The current overdraft facility is £50,000 and the bank has stated that it would not be willing to increase the facility at present, without a substantial increase in the interest rate charged, due to the lack of assets to offer as security.

The shareholders are concerned by the cash projections, and have sought advice from external consultants.

All figures, £'000						*Month*						
	J	*F*	*M*	*A*	*M*	*J*	*J*	*A*	*S*	*O*	*N*	*D*
Collections from customers	55	60	30	10	15	20	20	25	30	40	55	80
Dividend on investment						10						
Total inflows	55	60	30	10	15	30	20	25	30	40	55	80
Payments to suppliers		20		20		25		28		27		25
Wages and salaries	15	15	15	15	15	20	20	15	15	15	15	15
Payments for fixed assets			2		5	10		15				
Dividend payable				25								
Corporation tax									30			
Other operating expenses	5	5	5	5	7	7	7	7	7	7	8	8
Total outflows	20	40	22	65	27	62	27	65	52	49	23	48
Net in or (out)	35	20	8	(55)	(12)	(32)	(7)	(40)	(22)	(9)	32	32
Bank balance (overdraft)												
Opening	20	55	75	83	28	16	(16)	(23)	(63)	(85)	(94)	(62)
Closing	55	75	83	28	16	(16)	(23)	(63)	(85)	(94)	(62)	(30)

The following additional information relating to the cash budget has been provided by SF Ltd.

(i) All sales are on credit. Two months' credit on average is granted to customers.

(ii) Production is scheduled evenly throughout the year. Year-end stocks of finished goods are forecast to be £30,000 higher than at the beginning of the year.

(iii) Purchases of raw materials are made at two-monthly intervals. SF Ltd typically takes up to 90 days to pay for goods supplied. Other expenses are paid in the month in which they arise.

(iv) The capital expenditure budget comprises:

Office furniture	March	£2,000
Progress payments on building extensions	May	£5,000
Car	June	£10,000
New equipment	August	£15,000

Required

Assume you are an external consultant employed by SF Ltd. Prepare a report for the board advising on the possible actions it might take to improve its budgeted cash flow for the year, and consider the possible impact of these actions on the company's business. Your report should also identify possible short-term investment opportunities for the cash surpluses identified in the first part of the budget year.

27 HEADWATER PLC (25 marks) *45 mins*

It is now August 20X6. In 20X0, the current management team of Headwater plc, a manufacturer of car and motorcycle parts, bought the company from its conglomerate parent company in a management buyout deal. Six years on, the managers are considering the possibility of obtaining a listing for the company's shares on the stock market. The following information is available.

HEADWATER PLC
PROFIT AND LOSS ACCOUNT FOR THE YEAR ENDED 30 JUNE 20X6

	£ million
Turnover	36.5
Cost of sales	(31.6)
Profit before interest and taxation	4.9
Interest	(1.3)
Profit before taxation	3.6
Taxation	(0.5)
Profit attributable to ordinary shareholders	3.1
Dividends	(0.3)
Retained profit	2.8

BALANCE SHEET AS AT 30 JUNE 20X6

	£ million	£ million
Fixed assets (at cost less accumulated depreciation)		
Land and buildings		3.6
Plant and machinery		9.9
		13.5
Current assets		
Stocks	4.4	
Debtors	4.7	
Cash at bank	1.0	
	10.1	
Current liabilities		
Trade creditors	7.0	
Bank overdraft	2.0	
	9.0	
Net current assets		1.1
Total assets less current liabilities		14.6
Creditors due after more than one year: 12% Debenture 20X8		(2.2)
Net assets		12.4
Financed by		
Ordinary £1 shares		
Voting		1.8
'A' shares (non-voting)		0.9
Reserves		9.7
Shareholders' funds		12.4

Average performance ratios for the industry sector in which Headwater operates are given below.

Industry sector ratios

Return before tax on long-term capital employed	24%
Return after tax on equity	16%
Operating profit as percentage of sales	11%
Current ratio	1.6:1
Quick (acid test) ratio	1.0:1
Total debt: equity (gearing)	24%
Dividend cover	4.0
Interest cover	4.5
Price/earnings ratio	10.0

Required

(a) Evaluate the financial state and performance of Headwater by comparing it with that of its industry sector. (10 marks)

(b) Discuss the probable reasons why the management of Headwater is considering a Stock Exchange listing. (5 marks)

(c) Explain how you think Headwater should restructure its balance sheet before becoming a listed company. (6 marks)

(d) Discuss changes in financial policy which the company would be advised to adopt once it has been floated on the Stock Exchange. (4 marks)

28 KB (25 marks) *45 mins*

(a) KB plc has a paid-up ordinary share capital of £1,500,000 represented by 6 million shares of 25p each. It has no loan capital. Earnings after tax in the most recent year were £1,200,000. The P/E ratio of the company is 12.

The company is planning to make a large new investment which will cost £5,040,000, and is considering raising the necessary finance through a rights issue at 192p.

Required

(i) Calculate the current market price of KB plc's ordinary shares. (2 marks)

(ii) Calculate the theoretical ex-rights price, and state what factors in practice might invalidate your calculation. (8 marks)

(iii) Briefly explain what is meant by a deep-discounted rights issue, identifying the main reasons why a company might raise finance by this method and also the drawbacks of using it. (5 marks)

(b) As an alternative to a rights issue, KB plc might raise the £5,040,000 required by means of an issue of convertible loan stock at par, with a coupon rate of 6%. The loan stock would be redeemable in seven years' time. Prior to redemption, the loan stock may be converted at a rate of 35 ordinary shares per £100 nominal loan stock.

Required

(i) Explain the term *conversion premium* and calculate the conversion premium at the date of issue implicit in the data given. (5 marks)

(ii) Identify the advantages to KB plc of issuing convertible loan stock instead of the rights issue to raise the necessary finance. (5 marks)

29 RUMP (25 marks) *45 mins*

Rump Ltd is an all equity financed, listed company which operates in the food processing industry. The Rump family owns 40% of the ordinary shares; the remainder are held by large financial institutions. There are 10 million £1 ordinary shares currently in issue.

The company has just finalised a long-term contract to supply a large chain of restaurants with a variety of food products. The contract requires investment in new machinery costing £24 million. This machinery would become operational on 1 January 20X2, and payment would be made on the same date. Sales would commence immediately thereafter.

Company policy is to pay out all profits as dividends and, if Rump plc continues to be all equity financed, there will be an annual dividend of £9 million in perpetuity commencing 31 December 20X2.

There are two alternatives being considered to finance the required investment of £24 million:

(1) A 2-for-5 rights issue, in which case the annual dividend would be £9 million. The cum rights price per share would be £6.60.

(2) Issuing 7.5% irredeemable debentures at par with interest payable annually in arrears. For this alternative, interest would be paid out of the £9 million otherwise available to pay dividends.

For either alternative, the directors expect the cost of equity to remain at its present annual level of 10%.

Required

(a) Calculate the issue and ex rights share prices of Rump plc assuming a 2-for-5 rights issue is used to finance the new project at 1 January 20X2. Ignore taxation. (5 marks)

(b) Calculate the value per ordinary share in Rump plc at 1 January 20X2 if 7.5% irredeemable debentures are issued to finance the new project. Assume that the cost of equity remains at 10% each year. Ignore taxation. (4 marks)

(c) Write a report to the directors of Rump plc which:

(i) Compares and contrasts the rights issue and the debenture issue methods of raising finance – you may refer to the calculations in your answer to requirements (a) and (b) and to any assumptions made.

(ii) Explains and evaluates the appropriateness of the following alternative methods of issuing equity finance *in the specific circumstances* of Rump plc:

(1) A placing
(2) An offer for sale
(3) A public offer for subscription (16 marks)

30 DF (25 marks) *45 mins*

DF Ltd is a manufacturer of sports equipment. All of the shares of DF are held by the Wong family.

The company has recently won a major 3-year contract to supply FF plc with a range of sports equipment. FF plc is a large company with over 100 sports shops. The contract may be renewed after 3 years.

The new contract is expected to double DF Ltd's existing total annual sales, but demand from FF plc will vary considerably from month to month.

The contract will, however, mean a significant additional investment in both fixed and current assets. A loan from the bank is to be used to finance the additional fixed assets, as the Wong family is currently unable to supply any further share capital. Also, the Wong family does not wish to raise new capital by issuing shares to non-family members.

The financing of the additional current assets is yet to be decided. In particular, the contract with FF plc will require orders to be delivered within two days. This delivery period gives DF Ltd insufficient time to manufacture items, thus significant stocks need to be held at all times. Also, FF plc requires 90 days' credit from its suppliers. This will result in a significant additional investment in debtors by DF Ltd.

If the company borrows from the bank to finance current assets, either using a loan or an overdraft, it expects to be charged annual interest at 12%. Consequently, DF Ltd is considering alternative methods of financing current assets. These include debt factoring, invoice discounting and offering a 3% cash discount to FF plc for settlement within 10 days rather than the normal 90 days.

Required

(a) Calculate the annual equivalent rate of interest implicit in offering a 3% discount to FF plc for settlement of debts within 10 days rather than 90 days.

Briefly explain the factors, other than the rate of interest, that DF Ltd would need to consider before deciding on whether to offer a cash discount. (6 marks)

(b) Write a report to the Wong family shareholders explaining the various methods of financing available to DF Ltd to finance the additional current assets arising from the new FF plc contract. The report should include the following headings:

Bank loan
Overdraft
Debt factoring
Invoice discounting (14 marks)

(c) Discuss the factors that a venture capital organisation will take into account when deciding whether to invest in DF Ltd. (5 marks)

31 PROJECT APPRAISAL (25 marks) *45 mins*

(a) A company is considering two capital expenditure proposals. Both proposals are for similar products and both are expected to operate for four years. Only one proposal can be accepted.

The following information is available.

	Profit/(loss)	
	Proposal A	*Proposal B*
	£	£
Initial investment	46,000	46,000
Year 1	6,500	4,500
Year 2	3,500	2,500
Year 3	13,500	4,500
Year 4	(1,500)	14,500
Estimated scrap value at the end of year 4	4,000	4,000

Depreciation is charged on the straight line basis.

The company estimates its cost of capital at 20% pa.

	Discount factor
Year 1	0.833
Year 2	0.694
Year 3	0.579
Year 4	0.482

Required

(i) Calculate the following for both proposals.

(1) The payback period to one decimal place (5 marks)

(2) The return on capital employed on initial investment, to one decimal place (2 marks)

(ii) Give two advantages for each of the methods of appraisal used in (i) above. (5 marks)

(b) D'Arcy Toby Wise Ltd is a private family business of aluminium founders, incorporated in 1949. It makes castings by three processes of pressure die-casting, gravity die-casting and sand casting and serves a variety of customers and trades, though 40% of its output goes to one particular customer who makes do-it-yourself tools.

Profits have always been low, but liquidity has remained high, due to careful cash management. The company has invested its surplus cash in stocks and shares of quoted companies.

A new professional managing director was appointed two years ago after the retirement of the firm's founder. He has proposed to the Board that since the stocks and shares do not provide a satisfactory return and have shown little capital growth, they should be sold to provide funds to exploit other business opportunities. In particular, he has recommended either of the following.

(i) The purchase of a small aluminium foundry
(ii) Diversification into new products and new markets

Required

Describe the main factors to consider in deciding the strategy to be adopted by D'Arcy Toby Wise Ltd. (13 marks)

32 KNUCKLE DOWN LTD *45 mins*

The management of Knuckle Down Ltd are reviewing the company's capital investment options for the coming year, and are considering six projects.

Project A would cost £29,000 now, and would earn the following cash profits.

1st year	£8,000	3rd year	£10,000
2nd year	£12,000	4th year	£ 6,000

The capital equipment purchased at the start of the project could be resold for £5,000 at the start of the fifth year.

Project B would involve a current outlay of £44,000 on capital equipment and £20,000 on working capital. The profits from the project would be as follows.

Year	*Sales*	*Variable costs*	*Contribution*	*Fixed costs*	*Profit*
	£	£	£	£	£
1	75,000	50,000	25,000	10,000	15,000
2	90,000	60,000	30,000	10,000	20,000
3	42,000	28,000	14,000	8,000	6,000

Fixed costs include an annual charge of £4,000 for depreciation. At the end of the third year the working capital investment would be recovered and the equipment would be sold for £5,000.

Project C would involve a current outlay of £50,000 on equipment and £15,000 on working capital. The investment in working capital would be increased to £21,000 at the end of the first year. Annual cash profits would be £18,000 for five years, at the end of which the investment in working capital would be recovered.

Project D would involve an outlay of £20,000 now and a further outlay of £20,000 after one year. Cash profits thereafter would be as follows.

2nd year £15,000 3rd year £12,000 4th to 8th years £8,000 pa

Project E is a long-term project, involving an immediate outlay of £32,000 and annual cash profits of £4,500 in perpetuity.

Project F is another long-term project, involving an immediate outlay of £20,000 and annual cash profits as follows.

1st to 5th years £5,000 6th to 10th years £4,000 11th year onwards for ever £3,000

The company discounts all projects of ten years duration or less at a cost of capital of 12%, and all other projects at a cost of 15%.

Ignore taxation.

Required

(a) Calculate the NPV of each project, and determine which should be undertaken by the company on financial grounds.

(b) Calculate the IRR of projects A, C and E.

33 DINARD (25 marks) *45 mins*

(a) Explain the difference between real rates of return and money rates of return and outline the circumstances in which the use of each would be appropriate when appraising capital projects under inflationary conditions. (8 marks)

(b) Dinard plc has just developed a new product to be called Rance and is now considering whether to put it into production. The following information is available.

(i) Costs incurred in the development of Rance amount to £480,000.

(ii) Production of Rance will require the purchase of new machinery at a cost of £2,400,000 payable immediately. This machinery is specific to the production of Rance and will be obsolete and valueless when that production ceases. The machinery has a production life of four years and a production capacity of 30,000 units per annum.

(iii) Production costs of Rance (at year 1 prices) are estimated as follows.

	£
Variable materials	8.00
Variable labour	12.00
Variable overheads	12.00

In addition, fixed production costs (at year 1 prices), including straight line depreciation on plant and machinery, will amount to £800,000 per annum.

(iv) The selling price of Rance will be £80.00 per unit (at year 1 prices). Demand is expected to be 25,000 units per annum for the next four years.

(v) The retail price index is expected to increase at 5% per annum for the next four years and the selling price of Rance is expected to increase at the same rate. Annual inflation rates for production costs are expected to be as follows.

	%
Variable materials	4
Variable labour	10
Variable overheads	4
Fixed costs	5

(vi) The company's weighted average cost of capital in money terms is expected to be 15%.

Required

Advise the directors of Dinard plc whether it should produce Rance on the basis of the information above. (17 marks)

Notes

Unless otherwise specified all costs and revenues should be assumed to rise at the end of each year. Ignore taxation.

34 MUGGINS PLC *30 mins*

Muggins plc is evaluating a project to produce a new product. The product has an expected life of four years. Costs associated with the product are expected to be as follows.

Variable costs per unit
Labour: £30
Materials:
6 kg of material X at £1.64 per kg
3 units of component Y at £4.20 per unit
Other variable costs: £4.40

Indirect cost each year
Apportionment of head office salaries £118,000
Apportionment of general building occupancy £168,000
Other overheads £80,000, of which £60,000 represent additional cash expenditures (including rent of machinery)

To manufacture the product, a product manager will have to be recruited at an annual gross cost of £34,000, and one assistant manager, whose current annual salary is £30,000, will be transferred from another department, where he will be replaced by a new appointee at a cost of £27,000 a year.

The necessary machinery will be rented. It will be installed in the company's factory. This will take up space that would otherwise be rented to another local company for £135,000 a year. This rent (for the factory space) is not subject to any uncertainty, as a binding four-year lease would be created.

60,000 kg of material X are already in stock, at a purchase value of £98,400. They have no use other than the manufacture of the new product. Their disposal value is £50,000.

Expected sales volumes of the product, at the proposed selling price of £125 a unit, are as follows.

Year	*Expected sales*
	Units
1	10,000
2	18,000
3	18,000
4	19,000

All sales and costs will be on a cash basis and should be assumed to occur at the end of the year. Ignore taxation.

The company requires that certainty-equivalent cash flows have a positive NPV at a discount rate of 14%. Adjustment factors to arrive at certainty-equivalent amounts are as follows.

Year	*Costs*	*Benefits*
1	1.1	0.9
2	1.3	0.8
3	1.4	0.7
4	1.5	0.6

Required

Assess on financial grounds whether the project is acceptable.

35 BANDEN LTD (25 marks) *45 mins*

Banden Ltd is a highly geared company that wishes to expand its operations. Six possible capital investments have been identified, but the company only has access to a total of £620,000. The projects are not divisible and may not be postponed until a future period. After the project's end it is unlikely that similar investment opportunities will occur.

Expected net cash inflows (including salvage value)

Project	*Year 1*	*2*	*3*	*4*	*5*	*Initial outlay*
	£	£	£	£	£	£
A	70,000	70,000	70,000	70,000	70,000	246,000
B	75,000	87,000	64,000			180,000
C	48,000	48,000	63,000	73,000		175,000
D	62,000	62,000	62,000	62,000		180,000
E	40,000	50,000	60,000	70,000	40,000	180,000
F	35,000	82,000	82,000			150,000

Projects A and E are mutually exclusive. All projects are believed to be of similar risk to the company's existing capital investments.

Any surplus funds may be invested in the money market to earn a return of 9% per year. The money market may be assumed to be an efficient market.

Banden's cost of capital is 12% a year.

Required

(a) (i) Calculate the expected net present value for each of the six projects.

(ii) Calculate the expected profitability index associated with each of the six projects.

(iii) Rank the projects according to both of these investment appraisal methods. Explain briefly why these rankings differ. (10 marks)

(b) Give reasoned advice to Banden Ltd recommending which projects should be selected. (6 marks)

(c) A director of the company has suggested that using the company's normal cost of capital might not be appropriate in a capital rationing situation. Explain whether you agree with the director. (5 marks)

(d) The director has also suggested the use of linear programming to assist with the selection of projects. Discuss the advantages and disadvantages of this mathematical programming method to Banden Ltd. (4 marks)

36 FLOCKS LTD (25 marks) *45 mins*

The management of Flocks Ltd is trying to decide which of two machines to purchase, to help with production. Only one of the two machines will be purchased.

Machine X costs £63,000 and machine Y costs £110,000. Both machines would require a working capital investment of £12,500 throughout their operational life, which is four years for machine X and six years for machine Y. The expected scrap value of either machine would be zero.

The estimated pre-tax operating net cash inflows with each machine are as follows.

Year	Machine X	Machine Y
	£	£
1	25,900	40,300
2	28,800	32,900
3	30,500	32,000
4	29,500	32,700
5	-	48,500
6	-	44,200

With machine Y, there is some doubt about its design features, and consequently there is some risk that it might prove unsuitable. Because of the higher business risk with machine Y, the machine Y project cash flows should be discounted at 15%, whereas machine X cash flows should be discounted at only 13%.

Flocks Ltd intends to finance the machine it eventually selects, X or Y, by borrowing at 10%.

Tax is payable at 30% on operating cash flows one year in arrears. Capital allowances are available at 25% a year on a reducing balance basis.

Required

(a) For both machine X and machine Y, calculate:

(i) The (undiscounted) payback period
(ii) The net present value

and recommend which of the two machines Flocks Ltd should purchase. (16 marks)

(b) Suppose that Flocks Ltd has the opportunity to lease machine X under a finance lease arrangement, at an annual rent of £20,000 for four years, payable at the end of each year. Recommend whether the company should lease or buy the machine, assuming it chooses machine X. (9 marks)

37 MILBAO PLC (25 marks) *45 mins*

Milbao plc make and sell three types of electronic game for which the following budget/standard information and actual information is available for a four-week period.

Model	*Budget sales*	*Standard unit data* *Selling price*	*Variable cost*	*Actual sales*
	Units	£	£	Units
Superb	30,000	100	40	36,000
Excellent	50,000	80	25	42,000
Good	20,000	70	22	18,000

Required

(a) Calculate the *individual* sales quantity and sales mix variances for Milbao plc for the four-week period, using contribution as the valuation base. (5 marks)

(b) The following additional information is available for the four-week period.

The actual selling prices and variable costs of Milbao plc are 10% and 5% lower respectively than the original budget/standard.

General market prices have fallen by 6% from the original standard. Short-term strategy by Milbao plc accounts for the residual fall in selling price.

3% of the variable cost reduction from the original budget/standard is due to an over-estimation of a wage award, the remainder (ie 2%) is due to short-term operational improvements.

Prepare a summary for a four-week period for models 'Superb' and 'Good' *only,* which reconciles original budget contribution with actual contribution where planning and operational variances are taken into consideration. (15 marks)

(c) Comment on the usefulness to management of planning and operational variance analysis in feedback and feedforward control. (5 marks)

Approaching the answer

You should read through the requirement before working through and annotating the question as we have done so that you are aware of what things you are looking for.

Milbao plc make and sell three types of electronic game for which the following budget/standard information and actual information is available for a four-week period. [Note the time frame]

[This is in units, not £] [This is standard unit data in £] [This is actual data (in units)]

Model	*Budget sales*	*Standard unit data* *Selling price*	*Variable cost*	*Actual sales*
	Units	£	£	Units
Superb	30,000	100	40	36,000
Excellent	50,000	80	25	42,000
Good	20,000	70	22	18,000

Required [Not total variance] [Three models]

(a) Calculate the *individual* sales quantity and sales mix variances for Milbao plc for the four-week period, using contribution as the valuation base. (5 marks)

[Same time frame as above] [Very important] [It's that time frame again]

(b) The following additional information is available for the four-week period.

Differences between original budget and actual

The actual selling prices and variable costs of Milbao plc are 10% and 5% lower respectively than the original budget/standard.

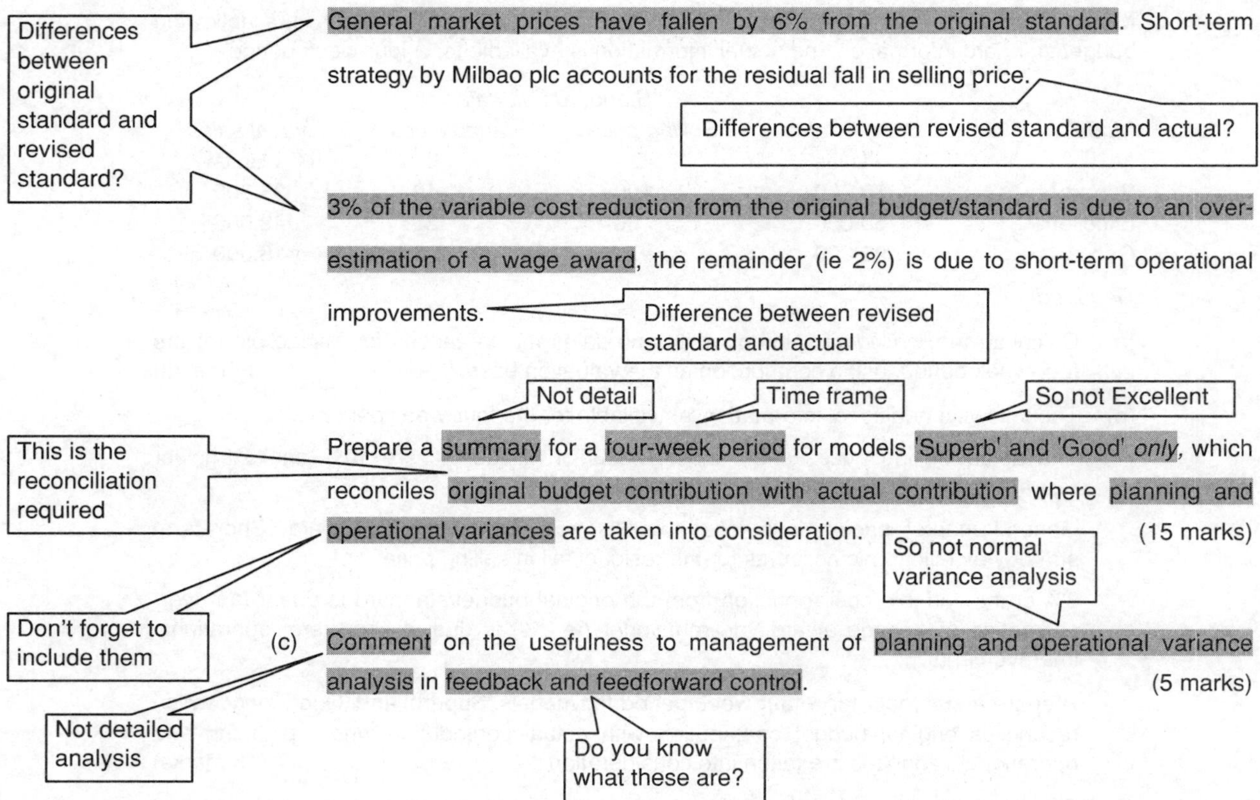
Differences between original standard and revised standard?
Differences between revised standard and actual?
Difference between revised standard and actual
Not detail
Time frame
So not Excellent
This is the reconciliation required
So not normal variance analysis
Don't forget to include them
Not detailed analysis
Do you know what these are?

General market prices have fallen by 6% from the original standard. Short-term strategy by Milbao plc accounts for the residual fall in selling price.

3% of the variable cost reduction from the original budget/standard is due to an over-estimation of a wage award, the remainder (ie 2%) is due to short-term operational improvements.

Prepare a summary for a four-week period for models 'Superb' and 'Good' *only*, which reconciles original budget contribution with actual contribution where planning and operational variances are taken into consideration. (15 marks)

(c) Comment on the usefulness to management of planning and operational variance analysis in feedback and feedforward control. (5 marks)

Framework for your answer

Part (a)

The **sales quantity variance** is calculated as the difference between the total actual sales quantity (given) in the budgeted proportions (you need to work out these proportions) and the budgeted sales quantities (given). You then need to value these differences at the standard contribution per unit (easy to calculate!)

The **sales mix variance** is calculated as the difference between the total actual sales quantity in the budgeted proportions (which you will have calculated already for the quantity variance) and the actual sales (given). You then need to value the difference at the standard contribution per unit (as above).

Part (b)

First reconcile **original budget contribution** (easy to calculate from information given in the question) to **revised budget contribution** via **planning variances**.

- The **selling price planning variance** is the difference between the original budget revenue and the revised budget revenue (based on original budget volumes).
- The **variable cost planning variance** is the difference between the original budget variable cost and the revised budget variable cost (based on original volumes).

Then take account of the **sales volume variance** (valued at the revised standard margin) to give the **revised standard contribution** (ie the contribution that should have been achieved for the actual activity level).

Lastly, calculate the **operational variances** (calculated using revised standards) to reconcile to actual contribution.

Part (c)

Useful for **feedback control** as operational variances can be controlled by management.

Useful for **feedforward control** as revised standards can be used when budgets next prepared.

38 SWANSEA PLC (50 marks) *90 mins*

(a) Swansea plc has entered into a long-term contract under which it will be required to make a number of cash payments (S) of £1 million each at a steady rate over the following twelve months. The company holds only a very small amount of cash at the present time.

Required

(i) Evaluate the following two alternative methods of providing for the payment of these amounts. (Ignore taxation and the time value of money.)

(1) *Sale of securities.* Swansea expects to make an average rate of return (i) of 10% on its holdings of securities over the next year. A sale of securities gives rise to a transaction cost (F) of £20, and following the sale the company will earn 4.5% per annum interest on the amount deposited. The optimal amount of cash raised by a sale of securities is given by the following formula.

$$Q = \sqrt{\frac{2FS}{i}}$$

(2) *Loan.* It would be possible for Swansea to borrow the £1 million required for payments at an interest rate of 13% of the amount loaned per annum. The arrangement fee of £6,000 for such a loan could be paid from existing cash resources. The amount borrowed would be placed as a term deposit at an interest rate of 8%, for drawing down when needed. (9 marks)

(ii) What are the possible limitations of the cash management model which Swansea plc is using in part (a)(i). (5 marks)

(b) Mumbles Ltd, a subsidiary of Swansea, wishes to install computerised equipment with a four year life which would involve an outlay of £5 million (residual value: nil). The Financial Director has carried out a study which shows that the project has a positive net present value when this is calculated using the shareholders' required rate of return as a discount rate.

Mumbles has asked Castles Leasing Limited ('Castles'), a subsidiary of a major bank, for a quotation for the acquisition of the equipment on a leasing contract under which maintenance of the equipment would be provided by Castles.

Castles has quoted an annual rental of £1,800,000. The maintenance services would cost Mumbles £190,000 annually if it had to obtain them from another source.

Mumbles pays corporate tax at a rate of 33%, and the tax becomes payable 12 months after the relevant cash flow. A writing down allowance can be claimed on a 25% reducing balance basis. A pre-tax borrowing rate of 18% applies to Mumbles.

Required

(i) Describe the key aspects of:

(1) Finance leases (2 marks)
(2) Hire purchase (2 marks)
(3) Sale and leaseback (2 marks)

(ii) Disregarding the savings in maintenance costs, evaluate whether Mumbles Ltd should lease the equipment from Castles or borrow money to purchase the equipment itself. (6 marks)

(iii) Calculate whether a different evaluation should be made if the savings in maintenance costs for Mumbles Ltd are accounted for. (2 marks)

(c) Gower Ltd is another subsidiary of Swansea plc and is required to make a rate of return on capital employed of at least 10% pa. For this purpose, capital employed is defined as fixed assets and investment in stocks. This rate of return is also applied as a hurdle rate for new investment projects. Gower has limited borrowing powers and all capital projects are centrally funded.

The following is an extract from Gower's accounts.

Profit and loss account for the year ended 31 December 20X4

	£m
Turnover	120
Cost of sales	(100)
Operating profit	20

Assets employed as at 31 December 20X4

	£m	£m
Fixed (net)		75
Current assets (including stocks £25m)	45	
Current liabilities	(32)	
		13
Net capital employed		88

Gower's production engineers wish to invest in a new computer-controlled press. The equipment cost is £14m. The residual value is expected to be £2m after four years operation, when the equipment will be shipped to a customer in South America.

The new machine is capable of improving the quality of the existing product and also of producing a higher volume. The firm's marketing team is confident of selling the increased volume by extending the credit period. The expected additional sales are:

Year 1	2,000,000 units
Year 2	1,800,000 units
Year 3	1,600,000 units
Year 4	1,600,000 units

Sales volume is expected to fall over time due to emerging competitive pressures. Competition will also necessitate a reduction in price by £0.5 each year from the £5 per unit proposed in the first year. Operating costs are expected to be steady at £1 per unit, and allocation of overheads (none of which are affected by the new project) by the central finance department is set at £0.75 per unit.

Higher production levels will require additional investment in stocks of £0.5m, which would be held at this level until the final stages of operation of the project. Customers at present settle accounts after 90 days on average, but some of the company's customers have recently been pressing for an extension to their credit period.

Required

(i) Determine whether the proposed capital investment is attractive to Gower, using the return on capital employed method, defined as average profit to average capital employed, ignoring debtors and creditors.
(*Note.* Ignore taxes.) (8 marks)

(ii) (1) Suggest *three* problems which arise with the use of the return on capital employed method for appraising new investments. (3 marks)

(2) In view of the problems associated with this method, explain why companies continue to use it in project appraisal. (3 marks)

(iii) Briefly discuss the dangers of offering more generous credit, and suggest ways of assessing customers' creditworthiness. (8 marks)

Approaching the answer

You should read through the requirement before working through and annotating the question as we have done so that you are aware of what things you are looking for.

(a) Swansea plc has entered into a long-term contract under which it will be required to make a number of cash payments (S) of £1 million each at a steady rate over the following twelve months. The company holds only a very small amount of cash at the present time.

This information will be significant

Can't use surplus cash holdings

Required

> Need to discuss other factors as well as calculation

(i) Evaluate the following two alternative methods of providing for the payment of these amounts. (Ignore taxation and the time value of money.)

(1) *Sale of securities.* Swansea expects to make an average rate of return (i) of 10% on its holdings of securities over the next year. A sale of securities gives rise to a transaction cost (F) of £20, and following the sale the company will earn 4.5% per annum interest on the amount deposited. The optimal amount of cash raised by a sale of securities is given by the following formula.

> What costs are involved? Is any income gained or lost?

> Inventory approach

$$Q = \sqrt{\frac{2FS}{i}}$$

(2) *Loan.* It would be possible for Swansea to borrow the £1 million required for payments at an interest rate of 13% of the amount loaned per annum. The arrangement fee of £6,000 for such a loan could be paid from existing cash resources. The amount borrowed would be placed as a term deposit at an interest rate of 8%, for drawing down when needed. (9 marks)

(ii) What are the possible limitations of the cash management model which Swansea plc is using (in part (a)(i)? (5 marks)

> What's wrong with its assumptions?

(b) Mumbles Ltd, a subsidiary of Swansea, wishes to install computerised equipment with a four year life which would involve an outlay of £5 million (residual value: nil). The Financial Director has carried out a study which shows that the project has a positive net present value when this is calculated using the shareholders' required rate of return as a discount rate.

> Investing decision been made

Mumbles has asked Castles Leasing Limited ('Castles'), a subsidiary of a major bank, for a quotation for the acquisition of the equipment on a leasing contract under which maintenance of the equipment would be provided by Castles.

Castles has quoted an annual rental of £1,800,000. The maintenance services would cost Mumbles £190,000 annually if it had to obtain them from another source.

> Should this be brought into calculation?

Mumbles pays corporate tax at a rate of 33%, and the tax becomes payable 12 months after the relevant cash flow. A writing down allowance can be claimed on a 25% reducing balance basis. A pre-tax borrowing rate of 18% applies to Mumbles.

> Cash effect

> Need to include tax cash flows

Required

(i) Describe the key aspects of:

> Lengthy discussion not required. Few quick points on each

(1) Finance leases (2 marks)
(2) Hire purchase (2 marks)
(3) Sale and leaseback (2 marks)

> Affect (iii)

(ii) Disregarding the savings in maintenance costs, evaluate whether Mumbles Ltd should lease the equipment from Castles or borrow money to purchase the equipment itself. (6 marks)

> Finance decision

(iii) Calculate whether a different evaluation should be made if the savings in maintenance costs for Mumbles Ltd are accounted for. (2 marks)

(c) Gower Ltd is another subsidiary of Swansea plc and is required to make a rate of return on capital employed of at least 10% pa. For this purpose, capital employed is

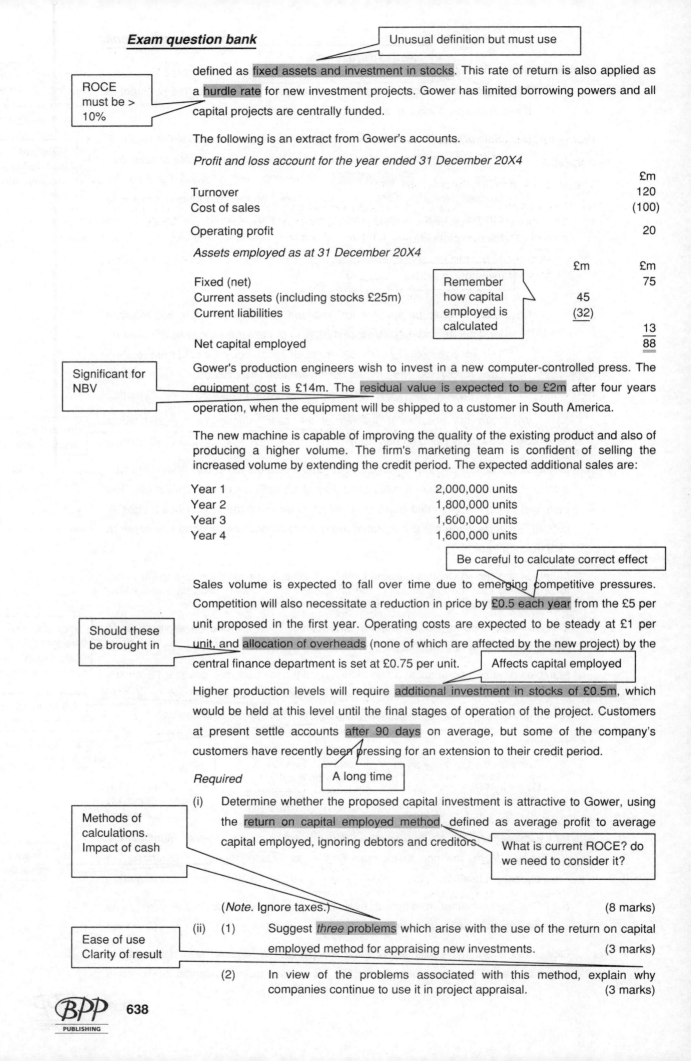

> Unusual definition but must use

> ROCE must be > 10%

defined as fixed assets and investment in stocks. This rate of return is also applied as a hurdle rate for new investment projects. Gower has limited borrowing powers and all capital projects are centrally funded.

The following is an extract from Gower's accounts.

Profit and loss account for the year ended 31 December 20X4

	£m
Turnover	120
Cost of sales	(100)
Operating profit	20

Assets employed as at 31 December 20X4

	£m	£m
Fixed (net)		75
Current assets (including stocks £25m)	45	
Current liabilities	(32)	
		13
Net capital employed		88

> Remember how capital employed is calculated

> Significant for NBV

Gower's production engineers wish to invest in a new computer-controlled press. The equipment cost is £14m. The residual value is expected to be £2m after four years operation, when the equipment will be shipped to a customer in South America.

The new machine is capable of improving the quality of the existing product and also of producing a higher volume. The firm's marketing team is confident of selling the increased volume by extending the credit period. The expected additional sales are:

Year 1	2,000,000 units
Year 2	1,800,000 units
Year 3	1,600,000 units
Year 4	1,600,000 units

> Be careful to calculate correct effect

> Should these be brought in

Sales volume is expected to fall over time due to emerging competitive pressures. Competition will also necessitate a reduction in price by £0.5 each year from the £5 per unit proposed in the first year. Operating costs are expected to be steady at £1 per unit, and allocation of overheads (none of which are affected by the new project) by the central finance department is set at £0.75 per unit.

> Affects capital employed

Higher production levels will require additional investment in stocks of £0.5m, which would be held at this level until the final stages of operation of the project. Customers at present settle accounts after 90 days on average, but some of the company's customers have recently been pressing for an extension to their credit period.

> A long time

Required

> Methods of calculations. Impact of cash

(i) Determine whether the proposed capital investment is attractive to Gower, using the return on capital employed method, defined as average profit to average capital employed, ignoring debtors and creditors.

> What is current ROCE? do we need to consider it?

(*Note.* Ignore taxes.) (8 marks)

> Ease of use Clarity of result

(ii) (1) Suggest *three* problems which arise with the use of the return on capital employed method for appraising new investments. (3 marks)

(2) In view of the problems associated with this method, explain why companies continue to use it in project appraisal. (3 marks)

(iii) Briefly discuss the dangers of offering more generous credit, and suggest ways of assessing customers' creditworthiness. (8 marks)

Potentially a lot of points for 8 marks. Need to make number of points, not spend too long on each

Framework for your answer

Part (a)(i)

The net costs of selling the securities are:

- Transaction costs (you need to calculate number of transactions using the formula)
- Less interest received on cash balances held (calculated on average balances)
- Plus interest foregone on securities (again calculated on average balance)

Answer also brings out problems of selling securities – the evaluation required is more than just financial calculations.

The net costs of using the loan finance are:

- Interest paid (on full loan balance)
- Less interest received on cash balance held (calculated on average balance)
- Plus arrangement fee

Again the answer mentions wider issues, in this case repayment problems.

Part (a)(ii)

The answer takes each element of the formula in turn, discusses the assumptions made and then considers whether the model misses anything out.

Part (b)(i)

Certain key considerations need to be discussed with all three methods:

- Who has ownership
- Responsibilities
- Taxation
- Effect on accounts

Part (b)(ii) and (iii)

It is easier to show the payments for each year in a single column. Bringing tax in means that you have to use an after tax discount rate and consider the tax implications of all revenues and payments. Don't assume that the sole tax implication is the ability to claim capital allowances. Your answer will be incomplete if you do not calculate the total net present value **and** make appropriate comparisons.

Part (c)(i)

You need first to calculate the current ROCE – all the information is used. A summary calculation, plus workings for each element, is the best way to show the impact of the press. Remember that you are after one average figure for the lifetime of the press. A conclusion comparing the ROCE of the press with the target rate and the current rate is essential.

Part (c)(ii)

The answer covers the elements contained in the calculation and discusses their nature (easy to manipulate) and how they are used. It also considers what the calculation does not contain (the cash movements). Different criteria apply though in practice – is it easy to do the calculation? Is its result easily understandable?

Part (c)(iii)

The first part involves assessment of the current position, and what will happen if the period is extended. The second part brings out the different types of evidence that can be obtained on prospective credit customers.

Exam answer bank

1 OVER EMPHASIS

Tutor's hint. You might think we're being a bit mean but we've given you an exam-standard question straight away. But don't panic! You could have probably made a fair attempt at this question before you had even opened this Study Text.

As well as using information from Chapter 1, you could **have introduced material from Paper 1.2** (such as on information, on the differences between financial accounting and management accounting and on non-financial indicators). It is important to remember that your studies are **cumulative**: knowledge from lower levels needs to be brought forward and applied as you progress through your ACCA exams.

Answers to this question would have been wide and varied so don't worry if yours is not too similar to ours! It would have been perfectly acceptable to draw upon your **own experience** where relevant.

Take note of the **layout** of our answer. The basic principles adopted here have been used throughout this answer bank where relevant and you should endeavour to use them too. They will make your answer much easier to mark than an uninterrupted flow of words covering two sheets of paper.

- **Short paragraphs**
- **Headings**
- **Emboldening** (you can underline) of key words and phrases
- **Reference in headings to key words/phrases in the question**

According to the CIMA's *Official Terminology*, the identification, generation, presentation, interpretation and use of information for planning, control and decision making are all important aspects of management accounting, along with providing information for formulating strategy, safeguarding assets, optimising the use of resources and so on.

Planning

Planning involves **establishing objectives** and **selecting appropriate strategies** to achieve those objectives. It forces management to **think ahead** systematically in both the short term (via the setting of budgets) and the long term (via strategic planning).

Decision making

Decision making is carried out at all levels of an organisation. At the **strategic** level, a decision might be taken to close down a division, at the **tactical** level to terminate a member of staff's employment and at the **operational** level to reduce a customer's credit limit.

Control

Control involves two stages. The performance of an organisation as set out in detailed operational plans is **compared** with actual performance on a regular and continuous basis. Any **deviations** from the plans are **identified** (variance analysis) and **corrective action** is taken by the manager responsible for the area in question as part of a system of responsibility accounting. The plans are then **reviewed** in the light of the first stage of control and modified to take account of any changes to the parameters upon which the plans were based.

Information required

Planning, control and decision making all require different types of information. **Planning information** must be essentially **forward looking** and must include **non-financial information** relating to personnel, markets and so on. The most important requirements of **decision-making information** are that it is **relevant, timely, accurate** and **appropriate**. **Control information**, on the other hand, is mostly **historic**.

The impact of the financial accounting system

As mentioned earlier, management accounting is concerned with the provision of information for planning, control and decision making. **In the past the most comprehensive information system was the financial accounting system**. As the **control** function relies on **historic** information, the **financial accounting system** provides a ready **source** of suitable information. Moreover, its suitability has only been reinforced in the past by the **concentration on the financial results** of an organisation.

Such information is entirely **unsuitable for planning and decision making**, however. The use of absorption costing to comply with the requirements of SSAP 9, for example, produces information which is totally misleading for product and output decisions.

It is because accounting information is so readily available from the financial accounting system that organisations have tended to **concentrate their efforts on control**, either disregarding the planning and decision making functions because of a lack of suitable information *or* using totally inappropriate information for planning and decision-making purposes.

The value of non-financial indicators

Financial results are no longer seen as the only way of assessing an organisation's performance, however, and it has recently become evident that **effective control** is possible using both **financial and non-financial information**. For example, there has been an increase in the use of non-financial indicators which are based on information more suited to planning and decision making. Moreover, the increase in the use of **activity based costing** and other activity based techniques means that information more relevant to planning and decision making is now available.

The impact of the nature of the organisation

The nature of an organisation may of course have an **impact on the relative importance of the control activity**. For example, public sector organisations may place more emphasis on control. This may be due to the need for greater accountability and is not necessarily to the detriment of the other functions of management accounting.

Other factors to consider

Other factors which may influence the relative importance of planning and decision- making activities compared with control activities include the following.

(a) The **nature of the environment in which the organisation operates**. Dynamic environments may require more emphasis on planning.

(b) The **management accounting resources** and the **sophistication of the information system** available. Some organisations may wish to spend more effort on planning but they may not have the resources available.

(c) The **complexity of the organisation**. More complex organisations may need to expend more effort on the control activity.

Conclusion

It is therefore **not necessarily detrimental** for an organisation to emphasise the control function in its management accounting activity.

However, it may be that organisations have **concentrated too much** on the control aspect of management accounting simply because of a **lack of suitable information** for planning and decision-making purposes. It is possible that as the importance of **non-financial results increases** and more **sophisticated management accounting techniques** are employed, the provision of information for planning, control and decision making will all become equally important for the management accountant.

2 RYMAN COUPLETS LTD

Tutor's hint. Although you need to do lots of calculations in the answer to this exam-standard question, you have already covered absorption costing and marginal costing in your earlier studies so you should have had no problem with the techniques and processes required.

When drawing up the marginal costing statement in (a)(i), don't forget that only variable costs are included in cost of production and sales, and stocks are valued at variable production cost. As well as the direct costs of production included in (a)(i), you also need to include the overheads absorbed (overhead cost per unit × number of units produced) in the absorption costing statement in (a)(ii). Closing stock is valued at full cost.

Because budget figures are being considered in **(a)(ii), over and under absorption does not occur**. There would be no under- or over-absorbed overhead if actual production volumes turned out to be the same as budgeted production volumes.

In part (a)(iii), you can use the same direct costs as in (a)(ii) but the overheads absorbed have changed.

Part (b) (the **comparison of absorption costing and marginal costing results**) is likely to be **examined fairly regularly** so if you made mistakes you must work through our answer carefully so that you can find out where you went wrong. There are three distinct parts to part (b), so make sure that you answer all of them.

Part (c)(i) of the question tests your understanding of a particular aspect of cost behaviour (that only variable costs increase if production increases within the relevant range). In part (c)(ii), total variable production costs will change (× 125%) because of the increase in production. Because sales levels have not increased, closing stock will increase by the additional production volumes (25% of the original production volumes).

In the 'real' exam, you may run out of time before you get to part (c)(ii), but it would have only have been worth about 5 marks.

(a) We begin by calculating the overhead cost per unit of the three products using the two different absorption bases.

Product		*Machine hours per annum*	*Labour hours per annum*
		Hours	Hours
X		60,000	40,000
Y		20,000	80,000
Z		20,000	20,000
		100,000	140,000
Budgeted annual overhead costs		£560,000	£560,000
Absorption rate		£5.60 per machine hour	£4 per direct labour hour
Overhead cost per unit	X	£16.80 per unit	£8 per unit
	Y	£5.60 per unit	£16 per unit
	Z	£11.20 per unit	£8 per unit

(i) **Marginal costing**

	X	*Y*	*Z*	*20X2 Total*	*X*	*Y*	*Z*	*20X3 Total*
	£'000	£'000	£'000	£'000	£'000	£'000	£'000	£'000
Opening stocks	0	0	0	0	96	72	84	252
Direct prod costs	320	360	120	800	320	360	120	800
	320	360	120	800	416	432	204	1,052
Closing stocks	96	72	84	252	192	216	36	444
Variable cost of production and sales	224	288	36	548	224	216	168	608
Sales	420	560	75	1,055	420	420	350	1,190
Contribution	196	272	39	507	196	204	182	582
Overheads				560				560
Profit/(loss)				(53)				22

(ii) **Absorption costing, using a machine hour rate of recovery**

	X	Y	Z	*20X2* Total	X	Y	Z	*20X3* Total
	£'000	£'000	£'000	£'000	£'000	£'000	£'000	£'000
Opening stock	0	0	0	0	196.8	94.4	162.4	453.6
Direct costs of production	320.0	360.0	120.0	800.0	320.0	360.0	120.0	800.0
O/hds absorbed	336.0	112.0	112.0	560.0	336.0	112.0	112.0	560.0
	656.0	472.0	232.0	1,360.0	852.8	566.4	394.4	1,813.6
Closing stock (W)	196.8	94.4	162.4	453.6	393.6	283.2	69.6	746.4
Full cost of sales	459.2	377.6	69.6	906.4	459.2	283.2	324.8	1,067.2
Sales	420.0	560.0	75.0	1,055.0	420.0	420.0	350.0	1,190.0
Profit	(39.2)	182.4	5.4	148.6	(39.2)	136.8	25.2	122.8

Working

Per unit: X £(16 + 16.8) = £32.80; Y £23.60; Z £23.20

(iii) **Absorption costing, using a direct labour hour rate of recovery**

	X	Y	Z	*20X2* Total	X	Y	Z	*20X3* Total
	£'000	£'000	£'000	£'000	£'000	£'000	£'000	£'000
Opening stock	0	0	0	0	144	136	140	420
Direct costs of prod	320	360	120	800	320	360	120	800
Overheads absorbed	160	320	80	560	160	320	80	560
	480	680	200	1,360	624	816	340	1,780
Closing stock (W)	144	136	140	420	288	408	60	756
Full cost of sales	336	544	60	940	336	408	280	1,024
Sales	420	560	75	1,055	420	420	350	1,190
Profit	84	16	15	115	84	12	70	166

Working

Per unit: X (£16 + £8) = £24; Y £34; Z £20

(b) The **figures differ because of the overhead content in stock carried forward or stock brought forward in each period, and thus in the valuation of opening and closing stocks.**

(i)

20X2	*Stock b/f*	*Stock c/f*	*Stock change*	*Profit/(loss)*
	£'000	£'000	£'000	£'000
Marginal costing	0	252.0	+ 252.0	(53.0)
Full costing - machine hr method	0	453.6	+ 453.6	148.6
Full costing - labour hr method	0	420.0	+ 420.0	115.0

The difference in the stock change between each method explains the difference in profit; for example the difference in the stock change with a machine hour recovery rate is (in £'000s) 453.6 – 252 = 201.6. The difference in profit is 148.6 – (–53) = 201.6.

(ii)

20X3	*Stock b/f*	*Stock c/f*	*Stock change*	*Profit/(loss)*
	£'000	£'000	£'000	£'000
Direct costing	252.0	444.0	+ 192.0	22.0
Full costing - machine hr method	453.6	746.4	+ 292.8	122.8
Full costing - labour hr method	420.0	756.0	+ 336.0	166.0

Once again, the difference in profit is explained by the difference in the value of stock changes; for example, the difference in profit between the two methods of absorption costing ((166 – 122.8) = £43,200) is the same as the difference in stock changes (336 – 292.8).

How to improve the absorption costing figures

The absorption costing method of stock valuations might be improved if separate departmental overhead absorption rates could be used for machining work (for which a machine hour rate would be applied) and for finishing work (for which a direct labour hour rate would be applied). Total overheads would need to be apportioned fairly between the two departments, so that the more equitable method of recovering fixed costs in product costs would be possible. This system of separate departmental rates is fairer because it would make allowance for both the machine hours and the labour hours worked on each product.

Which is correct?

Of the three costing systems, **none is more 'correct' than the other**. Each is equally 'right' or 'wrong'. Different costing principles have been applied to stock valuations, therefore different (short-term) period profits will be reported.

(c) (i) If production in 20X2 is increased by 25% the **extra costs** incurred in producing the additional stock would be the **variable costs** of production.

Total direct costs in original budget for 20X2	£800,000
A 25% increase in costs would be	£200,000
Interest rate per annum	14%
Annual interest cost of extra stocks	£28,000

(ii) If the increase in production is budgeted and fixed costs remain unaffected by the higher output, the **overhead recovery rates would be reduced**, as follows.

		Machine hours		*Labour hours*	
Budget		(125% of 100,000) = 125,000		(125% of 140,000) = 175,000	
Budgeted overheads		£560,000		£560,000	
Recovery rate		£4.48 per machine hour		£3.20 per labour hour	
Unit costs:	X	£(16 + 13.44)	= £29.44	£(16 + 6.40)	= £22.40
	Y	£(18 + 4.48)	= £22.48	£(18 +12.80)	= £30.80
	Z	£(12 + 8.96)	= £20.96	£(12 + 6.40)	= £18.40

	Marginal costing		**Absorption costing Machine hr method**		**Absorption costing Labour hr method**	
	£'000	£'000	£'000	£'000	£'000	£'000
20X2						
Opening stock		0		0		0
Production costs:						
Direct (800 × 125%)		1,000		1,000		1,000
Fixed		560		560		560
		1,560		1,560		1,560
Closing stocks						
X (6K + (20K × 25%))	176		324		246	
Y (4K + (20K × 25%))	162		202		277	
Z (7K + (10K × 25%))	114		199		175	
		452		725		698
Cost of sales		1,108		835		862
Sales		1,055		1,055		1,055
Profit		(53)		220		193

The loss in marginal costing would be unaffected, but with absorption costing a larger proportion of fixed costs would be carried forward in closing stock values, so that total profits in 20X2 would increase.

3 SOUTHCOTT LTD

> **Tutor's hint**. Because ABC is new to you, this first ABC question in the bank is **not exam standard.** Nevertheless, you need to be able to provide a good answer as it tests the key skills you need for the topic.
>
> Part (a) should have caused you no problems. The original absorption basis was course days and so you simply needed to calculate the number of course days (number of courses × duration of course) for each course and total the results. Dividing total overheads by this figure gives an overhead cost per course day. Overheads are included in the cost of a course on the basis of the course duration.
>
> Part (b) provides an example of the application of ABC to a **service organisation.** The **principles** to apply are the **same** as those you would apply when dealing with a manufacturing organisation.
>
> ***Step 1.*** Determine the cost driver for each category of overhead.
>
> ***Step 2.*** Calculate a cost per cost driver (cost/number of cost drivers)
>
> ***Step 3.*** Include overhead in the cost of a course on the basis of the number of cost drivers generated by a course.
>
> Don't forget to provide **reasons** for your choice of cost drivers. A 'tag-on' requirement like this might be worth the three marks that can make the difference between a pass and a fail.

(a)

	Auditing	*Taxation*	*Total*
No of courses sold	50	30	
Duration of course (days)	2	3	
No of course days	100	90	190

$$\text{Overhead cost per course day} = \frac{£152,625}{190} = £803.29$$

Overhead cost per course

Auditing £803.29 × 2 days = £1,606.58
Taxation £803.29 × 3 days = £2,409.87

(b) **Overhead costs per course using activity based costing**

		Auditing £ per course		*Taxation* £ per course
Centre hire at £328.95 per day	(× 2)	657.90	(× 3)	986.85
Enquiries administration at £2.50 per enquiry	(× 175)	437.50	(× 70)	175.00
Brochures at £3 per brochure	(× 300)	900.00	(× 200)	600.00
Overhead cost per course		1,995.40		1,761.85

Workings

1 $$\text{Centre hire cost per course day} = \frac{£62,500}{190} = £328.95$$

2 $$\text{Enquiries administration cost per enquiry} = \frac{£27,125}{(50 \times 175) + (30 \times 70)} = £2.50$$

3 $$\text{Brochure cost per brochure printed} = \frac{£63,000}{(50 \times 300) + (30 \times 200)} = £3 \text{ per brochure}$$

Reasons for the choice of cost drivers

(i) The cost driver for centre hire costs is the number of course days, since the centre is hired at a standard daily rate.

(ii) The cost driver for enquiries administration is the number of enquiries, since more enquiries would result in an increase in the cost of enquiries administration.

(iii) The cost driver for brochure costs is the number of brochures printed, since an increase in the number of brochures printed would lead to a higher cost.

4 ABC

> **Tutor's hint.** This is one of the questions from the pilot paper for 2.4, so it is definitely exam standard.
>
> In the exam you could face a written question or a calculation-based question on ABC. The calculations will never be too onerous but written question have an in-built danger - you might be tempted to write all you know about a topic. So **keep to the point** in this solution. Cover the areas required only. Notice how the headings in our solution tie in with the individual requirements of the question.
>
> Although not specifically asked for, we have also provided a brief introduction which explains what ABC is and why it was developed. Don't spend too much time on this – it simply sets the scene and provides a framework for your answer.
>
> The key issue to which you need to refer in part (b) is **controllability**: if a manager can control a cost driver then he should be responsible for the associated cost.

(a) **What is activity based costing (ABC)?**

Traditional absorption costing systems assume that all products **consume all resources in proportion to their production volumes.** While this may be true for overheads such as power costs, it does not necessarily hold for all overheads, or an increasing proportion of them, especially those connected with support services. Absorption costing **tends to allocate too great a proportion of such overheads to high volume products** (which cause relatively little diversity and hence use fewer support services) and too small a proportion of overheads to low volume products (which cause greater diversity and therefore use more support services).

ABC attempts to overcome this problem by **identifying the activities or transactions (cost drivers) which underlie an organisation's activities and which cause the incidence of the activity, and hence the cost of the activity, to increase.**

Although ABC has been introduced in a wide variety of organisations, there are a number of factors which impact on the effectiveness of ABC.

Product mix

ABC is basically a **way of apportioning overheads** between products so as to produce more accurate product costs for planning, control and decision-making purposes. In this respect there is no point in applying it unless an organisation's product mix contains at least two products (as all overheads are attributable to a product if that is the only one produced by an organisation).

ABC can still be useful in single product environment, however. Many decision-making situations rely on the **division of costs into fixed and variable components** (CVP analysis, for example). The more realistic analysis of costs using ABC claimed by its proponents allows more accurate decisions to be made.

Significance of overheads

The **traditional absorption costing approach** to dealing with overheads was developed at a time when most organisations produced only a narrow range of products and when **overhead costs** were only a very **small fraction of total costs**, direct labour and direct material costs accounting for the largest proportion of costs. Errors in attributing overheads to products were therefore not too significant.

Nowadays, however, the situation is very different.

(i) **Direct labour** may account for **as little as 5% of a product's cost.**

(ii) With the advent of **advanced manufacturing technology, support activities** such as setting-up, production scheduling, first item inspection and data processing have **increased**.

  (1) These support activities assist the efficient manufacture of a wide range of products and are not, in general, affected by changes in production volume. Instead, the level of such activities tends to vary in the long term according to the range and complexity of the products manufactured. The wider the range and the more complex the product, the more support services will be required. To allocate them to products on the basis of some measure of production volume (as would be the case if absorption costing were used) would therefore be entirely inappropriate.

(2) Support department costs have a tendency to increase. Management therefore need additional information to enable them to manage and control these costs.

In a today's modern organisations with significant levels of support department overheads, ABC can therefore be effectively introduced and is likely to have significant value.

ABC method of charging costs

Step 1. Identify an organisation's major activities

Step 2. Identify the factors which determine the size of the costs of an activity/cause the costs of an activity. These are known as cost drivers. For example, the costs of a credit investigations activity in a bank is likely to be driven by the number of credit investigations carried out.

Step 3. Collect the costs of each activity into cost pools.

Step 4. Charge costs to products on the basis of their usage of the activity. A product's usage of an activity is measured by the number of the activity's cost driver it generates. For example, if 1,000 credit investigations are carried out and a particular loan requires 5 credit investigations, that loan will be allocated 5/1000 of the costs in the credit investigations activity cost pool.

Availability of information collection procedures and resources

One of the principal disadvantages of ABC is that it may be **difficult to collect the information required** to enable ABC to be introduced.

The various activities within the organisation need to be established (possibly using observation and employee interviews) and cost drivers identified. A database of activities, their occurrence, their cost and cost drivers needs to be set up. This is a **huge wealth of information which may not have been recorded before**. Information collection and retrieval systems may therefore need to be expanded and improved. Although developments in information technology allow for more sophisticated information systems, the **cost** of required changes and improvements **may outweigh the anticipated benefits** of ABC and make its introduction unsuitable.

Other factors

ABC is likely to be more effective in an organisation in which **managers** embrace change. If there is resistance to change it may be difficult to sell the benefits of ABC to management and they may be unwilling to participate in its implementation.

(b) One of the principal problems in assessing management performance centres on ensuring that the costs and revenues upon which managers are being assessed are actually **controllable** by the manager.

It is claimed that ABC relates costs to products/departments/activities in **less arbitrary ways** than traditional absorption costing, however.

(i) The **reapportionment of service department costs** is avoided because ABC establishes separate cost pools for support activities and the costs of such activities are assigned directly to products/department/services through cost driver rates.

(ii) ABC uses **many cost drivers** as absorption bases instead of the two traditionally used under absorption costing. Absorption rates under ABC are therefore claimed to be closely linked to the causes of overhead costs and hence ABC should produce more realistic product costs.

The application of ABC should therefore provide a **more accurate information base** than absorption costing. The impact of management decisions should be more evident and it should be possible to establish more accurate spheres of responsibility upon which managers should be assessed. The assessment of management performance should therefore be more accurate.

5 JOBBING ENGINEERING COMPANY

Tutor's hint. Of exam standard, this question covers a range of topics all loosely tied together by the topic 'job costing'. The mixture of calculation and discursive requirements are a typical question format.

A Paper 1.2 exam question might require you to calculate a job cost or a job price. It is unlikely that you will encounter anything so straightforward in Paper 2.4, however. Part (a) of this question is a good example of the type of requirement you could face as it asks you to consider the **reasonableness of a particular management accounting technique**. In fact, your ability to criticise techniques is a key exam skill. You should by now have enough management accounting knowledge to make a reasoned judgement about the suitability of a particular approach in particular circumstances. Draw on your own experience if relevant.

In part (b) the 'better method' you suggest should overcome the problems you highlighted in part (a). Notice that we have provided two approaches for production overhead and do not be afraid to comment on the lack of information to enable you to make a more informed judgement.

Part (c) enables you to draw on a wide range of issues. There are two factors to cover – **controlling costs** and **pricing**. Although we have not yet covered budgeting in this Study Text, it is a topic you should have dealt with in your earlier studies. In terms of pricing, we have suggested the organisation take competition into account.

(a) The problem with the method adopted for estimating the costs lies with the **addition of a percentage to cover all costs** other than direct costs. The percentage used is based on the full year's figures ending in March of this year.

	£'000	
Overheads	383.0	
Administration costs	118.5	
Selling costs	192.0	
	693.5	47.5%
Direct costs	1,460.0	52.5%
Total costs	2,153.5	100.0%

This **assumes that overheads, administration costs and selling costs all stand in the same relationship to direct costs**. In practice this is extremely **unlikely** to be the case: overheads are probably partly fixed and partly variable; administration costs are perhaps mainly fixed but may need to be adjusted to allow for wage inflation; some selling costs will vary from item to item, others will fall under headings such as general advertising, which may be fairly stable.

In view of this there is a great danger that the size of the percentage uplift could result in **prices** that are seriously **over or understated.**

(b) **Production overheads**

These can reasonably be assumed to be related **to the cost of direct labour** such that the following costs would be allocated to job 878.

		£
Grinding	(175,000/200,000 × 2,000)	1,750
Finishing	(208,000/260,000 × 1,800)	1,440

Alternatively the total departmental hours can be calculated so as to give an **overhead rate per hour**, as follows.

		Hours
Grinding	(200,000/5)	40,000
Finishing	(260,000/6)	43,333
		83,333

		Overhead rate	*Total overhead*
Grinding	(175,000/40,000)	4.375	1,750
Finishing	(208,000/43,333)	4.800	1,440

Administration and selling costs

Administration and selling costs to be applied to job 878 are much more difficult to ascertain. The mere fact that this exercise is being performed by the company's first full-time accountant suggests that administration costs may be significantly different from last year's. The imminent recession could have a major impact on selling costs.

However, in the absence of the further information required estimates must be made on the **basis of the historical data**, as follows.

			Job 878	*Full year*
		£	£	£
Direct material (as stated)			9,000	1,000,000
Direct labour (as stated)			3,800	480,000
			12,800	1,480,000
Overhead (as above):	grinding	1,750		
	finishing	1,440		
			3,190	383,000
			15,990	1,843,000
Administration costs				
(118,500/1,843,000 × 15,990)			1,028	118,500
Selling costs			17,018	1,961,500
(192,000/1,961,500 × 17,018)			1,666	192,000
Total cost			18,684	2,153,500
Return required (balancing figure)			3,737	
Selling price (100/$83^1/_3$ × total cost)			22,421	

The revised cost is slightly lower than that originally calculated, but as indicated above it should be treated with extreme caution.

(c) **Improvements to the accounting information presently provided**

(i) The **nature of costs** should be further investigated to determine which are fixed and which are variable. This is particularly important in view of the imminence of a recession for the engineering industry. In such circumstances prices may need to be determined on the basis of the contribution generated towards fixed costs rather than on the existing 'cost plus' basis.

(ii) A **budget** should be drawn up for all figures, but in particular for administration costs and selling costs. The allocation of overheads should be based on what it is reasonable to expect in the current period rather than on historic figures.

Monitoring of actual costs, comparing them with budgeted figures and investigating variances will help to establish the level of understanding of cost behaviour which (i) indicates is necessary.

(iii) If possible the **pricing policies of competitors** should be ascertained so that management may be made aware of how the company's prices compare. It does not appear that prices much lower than those currently being charged are possible, but other companies may be significantly more expensive; it may be possible to earn greater premiums. Whatever the case the information will be useful for marketing.

(iv) In connection with (iii) above, the required return of $16^2/_3$% appears to be arbitrary and (in the light of the previous year's figures) over optimistic. As noted in (i) above, fixed costs should be covered first; thereafter the market is the main factor to consider. The aim should be to beat the competition before beating an **ideal profit margin**.

6 FERTILISER

Tutor's hint. Although not exam standard in terms of length, this question provides valuable practice in drawing up process accounts.

We'll analyse this question using the **four-step approach** to process costing questions set out in the Study Text. The first thing we need to establish, however, is the WIP valuation method adopted by the company. The definition of throughput indicates that ABC Ltd uses the **weighted average method** as no distinction is made between opening WIP and units introduced.

Step 1 for process 1 **Determine output and losses and prepare a statement of equivalent units**

You need to ensure that output + closing WIP + normal loss = material introduced. If it doesn't, there must be an abnormal loss or gain. Here the balancing figure is an abnormal loss. Units of normal loss are valued at zero equivalent units but units of abnormal loss are taken to be one full equivalent unit each.

Step 2 for process 1 **Calculate cost per unit of output, losses and WIP and prepare a statement of cost per equivalent unit**

Simply divide the costs by the appropriate number of equivalent units. Don't forget to include the production overhead at 150% of direct wages cost.

Step 3 for process 1 **Calculate total cost of output, losses and WIP and prepare a statement of evaluation**

Value the equivalent units derived in Step 1 at the cost per equivalent unit derived in Step 2. Remember that units of normal loss have no value.

Step 4 for process 1 **Complete account**

In this question you were only required to prepare process accounts but in other questions you may need to draw up accounts for scrap, abnormal loss and so on. The process account simply shows how the quantity and cost of the various inputs (on the debit side of the account) are spread across the various outputs (on the credit side). The figures for inputs are provided in the question, the figures for outputs are derived in step 3. Don't forget to include normal loss in terms of quantity.

Step 1 for process 2

For this process you have to include the opening WIP when calculating the normal loss. (There was no opening WIP in process 1.)

Step 2 for process 2

Again you need to include the various costs included in opening WIP and the cost of the material introduced from process 1.

Step 3 for process 2

The approach here is exactly as for process 1.

Step 4 for process 2

The inputs need to include the opening WIP and the material introduced from process 1.

PROCESS 1

Step 1. STATEMENT OF EQUIVALENT UNITS

	Total	*Material*	*Conversion costs*
	Kgs	Kgs	Kgs
Output to process 2	13,100	13,100	13,100
Closing WIP	2,000	2,000	1,000
Normal loss (15% × (10,500 + 7,200 – 2,000))	2,355	-	-
Abnormal loss (balancing figure)	245	245	245
Material introduced	17,700	15,345	14,345

Step 2. STATEMENT OF COST PER EQUIVALENT UNIT

		Material		Conversion costs
Costs incurred during period				
(£(4,960 + 14,700))		£19,660	(£(17,160 + 25,740))	£42,900
Equivalent units of production		15,345		14,345
Cost per equivalent unit		£1.2812		£2.9906

Step 3. STATEMENT OF EVALUATION

	Material		Conversion costs		Total
	Equiv units	£	Equiv units	£	£
Fully worked units	13,100	16,784	13,100	39,177	55,961
Closing WIP	2,000	2,562	1,000	2,990	5,552
Abnormal loss	245	314	245	733	1,047
	15,345	19,660	14,345	42,900	62,560

Step 4. PROCESS 1

	Kgs	£		Kgs	£
Raw material			Process 2 account	13,100	55,961
W	10,500	4,960	Normal loss	2,355	-
X	7,200	14,700	Abnormal loss	245	1,047
		19,660	Closing work in		
Wages		17,160	progress	2,000	5,552
Production overhead					
(150% × £17,160)		25,740			
	17,700	62,560		17,700	62,560

PROCESS 2

Step 1. STATEMENT OF EQUIVALENT UNITS

	Total	Process 1 material	Conversion costs
	Kgs	Kgs	Kgs
Finished goods	20,545	20,545	20,545
Closing WIP	1,500	1,500	750
Normal loss (10% × (8,400 + 13,100 + 4,050 – 1,500))	2,405	-	-
Abnormal loss (balancing figure)	1,100	1,100	1,100
	25,550	23,145	22,395

Step 2. STATEMENT OF COST PER EQUIVALENT UNIT

	Process 1/material		Conversion costs	
Opening WIP	£(8,720 + 2,000)	£10,720	£(3,600 + 7,200)	£10,800
Costs incurred during period	£(55,961 + 15,600)	£71,561	£(8,600 + 17,200)	£25,800
		£82,281		£36,600
Equivalent units		23,145		22,395
Cost per equivalent unit		£3.5550		£1.6343

Step 3. STATEMENT OF EVALUATION

	Process 1/Materials		Conversion costs		Total
	Equiv units	£	Equiv units	£	£
Fully worked units	20,545	73,037	20,545	33,577	106,614
Closing WIP	1,500	5,333	750	1,226	6,559
Abnormal loss	1,100	3,911	1,100	1,797	5,708
	23,145	82,281	22,395	36,600	118,881

Step 4. PROCESS 2

	Kgs	£		Kgs	£
Opening WIP	8,400	21,520	Finished goods control		
Process 1 account	13,100	55,961	account	20,545	106,614
Raw material	4,050	15,600	Normal loss	2,405	-
Wages		8,600	Abnormal loss	1,100	5,708
Production overhead			Closing WIP	1,500	6,559
(200% × £8,600)		17,200			
	25,550	118,881		25,550	118,881

7 PROCESS COSTING

Tutor's hint. A written question on process costing is perhaps more likely that a calculation-based one, and this exam-standard question is an indication of what you could encounter.

The first requirement of the question is to **define process costing**. Be careful that you do not cover the other requirements of the question in this introduction otherwise you will have less to say in later paragraphs.

The other requirements of the question are to explain how to account for three particular features associated with process accounting.

Accounting for incomplete production hinges on the idea of **equivalent units**, a concept that you must explain. The inclusion of a **simple numerical example** within a discursive question is often a quicker and clearer way of explaining a point than (what might become) long, rambling sentences. This is a perfect opportunity to do this. But don't make life difficult for yourself. Keep thing simple. Notice how our cost per equivalent unit is a nice round number. Don't decide on a figure for 'costs incurred during period' until you know the equivalent units produced. You can then choose a 'nice' cost per equivalent unit, with costs incurred as the balancing figure.

You need to cover **normal and abnormal losses and abnormal gains** in the next section and explain how they differ in terms of equivalent units, valuation and scrap.

As well as providing a simple definition of joint products, there are **four apportionment bases** to describe when explaining how to account for joint products. You could have provided simple examples here, but it is highly unlikely that you would have had enough time.

Process costing is the costing method which is used when goods or services are produced in a series of **continuous operations or processes**. It is **not possible to identify the costs associated with individual cost units** and therefore the costs are **averaged out** over all the units produced in a period.

This costing method can be contrasted with job costing, batch costing and contract costing. With each of these three methods it is possible to identify and allocate costs to individual cost units and very little averaging is involved.

Accounting for incomplete production

The averaging procedure in process costing results in a cost per unit produced in the period. However this unit rate would be distorted if no account was taken of units which are only part complete, ie work in progress.

This problem is overcome by using the concept of **equivalent units**, whereby work in progress is valued according to its degree of completion. A simple example will demonstrate the application of this concept.

Period 1

Opening work in progress	nil
Closing work in progress	1,000 units; 25% complete
Units transferred to next process	24,000
Cost incurred during period	£84,875

Equivalent units produced	=	24,000 + (1,000 × 25%)
	=	24,250
Cost per equivalent unit	=	£84,875/24,250
	=	£3.50

This unit cost would be applied to the completed units and to the incomplete units in progress, resulting in the following valuations.

Units transferred to next process = 24,000 × £3.50 = £84,000
Closing work in process = 250 equivalent units × £3.50 = £875

The 1,000 units in progress are therefore treated as the equivalent of 250 complete units, ie 1,000 × 25% = 250 equivalent units.

Process losses

When losses occur in the process they must be taken into account in calculating unit costs for the period. When a certain level of loss is expected, an allowance is made for **normal loss**, ie an expected level of loss for a given volume of activity. The normal loss does not absorb any of the production costs and it is not included in the calculation of equivalent units of production. The normal loss units have either zero value; or if they can be sold as scrap they are valued at their scrap value and this amount is subtracted from the total process costs for the period.

Abnormal losses and gains arise when process losses are higher or lower than the expected level of normal loss. Abnormal losses and gains are valued separately at the same cost as good units and their scrap value is not included in the calculation of process costs for the period. The full cost of abnormal losses and gains is transferred from the process account to a separate account. Their scrap value is then offset against this cost and the net balance on the account is transferred to the profit and loss account.

Joint products

Joint products arise when two or more products are manufactured in the same process and each of the products has a significant sales value compared with the others.

The cost of the joint process must be **apportioned** over the joint products as **fairly** as possible. These costs are called joint costs or common costs and the most common methods of apportionment use output volume or sales value as the basis.

The use of **output volume** as an apportionment basis is only appropriate if all joints products are in the same form, ie it would not be appropriate if the output consisted of a mixture of gases, solids and liquids. Alternatively, a **weighted average** approach can be used, if the outputs are different.

The use of sales value is only appropriate if all products are saleable at the split-off point, which is the point at which the products become separately identifiable. If the products are not all saleable at this point then it is possible to apportion joint costs on the basis of the final sales value for each product, less any costs incurred on each after the split-off point. This gives a form of 'proxy' sales value which can be used as the basis of joint cost apportionment.

8 STANDARD COSTING SYSTEM

> **Tutor's hint.** Part (a) of this question highlights the importance of reading the question carefully. You are told that you are a **member of your organisation's management accounting team**. So, when asked to describe how you would install a standard costing system you are not, as a management accountant, going to be too concerned with the specific computer hardware required. This would be the remit of the systems manager, say. Instead you need to consider issues such as how the standards will be set, the type of performance standard that will be used and the way in which costs will be collected. In all of these areas, the management accountant would be concerned with the **behavioural impact** of the standard costing system.
>
> This part of the question could have resulted in wide variety of answers, however, so don't be too despondent if yours wasn't exactly the same as ours.
>
> Again, in part (b), **behavioural issues** need to be mentioned, underlining the importance of the workforce to the successful implementation of a standard costing system. Other issues to consider here include inflation and changes in working practices.

(a) Before attempting to install a standard costing system it would be **essential to be familiar with a number of aspects of the organisation and its products.** In particular the following aspects would be important.

(i) A full understanding of the **structure of the organisation**: the cost centres in operation, the identity and ability of each cost centre manager, the reports and feedback information already available.

(ii) The **manufacturing processes** in use: how operations are carried out, the extent to which they can be standardised and monitored, and so on.

(iii) **How other operations are carried out**: the ordering and storage procedures for materials, any bonus schemes in operation for the payment of labour and so on.

Performance standards

Establishing a standard costing system involves calculating predetermined units costs for each cost element of each product. A decision must be taken as to **which type of performance standard** is to be used. For example an **ideal standard would not include any allowances for inefficiencies, breakdowns, losses and so on**. An **attainable standard** would allow an efficient level of breakdowns, losses and so on and this type of standard is **likely to have a more favourable motivational impact**. Motivation problems could arise if an ideal standard is used, since such a standard almost always results in adverse variances which can be demotivating.

Setting standards

(i) **Direct material costs**

It will be necessary to **establish a standard for material usage and for material price.** Standard material usage would take account of any allowances for breakages and losses and would be based on careful monitoring and observation of the production processes used. Standard material price would take account of a number of factors including desired quality, the availability of bulk discounts and any anticipated price inflation.

(ii) **Direct labour costs**

Standards must be established for labour times and for hourly rates of pay. The former would require the assistance of a work study specialist, who would investigate the method used and establish an efficient standard time. Employees may be suspicious of the reasons for which they are being observed and timed as they are doing their work. This problem can be overcome by involving them fully in the task of establishing standard times. They should understand that the standard times are to be used for cost control purposes and not as a device to reduce or affect their remuneration or job security. The personnel department would assist in establishing standard rates of pay, taking account of the skill levels required and the likely results of any future negotiations with trade unions.

(iii) **Production overhead**

The cost centre structure would be used to **allocate and apportion overheads to obtain cost centre totals for forecast overheads**. There may be a problem in identifying the most **appropriate basis for overhead absorption** but it is likely to be some form of time based method. An hourly rate could be determined for production overhead and this rate would be applied to the standard times identified in the work study exercise.

Collecting information

Once the standards have been established it will be necessary to install a **system for collecting the actual costs** for the purposes of monitoring and controlling costs. Once again there may be **resistance** from employees if they do not understand the reasons for the monitoring. For example they may not be willing to co-operate in completing the necessary documentation for the analysis of labour times. It will be important to **educate** and **communicate** with all employees involved in the monitoring of actual costs, to ensure the smooth and efficient installation and operation of the system.

(b) **Past performance** is **one possible guide to the ascertainment of standard costs but it is not necessarily the best guide**. For example, if it is known at the time when standards are being set that a new labour rate has been agreed, that new more efficient working methods are to be introduced, that materials prices are going to rise or that the materials specification of products is going to change then the standard should be revised accordingly. There is no point in measuring performance against out-of-date standards.

The point should also be made that **standards can be used as a psychological incentive** by giving employees a realistic but challenging target of efficiency. Standards based on past performance will not have any motivational impact.

The most that can be said, therefore, is that past performance may offer a starting point for ascertaining standard costs, but only in the absence of change will it provide the best available basis for doing so.

9 PAN CO LIMITED

Tutor's hint. As this is the first question on variance analysis in this bank, we have decided to start you off gently, as **parts (a) and (b)** of this question are possibly **slightly easier than potential variance analysis questions in the exam**. Part (c), however, is certainly exam standard.

You may have been confused by the requirement in **(a)(i)** to compute a variable production cost variance, but this simply means calculating a variance based on the **total variable cost made up of labour, materials and overhead**. The expected cost is easy to calculate (actual output × standard cost per unit of £210) but the calculation of the actual cost requires a little thought in terms of the direct materials cost. You need information about the **materials used in production**, not the materials purchased, as the variance is based on production levels and so you need to use opening stock + purchases – closing stock = materials used in production. (The material price variance, on the other hand will be based on materials purchased.)

Part (a)(ii) was straightforward. How did you do in part (a)(iii)? As we said above, the **material price variance** needs to be based on the quantity **purchased** while the **material usage variance** needs to be based on the quantity **used**. Variable production overhead variance is simply the difference between what the actual output should have cost in terms of overhead and what it did cost.

Once you have completed part (a)(iv) you can **compare** the **sum of the variances calculated in (a)(ii), (a)(iii) and (a)(iv)** with your answer to **(a)(i)** – they **should be the same**!

In the exam it is vital to present information in the **format requested**. **In part (b)** you were asked to use a report so make sure that you used appropriate headings (to, from and so on) as there will always be **marks for presentation.** Make sure you **take note of the recipient** of the information (the production manager in this case), and tailor your answer appropriately. A finance manager would be interested in monetary implications, whereas the production manager will want to know about resource implications too. You commentary should cover issues such as why the variances might have occurred and any possible interrelationships between them. Don't forget that you were also asked to indicate any **additional information** that you might require.

Part (c) is the trickiest part of the question and the key to a successful answer hinges on an issue we mentioned above, that of taking note of the recipient of the information. This is not to say that a production manager is only concerned with resource usage. The cost of the resource has an impact too. You also needed to mention the need for **comparability** across the organisation of various variances, achieved by converting quantity variances into monetary variances.

			£
(a)	(i)	Variable production cost should be (1,000 × £210)	210,000
		but was (W1)	224,160
		Variable production cost variance	14,160 (A)
		Check	£
		Wages (from (ii))	3,360 (A)
		Materials (from (iii))	9,000 (A)
		Overhead (from (iv))	1,800 (A)
			14,160 (A)
			£
	(ii)	5,200 hours should cost (× £9)	46,800
		but did cost	48,360
		Direct wages rate variance	1,560 (A)
		1,000 units should take (× 5 hours)	5,000 hrs
		but did take	5,200 hrs
		Direct wages efficiency variance	200 hrs (A)
		× standard rate	× £9
		Direct wages efficiency variance	1,800 (A)
		Summary	£
		Direct wages rate variance	1,560 (A)
		Direct wages efficiency variance	1,800 (A)
		Direct wages variance	3,360 (A)
	(iii)		£
		10,000 kg should cost (× £15)	150,000
		but did cost	144,000
		Direct materials price variance	6,000 (F)
		1,000 units should use (× 10 kg)	10,000 kg
		but did use (W)	11,000 kg
		Usage variance	1,000 kg (A)
			× £15
		× standard cost	£15,000 (A)
		Direct materials usage variance	
		Summary	
		Direct materials price variance	6,000 (F)
		Direct materials usage variance	15,000 (A)
		Direct materials variance	9,000 (A)
			£
	(iv)	Variable production overhead should cost (1,000 × £15)	15,000
		but did cost	16,800
		Variable production overhead variance	1,800 (A)

Workings

1 *Variable production cost*

	£
Total wages	48,360
Variable production overhead	16,800
Direct materials (W2)	159,000
	224,160

2 *Direct materials*

		Standard cost	
	kg	£	£
Opening stock	4,000	15	60,000
Purchases	10,000	-	144,000
	14,000		204,000
Closing stock	(3,000)	15	(45,000)
Production	11,000		159,000

(b) **REPORT**

To: Production manager
From: Management accountant
Date: 21 November 20X1
Subject: **Commentary on variances arising in the week ending 9 November 20X1**

Variable production cost variance.

The total variance is an adverse one of £14,160. This represents 6% of total standard production cost. Investigation is clearly warranted to identify what control action is required to bring costs back into line with budget. The total variance may be analysed into its different components to give a clearer idea of where problems are arising, as follows.

Direct wages rate variance

An adverse variance arises because the labour force were paid an average of (£48,360/5,200) = £9.30 per hour instead of the standard cost of £9 per hour. If this is a new agreed rate the standard should be revised. It may, however, be due to a short-term need to recruit temporary labour at rates more expensive than standard or to overtime working or bonus payments. The production manager and/or the personnel department should be contracted for further information.

Direct wages efficiency variance

An adverse variance of £1,800 has arisen because the labour force took 200 hours more to produce 1,000 units than the standard allowance. The production manager should be asked to explain the variance. Possible causes are lack of training or machine breakdown, but the material variances may also offer a clue as to the explanation.

Materials price variance

Materials were purchased for £14.40 per kg in the week, a price £0.60 less than standard giving rise to a favourable price variance of £6,000. However this appears to have been at the expense of quality, to judge from the usage variance.

Materials usage variance

1,000 kg more than standard were used to make 1,000 units. This seems most likely to be because cheaper, poor quality materials were purchased, probably resulting in excessive waste. It is possible that the need for rectification work due to poor materials also explains why the labour force was less efficient than standard.

Variable production overhead variance

An adverse variance of £1,800 has arisen. Variable overhead appears to vary in line with labour costs and thus 200 hours × £3 = £600 of the variance is explicable by reference to the extra labour hours worked. The remainder is due to an increase in variable overhead costs: the actual rate per hour was £16,800/5,200 hours = £3.23, as opposed to the standard rate of £3. For further explanation we need to know what the overhead comprises and who is responsible for the expenditure.

(c) The advantage of putting **money prices** to efficiency and usage variances is that they **indicate** the **effect on profit of that inefficiency**, provided that the standard prices for materials or labour are realistic. For example, an adverse usage variance of 2,000 units of material may appear more serious than an adverse efficiency variance of 500 hours. If the material only costs 30p per unit, and labour costs £6 per hour, however, the effect on costs and profits of each variance would be £600(A) and £3,000(A) respectively. The labour variance would be more significant.

Variances in production should also be **viewed in the context of the organisation as a whole.** A **comparison** must be possible between an adverse usage of 4,000 kg of material A in department A, an adverse usage of 3,000 kg of material B in department B, a shortfall in achieving the sales quota in sales department C and excess mileage travelled by lorries in distribution department D. The obvious basis for comparison is achieved by **converting all variances into a monetary value.**

On the other hand **many control measures** can be reported, at least in the **first instance**, in a non-financial **form as stated** by the production manager. Such information is **quicker** to produce for control purposes and may be **more easily understood** by the personnel responsible for day to day operational control.

10 RECONCILIATION STATEMENT

> **Tutor's hint**. This question in **unusual** because instead of being asked to calculate variances on the basis of budget and actual data provided in the question, you are given the variances and budget data and have to '**work backwards**' to determine the actual data. This type of question did come up once in an exam under the old syllabus version of Paper 2.4 so it is worth making sure that you can 'work backwards'.
>
> We think the easiest approach is to **lay out a variance calculation as normal** but to **use X,** say, **for the missing piece of actual data** and to insert the variance given in the question data as the final line of the calculation. You can then use algebra (don't panic at the mention of this word) to find the value of X by **equating the difference between the expected or standard data and actual data (which will contain X) with the variance**. It is important to **take account** of whether you are dealing with **favourable or adverse variances.** If the variance is adverse, the difference between the expected figure and the actual figure (say 300 kgs – X) will be negative because the actual figure is greater than the expected figure.
>
> Part (b) was a gift and you should have been able to earn full marks. It is vital that you check that the reasons you **provide make sense in the context of the question**. There is very little point in giving the activities of competitors as the reason for an adverse sales volume variance if you know that the organisation is a monopolist!
>
> You should also have been able to score full marks for part (c) by mentioning the **implications** on **sales volume and fixed overhead volume variances.**

(a) Budgeted profit = £4,250

∴ Budgeted profit per unit = £4,250 ÷ 1,500 = £17/6

(i)

Budgeted sales volume	1,500 units
Actual sales volume	X units
Sales volume variance in units (£850 ÷ £17/6)	300 units (A)

Note that the variance is adverse so actual volume must be less than budget volume.

∴1,500 – X = 300

∴1,500 – 300 = X = 1,200

∴Actual sales volume = 1,200 units

(ii)

1,550 units should have used (× (750 ÷ 1,500) kgs)	775 kgs
but did use	X kgs
Material usage variance in kgs	(775 – X) kgs (A)
× standard cost per kg (£4,500 ÷ 750 kgs)	× £6
Material usage variances in £	£150 (A)

Because the variance is **adverse**, X must be greater than 775 and hence 775 – X is **negative**.

$$\therefore -(775 - X) \times £6 = 150$$
$$-775 + X = 25$$
$$X = 800$$

∴ Actual material usage = 800 kgs

(iii)

	£
1,000 kgs should have cost (× £6)	6,000
but did cost	X
Material price variance	1,000 (F)

∴(6,000 – X) = £1,000

∴5,000 = X

∴Actual direct material cost = £5,000

(iv)

1,550 units should have taken (× (1,125 ÷ 1,500) hours)	1,162.5 hrs
but did take	X hrs
Labour efficiency variance in hrs	(1,162.5 – X) hrs (A)
× standard rate per hour (4,500 ÷ 1,125)	× £4
Labour efficiency variance	£150 (A)

Because the variance is **adverse**, 1,162.5 is less than X and so (1,162.5 – X) is **negative**.

$\therefore$ – (1,162.5 – X) × 4 = 150
– (1,162.5 – X) = 37.5
X = 37.5 + 1,162.5 = 1,200

(v)

	£
1,200 hours should have cost (× £4)	4,800
but did cost	X
Direct labour rate variance	200 (A)

$\therefore$ – (4,800 – X) = 200
X = 200 + 4,800 = £5,000

Actual direct labour cost = £5,000

(vi)

	£
1,200 hrs should have cost (× £(2,250 ÷ 1,125))	2,400
but did cost	X
Variable overhead expenditure variance	600 (A)

$\therefore$ – (2,400 – X) = 600
X = 600 + 2,400 = 3,000

Actual variable overhead cost = £3,000

(vii)

	£
Budgeted fixed overhead expenditure	4,500
Actual fixed overhead expenditure	X
Fixed overhead expenditure variance	2,500 (F)

$\therefore$ 4,500 – X = 2,500
X = 2,000

Actual fixed overhead cost = £2,000

(b) The **adverse direct materials usage variance** may have been caused by any of the following.

- Defective material
- Excessive waste
- Theft of material
- Stricter quality control (so that units had to be reworked)
- Errors in allocating material to jobs

The **adverse direct labour rate variance** may have been caused by any of the following.

- A wage rate increase
- The use of a higher grade labour than expected

The **adverse sales volume variance** may have been used by any of the following.

- The activities of competitors
- A general downturn in consumer spending
- Adverse reports about the product

(c) **In absorption costing fixed overheads** are **absorbed** into the cost of products. **Variances** will **arise** not only if actual fixed cost **expenditure differs** from budgeted fixed cost expenditure, (the **expenditure variance**), but also if **actual activity levels differ** from those **expected.** If there is a **difference** between actual and budgeted **activity level**, there will be over or under absorption of overheads as a result, and hence a **volume variance**.

By contrast **fixed overheads** are **not absorbed** into the cost of products under **marginal costing**. Hence no volume variance can arise, and the **only variance** that is therefore relevant will be the **fixed overhead expenditure variance**. This will be the **same** as the **expenditure variance** arising in **absorption costing**.

The other significant variance where differences arise is the **sales volume variance**. Under both marginal and absorption costing the variance will be calculated on the basis of the difference between expected sales and actual sales. However the difference in units will be **priced differently** under the two costing methods. Under marginal costing the difference in units will be priced at contribution per unit. Under absorption costing the difference in units will be priced at standard profit per unit. The standard profit figure will equal contribution less fixed overhead absorbed per unit.

11 MIX ETC

Tutor's hint. The only difficulty in part (a) of this pilot paper question was taking account of the **wastage rate**. Input of one kilogram does not produce output of one kilogram. This means that for the **usage variance** you need to calculate what the total input should have been for the total actual output (which is the output adjusted by the wastage rate). You then have to **split this standard input in the standard proportions for comparison with the actual quantities used**. You cannot work in terms of the total standard input and total actual input because each type of material has a different standard cost.

The **mix variance** compares what the mix should have been for the actual output with what it was. This means that you have to **apply the standard mix proportions to the actual total usage and compare these figures to the actual usage of each type of material**.

The **yield variance** compares what the yield should have been from the actual input with what the yield was. Whereas as the usage and mix variances are looking at the material input, here we are concerned with **output**. Output is not considered in terms of the three types of material input but in terms of Synthon and so we need to find the standard cost of a kilogram of Synthon to use to value the variance.

The **labour efficiency variance** calculation in (a)(ii) also needs to take into account the loss. The variance looks at **how long it takes to produce output**, not to process input, and so to determine how long it should have taken to produce the actual output, we need to work out how many kilograms of output can be produced in an hour.

You need to be able to answer (b) perfectly as this is an indication of your understanding of mix variances.

Don't forget to use a report format in (c) as this would earn you a few marks for presentation. Providing an introduction and conclusion is also good exam technique. For the mix and yield variances in particular, your comments should show the marker that you **understand what your calculations have highlighted about the organisation's performance**. Explain how mix and yield variances arise and then relate this to your calculations.

(a) (i) **Usage variance**

Output of 15,408 kgs should have used input of 15,408/90% = 17,120 kgs.

∴ Standard input should have been as follows.

			Kgs
S1	8/16 × 17,120	=	8,560
S2	5/16 × 17,120	=	5,350
S3	3/16 × 17,120	=	3,210
			17,120

	S1	*S2*	*S3*
Output of 15,408 kgs should have used	8,560 kgs	5,350 kgs	3,210 kgs
but did use	8,284 kgs	7,535 kgs	3,334 kgs
Usage variance in kgs	276 kgs (F)	2,185 kgs (A)	124 kgs (A)
× standard cost per kg	× £0.30	× £0.50	× £0.40
Usage variance	£82.80 (F)	£1,092.50 (A)	£49.60 (A)

∴ Total variance = £(82.80 (F) + 1,092.50 (A) + 49.60 (A))
= £1,059.30 (A)

Mix variance

Actual usage = (8,284 + 7,535 + 3,334) kgs
= 19,153 kgs

∴ Standard mix of actual usage is as follows.

			Kgs
S1	8/16 × 19,153	=	9,576.5
S2	5/16 × 19,153	=	5,985.3
S3	3/16 × 19,153	=	3,591.2
			19,153.0

	S1	*S2*	*S3*
Mix should have been	9,576.5 kgs	5,985.3 kgs	3,591.2 kgs
but was	8,284.0 kgs	7,535.0 kgs	3,334.0 kgs
Mix variance in kgs	1,292.5 kgs (F)	1,549.7 kgs (A)	257.2 kgs (F)
× standard cost per kg	× £0.30	× £0.50	× £0.40
Mix variance	£387.75 kgs (F)	£774.85 (A)	£102.88 (F)

∴ Total variance = £(387.75 (F) + 774.85 (A) + 102.88 (F))
= £284.22 (A)

Yield variance

Each batch of Synthon requires

		£
8 kg	of S1, costing (× £0.30)	2.40
5 kg	of S2, costing (× £0.50)	2.50
3 kg	of S3, costing (× £0.40)	1.20
16 kg		6.10

This will produce 16 × 90% = 14.4 kgs of output.

∴ Standard cost per kg of output = £6.10/14.4 = £0.4236

19,153 kg should have yielded (× 90%)	17,237.7 kgs
but did yield	15,408.0 kgs
Yield variance in kgs	1,829.7 kgs (A)
× standard cost per unit of output	× £0.4236
Yield variance	£775.08 (A)

(ii)

	£
1,235 hrs should have cost (× £5)	6,175
but did cost	6,916
Labour rate variance	741 (A)

Standard input per batch = (8 + 5 + 3) = 16 kgs

Standard output = 16 × 90% = 14.4 kgs

∴ 14.4 kgs of output are processed in 1 standard hour

15,408 kgs should have taken (÷ 14.4)	1,070 hrs
but did take	1,235 hrs
Efficiency variance in hrs	165 hrs (A)
× standard rate per hour	× £5
Labour efficiency variance	£825 (A)

(b) The total mix variance in quantity must be zero since the **expected mix is based on the total quantity actually used** and hence the difference between the total expected mix (total actual quantity) and the total actual mix (total actual quantity) is zero.

(c) **REPORT**

To: Management of Pan Ocean Chemicals
From: Management accountant
Date: 17 January 20X1
Subject: **Analysis of material and labour variances, week number 2**

This report explains and interprets the variance analysis carried out on material and labour for week 2 (set out in the Appendix to this report). It will consider in detail the materials mix and yield variances and will suggest reasons for the results of the variance analysis.

Materials variances

The total materials variance (the difference between what week 2 output should have cost in terms of material, and what it did cost) can be divided two variances, price and usage. Product Synthon uses three types of material and so the usage can then be divided into mix and yield components.

Mix variance

Although there is a standard mix of the three input materials to produce a batch of product Synthon, this standard mix is not always used as it is possible to use a range of different proportions of the input materials without affecting the quality of Synthon too adversely. If the **proportions of the input materials used differ from the standard proportions** a mix variance will occur. The effect of a mix variance on profit will depend on whether the particular mix used is **cheaper than the standard mix** (if the proportion of the cheaper materials in the mix has increased) or **more expensive**.

The mix variance for week 2 was £284 adverse as S2, the **most expensive input material, comprised a greater proportion of the actual mix** than standard (the proportions of the two cheaper input materials being less than standard). There may have been a **shortage** of S1 and S3 so that S2 had to be used as a replacement.

Yield variance

By changing the proportions in the mix, the **efficiency of the combined material usage may change**. The yield variance shows the **effect** on profit of **any difference between the actual input materials used and the amounts that should have been used given the actual output** of Synthon.

In week 2, more input material was required than expected given actual production of 15,408 kgs of Synthon. It may be that the **actual mix** of input materials was **unstable** or **difficult to use** and so **wastage levels were higher**. This had an adverse effect on profit of £775.

Labour variances

The total labour variance (the difference between what week 2 output should have cost in terms of labour and what it did cost) can be split into a rate variance and an efficiency variance.

Rate variance

The **actual hours** worked during week 2 **cost more than anticipated** as the labour rate variance for the period was £741 adverse. The variance was caused by payment of a rate of £5.60 compare with a standard rate of £5. There are a number of possible **reasons** for this.

(i) Overtime working may have been required, resulting in the payment of an overtime premium.

(ii) The standard rate may not have been updated to reflect a pay increase.

(iii) The mix of workers used may have differed from standard and incorporated a larger proportion of more skilled, and hence more expensive, workers.

Efficiency variance

The efficiency variance of £825 adverse reflects the fact that it **took longer to produce the given output than the standard time allowed**, at an additional cost of £825. This may be because the materials were difficult to work with (see comments on yield variance above), the introduction of new machinery or processes or possibly the use of new (and hence untrained) workers.

Conclusion

Management should carry out **investigative action** to determine the reasons for the occurrence of these variances. The standards used may no longer be appropriate and may need amending or additional control procedures may need adopting over, for example, wastage levels.

Analyses carried out over the last few weeks should also be reviewed to assess whether these poor results are part of a **trend** or a simply a one-off occurrence.

If I can provide any further information please do not hesitate to contact me.

12 TF PLC

> **Tutor's hint.** Even though there is not reams of information to absorb from this question, it required **careful reading**. The system under consideration is a **responsibility accounting system** rather than a budgetary control or standard costing system more frequently included in examination question scenarios. It would therefore be **inappropriate to refer to nothing but standards and/or variances** (although you could explain that only variances over which a manager has control should be included in any responsibility accounting system report). A responsibility accounting report could show divisional profit, for example, or the actual controllable costs incurred by a cost centre. Note, however, that budgetary control and standard costing systems can be part of a responsibility accounting system.
>
> And did you use a **report format**? If this were the exam you would have thrown away a vital mark or two if you had simply produced an essay.
>
> It's a good idea to use the questions raised by the managing director as the framework for your report, covering each question in turn. The second question is probably the most difficult to answer; you will probably need to provide simple **examples** to get your points across.

REPORT

To: The managing director
From: The management accountant
Date: xx.xx.xx
Subject: **Responsibility accounting system**

This report addresses the issues you have raised in respect of the proposed computerised responsibility accounting system.

Why does the report highlight controllable cost and profit?

A **responsibility centre** is a part of the organisation, the performance of which is the responsibility of a specific manager. **Controllable costs** are those which can be **influenced by the manager of the responsibility centre**. If the manager is also able to influence the centre's revenues then the resulting profits are referred to as controllable profits.

There are two main **reasons why such controllable items are highlighted.**

(a) **Busy managers' attention should be drawn to the areas over which it is possible to exercise control.** If managers cannot influence certain items, the report should not give prominence to these uncontrollable items. The result is that managers can quickly focus their attention on the most important information in the report.

(b) The report could have a **negative motivational impact if managers feel that their performance is being judged based on factors which are outside their control.** Highlighting controllable items and monitoring performance based on these factors will improve the motivational impact of the report.

How does one determine which costs are controllable?

Each cost should be considered separately in order to decide whether or not a responsibility centre manager is able to influence it and hence control it. A few examples should help to illustrate the considerations involved.

(a) Most **variable costs** within a division are usually controllable in the short term because managers can influence the efficiency with which resources are used.

(b) **Fixed costs** such as depreciation, rent and salaries are controllable if the divisional manager has influence over the factors which cause them to be incurred. For example, if the manager has the authority to decide whether or not to invest in a fixed asset then depreciation is a controllable cost. If the manager decides which premises to occupy and which staff to hire, then rent and salaries are controllable costs, and so on.

(c) **Discretionary fixed costs** such as advertising, training costs and consultancy fees may initially be authorised as a result of top management decisions, but the actual incurring of the expenditure may be within the control of the responsibility centre manager.

(d) **Apportioned costs of the central sales department** would have to be considered individually. The general rule is that any cost over which the manager has some influence is controllable. For example, it may be the responsibility of the sales department manager to control sales costs within budget allowances, but the sales costs in total will be partly fixed and partly variable, and the variable cost element will depend on the volume of demand for the sales department's services. If a particular division has some very demanding customers who require a great deal of sales effort we might expect higher sales costs, and the relevant divisional manager should therefore be made accountable for the extra sales costs that the central sales department incurs on the division's behalf.

What are cost centres, profit centres and investment centres?

Cost centres, profit centres and investment centres are all types of **responsibility centre**. The main difference between them lies in the amount of responsibility given to the manager of the centre.

A **cost centre** is a responsibility centre where the manager is responsible only for the costs incurred by the centre. Cost centres form the basis for building up cost records for cost measurement, budgeting and control.

A **profit centre** is a responsibility centre to which it is possible to assign revenues as well as costs, so that the profitability of the centre's activities can be determined. The revenues might come from external sales or from internal sales to other profit centres, or from work done for them, for which a notional selling price (a transfer price) can be charged.

Where a divisional manager is allowed some discretion about the amount of investment undertaken by the division, for example in working capital and fixed assets, the profit earned by the division can be related to the amount of capital invested. This type of centre is known as an **investment centre** and its performance can be measured by its return on investment (ROI).

What benefits are to be gained from a system of responsibility accounting?

The benefits to be gained from a system of responsibility accounting include the following.

(a) Each responsibility centre manager receives information on the performance of the centre so that they are aware of what is happening to all of the items within their area of authority.

(b) Management attention can be focused where action is needed by highlighting controllable items within the report.

(c) Senior managers have a basis for monitoring and rewarding the performance of the divisional managers.

(d) The authority to act to improve performance, combined with a well-designed reward structure linked to the system of responsibility accounting, can act as a valuable motivator to responsibility centre managers.

If you would like to discuss any of these items in more detail please do not hesitate to contact me.

13 FREEWHEEL LTD

Tutor's hint. It's a good idea to draw up **proformas** to begin with, into which you can insert figures either directly from the information in the question straight away or from each working as you complete it. You know what the balance sheet will look like (the same as the one in the question) but you may have to **leave spaces** within the cash budget and budgeted profit and loss account if you are not sure what the various expenses, payments and so on will be.

The trick to answering questions like this one is careful layout of **workings**. Never try to insert figures directly into the budgets as you run the risk of missing figures out, getting months wrong, forgetting debtors and creditors and so on.

Take the receipts from sales working, for example. By noting the total sales each month to begin with, you can then work on a month-by-month basis inserting the cash figure and credit figure under the appropriate month. For example, the receipts from the £27,600 of sales made in August are received half in August as cash (£13,800) and half in October when the debtors pay two months after the sales are made. If you had read through the question in advance you would know that a debtors figure is required (for the balance sheet) and this can also be noted on the same working (50% of November's and December's sales).

Remember that when you have **receipts or payments in different time periods to when the sales are made or the goods received/the labour cost incurred**, there will be **debtors and creditors**. Creditors are also incurred on the purchase of fixed assets (as in this question), not just on purchases for production.

One of the reasons for asking you to prepare both a cash budget and a budgeted profit and loss account is to see whether you appreciate the fact that the **cash budget** is prepared on a **receipts/payments basis**, **the profit and loss account** on an **accruals basis**. So don't make the mistake of adding up the receipts/payments in the cash budget and including the totals as the sales/purchases/expenses figures in the profit and loss account. The other reason is to determine whether you know not to include **certain non-cash items** like depreciation in the cash budget.

You are unlikely not to be asked to provide some sort of **analysis** of the budgets you have prepared, as in (b) here. Budgets are a form of **feedforward control**, giving management the opportunity to take control action now in an attempt to ensure actual results turn out as planned.

(a) (i) **CASH BUDGET JULY TO DECEMBER 20X2**

	July	*Aug*	*Sept*	*Oct*	*Nov*	*Dec*
	£	£	£	£	£	£
Receipts						
From sales (W1)	25,500	26,400	27,900	33,800	29,600	32,000
Share issue	-	-	20,000	-	-	-
	25,500	26,400	47,900	33,800	29,600	32,000
Payments						
Purchases (W2)	12,000	13,000	14,000	18,000	16,000	14,000
Wages/salaries (W3)	8,000	9,500	10,000	10,000	11,500	12,000
Overheads	7,000	7,000	7,000	7,000	8,000	8,000
Fixed assets (W5)	-	-	-	-	-	10,000
	27,000	29,500	31,000	35,000	35,500	44,000
Excess of receipts over payments	(1,500)	(3,100)	16,900	(1,200)	(5,900)	(12,000)
Balance b/f	3,000	1,500	(1,600)	15,300	14,100	8,200
Balance c/f	1,500	(1,600)	15,300	14,100	8,200	(3,800)

(ii) **BUDGETED PROFIT AND LOSS ACCOUNT JULY TO DECEMBER 20X2**

	£	£
Sales (W7)		177,800
Less cost of sales		
Opening stock	25,000	
Purchases	86,000	
Closing stock	(38,000)	
		(73,000)
Gross profit		104,800
Less expenses		
Wages and salaries	62,000	
Overheads	45,000	
Depreciation (W8)	8,500	
		(115,500)
Net loss		(10,700)
Profit and loss account balance b/f		44,600
Profits available for appropriation		33,900
Less dividends		(10,000)
Profit and loss account balance c/f		23,900

(iii) **BUDGETED BALANCE SHEET AS AT 31 DECEMBER 20X2**

	Cost	*Provision for depreciation*	*Net book value*
	£	£	£
Fixed assets	170,000	22,500	147,500
Current assets			
Stock	38,000		
Trade debtors (W1)	27,200		
		65,200	
Current liabilities			
Bank overdraft	3,800		
Trade creditors (W2)	24,000		
Other creditors (W9)	41,000		
		(68,800)	
Net current assets			(3,600)
Total assets less current liabilities			143,900
Capital and reserves			
Share capital			120,000
Profit and loss account			23,900
			143,900

Workings

1 **Receipts from sales**

	May	*June*	*July*	*Aug*	*Sept*	*Oct*	*Nov*	*Dec*	*Debtors*
	£'000	£'000	£'000	£'000	£'000	£'000	£'000	£'000	£'000
Total	24.0	25.2	27.0	27.6	28.8	40.0	30.4	24.0	NA
Cash	12.0	12.6	13.5	13.8	14.4	20.0	15.2	12.0	NA
Credit	NA	NA	12.0	12.6	13.5	13.8	14.4	20.0	*27.2
Receipts	NA	NA	25.5	26.4	27.9	33.8	29.6	32.0	

*(£15,200 + £12,000)

2 **Purchases**

	May	*June*	*July*	*Aug*	*Sept*	*Oct*	*Nov*	*Dec*	*Creditors*
	£'000	£'000	£'000	£'000	£'000	£'000	£'000	£'000	£'000
Purchases	12	13	14	18	16	14	12	12	NA
Payment	NA	NA	12	13	14	18	16	14	*24

*(£12,000 + £12,000)

3 **Wages and salaries**

	June	July	Aug	Sept	Oct	Nov	Dec	Creditors
	£'000	£'000	£'000	£'000	£'000	£'000	£'000	£'000
Total incurred	8	8	10	10	10	12	12	NA
75%	NA	6	7.5	7.5	7.5	9.0	9	NA
25%	NA	2	2.0	2.5	2.5	2.5	3	3
		8	9.5	10.0	10.0	11.5	12	

4 **Overheads**

Creditor at December of £8,000

5 **Fixed assets**

	November	December	Creditor
	£'000	£'000	£'000
Purchase	30		
Payment		10	
Creditor			20

6 **Dividends**

Declared October and therefore paid in January and to creditor at December of £10,000

7 **Sales**

	£
(4,500 + 4,600 + 4,800) × £6 =	83,400
(5,000 + 3,800 + 3,000) × £8 =	94,400
	177,800

8 **Depreciation**

	£
Assets owned at 30 June 20X2	140,000
Additions	30,000
	170,000
Depreciation = £170,000 × 10% × 0.5 =	£8,500

9 **Other creditors**

	£'000
Wages and salaries (W3)	3
Overheads (W4)	8
Fixed assets (W5)	20
Dividend (W6)	10
	41

(b) (i) The cash budget shows that there will be an overdraft at the end of August and at the end of December, despite the share issue in September. Payments in January and February 20X2 for the fixed asset and the payment of the dividend in January will only increase the overdraft. **Sufficient overdraft facilities must therefore be arranged or other action**, such as a reversal of the decision to purchase the fixed asset, should be considered.

(ii) A **reduction in sales quantities** in November and December results in a net loss of £10,700. If such a reduction is not part of a plan then ways of either cutting costs or increasing sales must be considered.

(iii) **Stock** at the end of the period represents three months' purchases whereas stock at the beginning of the period represents two months' purchases. If this is due to the reduction in sales quantities then it may be advisable to reduce purchases if the drop in sales is unavoidable.

14 PRESENTATION

Tutor's hint. The comparison of the actual results for 4,500 units with the budget data for 5,000 units is not particularly useful for the general manager. It is not possible to tell whether cost and revenue differences are caused by changes in activity or by changes in expenditure. So in part (a), a flexible budget presentation would be more relevant, presented **in marginal costing format** (showing variable costs, contribution and fixed costs) to highlight the more easily controlled variable costs. **Variable costs** are **flexed** by a ratio of 4,500/5,000. **Fixed costs do not change**.

The variances required in part (b) are calculated on marginal costing principles given that marginal costing was used in part (a). This means that there will be **no fixed overhead volume capacity and efficiency variances** as these two variances explain the reasons for under- or over-absorbed fixed production overhead, which cannot arise with marginal costing. The other main difference compared with absorption costing is that **the sales volume variance is valued at standard contribution per unit** (a figure that you need to calculate!).

To **reconcile actual results against the flexed budget does not require** the inclusion of the **sales volume variance** as the very process of flexing has removed any differences in volume (both the flexed budget and actual results being based on the actual volume). Once the sales volume variance is included, however, a reconciliation between actual results and the original budget is possible.

You might have been thrown by the fact that it was not possible to analyse the direct material cost variance into price and usage components but you simply did not have the appropriate information.

The key points for part (c) are that the use of **marginal costing** principles **highlights contribution**, which is a **more-easily controllable** performance measure, and that the use of a **flexible budget** provides more **realistic targets**.

(a)

	Original budget for 5,000 units		*Flexed budget for 4,500 units*	*Actual result*	*Variance against flexed budget*
	£'000		£'000	£'000	£'000
Sales	600		540.0	550	10
less variable costs					
Direct materials	150		135.0	130	5.0
Direct labour	200	$\times \frac{4,500}{5,000}$	180.0	189	(9.0)
Production overhead	50		45.0	46	(1.0)
Selling overhead	75		67.5	72	(4.5)
Total variable cost	475		427.5	437	(9.5)
Contribution	125		112.5	113	0.5
less fixed overhead:					
Production	25		25.0	29	(4.0)
Selling	50		50.0	46	4.0
Profit	50		37.5	38	0.5

Note. Variances in brackets are adverse.

(b) *Workings*

1 **Standard contribution per unit**

	For 5,000 units	*£ per unit*
Sales price	£600,000	120
Direct materials	£150,000	30
Direct labour	£200,000	40
Variable production overhead	£50,000	10
Variable selling overhead	£75,000	15
Standard contrib'n per unit		25

2 Standard labour rate per hour = £200,000/50,000 = £4 per hour

3 Standard variable production overhead per hour = £50,000/50,000 = £1 per hour

Variances (*Note.* Variances in brackets are adverse)

			Variance against flexed budget
(i)	**Selling price variance**		
		£	£
	Margin on 4,500 units should have been	112,500	
	but was (£(550,000 – 427,500))	122,500	
			10,000
(ii)	**Direct material cost variance**		
	No further analysis than that in (a) possible		5,000
(iii)	**Direct labour rate variance**		
		£	
	47,500 hrs should cost (× £4)	190,000	
	but did cost	189,000	
			1,000
	Direct labour efficiency variance		
	4,500 units should have taken (× 10 hrs)	45,000 hrs	
	but did take	47,500 hrs	
	Variance in hours	2,500 hrs	
	× standard rate per hour	× £4	
			(10,000)
(iv)	**Variable production overhead efficiency variance**		
	2,500 hrs × standard rate per hour (× £1)		(2,500)
	Variable production overhead expenditure variance		
		£	
	47,500 hrs should cost (× £1)	47,500	
	but did cost	46,000	
			1,500
(v)	**Variable selling overhead expenditure variance**		
		£	
	4,500 units should cost (× £15)	67,500	
	but did cost	72,000	
			(4,500)
Total contribution variance			500
(vi)	**Fixed production overhead expenditure variance**		
		= budget expenditure – actual expenditure	
		= £(25,000 – 29,000)	(4,000)
(vii)	**Fixed selling overhead expenditure variance**		
		= budget expenditure – actual expenditure	
		= £(50,000 – 46,000)	4,000
Profit variance against flexed budget			500
(viii)	**Sales volume variance**		
		= [actual units – budget units] × std contribution/unit	
		= (4,500 – 5,000) × £25	(12,500)
Variance against original budget			(12,000)

REPORT

(c) To: General manager
From: Management accountant
Date: 1 January 20Y1
Subject: **The principles upon which the redrafted statement is based**

As requested, I outline below the principles upon which the redrafted statement is based and the information it provides.

(i) **Marginal costing principles**

The report has been prepared using marginal costing principles. Marginal costing highlights the **variable costs**, which may be **more controllable than the fixed costs**.

The report concentrates management attention on **contribution**, which is often the more easily controlled performance measure. The contribution is so called because it contributes towards fixed costs and profits.

(ii) **Flexible budget principles**

The report has also used flexible budget principles. Flexible budgets use the available knowledge about **cost behaviour patterns** to 'flex' the budget. The resulting flexed budget contains **more realistic targets** for costs and revenues at the actual activity level for the period.

The report thus enables managers to **compare like with like**. There is little to be gained by comparing the actual costs and revenues for 4,500 units with the budget figures for 5,000 units. It would not be possible to tell which differences were caused by the volume change, and which were caused by over- and under-spending.

The most important piece of information in the re-drafted budget statement is the **large variance caused by the volume shortfall.** The net profit from sales was only £500 different from the flexed budget, but the large volume shortfall caused a major reduction of £12,500 in the profit result when compared with the original budget.

If I can provide any further information, please do not hesitate to contact me.

15 BUDGETS AND PEOPLE

Tutor's hint. You are **unlikely to get a full question on the behavioural aspects of budgeting**. The issue is more likely to be examined in the context of a wider question on budgeting. Under the old syllabus equivalent to Paper 2.4, the topic tended to appear in requirements worth five marks.

It is well worth attempting this 25-mark question, however, as it covers a wide range of the possible issues that you could encounter. Make sure that you **deal with both parts** of the question (the reasons for reluctance and the side effects of imposed budgets). Beware, however, of writing down everything you can possibly think of which is remotely related to the behavioural aspects of management accounting.

There is one major **reason why managers may be reluctant to participate** fully in setting up budgets and that is a **lack of education in the purposes of the budgeting process**. The budget's major role is to communicate the various motivations that exist among management so that everybody sees, understands and co-ordinates the goals of the organisation.

Specific reasons for the reluctance of managers to participate are as follows.

(a) Managers view budgets as **too rigid a constraint on their decision making.** For example, a manager may be unable to sanction an item of expenditure if it has not been budgeted for. The natural reaction to this supposed restriction of their autonomy is resistance and self defence.

(b) Managers feel that the top management **goals expressed by the budget will interfere with their personal goals** (for example their desire to 'build an empire' with substantial resources under their control, large personal income and so on). A successful budgetary system will harmonise the budget goals with the managers' personal goals, but it is by no means easy to achieve a successful system.

(c) Managers imagine that the purpose of budgets is to provide senior management with a **rod** with which to chastise those who do not stay within budget. They will be unwilling to help in the construction of such a rod.

(d) Managers view the budgeting process as one in which they must **fight for a fair share** of the organisation's **resources** in competition with colleagues with other responsibilities.

(e) Managers misinterpret the **control function** of the budgeting system to be a method whereby **blame** can be **attached**. By not participating in the budget setting process, they are able to blame an 'unattainable' or 'unrealistic' budget for any poor results they may have.

As a reaction to these uneducated notions, the behaviour of managers involved in budget preparation can conflict with the desires of senior management. Such behaviour is often described as **dysfunctional**; it is counter-productive because it is **not goal congruent.**

The **unwanted side effects** which may arise from the **imposition of budgets** by senior management (for example under an authoritative rather than a participative budgetary system) are examples of **dysfunctional behaviour** and include the following.

(a) There may be a **reluctance to reduce costs** for fear that future budget allowances may be reduced as a consequence of successful cost cutting.

(b) Managers may **spend up to their budget** in order to justify levels of expenditure. This is particularly the case in local government circles where there is a tendency to spend any available cash at the end of a financial year.

(c) There may be **padding**, whereby managers request inflated allowances. In turn senior management may cut budgets where they suspect padding exists. Padding is sometimes called slack and represents the difference between the budget allowance requested and the realistic costs necessary to accomplish the objective.

(d) In extreme cases of authoritative budgeting, the **'emotional' responses** of managers can be highly detrimental to the goals of the organisation, for example non-cooperation.

16 ROLLING

> **Tutor's hint.** The alternative approaches to budgeting are likely to be **examined as part of a wider question on budgeting**. For that reason we have not included a full question.
>
> Such parts of questions on non-core topics and techniques are often **'stand alone'**, in that they are not totally integrated within the main questions. They are therefore very important, as they provide you with the opportunity to **pick up marks** on questions even if you have struggled with the main requirement such as the preparation of a flexible or cash budget.
>
> You should have had little trouble with this question as it basically required you to regurgitate book knowledge. You are unlikely to be able to do this in the exam as you will probably have to apply your knowledge of, say, rolling budgets, to a particular scenario.
>
> In an exam **never provide more examples**/advantages/problems **than the number requested.** You are simply wasting your time as only the specified number will earn you marks, the additional ones will be ignored.

(a) A **rolling budget** is a budget which is **continuously updated** by adding a further accounting period (a month or quarter) when the earlier accounting period has expired. They are particularly **beneficial** when **future costs and/or activities cannot be forecast** with any degree of accuracy.

(b) The **system** operates as follows.

(i) A budget is prepared for the year ahead, broken down into suitable control periods (months or quarters).

(ii) At the end of the first control period, a comparison is made between that period's results and budget. The conclusions drawn are used to amend the budgets for the remaining control periods and to add a budget for a further period, so that the company once again has budgets available for a year ahead.

(iii) The process is repeated at the end of each control period.

(c) **Advantages** of a rolling budget system (three required)

(i) Budgets can be more realistic since they are continuously updated in the light of changing circumstances.

(ii) The arbitrary and artificial distinction between one financial year and the next is avoided, since budgets are always available for a year ahead.

(iii) The periodic disruption associated with annual budgeting is avoided.

(iv) Management feels more accountable because of the frequent review of budgets and the fact that budgets are more realistic.

(d) **Problems** likely to be encountered (three required)

(i) Greater work-load: will adequate staff be available; will management devote sufficient attention to preparing budgets which they know will shortly be revised?

(ii) If a standard costing system is in operation in conjunction with the budgetary control system, frequent changes of standard are necessitated.

(iii) Advantage (iii) above is only partly true as longer-term plans are still required.

(iv) What time period should be chosen as the control period? Monthly comparison of actual/budget will provide greater management control but can such frequent updating of budgets be justified in terms of the extra work involved?

17 DOMESTIC APPLIANCE

Tutor's hint. We think it unlikely that you will get a 25-mark question on forecasting. In the old syllabus version of Paper 2.4, forecasting was always examined as part of a wider question on budgeting, usually for about five marks. There is no guarantee that this pattern will continue, however, so you are well advised to attempt this forecasting question.

If, in part (a), you can't work out whether actual sales should be multiplied by (index for 20X0/index for current year) or by (index for current year/index for 20X0), remember that **deflated figures** should be **smaller**. Actual figures can be made smaller if the index multiplier is less than one, as opposed to greater than one. This means that the **smaller index number** (ie that for 20X0) needs to be **divided by the bigger index number.**

You are provided with the formula for r in the exam, so in part (b) you simply need to calculate r and square it. It **does not matter which variable you choose for x and which you choose for y when calculating r**, as you are simply determining the strength of the correlation between them. You choice does matter when it comes to **working out the values of a and b in a regression line**, however. The **independent variable must be x, the dependent variable y.** The question requires a regression equation that predicts insurance policy sales from deflated appliance sales, so the **dependent variable is policy sales as it depends on the level of appliance sales for its value.**

Take note of the units you are working in. We worked in £ millions and hundreds of policies, which means that we inserted a figure of 51 in the regression equation to represent sales of £51 million. Our prediction of 28.613 means 28.613 × 100 = 2,861 policies.

(a,b) **Deflated figures** for each year are calculated as follows.

$$\textbf{Actual figure} \times \frac{\textbf{Index for 20X0}}{\textbf{Index for current year}}$$

Deflation is needed so as to make appliance sales (given in cash terms, and therefore affected by inflation) comparable with policy sales (given in volume terms, and therefore not affected by inflation).

Deflated appliance sales *x* £m	*Policy sales* *y* Hundreds	x^2	y^2	*xy*
3	4	9	16	12
5	3	25	9	15
7	6	49	36	42
10	12	100	144	120
15	17	225	289	255
18	22	324	484	396
26	21	676	441	546
84	85	1,408	1,419	1,386

The formula for r is provided in the exam.

$$r = \frac{n\Sigma xy - \Sigma x\Sigma y}{\sqrt{[n\Sigma x^2 - (\Sigma x)^2][n\Sigma y^2 - (\Sigma y)^2]}}$$

$$r^2 = \frac{(7 \times 1{,}386 - 84 \times 85)^2}{(7 \times 1{,}408 - 84^2)(7 \times 1{,}419 - 85^2)} = 0.87$$

This shows that **87% of the variation in policy sales is explained by variation in appliance sales.**

(c) For a regression line y = a + bx

$$b = \frac{n\Sigma xy - \Sigma x\Sigma y}{n\Sigma x^2 - (\Sigma x)^2} \text{ and } a = \frac{\Sigma y}{n} - \frac{b\Sigma x}{n}$$

$$\therefore b = \frac{7 \times 1{,}386 - 84 \times 85}{7 \times 1{,}408 - 84^2} = 0.915$$

$$\therefore a = \frac{85}{7} - 0.915 \times \frac{84}{7} = 1.163$$

y = 1.163 + 0.915x

Note that y is in hundreds of policies and x in millions of pounds deflated to 20X0 prices.

(d) **Predicted policy sales**

$$= 1.163 + 0.915 \text{ x } \frac{51}{1.70} = 28.613 = 2{,}861 \text{ policies}$$

(e) This prediction is based on the **assumption** that there is a **linear relationship** between (deflated) appliance sales and policy sales. In fact, a non-linear relationship may exist, and there could well be other influences on policy sales.

18 PRODUCTION SHORTFALL

> **Tutor's hint.** This is a good example of an exam-style question as it contains both computational and discursive parts, although part (a) is possibly slightly easier than a requirement you might encounter in the exam.
>
> Part (a)(i) was fairly straightforward apart from the fact that you are not given information about the machine hours required per product so you need to use the absorption basis information.
>
> The make or buy decision in part (a)(ii) rests on a comparison of the cost per unit of saving an hour of Process N time (ie the cost per hour of process N time saved by buying in components). The product with the lowest cost per hour is the one which should be bought in.
>
> Don't ignore the discursive requirement of (a)(iii): four relevant factors will give you what could be four vital marks.
>
> The discursive requirement in (b) is more stretching. Make sure the you consider both financial and non-financial factors.

(a) (i) **Calculation of machine hours required**

	X	*Y*	*Z*
Fixed overhead absorbed per unit in M	£6	£6	£4.5
Hours per unit = fixed overhead absorbed/£3	2	2	1.5
Fixed overhead absorbed per unit in N	£10.50	£10.50	£3.50
Hours per unit = fixed overhead absorbed/£3.50	3	3	1

One year's requirements	*X*	*Y*	*Z*	*Total*
	Hrs	Hrs	Hrs	Hrs
M	(300 × 2) 600	(300 × 2) 600	(450 × 1.5) 675	1,875
N	(300 × 3) 900	(300 × 3) 900	(450 × 1) 450	2,250

	In M	*In N*
	Hrs	Hrs
Required	1,875	2,250
Available	2,000	2,000
Shortfall	-	250

(ii) **Variable cost comparison**

	Per unit X	*Per unit* Z
	£	£
Direct materials	15	4.5
Direct labour	12	8.0
Variable overhead	6	4.0
Variable cost of production	33	16.5
Outside cost	44	23.0
Extra cost incurred of buying in	11	6.5
Hours in N	3	1
Cost of saving an hour in N	11/3 = £3.67	6.5/1 = £6.5

X has a lower cost saving; it is better to buy in components of X from outside in order to make the best use of hours available in process N. (It would cost more to buy in Z.)

The shortfall in hours is 250, which represents 84 units of X (250/3 = 83.33). **84 units of X should therefore be bought in.**

(iii) **Factors to consider**

(1) Future forecasts of requirements (ie if demand patterns change)

(2) Variations in material or labour estimates

(3) Machine hour absorption rates - new machinery might improve efficiency and therefore make outside purchase unnecessary

(4) Price of components from outside suppliers and the likelihood that it could rise suddenly

(5) Assessment of objectives for production since costs are high in relation to outside costs

(6) Possibility of increasing capacity through shift work

(b) A **limiting factor** is any **factor which restricts an organisation's activities**. For many organisations the limiting factor is **sales demand** because they cannot sell as much as they would like to. However, it is possible for a factor of production to be a limiting factor, particularly in the short term. For example there may be a shortage of materials of the right quality or of labour with appropriate skills. There may not be sufficient production capacity to meet the anticipated demand or a company may have cash flow problems which limit the availability of cash.

The **first step** in any limiting factor decision is to **identify** what the limiting factor is, whether there is a single or multiple limiting factor situation and the likely availability of the scarce resource(s).

There are then several **factors that must be taken into account** when making limiting factor decisions.

(i) For **how long** will the availability of the limiting factor be restricted? The decision to be taken may be quite different if the restriction is to last, say, only three months compared with five years.

(ii) How much **contribution** per unit of limiting factor is earned by each product? For example, what is the contribution per labour hour earned by products A, B, C etc. The products would then be ranked according to the contribution earned per hour and the scarce labour hours would be allocated according to this ranking. This method can only be applied in single limiting factor situations. If there are multiple limiting factors then linear programming methods would be used to allocate the resources between the various products.

(iii) Are **fixed costs** affected by changes in the production mix? The methods outlined in (ii) assume that fixed costs are constant. This may not be a valid assumption.

(iv) **Commercial considerations** must be taken into account. A production mix recommended may involve the reduction or elimination of certain products from the production plan. This may have commercial implications which could affect the long-term profitability of the company. For example, a valued customer may go elsewhere if he wishes to obtain a supply of all the products in a range. Or perhaps products may be complementary so that eliminating the supply of one product will affect the demand for other products.

(v) Would the recommended production mix have any adverse **motivational** effects? It may be necessary to lay off some of the workforce or to make employees redundant. The effect on morale should be considered, as well as any longer-term problems of recruiting suitably qualified staff again when the constraint is alleviated in the future.

(vi) Is it possible to **alleviate** the constraint and what would it cost? For example it may be possible to purchase ready made components from another supplier, if internal capacity is limited. As well as cost considerations it would be necessary to ensure that quality and reliability of supply was acceptable and so on.

It is therefore clear that limiting factor decisions involve the consideration of a wide range of factors, both financial and non-financial, before the decision can be made.

19 SEDGEMAIR PARTNERS

> **Tutor's hint**. This question will test your ability to identify relevant and non-relevant costs. Work on the basis that **relevant costs** are **future, incremental cash flows.** Both costs that have **already been incurred**/will be **incurred regardless** of the decision taken and **non-cash flows** are **irrelevant**.
>
> As with all decision-making questions, remember to state your **assumptions**. It was ambiguous as to whether the office space freed by the removal of the filing cabinets required heating and lighting but whether the cost was included or not, the third option was still the most cost effective.
>
> The inclusion of a **simple example** may well help the clarity of your explanation in (c).

(a) (i) **Alternative 1 (cancel job)**

	£
Cost of cancelling job	47,000

Alternative 2 (sub-contract)

	£
Fee	35,000
Lost revenue from senior consultant's work (80 × £100)	8,000
	43,000

Alternative 3 (temporary staff)

	£
Temporary staff pay (£15 × 2,000)	30,000
Temporary staff employment tax (15% × £30,000)	4,500
Recruitment costs (£750 × 4)	3,000
Computers, lower of:	
Purchase cost = (4 × £(2,000 – 1,500)) = £2,000	
Lease cost = 4 × £750 = £3,000	2,000
Office space (and heat and light), lower of	
*Transfer to CD ROM = (£(1,300 – (20 × £20) + (40 × £50))) = £2,900	
Spare office = £1,500 + (£50 × 50) = £4,000	2,900
	42,400

*Assume space made free by removal of filing cabinets requires heating and lighting.

Alternative 3 is the most cost effective.

(ii) **Exclude (i)**. The costs associated with the employment of software development staff will be incurred regardless of the option chosen and hence they are not relevant to the decision.

Exclude (ii). Since the employment costs will be paid regardless of whether or not the job is cancelled, the information about the margin is irrelevant. It is the total fee income which is affected by the decision.

Include (iii). If the consultant has to oversee the contract he will be unable to work for other clients and hence the revenue from such work will be lost. The employment costs will be incurred regardless of the decision taken and so are not relevant.

Include (iv). Temporary staff will only be paid if the decision is taken to employ them.

Include (v). Employment tax is only payable if the decision is taken to employ the temporary staff.

Include (vi). Recruitment costs will only be incurred if the temporary staff are employed.

Include (vii). The costs associated with each alternative are relevant since they will only be incurred if temporary staff are employed. The following assumptions are made.

(1) The organisation will sell the computers after the work has been completed so as to recoup some of the cash outlay and hence the information about their life is not relevant.

(2) The organisation will choose the cheapest of the two alternatives.

Include (viii). The costs associated with both alternatives are relevant and it is assumed that the company would choose the cheapest alternative. Either the cost associated with the transfer to CD ROM or the rental cost of the spare office would only be incurred if temporary staff were employed.

Include (ix). If extra space is needed because of taking on the temporary staff then the heating and lighting costs will be incurred.

Exclude (x). The purchase price of the furniture is a sunk cost. The second-hand value has not been included as an opportunity cost since it is assumed that the furniture is not being sold if it is not required. Depreciation is not a cash flow and hence is never relevant in a decision-making situation.

(iii) **Non-cost factors relevant when considering the three options**

(1) Cancelling the job may have **commercial implications** which could affect the long-term profitability of the organisation. Potential customers may be loath to deal with Sedgemair, fearing that other jobs may be cancelled. Alternatively customers might demand that high cancellation penalty clauses be inserted into future contracts.

(2) The **reliability** of any firm subcontracted to do the work should be checked. Sedgemair will, of course, lose a certain degree of control over the work should it be sub-contracted.

(3) Sedgemair would need to ensure that the **temporary staff** had the necessary skills and expertise to perform the development work.

(4) The **effect** on the organisation's **software development staff** of the option chosen should be considered.

(b) **Opportunity costs** are **relevant** costs and can be defined as the **value of the next best alternative to that decided upon**. In other words, it is the net receipts foregone by not accepting the best alternative to the option chosen.

For example, suppose ABC Ltd makes product X and product Y. Labour is in short supply. If management decide to use the labour to make product X rather than product Y, the **opportunity cost** of that decision is the **contribution foregone from not making and selling product Y.**

When taking decisions it is necessary to identify all the relevant costs and benefits caused by that decision so that a rational conclusion can be drawn. **Including opportunity costs** in a decision model is a way of **ensuring that all the available alternatives are taken into account.**

Opportunity costs are **not stable;** they change as the external environment changes. In fact they are **usually estimates**. **Costing systems** contain **verifiable documented data** about transactions. '**Fuzzy**' **data**, such as opportunity costs, which are only **valid at a particular time**, **cannot** therefore **be included** in a costing system.

20 CORPORATE OBJECTIVES

> **Tutor's hint**. You may well get a part question on objectives in your exam, and the topic may need to be brought into discussions in other areas, for example how well does an investment that you have appraised fit in with the company's objectives.
>
> The question is answered with a clear structure:
>
> (a) The **extent** to which profit maximisation is the primary corporate objective
> (b) The **problems** with the objective
> (c) Other **financial** objectives
> (d) Other **non-financial** objectives
>
> The question is confined to what the directors of the company should seek. In practice they may pursue other objectives that are in their own, but not necessarily the company's best interests, for example maximisation of their own rewards.
>
> You were only allocated twenty minutes to answer the question, which is typical of the sort of timescale that you would get in the exam. The scope of the question is quite wide for the length of time available, so you must make sure your answer has sufficient breadth, and you do not spend all your time discussing profit maximisation.

As a general rule, increases in a company's profits will be in the interests of the shareholders. However, the maximisation of profits should not be the only goal, and it may be beneficial to aim for profits below the maximum possible.

The limitations of profit as a measure of performance

The profits shown in a company's accounts are not a wholly objective measure of the company's performance. The final figure depends on policies chosen on, for example, depreciation and the writing off of development expenditure. In the short term, profits can be increased by capitalising development expenditure, but such policies do not really increase the company's worth.

It is very hard to work out what profit could have been attained. **Comparisons** with an **industry average** may be useful, but comparisons with exceptional performers **in the industry** may be inappropriate. Profits need to be adjusted to reflect the **resources** used to earn them. A company which doubles its capital and increases its profits by 50% has probably done badly, not well.

Profits are computed annually, with half-yearly interim results. Investments which are highly profitable in the long term but are loss-makers initially could be rejected if management is concerned only with next year's profits.

Alternative financial objectives

A company must ensure its **financial stability** both in the short term and in the long term. Targets for the **reduction of gearing** or the **retention of profits** may therefore be appropriate. Of key importance is the solvency of the company. Profitable investments must be rejected if the expenditure required would leave the company unable to pay its debts.

Non-financial objectives

A company's directors may legitimately take into account a range of **non-financial objectives**, including the welfare of employees and of society, the provision of a service to the public and environmental goals. In some cases the pursuit of such objectives may lead to increased profits, for example when an environmentally responsible company attracts customers who share such concerns.

21 MARKET EFFICIENCY

> **Tutor's hint**. The efficient market hypothesis may be the subject of a part question in 2.4. An answer focusing on a technical concept should always start with a clear definition of that concept, including as appropriate the key assumptions. Here the answer goes on to discuss the various forms of the efficient market hypothesis, concentrating on the differences between them (the amount of information available).
>
> It is also important when discussing a theory that attempts to model actual behaviour to bring in evidence of how much it applies in practice. Here that is a key distinction between the strong form and other forms.
>
> If a theory does not appear to work in practice, you need to indicate why this might be so, or at least that there is no obvious explanation why the theory does not work. Here the strong form hypothesis does not work, so you consider why when discussing the hypothesis. In addition there is the general point that some financial institutions do perform better than expected. Because this applies to all forms of the efficient market hypothesis, and because the subject is highlighted in the question you need a separate paragraph covering why performance of financial institutions might deviate from what is anticipated.
>
> Generally written questions will benefit from a conclusion that sums up the answer and is supported by the preceding discussion.

The **efficient market hypothesis** contends that some capital markets (in the UK and US for instance) are 'efficient markets' in which the prices at which securities are traded reflect all the **relevant information** available. In other words, this information is freely available to all participants in the market and is fully reflected in share prices. Further, it is assumed that **transaction costs** are **insignificant** and do not discourage trading in shares, and that no single individual or group of individuals dominates the market.

The theory exists in three forms: weak form, semi-strong form and strong form.

Weak form efficiency

Weak form efficiency contends that prices only change when new factual information becomes available. Information about past prices is in the public domain and equally available to all players in the market, and thus if this form of the hypothesis is correct, no one player should be able to outperform the market consistently. Thus the fact that financial institutions rarely outperform the market on a regular basis lends weight to this form of the theory.

Semi strong efficiency

The semi-strong form of the theory holds that in addition to responding to information that is publicly available, the market also reflects all other knowledge that is publicly available and relevant to the share valuation. Thus to take the example used above, the share prices of companies involved in a takeover bid will change in **advance of the bid** being **formally announced** as the market anticipates the bid. Once again, this form of the theory is based upon the assumption that all the knowledge upon which share price movements are based is in **the public domain** and **freely available**. Thus no single player or group of players should be able consistently to outperform the market. This form of the theory is supported by empirical research which suggests that share price movements do anticipate merger announcements. The fact that the neither the financial institutions nor any other group of investors regularly beat the market also supports this version of the hypothesis.

Strong form efficiency

The strong form of the theory holds that the market price of securities reflects **all information** that is **available**. This includes knowledge of past performance and anticipated events as in the semi-strong form, and also '**insider**' **knowledge** not publicly available. This form can be tested by investigating the effect on the share price of the effect of releasing a piece of information previously confidential to the firm; if the strong form of the hypothesis is valid, then this should already be factored into the share value and a significant price movement should not result. The implication is that this sort of information is only available to specialists who are in regular contact with the company, such as investment trust managers, and that as a result they could use their privileged position to outperform other investors. Empirical work suggests that this form of the hypothesis is not valid, and this is what one would expect since insider dealing is illegal in the UK.

Why institutions may perform well

If an institution **does consistently perform well**, it is probably more related to the fund managers' understanding of the structure of the industries and markets in which they invest, and their ability to hold a more widely diversified portfolio than the small investor. This means that they are in a better

position to avoid the risk of large losses. The fact that they are in daily contact with the markets also means that they are in practice able to react more quickly to new information that becomes available than is the small investor.

Conclusion

Thus the fact that the financial institutions in general do **not consistently outperform** the **market supports** both the weak and semi-strong forms of the efficient market hypothesis.

22 MIXED ECONOMY

Tutor's hint. The question asks for an **identification** of general effects. This means that you have to mention a range of effects. This does not mean single line answers, but you should avoid spending too much time discussing individual effects. The fact that you are just asked to identify rather than carry out deeper analysis (discussion or evaluation) indicates the limits of the question-setter's expectations. Your answer should consist of short paragraphs saying just enough to make clear to the reader how the effects described will impact on businesses.

If you are asked about the general impact of government policy, consider the following areas:

- **Effect on profits**. This means effects on income (sales and also government grants). The impact on costs (especially wage and raw material costs) is critical.
- **Taxation implications**. These will affect the level of profits directly (through the taxing of those profits) and may also impact through the effects on consumer and investor behaviour.
- **Effect on capital structure**. This not only includes effects on the cost of capital, but also the impact upon the supply of funds (a favourite topic of the examiner).
- **Business environment effects**. This includes wider effects such as impact upon competitive environment or company ownership.

You will not get a full question on this subject area but the last part of a question may ask you to discuss the effects of a change in government policy on a specific firm. This will imply a more specific answer than we have given here, because the information you are given in the question should tell you that certain considerations will not apply. (For example a company that deals only with the private sector will not be directly affected by a reduction in government expenditure, as the government does not buy any of its goods.)

(a) **Minimising government borrowing requirements**

(i) A lower public sector borrowing requirement (PSBR) will **reduce the total market demand** for **long term funds**, since the government's demand for funds will be lower. This could result (through supply and demand) in lower long-term interest rates, and so make it cheaper for businesses to raise long-term debt capital.

(ii) In theory, if long-term debt capital is cheaper, a company's **overall cost of capital** should **fall**, and so companies might be encouraged to invest in more marginal capital expenditure projects.

(iii) Since investors, particularly institutional investors, might be **unable to invest** as much as before in gilts, **more investment capital** might be **diverted into shares**, thus pushing share prices up.

(iv) The purpose of reducing the PSBR *might* be to **control the growth in the money supply**, as a means towards keeping inflation under control. If such a policy is successful, lower inflation would affect **companies' costs and prices**, as well as the general state of the economy.

(v) If the PSBR is reduced to zero, and if the country has a balance of payments deficit on current account, the deficit would have to be financed by **private sector borrowing** from abroad, or by the sale of assets by the private sector. This would have implications for the ownership of some firms in the country and for divestments of foreign subsidiaries.

Reducing tax on incomes

(i) Lower income tax is thought by some economists to provide **greater incentives** to entrepreneurs and employees to **work harder**. If so, the consequences of lower taxes would include more new businesses, greater productivity and stronger industrial growth.

(ii) Lower income taxes would leave consumers with more income after tax. This could be saved, or invested in the stock market. Alternatively, the **extra income** might be **spent**, leading to a growth in consumer spending. Higher consumer spending will increase market demand for firms' goods and services. If a consumer spending boom is too fast, the rate of inflation will increase.

(iii) It is possible that if employees have more after-tax income because of lower taxation, **annual wage settlements** will be **lower** than they otherwise would be, because employees are already better off.

(iv) Lower taxes on the profits of companies will leave companies with **bigger after-tax profits** which they can either **re-invest** or pay out as **dividends**.

(b) **Reductions in public expenditure**

(i) If the government spends less, the firms that supply the government will suffer **a loss of business**; for example, a firm of defence equipment manufacturers might suffer a loss of orders. Firms suffering a loss of business will need to look to other markets for sales growth, perhaps by exporting more. If they fail to do this, their sales turnover and profits will fall.

(ii) A consequence of lower public expenditure is likely to be a **reduction of government assistance** for industry. Grants and subsidies might be cut, and government offices that provide specialist advice to industries might be closed.

(iii) It is conceivable that the cuts in public expenditure might persuade firms to **pay for services or benefits** that have been **lost**. This would increase firms' costs. (For example, a cut in public health services might persuade a firm to spend more on in-house medical services for its employees.)

(iv) Lower government spending will probably create **new competitive opportunities** for firms in the private sector. For example, lower government spending on schools and hospitals will create more market opportunities for private schools, private hospitals, private education funding schemes, medical insurance schemes and so on.

Increases in nationalised industries' prices

(i) While government finances will benefit from the increased revenue, for companies that buy the goods and services of nationalised industries, **higher prices** will **result in higher production costs**. Higher costs in turn mean lower profits, unless they put their own prices up.

(ii) Employees are likely to suffer from the **higher prices** of the **nationalised industries**, and there will be higher annual wage demands.

(iii) If demand for the goods and services of the nationalised industries falls, because of higher prices, **suppliers of materials** and services to the nationalised industries will **suffer a loss of business**. However, they might be able to raise their own unit prices.

(iv) Higher prices from nationalised industries will, in industries where there is private sector competition, make the **goods** of the **private sector firms more competitive**.

Selling nationalised assets

(i) The sale of nationalised assets could result in the creation of a **competitive private sector** market, such as in public transport in parts of the UK in recent years.

(ii) The opportunity might arise for firms to **purchase** some of the **assets** that are being **sold off**, or to **buy shares** in the **privatised business**.

(iii) The government will **benefit** from the **revenue generated** by asset sales. With large privatisations, there might be an effect on the general level of share prices, since the stock market will be flooded with new shares for sale.

(iv) One consequence of privatisation might be **higher prices** for customers. The nationalised industry, just before or just after privatisation, is likely to put up its prices, in order to become more profitable and so be more attractive to investors. This would result in higher costs for firms that buy goods and services from these industries.

(v) A further consequence of privatisation might be a **change in buying policy** by the privatised company, to a more commercial footing. There might, for example, be a greater willingness to buy from abroad. This would have implications for supplier firms.

23 MIDSOUTH ELECTRIC PLC

Tutor's hint. In (a) you need to mention the key differences between the two regimes. These are not just differences in **objectives** but also differences in **responsibility** (to shareholders and the regulator rather than the government). At the same time it is important not to give the impression that the public sector will not be concerned with financial targets – a target rate of return will need to be achieved. Therefore also as well as discussing differing objectives, you need to show that some objectives will stay the same – but be more or less important.

(b) signposts the **stakeholders** whose position you need to discuss. If you are asked for a general discussion on stakeholders, those mentioned in (b) will be important, but you would also need to consider other stakeholders whose connections with the organisation are less direct, for example pressure groups or local communities. (c) in fact highlights relationships with the government which itself is a stakeholder.

(b) also indicates key measures that will interest shareholders. It also shows how you need to bring together the various pieces of information you are given in the question. The sales per employee ratio's significant rise, together with the much smaller rise in average wage indicate the possibility of changes in the composition of the labour force.

(b) also brings out the importance of considering a range of plausible explanations. The increase in prices may be explained by reasons other than tougher pricing policies on core activities. It is valid to speculate on other possibilities and go on to say that more information will be required.

(a) (i) The primary objective prior to privatisation is likely to be to serve the public interest in the best possible way. Associated objectives are likely to include:

(1) Providing a **safe and reliable source of supply** to domestic and industrial consumers

(2) Keeping **supply and distribution costs as low as possible**

(3) Keeping **prices to consumers low**, often in response to political pressures

(4) Achieving the **target rate of return** on investment set for public sector organisations

(5) **Keeping capital expenditure within limits**, particularly during times of restraint on public sector capital investment

(ii) Following transfer to the private sector, the primary financial objective is likely to be the **maximisation** of the **wealth** of the **ordinary shareholders**. Although some of the objectives such as providing a safe and reliable supply of electricity are likely to remain the same after privatisation, the relative importance of the aims is likely to change, and further objectives will be introduced. These are likely to include:

(1) Establishing and maintaining a **good and reliable stream** of **dividends**

(2) Ensuring that the **use of available funds** is **maximised** in order to provide a good return to shareholders and to protect the company against hostile takeover bids

(3) Fulfilling the **requirements** of the **industry regulator**

The demands of the market may mean that there is a greater concern with short-term results to the detriment of long-term investment.

(b) (i) **Shareholders**

It is assumed that shareholders will demand that the company should operate so as to maximise their wealth accruing from the company. This can be measured in terms of the flow of dividends and the movement in the share price. The figures allow the market capitalisation (in £m) to be calculated. For analytical purposes, we use below the figures for alternate years.

	20X2	*20X4*	*20X6*
Profit after tax (£m)	52	74	80
P/E ratio	7.5	8.5	9.0
Market capitalisation (£m)	390	629	720
Dividends (£m)	12	17	24

The shareholders have seen a **rise of 84.6%** in the market capitalisation over the last four years together with a doubling in the level of dividends. If it is assumed that this has not involved the raising of additional equity, then this, together with the premium achieved on the first day of trading suggest that the shareholders have done very well out of the issue.

(ii) **Employees**

Sales per employee have risen from £60,700 in 20X2 to £75,400 in 20X6. However, the average salary has risen from £7,714 to £8,030, an increase of 4.1% compared with an increase of 5.8% in the RPI. Over the same period the number employed has fallen by 800, a reduction of 6.9%. The apparently poor rate of increase in remuneration, particularly when compared with the increase in the level of sales per employee, could partly reflect a move to a **less skilled workforce**, or perhaps a **greater proportion of part-time employees.**

The **directors' emoluments** have trebled since before the privatisation, and have doubled since 20X2. It is not known whether the number of directors has increased, or whether this increase has been solely in order to bring their remuneration into line with that in the private sector in order to retain quality management. It is also not known whether they also hold share options which could be a further valuable benefit.

(iii) **Customers**

Customers, as consumers, are primarily concerned with the quality and consistency of supply and the price that they have to pay for it. Information is not available to assess the service quality performance over the period, but the price levels can be evaluated, given that the output of electricity appears to have increased by an average of 2½% per annum. Figures for alternate years are shown below.

	20X0	*20X2*	*20X4*	*20X6*
Turnover (£m)	760	850	920	995
Projected turnover (£m) taking into account solely the increase in demand (2½% pa)	760	798	839	881
Increase due to price (£m)		52	29	28
Average annual increase in price (%)		3.4	1.8	2.0
Average annual RPI increase (%)		1.5	1.5	1.4

Thus the component of the growth in turnover due to price has been **rising** at an **increasing rate** over the period and at a **rate** in **excess of the rate of inflation**. At first sight this might appear to be due to weak regulation giving a bad deal to consumers, but there could be two other factors at work, as follows.

(1) The company could be **expanding** into **other unregulated areas** which are accounting for the growth in turnover, for example developing its laboratory facilities into a commercial business.

(2) The increase in price could be **needed to fund investment** in improved service quality and reliability of supply. There is no information available on this area.

(c) (i) The figures above suggest that prices have risen above the rate of inflation, although it is not known whether some of this increase is due to expansion into unregulated businesses. If this is the case then the **company** could have been **attempting to cooperate** with the government's desire for low inflation. At the same time, the **price of labour** as calculated above has been **kept very low** with increases below the rate of inflation, although the same has not been true for the directors. The effect of this is to transfer value to the directors and the shareholders rather than to society at large.

(ii) The company has **demonstrated** a **rapid rate of growth** in both turnover and operating profit over the period. The amount of revenue accruing to the government in the form of corporation tax has almost doubled since 20X2 to £19m in 20X6. Capital investment has increased by 2.57 times compared with 20X2 to £90m in 20X6. This will not only benefit the industry, but also the wider economy through the multiplier effect. (It is assumed that the money has not been spent outside the UK.)

24 GUSTAFFSON PLC

Tutor's hint. The eight marks available for (a) is a lot for a definition part question so your description in (a) needs to be fairly full. Although you are directed to describe the symptoms of overtrading, you would have mentioned them even if you had not been asked.

(b) should be approached by using your calculations to determine whether overtrading exists rather than just calculating random ratios. This means examining the short-term ratios in company finance, as well as sales growth, profit margins, liquidity ratios and working capital ratios. Do not be surprised however if not all the ratios show the same results; here the company is keeping up its payment schedule to creditors despite its other problems.

(b) concludes by highlighting the most important indicators of overtrading. It is important to do this in an answer where you have given a lot of detail, as you need to pick out where the greatest threats to the business lie. In this question the threats highlighted at the end of part (b) will be those for which remedies are identified in (c).

(a) **Overtrading**

'**Overtrading**' refers to the situation where a company is **over-reliant** on **short-term finance** to support its operations. This is risky because short-term finance may be withdrawn relatively quickly if creditors **lose confidence** in the business, or if there is a general tightening of credit in the economy, and this may result in a liquidity crisis and even bankruptcy, even though the firm is profitable. The fundamental solution to overtrading is to replace short term finance with longer term finance such as term loans or equity funds.

Problems of rapid expansion

The term overtrading is used because the condition commonly arises when a company is expanding rapidly. In this situation, because of increasing volumes, **more cash** is frequently **needed to pay input costs** such as wages or purchases than is currently being collected from debtors. The result is that the company runs up its overdraft to the limit and sometimes there is **insufficient time** to arrange an **increase in facilities** to pay other creditors on the due dates.

Lack of control

These problems are often compounded by a general lack of attention to **cost control** and **working capital management**, such as debt collection, because most management time is spent **organising selling or production**. The result is an unnecessary **drop in profit margins**.

Under-capitalisation

When the overdraft limit is reached the company frequently raises funds from other **expensive short term sources**, such as debt factoring or debtor's prompt payment discounts, and delays payment to creditors, instead of underpinning its financial position with equity funds or a longer term loan. The consequent under-capitalisation **delays investment in fixed assets and staff** and can further harm the quality of the firm's operations.

(b) (i) The company has become significantly more reliant on short term liabilities to finance its operations as shown by the following analysis:

	20X9		*20X8*	
	£'000		£'000	
Total assets	21,350		14,900	
Short-term liabilities	8,700	40.7%	5,000	33.6%
Long term funds (equity and debt)	12,650	59.3%	9,900	66.4%
	21,350		14,900	

Overtrading

A major reason for this is classic overtrading: sales increased by 50% in one year, but the operating profit margin fell from 9,000/20,000 = 45% in 20X8 to 10,000/30,000 = 33% in 20X9.

Refinancing

However, the effect is **compounded** by the **repayment** of £2.3 million (66%) of the 8% debentures and replacement with a £2 million bank overdraft and increased trade creditor finance. Although this may be because the interest rate on the overdraft is cheaper than on the debentures, it is generally not advisable in the context of the risk of short term debt.

However, if it is felt that the current sales volume is abnormal and that, when the Polly Playtime doll reaches the end of its product life cycle, sales will stabilise at a lower level, the use of shorter term debt is justified.

Liquidity ratios

As a result of overtrading, the company's **current ratio** has deteriorated from 13,500/5000 = 2.7 in 20X8 to 19,850/8700 = 2.28 in 20X9. The **quick assets ratio** (or 'acid test') has deteriorated from 10,500/5,000 = 2.1 to 12,500/8,700 = 1.44. However these figures are acceptable and only if they continue to deteriorate is there likely to be a liquidity problem. In the 20X9 accounts the company continues to have a healthy bank balance, although this has been achieved partly by halting dividend growth.

Investment in fixed assets

The company has **not maintained an investment in fixed assets** to match its sales growth. Sales/fixed assets has increased from 20,000/1,400 = 14.3 times to 30,000/1,500 = 20 times. This may be putting the quality of production at risk, but may be justified, however, if sales are expected to decline when the doll loses popularity.

Working capital ratios

An investigation of working capital ratios shows that:

(1) **Stock turnover** has **decreased** from 20,000/3,000 = 6.67 times to 30,000/7,350 = 4.08 times. This indicates that there has been a large investment in stock. The question of whether this is justified again depends on expected future sales, but the strategy appears to be the opposite of that adopted for fixed assets.

(2) The **average debtors payment period has increased** from 6,000/20,000 × 365 = 110 days to 10,000/30,000 × 365 = 122 days, indicating a lack of credit control. This has contributed to a weakening of the cash position. There appears to be no evidence of prompt payment discounts to debtors.

(3) The **payment period to creditors** (roughly estimated) has **decreased** from 2,500/11,000 × 365 = 83 days to 4,200/20,000 × 365 = 77 days. This result is unexpected, indicating that there has been no increase in delaying payment to creditors over the year. Creditors are being paid in a significantly shorter period than the period of credit taken by customers.

Conclusion

In summary, the main problem facing Gustaffson is its increasing overdependence on short term finance, caused in the main by:

(1) A major investment in stock to satisfy a rapid increase in sales volumes
(2) Deteriorating profit margins
(3) Poor credit control of debtors
(4) Repayment of debenture capital

(ii) **Future sales**

Possible solutions to the above problems depend on **future sales** and **product projections**. If the rapid increase in sales has been a one-product phenomenon, there is little point in over-capitalising by borrowing long term and investing in a major expansion of fixed assets. If, however, sales of this and future products are expected to continue increasing, and further investment is needed, the company's growth should be underpinned by an injection of equity capital and an issue of longer term debt.

Better working capital management

Regardless of the above, various working capital strategies could be improved. **Debtors** should be encouraged to **pay more promptly**. This is best done by instituting **proper credit control procedures**. **Longer credit periods** could probably be negotiated with creditors and quantity discounts should be investigated.

25 H FINANCE PLC

Tutor's hint. In the exam you probably would not get a complete question on factoring. The arrangement would most likely be examined in combination with other methods such as invoice discounting or credit insurance.

However the question is typical of the sort of things that might be asked about factoring, combining calculation with discussion of the general issues involved. When comparing the costs of two possibilities, sometimes as here you would calculate the total costs of each arrangement. On other occasions you would use the differences between each method in your calculation. (a) shows where the differences are likely to lie.

To answer (b) well you needed to bring out benefits in different areas (factoring as a source of finance, use of factors as means of improving working capital management and decreasing administration time and costs.) As far as the effect on the accounts is concerned, the gearing point is significant but note the uncertain effect on return on capital employed.

(a) Assuming that the historical data presented is a reasonable guide to what will happen in the future, we can calculate whether the factoring of the debts on the debtors' ledger of D Ltd would be worthwhile as follows. The 20Y0 figures are assumed below to be typical.

Cost of finance

The cost of the finance provided by the factor is 5% of sales, since 80% and then a further 15% is remitted by the factor. This is equivalent to around 23% of debtors (5 ÷ 0.22) based on the 20Y0 year end debtors' figure. However, it should be borne in mind that 15% of the finance is only received when the amounts due are received by the finance company: this delay of course makes the finance less attractive than if 95% were received straight away.

Administration costs

In addition, there would be administration costs of 0.5% × 98.7m = £0.5 million which amounts to considerably more than the amount of £80,000 saved in D Ltd's own administration costs.

Bad debts

There may be some saving through a reduction in bad debts, which in 20Y0 amounted to 0.6% of turnover (£0.6m). However there is against this a loss of contribution amounting to 18% × 10% × £98.7m ≈ £1.8m as a result of the factor's aggressive collection procedures. This will outweigh any savings in the cost of bad debts.

Considering:

(i) The **cost** of the **finance** provided
(ii) The **higher administration costs**, and
(iii) The **loss in contribution** from lost turnover

it would appear that factoring is not justified on the basis of any of these three elements.

(b) **Aspects of factoring**

The three main aspects of factoring are as follows.

(i) **Administration** of the client's invoicing, sales accounting and debt collection service.

(ii) **Credit protection** for the client's debts, whereby the factor takes over the risk of loss from bad debts and so 'insures' the client against such losses. This service is also referred to as 'debt underwriting' or the 'purchase of a client's debts'. The factor usually purchases these debts 'without recourse' to the client, which means that in the event that the client's debtors are unable to pay what they owe, the factor will not ask for his money back from the client.

(iii) **Making payments** to the client in **advance** of collecting the debts. This might be referred to as 'factor finance' because the factor is providing cash to the client against outstanding debts.

Benefits of factoring

The benefits of factoring for a business customer include the following.

(i) The business can **pay** its **suppliers promptly**, and so can take advantage of any early payment discounts that are available.

(ii) **Optimum stock** levels can be **maintained**, because the business will have enough cash to pay for the stocks it needs.

(iii) **Growth** can be **financed** through sales rather than by injecting fresh external capital.

(iv) The business gets **finance linked** to its **volume of sales**. In contrast, overdraft limits tend to be determined by historical balance sheets.

(v) The managers of the business do **not have to spend their time** on the **problems** of slow-paying debtors.

(vi) The business does **not incur the costs** of **running its own sales ledger department**.

Effect on accounts

Factoring of sales invoicing leads to a **reduction of debtors** and therefore of assets employed in the business, accompanied by a reduction in profit as a result of the costs involved. Part of these 'costs' are generally reflected in the fact that less than 100% of the debt is paid to the company by the factor. The effect on the **return on capital employed** will depend upon the cost of factoring and the level of profits without factoring relative to assets employed.

Since they reduce assets, the funds advanced by the factor do not show up as **borrowings** in the balance sheet. The apparent gearing will therefore improve. Factoring is attractive to some companies as a method of avoiding borrowing limits or covenants being breached. It provides a means of financing debtors, which are otherwise unsuitable for secured lending because of their volatility.

Disadvantages of factoring

The main disadvantage of factoring is that it is a **relatively expensive form** of finance compared to loan finance. Some businesses will also find it undesirable for customer relations if the administration of debt collection is passed to a third party.

26 SF

Tutor's hint. The first thing to pick up when you read part (a) of this question is that the company is a **small family owned private** company and not a large plc listed on the Stock Exchange. Your suggestions should reflect this and be ones that such a company might reasonably be expected to adopt.

You need to approach this question by making an assessment of the **underlying profitability** of the business, and trying to understand the key reasons for the cash flow problems before proposing possible solutions.

The solution works down the balance sheet suggesting possible ways of improving each element of working capital and obtaining further finance. The suggestions you put forward should make as much use as possible of the data given in the question, for example highlighting the implications of the seasonal nature of sales. At the same time there are also other general suggestions that can be made; a company in financial difficulties can almost always think about tightening its credit control procedures for example. Note that the answer includes assessment of how effective the various ways of improving the situation could be.

The conclusion highlights the most urgent action required as well as commenting on the company's overall state of health.

To: Board of Directors, SF Ltd
From: External consultant
Date: 12 November 20X1
Subject: Cash flow budget

Introduction

The budget shows that the company will experience a **positive cash position** for the first quarter of the year, there being a net inflow of cash during this time as well as no use of the overdraft facility. However, thereafter the position deteriorates, with the company being forecast to exceed its overdraft limit from August to November. By the end of the year, the company's cash reserves will be £50,000 lower than at the start of the period.

Possible remedial actions

1 **Production scheduling**

Sales show a cyclical movement, with receipts from customers being highest during the winter months. However, production is scheduled evenly throughout the year. If production could be **scheduled** to **match the pattern of demand**, the cash balance would remain more even throughout the year. Any resulting increase in the overall level of production costs could be quantified and compared with the savings in interest costs to assess the viability of such a proposal.

2 **Reduce the stockholding period**

At present it is forecast that stocks will be £30,000 higher by the end of the year. This represents three months' worth of purchases from suppliers. It is not clear to what extent this increase is predicated upon **increasing sales**, although since the building is being extended it is assumed that there will be some increase in the level of production and sales in the near future. However, the size of the increase seems excessive.

3 **Reducing the debt collection period**

SF Ltd currently allows its customers two months' credit. It is not known how this compares with the industry norms, but it is unlikely to be excessive. However, there may be some scope for **reducing the credit period** for at least some of the customers, and thereby reducing the average for the business as a whole.

4 **Tightening the credit control procedures**

It is not known what level of bad debts is incurred by SF Ltd, but even if it is low, **tightening up** the **credit control** and **debt collection procedures** could improve the speed with which money is collected.

5 **Factoring the sales ledger**

The use of a factor to administer the sales ledger might **reduce the collection period** and **save administration costs**. An **evaluation** of the **relevant costs and benefits** could be undertaken to see whether it is worth pursuing this option.

6 **Increase the credit period taken**

Since SF Ltd already takes 90 days credit, it is unlikely that it will be able to increase this further without **jeopardising** the **relationship** with its suppliers.

7 **Defer payment for fixed assets**

(a) Presumably the **purchase** of the **office furniture** could be deferred, although the sums involved are relatively insignificant.

(b) The **progress payment** on the **building extension** is likely to be a contractual commitment that cannot be deferred.

(c) The **purchase of the car** could reasonably be **deferred** until the cash position improves. If it is essential to the needs of the business, the company could consider spreading the cost through some form of leasing or hire purchase agreement.

(d) It is not clear why the new **equipment** is being **purchased**. Presumably some form of investment appraisal has been undertaken to establish the financial benefits of the acquisition. However, if it is being purchased in advance of an increase in production then it may be possible to defer it slightly. The company could also look at alternative methods of financing it, as have been suggested in the case of the car.

8 **Dividend**

SF Ltd is a private company, and therefore the shareholders could agree to **forego** or **defer the dividend**. The practicality of this will depend on the personal situation of the five shareholders.

9 **Defer the corporation tax payment**

This might be possible by **agreement with the Inland Revenue**. The company should consider the relative **costs of the interest** that would be charged if this were done, and the **cost of financing** the payment through some form of debt.

10 **Realise the investment**

The dividend from this is £10,000, and therefore assuming an interest rate of, say, 5%, it could be worth in the region of £200,000. It is not clear **what form** this takes or for **what purpose** it is being held, but it may be possible to dispose of a part of it without jeopardising the long-term strategic future of the business.

11 **Inject additional long-term capital**

The budget assumes that both fixed and working capital will increase by £30,000 during the year, and the directors should therefore consider seeking **additional long term capital** to finance at least the fixed asset acquisitions. Possible sources of capital include:

- Injection of funds from the existing shareholders
- The use of venture capital
- Long-term bank loan, debenture or mortgage

Conclusions

1 It can be seen that there are a number of avenues that SF could explore. It appears that the company is **fundamentally profitable**, given the size of the corporation tax bill, and the fact that were it not for the fixed asset additions and the investment in stock the cash balance would increase by £10,000 during the year. However, the liquidity issues must be addressed now to avoid exceeding the overdraft limit.

2 The company should also consider **investing its cash surpluses** during the first quarter of the year to earn at **least some interest**, although this will be restricted by the short periods for which funds are likely to be available . Possible investments include:

- Bank deposits
- Short-term gilts
- Bills of exchange

27 HEADWATER PLC

Tutor's hint. The bulk of the marks in (a) would be available for the written comparisons with the rest of the industry, particularly as you are told which ratios to calculate rather than having to select them yourself. You need to provide sensible explanations for differences with the industry and highlight areas for concern, in particular here the problems over sources of finance.

In (b) you need to show that the company can gain more funds not only because more investors can put money in, but also that listed status provides more reasons for investors to buy a stake (improved marketability of shares being probably the most important).

When answering (c) you should examine the balance sheet and consider how different elements might be made more attractive to investors. This includes looking at share capital and considering whether the issue price of each share is likely to be too high.

(d) brings out the primary pressure that will face the company after floating, to maintain or improve dividend levels. The market will also be sensitive to attempts to massage the balance sheet artificially, for example by using share proceeds to pay off debentures.

(a) The performance and financial health of Headwater in relation to that of the industry sector as a whole can be evaluated by comparing its financial ratios with the industry averages, as follows.

Headwater plc	*Industry average*
Return on (long-term) capital employed	
Operating profit (PBIT): Equity + long-term debt	
£4.9m: (£12.4m + £2.2m) = 33.6%	24%
Return on equity	
Profit attributable to ordinary shareholders: Equity	
£3.1m: £12.4m = 25%	16%
Operating profit margin	
Operating profit : Sales	
£4.9m: £36.5m = 13.4%	11%
Current ratio	
Current assets: Current liabilities	
£10.1m: £9.0m = 1.12:1	1.6:1

Headwater plc	*Industry average*
Acid test	
Current assets excluding stock: Current liabilities	
£5.7m: £9.0m = 0.63:1	1.0:1
Gearing	
Debt: Equity	
(£2m + £2.2m): £12.4m = 33.9%	24%
Dividend cover	
Profit attributable to equity: Dividends	
£3.1m: £0.3m = 10.3 times	4.0
Interest cover	
Profit before interest and tax (PBIT): Interest	
£4.9m: £1.3m = 3.77 times	4.5

These ratios can be used to evaluate performance in terms of profitability, liquidity and financial security.

Profitability

Headwater's return on capital employed, return on equity and operating profit margin are all significantly above the industry averages. Although the first two measures could be inflated due to assets being shown at low book values, the profit margin indicates that Headwater is managing to make good profits, which could be due to successful marketing, a low cost base or to its occupation of a particularly profitable niche in the market.

Liquidity

Both the current and the quick (acid test) ratios are well below the industry averages. This suggests that Headwater is either short of liquid resources or is managing its working capital poorly. However, the three key working capital ratios modify this impression.

Debtor days:	365 × 4.7/36.5	=	47 days
Stock turnover:	365 × 4.4/31.6	=	51 days
Payment period:	365 × 7.0/31.6	=	81 days

Although the industry averages are not known, these ratios appear to be very good by general standards. It therefore appears that Headwater has become under-capitalised, perhaps through the use of working capital to finance growth.

Financial security

Gearing is **high** in comparison with the rest of the industry, and 48% of the debt is in the form of overdraft which is generally repayable on demand. This is therefore a risky form of debt to use in large amounts. The debenture is repayable in two years and will need to be refinanced since Headwater cannot redeem it out of existing resources. Interest cover is also poor, and this together with the poor liquidity probably account for the low payout ratio (the inverse of the dividend cover).

In summary, profit performance is strong, but there are significant weaknesses in both the liquidity and the financial structure. These problems need to be addressed if Headwater is to be able to maintain its record of strong and consistent growth.

(b) A company such as Headwater may seek a stock market listing for the following reasons.

(i) To **allow access** to a **wider pool of finance:** companies that are growing fast may need to raise larger sums than is possible privately. Obtaining a listing widens the potential number of equity investors, and may also result in an improved credit rating, thus reducing the cost of additional debt finance.

(ii) To **improve the marketability of the shares:** shares that are traded on the stock market can be bought and sold in relatively small quantities at any time. This means that it is easier for existing investors to realise a part of their holding.

(iii) To **allow capital to be transferred** to other ventures: founder owners may wish to liquidate the major part of their holding either for personal reasons or for investment in other new business opportunities.

(iv) To **improve the company image:** quoted companies are commonly believed to be more financially stable, and this may improve the image of the company with its customers and suppliers, allowing it to gain additional business and to improve its buying power.

(v) **Growth by acquisition** is easier: a listed company is in a better position to make a paper offer for a target company than an unlisted one.

(c) Restructuring its balance sheet prior to flotation will help to make Headwater appear a sounder prospect to potential investors who know little about its past performance. Methods available include the following.

Disposal of surplus assets. This will improve both gearing and liquidity.

Fixed asset revaluation. Land and buildings may well be shown in the accounts at values that are significantly below the current market valuation. Adjustment to market values will improve the gearing ratio and the value of shareholders' funds, although the effect of this will be to depress the reported return on capital employed and return on equity. However, since these are currently well above industry averages this should not present too much of a problem.

Liquidity improvement. Although there does not appear to be much scope for tightening the control of working capital, Headwater may be able to improve its cash flow by other means, for example by reducing overheads and delaying the purchase of additional fixed assets.

Sale and leaseback. If Headwater owns valuable freehold premises it may be able to release cash by selling them and exchanging the freehold for an operating lease. This would improve both the liquidity position and the reported return on capital employed although the gearing would be little affected.

Elimination of non-voting 'A' shares. These are not permitted by the Stock Exchange for companies newly entering the market.

Share split. On the basis of the industry average P/E of 10, the shares would be priced at £11.48 (= 10 × 3.1m/(1.8m + 0.9m)). A highly priced new issue is likely to deter potential small investors. This problem could be overcome by reducing the nominal value of the shares by means of a share split.

(d) Following the flotation Headwater is likely to come under pressure to **improve** the **payout ratio** and **dividend performance** of the shares. If it wishes to maintain a good share price and the ability to raise further finance in the future then it would be well advised to consider this seriously. It could also work towards **lowering the gearing ratio**, perhaps by using a part of the issue proceeds to **redeem some** or all of the **debentures**. However this should not appear to be the prime reason for the float or the attractiveness of the issue will be diminished.

28 KB

> **Tutor's hint.** Don't forget in (a) (ii) that you need to use the issue price to calculate how many shares should be issued and not the current market price. The answer to (a) (i) is a red herring. The discussion in (a) (ii) takes into account external market factors as well as the performance of the company. Focus on the assumptions made. What are the costs (assumed to be none)? What else might influence the share price? Will the rights issue itself change investors' views of the company?
>
> The key feature that your answer to (a) (iii) should bring out is that issuing shares at a large discount provides **security** that all the shares will be taken up.
>
> Your answer to (b) (ii) should show clearly what an issue of convertible loan stock will achieve that a rights issue will not.

(a) (i) The **current market price** can be found by multiplying the earnings per share (EPS) by the price/earnings (P/E) ratio.

EPS is £1.2m/6m = 20 pence per share
P/E ratio is 12
Market price of shares is 12 × 20p = **£2.40 per share**

(ii) In order to raise £5,040,000 at a price of 192 pence, the company will need to issue an additional 2,625,000 (£5,040,000/£1.92) shares.

Following the investment, the total number of shares in issue will be 8,625,000 (6,000,000 + 2,625,000).

At this point, the total value of the company will be:

($6m \times £2.40$) + £5,040,000 = £19,440,000

The **theoretical ex-rights price** will therefore be £19.44m/8.625m = **£2.25**.

Problems with calculations

(1) The **costs of arranging the issue** have not been included in the calculations.

(2) The **market view** of the **quality of the new investment** will affect the actual price of the company's shares.

(3) If the **issue** is **not fully subscribed** and a significant number of shares remain with the underwriters, this will **depress the share price**.

(4) The effect of the new investment on the **risk profile** of the company and the expected **future dividend stream** could also cause the share price to differ from that predicted.

(5) The price of the shares depends not only on the financial performance of the company, but also on the **overall level of demand** in the stock market. If the market moves significantly following the announcement of the issue, this will affect the actual price at which the shares are traded.

(iii) **Features of deep discounted rights issue**

In a **deep-discounted** rights issue, the new shares are priced at a **large discount** to the current market price of the shares. The purpose of this is to ensure that the issue is **well subscribed** and that shares are not left with the underwriters, and thus this form of issue pricing is attractive when the stock market is particularly **volatile**. However, the shares cannot be issued at a price which is below their nominal value.

Disadvantage of deep discounted rights issue

The main drawback to this approach is that a **larger number of shares** will need to be **issued** in order to raise the required amount of finance, and this will lead to a larger dilution of earnings per share and dividends per share.

(b) (i) **Conversion premium**

The **conversion premium** is the **difference** between the **issue value** of the **stock** and the **conversion value** as at the date of issue. In other words it is the measure of the additional expense involved in buying shares via the convertible stock as compared with buying the shares on the open market immediately.

In this case, £100 loan stock can be converted into 35 ordinary shares. The **effective price** of these shares is therefore £2.86 (£100/35) per share.

The **current market price** of the shares is £2.40. The **conversion premium** is therefore £2.86 − £2.40 = **46 pence**. This can also be expressed in percentage terms as **19%** (0.46/2.40).

(ii) **Advantages of issuing convertible loan stock**

(1) **Convertibles** should be **cheaper than equity** because they offer greater security to the investor. This may make them particularly attractive in fast growing but high-risk companies.

(2) **Issue costs** are **lower** for loan stock than for equity.

(3) **Interest** on the **loan stock** is **tax deductible**, unlike dividends on ordinary shares.

(4) There is **no immediate change** in the **existing structure** of control, although this will change over time as conversion rights are exercised.

(5) There is no **immediate dilution** in **earnings** and **dividends per share**.

29 RUMP

Tutor's hint. Note the step by step approach in (a).

Step 1.	Calculate number of shares
Step 2.	Calculate issue price
Step 3.	Calculate ex-rights price

In part (c) you need to do more than describe the various alternatives. You must compare and contrast the merits of the rights issue and the debenture, and ensure that all your discussions are related to the circumstances of Rump plc. Your answer needs to bring out the potential difficulties with whatever choice the directors make. Note how the change in financing can have quite wide implications (the impact on strategy of restrictive covenants and a change in the ownership structure). The issue of change in control is also important when we consider the alternative methods of issuing shares.

The conclusion here brings out that the other methods suggested are unlikely to be used and in practice the choice would be between a rights issue and a debenture issue.

(a) There are currently 10m shares in issue. A 2 for 5 rights issue would mean that **4m additional shares** would have to be issued (10m × 2/5).

The rights issue must raise £24m. Therefore the new shares must be issued at a price of **£6 per share** (£24m/4m).

Using the formula

$$\text{Theoretical ex rights price} = \frac{1}{N+1}((N \times \text{rights price}) + \text{issue price})$$

$$= \frac{1}{2.5+1}((2.5 \times 6.60) + 6.00)$$

$$= 6.43$$

(b) If the debenture issue is made, the number of equity shares in issue will be unchanged at 10m.

The **profit available** for **dividend** will be reduced by the amount of the debenture interest, which is £1.8m per year (£24m × 7.5%), giving an annual dividend of £7.2 million.

The theoretical share price can be found using the dividend valuation model:

$k_e = d/p_0$

$10\% = £0.72/p_0$

$\mathbf{p_0 = £7.20}$

(c) To: Chairman
From: Finance Director
Date: 20 November 20X1
Subject: Financing alternatives for the new investment

Introduction

The new contract is large in relation to the size of the company, and therefore the new external source of finance could have a **significant effect** on the existing **capital structure** of the business, and on its **ownership and control**. There are two main sources of finance that are being considered, namely a rights issue and a debenture issue, and these will be considered in more detail below. The final section of the report will consider some further methods of raising equity finance that are available to Rump plc.

Rights issue versus debenture issue

Ownership

The rights issue is large in relation to the existing equity in issue, and requires a significant additional investment on the part of the shareholders. If shareholders are likely to be unwilling or unable to exercise their rights, the company should consider underwriting the issue. The underwriters will then take up any shares that remain unsold, but this could result in a **change** in the **balance of control**. A debenture issue by contrast would result in no change in control.

Problems with all equity financing

The company is currently 100% equity financed, and this would continue to be the case in the event of a rights issue. This means that the **level of financial risk** faced by the shareholders is

low. However, it also means that they cannot take advantage of the **lower cost and tax benefits** of debt finance, and that therefore the potential returns to equity are lower than they might be if some debt were to be used.

Introduction of gearing

A **debenture issue** of this size would introduce a significant element of **gearing** into the company. The value of debt in the company structure would be £24m, and the value of equity would be £72m (10m × £7.20). This gives a gearing ratio of 25% (ratio of prior charge capital to total capital). This represents a significant change in the **level of financial risk** faced by shareholders, and their attitude to this must be taken into account in making the financing decision.

Issue costs

The calculations ignore issue costs. These may be **significant** for a **rights issue,** amounting on average to 4% of the finance raised, although this percentage rises for small issues. The issue costs of debentures would be less than for a rights issue.

Flexibility

Debenture issues are commonly linked to **restrictive covenants** that limit the company's further ability to borrow. The effect of such covenants on the future needs of the company must be taken into account. Equity funding would impose no such restriction.

(ii) **Further methods of raising equity finance**

(1) **A placing**

This is an arrangement whereby the shares are not all offered to the public, but instead, the sponsoring market maker arranges for **most of the issue** to be **bought by a small number of investors**, usually institutional investors such as pension funds and insurance companies. The **issuing costs** would be **lower** than for a **rights issue**, but the position with regard to **pre-emption rights** of the existing shareholders may have to be resolved. There could be a significant effect on the **control** of the business if the new shares are concentrated in the hands of a small number of institutional investors.

(2) **Offer for sale**

This means that Rump plc would **allot new shares** to an **issuing house**. The issuing house would then offer the **shares for sale** on the basis of a prospectus, either at a **fixed price** or by **tender**. The **issuing costs** would be significantly **higher** than for a rights issue. This is particularly true for fixed price offers where there is a higher risk that not all the shares will be subscribed. However, the **effect** on the **control of the company** is likely to be less than for a placing.

(3) **Public offer for subscription**

This is the **direct offer** of shares to the **public** by the company using a **prospectus**. **Issuing costs**, **underwriting** and **publicity costs** are **high**. It is only appropriate for **large issues** of shares.

Conclusion

Although alternative routes are available for raising equity, in this case the choice is really between a rights issue and a debenture issue. The key factors influencing the decision have been summarised above, but probably the major consideration will be the company's **attitude to financial risk**. This will be significantly increased if the debenture is used, but on the other hand, the **cost** of this will be **less** than if more **equity** is issued, and the potential returns to equity are greater.

30 DF

Tutor's hint. The nature of the calculation in (a) should have suggested to you that the majority of marks would be available for the discussion. The answer looks well beyond the relationship with FF plc, considering the effect on relations with other customers, the effect on DF itself, and whether there are alternative sources of finance for DF.

(b) goes on to cover those alternative sources of finance. Various criteria can be used to consider them:

- **Costs** (including costs saved)
- **Flexibility** (a company knows when and how much interest and principal it has to pay on a loan but still has to pay it; by contrast an overdraft facility only has interest charged on it if it is used, but it is repayable on demand.)
- **Commitment** (security that has to be given, how much the company is tied into the arrangement)
- **Appearances** (effect on gearing, effect on debtors if factor organisation is employed)

Although the question directs you towards discussing certain sources of finance, it does not confine you to those sources. Therefore, although the bulk of your answer to (b) should discuss the sources listed, a section briefly mentioning other sources should also be included.

Don't forget also in (b) to bear in mind the likely level of financial knowledge of the recipients of your report; don't assume a high level of understanding.

(c) is a summary list of the key factors venture capitalists will take into account. As well as the company's market prospects, venture capitalists are also interested in the involvement of management (level of commitment and expertise).

(a) **Cost of discount**

The **percentage cost** of an **early settlement discount** to the company giving it can be estimated by the formula:

$$\frac{d}{100 - d} \times \frac{365}{t}$$

Where d is the size of discount (%)

t is the reduction in payment period in days necessary to achieve discount

d = 3%

t = 90 – 10 = 80

$$\% \text{ cost} = \frac{3}{100-3} \times \frac{365}{80}$$

$$= 14.1\%$$

The **annual equivalent rate of interest** in offering a 3% cash discount is therefore 14.9%.

Offer of discount

Other factors that DF should take into account before deciding on whether to offer a discount include:

(i) The **attractiveness** of the **discount** to FF plc, and the probability that it will be taken up

(ii) Whether the **discount** will encourage FF plc to **purchase larger volumes** than it would if the discount was not available

(iii) The **relative effect** of the **different financing alternatives** on the administration costs of DF plc

(iv) The **ease** with which DF plc will be **able to raise alternative sources of finance,** the effect on **gearing** of these sources and the need for **security**

(v) The interest **other customers** might show in taking a discount

(vi) The possibility of **withdrawing** from the discount arrangement without loss of FF's goodwill in the future

(b) To: Shareholders in DF Ltd
From: Management Accountant
Date: 11 December 20X1
Subject: Alternative methods of financing current assets

Introduction

The contract to supply FF plc means that DF Ltd will need to make a **significant additional permanent investment** in **current assets** (in the form of additional stocks and higher debtors). There will also be an additional temporary element which **fluctuates** with the level of sales. This will increase the amount of money needed by the company to finance these assets. There are a number of different sources of finance that could be considered.

Bank loan

A bank loan would normally be for a **fixed amount of money** for a fixed term and at a fixed rate of interest. It is not clear whether or not the company has any existing debt finance. However, it has already been decided to use a bank loan to fund the purchase of the additional fixed assets. The **size of this loan** and the **quality of security** available will be key factors in determining whether the bank is willing to make a further advance to cover the investment in current assets. Assuming that a further loan is forthcoming, the company will need to evaluate the effect of this in terms of **cost** and the **effect on the capital structure**.

Advantages of bank loan

(i) **Bank finance** is **cheaper** than the cost of allowing a 3% **settlement discount**, and is also likely to be cheaper than using debt factoring or invoice discounting.

(ii) The **loan** can be **negotiated** for a **fixed term** and a **fixed amount**, and this is less risky than for example using an overdraft, which is repayable on demand.

Disadvantages of bank loan

(i) The company will have to **pay interest** on the **full amount of the loan** for the entire period. This could make it more expensive in absolute terms than using an alternative source of finance where interest is only payable on the amount outstanding.

(ii) The loan will **increase the level** of the company's **financial gearing**. This means that there could be greater volatility in the returns attributable to the ordinary shareholders.

(iii) The bank is likely to **require security**. If there are questions as to the quality of the asset base, the bank may also require personal guarantees or additional security from the directors or shareholders.

Overdraft

An overdraft is a form of lending that is **repayable on demand**. The bank grants the customer a **facility** up to a certain limit, and the customer can take advantage of this as necessary. Overdrafts are essentially short-term finance, but are renewable and may become a near-permanent source.

Advantages of overdraft

The attraction of using an overdraft to finance current assets is that **interest** is only **payable** on the **amount of the facility actually in use** at any one time. This means that the **effective cost of the overdraft** will be **lower** than that of the **bank loan**. This is particularly attractive for a company such as DF Ltd, where demand is expected to fluctuate significantly from month to month, and consequently there are likely to be large variations in the level of working capital. It is also likely to be cheaper than the other alternatives being considered.

Disadvantages of overdraft

The main drawback to using an overdraft is that it will be **repayable on demand**, and therefore the company is in a more vulnerable position than it would be if a bank loan were used instead. A long-term overdraft may be included in the **gearing** calculations, and the bank may require **security.**

Debt factoring

Factoring is an arrangement to have **debts collected** by a **factor company**, which advances a proportion of the money it is due to collect. Services offered by the factor would normally include the following:

(i) **Administration** of the client's invoicing, sales accounting and debt collection service.

(ii) **Credit protection** for the client's debts, whereby the factor takes over the risk of loss from bad debts and so 'insures' the client against such losses.

(iii) **Making advance payments** to the client before the debts are collected.

Benefits of factoring

(i) **Growth** is **effectively financed through sales**, which provide the security to the factor. DF would not have to provide the additional security that might be required by the bank.

(ii) The **managers** of the business will **not** have to **spend time** on the problem of **slow paying debtors**.

(iii) **Administration costs** will be **reduced** since the company will not have to run its own sales ledger department.

Disadvantages of factoring

(i) The **level of finance** is **geared** to the **level of sales**; in other words, finance lags sales. In practice, DF will need finance ahead of sales in order to build up sufficient stocks to meet demand.

(ii) Factoring may be **more expensive** than bank finance. Service charges are generally around 2% of total invoice value, in addition to finance charges at levels comparable to bank overdraft rates.

(iii) The fact that debtors will be making payments direct to the factor may present a **negative picture** of the firm.

Invoice discounting

Invoice discounting is related to factoring and many factors will provide an invoice discounting service. Invoice discounting is the **purchase of a selection of invoices**, at a discount. The discounter does **not take over** the **administration** of the client's sales ledger, and the arrangement is purely for the advance of cash.

Advantages of discounting

The arrangement is thus a **purely financial transaction** that can be used to release working capital, and therefore shares some of the benefits of factoring in that **further security** is **not required**. The discounter will make an assessment of the risk involved, and only good quality invoices will be purchased, but this should not be a problem to DF since FF plc is a large well established company.

Disadvantages of discounting

The main disadvantage is that **invoice discounting** is likely to be **more expensive** than any of the other alternatives. It is normally only used to cover a temporary cash shortage, and not for the routine provision of working capital.

Other options

(i) Finance can be obtained by **delaying payment to creditors.** In theory this is potentially a **cheap source of finance.** The main disadvantage may be a **loss of supplier goodwill,** at a time when the company needs supplier co-operation to fulfil the new order.

(ii) Other methods of loan finance, notably debenture issue, are not appropriate as they are essentially **long-term,** and the **debentureholders** may require **security** that the company is unable to give.

(iii) Although we are told that **increased stock levels** will be needed to **fulfil FF's requirements,** there may be scope for **reducing the stock levels** necessary to fulfil other customers' requirements.

Conclusions

Of the options considered, factoring or some form of bank finance is likely to be the most appropriate. The final decision must take into account the full cost implications, and not just the relative rates of interest on the finance. DF Ltd must also consider the effect of the type of finance selected on the balance sheet, and the type of security that will be required. This could also impact on the ability of the company to raise further finance in the future.

(c) A **venture capital organisation** (below, 'VC') is likely to take the following factors into account when deciding whether or not to invest in Fashions Ltd.

The nature of the company's product

The VC will consider whether the good or service can be produced viably and has potential to sell, in the light of any market research which the company has carried out.

Expertise in production

The VC will want to be sure that the company has the necessary technical ability to implement production plans with efficiency.

Expertise in management

Venture capitalists pay much attention to the quality of management, since they believe that this is crucial to the success of the enterprise. Not only should the management team be committed to the enterprise; they should also have appropriate skills and experience.

The market and competition

The nature of the market for the product will be considered, including the threat which rival producers or future new entrants to the market may present.

Future prospects

The VC will want to be sure that the possible prospects of profits in the future compensate for the risks involved in the enterprise. The VC will expect the company to have prepared a detailed business plan detailing its future strategy.

Board membership

The VC is likely to require a place on the Board of Directors. Board representation will ensure that the VC's interests will be taken account of, and that the VC has a say in matters relating to the future strategy of the business.

Risk borne by the existing owners

The VC is likely to wish to ensure that the existing owners of the business bear a significant part of the investment risk relating to the expansion. If they are owner-managers, bearing part of the risk will provide an incentive for them to ensure the success of the venture. Although the VC may be providing most of the investment, the amounts provided by the owners should be significant in relation to their overall personal wealth.

Exit routes

The means by which the VC can eventually realise its investment are called 'exit routes'. Ideally, the VC will try to ensure that there are a number of exit routes.

31 PROJECT APPRAISAL

Tutor's hint. (a) would be a typical part question on these methods of investment appraisal; the rest of the question might well go on to cover net present value and internal rate of return (covered in the next chapter).

It is unlikely that you would get a question on SWOT analysis for as many marks as part (b) gives. However the technique can be used to help you decide **quickly** what strategy a company should follow in a given set of circumstances. As previous questions have demonstrated, you need to do more than just decide which solution has the lowest cost when making decisions. SWOT analysis helps you focus on all relevant aspects of a business (production, sales/marketing, research and development, management), and how external factors impact upon a business (not just impact upon markets, but also impact upon internal costs).

Note in (b) how the financial position of the company has a significant impact upon the means used to purchase the foundry.

The conclusion in (b) highlights the key decisions that need to be made. You can legitimately say that the absence of strategic objectives means that no long-term decision can be made. What the conclusion does is highlight the principal appeal of each option.

(a) (i) Depreciation must first be **added back** to the **annual profit figures**, to arrive at the annual cash flows.

$$\text{Depreciation} = \frac{\text{Initial investment £46,000 – scrap value £4,000}}{\text{4 years}}$$

$$= £10,500$$

Adding £10,500 per annum to the profit figures produces the cash flows for each proposal.

	Proposal A		*Proposal B*	
Year	*Annual cash flow*	*Cumulative cash flow*	*Annual cash flow*	*Cumulative cash flow*
	£	£	£	£
0	(46,000)	(46,000)	(46,000)	(46,000)
1	17,000	(29,000)	15,000	31,000
2	14,000	(15,000)	13,000	(18,000)
3	24,000	9,000	15,000	(3,000)
4	9,000	18,000	25,000	22,000
4	4,000	22,000	4,000	26,000

(1) *Proposal A*

Payback period =

$$2 + \left(\frac{15,000}{24,000} \times 1\text{ year}\right)$$

= 2.6 years

Proposal B

Payback period =

$$3 + \left(\frac{3,000}{25,000} \times 1\text{ year}\right)$$

= 3.1 years

(2) The return on capital employed (ROCE) is calculated using the accounting profits given in the question.

Proposal A Average profit

$$= \frac{£(6,500 + 3,500 + 13,500 - 1,500)}{4}$$

$$= \frac{£22,000}{4}$$

$$= £5,500$$

ROCE

$$= \frac{£5,500}{£46,000} \times 100\%$$

$$= 12.0\%$$

Proposal B Average profit $= \frac{£(4,500 + 2,500 + 4,500 + 14,500)}{4}$

$= \frac{£26,000}{4}$

$= £6,500$

ROCE on initial investment $= \frac{£6,500}{£46,000} \times 100\%$

$= 14.1\%$

(ii) Two advantages of each of the methods of appraisal can be selected from the following.

Payback period

(1) It is **simple** to **calculate**.
(2) It **preserves liquidity** by preferring early cash flows.
(3) It **uses cash flows** instead of more arbitrary accounting profits.
(4) It **reduces risk** by preferring early cash flows.

Return on capital employed

(1) It uses readily available **accounting profits**.

(2) It is **understood** by **non-financial managers**.

(3) It is a measure used by **external analysts** which should therefore be monitored by the company.

(b) A general interpretation might be as follows.

(i) **Objectives**. The company does not have any stated objectives. In view of the probable high (100%) shareholding by the family, it may be that a high level of **liquidity** is required to meet future dividend expectations. There is a clear necessity to agree stated objectives with regard to earnings and dividend payments.

(ii)

Strengths High liquidity. A wide range of products and markets.	*Weaknesses* Low profits due to poor returns from investments and possibly high unit costs, low sales or low prices. Family business, therefore possibly weak management. Heavy reliance on one customer. Poor growth due to limited markets or poor R & D.
Threats Unknown future for the market for aluminium products.	*Opportunities* Investment in stocks and shares. Purchase of a small foundry. Product-market diversification. Major customer involved in the do-it-yourself industry, which still has buoyant markets.

(iii) **Strengths**. The high liquidity is the clearest source of strength. Although the company offers a wide range of products to a variety of customers, growth is poor.

(iv) **Weaknesses**. **Low growth** and **profitability** in current markets and with current products should be a matter of some concern. The reasons for poor performance might range from high variable costs, low output (therefore high unit fixed costs), sluggish demand, weak marketing, high prices, inadequate R & D, ageing machinery and out-of-date technology, poor management, inefficient purchasing and so on. Weaknesses need to be identified more specifically.

(v) **Threats**. None are known, and the future for the aluminium products market may be reasonable if the managing director is correct in his assessment that the purchase of a new foundry would be a viable proposition.

(vi) **Opportunities**

(1) **Stocks and shares**. The **return** from **existing stocks** and shares has been **poor**, which might be the result of **poor investment management** which should be dealt with. There should be a **prospect of improvement** in the **future**, especially if professional advice is taken to sell parts of the existing portfolio and to re-invest in securities offering a higher return or better capital growth. If high liquidity remains a top priority, this strategy has clear merits.

(2) **Purchase of an aluminium foundry**. This policy of market penetration through the acquisition of a competitor offers several advantages:

- Increased market share (and new customers)
- Perhaps improved technology
- Joint fixed costs of administration and marketing, therefore lower unit costs of output
- Rationalisation of production and distribution
- Possibly, management expertise will be acquired

The **purchase consideration** might be for **cash only**, although it might be possible to obtain agreement to a share exchange deal, or a shares plus cash deal. Because the company is a private company, a share exchange arrangement is unlikely to be attractive (and the poor profit record of the company makes a launch on to the Alternative Investment Market an unlikely prospect).

Although the company already has knowledge of the aluminium industry, a **close investigation** of the **past performance and history** (and the future prospects) of the new foundry would be required.

(3) **Diversification into new products and markets.** This would be a difficult step into the unknown, especially in view of the lack of management experience in the company. It is **not recommended strategy**, unless clear opportunities for profits and growth present themselves since the company has **no obvious strengths** to exploit apart from its cash. However, there is a possibility of vertical integration, by attempting the acquisition of the do-it-yourself tools manufacturer. Leisure industries are prospective growth markets and a closer investigation of this possibility may be worthwhile.

(vii) **Conclusion**. No recommendation is possible, except that a strategic planning exercise should be carried out to recommend a long-term strategy. It is perhaps significant that in a comparison of the three opportunities mentioned the following conclusions can be drawn.

(1) The **continued investment in stocks and shares** promises high liquidity and returns in the long and short term.

(2) The **acquisition** of the **aluminium foundry** offers the prospect of a timescale for achieving profits which might be relatively short.

(3) **Diversification offers** no clear prospects, and the timescale required to earn profits might be long. Carefully chosen acquisitions, however, might yield the greatest long-term profits.

32 KNUCKLE DOWN LTD

> **Tutor's hint**. Although this question should take you 45 minutes (the amount of time a question in the exam will take you), an exam question would not consist purely of calculations; it would also most likely include discussion of the benefits and drawbacks of the NPV and IRR methods.
>
> The question nevertheless does give you lots of practice in the techniques and highlights common traps. Depreciation is not a cash flow and should be eliminated. If you have to deal with working capital you need to read the question very carefully. In C the increase in working capital from £15,000 to £21,000 at the end of year 1 is an increase of the **difference** between the figures (£6,000) at the end of year 1. The question also tells you that the working capital investment will be recovered, so that figure ultimately has to be included as a receipt.
>
> The question also requires you to calculate annuities and perpetuities, and deal with cash flows that are constant over a number of years but do not start at year 1. The treatment of the discount rate may have caught you out if you didn't read the question carefully. The discount rate of 15% should be used throughout the duration of all projects lasting more than ten years, and not just from year 10 onwards.
>
> You can use the NPV calculations for A and C as the first rates in the IRR estimation process. The fact that the NPV for C was rather larger than A indicates that you should try a different second rate. The main thing is to pick two higher rates as the NPVs were positive; you would get equal credit if you had chosen any rate in the 15 - 20% band for your second IRR calculation. (Below 15% would probably be a bit too near to the 12%, but you would be unlikely to be penalised very heavily for using 13% or 14%).

(a) (i) *Project A*

Year	*Cash flow*	*Discount factor*	*Present value*
	£	12%	£
0	(29,000)	1.000	(29,000)
1	8,000	0.893	7,144
2	12,000	0.797	9,566
3	10,000	0.712	7,120
4	11,000	0.636	6,996
		Net present value	1,826

(ii) *Project B*

Year	*Equipment*	*Working capital*	*Cash profit*	*Net cash flow*	*Discount factor*	*Present value*
	£	£	£	£	12%	£
0	(44,000)	(20,000)		(64,000)	1.000	(64,000)
1			19,000	19,000	0.893	16,967
2			24,000	24,000	0.797	19,128
3	5,000	20,000	10,000	35,000	0.712	24,920
					Net present value	(2,985)

(iii) *Project C*

Year	*Equipment*	*Working capital*	*Cash profit*	*Net cash flow*	*Discount factor*	*Present value*
	£	£	£	£	12%	£
0	(50,000)	(15,000)		(65,000)	1.000	(65,000)
1		(6,000)		(6,000)	0.893	(5,358)
1-5			18,000	18,000	3.605	64,890
5		21,000		21,000	0.567	11,907
					Net present value	6,439

(iv) *Project D*

Year	*Cash flow*	*Discount factor*	*Present value*
	£	12%	£
0	(20,000)	1.000	(20,000)
1	(20,000)	0.893	(17,860)
2	15,000	0.797	11,958
3	12,000	0.712	8,544
4-8	8,000	2.566	20,528
		Net present value	3,170

Discount factor at 12%, years 1 to 8	4.968
Less discount factor at 12%, years 1 to 3	2.402
Discount factor at 12%, years 4 to 8	2.566

(v) *Project E*

The cumulative discount factor for a perpetuity at 15% is 1/0.15 = 6.667.

Year	*Cash flow*	*Discount factor*	*Present value*
	£	15%	£
0	(32,000)	1.000	(32,000)
1-∞	4,500	6.667	30,000
		Net present value	(2,000)

(vi) *Project F*

		£
1	Present value (at 15%) of £3,000 a year from year 1 in perpetuity	20,000
	Less present value of £3,000 a year for years 1 to 10 (× 5.019)	15,057
	Present value of £3,000 a year from year 11 in perpetuity	4,943
2	Discount factor at 15%, years 1 to 10	5.019
	Less discount factor at 15%, years 1 to 5	3.352
	Discount factor at 15%, years 6 to 10	1.667

3

Year	*Net cash flow*	*Discount factor*	*Present value*
	£	15%	£
0	(20,000)	1.000	(20,000)
1-5	5,000	3.352	16,760
6-10	4,000	1.667	6,668
11-∞	3,000	See above	4,943
		Net present value	8,371

(vii) Projects A, C, D and F have positive net present values and should be undertaken. Projects B and E should not be undertaken.

(b) (i) The IRR of project A is above 12% (where the NPV is £1,826). We will calculate the NPV at 15%.

Year	*Cash flow*	*Discount factor*	*Present value*
	£	15%	£
0	(29,000)	1.000	(29,000)
1	8,000	0.870	6,960
2	12,000	0.756	9,072
3	10,000	0.658	6,580
4	11,000	0.572	6,292
		Net present value	(96)

The IRR is between 12% and 15%. By interpolation, we can estimate the IRR as about

$$12\% + \left[\frac{1,826}{(1,826 - -96)} \times (15 - 12)\right] \%$$

= 14.85%

(ii) The IRR of project C is above 12%, where the NPV is £6,439. Try 20%.

Year	Net cash flow	Discount factor	Present value
	£	20%	£
0	(65,000)	1.000	(65,000)
1	(6,000)	0.833	(4,998)
1-5	18,000	2.991	53,838
5	21,000	0.402	8,442
		Net present value	(7,718)

$$\text{The IRR is approximately } 12\% + \left[\frac{6{,}439}{(6{,}439 - -7{,}718)} \times (20 - 12)\right]\% = 15.6\%$$

(iii) The IRR, r, of project E is found as follows.

PV of cost = PV of benefits

$$(32{,}000) = \frac{4{,}500}{r}$$

$$r = \frac{4{,}500}{32{,}000} = 0.140625$$

IRR = 14.0625%

33 DINARD

Tutor's hint. (a) allows you to demonstrate that you understand the topic of real and money returns by explaining the difference between them.

(b) introduces the complication of what you should do if you are told what current (or year 1) prices are but are also given information about price increases over the period of investment. Because the costs are increasing at different rates, the money rate (which you are given) has to be used, and the revenues and costs inflated each year. If the rate of increase for everything had been the same, you could either have used the money rate (and inflated costs and revenues), or calculated the real rate (and used uninflated costs and revenues). Since calculating the real rate only involves one calculation, you should really have chosen that option.

Again don't forget to exclude depreciation as it is not a cash flow. Development costs of £480,000 are sunk costs and should also be excluded from the calculation. Because you are told to confine your answer to the information given, you should not discuss any wider issues that might be involved in the investment.

(a) The **real rate of return** is the rate of return which an investment would show in the **absence of inflation**. For example, if a company invests £100, inflation is 0%, and the investment at the end of the year is worth £110, then the real rate of return is 10%.

In reality however, there is likely to be an element of inflation in the returns due to the change in the purchasing power of money over the period. In the example above, if inflation was running at 5%, then to show a real rate of return of 10%, the investment would need to be worth £115.50 at the end of the year. In this case the money rate of return is 15.5% which is made up of the real return of 10% and inflation at 5%.

The relationship between the nominal ('money') rate of return and the real rate of return can be expressed as follows:

$$(1 + \text{nominal rate}) = (1 + \text{real rate}) \times (1 + \text{inflation rate})$$

The rate to be used in discounting cash flows for capital project appraisal will depend on the **way** in which the **expected cash flows** are calculated. If the cash flows are expressed in terms of the **actual number of pounds** that will be received or paid on the various future dates, then the **nominal rate** must be used. If however they are expressed in **terms** of the **value of the pound at year 0**, then the **real rate must be used**.

(b) *Workings*

	Year 1	*Year 2*	*Year 3*	*Year 4*
Sales volume	25,000	25,000	25,000	25,000
Unit price (£)	80	84	88	93
Variable material cost (£)	8.00	8.32	8.65	9.00
Variable labour cost (£)	12.00	13.20	14.52	15.97
Variable overhead (£)	12.00	12.48	12.98	13.50

Notes

Evaluation of investment
(All figures £'000)

	Year 0	*Year 1*	*Year 2*	*Year 3*	*Year 4*
Capital outlay	(2,400)				
Sales		2,000	2,100	2,205	2,315
Direct costs					
Materials		(200)	(208)	(216)	(225)
Labour		(300)	(330)	(363)	(399)
Overhead		(300)	(312)	(324)	(337)
Fixed overheads		(200)	(210)	(221)	(232)
Gross cash flow	(2,400)	1,000	1,040	1,081	1,122
Discount at 15%	1.000	0.870	0.756	0.658	0.572
Present value	(2,400)	870	786	711	642
Cumulative PV	(2,400)	(1,530)	(744)	(33)	608

The investment yields a net present value at the end of four years of £608,000. In the absence of other factors such as a capital rationing situation, production of the Rance should be undertaken.

34 MUGGINS PLC

Tutor's hint. A methodical set of workings is key to answering this question well (also not confusing the adjustment factors for costs and benefits).

Apart from testing your ability to use the certainty-equivalent approach, the question is a good test of your understanding of relevant costs and opportunity costs.

- Apportioned costs are not incurred by the project and should not be included.
- Only the additional element of other overheads should be included.
- The current assistant manager's salary of £30,000 will be incurred anyway and should not be included; the £27,000 salary of the new manager should however be included since it has been incurred because the current assistant manager is needed on the project.
- The company will not be able to obtain the rental of £135,000 on the factory space if it undertakes the project; thus the rental is an opportunity cost which should be included.
- The 60,000 kg of material X currently in stock should not be included at purchase price since this is a sunk cost. However by undertaking the project, the company forgoes the opportunity to sell the raw materials in stock, and they should thus be included at selling price.

Certainty-equivalent cash flows

	Year 1	*Year 2*	*Year 3*	*Year 4*
	£'000	£'000	£'000	£'000
Sales (W1)	1,125	1,800	1,575	1,425
Material X (W2)	50	230	248	280
Other variable costs (W3)	517	1,100	1,184	1,340
Management salaries (W4)	67	79	85	92
Rental: opportunity cost	135	135	135	135
Other overheads (× 1.1, 1.3, 1.4, 1.5)	66	78	84	90
	835	1,622	1,736	1,937
Sales less cash costs	290	178	(161)	(512)
Discount factor at 14%	0.877	0.769	0.675	0.592
Present value	254	137	(109)	(303)

The net present value is -£21,000, so the project is not acceptable.

Workings

1 *Sales*
Year 1 10,000 × £125 × 0.9
Year 2 18,000 × £125 × 0.8
Year 3 18,000 × £125 × 0.7
Year 4 19,000 × £125 × 0.6

2 *Material X*
Year 1 £50,000 opportunity cost
Year 2 18,000 × 6 × £1.64 × 1.3
Year 3 18,000 × 6 × £1.64 × 1.4
Year 4 19,000 × 6 × £1.64 × 1.5

3 *Other variable costs*
Per unit: £30 + (3 × £4.20) + £4.40 = £47
Year 1 10,000 × £47 × 1.1
Year 2 18,000 × £47 × 1.3
Year 3 18,000 × £47 × 1.4
Year 4 19,000 × £47 × 1.5

4 *Management salaries*
Year 1 £34,000 + £27,000 = £61,000 x 1.1
Year 2 £61,000 × 1.3
Year 3 £61,000 × 1.4
Year 4 £61,000 × 1.5

35 BANDEN LTD

Tutor's hint. This question gives you practice in doing NPV calculations rapidly. Note how the NPV calculations are laid out in a way that enables you to show clearly how the profitability index is calculated. It would be less time consuming to use the proforma we have used than to do the NPV calculations, and then separately to do the profitability index calculations. What this emphasises is the usefulness of taking a few moments to plan the most efficient way of carrying out calculations.

In (b) because of the constraints you have to calculate the combined NPV of various possible combinations. It is obvious looking at the figures that the company will be undertaking some combination of three of the projects. However you would be penalised (and waste time) if you calculated the NPV of all combinations of three of the six. Any combinations including C should be excluded as the project makes a loss. It is also not possible for a combination to include A and E as they are mutually exclusive.

Our answer shows only those possible combinations of projects that cost less than £620,000. It would also be fine if you showed the cost of combinations that cost more than £620,000; however you should have then stated that they could not be undertaken, and should not have calculated their NPV.

(c) demonstrates why the cost of capital is used as an approximation, but you also need to demonstrate your understanding of its theoretical limitations. In (d) you need to show that linear programming is underpinned by significant simplifying assumptions.

(a) The profitability index will be calculated as the ratio of the PV of net cash inflows to the year 0 capital outlay.

	Year	Cash flow £	Discount factor 12%	Present value £	Profitability index
Project A	1-5	70,000	3.605	252,350	6,350
	0	(246,000)	1.000	(246,000)	246,000
				NPV = 6,350	= 0.026
Project B	1	75,000	0.893	66,975	
	2	87,000	0.797	69,339	
	3	64,000	0.712	45,568	
				181,882	1,882
	0	(180,000)	1.000	(180,000)	180,000
				NPV = 1,882	= 0.010
Project C	1	48,000	0.893	42,864	
	2	48,000	0.797	38,256	
	3	63,000	0.712	44,856	
	4	73,000	0.636	46,428	
				172,404	(2,596)
	0	(175,000)	1.000	(175,000)	175,000
				NPV = (2,596)	= (0.015)
Project D	1-4	62,000	3.037	188,294	8,294
	0	(180,000)	1.000	(180,000)	180,000
				NPV = 8,294	= 0.046
Project E	1	40,000	0.893	35,720	
	2	50,000	0.797	39,850	
	3	60,000	0.712	42,720	
	4	70,000	0.636	44,520	
	5	40,000	0.567	22,680	
				185,490	5,490
	0	(180,000)	1.000	(180,000)	180,000
				NPV = 5,490	= 0.031
Project F	1	35,000	0.893	31,255	
	2	82,000	0.797	65,354	
	3	82,000	0.712	58,384	
				154,993	4,993
	0	(150,000)	1.000	(150,000)	150,000
				NPV = 4,993	= 0.033

Ranking	*NPV*	*Profitability index*
1st	D	D
2nd	A	F
3rd	E	E
4th	F	A
5th	B	B
6th	C	C

The rankings differ because the project's capital outlays differ. NPV shows the absolute benefit from a project, while profitability index scales that benefit according to the project's size.

(b) Project C comes sixth and last in the ranking according to both NPV and profitability index. It has a negative NPV and should not be undertaken.

Banden Ltd cannot afford to undertake more than three projects, given the maximum available capital of £620,000. It should not undertake project C, and it cannot undertake A and E simultaneously. The various feasible options are as follows.

Capital outlay

Projects	*In total*	*NPV in total*
	£	£
D, F, E	510,000	18,777
D, F, A	576,000	19,637
D, F, B	510,000	15,169
D, E, B	540,000	15,666
D, A, B	606,000	16,526
F, A, B	576,000	13,225
F, E, B	510,000	12,365

Banden Ltd should not invest any funds in the money markets, because the return would only be 9% pa and the cost of capital for Banden is higher, at 12% pa.

It is assumed that the company does not have to use more funds than it needs to, and so there will not be any surplus funds which have to be invested somewhere.

Recommendation. The company should use £576,000 and invest in projects D, F and A.

(c) When there is **capital rationing**, there is **not enough capital to invest** in all the projects which have a positive NPV, when their NPVs are calculated by discounting the estimated cash flows at the company's cost of capital. The financial director is correct in theory to say that the company's cost of capital is inappropriate. The marginal opportunity cost of capital, which will be higher than the company's cost of capital, would be more appropriate for calculating project NPVs and deciding which projects would yield the best returns, given the shortage of capital.

However, the marginal cost of capital cannot be calculated easily, and a practical way of making decisions in a capital rationing situation is to **calculate** the **NPV** of **each project** using the company's normal cost of capital, and then to rank the projects in order of desirability, as in parts (a) and (b) of this solution.

(d) **Advantages of linear programming**

Linear programming has the advantages of helping management:

(i) To **identify** the **optimal capital expenditure programme** in a capital rationing situation

(ii) To **establish the opportunity cost of capital**, from the shadow price for capital in the solution to the linear programming problem

Once the model has been set up, it can be used for sensitivity tests, for example by varying the estimated cash flows of any projects.

Disadvantages of linear programming

Linear programming has the very serious drawback, however, that **projects** are assumed to be **divisible**, and so the optimal solution obtained from a model might be to undertake fractions of one or more projects. This is often unrealistic and impractical.

A second disadvantage of linear programming is that although sensitivity analysis is possible, the **data** used in the model are initially treated as being **certain** and the **constraints as fixed**. In reality, neither of these is the case. For example, when capital is a constraint, management will often be able to raise some extra capital from one source or other.

For Banden Ltd, linear programming seems unnecessarily complex, since there are only seven sensible combinations of projects. A simpler mathematical approach, as illustrated in part (b) of this solution, would seem to be suitable for making the investment decision.

36 FLOCKS LTD

Tutor's hint. This question splits clearly the investment decision ((a)) and the finance decision (b).

(a) requires careful planning of layout. Having separate columns for the items of income and expenditure and including a net cash flow column means you only have to do one net present value calculation per year. This is clearer and more economical than listing in one column all the year 0 figures, then all the year 1 figures, and having to do a net present value calculation for each figure.

The layout of the main calculations can also be simplified by just including the net tax payable figure rather than separate figures for tax on profits and tax saved on capital allowances.

The cumulative cash flow column enables you to work out the payback period easily.

You should not have calculated a writing down allowance for the years of disposal (4 and 6), but a balancing allowance.

In (b) the relevant items are the lease/buy costs and the tax savings.

An exam question on this area might well include a written part asking you to discuss other implications of the choice between leasing and buying.

(a) *Workings*

(i) *Capital allowances*

Year		*Machine X allowance*	*Year*		*Machine Y allowance*
		£			£
1	(25% of £63,000)	15,750	1	(25% of £110,000)	27,500
2	(75% of £15,750)	11,813	2	(75% of £27,500)	20,625
3	(75% of £11,813)	8,859	3	(75% of £20,625)	15,469
		36,422	4	(75% of £15,469)	11,602
4	(£63,000 - £36,422)	26,578	5	(75% of £11,602)	8,702
					83,898
			6	(£110,000 - £83,898)	26,102

(ii) *Taxable profits and tax liabilities*

Machine X

Year	*Cash profits*	*Allowance*	*Taxable profits*	*Tax at 30% (one year later)*
	£	£	£	£
1	25,900	15,750	10,150	3,045
2	28,800	11,813	16,987	5,096
3	30,500	8,859	21,641	6,492
4	29,500	26,578	2,922	877

Machine Y

Year	*Cash profits*	*Allowance*	*Taxable profits*	*Tax at 30% (one year later)*
	£	£	£	£
1	40,300	27,500	12,800	3,840
2	32,900	20,625	12,275	3,683
3	32,000	15,469	16,531	4,905
4	32,700	11,602	21,098	6,329
5	48,500	8,702	39,798	11,939
6	44,200	26,102	18,098	5,429

NPV and payback calculations

Machine X

Year	*Machine cost* £	*Working capital* £	*Cash profits* £	*Tax* £	*Net cash flow* £	*Discount factor* 13%	*Present value* £	*Cumulative cash flow* £
0	(63,000)	(12,500)			(75,500)	1.000	(75,500)	(75,500)
1			25,900		25,900	0.885	22,922	(49,600)
2			28,800	(3,045)	25,755	0.783	20,166	(23,845)
3			30,500	(5,096)	25,404	0.693	17,605	1,559
4		12,500	29,500	(6,492)	35,508	0.613	21,766	
5				(877)	(877)	0.543	(476)	
						NPV =	6,483	

The NPV for machine X is + £6,483, and the payback period is about three years.

Machine Y

Year	*Machine cost* £	*Working capital* £	*Cash profits* £	*Tax* £	*Net cash flow* £	*Discount factor* 15%	*Present value* £	*Cumulative cash flow* £
0	(110,000)	(12,500)			(122,500)	1.000	(122,500)	(122,500)
1			40,300		40,300	0.870	35,061	(82,200)
2			32,900	(3,840)	29,060	0.756	21,969	(53,140)
3			32,000	(3,683)	28,317	0.658	18,633	(24,823)
4			32,700	(4,905)	27,795	0.572	15,899	2,972
5			48,500	(6,329)	42,171	0.497	20,959	
6		12,500	44,200	(11,939)	44,761	0.432	19,337	
7				(5,429)	(5,429)	0.376	(2,041)	
						NPV =	7,317	

The NPV for machine Y is + £7,317 and the payback period is about four years.

Machine X would appear to be the preferable option.

(b) The financing decision will be appraised by discounting the relevant cash flows at the after-tax cost of borrowing, which is 10% × 70% = 7%.

(i) *Purchase option*

Year	*Item*	*Cash flow* £	*Discount factor* 7%	*Present value* £
0	Cost of machine	(63,000)	1.000	(63,000)
	Tax saved from capital allowances			
2	30% × £15,750	4,725	0.873	4,125
3	30% × £11,813	3,544	0.816	2,892
4	30% × £8,859	2,658	0.763	2,028
5	30% × £26,578	7,973	0.713	5,685
				(48,270)

(ii) *Leasing option*

Years	*Item*	*Cash flow* £	*Discount factor* 7%	*Present value* £
1 - 4	Lease costs	(20,000)	3.387	(67,740)
2 - 5	Tax savings on lease costs (× 30%)	6,000	3.165	18,990
				(48,750)

The purchase option is marginally cheaper, using a cost of capital based on the after-tax cost of borrowing.

On the assumption that investors would regard borrowing and leasing as equally risky finance options, the purchase option is recommended.

37 MILBAO PLC

(a)

Model		Actual sales quantity in budgeted proportions	Budgeted sales quantity	Sales quantity variance		Standard contribution	Sales quantity variance	
		Units	Units	Units		£	£	
Superb	(3/10)	28,800	30,000	1,200	(A)	60	72,000	(A)
Excellent	(1/2)	48,000	50,000	2,000	(A)	55	110,000	(A)
Good	(1/5)	19,200	20,000	800	(A)	48	38,400	(A)
		96,000	100,000	4,000	(A)		220,400	(A)

For example, actual sales quantity in budget proportions for Superb = 3/10 of 96,000 =

Sales quantity variance in total: 4,000 units (A)
£220,400 (A)

Model		Std mix of actual sales	Actual mix	Sales mix variance		Std contribution	Sales mix variance	
		Units	Units	Units		£	£	
Superb	(3/10)	28,800	36,000	7,200	(F)	60	432,000	(F)
Excellent	(1/2)	48,000	42,000	6,000	(A)	55	330,000	(A)
Good	(1/5)	19,200	18,000	1,200	(A)	48	57,600	(A)
		96,000	96,000	-			44,400	(F)

The mix variance is always zero in quantity

Sales mix variance in total: 0 units
£44,400 (F)

(b)

	Superb £		Superb £		Good £		Good £	
Original budget contribution (W1)			1,800,000				960,000	
Planning variances								
Selling price (W2)	180,000	(A)			84,000	(A)		
Variable cost (W3)	36,000	(F)			13,200	(F)		
			144,000	(A)			70,800	(A)
Revised budget contribution			1,656,000				889,200	
Sales volume variance (W4)			331,200	(F)			88,920	(A)
Revised std contribution			1,987,200				800,280	
Operational variances								
Selling price (W5)	144,000	(A)			50,400	(A)		
Variable cost (W6)	28,800	(F)			7,920	(F)		
			115,200	(A)			42,480	(A)
Actual contribution			1,872,000				757,800	

The inclusion of the sales volume variance results in a figure showing what contribution should have been for actual activity level

Workings

1 Superb $30,000 \times £60 = £1,800,000$
Good $20,000 \times £48 = £960,000$

2 The 6% fall in general market prices results in a planning variance as operational managers could not have controlled the fall.

The other 4% was controllable

Superb

	£
Original budget revenue (30,000 × £100)	3,000,000
Revised budget revenue (30,000 × £100 × 94%)	2,820,000
	180,000 (A)

Based on original budget of 30,000 units

Good

	£
Original budget revenue (20,000 × £70)	1,400,000
Revised budget revenue (20,000 × £70 × 94%)	1,316,000
	84,000 (A)

3 The 3% over estimation of the wage award results in a planning variance as this was a poor piece of planning rather than an operational efficiency or inefficiency.

Again, uses original budgets of 30,000 and 20,000 units

Superb

	£
Original budget variable cost (30,000 × £40)	1,200,000
Revised budget variable cost (30,000 × £40 × 97%)	1,164,000
	36,000 (F)

Good

	£
Original budget variable cost (20,000 × £22)	440,000
Revised budget variable cost (20,000 × £22 × 97%)	426,800
	13,200 (F)

4 The sales volume variances are based on the differences between actual and budget sales units.

	Actual units	*Budget units*	*Sales volume variance*
Superb	36,000	30,000	6,000 units (F)
Good	18,000	20,000	2,000 units (A)

Note how the revised standard margin is calculated

The variances are then valued at the revised standard margin, with prices reduced by 6% and costs by 3%.

Superb	Variance in units	6,000 units (F)
	× revised standard margin	
	(× £((100 × 94%) – (40 × 97%))	× £55.20
		£331,200 (F)
Good	Variance in units	2,000 units (A)
	× revised standard margin	
	(× £((70 × 94%) – (22 × 97%))	× £44.46
		£88,920 (A)

5 *Superb*

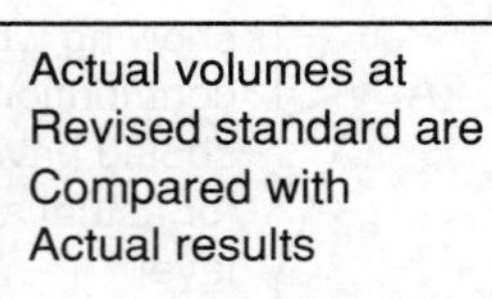

	£
Sales revenue for actual volume of 36,000 units	
should have been (using revised standard of £100 × 94%)	3,384,000
but was (£100 × 90% × 36,000)	3,240,000
	144,000 (A)

Good

	£
Sales revenue for actual volume of 18,000 units	
should have been (using revised standard of £70 × 94%)	1,184,400
but was (£70 × 90% × 18,000)	1,134,000
	50,400 (A)

6 Variances are 2% of original budget costs for actual volume.

Superb

36,000 × £40 × 2% = £28,800 (F)

Good

18,000 × £22 × 2% = £7,920 (F)

Note. You may find it useful to calculate revised budget contribution using the revised standard figures.

	Superb	*Good*
Revised selling price (W1)	£94.0	£65.80
Revised variable cost (W2)	£38.8	£21.34
Revised contribution	£55.2	£44.46
Budgeted sales	× 30,000	× 20,000
Revised budget contribution	£1,656,000	£889,200

Workings

1 Superb £100 × 94% = £94
Good £70 × 94% = £65.80

2 Superb £40 × 97% = £38.80
Good £22 × 97% = £21.34

(c) By analysing the variances in this way management are able to see how well the business has performed against what should in hindsight have been the standard. Otherwise part of each variance identified would simply reflect the fact that the original budget was wrong, perhaps through factors beyond the control of management. The analysis into planning and operational variances thus provides more useful **feedback** about operational performance, and this can be used to prompt investigation, cost benefit analysis and control action where possible.

No need to define feedback and feedforward control here

This approach is also useful for **feedforward control**. When budgets are next prepared the revised standards can be used. If it is not possible to set right all of the operational problems, the relevant proportion of operational variances can also be taken into account in future plans.

38 SWANSEA PLC

(a) (i) The two alternative policies will be evaluated separately to determine the most beneficial choice in financial terms.

(1) **Selling securities**

The first step is to determine the optimal amount of cash that will be raised in each transaction, and hence the number of transactions and the level of transaction costs.

Work out best cash management policy

$$Q = \sqrt{\frac{2FS}{i}}$$

where: i = average % rate of return 10%

S = cash payments £1m

F = transaction fee £20

$$Q = \sqrt{\frac{2 \times £20 \times £1m}{10\%}}$$

$$= £20,000$$

Sales made $= \dfrac{£1\text{ million}}{20,000}$

= 50

Transaction costs = 50 × £20
= £1,000

Average level of cash balances $= \dfrac{£20,000}{2}$
= £10,000

Interest on cash balances = £10,000 × 4.5%
= £450

Average portfolio balances $= \dfrac{£1,000,000}{2}$
= £500,000

Income lost on portfolio securities = 10% × £500,000
= £50,000

Total costs

	£
Transaction costs	1,000
Interest received on cash balances	(450)
Income lost on portfolio securities	50,000
	50,550

(2) **Secured loan**

Average value of remaining cash $= \frac{£1{,}000{,}000}{2}$

$= £500{,}000$

Interest received $= £500{,}000 \times 8\%$

$= £40{,}000$

Total costs

	£
Interest paid (£1 million × 13%)	130,000
Interest received	(40,000)
Arrangement fee	6,000
	96,000

The figures suggest that the policy of **selling securities** is to be preferred since this has a net cost of £50,550, which is £45,450 less than the cost of taking out a secured loan for the period.

The company should also take into account the following other factors associated with the policies.

(1) The **value of the short-term securities** is likely to **fluctuate** and Swansea must consider the possibility that the **value** could **fall** to below that required to meet the cash payments.

(2) **Use of the securities** will **eliminate them** as a future source of finance.

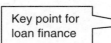

Key point for loan finance

(3) If Swansea takes out the loan it must have **funds available** with which to repay it at the end of the period.

(ii) **Limitations** of the model include the following.

(1) It assumes that the **level of transaction costs** is **independent** of the size of the transaction. Again this is unlikely to be true in practice.

(2) In reality, **payments** will **not be made continuously** but at regular intervals. The effect of this 'stepped' effect on the operation of the model should be considered.

(3) It **assumes a steady rate of return** from the securities although this may be very uncertain. Swansea should consider the effect of fluctuations in this rate on the model.

(4) It **does not allow** for a **buffer stock of cash** but assumes that further securities will only be sold when the cash balance reduces to zero. This is unlikely to be realistic in practice.

(b) (i) (1) **Finance leases** are **similar** to **hire purchase contracts** in that the asset is sold not to the user but to an intermediary who then leases the asset to the user in return for periodic payments.

The main differences are as follows:

- Unlike the hire purchase contract, **ownership** of the asset **does not transfer** to the user at the end of the lease period, but is retained by the purchaser.
- The **purchaser** and not the user is able to **claim** the **capital allowances,** which may be passed on to the user in the form of a reduction in the periodic payments.

- Although the user does not own the asset, entries appear in the user's **balance sheet** and **profit and loss account** to reflect the **capital element** of the lease, the **interest element** of the payments, and the **remaining lease commitment**. This is to ensure that all forms of long-term debt are fully reflected in the balance sheet.

Many finance leases are structured into a '**primary period**' which covers the major part of the economic life of the asset, and a '**secondary period**' during which the user continues to lease the asset, but at a much lower (often only nominal) rate.

(2) **Hire purchase** is a form of **instalment credit** whereby the business purchases goods on credit and pays for them by instalments. The goods are accounted for when purchased. The periodic payments include both an **interest element** on the initial price and a **capital repayment** element. At the end of the hire purchase period, ownership of the asset passes to the user, who is also able to claim **capital allowances** on the basic purchase cost of the asset. The mechanics of the transaction are as follows.

- The **supplier** of the **asset sells** it to a **finance house**.
- The **supplier of the asset delivers** it to the **customer** who will be the user and the eventual owner.
- The **hire purchase agreement** is made between the **finance house** and the **customer**.

(3) **Sale and leaseback** is an arrangement which is similar to **mortgaging**. A business which already owns an asset, for example a building or an item of equipment, agrees to sell the asset to a financial institution and then immediately to lease it back on terms specified in the agreement. The business has the benefit of the **funds from the sale** while retaining use of the asset, in return for regular payments to the financial institution.

The principal benefit is that the **business** gains **immediate access to liquid funds**; however this is at the expense of the **ability to profit** from any capital appreciation (potentially significant in the case of property) and **tax allowances.** The capacity to borrow elsewhere may be reduced since the balance sheet value of assets will fall.

(ii) The approach is to calculate the net of tax present value of the two options available to Mumbles. The discount rate to be used will be the cost of borrowing net of tax. 18% × (1 – 0.33) = 12%.

Easier to show each year's payments in single column

Purchasing outright

Year	*0*	*1*	*2*	*3*	*4*	*5*
	£'000	£'000	£'000	£'000	£'000	£'000
Initial outlay	5,000					
Tax savings on capital allowances (W)		413	310	232	174	522
Net cash flow	(5,000)	413	310	232	174	522
Discount factor at 12%	1.000	0.893	0.797	0.712	0.636	0.567
PV of cash flow	(5,000)	369	247	165	111	296

Working

Year of claim	*Allowance*	*Tax saved*	*Year of tax payment*
	5,000		
	(1,250)	413	
0	3,750		1
	(938)	309	
1	2,812		2
	(703)	232	
2	2,109		3
	(527)	174	
3	1,582		4
	(1,582)	522	
4			5
	-		

Thus the **NPV cost of purchasing** outright is £3,812,000.

Leasing

Tax implications of rental

Year	*0*	*1*	*2*	*3*	*4*
	£'000	£'000	£'000	£'000	£'000
Annual rental	(1,800)	(1,800)	(1,800)	(1,800)	-
Tax savings (rental × 33%)	-	594	594	594	594
Net cash flow	(1,800)	(1,206)	(1,206)	(1,206)	594
Discount factor at 12%	1.000	0.893	0.797	0.712	0.636
PV of cash flow	(1,800)	(1,077)	(961)	(859)	378

Comparison and conclusion

Thus the **NPV cost of leasing** is **£4,319,000**. This is £506,000 more than the NPV cost of direct purchase over the life of the equipment, and direct purchase therefore appears more attractive on financial grounds.

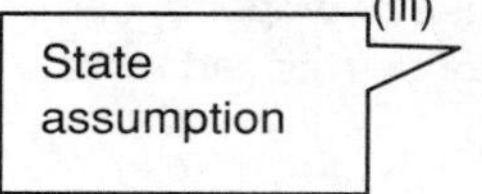

(iii) The cost of purchase can be re-evaluated to take into account the **additional maintenance costs** of £190,000 per year. These costs are assumed to start in year 1, with the associated tax saving coming through in the subsequent year.

Tax implications of maintenance

Year	*0*	*1*	*2*	*3*	*4*	*5*
	£'000	£'000	£'000	£'000	£'000	£'000
Initial outlay	(5,000)					
Tax savings on capital allowances (above)		413	310	232	174	522
Maintenance costs		(190)	(190)	(190)	(190)	
Tax saving			63	63	63	63
Net cash flow	(5,000)	223	183	105	47	585
Discount factor at 12%	1.000	0.893	0.797	0.712	0.636	0.567
PV of cash flow	(5,000)	199	146	75	30	332

Comparison and conclusion

If the maintenance costs are taken into account, the NPV cost of purchase rises to £4,218,000, which is slightly less (by £100,000) than the cost of leasing. Although the decision is not reversed, the **relative costs** are **marginal**, and other factors should also be considered, for instance the **reliability** and **availability** of the **different maintenance options**.

(c) (i) Current rate of return on capital employed

		£'000
Operating profit		20,000
Fixed assets	(a)	75,000
Stocks	(b)	25,000
Capital employed	(a) + (b)	100,000
Rate of return	£20m/£100m =	20%

Incremental profits and investments arising from the project

	Year 1	Year 2	Year 3	Year 4
	£'000	£'000	£'000	£'000
Sales (W)	10,000	8,100	6,400	5,600
Operating costs (W)	(2,000)	(1,800)	(1,600)	(1,600)
Overheads (W)	(1,500)	(1,350)	(1,200)	(1,200)
Depreciation (W)	(3,000)	(3,000)	(3,000)	(3,000)
Profit	3,500	1,950	600	(200)

Average profit = £1,463,000

Workings

	Year 1	Year 2	Year 3	Year 4
Sales ('000 units)	2,000	1,800	1,600	1,600
Price per unit (£)	5.00	4.50	4.00	3.50
	£'000	£'000	£'000	£'000
Sales value	10,000	8,100	6,400	5,600
Operating costs at £1/unit	2,000	1,800	1,600	1,600
Overheads at £0.75/unit	1,500	1,350	1,200	1,200
NBV at start of year	14,000	11,000	8,000	5,000
Depreciation: (£14m – £2m)/4	3,000	3,000	3,000	3,000
NBV at end of year	11,000	8,000	5,000	2,000
Average NBV	12,500	9,500	6,500	3,500

Include allocated overheads

Residual value

Average capital employed

Fixed assets (average NBV)(W)	12,500	9,500	6,500	3,500
Stock	500	500	500	500
Total	13,000	10,000	7,000	4,000

Must use average

Average capital employed = £8,500,000

Average return = Average profit/Average capital employed during each year

In this case the average return (ROCE) is 17.2%.

The project shows an **ROCE** of 17.2% which is in excess of the hurdle rate of 10%. However, since the current rate of return achieved by Gower is 20%, acceptance of the project would result in a **small depression** of the overall ROCE. It is therefore unlikely that the management of Gower would find the project attractive since its acceptance would mean that their performance would **appear** to have **deteriorated.**

Comment and conclusion

(ii) (1) The main problems are as follows.

- The ROCE approach can easily be **manipulated** to put project returns in a good light, for example by changing the method of depreciation or the estimate of the terminal value.
- There is an element of **double counting** in that depreciation is deducted from the profit figure in full, but the use of the average assets figure means that part of this is also included in the denominator. The effect of this is to depress the calculated returns.
- It **ignores** the **actual cashflows** associated with the project, and ignores the effect of the timing of those cashflows on the real return of the project.

Not cash flow based measure

(2) The ROCE approach remains popular because it is expressed in terms with which **managers are familiar**, namely **profit** and **capital employed**. It is also **easy** to **calculate the effect** that the project is likely to have on the reported profit and loss account and balance sheet. Since managers are frequently rewarded in relation to performance against these variables

Manager self interest

they will be concerned to see the effect on them of undertaking a new project.

Very long

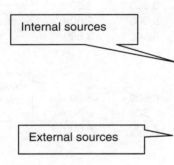

(iii) The dangers of extending the credit period include the following.

(1) The **average collection period** at present is 90 days which is already **long** by the standards of most industries. It is questionable whether extending it further will really achieve the anticipated improvement in sales volume.

(2) Any **additional customers** attracted to Gower will be those to whom **extended credit** is **important**, and these are likely to be firms which are less financially secure. It is therefore likely that there will be an increased risk of both slow payment and bad debts, and such customers may have a greater tendency to demand discounts.

(3) Where the credit period is very long, the **absolute amount** of any **bad debt** will be **larger** than if the collection period is short since there will be a greater number of months of supply outstanding.

Ways of assessing customers' creditworthiness are as follows.

(1) Offering a cash-only **trial period** could help to establish the **likely volume** of trade, and **demonstrate** that the customer is capable of paying reliably.

(2) An **analysis** can be made of **their published accounts** to establish their **liquidity** and **financial security.**

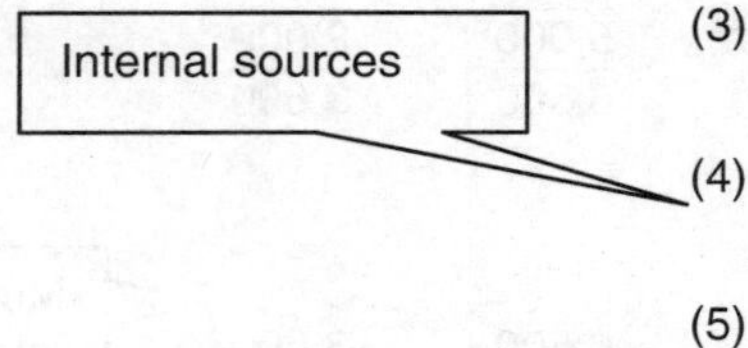

(3) **Visits** to the **customers' premises** are useful in gaining a view of the company and its prospects.

(4) Potential new customers should **supply two good references** including one from a bank before credit is granted.

(5) **Credit ratings** can be **checked** using an agency such as Dun and Bradstreet.

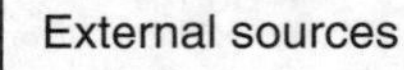

(6) For export customers, **advice** may be **obtained** from the **DTI** and the **ECGD.**

(7) Information relevant to the company and the industry may be gained from the **trade press** and from newspapers.

(8) The **credit limit** should be **low** for an initial period to allow the payment performance to be checked.

List of key terms and index

Note: **Key Terms** and their page references are given in **bold.**

ABC, 38
Abnormal gain, 66
Abnormal loss, 66
Absorption base, 22
Absorption costing, 14, 16, 17
Absorption rate, 22
Absorption, 17
Acceptance credits, 418
Accepting or rejecting orders, 289
Accounting rate of return method, 522
Acid rain, 378
Acid test ratio, 387
Acquisition, 520
Activity based budgeting (ABB), 236
Activity based budgets, 236
Activity based costing, 38
Additive model, 253
Agency relationship, 318
Aggregate demand, 354
Algebraic method, 19
Allocation, 17
Allocative efficiency, 376
Alternative Investment Market (AIM), 334
Altman, 394
Annuity tables, 536
Ansoff, 516
Apportionment, 17
ARR and the comparison of mutually
exclusive projects, 523
Aspiration level, 225
Aspirations budget, 225
Asset replacement decisions, 545
Asset turnover, 323
Attainable standard, 112
Attributable fixed costs, 270
Average stock, 425, **426**
Avoidable costs, 268

BACS, 431
Bad debt risk, 405
Bad debts, 400
Balance of payments, 366
Balance sheet valuation, 312
Balanced scorecard approach, 88
Balancing transactions, 40
Bank lending, 333
Bank of England, 340
Base package, 232
Basic standard, 112
Batch costing, 55
Batch, 55
Behavioural implications of budgeting, 219
Bills of exchange, 417
Boston classification, 519
Boston matrix, 519
Bought deal, 457
Breakeven analysis, 291
Breakeven chart, 291
Breakeven point, 291
Break-up basis, 312
Budget centre, 175
Budget committee, 186
Budget constrained style of evaluation, 223
Budget cost allowance, 213, 215
Budget deficit, 355
Budget development, 186
Budget documentation, 185
Budget implementation, 186
Budget manual, 185
Budget period, 185
Budget preparation timetable, 186
Budget review, 189
Budget surplus, 355
Budget variance, 215
Budget, 171, 179, 186, 188, 189, 200 202
sales, 187
Budgetary control, 214
Budgetary planning and control systems, 179
Budgetary slack, 224
Budgeted balance sheet, 200, 202
Budgeted capacity, 110
Budgeted profit and loss account, 200, 202
Budgets as targets, 224
Buffer, 429
Bulk discounts, 426
Business angel financing, 507
Business failure, 394
Business risk, 533
By-product, 80

C/S ratio, 291
Cadbury report, 379
Capacity levels, 110
Capacity ratio, 111
Capacity, 190
Capacity levels
budgeted capacity, 110
full capacity, 110
idle capacity, 110
practical capacity, 110
Capital allowances, 559
Capital employed, 322
Capital expenditure, 515
Capital markets, 333
Capital rationing, 584
Capital structure, 493, 498, 509
Capitalisation issue, 464

BPP PUBLISHING

Cash budget, 194, 195, 430
Cash cows, 519
Cash cycle, 386
Cash flow forecasts, 395
Cash flow planning, 394
Cash flow problems, 429
Cash flow, 386
Centralised treasury department, 445
Certainty-equivalent approach, 571
Certificates of deposit (CDs), 438
Change transactions, 40
Code of Best Practice, 380
Coefficient of correlation, 248
Coefficient of determination, 249
Combined Code, 381
Commercial banks, 333
Committed cost, 269
Competition Commission, 373
Competition policy, 373
Competition, 297
Competitive performance, 87
Compounding, 529
Consensus theory, 311
Consumer price indices, 367
Continuous budget, 234, **235**
Contract, 59
Contract costing, 59
Contribution (contribution breakeven) chart, 291
Contribution, 25, 291
Contribution/sales (C/S) ratio, 291
Control chart, 136
Control cycle, 171
Control process, 171
Control reporting, 179
Control, 169
Controllability, 175, 178
Controllable costs, 177
Controlling, 5, 6
Conversion premium, 485
Conversion value, 485
Convertible debentures, 486
Convertible loan stock, 484
Convertible securities, 484
Corporate appraisal, 517
Corporate governance, 379
Corporation tax, 562
Correlation, 246, 245
  and causation, 249
  curvilinear, 247
  negative, 248
  non-linear, 247
  partial, 247
  perfect, 246
  positive, 248
Cost accounting, 7, 8
Cost centre, 177
Cost driver, 39, 42
Cost gap, 50
Cost of capital, 498, 530, **534**
Cost of debt capital, 531
Cost of preference shares, 531
Cost of share capital, 531
Cost pools, 39
Costing, 8
Cost-push inflation, 367
Cost-volume-profit analysis, 291
Count-back method, 399
Countertrade, 415
Coupon, 466, 480
Credit control, 401
Credit creation, 332
Credit insurance, 406
Credit ratings, 409
Credit reviews, 410
Credit utilisation report, 413
Creditors' turnover, 388, 419
Creditors, 317, 416
Creditworthiness, 402
Currency of invoice, 440
Current ratio, 387
Current standard, 112
Cusum chart, 136
Cyclical variations, 253

Days sales outstanding, 400
DCF yield method, 533
Debentures, 481
Debt collection policy, 401
Debt ratio, 324, 497
Debtors age analysis, 411
Debtors' days ratio, 387
Debtors' payment period, 387
Debtors turnover, 399
Debtors, 401
Decision making, 5, 6, 267, 299
Decision packages, 232
Decision trees, 575
Decisions, 5
Deep discount bonds, 482
Deferred ordinary shares, 452
Demand management, 355, 356
Demand, 296
Demand-pull inflation, 367
Denationalisation, 376
Departmental budget, 190
Dependent variable, 241
Dependent variable, 241
Deregulation, 375
Direct cost, 15
Directly attributable fixed costs, 270
Directly attributable overhead, 178
Discount rate computation, 531
Discount tables, 535

Discounted cash flow, 529
Discounts, 426
Discretionary fixed costs, 178
Dividend cover, 471
Dividend decision, 309
Dividend growth model, 473
Dividend payout ratio, 471
Dividend policy, 471
Dividend valuation model, 473
Dividend yield, 465
Dividends, 437
Double loop feedback, 174
Du Pont system of ratio analysis, 322
Dual price, 280
Dual responsibility, 179
Dynamic conditions, 234

Earnings per share, 467
Economic order quantity (EOQ), 423
Economic policy, 319, 351
Economy, 89
Effectiveness, 89
Efficiency, 89
Efficiency ratio, 111
Efficiency targets, 326
Efficient market hypothesis, 336
Efficient portfolios, 344
Elimination method, 19
Employee share option schemes, 464
Employees, 317
Enterprise Initiative, 377, 510
Enterprise Investment Scheme, 511
Environmental ('green') policies, 378
Environmental reporting, 325
Environmentally friendly policies, 379
Equity finance, 507
Equity shares, 452
Equivalent units, 70
Ethical investment funds, 379
Eurobond, 347
Eurocurrency, 346
Euro-equity, 347
European Union, 375
Exchange rate, 360
Exchange rate policy, 352
Exchange rate risk, 440
Exchange rate stability, 364
Executive agencies, 326
Exercise price, 488
Expectational inflation, 368
Expectations budget, 225
Expectations, 340
Expected cash flows, 430, 572
Export credit insurance, 415
External trade policy, 353
Externalities, 378
Extra shift decisions, 288
Extrapolation, 244

Factoring, 407, **406**
Feedback, 171, **174**
negative, 174
positive, 174
Feedforward control, 174
FIFO, 71
Finance house deposits, 438
Finance lease, 594
Financial accounts, 310
Financial control, 308
Financial gearing, 494
Financial intermediary, 331
Financial management, 308
Financial performance targets, 326
Financial performance, 87, 321
Financial planning, 308
Financial risk, 493, 533
Financial targets, 313
Financing decision, 309
Fiscal policy, 352, **354**
Fixed asset investment, 515
Fixed budget, 211
Fixed charge, 482
Fixed contracts, 441
Fixed costs, 270
Fixed exchange rates, 362
Fixed production overhead expenditure variance, 125
Fixed production overhead total variance, 124, 125
Fixed production overhead volume capacity variance, 125
Fixed production overhead volume efficiency variance, 125
Fixed production overhead volume variance, 125
Flexed budget, 213
Flexibility, 87
Flexible budget, 211
using absorption costing, 217
Float, 431
Floating charge, 482
Floating exchange rates, 363
Floating rate debentures, 481
Floating rate debt capital, 533
Forecasting, 240, 241, 250, 260
Foreign exchange risk management, 445
Foreign exchange risk, 438
Forward discount, 442
Forward exchange contract, 440
Forward premium, 442
Full capacity, 110
Full cost plus pricing, 297
Fully diluted earnings per share , 468
Functional budget, 190

Funding policy, 355
Further processing decisions, 294

Gearing ratios, 324, 494
Gearing, 314
Goal congruence, 223
Golden rule, 356
Government aid, 510
Government incentives, 377
Government, 317, 319
Grants, 377
Graphical approach to linear programming, 589
Greenbury report, 380
Growth in dividends, 473

Hampel report, 380
Hard capital rationing, 584
Hedging, 438, 445
Hierarchy of costs, 45
Higher-level feedback, 174
High-low method, 212
Hire purchase, 596
Historical costs, 269
Historigram, 251

Ideal standard, 112
Idle capacity, 110, 111
Idle production capacity, 288
Idle time variance, 121
Import cost-push inflation, 367
Imputed cost, 269
Imputed interest, 37
Incremental budgeting, 230
Incremental costs, 268
Incremental packages, 232
Independent variable, 241
Indirect cost, 15
Inflation, 297, 366, 554
In-house credit ratings, 409
Innovation, 87
Institutional investors, 336
Interdependence between variances, 133
Interest cover, 325, 496
Interest rates, 338
Interest yield, 466
Internal opportunity cost, 281
Internal rate of return (IRR) method, 538
International capital markets, 346
International money markets, 346
Interpolation, 244
Inter-relationships beween variances, 133
Inventories, 423
Inventory approach to cash management, 432
Investing surplus cash, 437
Investment by not-for-profit organisations, 515
Investment by the commercial sector, 515
Investment centre, 177
Investment decisions, 309
Investment, 514
Invoice discounting, 408
Issue price for a rights issue, 458

Job costing, 55
for internal services, 59
Job, 55
Joint product decisions, 294
Joint products, 80, 294
Just-in-time procurement, 427

Key budget factor, 187
Key factor, 275
Keynes, 428

Labour efficiency variance, 120
Labour rate variance, 120
Labour total variance, 120
Labour variances, 120
Labour, 274
Lagged payments, 439
Lease or buy decisions, 597
Leasing, 593
Least squares technique, 242
Legislation, 319
Lessee, 593
Lessor, 593
Life cycle costing, 46
Limited freedom of action, 278
Limiting budget factor, 187
Limiting factor analysis, 275
Limiting factor, 275
Line of best fit, 242, 245
Linear programming approach to capital rationing, 591
Linear regression analysis, 242
Linear relationships, 241
Liquidity ratios, 325, 394
Listing, 453
Loan Guarantee Scheme, 510
Loan stock, 480
Local authority deposits, 438
Logistical transactions, 40
Long range planning, 313
Long-term capital, 318, **334**
Long-term plan, 171

Macroeconomics, 351
Make or buy decisions, 282, 284

Management accounting, 7, 310
Management control action, 137
Management, 317
Managerial model, 311
Managerial performance, 223
Margin of safety, 291
Marginal cost plus pricing, 298
Marginal cost, 25
Marginal costing, 14, 17, 25
Market failure, 372
Market portfolio, 346
Market segmentation theory of interest rates, 340
Market values, 312
Marketing, 296
Mark-up pricing, 298
Master budget, 200, **202**
Matching receipts and payments, 439
Material price variance, 118
Material usage variance, 118
Material variances, 118
Materials mix and yield variances, 148
Maximum level, 425
Mergers, 373
Microeconomics, 351
Miller-Orr model, 433
Minimum level, 425
Minimum pricing, 298
Mix variance (sales), 153
Mix variance (materials), 148
Mix variance, 149
Models, 260
Modigliani and Miller, 498
Monetary Policy Committee, 340
Monetary policy, 352, **357**
Money market hedges, 442
Money markets, 333
Monopolist, 296
Monopoly, 373
Mortgages, 484
Motivating, 5, 6, 219, 221, 225
Moving averages, 254
Multi-period capital rationing, 589
Multiplicative model, 257
Mutually exclusive packages, 232

Nationalised industries, 320
Negative correlation, 248
Net present value (NPV) method, 533, 534
Net working capital, 385
Non-accounting style of evaluation, 223
Non-controllable costs, 178
Non-financial indicators, 88
Non-financial objectives, 315
Non-relevant costs, 268
Normal loss, 66
Not-for-profit organisations, 89, 90, 320, 515
Notional cost, 269
Notional interest, 37

Objectives, 170
OFEX, 336
Offer for sale, 454
Offers for sale by tender, 454
Official aid schemes, 377
Oligopoly, 296
Open offer, 464
Operating and measurement, 173
Operating gearing, 496
Operating lease, 594
Operating statement, 142
Operating variance, 155
Operational variance, 155, 156
Operational-level decisions, 6
Opportunity cost, 36, 268, 269
Options, 441
Ordinary shares, 452
Organic growth, 520
Organising, 5, 6
Over absorption, 23
Over-capitalisation, 389
Overdraft facility, 429
Overdraft financing, 505
Overdraft, 333, 505
Overhead absorption, 17, 22
Overhead apportionment, 19
Overhead recovery rates, 22
Overhead, 15
Overseas factor, 414
Overtrading, 390

Partial month method, 399
Participation, 221
Payback, 521
Pearsonian coefficient of correlation, 248
Perfect competition, 296
Performance evaluation, 223
Performance measurement in central government, 326
Performance measurement in local government, 327
Periodic budget, 235
Personal taxation, 475
Placing, 456
Planning and control cycle, 169
Planning variance, 155, 156
Planning, 5, 6, 169
Polluter pays principle, 378
Pollution, 378
Position audit, 170
Positive correlation, 248
Practical capacity, 110
Precautionary motive, 429

Predetermined absorption rate, 22
Pre-emption rights, 458
Preference shares, 479
Present value, 529
Price earnings ratio, 469
Price elasticity of demand, 296
Prices and incomes policy, 352
Pricing decisions, 296
Principal budget factor, 187
Prior charge capital, 324
Private Finance Initiative, 356
Privatisation, 376
Probability distribution, 572
Process costing, 64
Product life cycle, 47, 296
Product moment correlation coefficient, 248
Production capacity, 109
Production volume ratio, 111
Product-market mix, 518
Profit centre, 177
Profit conscious style of evaluation, 223
Profit margin, 323
Profit maximisation, 310
Profit/volume (P/V) chart, 291
Profitability, 313, 322
Profitability index, 586
Programming, 173
Progress payments, 59
Proportional model, 257
Prospectus issue, 456
Public expenditure, 354
Public sector borrowing requirement, 355
Public sector debt repayment, 355
Public sector, 326, 533
Purchasing power parity theory, 361

Qualitative controls, 359
Quality of service targets, 326
Quality transactions, 40
Quality, 296
Quantitative controls, 358, 359
Quantity discounts, 426
Quantity variance, 153
Quarterly accounting, 562
Quick ratio, 387

Random variations, 252
Ratio analysis, 321
Ratio pyramids, 322
Reciprocal services, 19
Reconciling profits, 28
Rectification costs, 55
Redemption, 483
Redistribution of wealth, 366
Regional Enterprise Grants, 510
Regression, 250
Regulation of markets, 373
Relevant cost, 268
of materials, 271
some rules for identifying, 271
Reorder level, 424
Repeated distribution method, 19
Replacement decisions, 545
Reporting and analysis, 173
Resource utilisation, 87
Responsibility accounting, 176
Responsibility centre, 176
Responsibility reporting, 175
Restricted freedom of action, 278
Restrictive practices, 375
Retention monies, 59
Retentions policy, 473
Return on Capital Employed (ROCE), 313, 322, 522
Return on investment (ROI) method, 522
Revenue expenditure, 515
Reverse yield gap, 342
Revision variance, 155
Rights issue, 458
Risk-return trade-off, 341
Rolling budget, 234, 235
Rule-of-thumb models, 134

Safety stock, 425
Sale and leaseback, 595
Sales budget, 187
Sales forecasting, 250
Sales mix and quantity variances, 153
Sales variances, 129
Sales volume variance, 129
Scarce resources, 284
Scatter diagrams, 245
Scrap value of loss, 66
Scrip dividend, 464
Scrip issue (bonus issue), 465
Seasonal variations, 252
Secondary ratios, 323
Selling price variance, 129
Sensitivity analysis, 568
Separation point, 81
Separation theorem, 342
Service costing, 85, 94
for internal services, 94
Service quality, 87
Service/function costing, 85
Settlement discount, 404
Shadow price, 280, 281
Share ownership, 319
Shareholders and management, 317
Shareholders, 316
Short-term capital, 334
Short-term debt instruments, 438

Short-term deposits, 437
Short-term finance, 416
Short-term investments, 437
Shutdown problems, 286
Signalling, 472
Simulation model, 580
Simultaneous equation (algebraic) method, 20
Single loop feedback, 174
Single period capital rationing, 586
Small and medium-sized enterprises, 503
Soft capital rationing, 584, 585
Sources of funds, 452
Special dividend payment, 437
Specific order costing
Specific order costing, 54, 55
Speculation, 360
Speculative motive, 429
Split-off point, 81
Spreadsheet packages, 260
Stakeholders, 316
Standard cost, 106, 107
  as a control technique, 107
  in the modern organisation, 113
  uses of, 106
Standard hour, 109, **192**
Standards, 105, 108
  behavioural impact, 112
  deriving, 108
  reviewing, 113
  types of, 112
Statistical control charts, 136
Statistical significance model, 135
Step-wise (elimination) method, 20
Stock days, 388, 428
Stock Exchange, 334
Stock Exchange introduction, 456
Stock Exchange requirements, 381
Stock market ratios, 465
Stock splits, 464
Stock turnover, 388, 428
Stockless production, 427
Stocks, 423
Strategic analysis, 170
Strategic fund management, 395
Strategic-level decisions, 5
Strategies, 170
Subjective judgement, 90
Substitutes, 297
Sunk cost, 269
Supply side policies, 377
Surplus cash, 437
SWOT analysis, 517
Tactical-level decisions, 5

Target cost, 48, **49**
Taxation, 559
Temporary closure, 287
Theoretical ex rights price, 459
Time series analysis, 251
Time series, 251
Time value of money, 544
Timing of cash flows, 535
Trade bill, 417
Trade credit, 416, 507
Trading cycle, 386
Transactions motive, 428
Treasury bills, 438
Treasury management, 444
Trend, 252

Under absorption of overheads, 23
Underwriters, 456
Unit cost measurements, 90
Unit cost measures, 86
Updated annual budgets, 236
User costs, 273

Valuation, 312
Value of rights, 460
Variable costs, 270
Variable production overhead efficiency variance, 123
Variable production overhead expenditure variance, 123
Variable production overhead total variance, 123
Variable production overhead variances, 123
Variance analysis, 107, 118
Variance investigation models, 134
Variance trend, 133
Variance, 107, 118, 119, 120, 121, 123, 124, 129, 148, **214**
  in a standard absorption costing system, 144
  in a standard marginal costing system, 144
  interdependence between, 133
  investigating, 132
  reasons for, 131
  significance of, 132, 134
Vendor consideration issue, 464
Vendor placing, 463
Venture capital trusts, 508, 509, 511
Venture capital, 508
Volume capacity, 109
Volume of output targets, 326

Wage-price spiral, 368
Warhorses, 520
Warrant, 488
Warrant conversion premium, 489
Weighted average cost of capital, 498, 531

Weighted average costing, 72
'What' if analysis, 262
Without recourse, 408
Working capital cycle, 386
Working capital investment, 515
Working capital requirement, 392

Yield curve, 339
Yield variance, 148, 149

Z scores, 394
Zero based budgeting (ZBB), 231, 233
Zero coupon bonds, 482

See overleaf for information on other
BPP products and how to order

Mr/Mrs/Ms (Full name)

Daytime delivery address

Postcode

Daytime Tel

Date of exam (month/year)

ACCA Order

To BPP Publishing Ltd, Aldine Place, London W12 8AW

Tel: 020 8740 2211 Fax: 020 8740 1184

email: publishing@bpp.com online: www.bpp.com

	6/02 Texts	1/02 Kits	9/01 Passcards	MCQ Cards	Tapes	Videos	7/02 i-Learn	7/02 i-Pass	Virtual Campus
PART 1									
1.1 Preparing Financial Statements	£20.95 ☐	£10.95 ☐	£5.95 ☐	£5.95 ☐	£12.95 ☐	£25.00 ☐	£34.95 ☐	£24.95 ☐	£90.00 ☐
1.2 Financial Information for Management	£20.95 ☐	£10.95 ☐	£5.95 ☐	£5.95 ☐	£12.95 ☐	£25.00 ☐	£34.95 ☐	£24.95 ☐	£90.00 ☐
1.3 Managing people	£20.95 ☐	£10.95 ☐	£5.95 ☐		£12.95 ☐	£25.00 ☐	£34.95 ☐	£24.95 ☐	£90.00 ☐
PART 2									
2.1 Information Systems	£20.95 ☐	£10.95 ☐	£5.95 ☐		£12.95 ☐	£25.00 ☐	£34.95 ☐	£24.95 ☐	£90.00 ☐
2.2 Corporate and Business Law	£20.95 ☐	£10.95 ☐	£5.95 ☐		£12.95 ☐	£25.00 ☐	£34.95 ☐	£24.95 ☐	£90.00 ☐
2.3 Business Taxation FA 2001 (for 12/02 exam)	£20.95 ☐	£10.95 ☐	£5.95 ☐		£12.95 ☐	£25.00 ☐	£34.95 ☐	£24.95 ☐	£90.00 ☐
2.4 Financial Management and Control	£20.95 ☐	£10.95 ☐	£5.95 ☐		£12.95 ☐	£25.00 ☐	£34.95 ☐	£24.95 ☐	£90.00 ☐
2.5 Financial Reporting	£20.95 ☐	£10.95 ☐	£5.95 ☐		£12.95 ☐	£25.00 ☐	£34.95 ☐	£24.95 ☐	£90.00 ☐
2.6 Audit and Internal Review	£20.95 ☐	£10.95 ☐	£5.95 ☐		£12.95 ☐	£25.00 ☐	£34.95 ☐	£24.95 ☐	£90.00 ☐
PART 3									
3.1 Audit and Assurance Services	£20.95 ☐	£10.95 ☐	£5.95 ☐		£12.95 ☐	£25.00 ☐			
3.2 Advanced Taxation FA 2001 (for 12/02 exam)	£20.95 ☐	£10.95 ☐	£5.95 ☐		£12.95 ☐	£25.00 ☐			
3.3 Performance Management	£20.95 ☐	£10.95 ☐	£5.95 ☐		£12.95 ☐	£25.00 ☐			
3.4 Business Information Management	£20.95 ☐	£10.95 ☐	£5.95 ☐		£12.95 ☐	£25.00 ☐			
3.5 Strategic Business Planning and Development	£20.95 ☐	£10.95 ☐	£5.95 ☐		£12.95 ☐	£25.00 ☐			
3.6 Advanced Corporate Reporting	£20.95 ☐	£10.95 ☐	£5.95 ☐		£12.95 ☐	£25.00 ☐			
3.7 Strategic Financial Management	£20.95 ☐	£10.95 ☐	£5.95 ☐		£12.95 ☐	£25.00 ☐			
INTERNATIONAL STREAM									
1.1 Preparing Financial Statements	£20.95 ☐	£10.95 ☐	£5.95 ☐	£5.95 ☐					
2.5 Financial Reporting	£20.95 ☐	£10.95 ☐	£5.95 ☐						
2.6 Audit and Internal Review	£20.95 ☐	£10.95 ☐	£5.95 ☐						
3.1 Audit and Assurance Services	£20.95 ☐	£10.95 ☐	£5.95 ☐						
3.6 Advance Corporate Reporting	£20.95 ☐	£10.95 ☐	£5.95 ☐						
Success in your Research and Analysis Project – Tutorial Text (8/02)	£20.95 ☐								
Learning to Learn (7/02)	£9.95 ☐								

Subtotal £

POSTAGE & PACKING

Study Texts

	First	*Each extra*	
UK	£3.00	£2.00	£
Europe*	£5.00	£4.00	£
Rest of world	£20.00	£10.00	£

Kits/Passcards/Success Tapes

	First	*Each extra*	
UK	£2.00	£1.00	£
Europe*	£2.50	£1.00	£
Rest of world	£15.00	£8.00	£

MCQ cards	£1.00	£1.00	£

CDs each

UK	£2.00	£
Europe*	£2.00	£
Rest of world	£10.00	£

Breakthrough Videos

	First	*Each extra*	
UK	£2.00	£2.00	£
Europe*	£2.00	£2.00	£
Rest of world	£20.00	£10.00	£

Grand Total (incl. Postage)

I enclose a cheque for £

(Cheques to *BPP Publishing*)

Or charge to Visa/Mastercard/Switch

Card Number

Expiry date Start Date

Issue Number (Switch Only)

Signature

We aim to deliver to all UK addressess inside 5 working days; a signature will be required. Orders to all EU addresses should be delivered within 6 working days. All other orders to overseas addresses should be delivered within 8 working days.

* Europe includes the Republic of Ireland and the Channel Islands.

REVIEW FORM & FREE PRIZE DRAW

All original review forms from the entire BPP range, completed with genuine comments, will be entered into a draw on 31 January 2003 and 31 July 2003. The names on the first four forms picked out will be sent a cheque for £50.

Name: ____________________ **Address:** ____________________

____

How have you used this Text?
(Tick one box only)

☐ Home study (book only)
☐ On a course: college ____________
☐ With 'correspondence' package
☐ Other ____________

Why did you decide to purchase this Text?
(Tick one box only)

☐ Have used complementary Study Text
☐ Have used BPP Texts in the past
☐ Recommendation by friend/colleague
☐ Recommendation by a lecturer at college
☐ Saw advertising
☐ Other ____________

During the past six months do you recall seeing/receiving any of the following?
(Tick as many boxes as are relevant)

☐ Our advertisement in *ACCA Student Accountant*
☐ Our advertisement in *Pass*
☐ Our brochure with a letter through the post

Which (if any) aspects of our advertising do you find useful?
(Tick as many boxes as are relevant)

☐ Prices and publication dates of new editions
☐ Information on Text content
☐ Facility to order books off-the-page
☐ None of the above

Which BPP products have you used?

Text	☑	**MCQ cards**	☐	**i-Learn**	☐
Kit	☐	**Tape**	☐	**i-Pass**	☐
Passcard	☐	**Video**	☐	**Virtual Campus**	☐

Your ratings, comments and suggestions would be appreciated on the following areas.

	Very useful	*Useful*	*Not useful*
Introductory section (Key study steps, personal study)	☐	☐	☐
Chapter introductions	☐	☐	☐
Key terms	☐	☐	☐
Quality of explanations	☐	☐	☐
Case examples and other examples	☐	☐	☐
Questions and answers in each chapter	☐	☐	☐
Chapter roundups	☐	☐	☐
Quick quizzes	☐	☐	☐
Exam focus points	☐	☐	☐
Question bank	☐	☐	☐
Answer bank	☐	☐	☐
List of key terms and index	☐	☐	☐
Icons	☐	☐	☐
Mind maps	☐	☐	☐

	Excellent	*Good*	*Adequate*	*Poor*
Overall opinion of this Text	☐	☐	☐	☐

Do you intend to continue using BPP Products? ☐ Yes ☐ No

Please note any further comments and suggestions/errors on the reverse of this page. The BPP author of this edition can be e-mailed at: nickweller@bpp.com

Please return to: Katy Hibbert, ACCA Range Manager, BPP Publishing Ltd, FREEPOST, London, W12 8BR

REVIEW FORM & FREE PRIZE DRAW (continued)

TELL US WHAT YOU THINK

Please note any further comments and suggestions/errors below.

FREE PRIZE DRAW RULES

1 Closing date for 31 July 2003 draw is 30 June 2003. Closing date for 31 January 2003 draw is 31 December 2002.

2 No purchase necessary. Entry forms are available upon request from BPP Publishing. No more than one entry per title, per person. Draw restricted to persons aged 16 and over.

3 Winners will be notified by post and receive their cheques not later than 6 weeks after the draw date.

4 The decision of the promoter in all matters is final and binding. No correspondence will be entered int